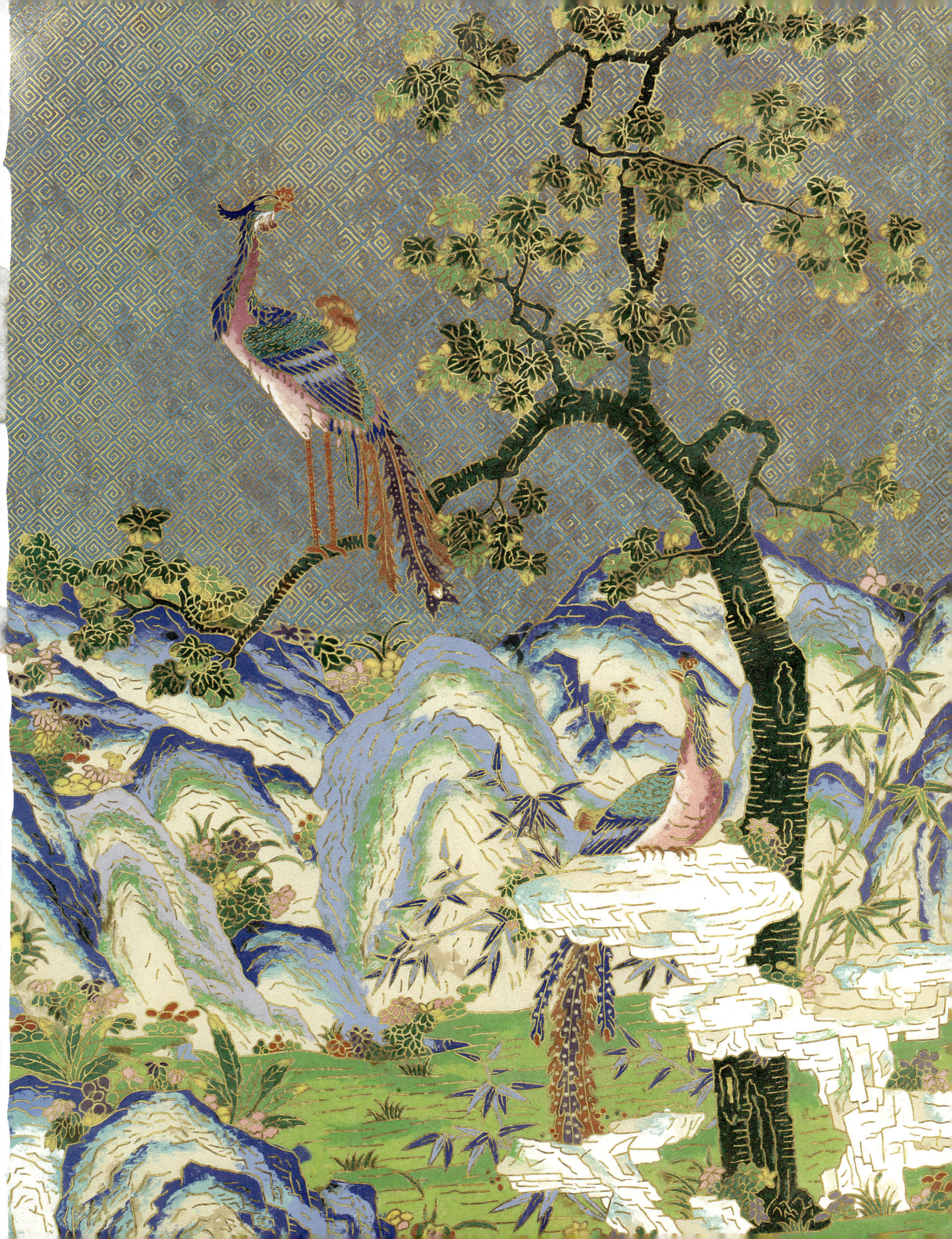

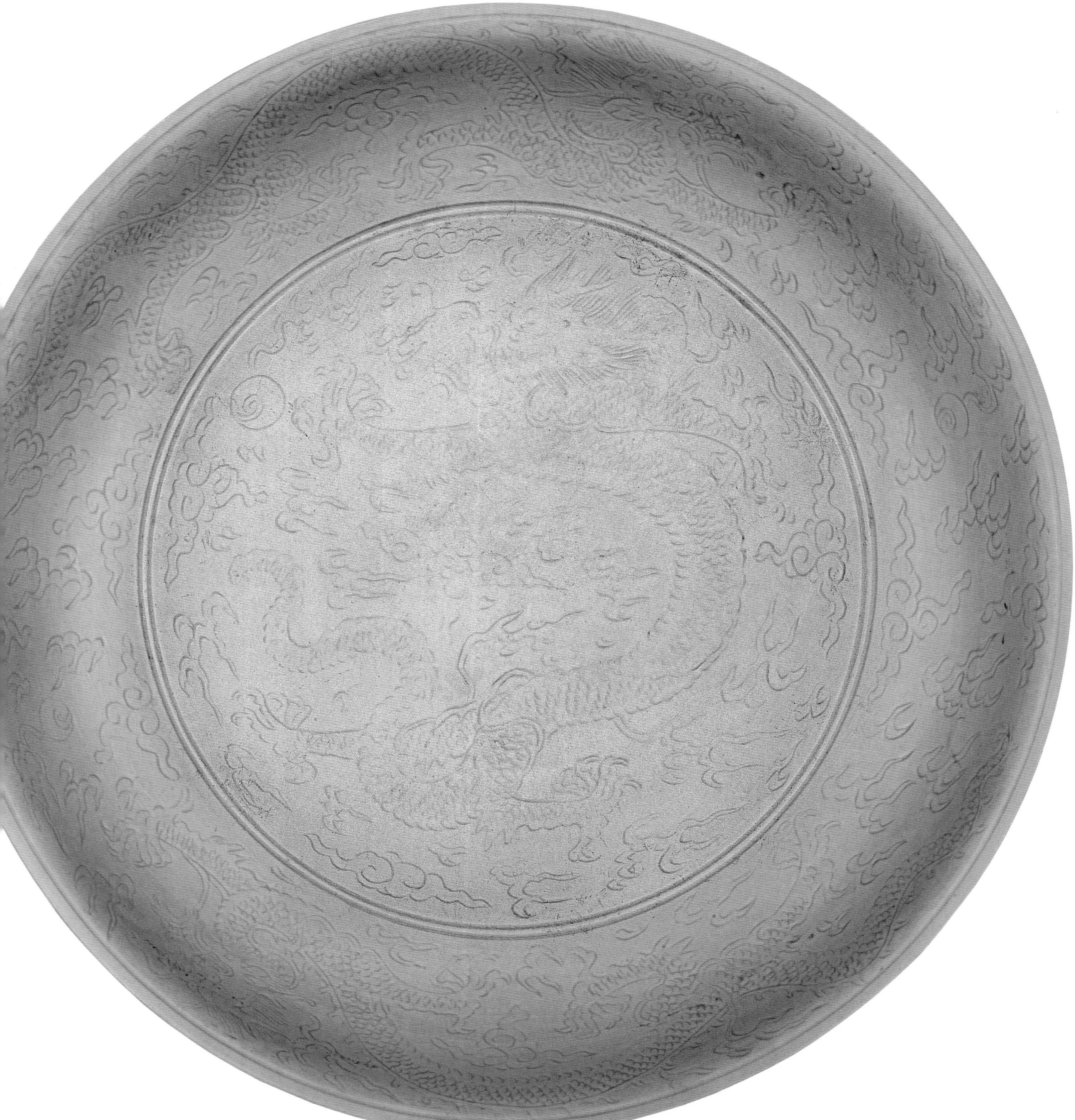

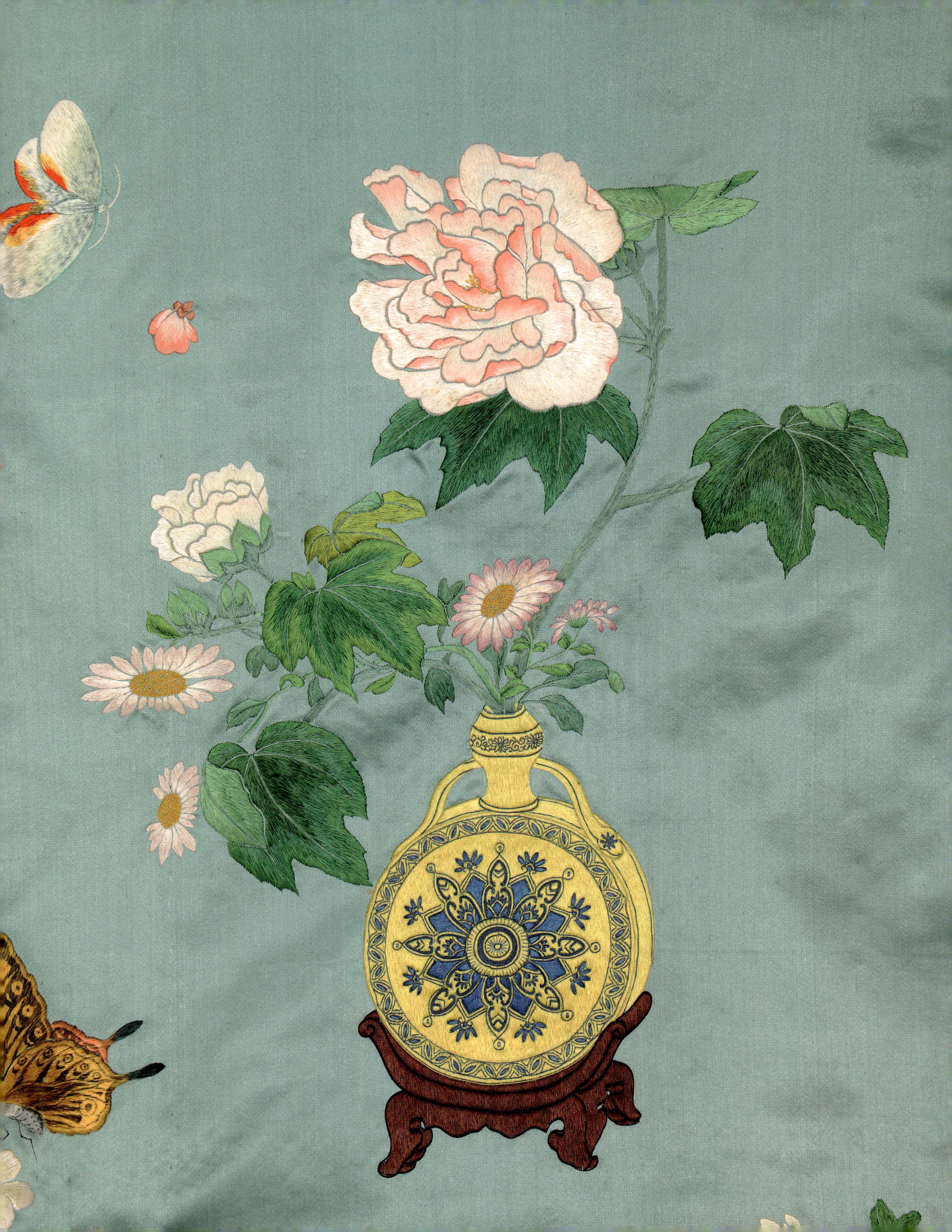

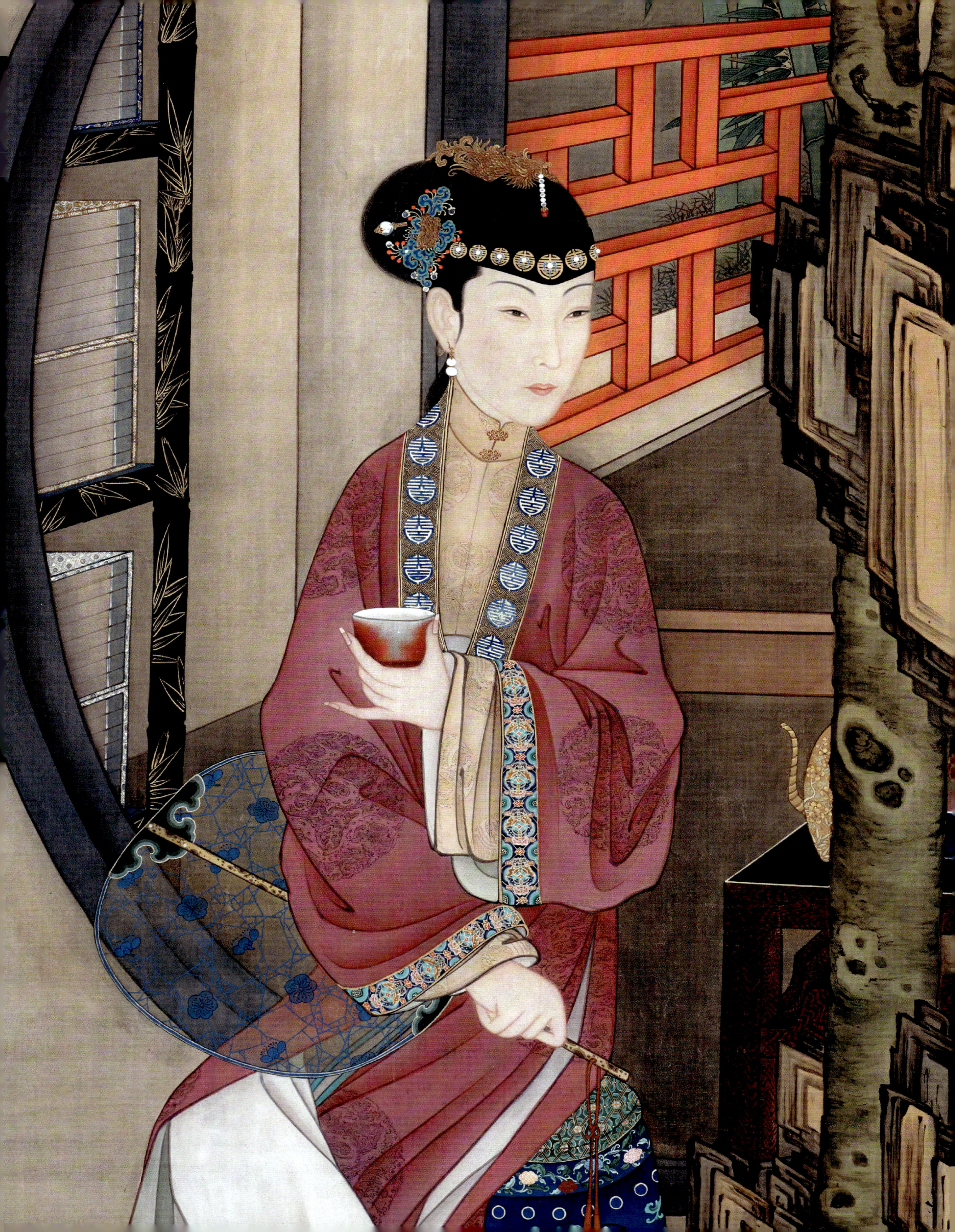

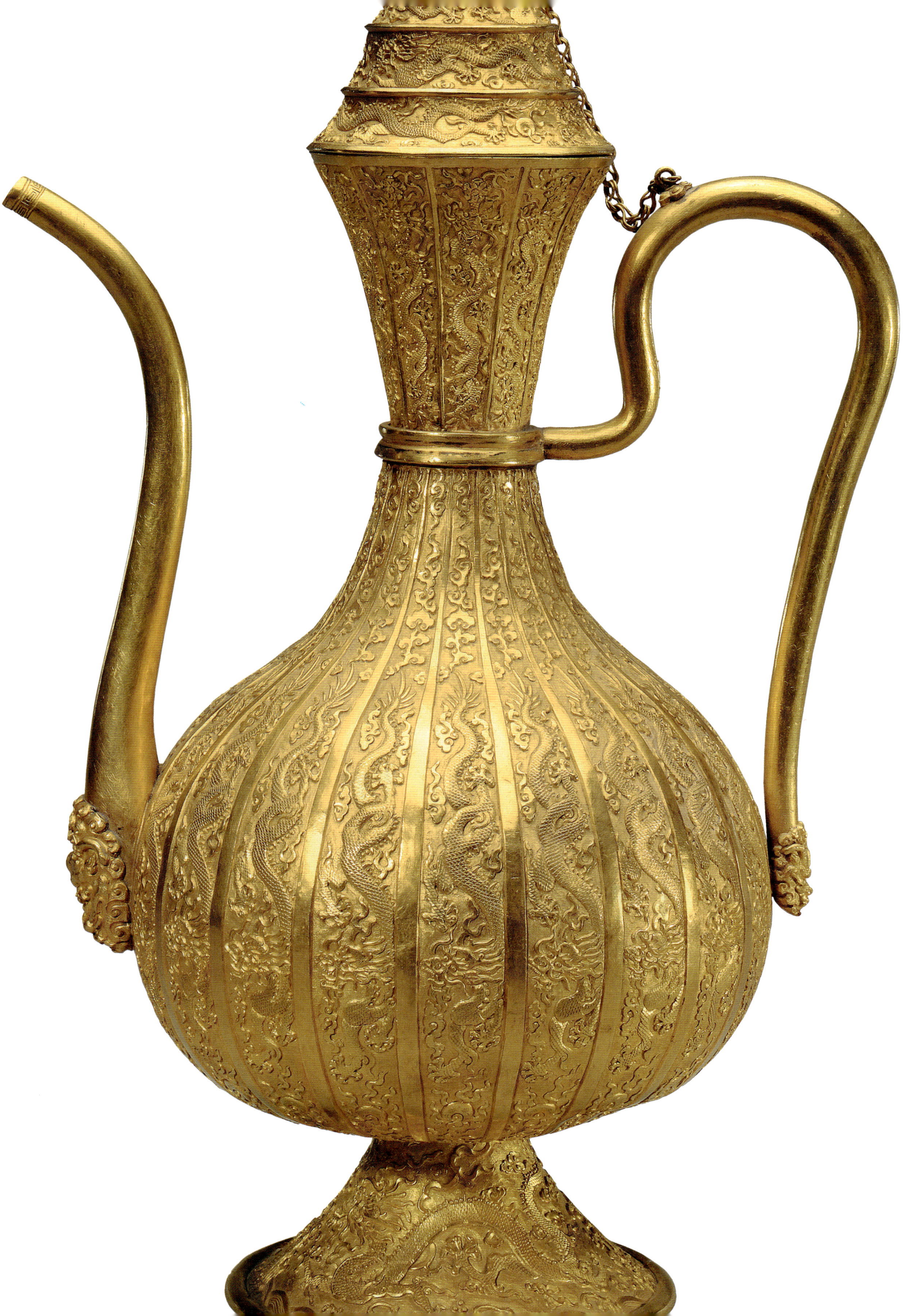

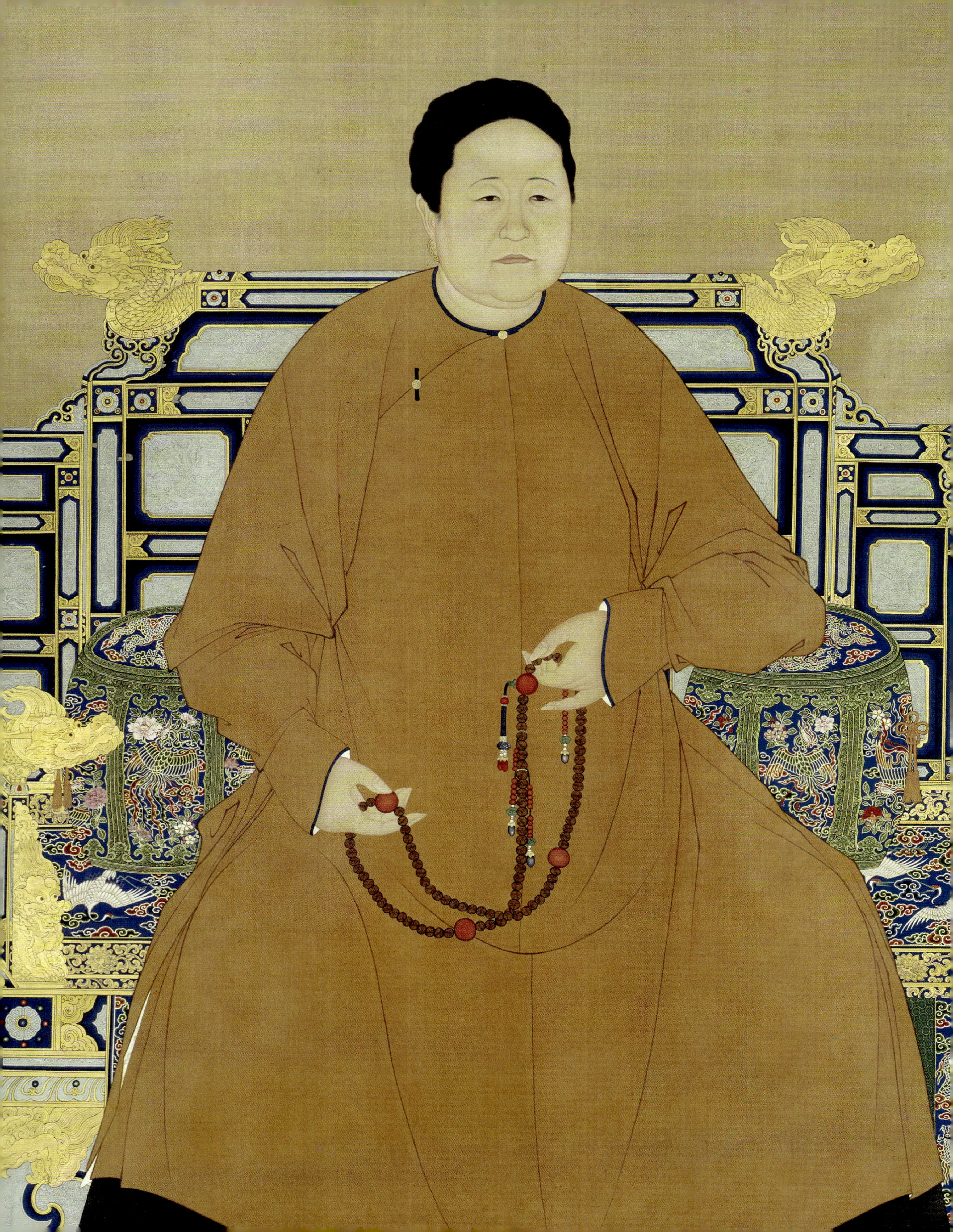

EMPRESSES OF CHINA'S FORBIDDEN CITY 1644–1912

EDITED BY

Daisy Yiyou Wang and Jan Stuart

WITH ESSAYS AND ENTRIES BY

Daisy Yiyou Wang, Jan Stuart, Lin Shu, Luk Yu-ping, Ying-chen Peng, Evelyn S. Rawski, Ren Wanping, and additional entries by curators at the Palace Museum, the Peabody Essex Museum, and the Freer|Sackler, Smithsonian Institution

Peabody Essex Museum SALEM, MASSACHUSETTS

Freer|Sackler, Smithsonian Institution WASHINGTON, DC

DISTRIBUTED BY Yale University Press NEW HAVEN AND LONDON

CONTENTS

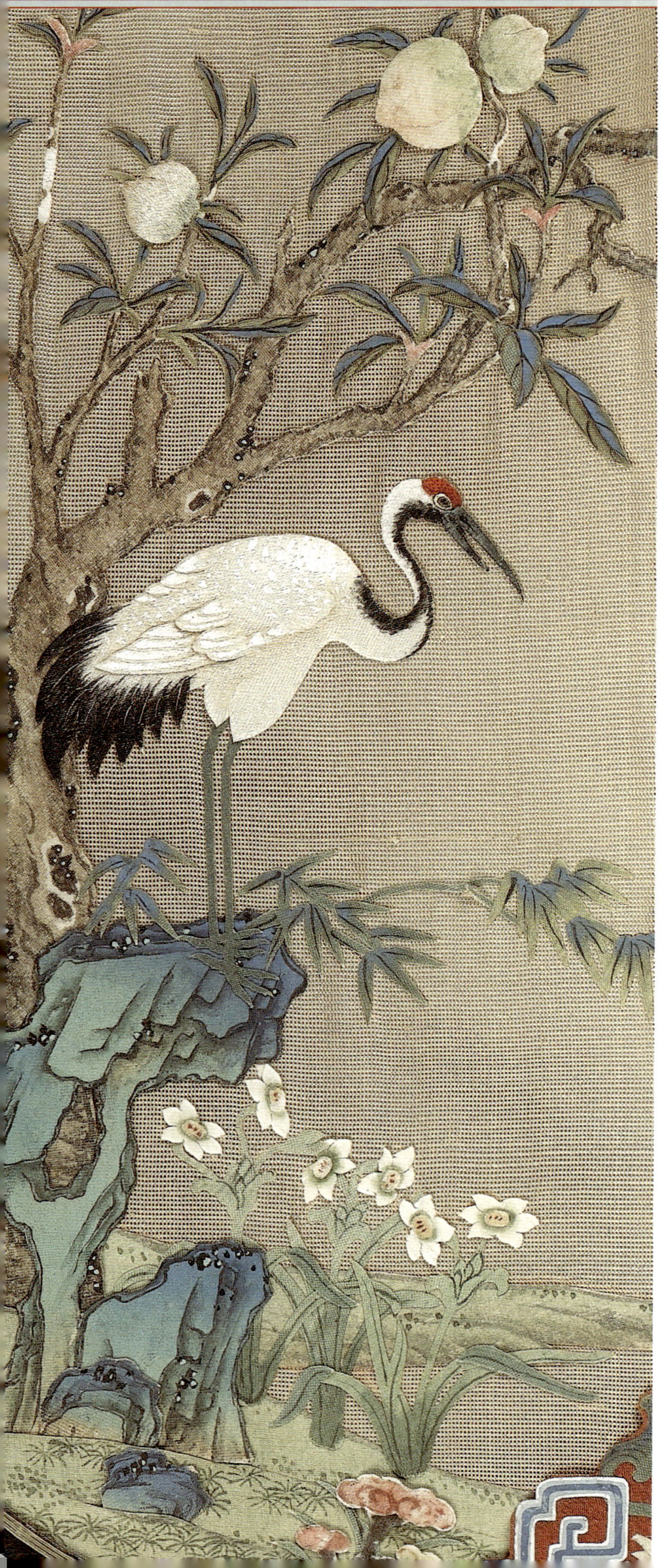

DIRECTORS' FOREWORDS

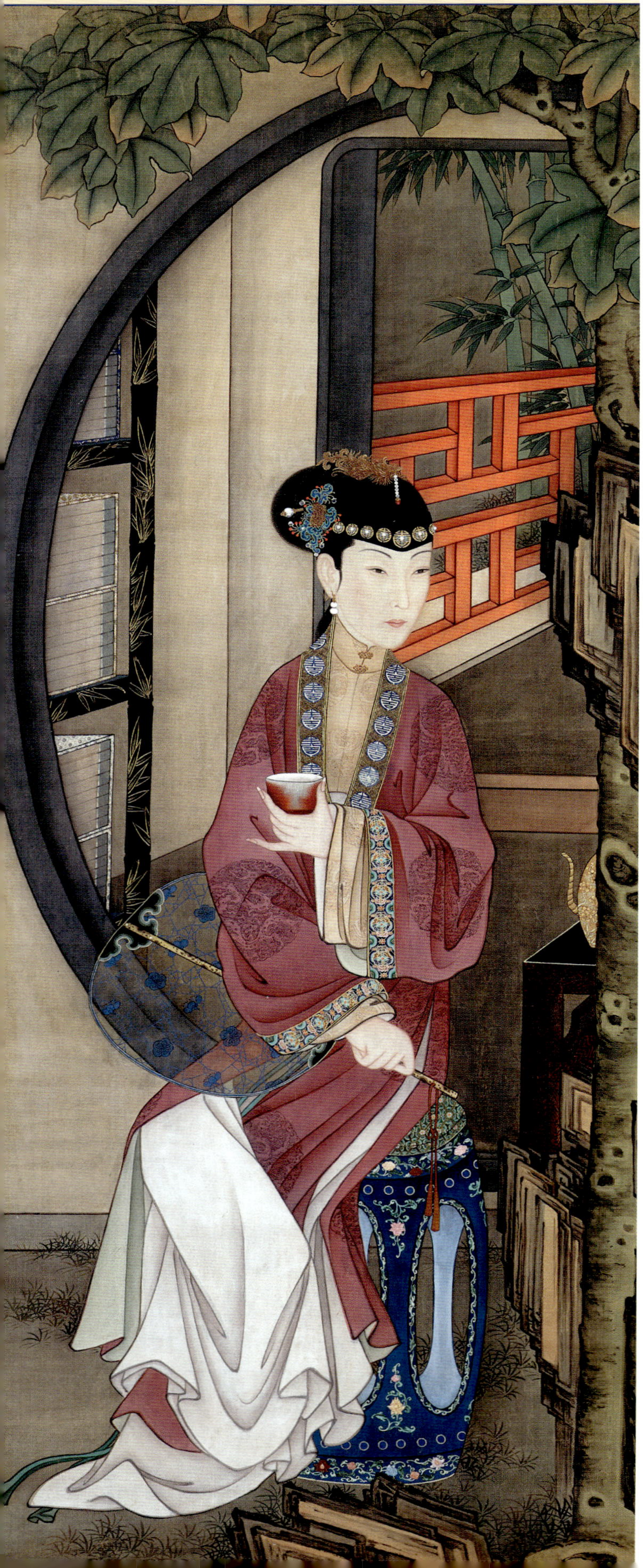

The Peabody Essex Museum (PEM) and the Smithsonian's Freer Gallery of Art and Arthur M. Sackler Gallery (F|S) are gratified to organize with the Palace Museum, Beijing, the exhibition and book *Empresses of China's Forbidden City, 1644–1912*. Through the detailed study and dazzling display of artworks associated with the lives of Qing dynasty empresses, our international project team has elucidated the multidimensional role the empresses played in shaping the history of the Qing court. Given the rich visual experience this material provides, it is rather surprising that this is the first international exhibition on the topic. All three museums are proud to reclaim the presence and influence of these prominent women, about whom history has largely been silent. The empresses' significance in court dynamics—including art, religion, politics, and diplomacy—as well as their contributions to the multiethnic cosmopolitanism of the Qing, create a compelling narrative about China during its last dynasty, before its transition to the modern world power it is today. It is clear that the stories of these empresses are worth engaging with, and while this project focuses on the past, we hope it can also encourage broader reflection on issues of women and power around the world today.

This exhibition and publication, involving more than 200 significant loans from the Palace Museum, marks the fortieth anniversary of the establishment of US-China diplomatic relations in an unforgettable way. The project required the full cooperation and welcome expertise of many dedicated and talented colleagues at the Palace Museum, especially Director Shan Jixiang and Deputy Directors Lou Wei, Ren Wanping and Feng Nai'en, whose support made the endeavor possible. We also value the encouragement we received from the diplomatic community in both countries. At an early stage, the project was highlighted as a key example of cultural and art exchange at the 2016 China-US High-Level Consultation on People-to-People Exchange in Beijing, chaired by Chinese Vice Premier Liu Yandong and Secretary of State John Kerry.

Daisy Yiyou Wang, The Robert N. Shapiro Curator of Chinese and East Asian Art at PEM, and Jan Stuart, the Melvin R. Seiden Curator of Chinese Art at F|S, co-curated the exhibition and co-edited the book and have tirelessly pooled their deep knowledge of China and its art. In working closely with the learned curators and scholars at the Palace Museum and by tapping other top experts to contribute to this publication, they have raised the bar for scholarly exchanges between Chinese and American museums.

We are profoundly grateful to the many sponsors and patrons who provided generous support for the exhibition and book. We wish to thank the Bei Shan Tang Foundation and Furthermore, a program of the J. M. Kaplan Fund, for funding the publication. Exhibition supporters include Liu Dan; the Henry Luce Foundation; the National Endowment for the Humanities; Carolyn and Peter S. Lynch and the Lynch Foundation; Shirley Z. Johnson and Charles Rumph; Susan and Michael Pillsbury; the Richard C. von Hess Foundation; the AMG Foundation; the Coby Foundation Ltd.; Eaton Vance; American Friends of the Shanghai Museum; and the Blakemore Foundation. Additionally, we would like to thank Rose-Marie and Eijk van Otterloo; Quan Zhou and Dr. Xiaohua Zhang; Skinner, Inc.; the Ellen Bayard Weedon Foundation; Sandra Urie and Frank Herron; Robert N. Shapiro; and those individuals who wish to remain anonymous. We would also like to thank Mr. and Mrs. James B. Hawkes for the support of seminar programming around the exhibition.

Empresses of China's Forbidden City, 1644–1912 is not only the first three-way collaboration of the organizing museums, it is also the first time that PEM and F|S have co-curated and co-organized an exhibition, and we want to acknowledge the special role that PEM has undertaken as the project's administrative leader. In 2010 and 2011 PEM partnered with the Palace Museum to organize *The Emperor's Private Paradise: Treasures from the Forbidden City*, a nationally touring exhibition that attracted nearly half a million visitors. *Empresses of China's Forbidden City, 1644–1912* expands an important tradition of collaboration between PEM and the Palace Museum. For F|S, it is the first exhibition and publication agreement with the Palace Museum, and an exciting beginning. The exceptional loans from the Palace Museum are at the heart of this project, but we also thank the Art Institute of Chicago; the Chazen Museum of Art, University of Wisconsin-Madison; the Minneapolis Institute of Art; the Museum of Fine Arts, Boston; the Rhode Island School of Design Museum; and the University of Alberta Museums; as well as PEM and F|S for sharing key objects.

Mounting this exhibition and creating this book has involved sharing many types of experiences and expertise, including the Palace Museum's state-of-the-art photography studios and innovative digitization projects. We were thrilled that the project team produced special photography of objects and the palace environment for the publication, in-gallery images, and interactive materials. All three museums shared best practices for registration, conservation, exhibition management, design, and installation.

PEM and F|S each have a long history of engagement with China. The Peabody Essex Museum, located in Salem, Massachusetts, is a birthplace of US-China commercial and cultural exchanges, reaching back to 1786 when the *Grand Turk*, one of the first American ships to trade directly with China, reached the Qing empire. As the first American museum to collect and present Chinese art and culture, PEM has been a leader in preserving and promoting Chinese art and architecture. In addition to its strengths in Chinese photographic, vernacular, decorative, and export arts, PEM is home to Yin Yu Tang, a 200-year-old house that is the only example of an entire Chinese vernacular building on display in the United States. PEM's mission focuses on providing transformative experiences and unexpected perspectives to enhance our understanding of the relationship between the past and the present and our place in the world. In celebrating global art, culture, and creative expression, the museum aspires to increase knowledge, enrich the spirit, engage the mind, and stimulate the senses.

The Freer Gallery of Art and the Arthur M. Sackler Gallery, located in Washington, DC, on the National Mall, are the Smithsonian Institution's Asian art museums and hold in trust for the nation stellar collections of Asian art and art from the American Aesthetic movement. F|S exists to further scholarship, foster empathy across cultures, and promote understanding of Asian art and culture. Since merging in 1987, the two museums have become a single destination where Asia meets America. Through its many exhibitions and publications on Chinese art, F|S has enjoyed a history of bringing China and America together, including through diplomatic visits. On January 30, 1979, Zhuo Lin, dignitary and wife of China's Vice Premier Deng Xiaoping, visited the Freer during her husband's state visit to Washington. The value diplomats place on art as a common ground for people to communicate across different cultures continues today. *Empresses of China's Forbidden City, 1644–1912* comes forty years after Zhuo Lin's visit, enacting a historic three-way international partnership that was only a dream then.

The fresh research and interpretation that *Empresses of China's Forbidden City, 1644–1912* embodies amply fulfill our shared commitment to expanding appreciation of China's rich culture, in this instance by recovering the preeminence of the Qing empresses through the stunning and rare objects in this exhibition and book.

Dan L. Monroe
THE ROSE-MARIE AND EIJK VAN OTTERLOO DIRECTOR AND CEO
PEABODY ESSEX MUSEUM

Julian Raby
DIRECTOR EMERITUS
FREER GALLERY OF ART AND ARTHUR M. SACKLER GALLERY
SMITHSONIAN INSTITUTION

When visitors come to the Palace Museum for the first time, they may feel overwhelmed by a myriad of buildings and exhibitions. The museum, known as the Forbidden City, is a unique palatial complex and a labyrinth of history. For nearly five hundred years, it was the seat of government during the Ming and Qing dynasties, a central repository of Chinese cultural heritage, and an encyclopedia of Chinese political history, philosophy, art, and life.

With a rich collection of millions of objects, rare books, and archival documents, the Palace Museum plays an indispensable role in broadening our understanding of Chinese and Asian history and culture. Since the founding of the museum, our dedicated staff has worked tirelessly to organize, conserve, present, and research this immense treasure house of Chinese cultural heritage. Today we are proud to lead many innovative projects in collection access, exhibitions, publications, and digital media in our effort to reach out to new audiences nationally and globally. Over the years, special exhibitions featuring the Palace Museum's collection have presented Chinese culture to countries around the world.

The year 2019 marks the fortieth anniversary of the establishment of diplomatic relations between China and the United States. Since 1980 the Palace Museum has worked closely with many American museums, including the Peabody Essex Museum, the Arthur M. Sackler Gallery, the Metropolitan Museum of Art, and the Virginia Museum of Fine Arts, etc. The fruition of these partnerships includes more than twenty highly successful exhibitions of the Palace Museum's collection in America and vital scholarly and personnel exchanges. I firmly believe *Empresses of China's Forbidden City, 1644–1912* will be yet another great success.

To many people, Qing imperial women lived in a mysterious, yet colorful world. In the official history and archives of the Qing imperial court, empresses and other consorts were largely overshadowed by emperors, who were often judged by their political achievements. Despite the patriarchal structure of the Qing imperial court, a few women stood out and played an important role in history. The empress headed the affairs of the imperial family and could exert an influence on the emperor. She was therefore regarded as the "mother of the state." Empress Xiaozhuang (1613–1688), at the beginning of the dynasty, and Empress Dowager Cixi (1835–1908), toward its end, directly influenced the reigning monarchs and played a critical part in shaping the course of history. Many important artworks and historical documents in the Palace Museum's collection testify to their lives and achievements.

The Palace Museum has exhibited and published in China extensive materials related to the life of imperial women, which has helped draw scholarly and public attention to this important field. It is particularly meaningful that *Empresses of China's Forbidden City, 1644–1912* is curated by two very special friends and colleagues: Jan Stuart and Daisy Yiyou Wang. Over the years my colleagues and I have had the great pleasure to get to know and work closely with them. Gracious and tireless, these two curators have made major contributions to deepening mutual understanding and advancing the museum profession in China and the United States.

The Palace Museum explores new approaches and themes in organizing special exhibitions, many of which have emerged from findings uncovered by our staff as they catalogue and research the museum's collection. These discoveries have informed the curatorial concepts and object selection of *Empresses of China's Forbidden City, 1644–1912*. For the past three years, Stuart and Wang have researched the collection with Palace Museum staff, including researchers and collection managers. This has resulted in an impressive assemblage of spectacular objects as well as new scholarship on imperial women. Further, it establishes a new model for future international research and exhibition collaborations.

The Forbidden City will celebrate its 600th anniversary in 2020. Since it opened to the public in 1925, the Palace Museum has continually broadened its outreach and deepened its impact. *Empresses of China's Forbidden City, 1644–1912* not only features treasures from the Palace Museum but also draws on collections of American museums, enabling visitors to appreciate the richness and diversity of Chinese art and culture. The museum is committed to sharing its exhibitions and collections with audiences outside of China and to presenting great traveling exhibitions from around the globe inside the Forbidden City. I look forward to more exchanges and collaborations with colleagues in America.

Shan Jixiang
DIRECTOR
PALACE MUSEUM

SPONSORS

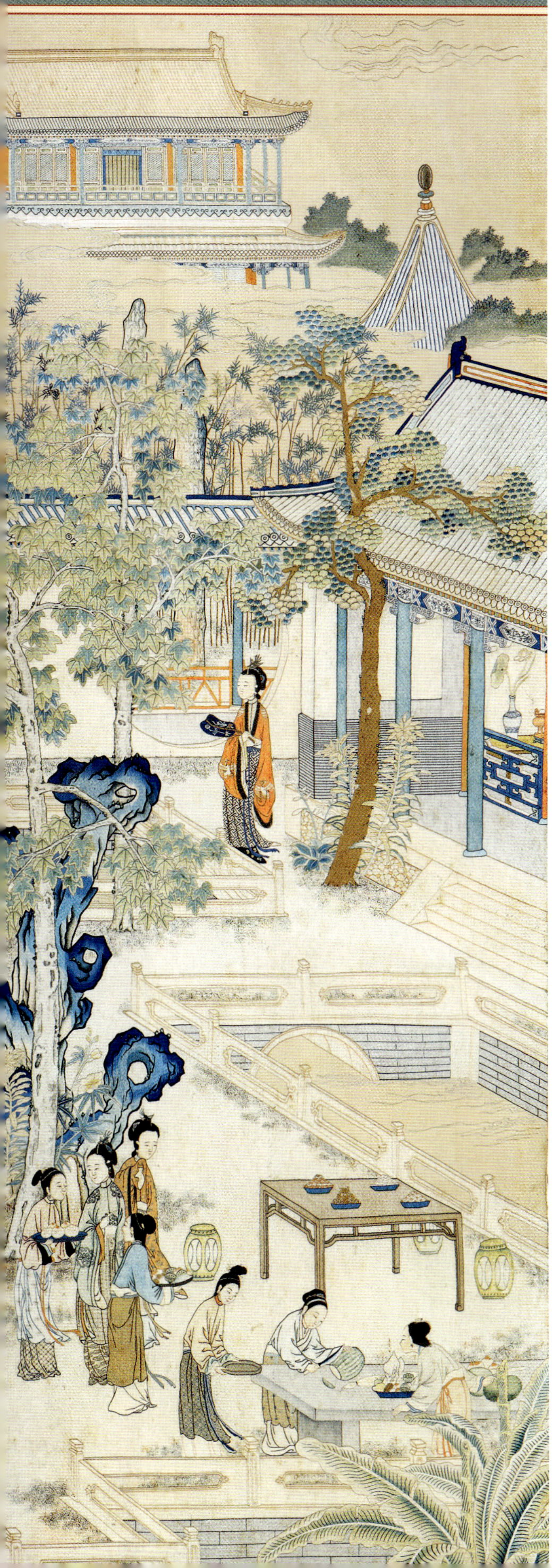

FOR MAJOR SUPPORT OF *EMPRESSES OF CHINA'S FORBIDDEN CITY, 1644–1912*, WE WOULD LIKE TO THANK

Liu Dan

Henry Luce Foundation

National Endowment for the Humanities

Carolyn and Peter S. Lynch and the Lynch Foundation

Shirley Z. Johnson and Charles Rumph

The Richard C. von Hess Foundation

Anonymous

The AMG Foundation

The Coby Foundation, Ltd.

Eaton Vance

American Friends of the Shanghai Museum

Blakemore Foundation

Rose-Marie and Eijk van Otterloo

Quan Zhou and Dr. Xiaohua Zhang

Skinner, Inc.

Ellen Bayard Weedon Foundation

Sandra Urie and Frank Herron

Robert N. Shapiro

The East India Marine Associates of the Peabody Essex Museum

The Empresses Leadership Council of the Freer|Sackler, Smithsonian Institution, co-chaired by Liu Dan, Shirley Z. Johnson, and Susan and Michael Pillsbury

GENEROUS FUNDING FOR THE PUBLICATION IS PROVIDED BY

Bei Shan Tang Foundation

WITH ADDITIONAL FUNDING BY

Furthermore: a program of the J. M. Kaplan Fund

Mr. and Mrs. James B. Hawkes for their support of seminar programming around the exhibition

ACKNOWLEDGMENTS

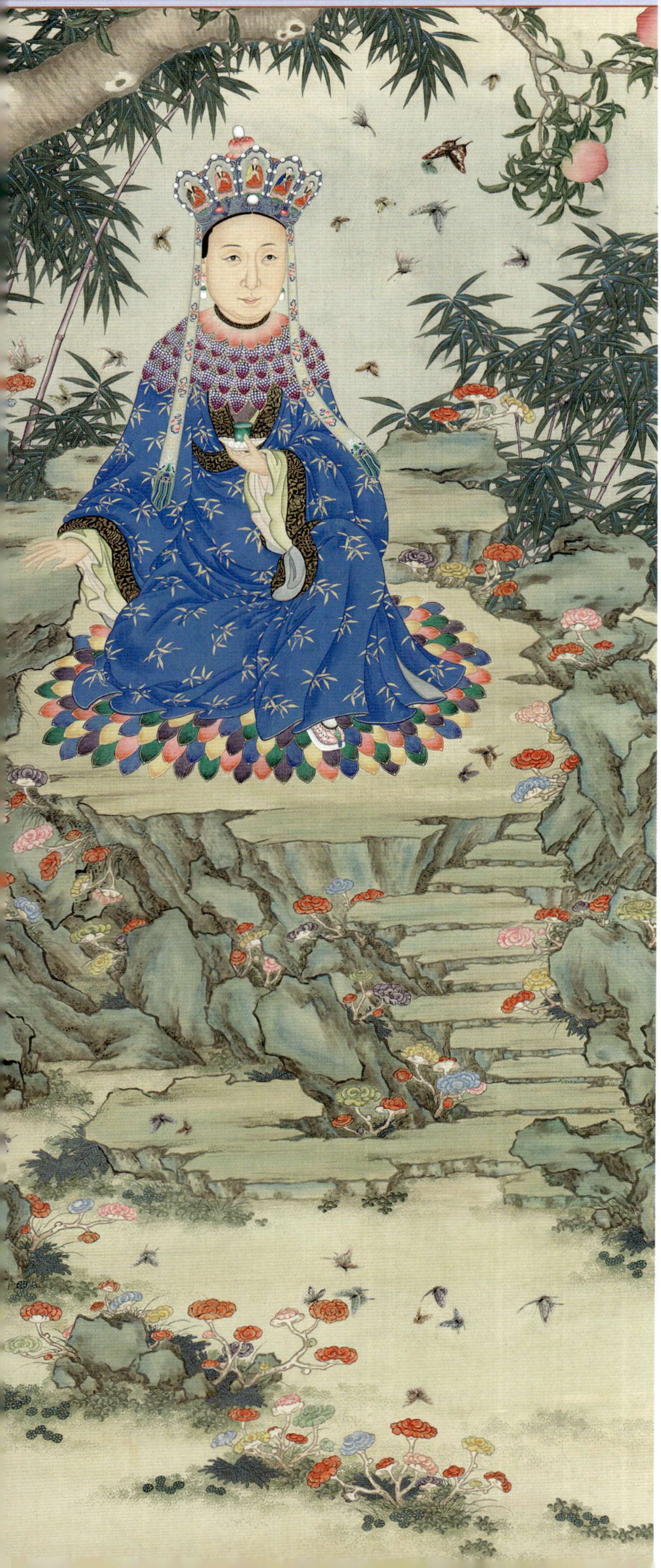

IF IT TAKES A VILLAGE to raise a child, it takes a city to make *Empresses of China's Forbidden City, 1644–1912.* This exhibition and its associated book have been built on the collaboration of many talented and dedicated individuals at the three organizing institutions: the Peabody Essex Museum (PEM), the Freer|Sackler, Smithsonian Institution (F|S), and the Palace Museum. We also benefited from other experts, supporters, and museums, and are equally indebted to the profound professionalism and commitment of a broad range of staff members at our home institutions and the Palace Museum. The sum of everyone's individual contributions has yielded a project stronger than we could have initially dreamed, bringing concentrated attention to the neglected history of Qing dynasty empresses—their lives and the compelling art that surrounded them.

It is not typical for co-editors to acknowledge each other, but since we took such delight and mutual inspiration in working together, we ask for the indulgence of thanking each other here. We also jointly take responsibility for any errors or infelicities that may occur in the exhibition or book.

We first draw attention to the inestimably capable and indefatigable staff of our Chinese co-organizer, the Palace Museum, whose efforts underpin the project. Our respect for and gratitude to all of our colleagues there is heartfelt, starting with the executive leadership whose wisdom and support shaped the project. Director Shan Jixiang and Deputy Directors Lou Wei, Ren Wanping, and Feng Nai'en have, from beginning to end, been crucial in ensuring the outstanding quality of the loans and offering scholarly guidance. Lou Wei graciously hosted several of our meetings in Beijing. Special acknowledgment is due to the museum's Foreign Affairs Department, whose staff tirelessly executed the numerous details necessary to bringing the exhibition to fruition. In this department, Director Li Shaoyi, Deputy Director Yuan Hong, and Liu Yufeng bore a heavy burden in actualizing the exhibition and book; beyond their professionalism, we will always remember their good cheer, even when we went back to them with yet one more question.

Led by Wang Yuegong, Director of the Court History Department, the Palace Museum curatorial team consisted of Zhang Xin, Gao Xiaoran, and Wang Zhongxu. Along with other colleagues at the Palace Museum, they provided key research as well as expert advice and support. This project would have been impossible without their unstinting efforts to coordinate object study sessions, manage the checklist, and facilitate communication across the ocean and between multiple departments in the Palace Museum. And no matter how tiring his work was, Zhang Xin—whom we saw more often than others—always offered us a welcoming smile while executing all matters with perfection.

We also offer sincere thanks for the leadership of Lü Chenglong, Director of the Antiquities Department; Zeng Jun, Director of the Painting and Calligraphy Department; Zhang Rong, Director of the Library; Li Yongxin, Director of the Collection Management Department; Shi Mingchang, Director of the Conservation Department; and Su Yi, Director of the Information Department. The following staff has provided assistance and shared their expertise: Cao Lianming, Chun Hua, Fu Chong, Gao Fei, Guan Xueling, Guo Fuxiang, Han Qian, Hao Yanfeng, Hua Ning, Huang Jian, Huang Weiwen, Ji Luoyuan, Jiang Tong, Jing Wen, Lei Yong, Li Huan, Li Lili, Li Shi, Li Tianyin, Liang Ke, Liu Jingying, Liu Liyong, Liu Yue, Liu Yuxian, Liu Zhenghong, Ma Chengnan, Nie Hui, Peng Tiandi, Qian Jiuru, Qiu Taige, Ruan Weiping, Rui Qian, Shan Yingying, Si Bing, Song Yongji, Sun Jing, Sun Zhiyuan, Tao Jing, Teng Deyong, Tian Yimin, Wan Xiufeng, Wang He, Wang Hebei, Wang Hu, Wang Jin, Wang Zilin, Wei Chen, Wen Ming, Xing Na, Xu Kai, Xu Lin, Xu Tong, Yan Yong, Yang Danxia, Yang Fan, Yang Guopeng, Yang Liwei, Yu Ningchuan, Yu Zhuang, Yun Limei, Zhan Mengxia, Zhang Li, Zhang Lifang, Zhang Lin, Zhang Linjie, Zhang Yuntian, Zhang Zhen, Zhao Bingwen, Zhao Guiling, Zhao Xiaochun, and Zhou Yaoqin.

Our own museum "top brass" also deserves appreciation and credit for their steady belief in our project and vision to help mold it. We give heartfelt thanks to Dan L. Monroe, The Rose-Marie and Eijk van Otterloo Director and CEO, and Lynda Roscoe Hartigan, The James B. and Mary Lou Hawkes Deputy Director, at PEM, and to Julian Raby, Director Emeritus at F|S. PEM staff took a lead role in coordinating the exhibition and publication on the US side, and the F|S wishes to add a special note of appreciation for that effort.

We hold the funders of the project in esteem, ardently reiterating the directors' thanks. Here, we wish to repeat the name of our first and largest individual donor, Liu Dan, without whose early belief this project might never have happened. Wonderful staff members at PEM and F|S spearheaded and managed complex efforts to build the financial support that undergirds the project. Accolades go to Nathalie Apchin, Chief Financial Officer; Amanda Clark MacMullan, Chief Philanthropy Officer; Kathleen Corcoran, Director of Institutional Giving; Rebecca Ehrhardt, Senior Director of Development; and Julie Fentin, Development Business Analyst at PEM; and Elisa Glazer, Director of External Affairs; Jessica Duby, Individual Gifts Officer; Alice Tracy, Institutional Gifts Officer; and Anna Troein, Assistant Manager for Advancement and Special Projects at F|S.

This book gives the exhibition a lasting presence, and the Bei Shan Tang Foundation, its primary funder, deserves our special gratitude as editors and authors. Kathy Fredrickson, Chief of Curatorial Affairs at PEM, has championed the publication, orchestrating details big and small with exceptional finesse that has ensured the book's success. The intelligibility of the text owes a huge debt to the "quiet man behind the scenes," our tireless editor, Tom Fredrickson, who was always gentle in working with the authors but never dropped a stitch. His clarity and depth of thought have immeasurably improved every aspect of the book, from its structure to its text. This volume's visual pleasure is due to the design of Joan Sommers and the production of Amanda Freymann of Glue + Paper Workshop. Paula Richter, Curator for Exhibitions and Research, and Doris Sung, Assistant Curator for Exhibitions and Research, at PEM have provided critical curatorial support and contributed significantly to the publication and many other aspects of this exhibition. Also at PEM, Rebecca Bednarz, Editor for Exhibition Research and Publishing, and Claire Blechman, Digital Asset Manager, Exhibition Research and Publishing, unstintingly contributed their hard work, expertise, and professional talents. Some of the captivating images in this publication attest to the talent of Bob Packert, Senior Photographer at PEM.

The authors of the book are listed in the table of contents, but here we want to recognize their uniformly high scholarship and expertise as well as to note their incredible goodwill in writing to an unforgiving deadline and compromising neither their academic standards nor their literary fluency. Additional recognition is due to the author Evelyn S. Rawski, who also generously read the entire manuscript and made invaluable suggestions. We benefited greatly from distinguished scholars Karina Corrigan, Mark C. Elliott, Grant Hayter-Menzies, Sarah Kennel, Stacey Lambrow, Yuhang Li, Liu Xinling, Keith McMahon, Julia Murray, Susan Naquin,

Anne Walthall, Dorothy C. Wong, and Wu Hung, who provided discerning comments to guide our research and frame the questions we wanted to explore.

For research assistance, we are grateful to the librarians and archivists Catherine Robertson at PEM and Shu Yue and David Hogge at F|S. The work of interns is sometimes invisible, but the following participants in the project aided us immensely. At PEM, Huang Yufu, Zhao Hejun, Jiang Yuqing, Xu Tingting, Fiona Collins, and Rosemarie Mele worked diligently to help lay a foundation for the exhibition checklist and support our writing. Gabrielle Niu and Jiang Kailun helped in implementing the project as well as working on interactives in the gallery and marketing. At F|S, Guoshi (Cedric) Li's bilingual research, draft texts, and nuanced academic questions immeasurably improved his supervising curator's work, and Weixun (Leslie) Qu's knowledge of and research on textiles as well as patience in checking details were inspiring.

The framework for this large exhibition and book depended on the perspicacity of our museums' exhibitions departments, which carry out all details from negotiating the exhibition contract to managing the budget and arranging the transport of artwork from China to the United States, as well as overseeing the exhibition installations at both venues. Priscilla Danforth, Director of Exhibition Planning at PEM, took a terrific leading role in consultation with the eagle-eyed Cheryl Sobas at F|S. Sarah Otto and Beth Dion, at PEM and F|S, respectively, have been exceptional project managers. The registrars have been exemplary, and we thank Francesca Williams, Registrar for Exhibitions, and Suzanne Inge, Associate Registrar for Exhibitions, at PEM, and Alan Francisco, Exhibitions Registrar at F|S, for their considerable expertise. Conservators and exhibition installers who ensure the safety of the art on display are essential. At PEM, Robert Monk, Chief of Security, Facilities Operations and Planning; John Childs, Chief of Collection Services and the Ann C. Pingree Director of the Phillips Library; Dave O'Ryan, Preparator; and conservators Mimi Leveque and Kathryn Carey are to be thanked. At F|S, Donna Strahan, head of the Department of Conservation and Scientific Research; Gu Xiangmei, Conservator, East Asian Painting Conservation Studio; Andrew Hare, Supervisory Conservator of the Studio; and Jennifer Bosworth, Exhibits Conservator, have been instrumental in caring for the artworks.

The visual form and expressive vision of an exhibition relies on the creativity and lucidity of the exhibition designers and the experts in interpretation and educational programs. At PEM, our sincere gratitude goes to Dave Seibert, Director of Exhibition Design, assisted by Rich Pepin, Exhibit Designer/Draftsperson; Karen Moreau Ceballos, Exhibition Design Manager; and Jackie Traynor, Graphic Designer. At F|S special thanks go to Jeremiah Gallay, Exhibitions Designer, and to Nancy Hacskaylo for graphic design. The designers' inspirational work and energy—the latter especially evident in a trip we took together to Beijing—sparked many important ideas. The project's educational programming and interpretation strategies reflect the creativity and visitor-centric understanding of Gavin Andrews, Chief Learning Officer; Liz Gardner, Interpretation Planner; Bridget Devlin, Evaluation and Interpretation Planner; with assistance from Cristy Hebert at PEM; and at F|S Elizabeth Eder, Head of Education, in particular, as well as Nancy Micklewright, Head, Public and Scholarly Engagement; Grace Murray, Head of Public Programs; and Matthew Lasnoski, Educator, Youth and Family Programs.

Jay Finney, Chief Marketing Officer at PEM, and Elisa Glazer with Megan Krefting and Ginny Maycock at F|S spearheaded our creative marketing initiatives and have played a major role in broadening this exhibition's local and international reach. We are deeply grateful to Whitney Van Dyke, Director of Communications, and Derek O'Brien, Director of Creative Services, at PEM. Ed Rodley, Associate Director of Integrated Media at PEM, took the lead in developing innovative in-gallery video and interactives. We also thank Jim Olson, Director of Integrated Media; Caroline Herr, Digital Media Designer; and Chip Van Dyke, Manager of Media Productions, at PEM; and Courtney O'Callaghan, Chief of Technology, Hutomo Wicaksono, Audio Visual and Media Specialist, and Sana Mirza, Education Specialist, at F|S for their commitment to widening and deepening our visitors' experience.

Lending institutions in addition to the Palace Museum have enriched the project. We thank colleagues at the Art Institute of Chicago; the Chazen Museum of Art, University of Wisconsin–Madison; the Minneapolis Institute of Art; the Museum of Fine Arts, Boston; the Rhode Island School of Design Museum; and University of Alberta Museums. We are grateful to the Department of Asian Art and the Antonio Ratti Textile Center at the Metropolitan Museum of Art, the Asian Art Department at the Cleveland Museum of Art, and Stephan Loewentheil for granting us access to their wonderful collections. The Shanghai Museum, the White Cloud Monastery, the Potala Palace, and the Palace of Harmony and Peace generously allowed us to reproduce images in the catalogue. We rely on the expertise of Masterpiece International and Huaxie International Fine Art Freight Service Company, Ltd., China, in ensuring the safe shipping of the objects.

On the occasion of a project celebrating the fortieth anniversary of US-China diplomatic relations, we extend our deepest appreciation to His Excellency, Ambassador Cui Tiankai at the Embassy of the People's Republic of China in the United States for guidance on and encouragement for the project. We also acknowledge Ambassador and Consul General Zhang Qiyue at the Chinese Consulate General in New York. This project benefited greatly from the advice of Guan Qiang, Deputy Administrator, and Wen Dayan, Head of Foreign Affairs, at China's State Administration of Cultural Heritage, and Chen Chunmei, former Director of America and Oceania Division, Bureau for External Cultural Relations, Ministry of Culture in China.

This project was enthusiastically welcomed and assisted by Frank Whitaker, Minister Counselor for Public Affairs; Lisa Heller, the former Minister Counselor for Public Affairs; and Anne E. Grimes, Deputy Public Affairs Officer, of the Embassy of the United States of America in China.

On a personal note, friends worldwide have shared their knowledge and expertise with us and have always spurred us on to realize this project, but without a doubt it is our families and partners who have provided the bedrock support that advanced our realization of *Empresses of China's Forbidden City, 1644–1912*.

Daisy Yiyou Wang
THE ROBERT N. SHAPIRO CURATOR OF CHINESE AND EAST ASIAN ART
PEABODY ESSEX MUSEUM

Jan Stuart
MELVIN R. SEIDEN CURATOR OF CHINESE ART
FREER GALLERY OF ART AND ARTHUR M. SACKLER GALLERY
SMITHSONIAN INSTITUTION

NOTE TO THE READER

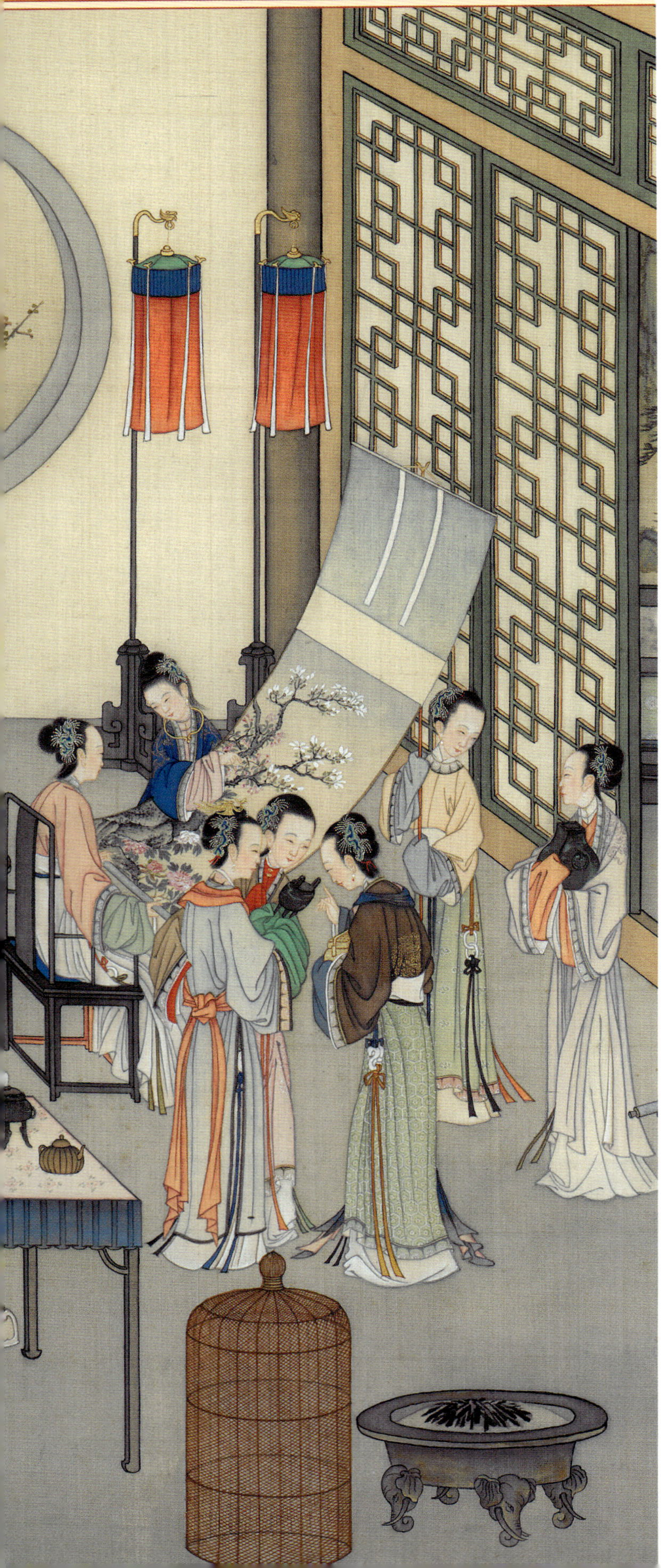

INFORMATION ON ARTWORKS

The Palace Museum (Gugong bowuyuan) in Beijing is the largest lender to the exhibition. Unless otherwise noted, all artworks are from its collection and all images have been provided courtesy of the Palace Museum.

Most works in this publication were made in China, therefore no country of origin is listed unless otherwise noted. Dimensions are given height before width before depth. The dimensions for paintings, calligraphies, and photographic prints are for the image proper (without the mounting) unless otherwise noted.

DATES

For this publication 1912 is given as the end of the Qing dynasty, as the formal abdication of the last emperor took place on February 12, 1912.

Reign periods correspond to the dates that Qing emperors ruled under their own reign, or era, names, but an emperor was usually enthroned about a year before his reign name was chosen. Until that time, a new emperor served under his father's reign name. Reign periods appear in parentheses at the first appearance of an emperor's name in the text: Qianlong emperor (r. 1736–95).

QING DYNASTY (1644–1912)
Shunzhi period (1644–61)
Kangxi period (1662–1722)
Yongzheng period (1723–35)
Qianlong period (1736–95)
Jiaqing period (1796–1820)
Daoguang period (1821–50)
Xianfeng period (1851–61)
Tongzhi period (1862–74)
Guangxu period (1875–1908)
Xuantong period (1909–12)

The ages of Chinese people correspond to Chinese convention, whereby a person was one year old at birth. For example, a person who was sixty-nine years of age by Western reckoning was considered to be seventy in China.

PLACE-NAMES

The names of certain places in China have changed over time. When a place is cited by its historical name, it is followed by its present-day name. For the sake of convenience, we use "Beijing" to refer to the city in modern and Qing times, although in the Qing it was usually called Jingshi (Capital).

NAMES OF PERSONS

The appellations of empresses and other consorts are complicated. For example, although each empress had a birth name, she was given a new title when she became a consort—and that title might change several times during her lifetime if she was promoted within the eight ranks of consorts. If a consort became an empress or empress dowager, she again received new titles. Empresses and empress dowagers were also given new names posthumously, all of which begin with the Chinese character for filiality (*xiao*).

In this publication we (usually) refer to each woman by the name most widely known in historical accounts, and—in an acknowledged anachronism—we use that name across different periods in her life to avoid the confusion of calling the same woman by multiple names.

Emperors also had multiple names and are referred to by their reign names. For example, we refer to the Qianlong emperor using his reign name—Qianlong, meaning "supernal eminence"—and Qianlong for short, though in Qing China he would not have been called Qianlong as a personal name.

The names of Chinese artists and authors of Chinese language books and articles are generally given family name first followed by given name, according to Chinese convention, unless otherwise noted. If a Chinese person has a personal style of romanization for his or her name, we follow that convention.

WORKSHOPS AND UNIDENTIFIED ARTISTS

When no maker or workshop is mentioned in a caption, no maker has been identified. The Imperial Workshop (Zaoban chu) under the Imperial Household Department (Neiwu fu) was located in Beijing. Other workshops in other cities also served the Qing court.

ROMANIZATION AND PRONUNCIATION OF CHINESE WORDS

Unless otherwise indicated, all Chinese romanization is given in pinyin, the system used by the US Library of Congress. Terms and place-names appearing in parentheses in the text are Chinese unless otherwise noted. Readers who wish to know the Chinese characters for selected terms and names should refer to the glossary at the back of this book (pp. 240–43).

The pronunciation of many consonants and vowels in pinyin is similar to their English equivalents; however, some common exceptions are

Qing is pronounced like "Ching," with the initial "ch" like that in *cheer* and "ing" like that in *sing*.
X sounds like the "sh" in *she*.
Q sounds like the "ch" in *cheer*.
C sounds like the "ts" in *beets*.
Zh sounds like the "dg" in *judge*.
Ü sounds like German "ü" in *über* or French "u" in *tu*.
Ai sounds like "ie" in *pie*.
Ang sounds like "ong" in *long*.
Ao sounds like "ow" in *how*.
Ei sounds like the "ay" in *say*.
Ou sounds like "oh."
Ua sounds like "wa."
Ue sounds like "weh."
Ui sounds like "way."

PLATE ENTRIES

Plate entries have been written by the following authors:

Huang Ying, Palace Museum—HY
Li Li, Palace Museum—LL
Lin Shu, Palace Museum—LS
Liu Guilin, Palace Museum—LGL
Lu Ying, Palace Museum—LY
Luk Yu-ping, British Museum, London—LYP
Ying-chen Peng, American University, Washington, DC—YCP
Evelyn S. Rawski, University of Pittsburgh—ESR
Jan Stuart, Freer|Sackler—JS
Sun Zhaohua, Palace Museum—SZH
Doris Sung, Peabody Essex Museum—DS
Daisy Yiyou Wang, Peabody Essex Museum—DYW
Wen Jinxiang, Palace Museum—WJX
Xie Li, Palace Museum—XL
Xu Qixian, Palace Museum—XQX
Yang Guopeng, Palace Museum—YGP
Yang Zitong, Palace Museum—YZT
Zhao Yingying, Palace Museum—ZYY

INTRODUCTION

Rediscovering the Empresses of Qing China, 1644–1912

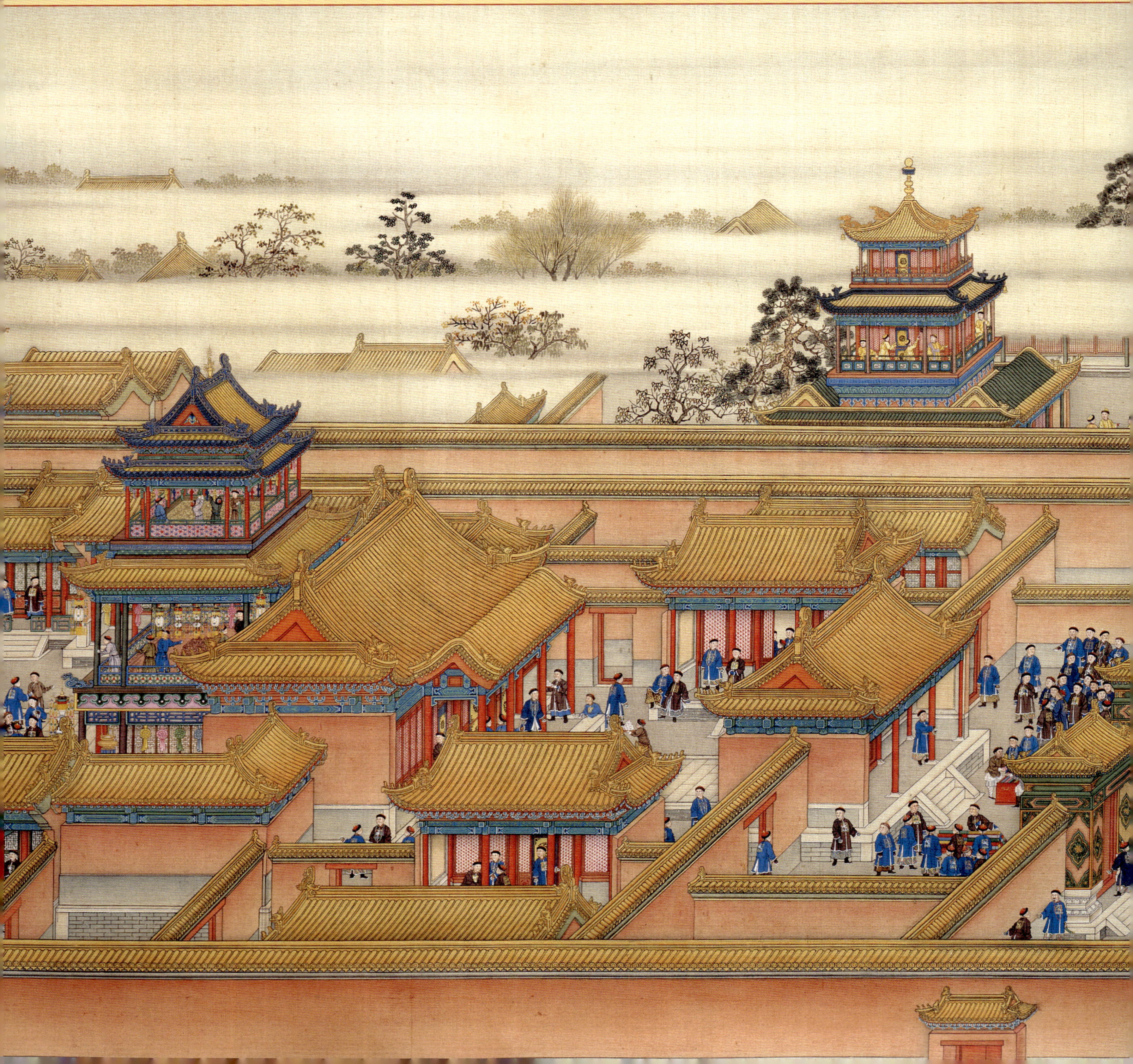

DAISY YIYOU WANG AND JAN STUART

BY TODAY'S STANDARDS, the restrictions imposed on empresses in China's last dynasty are shocking. The more than two dozen empresses and numerous other women of the Qing imperial court were technically "inalienable possessions" of the monarchy and lived within stringent codes that kept them sequestered from public view and curtailed their freedom and opportunities. Yet, if you engage with these palace women on their own terms and within their historical context and don't try to pull them into the present, their experiences prove enlightening as they made meaningful lives for themselves within—and sometimes beyond—the formal strictures of the court. Their stories form the narrative spine of this book and its companion exhibition, *Empresses of China's Forbidden City, 1644–1912*, and, when considered against the backdrop of Qing culture and society, are nothing short of inspirational.

Qing empresses helped shape the long, cosmopolitan history of the dynasty, with strong personalities marking its rise and fall at key moments. Empress Xiaozhuang (1613–1688) escorted her young son, the Shunzhi emperor (r. 1644–61), into Beijing as it became the new dynasty's capital in 1644. Empress Dowager Cixi (1835–1908) assumed unprecedented power when she boldly overturned the long-standing tradition in China that "women shall not rule." Taking direct control of state and international affairs near the end of the dynasty and on the eve of China's transformation into a modern polity, she embodied unprecedented ambition and achievement for an imperial woman. Empress Xiaoding (1868–1913) signed abdication papers on behalf of the child emperor Xuantong (r. 1909–12), officially ending the dynasty in 1912.

The emperor-centric Qing court recorded only skeletal outlines of these women's lives, and not until recently have historians begun to fill in a more complete picture. The premise of this book is that the objects made for, by, and about the empresses—clothing, devotional objects, art, even tableware—offer perhaps the richest means for engaging with these intriguing women and their veiled world. Scrutiny of these objects along with textual evidence found in court archives, inventories, and other historical sources come together to elucidate the largely hidden activities of the empresses. Each of the book's authors focuses on a different facet of their lives, and together the essays and object entries present a picture of Qing imperial women far more nuanced and dynamic than is common. All the authors have been inspired by recent scholarship focused on issues of women and gender in Chinese society, especially that of Ding Yizhuang, Du Fangqin, Mark Elliott, Dorothy Ko, Susan Mann, Keith McMahon, and Evelyn S. Rawski.

The relative paucity of in-depth information about Qing empresses has led us to concentrate on five women for whom the historical and visual records are more complete: Empress Xiaozhuang, Empress Dowager Chongqing (1693–1777),

Empress Xiaoxian (1712–1748), Empress Dowager Cixi, and Empress Dowager Ci'an (1837–1881). Some of the artworks in this exhibition and book are firmly associated with a particular empress, but due to the complex "life history" of some objects—those that have changed hands and locations within the palace—it is not always possible to establish such a direct association between object and empress. Sometimes the textual descriptions found in imperial archives or Palace Museum inventories are too brief to be convincingly matched with a specific object, leaving us uncertain as to who actually used it. Nonetheless, all the artworks in this project help reconstruct the world the empresses inhabited and together offer strong evidence of their general life experiences.

On Becoming an Empress

As Evelyn S. Rawski explains in her opening essay, the Qing dynasty was an explicitly multiethnic and multicultural state founded in 1644 by a small northeast Asian group who came to call themselves Manchus. These conquering rulers adopted the Forbidden City in Beijing as the seat of the Qing government. The Manchu ruling house differed from their populous Han Chinese subjects—and the emperors and empresses of the previous Ming dynasty (1368–1644)—by language, history, and culture. Determined to retain their unique identity, the Qing rulers prohibited the palace elite from marrying members of the subjugated Chinese population. The emperors chose their wives from women born into the hereditary lineage of the conquering elite, a diverse coalition of peoples who had joined the Manchu cause before 1644.

An emperor was simultaneously married to multiple women (called consorts) but had only one empress, or primary wife, at a time. The empress stood at the pinnacle of eight ranks of consorts, each granted its own privileges and prestige. Every three years, as they approached the age of thirteen, daughters of qualified families—mostly Manchus or Mongols—presented themselves as candidates to be chosen as consorts for the emperor and his sons. As Ren Wanping's essay on grand imperial weddings shows, a few entered the imperial household as the empress via marriage that severed the woman's tie with her natal family, signaling her new status as a key member of the imperial family who was loyal to the ruling house. Some were chosen to be the primary wife of a prince and later received the title of empress after her husband was enthroned as emperor. Others were lower-ranking consorts who were promoted to replace a deceased or demoted empress. The title of empress could also be granted posthumously to the mother of an emperor or to the deceased primary wife of the heir to the throne.

A consort's rank determined her stipend, the number of servants attending her, and the amount and sort of food and garments she received. It was possible to advance to a higher rank—just as it was possible to be promoted from a palace maid (who entered the palace through a special draft for servants) to a consort—usually by bearing a son. The Qing court determined heirs based on merit rather than by birth order or the status of the mother, creating a system in which an empress's son was, in theory, no better positioned to become emperor than any other consort's. Thus, fertility was key to female power and influence, resulting in intense competition among mothers vying for their son to be named emperor. Consorts could also be demoted for serious misbehavior or by greatly displeasing the emperor; a consequence of which was loss of privilege in life and near oblivion in the court genealogies. While such a harsh fall was rare among those with the rank of empress, it was not unknown. But just as an empress could almost disappear from history, some had an outsize influence. By nature of their intimate relationship with an emperor—husband, son, or grandson—they had special access to the heart of the court and could indirectly, and occasionally openly, shape the course of events, as when a regent of the Kangxi emperor (r. 1662–1722) was jailed on the advice of his grandmother, Empress Xiaozhuang.

With motherhood inextricably connected to the power of imperial women, empresses' stories inevitably revolve around their place in the imperial family, largely defined by the notion of filial piety, a core Confucian virtue underpinning the stability of Chinese society at large. In it most basic form, filial piety is the respect, devotion, and care that children give their parents and family elders. As it developed in China, it became a defining social structure with strict principles of hierarchy, obligation, and obedience. As nearly all the essays here note, filial behavior played a prominent role in consorts' lives—as a framework for how they were expected to act, and also as a mechanism through which they achieved status, resources, and influence. An emperor's filial devotion was primarily directed toward the memory of his father, the previous emperor, but also to an empress dowager, often his birth mother but sometimes his father's widowed primary wife (and thus the effective mother of the entire imperial family). Indeed, the empress dowager was second only to the emperor himself in the hierarchy of the imperial family, presiding above all eight ranks of consorts, including the empress. The empress dowager's eminence was reflected in the emperor's willingness to ritually bow to her (but not to other men), reflecting the complexities of gender and status in Qing times. Many of the artworks in this publication embody an emperor's devotion to an imperial matriarch, either as elaborate gifts given on occasions such as birthdays or as paintings depicting such events. In these objects the emperor's respect for his mother or grandmother was made manifest and served as a model to be emulated by his subjects. Paintings of this nature often portray a happy, harmonious imperial family and suggested that a similar condition, extending from the Qing rulers' beneficent example, could be achieved throughout the empire.

While the Qing court was strictly patriarchal and hierarchical, there was room for strong empresses. Evelyn S. Rawski draws attention to the persistence of Manchu customs proscribing the binding of feet and encouraging women to learn to ride and hunt. In general, Manchu women enjoyed more freedom and rights than their Han Chinese counterparts. Qing empresses clearly were not empowered in a contemporary sense, but, given the Manchu emphasis on the importance of a mother's descent line, they were clearly valued as more than reproductive vessels who served merely to continue the imperial bloodline: their own contribution to that bloodline mattered. And the court formally recognized their indispensability as mother of the empire and a role model for all women, with some empresses dowager called Sage Mother (*shengmu*). Beginning with Xiaoxian, Qing empresses presided over the state ritual promoting silk production. The ceremony symbolized women's role in the making of cloth and clothing, one that complemented men's role in rice cultivation, and showed that women played a vital part in the economic health of the state.

The degree of influence an empress might exert was keyed to her talents and character as well as opportunity. Research shows that imperial females were praised for their talents and skills (*cai*) and offered as exemplars. In Qing times, the well-read Empress Xiaozhuang's mentorship of the Shunzhi and Kangxi emperors followed a paradigm of erudite court women, such as Empress Deng (81–121 CE; see pl. 58).[1] Similarly, the Qianlong emperor praised his wife Empress Xiaoxian as an adept manager of family affairs, noting her thoughtfulness, diligence, and moral strength as a source of harmony at the inner court.[2] Yet just as notably, he praised her for brewing tea and sewing for him. So while the strongest empresses deployed sophisticated interpersonal and managerial skills to navigate the intricate web of court relations, they were always expected to heed the importance of pleasing and remaining obedient to the emperor.

Art, Architecture, and Lifestyle

Many Qing empresses were enthusiastic consumers and learned appreciators of art, with Empress Dowager Cixi at the end of the dynasty being an especially active patron and amateur painter and calligrapher herself. Given their place at the center of the Qing court and culture, imperial women were often depicted in court arts. These works provide a key that unlocks the empresses' world behind the walls of the Forbidden City. Recent research has uncovered a range of objects newly identified as belonging to this world, including two little-known portraits in the Peabody Essex Museum's collection and a sketch of Empress Dowager Cixi in the Palace Museum Library, which are featured in Daisy Yiyou Wang's essay examining posthumous portraits of empresses for ancestral rites. By comparing empress portraits with those of emperors, she sheds new light on the iconography, production, and display of empress portraits as well as women's roles in the imperial family.

Our object-based approach also reveals that the artworks and furnishings in the empresses' and other top consorts' residences were of the same superlative quality as the emperors'. Many objects in women's quarters cannily interweave a range of artistic styles and traditions, demonstrating that Qing empresses—like their male counterparts—cultivated cosmopolitan tastes. Moreover, the art they enjoyed carried the same intent as the emperor's possessions: a desire to demonstrate the glory and legitimacy of Qing rule through its inclusive embrace of multiple cultures and ethnicities. References to Manchu and Tibetan heritage, Chinese culture from antiquity onward, and Japanese and European influences enliven the art in these pages. In her essay and entries, Jan Stuart demonstrates that some artifacts previously considered "male," such as an elaborate cabinet for displaying art (pl. 24), actually belonged to empresses, defying the androcentric tendency that envisions the best court art being exclusively for men. Court residences were decorated as "gender neutral" spaces suggestive of respect for the empresses, and the discovery of important art in the women's quarters counters the theoretical stance that those genre paintings that depict a consort viewing antiquities were meant to imply an "objectification" of palace women as possessions of the emperor the same way the bronzes and porcelains were his. In fact, the environments of high-ranking consorts were filled with beautiful things. At the same time, art objects in women's quarters carried many more messages relating to fertility than those in men's, reminding us of an essential and inescapable facet of their lives in the desire to bear a son.

In writing about the Palace of Longevity and Health (Shoukang gong), the residence of Empress Dowager Chongqing, Lin Shu shares discoveries gained during a seven-year project dedicated to reconstructing the palace, down to its interior furnishings. She details the construction of the palace and how it was used, providing concrete evidence of the revered position of Chongqing and how her son, the Qianlong emperor, honored her in the most extreme examples of filial piety witnessed during the Qing.

Religion and Court Politics

Recent research has revealed the degree to which Qing empresses shaped the pluralistic spiritual traditions of the Qing court. In her essay Luk Yu-ping traces the empresses' influence in this sphere, beginning with Empress Xiaozhuang, the first major Qing imperial figure to patronize Tibetan Buddhism. She created several worship sites at her residence, establishing a powerful precedent followed by later emperors and empresses, yet she is strangely absent from most discussions of Tibetan Buddhism at the court, perhaps having fallen prey to skepticism that a woman could play such a critical role in shaping court religion. Her promotion of the faith helped the Manchu rulers to claim political and spiritual legitimacy over the Mongols, believers in Tibetan Buddhism and the Manchu's greatest contenders early in the dynasty.

Luk also highlights the manner in which empresses negotiated the boundaries between sacred and secular power in the imperium. For example, empresses adopted dimensions of multiple faiths in order to further the court's political agenda. Empress Dowager Cixi often dressed as Guanyin, the Buddhist deity associated with benevolence and worshipped by the Chinese population. With this act, she continued a practice of earlier Qing emperors in adopting a Buddhist persona to claim legitimacy and project authority to a multicultural populace—one more example of how she saw herself on a par with the dynasty's male rulers.

As the most powerful empress in the history of China, Cixi challenged the gender rules and political norms that were designed to distance imperial women from political power at the Qing court. Under her leadership, the Qing government initiated economic and diplomatic policies that, while controversial, nonetheless presaged China's transformation into a modern nation soon after her death in 1908. In charting the ways empresses accrued and deployed their power, Ying-chen Peng compares and contrasts Empress Xiaozhuang at the beginning of the dynasty with Cixi and her co-regent, Empress Dowager Ci'an, at its end. Peng vividly illustrates the exceptional intelligence and dexterity of Cixi in handling affairs of state, becoming in the process a new—and often unjustly vilified—female leader on the threshold of modern China.

Conclusion

The study of women in history is exciting, timely, and necessary. From the outset of this project, our goal has been to reclaim the significance of Qing empresses and to convey something of the texture of their lives. Existing at the intersection of family and state, empresses occupied roles at court that offer a unique lens on the fundamental social structures and moral values that made the Qing dynasty the strong and expansive empire it indisputably was. By focusing on the material and spiritual world of these women, this collective study begins to fill in details absent from previous accounts of women in Chinese history; we also believe it opens a door to future research. To the extent that the empresses' experience of the expectations and constraints of gender finds echo in our own world, we hope this book prompts broader reflection on the position of women in society and fosters a sense of commonality and connection across time and cultures.

Notes

1 Yang Zhen 1994, 14.

2 ZGDYLSDAG 2002, 7:182.

Key Empresses in the Qing Imperial Family

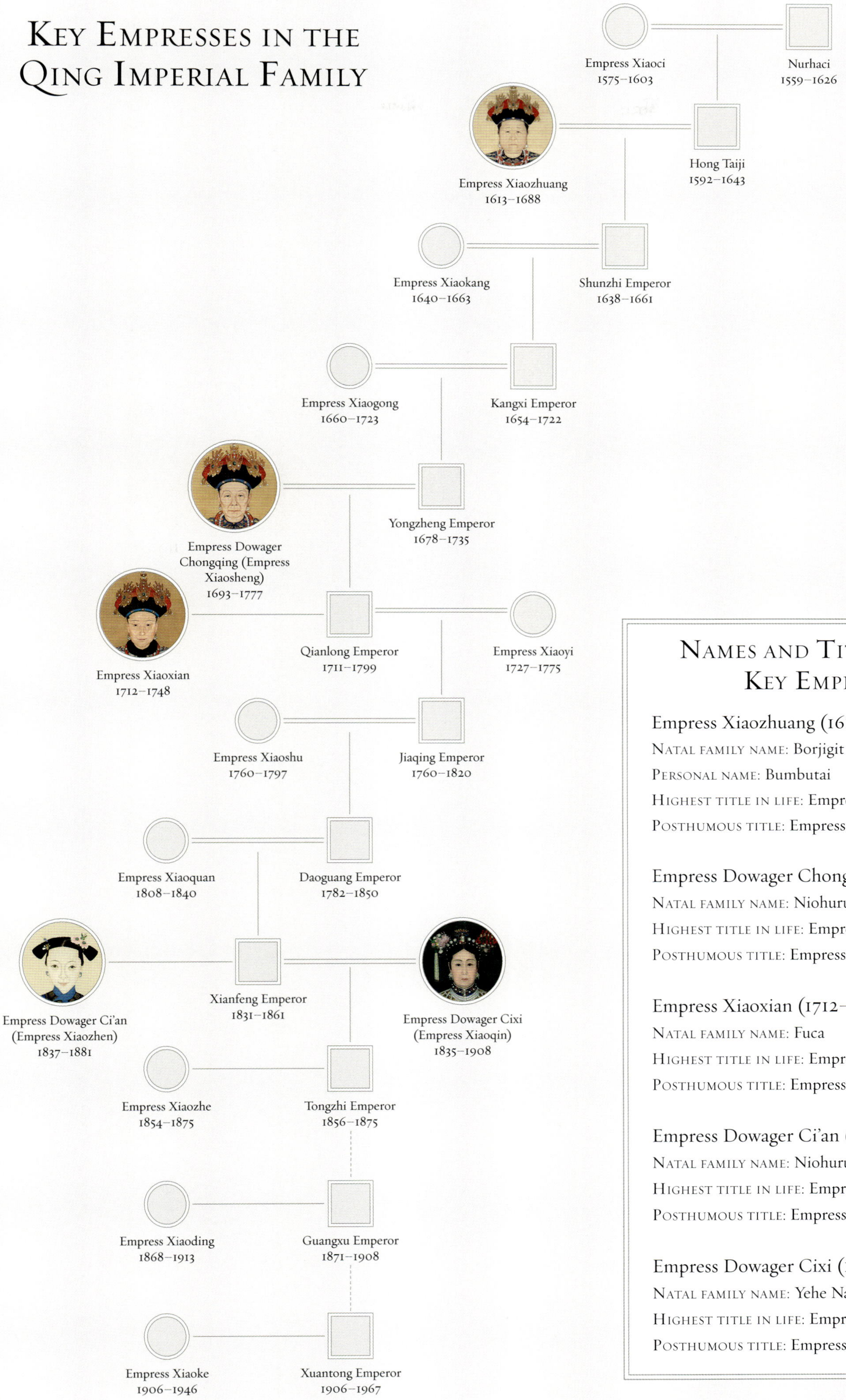

Names and Titles of the Key Empresses

Empress Xiaozhuang (1613–1688)

Natal family name: Borjigit
Personal name: Bumbutai
Highest title in life: Empress Dowager Zhaosheng
Posthumous title: Empress Xiaozhuang Wen

Empress Dowager Chongqing (1693–1777)

Natal family name: Niohuru
Highest title in life: Empress Dowager Chongqing
Posthumous title: Empress Xiaosheng Xian

Empress Xiaoxian (1712–1748)

Natal family name: Fuca
Highest title in life: Empress
Posthumous title: Empress Xiaoxian Chun

Empress Dowager Ci'an (1837–1881)

Natal family name: Niohuru
Highest title in life: Empress Dowager Ci'an
Posthumous title: Empress Xiaozhen Xian

Empress Dowager Cixi (1835–1908)

Natal family name: Yehe Nara
Highest title in life: Empress Dowager Cixi
Posthumous title: Empress Xiaoqin Xian

TIMELINE OF QING EMPRESSES IN WORLD CONTEXT

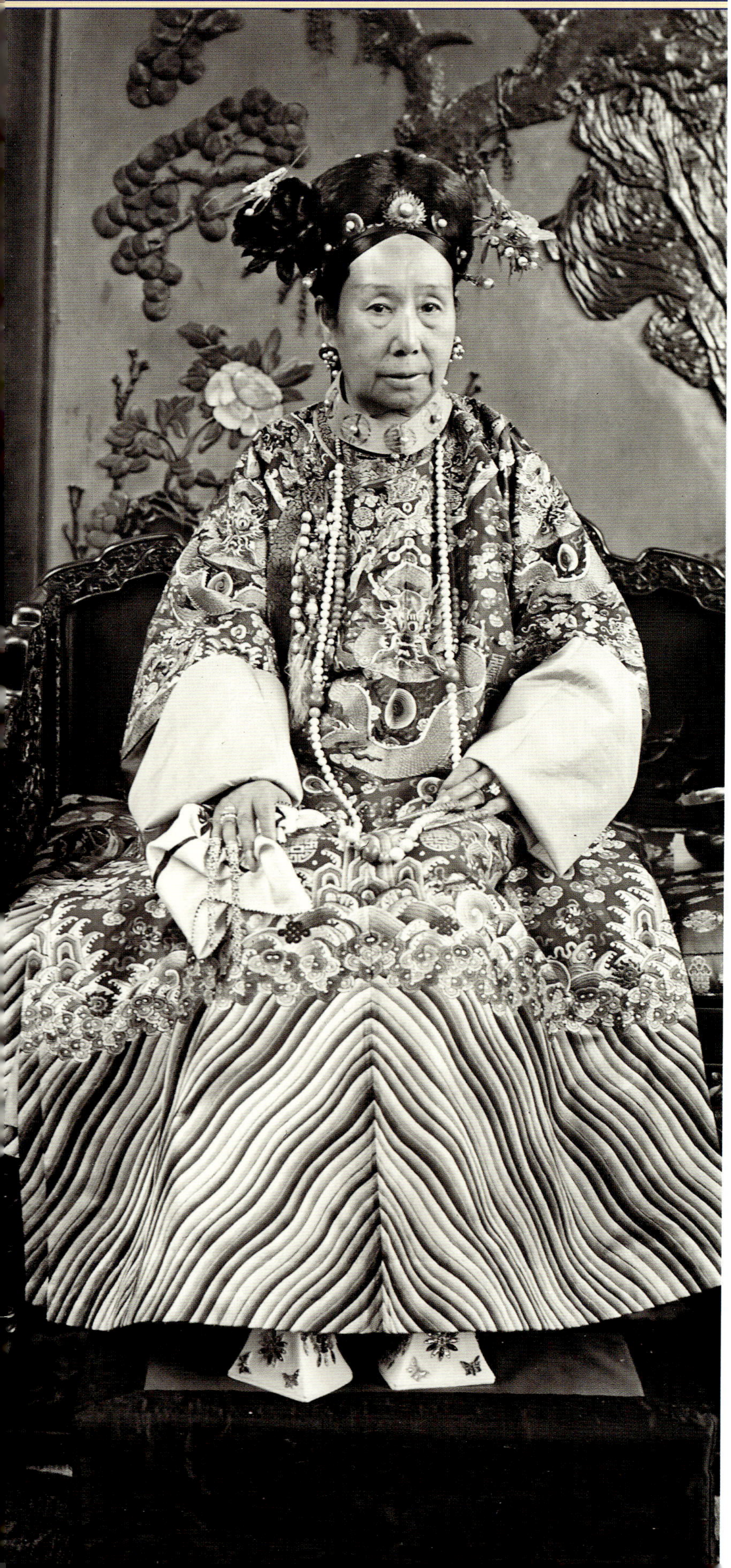

Significant moments in Chinese history, including those most relevant to the empresses featured in this book, are featured here along with major events in world history, especially those involving women of note.

1616
The chieftain Nurhaci (r. 1616–26) unites various Jurchen tribes and proclaims his rulership of the Later Jin dynasty.

1625
Bumbutai (1613–1688), a descendant of a Mongol royal line, marries Hong Taiji (r. 1626–43), Nurhaci's son and successor. She subsequently is named **Empress Xiaozhuang**.

1636
Hong Taiji adopts "Manchu" as a new name for his people and changes the name of the Jin to the Qing dynasty.

1644
The Manchus conquer Beijing and formally establish their seat of government in the Forbidden City.

Empress Xiaozhuang is promoted to empress dowager after her five-year-old son is enthroned as the Shunzhi emperor (r. 1644–61).

1600s

1600
Elizabeth I (r. 1558–1603) grants a charter to the British East India Company expanding trade with the East Indies, the Indian subcontinent, and China.

1618–48
Religious conflict between Catholics and Protestants convulses Europe in the Thirty Years War.

1644
Christina (1626–1689) becomes queen of Sweden and reigns until her abdication in 1654.

1653
Empress Xiaozhuang takes up residence at the Palace of Compassion and Tranquility (Cining gong), later using it as a site for Buddhist worship.

1661
The Shunzhi emperor dies and is succeeded by his son, known as the Kangxi emperor (r. 1662–1722).

1661
Empress Xiaozhuang receives the title of grand empress dowager and serves as her grandson's adviser and mentor until her death in 1688.

1704
Lady Niohuru (1693–1777), a member of a prominent Manchu family, enters the household of the future Yongzheng emperor (r. 1723–35) as a low-ranking consort. She is later known as **Empress Dowager Chongqing** and Empress Xiaosheng.

1716
Italian Jesuit missionary Giuseppe Castiglione (Lang Shining; 1688–1766) becomes the first European court painter in China.

1722
The Yongzheng emperor ascends the throne after the death of his father.

1727
The future Qianlong emperor (r. 1736–95) marries Lady Fuca (1712–1748), who becomes his primary consort and is later named **Empress Xiaoxian**.

1735
The Qianlong emperor begins his reign following the death of his father.

1736
Qianlong grants his mother, Chongqing, the title of empress dowager. She enters her newly built residence, the Palace of Longevity and Health (Shoukang gong).

1744
Empress Xiaoxian presides over the Qing dynasty's first state sericulture ceremony at the Altar of the Goddess of Silkworms in Beijing.

1748
Empress Xiaoxian dies, plunging the Qianlong emperor into grief.

1750
The Qianlong emperor commissions the Garden of Clear Ripples (Qingyi yuan) for Empress Dowager Chongqing's sixtieth birthday.

1765
The Garden of the Palace of Compassion and Tranquility is expanded for Empress Dowager Chongqing as a space for her Buddhist devotional activities.

1700s

1646
Queen Nzinga (r. 1624–63) of the Kingdoms of Ndongo and Matamba (present-day Angola) battles the Portuguese in an effort to stave off colonization and the slave trade in southwest Africa.

1689
Queen Mary II (r. 1689–94) assumes the throne as joint sovereign of England, Scotland, and Ireland with her husband, King William III (r. 1689–1702).

1702
Anne (r. 1702–14) becomes queen of England, Scotland, and Ireland following the death of her brother-in-law, William III. In 1707, she becomes ruler of the United Kingdom of Great Britain following the joining of England (including Wales) and Scotland.

1740
Maria Theresa (r. 1740–80) begins her rule of the Hapsburg empire.

1762
Empress Catherine II (r. 1762–96) ascends the throne of Russia.

1776
Abigail Adams (1744–1818) urges her husband, John Adams (1735–1826), to include rights for women in laws being drafted for what will soon be proclaimed the United States of America. No such rights are enumerated in the Declaration of Independence, issued on July 4.

1780s
Rani Velu Nachiyar (r. about 1780–90), queen of Sivaganga estate (present-day Tamil Nadu, India), is the first queen to fight against British colonial rule in India.

1793
The Qianlong emperor receives diplomats from the court of King George III (r. 1760–1820), the first such mission from Great Britain.

1795
The Qianlong emperor retires, and his son ascends the throne, taking the reign name of the Jiaqing emperor (r. 1796–1820).

1796
Lady Niohuru marries the future Daoguang emperor (r. 1821–50). She dies in 1808, receives the posthumous title of empress when Daoguang ascends the throne, and is later known as **Empress Xiaomu**.

1820
The Jiaqing emperor dies and is succeeded by his son, the Daoguang emperor.

1839–42
Conflicts initiated by Great Britain over trade rights in China erupt into military actions known as the First Opium War. Hostilities end with the Treaty of Nanjing, in which the Qing agree to open five ports for trade, thus weakening control over its social, economic, and foreign policies.

1850
The Xianfeng emperor (r. 1851–61) succeeds his father, the Daoguang emperor, after the latter dies.

1851–64
Rebels occupy much of the Yangzi River heartland with the goal of overthrowing Manchu rule. Known as the Taiping Rebellion, the civil war costs more than 20 million lives.

1852
Lady Niohuru (1837–1881) becomes the empress of the Xianfeng emperor. She later is named **Empress Dowager Ci'an**.

1852
Lady Yehe Nara (1835–1908) enters the household of the Xianfeng emperor as a sixth-rank consort. After giving birth to a son in 1856 she is promoted to the fourth rank. She is later named **Empress Dowager Cixi**.

1856–60
The Second Opium War breaks out as Western powers seek to expand trade in China, including the right to deal in opium. The war weakens Qing imperial rule.

1860
French and British troops invade Beijing, looting the Garden of Perfect Brightness (Yuanming yuan) and the Garden of Clear Ripples. Empresses Dowager Ci'an and Cixi flee to Rehe (present-day Chengde) with the Xianfeng emperor.

1861
The Xianfeng emperor dies. Having each been granted the title of empress dowager, Ci'an and Cixi launch a coup d'état with the help of Xianfeng's brother, Prince Gong (1833–1898). The resulting co-regency of Ci'an and Cixi lasts until 1875, a period of relative stability.

1862
Empress Dowager Cixi's five-year-old son adopts his reign name as the Tongzhi emperor (r. 1862–74).

1700s

1800s

1784
The *Empress of China* departs New York and becomes the first American ship to sail to China, opening trade between China and the United States.

1793
The French Revolution overthrows the monarchy, resulting in the execution of King Louis XVI (r. 1774–92) and Queen Marie Antoinette (1755–1793), daughter of Maria Theresa of the Hapsburg empire.

1804
Napoléon Bonaparte (1769–1821) crowns himself emperor of France and his wife, Josephine (1763–1814), empress.

1837
Coronation of Queen Victoria of the United Kingdom (r. 1837–1901).

1861–65
Approximately 750,000 people die in the US Civil War.

1867
Queen Min (Empress Myeongseong, 1851–1895) becomes consort of King Gojong (r. 1863–97) of the Joseon dynasty of Korea. The couple pursue progressive policies modernizing and opening Korea to the West.

1868
Japan's Meiji emperor (r. 1867–1912) initiates steps to modernize and Westernize his nation. They provide models for reforms later implemented in China.

1875
The Tongzhi emperor dies; Empress Dowager Cixi chooses her four-year-old nephew to become the Guangxu emperor (r. 1875–1908).

1881
Empress Dowager Ci'an dies. Empress Dowager Cixi continues as sole regent to the Guangxu emperor.

1884
Empress Dowager Cixi retires from the regency and resides in the lavishly refurbished Palace of Gathered Elegance (Chuxiu gong).

1886
Empress Dowager Cixi orders the restoration of the Garden of Clear Ripples, damaged by the French and English troops in 1860, using funds originally designated for the Qing navy.

1889
The grand imperial wedding of the Guangxu emperor and **Empress Xiaoding**, Empress Dowager Cixi's niece, takes place.

1894
Sino-Japanese War breaks out.

1898
Empress Dowager Cixi halts the Guangxu emperor's modernizing "Hundred Days Reform," puts him under house arrest, and resumes her regency and direct control of the court.

1900–01
Fearing foreign influence, Empress Dowager Cixi backs the forces known as the Boxers who lay siege to Western diplomatic quarters in Beijing. In the ensuing conflict, known as the Boxer Uprising, Cixi and the Qing court flee Beijing to Xi'an as an eight-nation military force invades and loots Beijing. The Xinchou Treaty ending the fighting requires China to pay reparations.

1902
Empress Dowager Cixi and the court return to Beijing. She implements a series of "New Policies" that institute modernizing law, government, education, and social reforms.

1904
Empress Dowager Cixi's portrait, by the American painter Katharine A. Carl (1865–1938), is shown at the St. Louis Exposition.

1905–06
After failing to reach an agreement on an immigration treaty in 1904, China boycotts US products and businesses.

1908
The Guangxu emperor and Empress Dowager Cixi die. Cixi's infant grandnephew—known as Puyi—is chosen to reign as the Xuantong emperor (r. 1909–12). Guangxu's wife, Empress Xiaoding, becomes **Empress Dowager Longyu**.

1911
The Xinhai Revolution overthrows the Qing dynasty and ends imperial rule in China. The Republic of China is established a year later.

1912
Empress Dowager Longyu signs abdication papers on behalf of the five-year-old Xuantong emperor, who continues to live in the Forbidden City until 1924.

1922
The Xuantong emperor marries **Empress Xiaoke**.

1925
The Forbidden City opens to the public as the Palace Museum.

1900s

1891
Liliuokalani becomes the first queen and last monarch of Hawaii, reigning until 1895, when she is forced to abdicate the throne prior to the US annexation of the Hawaiian Islands.

1899
The US government pursues an "Open Door" policy, promoting international trade and commerce in China.

1905
Alice Roosevelt (1884–1980), daughter of President Theodore Roosevelt, visits the Forbidden City, where she meets Empress Dowager Cixi.

1914–18
World War I starts in Europe and evolves into a global conflict.

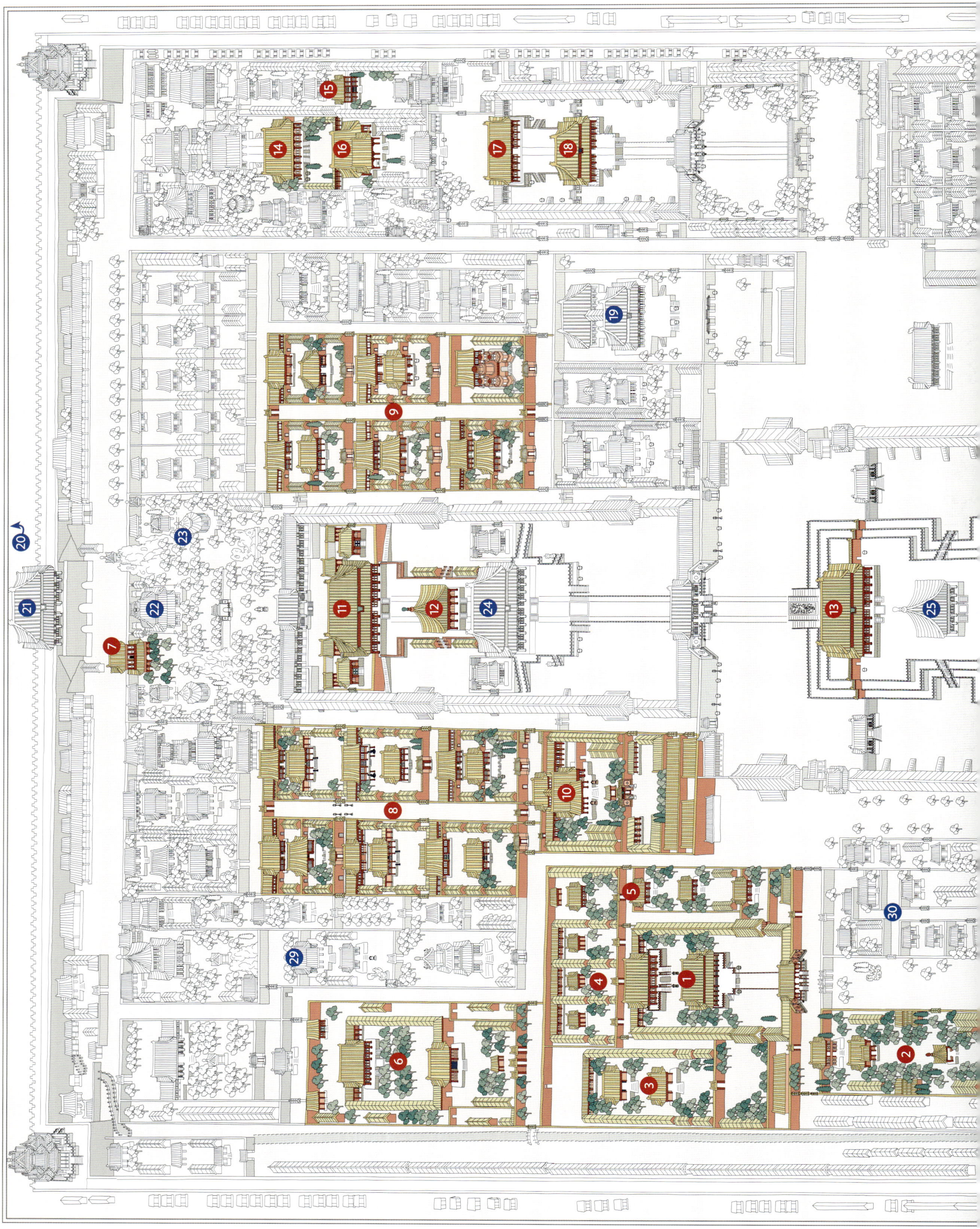
1
2
3
4
5
6
7
8
9
10
11
12
13
14
15
16
17
18
19
20
21
22
23
24
25
29
30

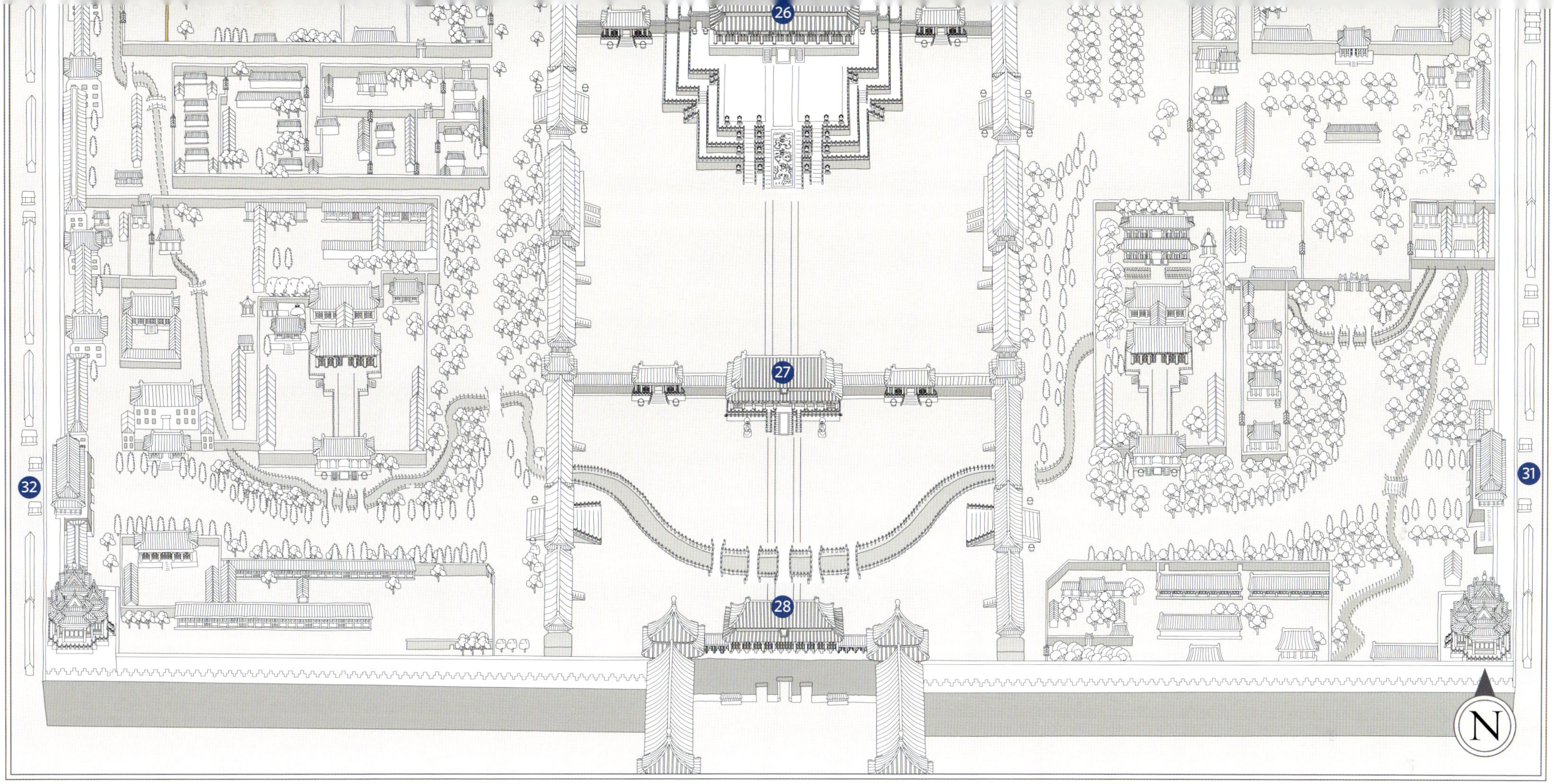

Map of the Forbidden City

Main Living Quarters of and Sites Visited by Imperial Women

1 Palace of Compassion and Tranquility 慈寧宮
2 Garden of the Palace of Compassion and Tranquility 慈寧宮花園
3 Palace of Longevity and Health 壽康宮
4 The Three Rear Palaces 後三宮
5 The Three Lodges 三所
6 Palace of Longevity and Peace 壽安宮
7 Pavilion of Prolonged Splendor 延暉閣
8 Area of the West Six Palaces 西六宮
Palace of Shared Fortune 咸福宮
Palace of Eternal Spring 長春宮
Hall of Supreme Principle 太極殿
Palace of Gathered Elegance 儲秀宮
Palace of Earthly Honor 翊坤宮
Palace of Eternal Longevity 永壽宮
Bower of Enchanting Scenery 麗景軒
9 Area of the East Six Palaces 東六宮
Palace of Accumulated Purity 鍾粹宮
Palace of Heavenly Favor 承乾宮
Palace of Great Benevolence 景仁宮
Palace of Great Brilliance 景陽宮
Palace of Eternal Harmony 永和宮
Palace of Prolonged Happiness 延禧宮
10 Hall of Mental Cultivation 養心殿
Hall of Harmony and Joy 燕禧堂
East Warm Chamber 養心殿東暖閣
11 Palace of Earthly Tranquility 坤寧宮
12 Hall of Harmonious Union 交泰殿
13 Hall of Preserved Harmony 保和殿
14 Hall of Happiness and Longevity 樂壽堂
15 Tower for Viewing Opera 閱是樓
16 Hall of Spiritual Cultivation 養性殿
17 Palace of Tranquility and Longevity 寧壽宮
18 Hall of Imperial Supremacy 皇極殿

Additional Sites

19 Hall of the Ancestors 奉先殿
20 Prospect Hill 景山
21 Gate of Divine Prowess 神武門
22 Hall of Imperial Peace 欽安殿
23 Imperial Garden 御花園
24 Hall of Heavenly Purity 乾清宮
25 Hall of Central Harmony 中和殿
26 Hall of Supreme Harmony 太和殿
27 Gate of Supreme Harmony 太和門
28 Meridian Gate 午門
29 Hall of Central Uprightness 中正殿
30 Imperial Workshop 造辦處
31 East Gate of Glory 東華門
32 West Gate of Glory 西華門

Based on illustration by Chiu Kwong-chiu, Design and Cultural Studies Workshop, Hong Kong

ONE

Qing Empresses and Their Place in History

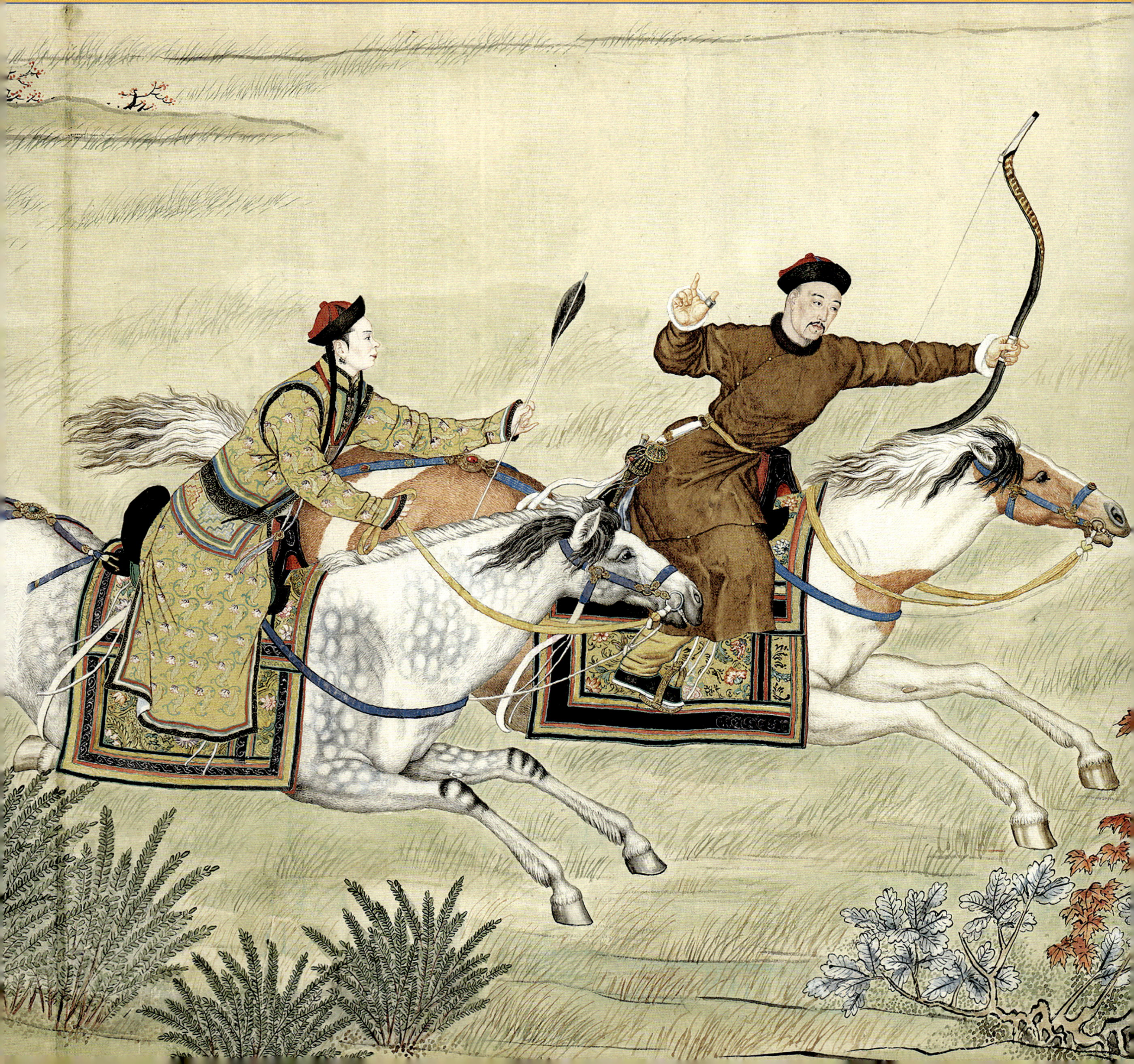

EVELYN S. RAWSKI

THE QING DYNASTY (1644–1912) was the last regime organized along traditional dynastic lines to rule China before it became a modern nation-state. Forced by foreign military powers to sign the "unequal treaties" during the mid-nineteenth and early twentieth centuries, the Qing was repudiated by Chinese nationalist leaders in the Revolution of 1911. An interval of civil war and foreign invasion followed before the country reemerged as a unified nation in 1949, when the Chinese Communist Party established the People's Republic of China.

The Legacy of China's Last Dynasty

China today, a prosperous global power, seems a world apart from that of emperors and empresses, but the Qing legacy continues to affect the behavior of leaders and ordinary Chinese in complex ways—including the treatment of women. The Qing bequeathed contemporary China its current borders. The territory of the Ming empire (1368–1644), primarily inhabited by Chinese-speaking subjects, was only part of the Qing realm; the provinces of Liaoning, Jilin, Heilongjiang, Tibet, and Xinjiang are currently part of the People's Republic of China because of Qing conquests. The Qing empire was indeed bigger than China's current borders, as it included what is now the independent state of Mongolia (fig. 1).

Modern Chinese governments have confronted another consequence of the Qing imperium: ruling over a diverse multiethnic population. The Qing emperors were Jurchen from Jianzhou, a northeast Asian people with a history, language, culture, and identity that had evolved outside the Great Wall, which separated them from the Chinese-speaking people who are today designated as Han Chinese.[1] In the late sixteenth and early seventeenth centuries, Nurhaci (r. 1616–26), a petty chieftain, and his son Hong Taiji (r. 1626–43) united the loosely organized Jurchen tribes in the northeastern provinces to create the Later Jin state.[2] They named their lineage "Aisin Gioro" (literally, the clan of "gold"—*jin*) to reinforce their claim to have descended from the rulers of the Jurchen Jin dynasty that had ruled parts of north China from 1115 to 1260. Nurhaci, his sons, and his brothers formed alliances with Mongol tribes and Han Chinese transfrontiersmen (long-time residents of the northeast), organizing their followers into disciplined military units called "banners" to fight their foes. The banners were marshaled for the registration, conscription, taxation, and mobilization of the tribes and peoples who enlisted in the Jurchen cause before 1644, when banner troops moved into China proper.[3] In 1636 Hong Taiji ordered that the Jurchen would henceforth be called "Manchu." With a population that was minuscule compared to that of the Ming, the Manchus were successful in binding warriors from a variety of cultural backgrounds to their cause. The eight banners formed in 1616 eventually expanded by 1642 to include Manchu, Mongol, and Han units in a total of twenty-four banners. These forces were key to the Qing conquest of Ming China.[4]

FIGURE 1
The Qing empire around 1820.
Adapted from Rawski 1998, xiii.

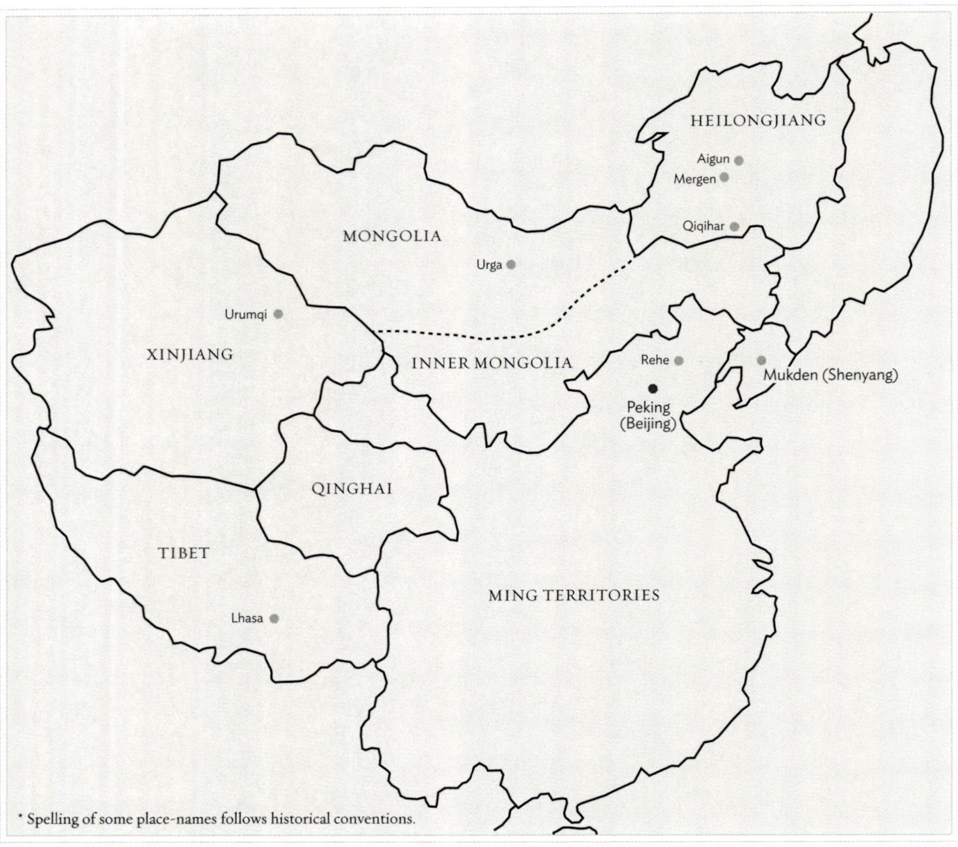

FIGURE 2
Daughters of Yellow Bannermen present themselves for recruitment as imperial consorts in front of the Pavilion of Prolonged Splendor (Yanhui ge) in the Forbidden City; younger girls are also in attendance. Probably Xuantong period, silver gelatin print.

Centuries of economic and cultural contact with China gave the ancestors of the Qing rulers a keen appreciation of Chinese culture but also a determination to preserve their own identity. The idea that the Qing ruling house strived to perpetuate a self-identity that distinguished it from the majority of its subjects is now widely accepted. Hong Taiji blamed the decline of earlier conquest dynasties in China on their sinicization, or assimilation into the Han majority, and he exhorted his descendants not to forget their origins.[5] In the seventeenth and eighteenth centuries Qing rulers followed his lead and issued stern injunctions on retaining Manchu dress at court, reminded their followers to perpetuate the martial virtues of their forebears, and attempted to enforce Manchu language competency among imperial kinsmen.

Although the Qing dynasty officially began in 1644, the military conquest of the Ming was not completed until 1683. The Qing also embarked on military actions against potential challengers to the north. The most weighty and sustained campaign, against the Zunghar leader Galdan (1644–1697), began in the 1690s and culminated in 1759 with the consolidation of Qing control of the region known today as Xinjiang. In the process of subjugating the Zunghars, the court also invaded Lhasa and established a Qing military presence in the Tibetan capital. By 1760 the Qing empire had expanded to incorporate significant parts of Inner Asia, a region inhabited by people whose languages and cultures were not Han Chinese. The Qianlong emperor (r. 1736–95) saw himself as the ruler of the five peoples—Manchus, Mongols, Chinese, Tibetans, and Uyghurs—and he articulated a policy designed to accommodate the religions, cultural traditions, and histories of his diverse subjects.[6] This explicit embrace of China as a multiethnic state was a Qing legacy that appeared in the first constitution devised by the Republic of China in 1912 and in all subsequent Chinese constitutions. Understanding how its non-Han origins affected Qing rule is an important first step in understanding the social contours of contemporary China.

Ethnicity and Imperial Women

This study of Qing empresses begins with their northeastern origins. At that place and time it was customary for wealthy male commoners and rulers to have multiple spouses.[7] Nurhaci and Hong Taiji, the first two leaders of the Aisin Gioro lineage, followed the pattern of earlier conquest dynasties in China in using their marriages to cement political alliances.[8] For example, fourteen of Nurhaci's sixteen wives were sisters and daughters of prominent Jurchen chieftains, marking his successful subjugation of the northeast tribes, and the other two were Mongols.[9] Six of Hong Taiji's fifteen wives were Jurchen, while seven were Mongol, reflecting the chieftain's focus on bringing those tribes into alliance with the Manchus.[10] In 1636 Hong Taiji declared the establishment of

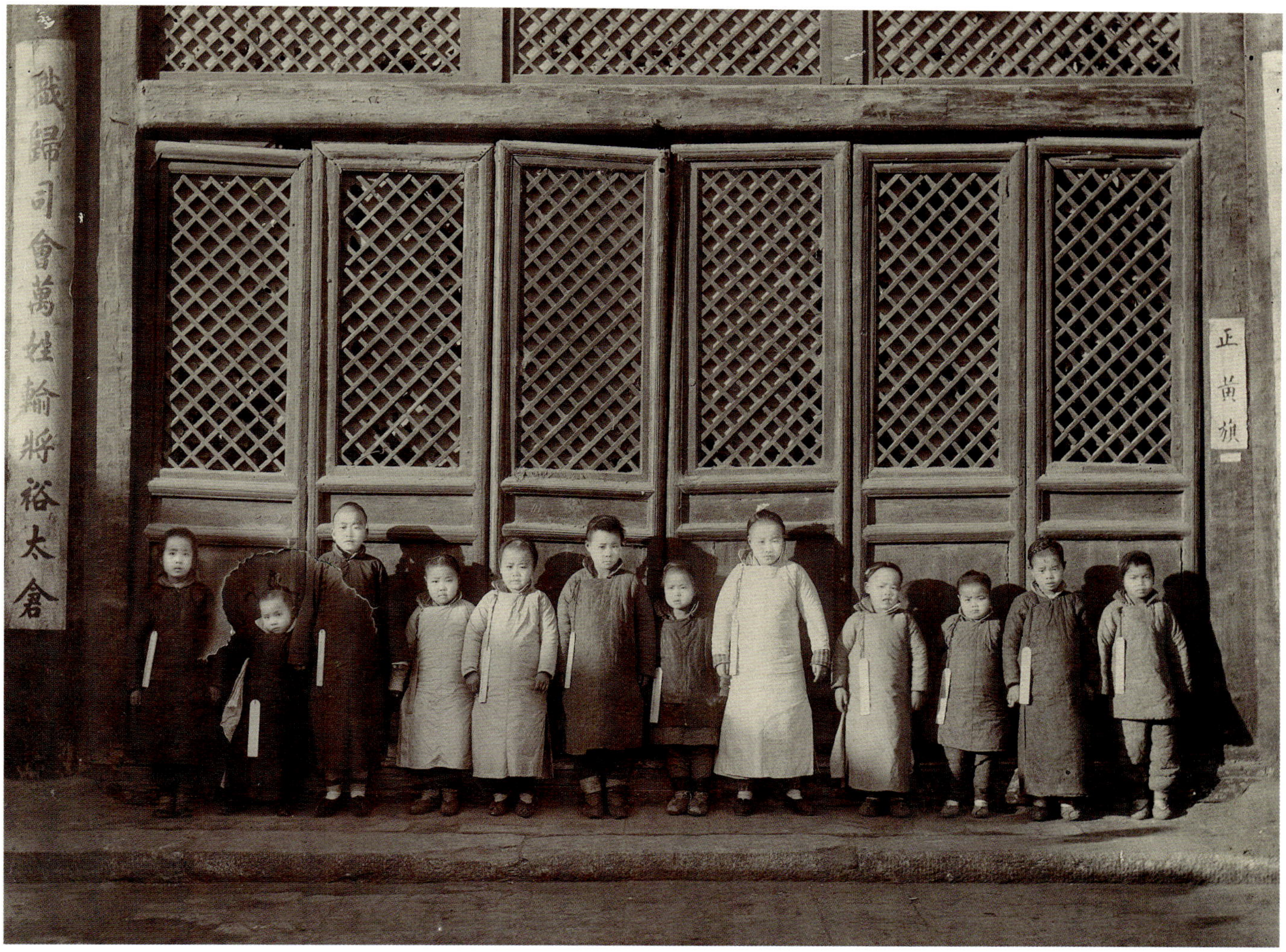

the Qing dynasty and began his formal challenge to Ming rule, which culminated in its conquest.

After the installation of the Shunzhi emperor (r. 1644–61) on the throne in Beijing in 1644, the fluidity that had marked the organization of the banners began to tighten. The most important dividing line in Qing society was that separating the conquerors and their allies—we call them the "conquest elite"—from the subjugated population, most of whom were descended from subjects of the Ming dynasty. The term "Han" was a Qing designation for former subjects of the Ming, differentiating them from the Chinese transfrontiersmen who had come over to the Manchu side before 1644. Members of this latter group were enrolled in martial banners (*Hanjun*) and were known as bannermen.[11] In the Qing period, their lives were governed by Manchu regulations that applied to all bannermen, while Han Chinese were governed by laws based on Ming precedent.

Following an imperial edict in 1655, bannermen (including emperors) were prohibited from marrying Han Chinese women.[12] In reality, the ban on intermarriage was enforced for women but not men, many of whom took Han Chinese women as secondary wives.[13] After 1653 brides for the imperial family were selected from banner officials' daughters who had attained the age of twelve or thirteen (fig. 2).[14] These girls were required to present themselves at the palace in Beijing before they could be betrothed to others; in short, the palace had first pick. At this triennial draft of "beautiful women" (*xiunü*), some girls were immediately chosen to be a primary wife or a lower-ranking consort for imperial sons or the emperor himself. Others were appointed to serve a five-year term as ladies-in-waiting, in the course of which those who caught the emperor's eye might be promoted into the harem (others served their term and left the palace service). A painting of Yinzhen, the future Yongzheng emperor (r. 1723–35), shows him with consorts who entered his household through these avenues (fig. 3). Another draft, held every year, picked palace maids from the daughters of officials in the Imperial Household Department (Neiwu fu), the agency that managed palace affairs.[15] These maids might be promoted into the harem as well; 16 percent of the imperial consorts of the ten Qing emperors were originally palace maids.[16]

Since empresses and other consorts were born into the conquest elite, these palace women were distinguished from Han Chinese commoners by their distinctive dress

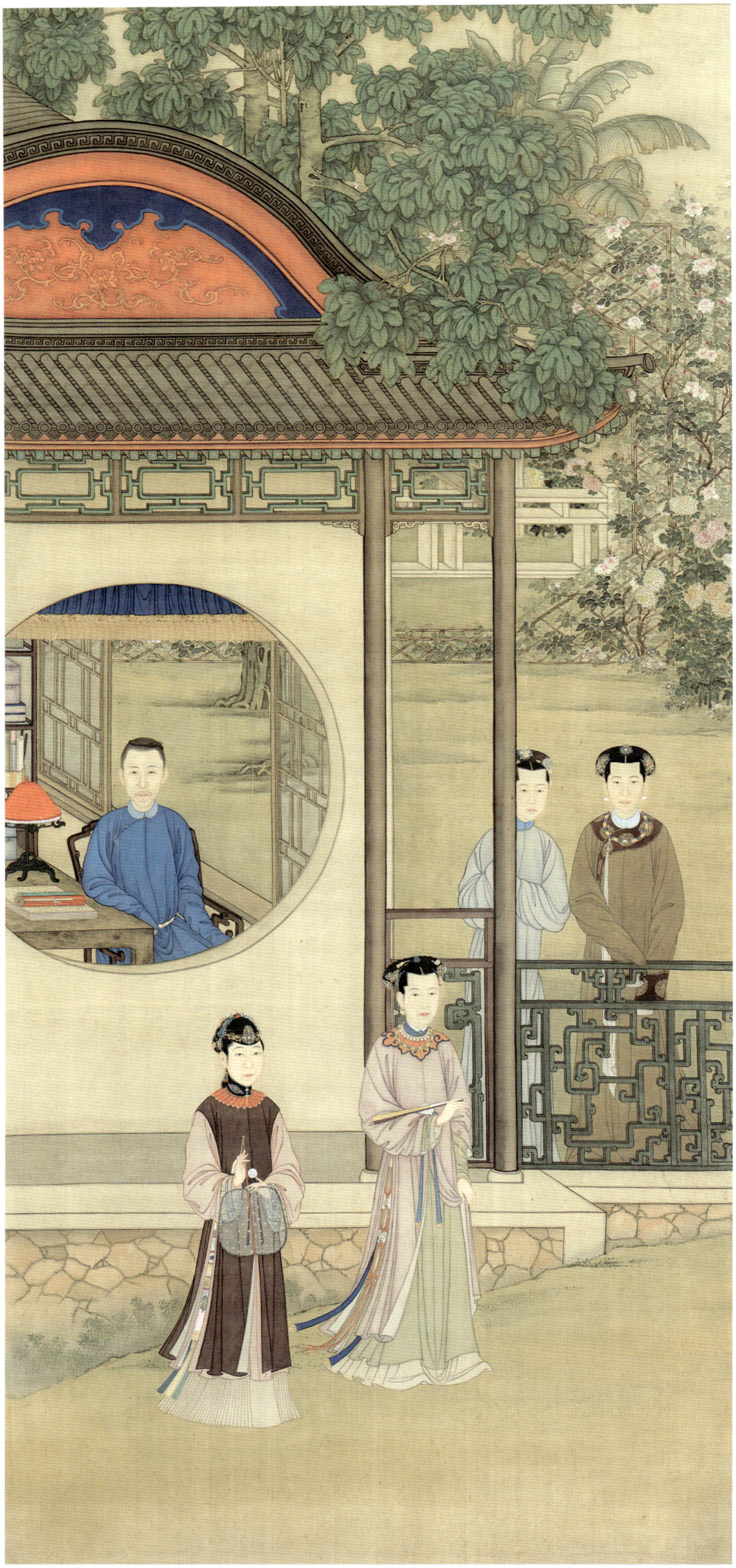

FIGURE 3

Yinzhen and Consorts. Court painters, Beijing, Kangxi period, early 18th century, hanging scroll, ink and color on silk, cat. 1.

FIGURE 4

Empress Dowager Cixi (center) and consorts of the Guangxu emperor: Consort Jin (1873–1924; front left) and Empress Xiaoding (1868–1913; front right). Photographed by Yu Xunling (1874–1943), Guangxu period, 1903, print from glass-plate negative.

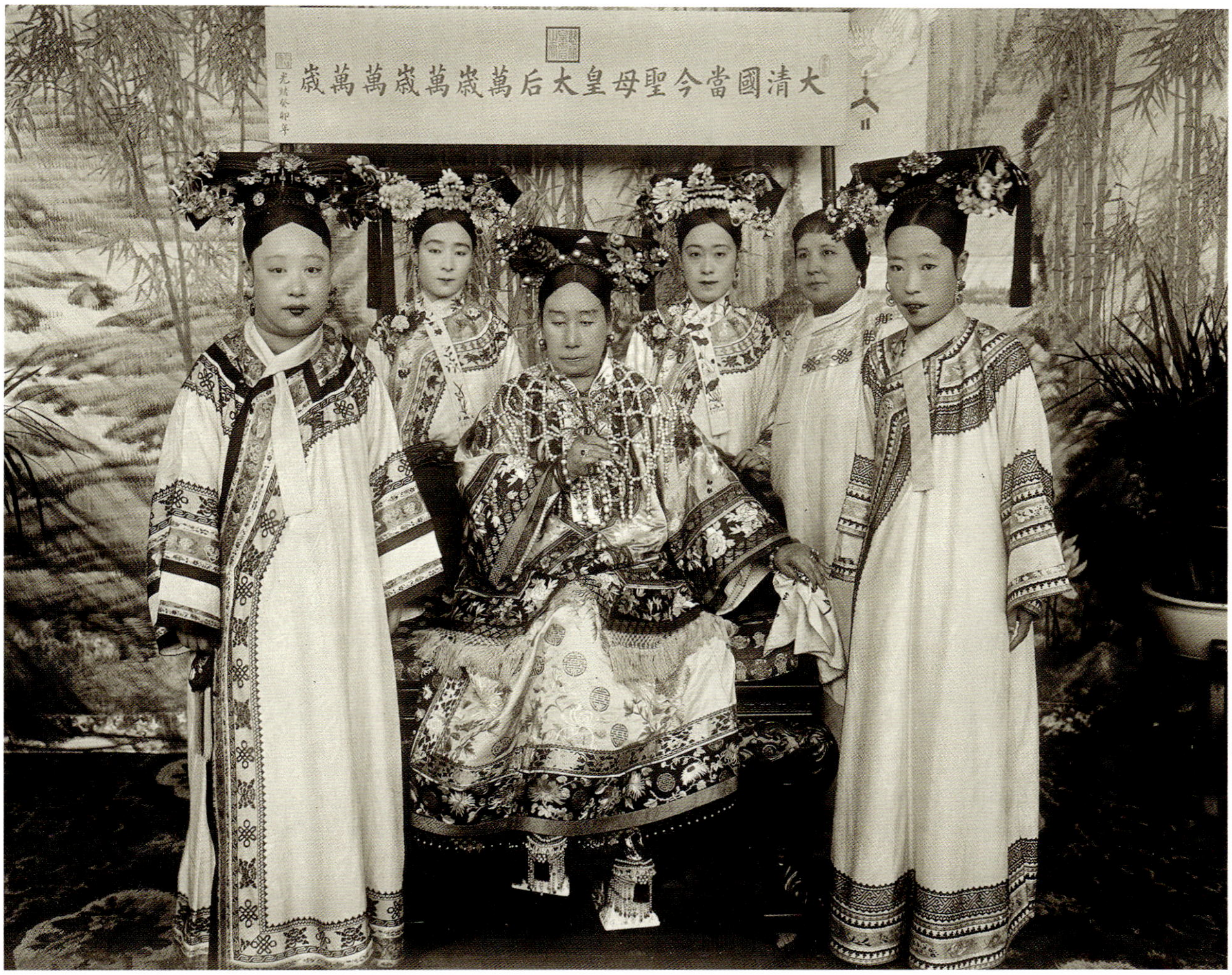

and cultural practices. For example, Manchu women did not bind their feet, so instead of being physically confined to the inner quarters of their residences, they traveled widely, rode horses, practiced archery, and participated in hunts alongside men (see pl. 15). Written records even mention some women participating in battle, with a few rising to the level of lieutenant. Nor were women excluded from the ritual arena, as female shamans held key roles in the sacrifices performed at court.[17] Seventeenth-century accounts also show that Mongol and Manchu women of elite backgrounds had personal names, which Han Chinese women often lacked.[18]

In the early seventeenth century, Manchu and Mongol noblewomen possessed the right to divorce. In addition, widows often married their husband's younger brother, a practice forbidden in Han Chinese society.[19] This custom, the levirate, allowed the husband's family to keep the property a bride brought to the household. Hong Taiji prohibited the levirate in 1631 and 1636 but ignored his own ban by remarrying his daughter Maketa to her first husband's younger brother in 1648.[20] Nonetheless, the regulations governing the selection of brides for princes were gradually put in place during the 1650s and 1660s as Qing rulers replaced Inner Asian customs with Han Chinese ones. Earlier texts referring to customs that deviated from the Han Chinese norm (for example, shamanic rites and the cremation of deceased imperial figures) were often excised from the written record.

Hong Taiji himself engaged in cross-generational marriage, a practice regarded with disfavor by the Han Chinese. His wives included two sisters and their aunt, which complicated Hong Taiji's relationships with his in-laws but added a more intimate dimension to life in the women's chambers of the palace.[21] The women residing in the inner court were often linked to one another by fairly dense and interwoven family ties. Two hundred years later, in the late nineteenth century, Isaac Headland noted that among the ladies-in-waiting at the court of Empress Dowager Cixi (Empress Xiaoqin; 1835–1908) were an adopted daughter fathered by her brother-in-law; a niece; and another niece by marriage (fig. 4).[22]

The Manchus were vastly outnumbered by the former subjects of the Ming. While cultivating Ming officials who transferred their loyalties with rewards of titles, wives, and gifts, they were keenly aware of the need to adopt policies that would enable them to enjoy harmonious relations with the subjugated population. Beginning with the Shunzhi reign

(1644–61), emperors learned to speak and write Chinese, patronized Chinese art, issued hortatory edicts supporting Confucian values, continued Ming sacrifices at state altars, and performed Chinese rituals at marriage and death.

Hierarchy and Status

A hierarchical system for imperial consorts, modeled on those of prior Han Chinese dynasties, emerged only in the second half of the seventeenth century, accompanied by a political shift from the Manchu form of collegial rule to one-man rule in the Chinese imperial tradition. Existing records suggest that the spouses of Nurhaci and Hong Taiji lived in circumstances that were much less stratified than those encountered by later imperial women. Before 1636 the Manchu term applied to Hong Taiji's consorts was *fujin*, designating the wife of a prince (*beile* in Manchu). The women in Nurhaci's harem bore simple titles such as "first consort" (*yuanfei*), "successor consort" (*jifei*), "side-chamber consort" (*cefei*), and "ordinary consort" (*shufei*). Indeed, the wives of Nurhaci and Hong Taiji do not seem to have been inserted into the formal hierarchy of the postconquest period except when the records were retroactively edited.[23] The same holds true for the imperial women of the Shunzhi reign. The majority of the women buried in the Shunzhi emperor's tomb complex were identified as *gege*, a Manchu term for "lady" that was only later limited to princesses. Into the late seventeenth century, some women buried in the tomb of the Kangxi emperor (r. 1662–1722) were identified only as ordinary consorts (*shufei*).

From the late seventeenth century on, women in the imperial harem were placed in eight ranks, at the top of which was the empress. Yet, at an even higher pinnacle was her mother-in-law, the empress dowager. Below the empress, who occupied the position of the emperor's primary wife, were the seven remaining ranks of consorts:

Empress dowager	*huangtaihou*	皇太后
Empress	*huanghou*	皇后
Second-rank imperial consort	*huangguifei*	皇貴妃
Third-rank imperial consort	*guifei*	貴妃
Fourth-rank imperial consort	*fei*	妃
Fifth-rank imperial consort	*pin*	嬪
Sixth-rank imperial consort	*guiren*	貴人
Seventh-rank imperial consort	*changzai*	常在
Eighth-rank imperial consort	*daying*	答應

In general, women recruited through the draft of "beautiful women" joined the four highest ranks and came from the same social stratum as the empress: daughters born into Manchu lineages descended from prominent generals of the early seventeenth century.[24] Han Chinese commoners customarily made a sharp distinction between wives, who came as brides with dowries, and concubines, who were purchased. Even though the emperor refused to accept a dowry from his consorts, there was a tacit recognition of the family background of higher-ranking brides in the recording of their father's clan, personal name, and official title in the imperial genealogy (see Ren Wanping's essay, pp. 51–59). By contrast, consorts in ranks five through seven were often referred to only by their clan name and rank. Women at the lowest level, the eighth rank, did not receive the formal documents called patents of investiture, inscribed with their clan name and rank; they were often recruited through the palace maid draft and entered the palace without performing sacrifices at the ancestral altars, a ritual performed by wives (and not concubines) in commoner households. When they died, many of these lower-ranking consorts went uncommemorated.

Just as women in Chinese commoner society were confined to the "inner quarters" of their homes, imperial consorts were assigned residences in the "Great Interior" of the palace, which was separated by a wall from the public halls for governmental affairs. The actual living spaces for most consorts were quite small, certainly in comparison with the great palaces of Western Europe—but then, even emperors' sleeping quarters were very modest in size, especially when compared to the massive Hall of Supreme Harmony (Taihe dian) in which public audiences were held. Consorts' rooms faced south toward a small courtyard surrounded by a wall.[25] These were arrayed in a dense mass of room-courtyard units along narrow alleys arranged in a grid pattern (fig. 5).

A consort's rank determined the quantities of robes, jewelry, stipends, and servants allocated to her, with minute gradations marking status distinctions. For example, the empress dowager was given twelve "palace maids" (*gongnü*); the empress ten maids, and so on down to the lowest-ranking consort, who might have only one. There were exceptions to the rule—Empress Dowager Cixi, for instance, had twenty maids—but these regulations were observed most of the time.[26] In addition, each consort was assigned eunuchs and nurses (*baomu*), along with "slave" (*sinjeku* in Manchu) women who performed menial tasks such as lighting lamps, fetching water, doing needlework, and preparing offerings for altars, the number varying with her rank.[27] Status also determined food rations, such as the milk, cream, and sour milk that were distinctive features of the Qing imperial cuisine (and absent from the Han Chinese diet; fig. 6). In Beijing, the court drank milk supplied by cows paddocked in Nanyuan, a hunting preserve south of the capital. When the emperor traveled north to the summer villa at Rehe (present-day Chengde) and the autumn

FIGURE 5

An alleyway in a residential complex for imperial women, East Six Palaces, in the Forbidden City.

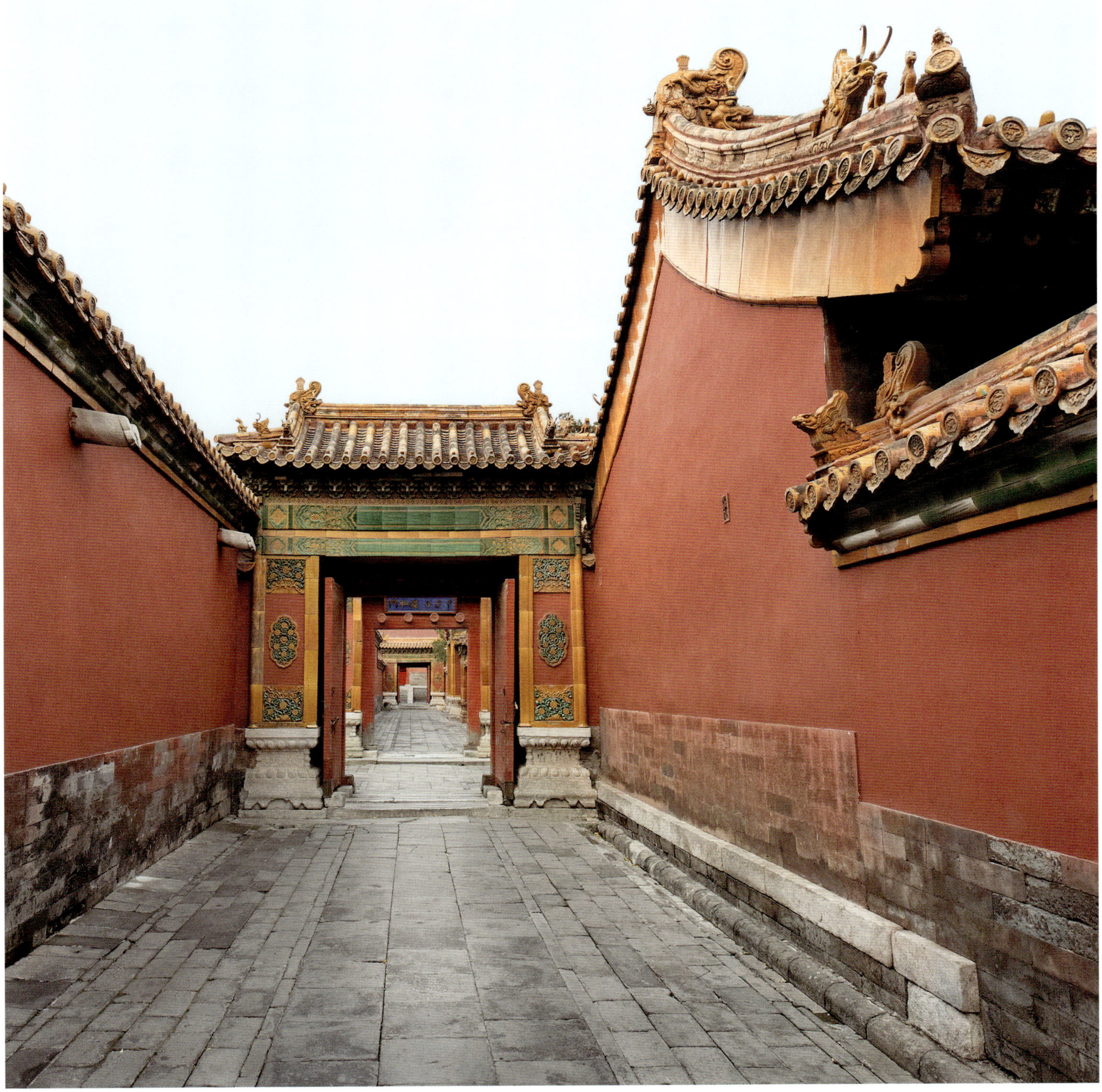

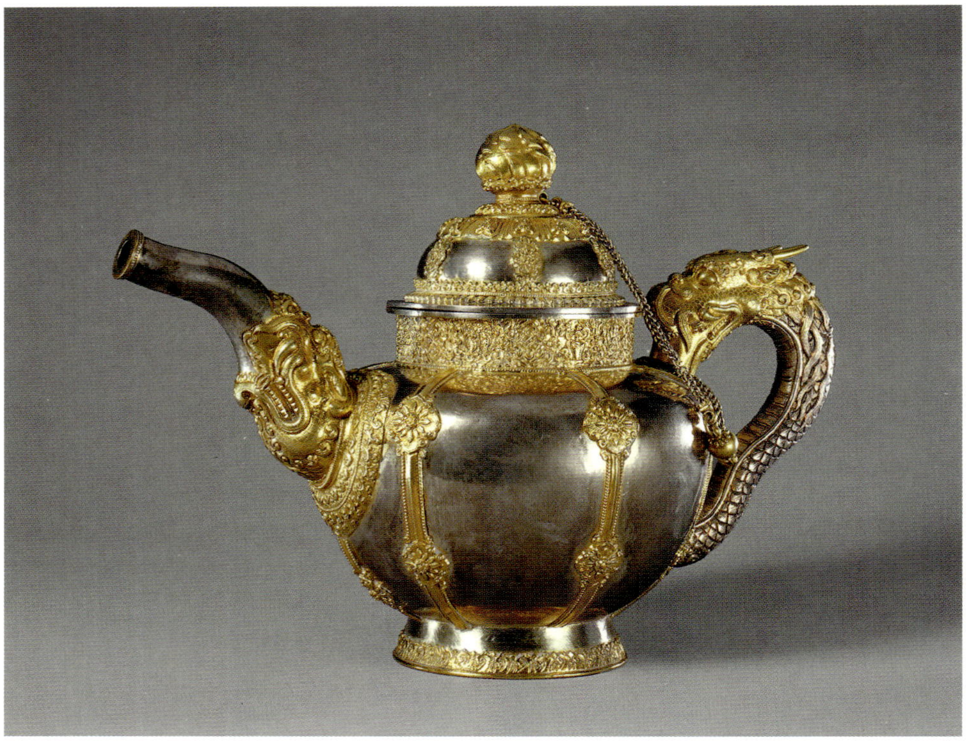

FIGURE 6
Pot with dragons for milk tea. 18th to 19th century, silver with gilding, cat. 158.

hunting grounds at Mulan, two hundred milk cows, each supplying two catties of milk a day, were reserved for the emperor and empress, twenty-four for the empress dowager, and so on down to the two cows designated for a fifth-rank imperial consort.[28]

Whereas marriage and divorce had been relatively frequent in the period up to the 1650s, the women who entered the imperial household as wives thereafter found it very difficult to leave the inner quarters of the palace. The great Qing novel *The Story of the Stone* (*Hongloumeng*; also known as *The Dream of the Red Chamber*) describes how the Jia family's daughter, an imperial consort, is able to make a rare visit to her natal home: this is regarded as a great honor bestowed upon her family, whose visits with her are otherwise severely limited.[29] Documents from the Imperial Household Department provide us with the Qianlong emperor's firm rejection of a request by one of his half-brothers that the prince's birth mother, an aged widow of the previous ruler, be permitted to leave the inner quarters of the palace to join her son in his own mansion. While acknowledging and praising the filiality behind this request, the emperor argued that such a move would violate dynastic principles. Qianlong fretted over his decision and came to a compromise: widowed consorts could reside with their sons during the summer and winter festivals and on birthdays, a total of several months each year; the rest of the time they were required to live in the palace.[30]

An imperial consort's standing was very closely linked to her ability to produce sons. Unlike the Ming dynasty, where the eldest son of the empress was designated as the heir to the throne from a very young age, the Qing (after a brief experiment with the eldest-son principle during the late seventeenth and early eighteenth centuries) decided instead that all sons were eligible to inherit the throne. This meant that the menial status of former maidservants in the harem did not bar their sons from ascending to the throne. Indeed, three women from such lowly backgrounds became empresses as a result of giving birth to a future emperor.[31]

By the same token, infertility was a black mark affecting a woman's status. Information on imperial consorts is recorded in the *Imperial Genealogy of the Great Qing (Da Qing yudie)*; *Aisin Gioro Clan Records (Aixin jueluo zongpu)*, the last published imperial genealogy; and Tang Bangzhi's reconstitution of the imperial descent group.[32] When we compare these texts against archival records listing the annual distribution of imperial gifts to palace residents (*gongfen*) and to the records of consorts buried in imperial graves, we find that in many cases the actual number of consort burials significantly exceeded the number recorded in the imperial genealogy. Those missing from the genealogy seem to have been lower-ranking consorts who did not bear children. Other kinds of written records suggest, moreover, that lower-ranking consorts listed in the genealogy are missing from the rolls of women interred in the graves.[33] These findings parallel the situation that prevailed in Qing society among commoners, namely the social oblivion awaiting poor or low-status infertile women without descendants to commemorate them in ancestral rituals. They also underline a reality of palace life: many consorts—in most reigns, the majority of consorts—bore the stigma of infertility. Of the Kangxi emperor's fifty-four consorts, for example, only thirty (55 percent) gave him children; only nine (22 percent) of the Qianlong emperor's forty-one consorts were fertile.[34] While a high-ranking mother-consort remained "on the record," some low-ranking childless consorts faded into oblivion, lying in unmarked graves, leaving nothing—not even their names—in the imperial genealogy.

The ultimate prize for a consort was to bear a son who became emperor. As soon as a consort became pregnant, special measures were put in place to ensure her health and that of the unborn child. The expectant mother's food rations were increased, imperial physicians and midwives visited her at least once a month during the course of her pregnancy and more frequently in its final phases, baby clothes were prepared, and wet nurses and staff for the newborn child were hired. Archival reports on the 1821 pregnancy of the woman who gave birth to the future Xianfeng emperor (r. 1851–61) suggest that the last five weeks before his birth, a physician and a midwife were in constant attendance to await the onset of labor. When the future Empress Dowager Cixi became pregnant, her husband, Xianfeng, issued an edict authorizing Cixi's mother to reside with her in the palace until the birth. The Imperial Household Department recruited additional staff for Cixi, adding two nurses and four additional workers for domestic chores. As her pregnancy entered the ninth month, two midwives were assigned to watch over her, with two imperial physicians on call. Later, four other physicians were assigned and put on rotations to provide around-the-clock staffing.[35]

With the exception of women who entered the harem as empress, the status of most consorts changed as they won or lost imperial favor. For example, when Cixi first entered the palace in 1853, she was given the name Lan (orchid) and the sixth rank (*guiren*). After her promotion in 1854 to the fifth rank (*pin*), her name was changed to Yi (virtuous). The birth of her son in 1856 caused her to be promoted to Yi *fei* (fourth rank) and then Yi *guifei* (third rank). Cixi, the name by which she is best known, was conferred on her after the Xianfeng emperor's death, when she finally became empress dowager.[36] Empress Dowager Ci'an (Empress Xiaozhen; 1837–1881) entered the palace as a consort of the fifth rank and was promoted to empress after the death of the Xianfeng emperor's first wife. Neither Empress Xiaozhuang (1613–1688) nor Empress Dowager Chongqing (Empress Xiaosheng; 1693–1777) attained their exalted positions while their spouses were alive.[37] Of the five empresses most frequently mentioned in this book, only Empress Xiaoxian (1712–1748) entered the palace's inner quarters as the emperor's primary wife. She married the prince who became the Qianlong emperor, and after he ascended to the throne, he invested her as his empress in 1738 (see pl. 1). A member of the prominent Fuca clan, Xiaoxian bore him two sons and two daughters before her untimely death in 1748 while accompanying the emperor and his mother on a tour of Mount Tai and Confucius's birthplace, Qufu, in Shandong province. Historians have commented on the intensity of Qianlong's grief, displayed in the national mourning rituals that were ordered on her behalf: the stoppage of all official business for nine days; three days of public lamentation at provincial government offices; and the donning of white mourning dress by palace residents, nobles, and high officials for one month. Mark Elliott notes that fifty-three persons were punished for neglecting to submit condolences, two imperial sons were denounced for insincerity in mourning, and Manchu officials who flouted the mourning regulations were purged for their offenses.[38]

Although an empress stood at the pinnacle of the ranked hierarchy of women sharing the emperor's sexual favors, her position was much less secure than her nominal preeminence would suggest. Paralleling Han Chinese commoner household arrangements between husbands, wives, and concubines, the choice of who became empress was usually made by the emperor's parents or senior kinsmen; other consorts were more likely to have been chosen by the ruler himself. In commoner families, a man's interactions with his wife might be rather distant, while his relations with women of his own choice could be much more intimate and deep. Although a wife was by definition superior to a concubine (concubines' children called the wife "mother" and were taught that she was the proper object of filial devotion, not the birth mother), in practice a man—even the emperor—might favor a concubine (consort) above all others. Beloved concubines and unloved wives provided the emotional dynamics of domestic life as frequently depicted in fictions and plays.[39]

Such dramas were not unknown in the imperial family. Some were prompted by a son's opposition to his mother's choice of a bride. Empress Xiaozhuang seems to have had a rather tense relationship with her own son, the Shunzhi emperor (figs. 7 and 8). In 1653 he divorced his first and then his second empress, Xiaozhuang's niece and grandniece. When Shunzhi instead became infatuated with a consort from the Donggo clan (1639–1660), the mother-son relationship must have become even more strained, heightening the empress's disapproval of the emperor's widespread use of eunuchs in palace affairs. After Shunzhi's death, Empress Xiaozhuang and four Manchu regents issued a self-criticism in the emperor's name that addressed his favoritism toward the consort from the Donggo clan.[40] And shortly after the death of Empress Xiaoxian, the Qianlong emperor's mother pressed him to

FIGURE 7

Empress Xiaozhuang. Court painters, Beijing, probably Qianlong period, about 1750, sketch, ink and color on paper, 22⅛ × 13 15/16 in. (56.2 × 35.5 cm), Gu6380.

FIGURE 8

The Shunzhi emperor. Court painters, Beijing, probably 18th century, hanging scroll, ink and color on silk, 130¾ × 70⅝ in. (332 × 179.5 cm), Gu6386.

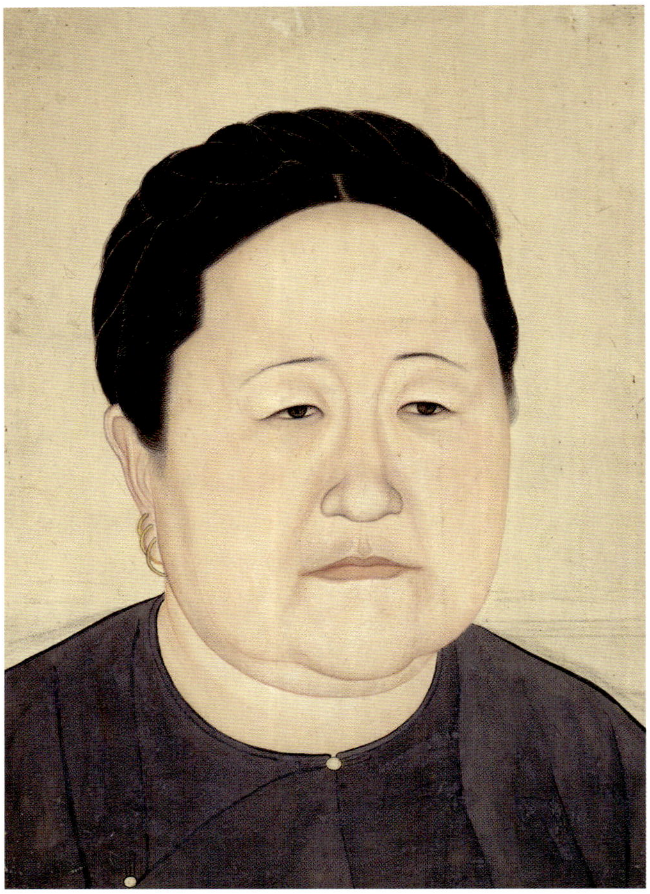

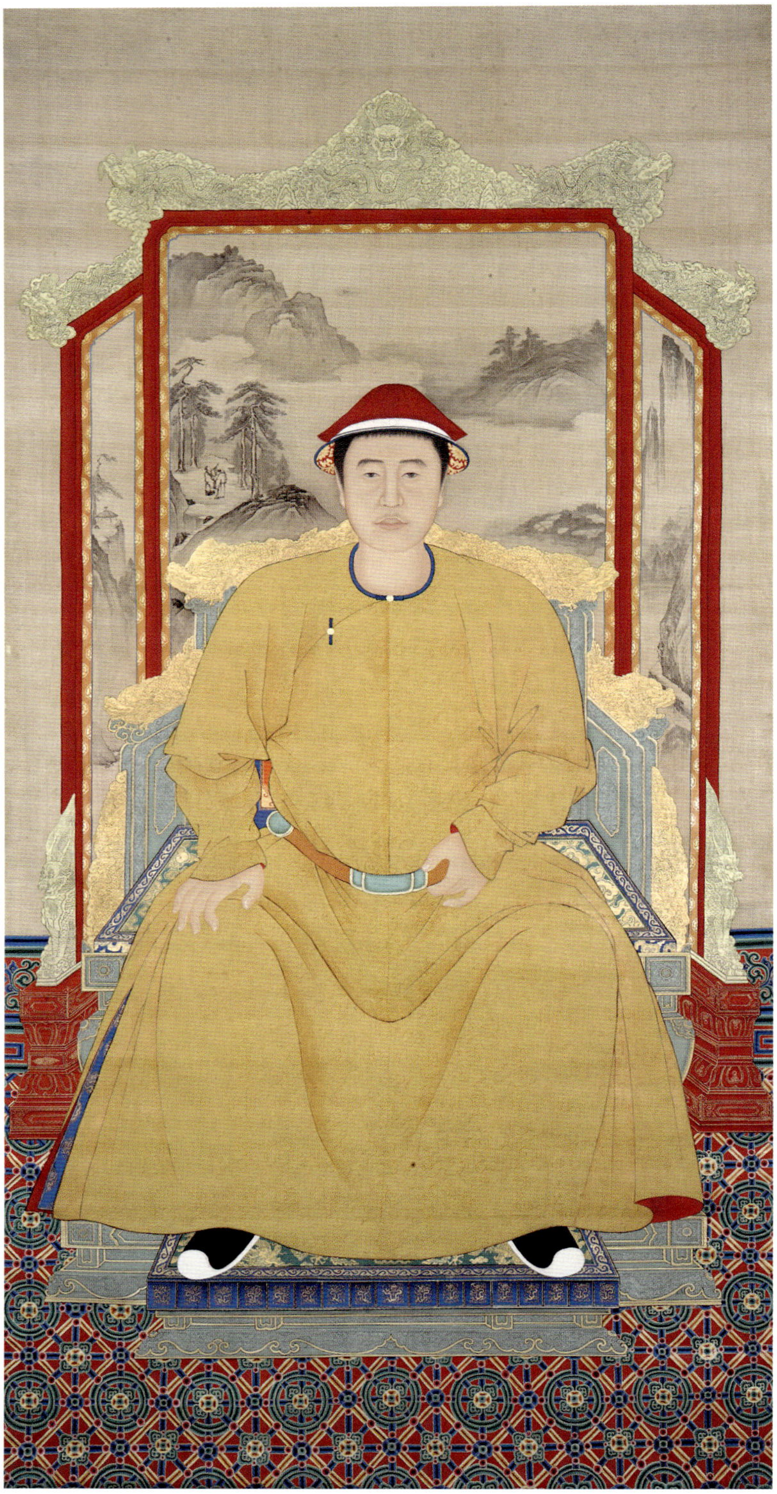

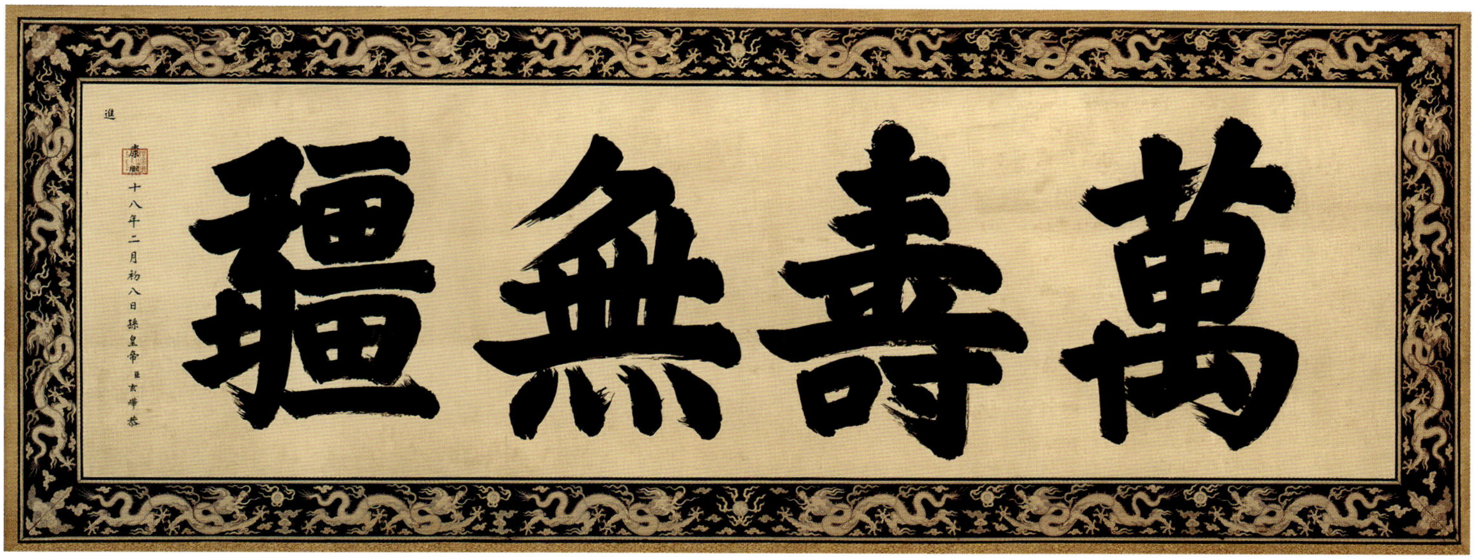

FIGURE 9
Plaque reading "[Wishing you] boundless longevity" after the Kangxi emperor's calligraphy. Kangxi period, 1679, embroidery, silk and metallic-wrapped threads on silk satin, 56 11/16 × 152 in. (144 × 386 cm), Gu202329.

elevate a consort of the Ula Nara clan to empress, which he did in 1750. This empress provided Qianlong with two sons and a daughter, only to fall ignominiously from grace in 1765 when she and the emperor quarreled, and she cut her hair in protest. The emperor put her under house arrest, and when she died, he ordered that she be buried as a second-rank consort.[41]

Mother-Empresses

Xiaozhuang gave Hong Taiji three daughters and his ninth son, the Shunzhi emperor. She was named empress after the death of her aunt, Jere, who had held that position. As mother of the emperor, Xiaozhuang worked closely with her brother-in-law, the regent Dorgon (1612–1650).[42] Her relations with her son became strained after he reached adulthood and began to rule in his own right. His death in 1661, however, brought Xiaozhuang back into prominence: she cooperated again with regents, this time for her grandson the Kangxi emperor. Xiaozhuang took charge of the emperor's upbringing after his birth mother died in 1663. When Kangxi was eleven, he was wed to his first empress, the granddaughter of the senior regent, Soni, who was selected by his grandmother.[43] She also seems to have played a decisive role in enabling Kangxi to take power away from the regents and into his own hands.[44] After the regents were deposed in 1669, Xiaozhuang continued to wield a strong influence over the emperor until her death in 1688. For his part, the emperor, out of respect and devotion, honored his grandmother with extraordinary birthday gifts, such as a plaque reading "[Wishing you] boundless longevity" (fig. 9). In later life Kangxi recalled her "kind discipline," citing the lessons he learned from her as crucial to his character formation and concluding, "I credit her with the accomplishments of my entire career."[45]

Honoring one's mother was an especially popular act for newly enthroned emperors. Obeying the Kangxi emperor's pronouncement "We rule the empire with filial piety," Qing rulers performed "veritable orgies of filial solicitude."[46] It was the Qianlong emperor's active mother-devotion that brought his birth mother, Empress Dowager Chongqing, to historical notice. Despite her illustrious ancestry (she was a great-granddaughter of Eidu, the great general of the Qing conquest), Chongqing entered the establishment of the future Yongzheng emperor in 1704 as a servant when she was eleven years old. Seven years later she gave birth to her only child, the future Qianlong emperor. During the life of her husband, Yongzheng, Chongqing attained only the third rank of consorts, receiving this promotion after the emperor had secretly selected her son as his successor.[47] It fell to her son to invest her as empress and empress dowager. From 1736 until her death in 1777, she was the object of Qianlong's filial attention. He took her on four of his six southern tours (fig. 10); three of his five official visits to the famous Buddhist pilgrimage site Mount Wutai (Wutai

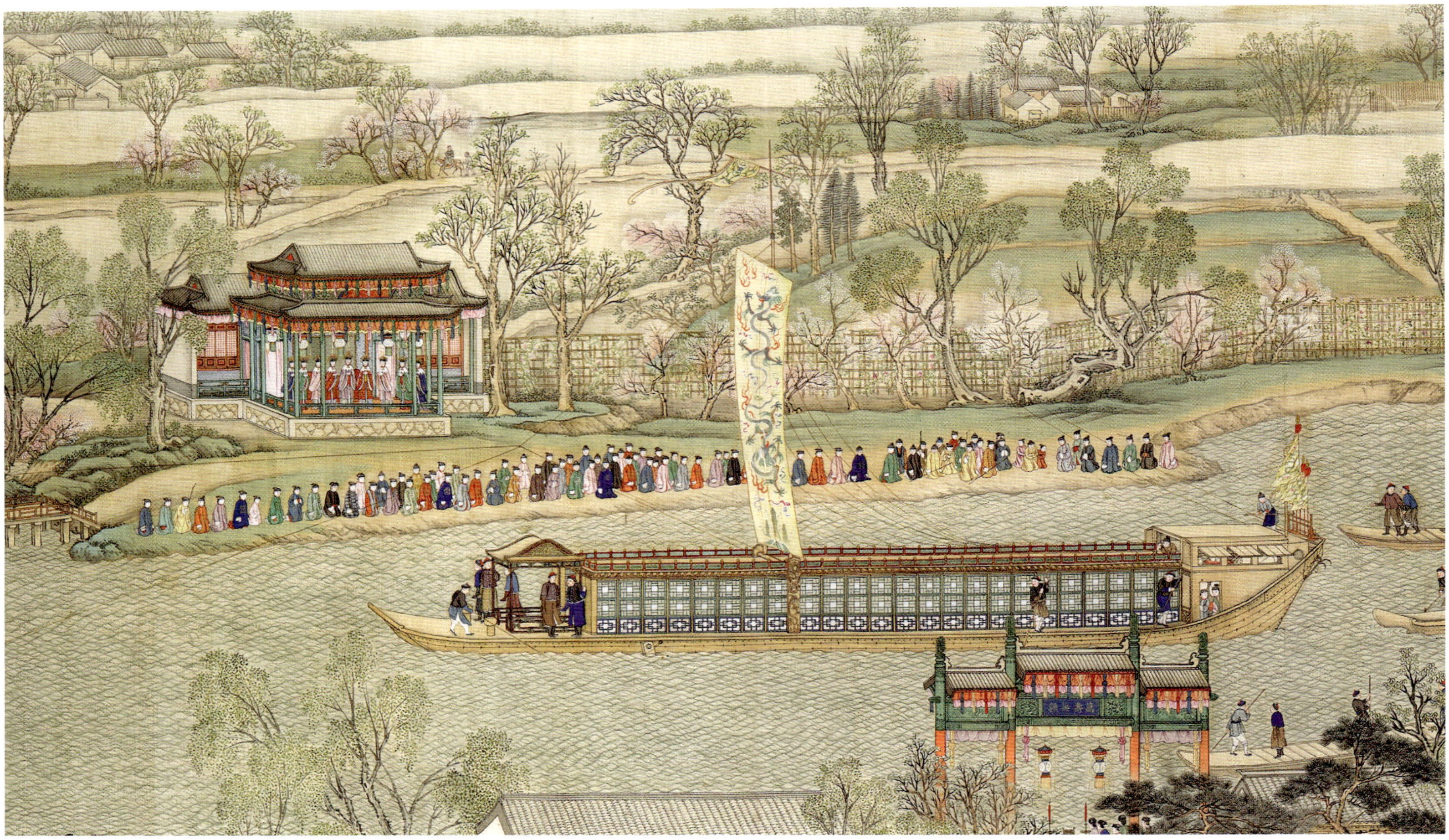

FIGURE 10
Entering Suzhou along the Grand Canal (detail), scroll six of The Qianlong Emperor's Southern Inspection Tour. Xu Yang (active about 1750–after 1776), Qianlong period, 1770, handscroll, ink and color on silk, 27⅛ × 784½ in. (68.8 × 1,994 cm), Metropolitan Museum of Art, purchase, The Dillon Fund Gift, 1988, 1988.350a–d.

shan); and three of his five pilgrimages to Qufu. She accompanied him on his summer sojourns in Rehe and autumn hunts at Mulan. He visited her each morning whenever possible to inquire after her health and celebrated her birthdays with lavish gifts and festivities. His exemplary devotion was a public manifestation of the idea that by carrying out his role as son, he inspired his subjects to fulfill their obligations as fathers, sons, and subjects (see Lin Shu's essay, pp. 78–87).

Emperors promoted not only their birth mothers but also kind senior consorts who had befriended them in childhood. In later life Qianlong often gave special tokens of affection and gratitude to the consorts who had cared for him when, as a child of ten, he left his father's house to move into the Kangxi emperor's palace inside the Forbidden City. When the future Xianfeng emperor was not yet nine years old his mother died, and he was handed over to a third-ranked consort, Jing *guifei* (1812–1855). She had entered the palace as a sixth-ranked consort and was promoted after presenting the Daoguang emperor (r. 1821–50) with a son, the future Prince Gong (Yixin; 1833–1898; fig. 11). After the Xianfeng emperor

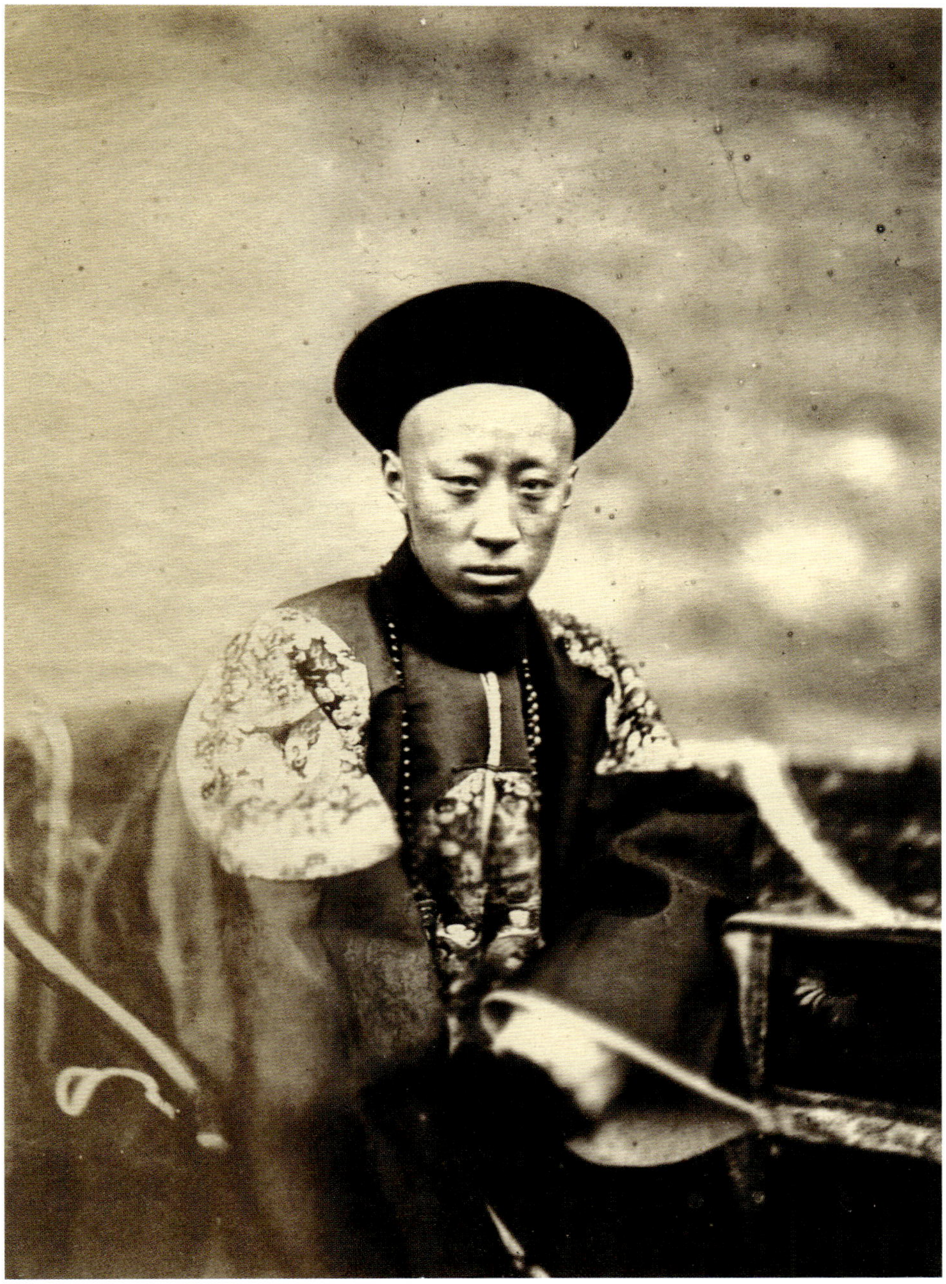

FIGURE 11
Portrait of Prince Kung [Gong], Brother of the Emperor of China; Who Signed the Treaty, 1860. Felice Beato (Italy, 1832–1909), 1860, albumen print, cat. 189.

ascended the throne eleven years later, he treated Jing *guifei* as he would have his real mother: he visited her every day and, in her last illness, promoted her to the rank of empress dowager. Her funeral arrangements were managed by two princes, one of them being her own son, Prince Gong. The emperor observed mourning as if she were his own mother, and she received ancestral rites within the palace for the rest of the nineteenth century.[48]

A more generalized expression of filiality developed whereby a new emperor would promote his father's consorts to a higher rank. This practice seems to have begun with the Kangxi emperor and was continued by Yongzheng and Qianlong. Later rulers also seem to have promoted their father's consorts, including those who had never had children.[49]

Empress Dowager Cixi: The De Facto Ruler of the Late Qing Period

As we have seen, most of the Manchu and Mongol women who occupied leading positions at the Qing court were the mothers of emperors. Empress Xiaozhuang, in the middle of the seventeenth century, and Cixi, in the late nineteenth century, had a strong voice in selecting brides for the imperial princes, and, as the senior imperial women, assumed an important role in determining the successor in moments of crisis. Both Xiaozhuang and Cixi cooperated with their deceased spouse's male kinsmen during the period before their young sons matured and governed in their own right. Cixi's actions after the death of her spouse, the Xianfeng emperor, provide a striking example of how she used her position as an imperial mother to attain broad power during the last decades of the Qing dynasty.

The fascinating story of how the two empresses dowager, Ci'an and Cixi, came to power through a successful coup following the death of their spouse is well-known (see Ying-chen Peng's essay, pp. 128–41). The two women served as co-regents from 1861 through most of the 1870s, but long before Ci'an's death in 1881, Cixi had emerged as the more powerful figure. With the exception of the period from 1889 to 1898, when the Guangxu emperor (r. 1875–1908) came of age and she went into retirement, Cixi was the de facto ruler at the Qing court.

Cixi dominated the Qing court and policies from 1861 until her death in 1908.[50] As one of her biographers, Zuo Shu'e, points out, this period is virtually coterminous with China's modern era, which begins with China's defeat at the hands of Great Britain in the First Opium War (1839–42).[51] Historians still differ in their evaluations of Cixi's role, but that she wielded significant political authority in a crucial era is undeniable. She did not exercise this power alone but in concert with imperial princes, her brothers-in-law. During the 1860s, the most influential such figure was Prince Gong.[52]

When the Xianfeng emperor died in 1861, the empire was in the midst of extraordinary crises precipitated by Qing attempts to suppress the illegal importation of opium grown in British India. In 1842 British military pressure forced the Qing to sign the Treaty of Nanjing, the first in a series of "unequal treaties" that opened foreign trade beyond the southern port city of Guangzhou (often called Canton), to which it had previously been confined, and established a structure of fixed tariffs on this trade to be collected by a new Sino-foreign institution, the Imperial Maritime Customs Service.[53] The Treaty of Nanking was followed by similar treaties with Japan, the United States, France, and other Western European nations.

The stage was set for another diplomatic stand-off in 1856, when Qing naval forces boarded the *Arrow*, a Chinese-owned vessel sailing under British registry, searched for contraband opium, and took several Chinese crew members off the ship.[54] The British, frustrated by Qing officials who had done everything in their power to halt the European economic and cultural penetration into China, seized on the incident to demand further concessions, notably permission to open diplomatic legations in Beijing, a step that undermined the Qing commitment to a Sinocentric world order. The arrest and execution of a French Catholic missionary who had illegally traveled into the interior of China provided the French with an opening to pursue their goal: the removal of the regulation that confined foreigners to the treaty ports. Hostilities in what became known as the Second Opium War began in 1856 and escalated as the British occupied Guangzhou in 1857.

The pattern of foreign action and Qing reaction followed earlier precedent: the court would oppose foreign demands until compelled to submit by force of arms. An initial agreement, negotiated in 1858 when British and French ships bombarded the forts guarding the northern port of Tianjin, close to the capital, was repudiated by the Xianfeng emperor under the influence of an extreme antiforeign faction at court. British and French troops, returning in 1859 to exchange ratifications of the treaties, were met with artillery fire from the forts at Tianjin and forced to retire from the field. When these troops returned the following year, they bypassed the forts and marched toward Beijing, causing the emperor to flee the capital and seek refuge in Rehe, a favored imperial summer destination in the northeast. In his absence, the emperor appointed his half-brother, Prince Gong, to negotiate with the foreigners. In 1861 the Xianfeng emperor died in Rehe.

The resulting coup that put Empresses Dowager Cixi and Ci'an and Prince Gong at the helm of government affairs had significant historical consequences. The reign of Cixi's son, known as the Tongzhi Restoration (1862–74), was marked by a radical turnabout in Qing responses to Western imperialism. Though he had been strongly anti-Occidental before his contact with British and French diplomats in 1860, Prince Gong observed that the foreigners respected the law. He concluded that the best way for the Qing to counter Western pressure was to sign the treaties and then demand that the foreigners uphold their provisions. Prince Gong's firsthand contact with the British and French may also have persuaded him that institutional change was necessary. He established the Zongli Yamen, an early ministry of foreign affairs, in 1862. As co-regents, Cixi and Ci'an presided over the "Self-Strengthening Reforms" that addressed military modernization, infrastructure investment (railroads and telegraph systems), and the creation of an agency to translate foreign technical and scientific works into Chinese (Tongwen guan).[55] One scholar has called this era China's "most innovative period of state-making" since the beginning of the dynasty.[56]

The 1860s and 1870s marked the zenith of Prince Gong's authority at court. Prince Chun (Yihuan; 1840–1891), a member of the inner circle after 1861, saw his influence increase after 1875, when Empress Dowager Cixi selected his son to serve as the Guangxu emperor after the death of the Tongzhi emperor, who left no heir. When Guangxu reached his majority in 1889, Cixi stepped back from her active role in politics. The 1880s and 1890s were marked by the expansion of the treaty-port system and a succession of military defeats

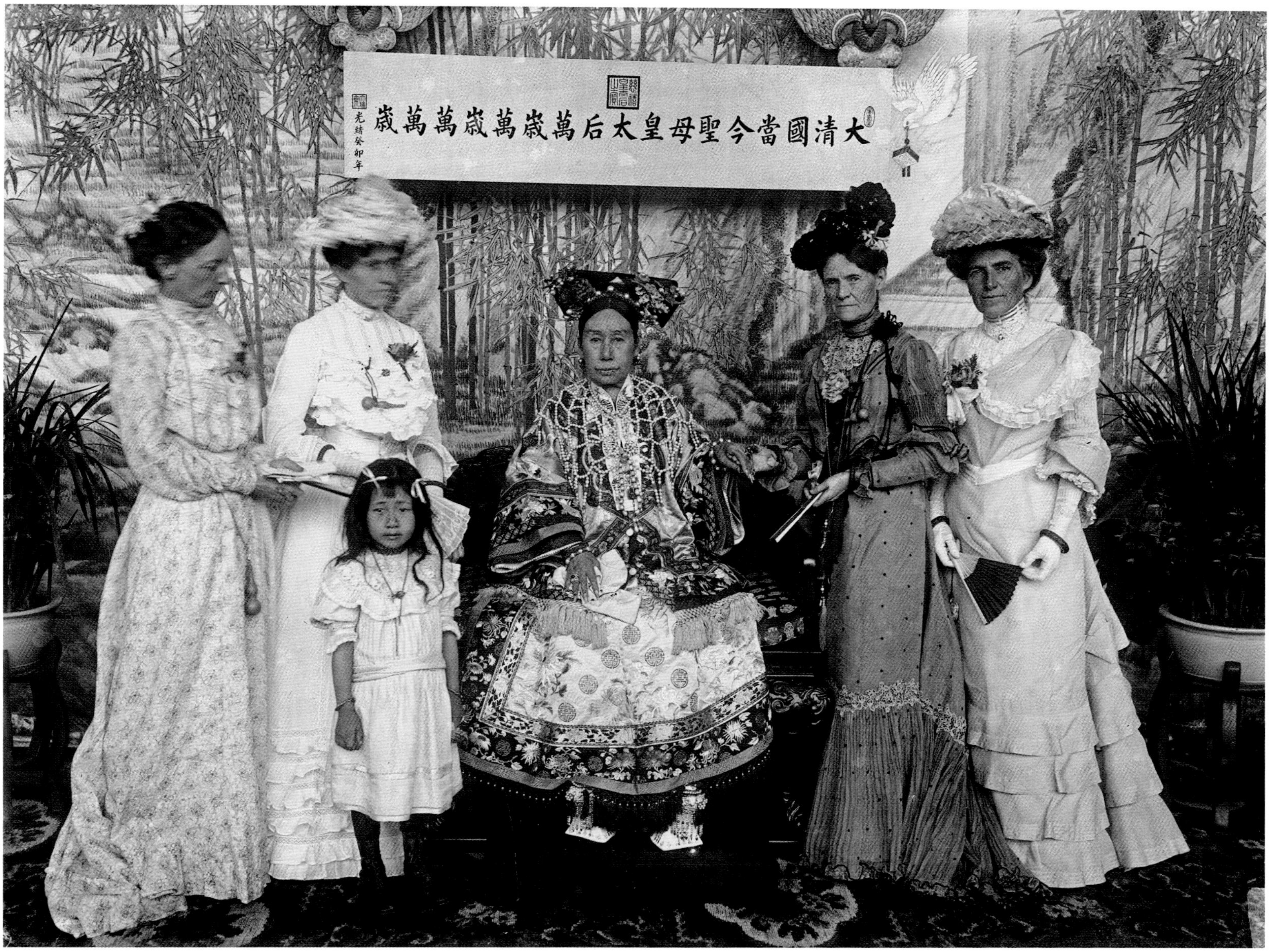

FIGURE 12
Empress Dowager Cixi with foreign envoys' wives in the Hall of Happiness and Longevity (Leshou tang) in the Garden of Nurturing Harmony (Yihe yuan). Photographed by Yu Xunling (1874–1943), Guangxu period, 1903–05, print from glass-plate negative, 9½ × 7 in. (24.1 × 17.8 cm), Freer Gallery of Art and Arthur M. Sackler Gallery Archives, FSA A.13 SC-GR-249. Smithsonian Institution, Washington, DC, purchase.

at the hands of foreign powers. This trend culminated in the Qing defeat by a modernizing Japan in the Sino-Japanese War of 1894–95, called "a major watershed in Chinese imperial history."[57] It galvanized Chinese intellectuals and stimulated the Guangxu emperor to issue a number of reform edicts, the first in decades to emanate from the center of the empire and not the provinces. But what historians have called the "Hundred Days Reform Movement" was quashed by Empress Dowager Cixi, who emerged from retirement in 1898 and put the emperor under house arrest.[58]

The last decade of Cixi's life was marked by the repercussions of her decision in 1900 to launch an attack on foreign powers, euphemistically called the Boxer Uprising.[59] As the Allied Expeditionary Force (including troops from Britain, Germany, France, Japan, and the United States) advanced on Beijing to liberate the foreign legations under siege by the

Chinese antiforeign forces known as the Boxers, the empress dowager fled the capital and sought refuge in western China. After she returned to Beijing in 1902, she had a new agenda. She embraced the very modernization measures that she had repudiated in 1898: constitutional reform, the abolition of the civil service examinations, adoption of a Western curriculum in new schools, and economic infrastructural development. She not only received the wives of foreign diplomats at court but cultivated their acquaintance (fig. 12), and she used images of herself to participate in the diplomatic exchanges that were customary in the international circles of the day (see pl. 46). Before her death in 1908, China's last true ruler, a female, had transformed herself into a modernizing monarch, inaugurating a series of "New Policies" that promised hitherto unprecedented "far-reaching and fundamental" change for China.[60]

Any evaluation of Empress Dowager Cixi's rule should place her within the Manchu political tradition. She was not a female usurper but ruled—like the Qing emperors who preceded her—in collaboration with imperial princes.[61] Despite outward similarities in espousing patrilineal principles, the Han Chinese and Manchus differed sharply in their treatment of women. A Han Chinese bride was never fully a member of her husband's descent group; daughters were regarded as individuals who belonged to their father's line only until they married.[62] The situation in non-Han ruling circles was quite different. Jennifer Holmgren has noted that ruler's wives in conquest regimes became permanent members of the ruling house and often collaborated with the ruler's sisters and brothers in governance. Although regencies were relatively rare, there being a strong preference for adult rulers, when they did occur "the empress in the Mongol-Yuan dynasty (1279–1368) was seen as an individual to be entrusted with power and authority in the same manner as an imperial sister or brother."[63] The career of Empress Dowager Cixi is an excellent example of this principle at work.

Like Empress Xiaozhuang, Cixi's authority was based on her role as mother, not as wife. The Inner Asian traditions shaping Qing court society gave both women greater opportunities to participate in governance when an infant ascended the throne, and both governed in collaboration with their brothers-in-law, the imperial princes. When Prince Gong fell out of favor, Empress Dowager Cixi consulted Prince Chun; his son Zaifeng (1888–1953; also known as Prince Chun and the father of the Xuantong emperor, r. 1909–12); Prince Qing (Yikuang; 1838–1917); and Prince Li (Shiduo; 1843–1914). This inner council of imperial princes continued to be a key decision-making body into the last decade of Qing rule.[64]

Historians have blamed Empress Dowager Cixi for the dynasty's failure to respond effectively to Western demands. One scholar has called her a "feudal autocrat" who presided over an increasingly unsustainable political position that gave rise to the Revolution of 1911: "The good things she did were few, and the bad things that harmed the nation and brought calamity to the people were many."[65] Scholars have pointed out numerous instances in which the empress dowager acted to preserve her own political preeminence instead of putting the interests of the country first. Nonetheless, as the Self-Strengthening Movement and the reforms of the last decade of Qing rule are reevaluated, future researchers may cast a kindlier eye on her actions. The sharp policy reversals that occurred under her suggest that she was a pragmatic ruler and not a conservative ideologue. Regardless of how scholars evaluate her actions, Cixi's significance in Chinese history cannot be denied. For good or ill, she was the de facto ruler during several tumultuous decades whose historical legacy has not yet been fully examined.

Notes

1 The term "Han Chinese" has a long and complex history; see Mullaney 2012.

2 Although the name "Manchu" was only coined in 1636, it is used throughout the essay to refer to the followers of Nurhaci and Hong Taiji before that date.

3 For more information on the origins of the Qing ruling house, see Crossley 1997.

4 On the banner system, see Elliott 2001.

5 "Sinicization"—the idea that non-Chinese groups were all incorporated into Chinese culture and identified themselves as "Chinese"—was first challenged by Pamela K. Crossley in Crossley 1990. The issue of sinicization is closely linked to questions of Han identity, touched upon earlier.

6 For the ramifications of Qing policy on major groups incorporated into the empire, see Crossley, Siu, and Sutton 2006; and Schorkowitz and Chia 2017.

7 Before the late seventeenth century, Manchu chieftains had multiple spouses whose status was often not clearly differentiated. The term "imperial consorts" can refer to all the emperor's wives, including the empress; that is the convention this books follows. It can also refer to women in the harem who did not enjoy the rank of empress.

8 The Khitan Liao (907–1115), the Jurchen Jin, and the Mongol-Yuan (1279–1368) are examples of earlier conquest dynasties that used marriage to build political alliances.

9 Although these sisters and daughters of prominent tribal chieftains may not have chosen to enter Nurhaci's household, their high status ensured that maltreatment would not be tolerated by their male kinsmen. Nurhaci himself cited his daughter's mistreatment as the cause of his 1613 campaign against her husband, the Ula chieftain Bujanai; see Hummel 1943, 1:16.

10 Hong Taiji subjugated the Chakhar Mongols, led by Ligdan Khan, in 1634.

11 The "conquest elite" eventually included Khalka Mongol noblemen, Uyghur elites, and Tibetan prelates who were not registered in the eight banners; bannermen were thus a subset of the conquest elite.

12 Although scholars have failed to locate the document supporting this statement, imperial edicts from the late seventeenth century reiterate the existence of such a regulation; see Rawski 2009, 130–31; and S. Wang 2004.

13 Ding Yizhuang 1999. Ding's investigation jibes with those of other scholars, who conclude that the principle of emperors taking only Mongol noble and banner daughters into their harems was actually implemented with a few exceptions. Ding shows that intermarriage between Manchus and Han Chinese did occur, but mostly involved bannermen taking Han Chinese women as secondary wives. The prohibition on intermarriage was implemented more strictly for daughters of bannermen, who rarely married outside the conquest elite. Mark Elliott comments that the more rigorous enforcement of the ban on intermarriage for women reflected Qing imperial anxieties about maintenance of their self-identity; see Elliott 1999, 70.

14 Their age was twelve or thirteen by Western reckoning, but according to Chinese calculation, which held that a child was one *sui* at birth, thirteen to fourteen *sui*. While girls usually presented themselves at the palace at this age, as fig. 2 suggests, some families toward the end of the Qing dynasty presented their daughters before they had reached the required age with the intent of disqualifying the girls from the draft.

15 The Imperial Household Department was staffed by bondservants (*booi* in Manchu), a hereditarily servile group of people who were enrolled in the banners. Most descended from persons who, captured in battle, became the property of the banner nobles. Bondservants of the upper three banners (the Bordered Yellow, Plain Yellow, and Plain White) were the emperor's household servants and staffed the Imperial Household Department. See Rawski 2009, 167.

16 See Table 5.3 in Rawski 1991, 188.

17 Rawski 2009, 129.

18 Watson 1986. Although they lacked personal names, empresses and other high-ranking consorts received names with rank titles as well as posthumous names, which were inscribed on graves and the spirit tablets placed on altars to receive periodic sacrifices; see Rawski 1988, 141.

19 On evolving Qing policies concerning widow remarriage, see Elliott 1999.

20 *AJZP*. Both men were sons of Ligdan Khan (1588–1634), the Caqar (Chakhar) Mongol chieftain defeated by Hong Taiji in 1634. This defeat was a major milestone in the development of the pre-1644 Jurchen state.

21 *AJZP*.

22 Headland 1909, 205.

23 For more on Hong Taiji's posthumous promotion of his mother, see Rawski 2009, 132.

24 Details are provided in Table 5.2 in Rawski 1991, 176. The Fuca, Niohuru, and Yehe Nara lineages, which provided four of the five empresses featured in this book, belonged to the elite "Eight Great Houses" of bannerman society.

25 "Facing south" was both symbolic and practical: symbolic in that "facing south" meant to take the ruling position in China; practical in that orienting houses with their doors opening on the south-facing plane allowed the residents to take full advantage of the sun. Rawski 2009, 203–04.

26 *Qinding gongzhong xianxing zeli*, 3.1; on Cixi's staff, see archival document 467-4-85/246, n.d.

27 Rawski 2009, 164, 172, 174.

28 The regulations for Beijing are in *Qinding zongguan neiwufu tang xianxing zeli*. For further details see Rawski 2009, 318–19n109.

29 Cao Xueqin 1973, vol. 1, chap. 16, 302–23.

30 Rawski 2009, 139.

31 The birth mothers of the Yongzheng, Qianlong, and Jiaqing (r. 1796–1820) emperors came from bondservant families.

32 Tang Bangzhi 1967.

33 Rawski 2009, 149–52.

34 Rawski 2009, Table 6, 142.

35 Wang Peihuan 1993, 140–43; Wan Yi 1985, 63–70.

36 Yu Bingkun 1985, 58; Wan Yi 1985, 63.

37 Empress Xiaozhuang was given the title after her son mounted the throne in 1644; Empress Dowager Chongqing was promoted by her son the Qianlong emperor after he ascended the throne, in 1735.

38 Elliott 2009, 41–44.

39 For a full presentation of the complex family dramas played out between wife and concubine, see Pruitt 1979.

40 Hummel 1943, 1:255–59.

41 Elliott 2009, 44–45.

42 Yun Limei observed that Empress Xiaozhuang "did not have the reputation of taking part in decision-making, although the reality was that she did" (*wu chuilian zhi ming, hou tingzhi zhi shi*). Yun Limei 2011, 73.

43 Kessler 1976, 56–57. Empress Xiaocheng (1653–1674) gave the emperor two sons before her death in 1674.

44 See Oxnam 1970, chap. 8.

45 S. Wu 1979, 17.

46 Quoting Kahn 1971, 89.

47 Kahn 1971, 88. Much of the information in this paragraph is drawn from Kahn 1971, chap. 5.

48 Rawski 2009, 138.

49 Rawski 2009, 139.

50 Biographies of Cixi include Chung 1975; Zuo Shu'e 1993; Yu Bingkun et al. 1985; and Bao Chengguan 1980.

51 Zuo Shu'e 1993, 4. Rather than presenting Cixi as an illegitimate usurper of the imperial prerogative, Zuo treats her as a female ruler whose actions need to be studied precisely because they were at the center of affairs of state.

52 For Prince Gong's biography, see Hummel 1943, 1:380–84. The prince was close to Xianfeng because of the attention Gong's birth mother, Jing *guifei*, had given to the future emperor.

53 For a description of the major articles in the treaty and the bilateral treaties with the Americans and the French, see Spence 2013, 158–62.

54 The events of 1856–60 are covered in Spence 2013, 176–77; and Porter 2016, 312–15.

55 See Rudolph 2008 for a full analysis of the Zongli Yamen and Prince Gong's role in the creation of this government agency.

56 Halsey 2015.

57 Rowe 2009, 230.

58 For more information on this movement, see Kwong 1984.

59 See Esherick 1987.

60 Quotations from Rowe 2009, 255–56; see 256–62 for details on the New Policies.

61 For example, the Xianfeng emperor was advised by several imperial princes, who were divided in their policy recommendations: three of the eight regents named by him on his deathbed were imperial kinsmen who had held high office under him, as is evident in Wright 1957, chap. 2. In addition, the emperor had assigned Prince Gong the major task of negotiating with the foreigners occupying Beijing on his behalf.

62 See Wolf 1972; and Patricia B. Ebrey's introduction to Watson and Ebrey 1991, 1–24.

63 Holmgren 1991, 86.

64 This is the central argument of Rhoads 2000.

65 Liu Beisi, preface to Yu Bingkun 1985, 6. See also Zuo Shu'e 1993, chap. 12.

Qing Empresses and Grand Imperial Weddings

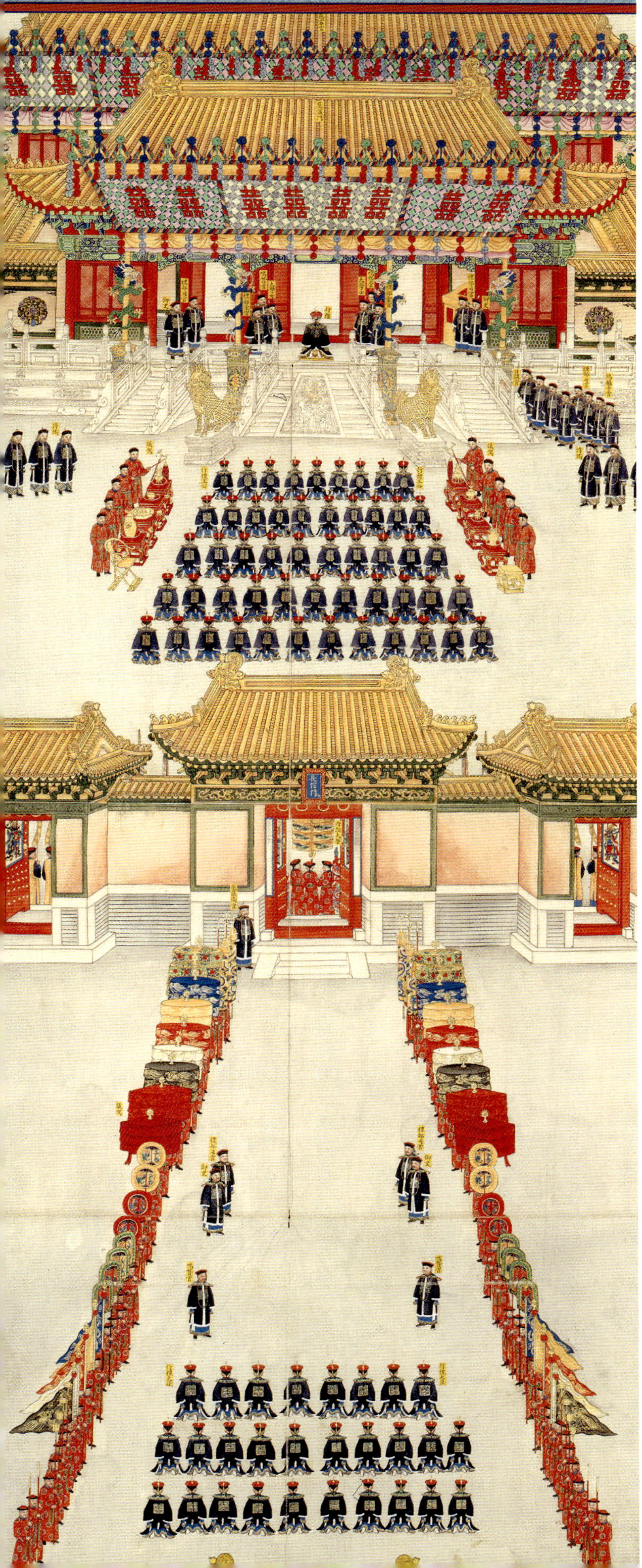

REN WANPING

Five of the ten Qing emperors who reigned between 1644 and 1912 were married before they took the throne. Four of the remaining five—Shunzhi (r. 1644–61), Kangxi (r. 1662–1722), Tongzhi (r. 1862–74), and Guangxu (r. 1875–1908)—ascended the throne before they reached adulthood and were, therefore, married in ceremonies held inside the Forbidden City.[1] Out of more than two dozen Qing empresses, just four experienced these "grand imperial weddings" (*dahun*): Empresses Xiaohui (1641–1717), Xiaocheng (1653–1674), Xiaozhe (1854–1875), and Xiaoding (1868–1913). These events were important state ceremonies and differed in important ways from the nuptials of commoners and other imperial clansmen, involving rituals that emphasized the status and ethnicity of Qing empresses and emperors.

Before the Wedding

Whereas commoner weddings involved formalized negotiations between the prospective bridegroom and his future in-laws, Qing imperial wives were selected through the triennial draft of "beautiful women" (*xiunü*; see Evelyn S. Rawski's essay, pp. 32–50).[2] Qualified banner women were required to present themselves at the palace and had their age, banner, and paternal lineage (father, grandfather, and great-grandfather and their titles) recorded in registers (fig. 1). From these candidates the empress dowager and emperor chose an empress and other consorts for the emperor and wives for princes.

Having selected a prospective empress, the emperor then initiated a gift-giving ceremony (*nacai li*) with his future in-laws. As the Manchus defined themselves in part by their reputation for horsemanship and martial prowess, many of the items given to the bride's family reflected this heritage. For example, a key part of the ceremony involved a gift of ten horses, with saddles and halters, and ten pieces of armor. Further, a lance, quiver, bow, and arrows were placed above the main entrance of the bride's family home, where she remained until she entered the Forbidden City during the wedding.[3] Gold and silver pots for milk tea were also among the offerings to the bride's family. The prototypes for these vessels were probably Tibetan silver containers for milk tea or wine, reflecting not only the Manchu custom of drinking milk tea, an

FIGURE 1
Registers with names and family background of candidates being recruited for the palace. Tongzhi period, about 1870.

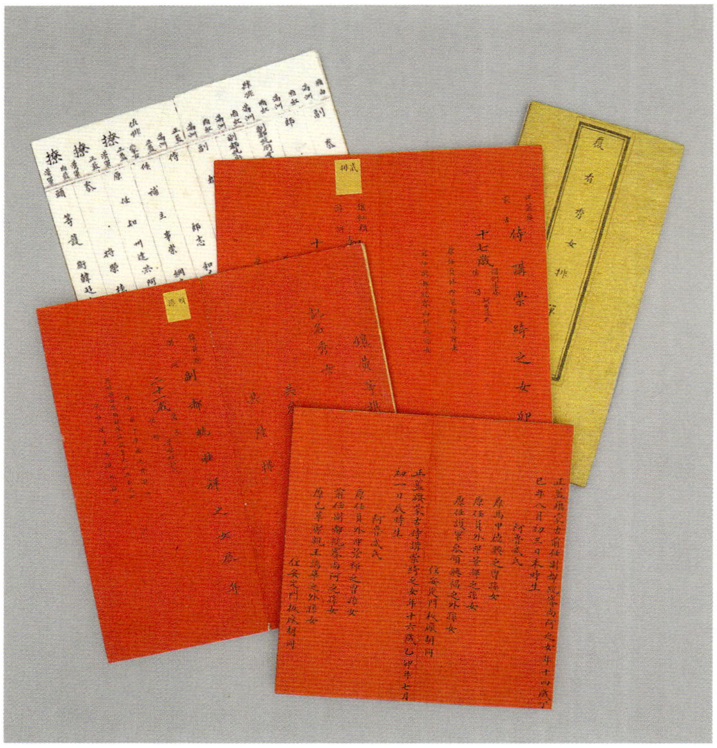

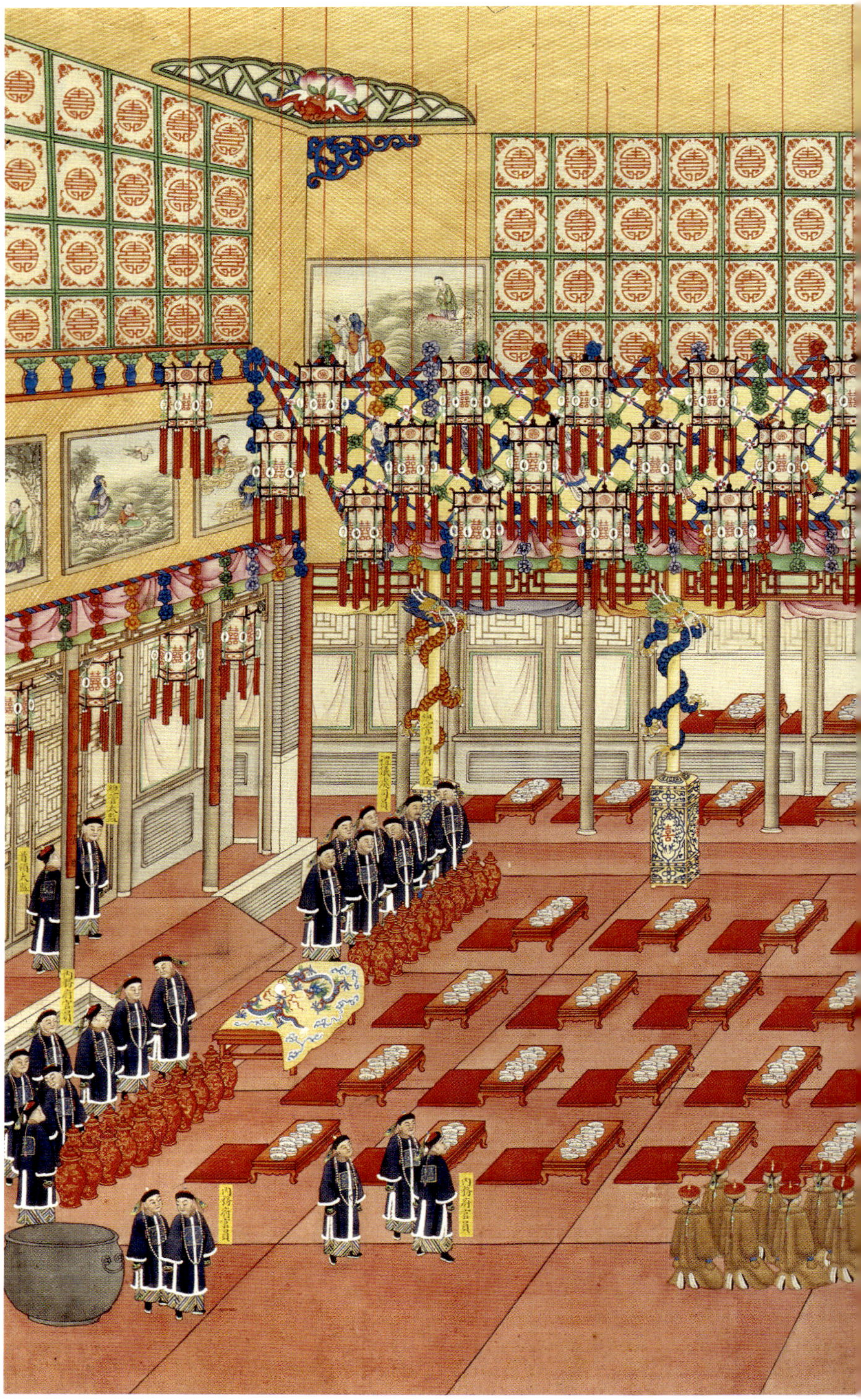

indispensable part of both daily life and formal banquets, but also their incorporation of Tibetan traditions, thus signaling the empire's multicultural nature.

After the gift-giving ceremony, the bride's family received additional gifts, including a large sum of money and textiles to acknowledge the prospective marriage (*dazheng li*). The empress was given similar gifts—though, unlike the items given to her parents, which remained in their possession, her presents were returned to the palace as the property of the imperial household.

The gift giving was then followed by a banquet (fig. 2). In commoner marriages the bride's father would host this banquet, but for imperial weddings, the emperor's representatives (ministers, bodyguards, and nobles) hosted it on his behalf in the residence of the bride's family. Even though the event took place in his own home, the bride's father occupied the seat of a guest at the banquet—a reflection of the supreme power of the Qing monarch, who would not accept a dowry or deign to be a guest of the bride's family. The purpose of this banquet was to honor and thank the bride's father for raising a wise and virtuous woman: one who would help the emperor manage the affairs of the inner court, whose exemplary womanly values would influence him positively, and who could rightfully be regarded as the mother of the state. Princesses and wives of court officials similarly feted the future empress's mother at the bride's family home. The Imperial Astronomical Bureau (Qintianjian), which oversaw calendar making, chose auspicious dates for these rites and all events connected with the wedding.

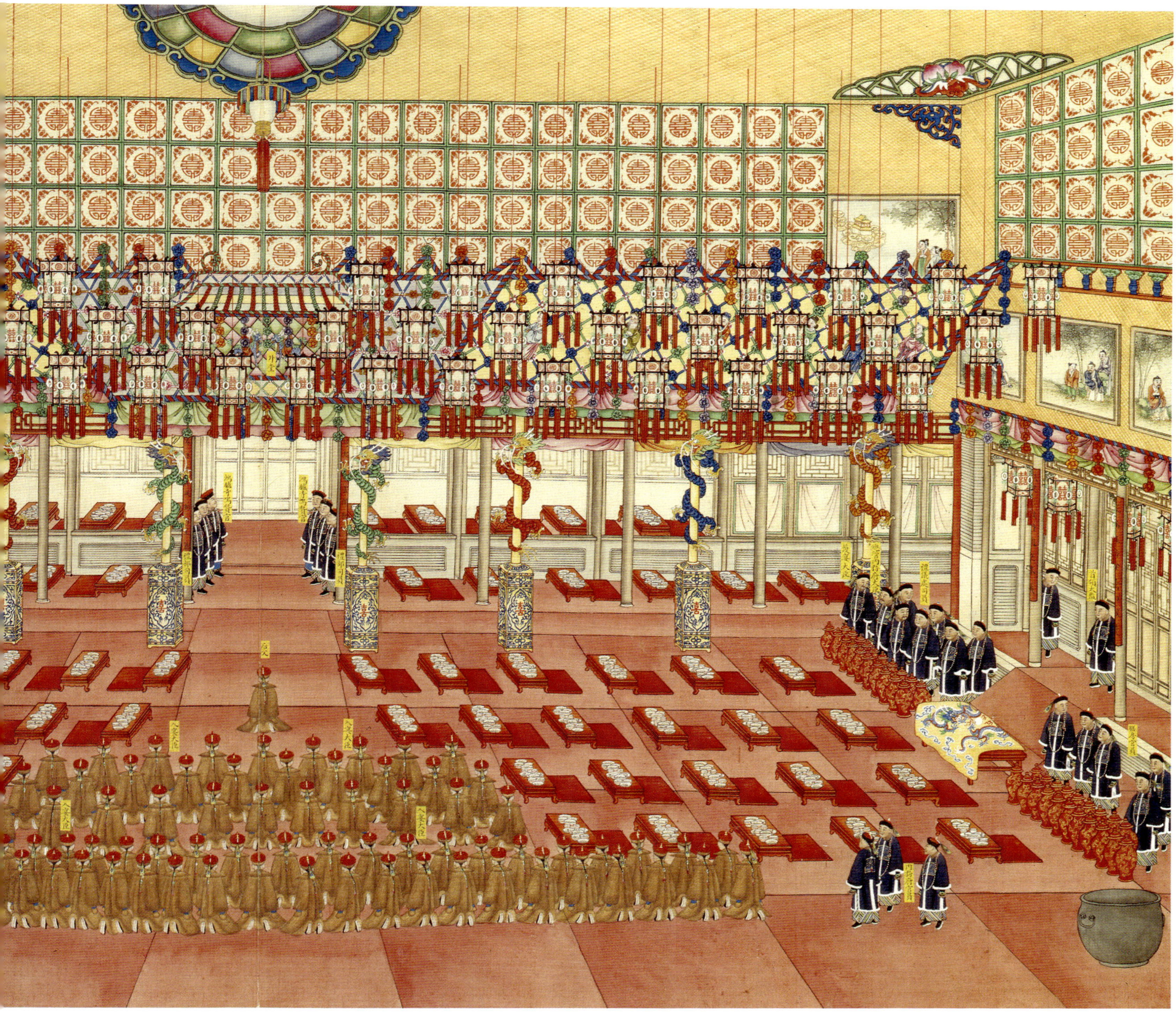

FIGURE 2
The Guangxu emperor's envoys banqueting his bride's father and family after the gift-giving ceremony, detail of leaf 29, volume 2, from The Grand Imperial Wedding of the Guangxu Emperor. Qing Kuan (1848–1927) and other court painters, Beijing, Guangxu period, about 1889, album leaf, ink and color on silk, cat. 36.

FIGURE 3
Phoenix Palanquin for the Empress from Illustrated Precedents for the Ritual Paraphernalia of the Qing Imperial Court. Leng Jian (active 18th century), Huang Men (active 18th century), and other court painters, Beijing, Qianlong period, probably 1772, album leaf, ink and color on silk, cat. 35.

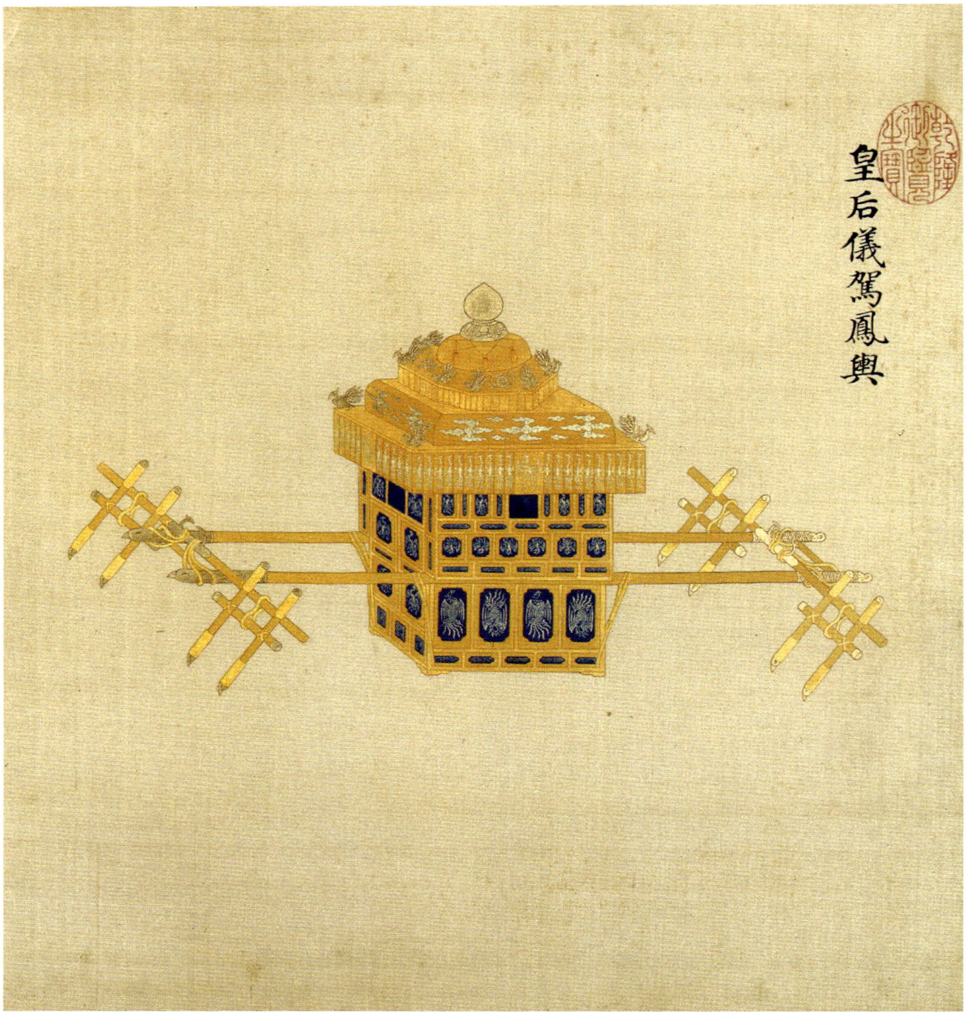

The Wedding Ceremony

In commoner weddings, which traditionally began at dusk, the bridegroom visited the bride's home to escort her to his home. Such a task, however, was beneath the station of the Qing emperor, so he sent a representative to his bride's residence to confer on her the title of empress. This involved presenting the empress-to-be with the emblems of her new position: a book consisting of gold tablets and a gold seal (both inscribed in Manchu and Chinese; see pl. 47). Only after this rite was completed would the emperor's representative formally usher the empress to the Forbidden City. The empress began this journey from her natal home in a palanquin decorated with phoenixes and painted bright yellow, a color reserved for the emperor and high-ranking imperial women (fig. 3).

Qing imperial wedding ceremonies started between 11 pm and 1 am, a time, according to the *Book of Changes* (*Yijing* or *I Ching*), when male and female forces were united, and thus an auspicious time for the emperor and the empress to become husband and wife. Archival records describe the progress of Empress Xiaoding, bride of the Guangxu emperor, at her wedding in 1889: "Just before midnight the empress started her journey from the main building of her natal family's residence. . . . After 3:15 am she arrived at the Gate of Heavenly Purity [Qianqing men in the Forbidden City]. . . . At 4:45 am she arrived at the Palace of Heavenly Purity [Qianqing gong]."[4] The palace staff escorted the procession using lanterns to light the empress's way (fig. 4).

When the palanquin reached the Gate of Heavenly Purity, the entry point to the inner court of the Forbidden City, the empress exited the palanquin holding a gold wish-granting scepter (*ruyi*; fig. 5) in one hand and an apple, a symbol of peace, in the other. When Xiaoding was married, she traveled in a palanquin along with a calligraphy piece bearing the character for dragon (*long*) that her mother-in-law, Empress Dowager Cixi (Empress Xiaoqin; 1835–1908), had created. Meeting a group of wives of Manchu noblemen, the empress exchanged the gold scepter for a vase containing pearls, gemstones, and gold and silver coins and ingots conveying wishes for wealth.[5] Within the Palace of Heavenly Purity

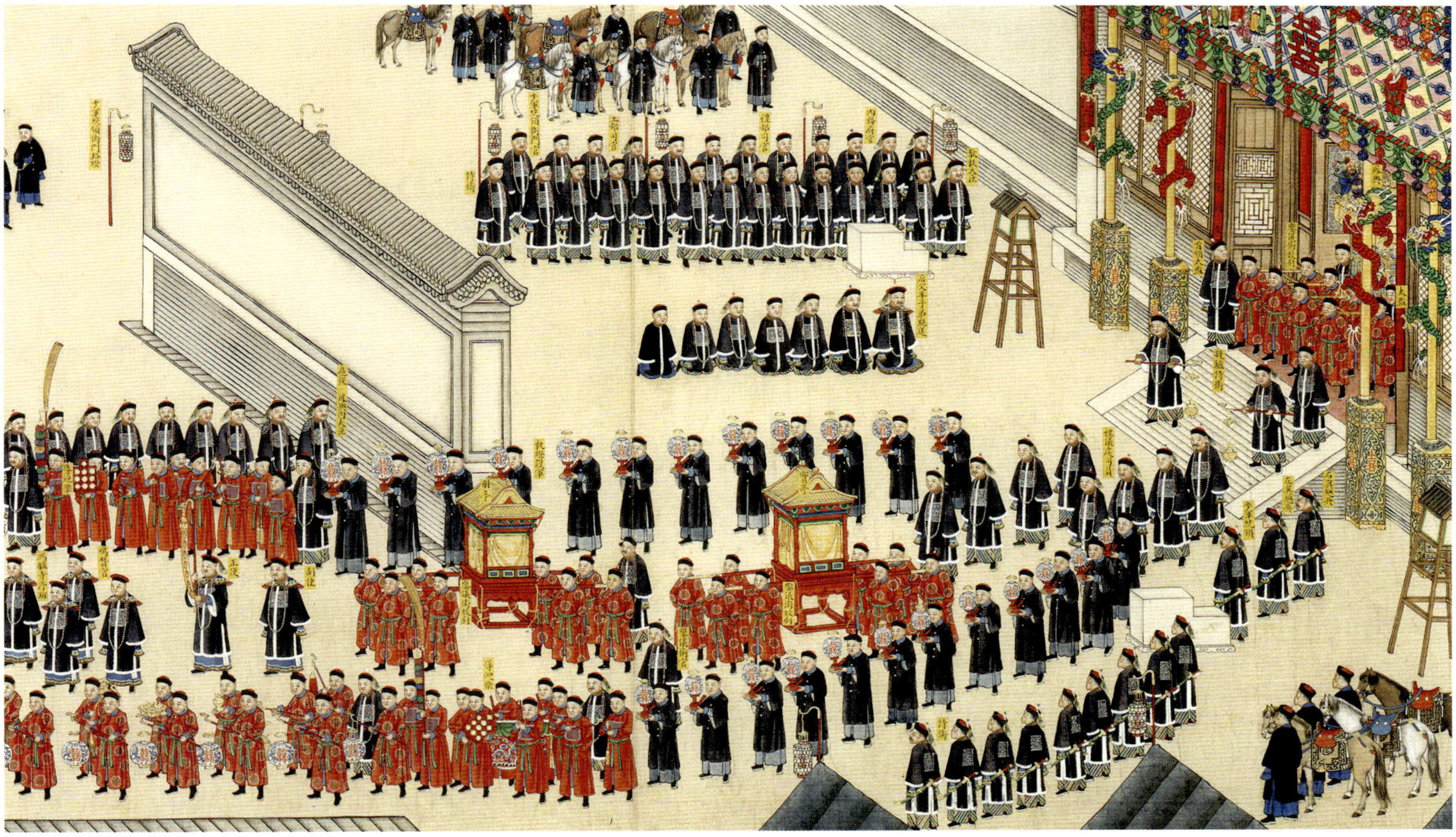

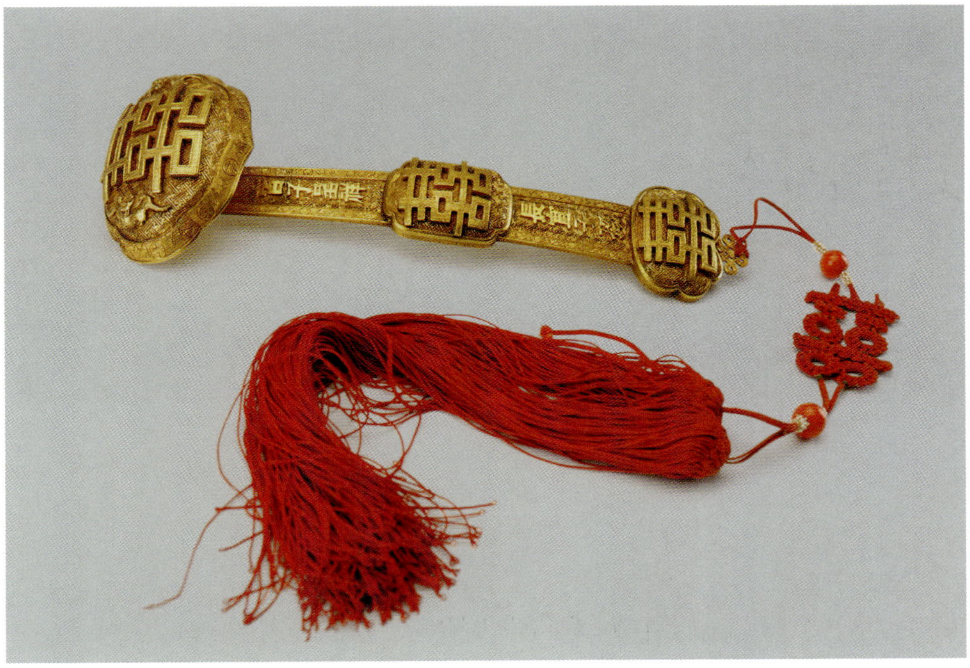

FIGURE 4

Empress Xiaoding's entourage leaving her parents' residence en route to the palace (detail), leaf 2, volume 7, from The Grand Imperial Wedding of the Guangxu Emperor. Qing Kuan (1848–1927) and other court painters, Beijing, Guangxu period, about 1889, album leaf, ink and color on silk, cat. 36.

FIGURE 5

Wish-granting scepter (*ruyi*) with the character for double happiness. Imperial Workshop, Beijing, Guangxu period, about 1888–89, gold alloy with silk tassels, cat. 161.

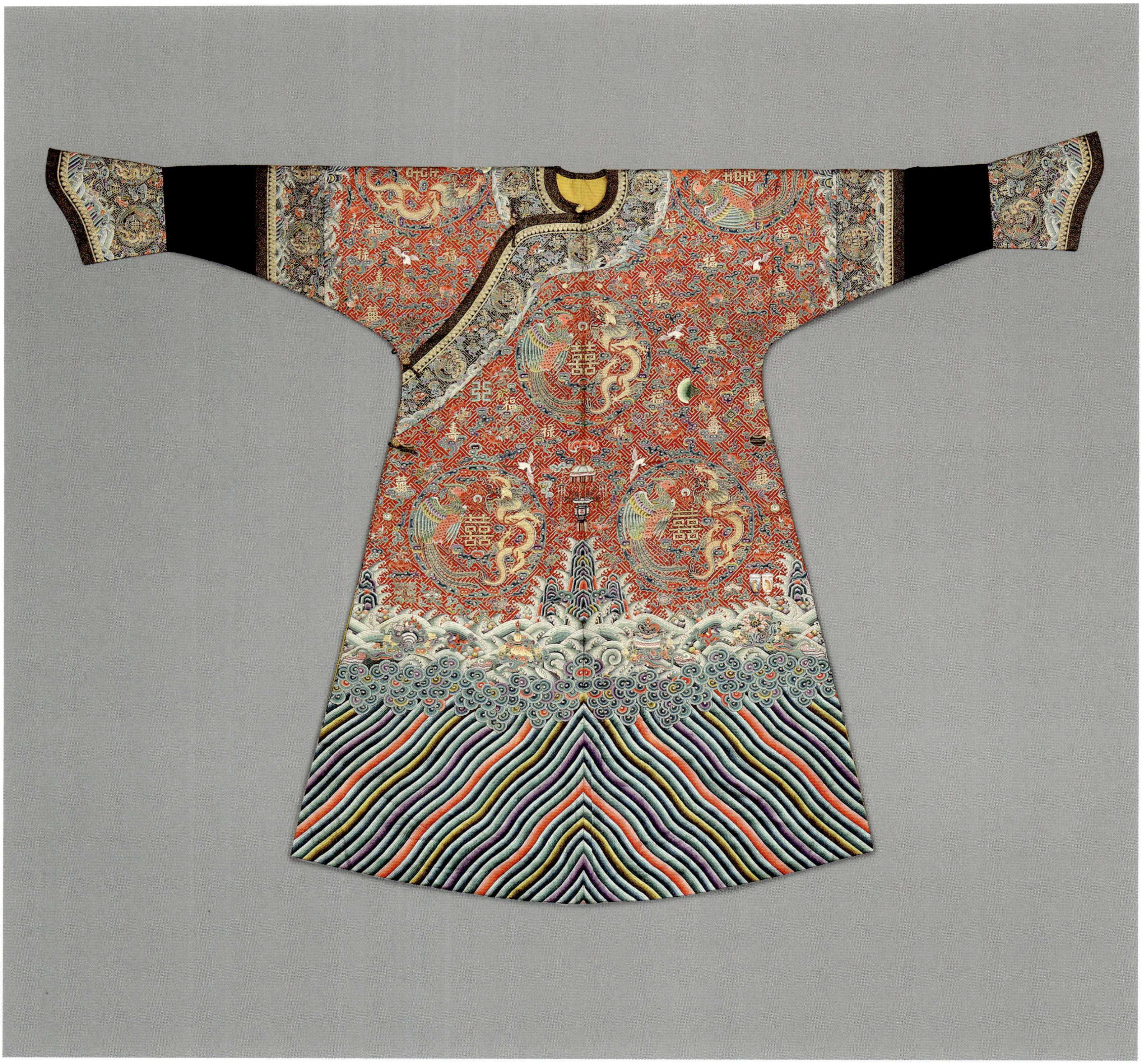

FIGURE 6

Festive robe with eight dragon-phoenix roundels and twelve imperial symbols. Imperial Silk Manufactory, Suzhou (embroidery), and Imperial Workshop, Beijing (tailoring), Guangxu period, about 1888–89, embroidery, polychrome and metallic-wrapped silk threads on silk tabby, cat. 59.

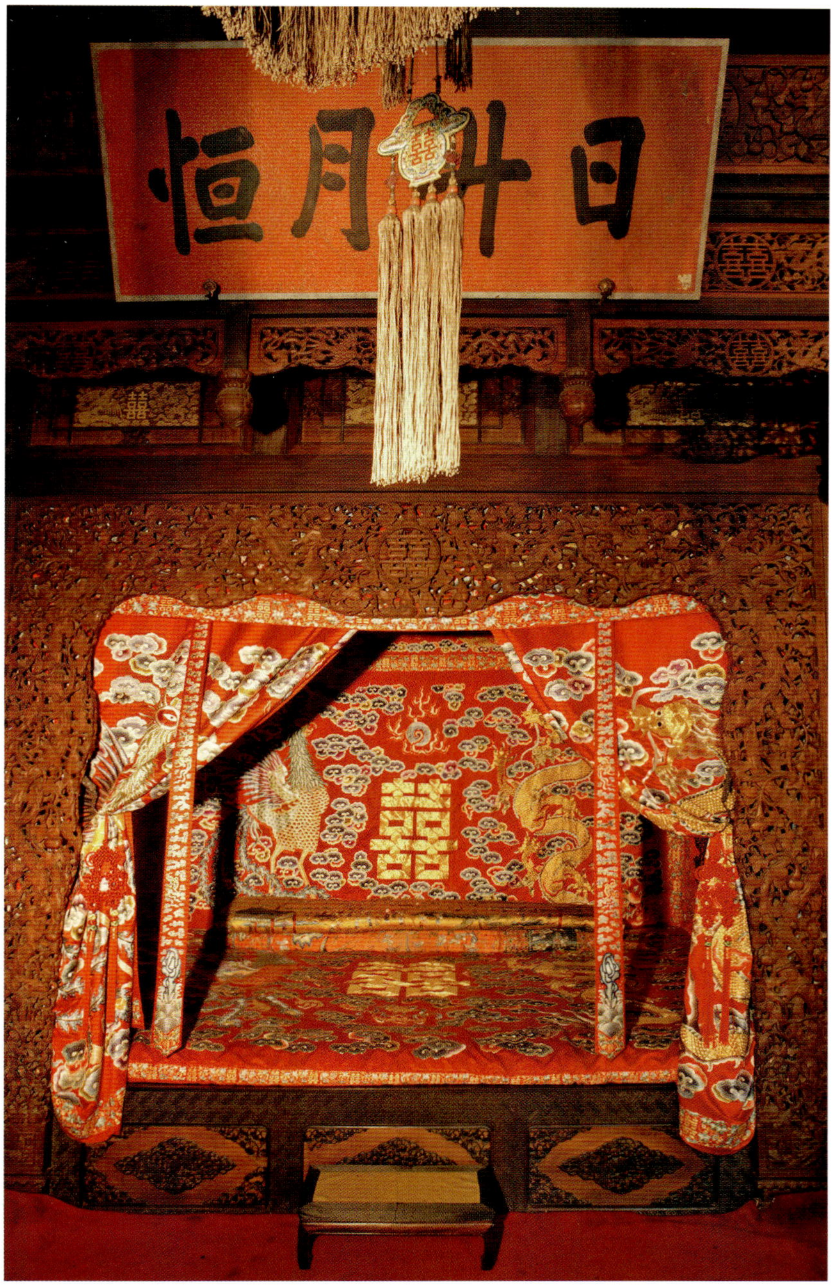

FIGURE 7
Interior view of the East Warm Chamber in the Palace of Earthly Tranquility, where the emperor and the empress consummated their marriage.

the empress stepped over a lit brazier—a Manchu ritual likely intended to exorcise any evil spirits she might have brought from her family.[6] As she crossed the threshold of the Palace of Earthly Tranquility—site of the bride's first night with the emperor—the empress stepped over a saddle beneath which were placed two apples; the Chinese words for "apple" and "saddle" form a rebus communicating good wishes for peace (*ping'an*).

After entering the Palace of Earthly Tranquility, the symbolic abode of empresses, the new empress changed her festive red robe decorated with roundels of dragons and phoenixes for a dragon robe, signaling her status as a married woman and empress (fig. 6). Inside the wedding chamber (fig. 7) she met the emperor, sat to his right on the floor near the bed, faced him, and performed the rite of drinking and eating together (*tonglao hejin li*).[7] After eating undercooked dumplings prepared by the empress's family to express the wish for children—"undercooked dumplings" in Chinese is a pun for "having children" (*shengzi*)—they drank from the wedding cup, an act representing the perfect union of man and woman who share both happiness and hardship, which is a ritual practiced by nearly all ethnic groups in China since antiquity.[8] After this, they ate noodles symbolizing many future years of happily married life.

After the Wedding

There then came a series of ceremonies formalizing the new empress's acceptance into the emperor's family. First, she made sacrificial offerings to the imperial ancestors (*miaojian li*). Before the Tongzhi reign (1862–74) this ritual was held at the Hall of the Ancestors (Fengxian dian), where spirit tablets of ancestors were kept. However, Empress Xiaozhe, wife of the Tongzhi emperor, and Empress Xiaoding, wife of the Guangxu emperor, conducted these rituals before ancestral portraits in the Hall of Imperial Longevity (Shouhuang dian) and other halls within the Forbidden City where portraits were displayed on the day after the wedding (see Daisy Yiyou Wang's essay, pp. 88–109).[9]

A rite honoring the emperor's mother (*chaojian li*) followed.[10] Here the empress and other consorts of the emperor presented the empress dowager with wish-granting scepters betokening good wishes. At the residence of the empress dowager, the empress symbolically served her mother-in-law food and wine, a practice similar to the commoner tradition whereby a new wife cooked for her in-laws two days after the wedding. This ritual manifested the empress's respect for her mother-in-law, an imperial woman of the highest status, as well as the filial duties of the empress as the maternal model

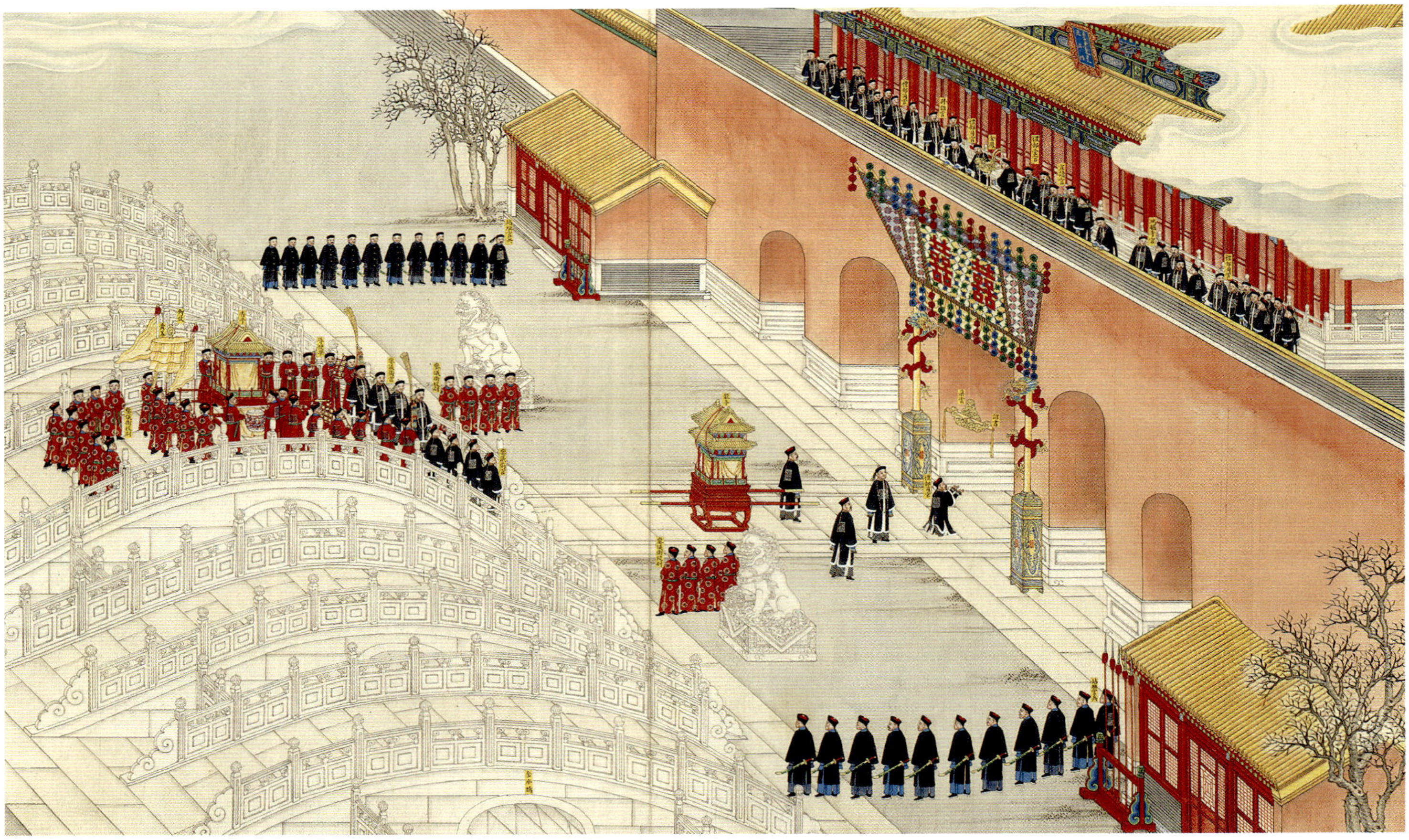

for the state. The commoner homecoming ritual (*guining li*), in which the bride visited her parents, was omitted from the imperial rituals as a way to sever the new empress's ties with her natal family and exact her loyalty to her husband's family.

Given that the imperial wedding was considered a state ceremony, an auspicious day was then chosen to issue an imperial edict publicly announcing the nuptials (*banzhao li*). On that day officials gathered at the Gate of Heavenly Peace (Tian'an men), where important imperial announcements were made. One official stood atop the gate and read the edict aloud in Manchu and Chinese as other attendees prostrated themselves. Then the edict was placed on a cloud-shaped tray suspended from the mouth of a phoenix-shaped ornament and lowered to an official from the Board of Rites (Libu) below so it could be transcribed and promulgated to the entire country (fig. 8).[11]

The ensuing celebration and banquet (*qinghe yanyan li*) saw princes and officials presenting written congratulations to the emperor in a manner consistent with other court celebratory rites. This magnificent ritual received a notable twist when it came to the marriages of Tongzhi and Guangxu. Because they had ascended the throne as young children, Empresses Dowager Ci'an (Empress Xiaozhen; 1837–1881) and Cixi served as their co-regents and handled court affairs. According to convention, marriage marked an emperor's transition to adulthood and the end of the regency. But Tongzhi and Guangxu led ceremonies honoring the empresses dowager, only after which did the emperors receive the congratulations of their subjects—a striking acknowledgment of the unique power these empresses dowager had gathered as regents.[12] Significantly, the painting of the rite honoring Cixi at the Palace of Compassion and Tranquility (Cining gong) is the largest in the set depicting Guangxu's wedding (fig. 9).

Finally, the emperor prepared a feast at the Hall of Supreme Harmony (Taihe dian) to express his gratitude to the bride's father and other male members of her clan. Ritual paraphernalia, imperial-yellow canopies, and stands for wine vessels were set up and musicians performed, signaling the importance and solemnity of the occasion. Meanwhile, at another feast the empress dowager honored the bride's mother and other female members of the family.[13]

The grand imperial weddings of the Qing dynasty were important state ceremonies whose complexity and grandeur expressed the couple's ethnicity, the role of the empress as the mother of the state, and the unassailable power of the emperor.

Translated by Daniel M. Greenberg with Daisy Yiyou Wang

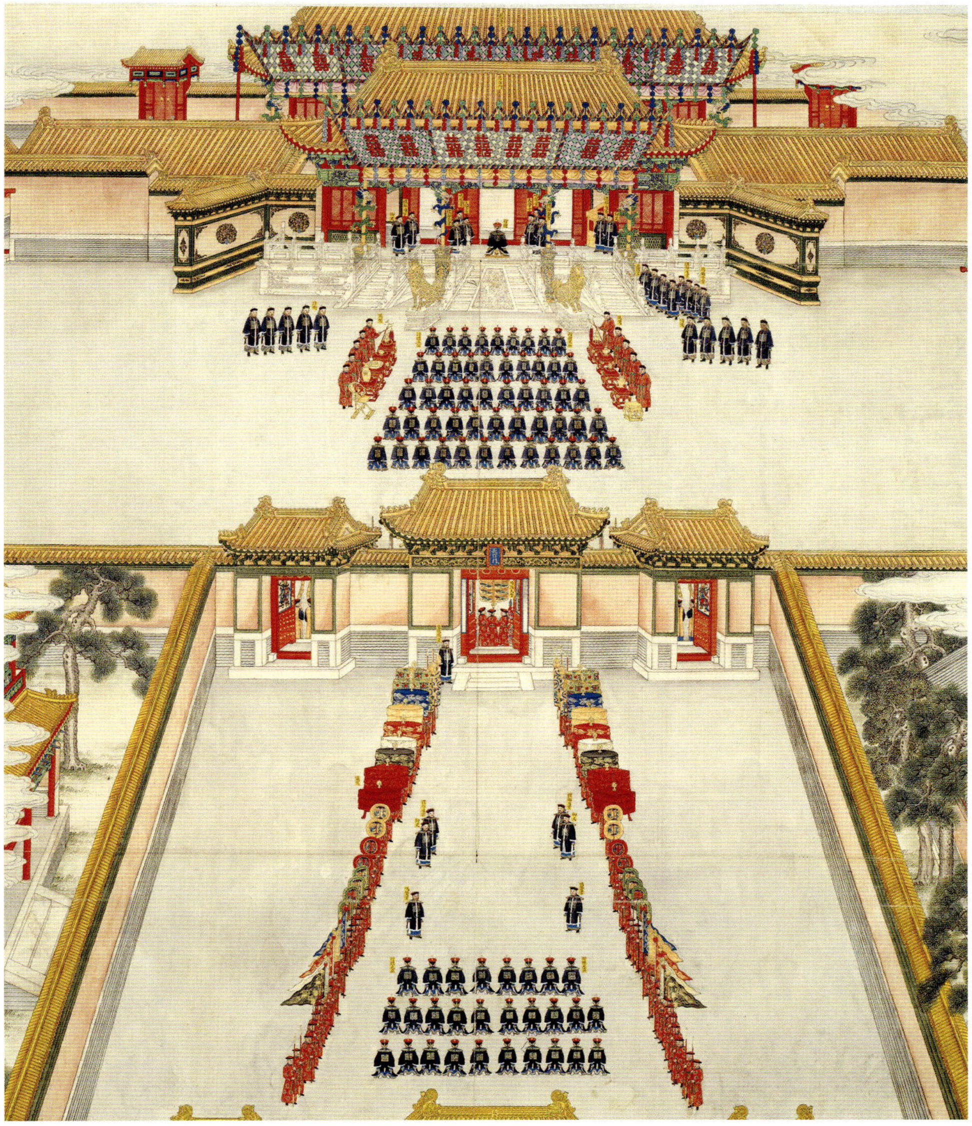

FIGURE 8

Public announcement of the wedding of the Guangxu emperor and Empress Xiaoding (detail), leaf 8, volume 8, from The Grand Imperial Wedding of the Guangxu Emperor. Qing Kuan (1848–1927) and other court painters, Beijing, Guangxu period, about 1889, album leaf, ink and color on silk, cat. 36.

FIGURE 9

The Guangxu emperor leading the ceremony honoring Empress Dowager Cixi (detail), leaf 3, volume 8, from The Grand Imperial Wedding of the Guangxu Emperor. Qing Kuan (1848–1927) and other court painters, Beijing, Guangxu period, about 1889, album leaf, ink and color on silk, cat. 36.

Notes

1 The last Qing emperor, Xuantong (1906–1967), came to the throne as a boy in 1908 and married in 1922 after the fall of the dynasty. His wedding is not discussed in this essay.

2 In commoner weddings, the bridegroom's family traditionally sent a go-between to the bride's family to propose a match. Having secured the consent of the bride's family, the bridegroom would then officially send another intermediary with gifts to ask the bride's family to formally accept his offer.

3 *Tongzhi dahun dianli hongdang*.

4 *Guangxu dahun dianli hongdang*.

5 *Tongzhi dahun dianli hongdang*.

6 *Tongzhi dahun dianli hongdang*.

7 *Tongzhi dahun dianli hongdang*.

8 According to Zhang Mengyuan (1825–1896) in *Collected Writings of Origins* (*Yuanqi huichao*), the use of the wedding cup has two meanings. First, it is made from a calabash gourd, which is not edible and is only used as a vessel for drinking. It symbolizes the husband and wife sharing both joy and bitterness. Second, the calabash gourd was one of the eight basic materials for Chinese traditional musical instruments and was used to make the wind instruments the *sheng* and the *yu*, symbolizing harmony embodied in the music produced when two instruments are played together.

9 *Tongzhi dahun dianli hongdang*.

10 According to Qing succession rules, the emperor could take the throne only after his father's death. Thus, this rite generally involved the empress and her mother-in-law.

11 *Guangxu dahun yizhu*.

12 Yang Zhen 2001.

13 Toward the end of the dynasty, this banquet was replaced by a gift of food to the bride's mother.

TWO

Tracing the Lives of Qing Court Women

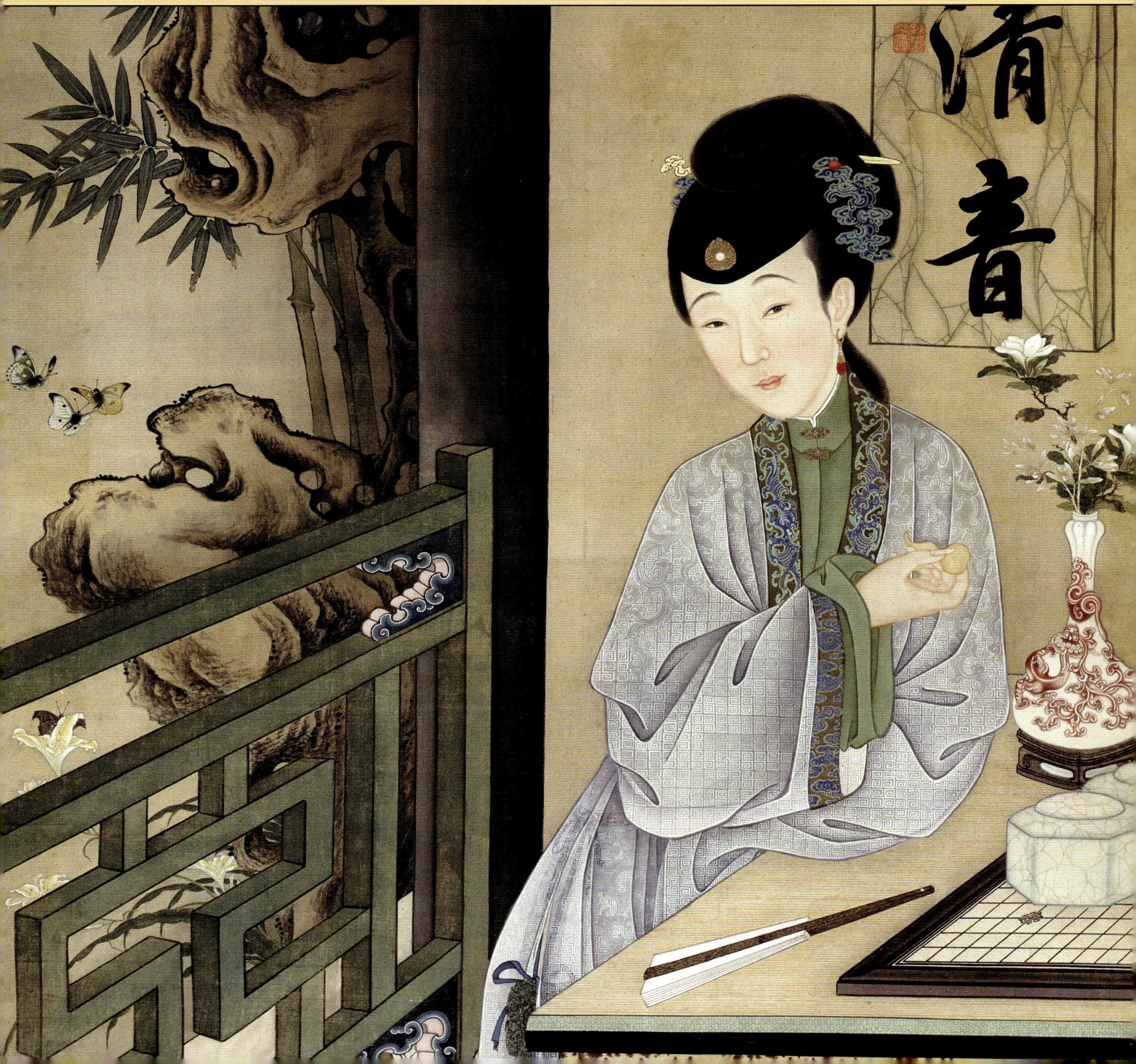

JAN STUART

THE LIFE OF A QING EMPEROR was thoroughly documented, even down to particulars as inconsequential as a favored cake recipe.[1] By contrast, little was recorded about the lives of consorts—including empresses—beyond official accounts of ritual duties, court entitlements, gifts, celebrations held in their honor, or varia such as prescriptions. Nor did these women leave behind poems or diaries to fill in the details of their story. While it is possible to recapture quite a lot of factual information for a few exceptional palace women—such as Empress Dowager Chongqing (Empress Xiaosheng; 1693–1777), the beloved mother of the Qianlong emperor (r. 1736–95; see Lin Shu's essay, pp. 78–87)—and make some generalizations about empresses' lives, most information about imperial wives is refracted through the male perspective of the emperor in the meticulous records kept about or written by him. Thus, it is a challenge to imagine the actual texture of any empress's life.

Fortunately, the relative silence of history about empresses and other consorts has a partial remedy in the vast and lavish art produced by the Qing court. Through the study of paintings, household furnishings, tableware, clothing, and jewelry it is possible to reconstruct—or at least speculate within reason—what the general tenor of the imperial women's lifestyle was like. Through this lens we can see their lives as purposeful and fulfilling, not just in the sense of serving the state by producing and educating future emperors but also in personal ways.

The Imperial Household Department (Neiwu fu) managed the domestic affairs of the emperors and empresses, with the significant distinction that the consorts were under the emperor's direct control and considered his property. Everyone knew at a glance a consort's status based on the size of her residence and stipend; the number of her servants; and the quantity, quality, and design of her every possession. Tableware is but one such example: the emperor, empress dowager, and empress had the privilege of using dishes glazed inside and out with monochrome yellow, the imperial color (fig. 1), while a second-rank imperial consort was entitled to dishes yellow on the outside but plain white inside. Lower-status consorts dined from dragon-patterned dishes in two colors, such as the yellow-and-blue combination for consorts of the fourth to seventh ranks (fig. 2).

A strain of modern scholarship has viewed the lives of palace women as an almost "tormented" existence.[2] One assessment reduces the empresses to being little more than political tools, presented by the court as "identical puppets" bearing signs of "Manchu ethnic and political identity."[3] Yet, as *Portraits of Emperor Qianlong and His Twelve Consorts* (see p. 103, fig. 18) makes clear, emperors did not attempt to erase their consorts' individuality. Writing about this handscroll, the scholar Chen Pao-chen has noted that court artists managed to insinuate subtle differences and capture the "ladies' concealed personalities" in the depiction of their faces.[4] As Qianlong inspected drafts of every artwork he commissioned, the hints of individuality in his consorts' faces must have been initiated or at least encouraged by him. It is true

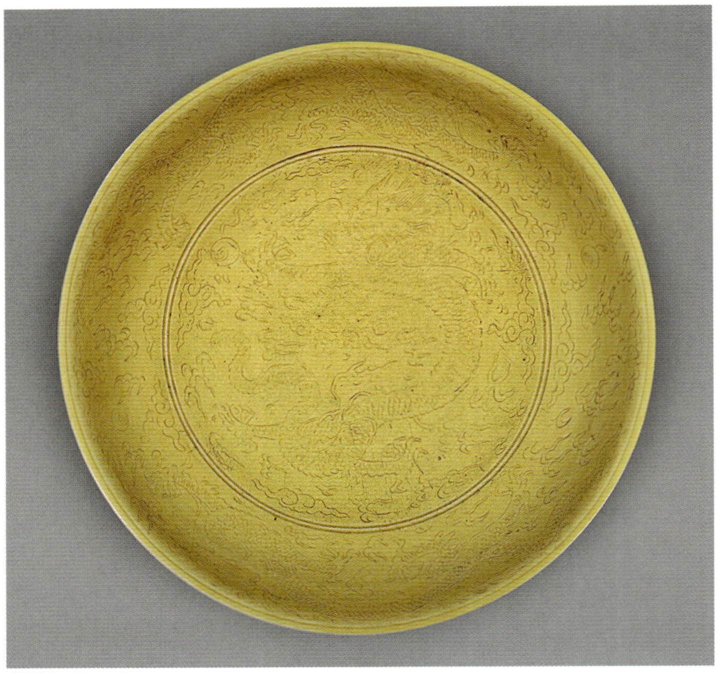

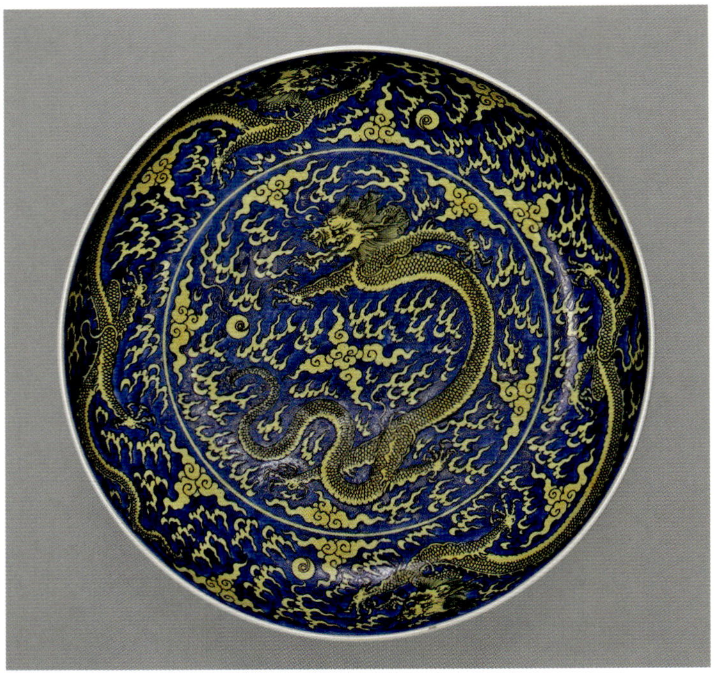

that outward expression of personality for palace women was always subordinated to display of court decorum and standard protocol. Yet just because the empress and other consorts were subject to constraints in their formal appearance and were expected to follow conventional standards of virtue—or because we lack the records to fully reanimate them—we should not assume that these women were robbed of personal identity or that they led bleak lives.

Activities

The empress dowager, empress, and other consorts were largely sequestered from male view (except for close family and eunuchs), but they were physically and socially active. Among an empress's preeminent duties were rites that paralleled or were combined with those of the emperor. One such example involved the royal couple's promotion of agriculture and sericulture, which formed the economic foundation of the empire. Following Chinese tradition, Qing emperors personally ploughed and seeded a furrow in the soil once a year, while empresses (or other consorts serving as substitutes) fed handpicked mulberry leaves to silkworms at the Altar of the Silkworm Deity.[5] The tasks of tilling and weaving were depicted in many imperial artworks to express benevolent concern for the hard labor of the dynasty's subjects. Illustrations of the stages of sericulture—from raising silkworms to spinning and weaving—were promulgated among court women to encourage and instill virtuous behavior.[6] An album of delicate porcelain tiles painted in black enamel and showing women toiling at silk production represents this type

FIGURE 1
Dish with incised dragons. Imperial Porcelain Factory, Jingdezhen, Kangxi period, 1662–1722, porcelain with cobalt reign mark beneath colorless glaze (on base) and yellow enamel over colorless glaze, cat. 124.

FIGURE 2
Dish with dragons. Imperial Porcelain Factory, Jingdezhen, Kangxi period, 1662–1722, porcelain with cobalt reign mark beneath colorless glaze (on base) and cobalt ground under colorless glaze with yellow enamels over colorless glaze, cat. 125.

FIGURE 3
Scene of sericulture from volume 4 of Pictures of Tilling and Weaving with poems by the Qianlong emperor. Imperial Porcelain Factory, Jingdezhen, Qianlong period, 1736–95, porcelain with gray, black, and red enamels over colorless glaze, silk damask binding added in the Imperial Workshop, Beijing, cat. 130.

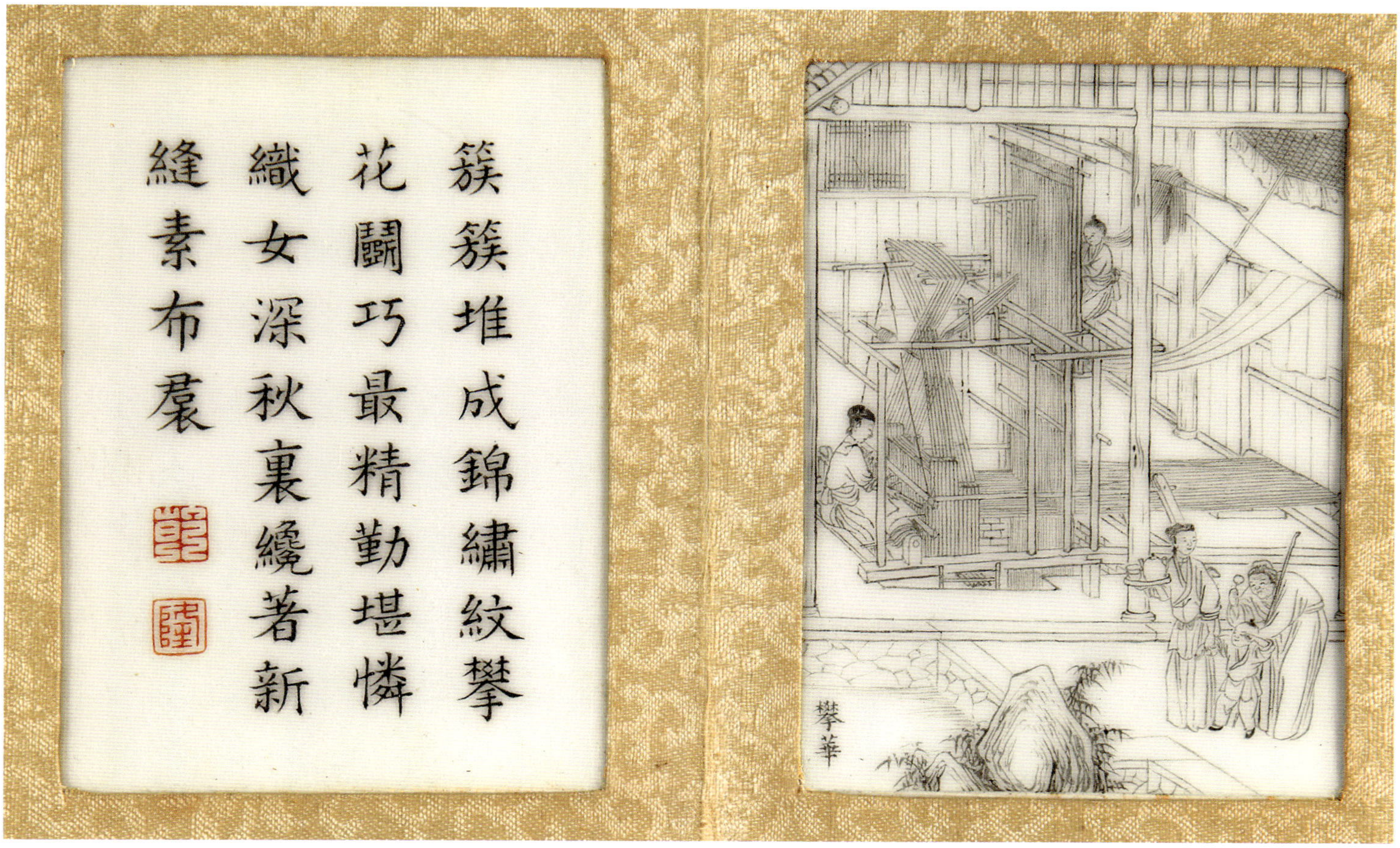

of imagery (fig. 3). Qing empresses also performed numerous minor symbolic rites as part of their duty. For example, they marked the passing of the seasons by switching from gold to jade hairpins in the third lunar month (just as the emperor traded a fur hat for one of silk) and switching back again in the eighth lunar month.[7] These small gestures exemplify the series of similar demands that filled the empresses' days, sometimes rather pleasurably, and, most important, gave them purpose in maintaining imperial decorum.

The lives of imperial women were punctuated by lighthearted seasonal entertainments, including annual festivals, and special occasions such as birthdays. Some of these activities coincided with travel beyond the Forbidden City—for example, to the suburban palace of the Garden of Perfect Brightness (Yuanming yuan), which offered a variety of diversions, including all-female outings to temples within the complex or boating parties among the lotuses on its lakes. Boating on small skiffs was a common activity among the females at court: an early eighteenth-century album depicting monthly pastimes (see pl. 22) and a photograph of Empress Dowager Cixi (Empress Xiaoqin; 1835–1908; see p. 120, fig. 8) confirm its enduring popularity.[8] Birthday celebrations, especially the grand ones that Qianlong arranged for his mother, brought special delights. For Empress Dowager Chongqing's eightieth birthday, the emperor transformed part of the route from the Forbidden City to the Garden of Perfect Brightness and an area within that compound into a re-creation of Suzhou's buzzing commercial district. The emperor commanded costumed eunuchs to staff the ersatz stores for the imperial women's "play" shopping sprees.[9] Opera was another great pleasure for women, with lavish performances produced by Qianlong for his mother's birthday; she and other empresses also initiated performances to which they invited other women as guests on many other occasions.

Annual festivals celebrated throughout the empire were also enjoyed at the court by both sexes. For example, Qianlong invited his mother to view ice skating with him at the winter solstice, and he hosted a family banquet at the end of the New Year season that included the empress dowager, selected daughters, and favored consorts of the moment (a reminder of his mutable affections). Some celebrations catered specifically to women, especially the Double Seventh Festival occurring on the seventh day of the seventh lunar month. Its formal name, Qiqiao, literally means "pleading for skills [in needlework]"—a talent deemed essential for attracting and pleasing a spouse. Double Seventh also invoked a legend of enduring love: Zhinü, a celestial weaving maiden weary of fashioning colorful clouds in heaven, escaped to earth and married Niulang, a mortal cowherd, bearing his children. Angered by her defection, the Heavenly Goddess forced Zhinü to return to her divine

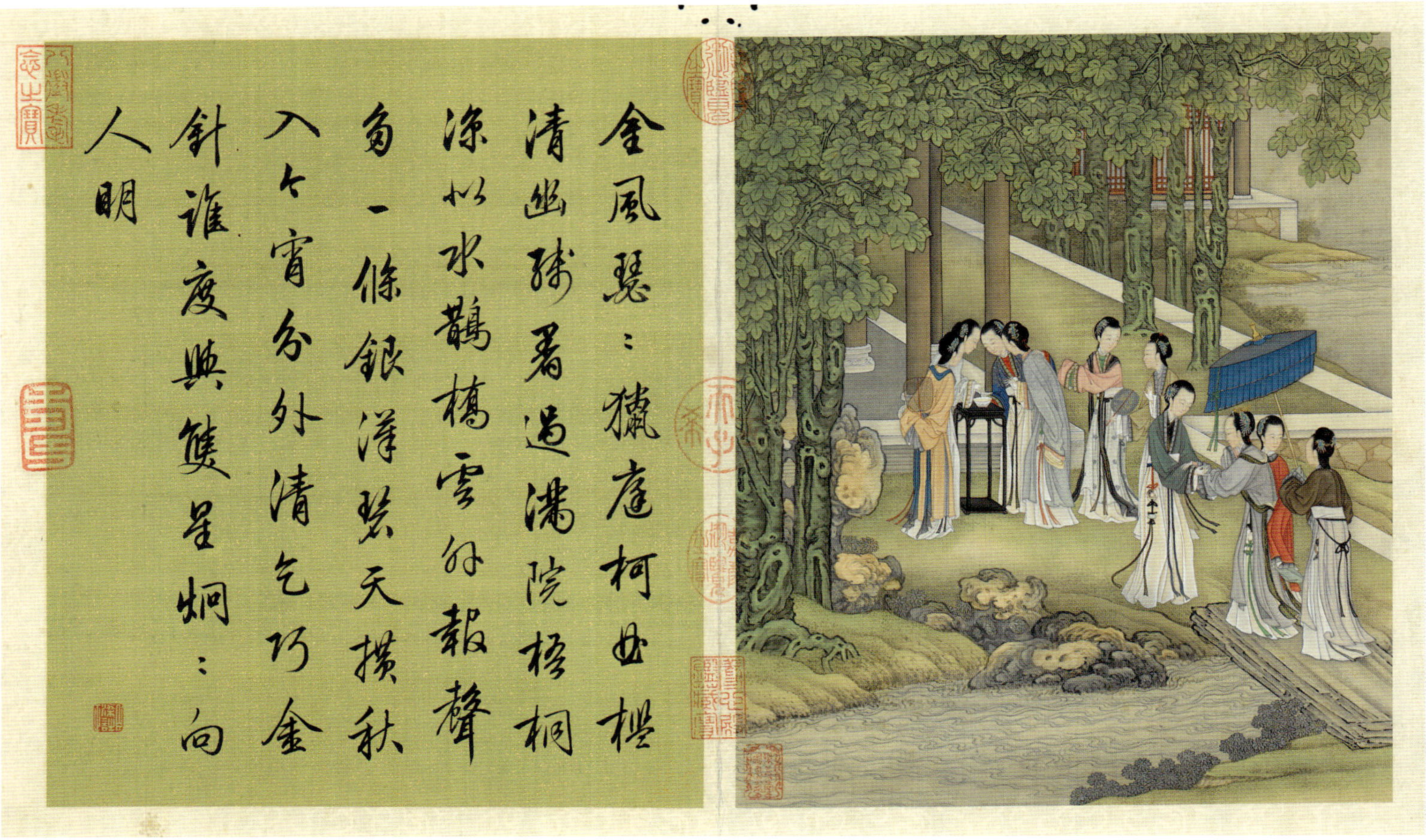

station. Availing himself of magic, Niulang tried to follow, but the goddess created a "river of stars" in the sky (i.e., the Milky Way) to separate them forever. Their anguish was said to bring all the world's magpies together every Double Seventh to form a bridge to connect the lovers for that one night, while throughout China commoners and palace women, including servants, engaged in festivities.

Typical features of the imperial celebration of Double Seventh included women dining al fresco and competitions to prove dexterity in sewing, including threading a needle by candlelight. Another contest had a girl throwing a needle in a bowl of water; if it floated, she was deemed ready for matrimony (fig. 4). The ultimate event of the evening was placing offerings of fruit, tea, and wine on an altar to pray for prowess in needlework and a happy marriage—one of many Double Seventh festivities captured for the Qianlong emperor by the court painter Ding Guanpeng (fig. 5).

Qianlong also commissioned special decorations for Double Seventh, perhaps to underscore the importance of needlework and sericulture as virtuous occupations for women. Yet the grandeur of some of these objects—such as a screen with an expensive *zitan* wood frame and delicate embroidery on the front and painting on the back (fig. 6)—suggests genuine affection for his consorts in his desire to present them with

FIGURE 4

Floating a needle from The Pursuit of Pleasures in the Course of the Seasons. Painting by Chen Mei (1697–1745); calligraphy by Liang Shizheng (1697–1763), Beijing, painting: Yongzheng period, 1723–35; calligraphy: Qianlong period, 1738, album leaf, ink and color on silk, cat. 33.

FIGURE 5

Ladies celebrating the Double Seventh Festival, pleading for skills in needlework (detail). Ding Guanpeng (d. after 1770), Qianlong period, 1748, handscroll, ink on paper, 11¼ × 151⅜ in. (28.7 × 384.5 cm), Shanghai Museum.

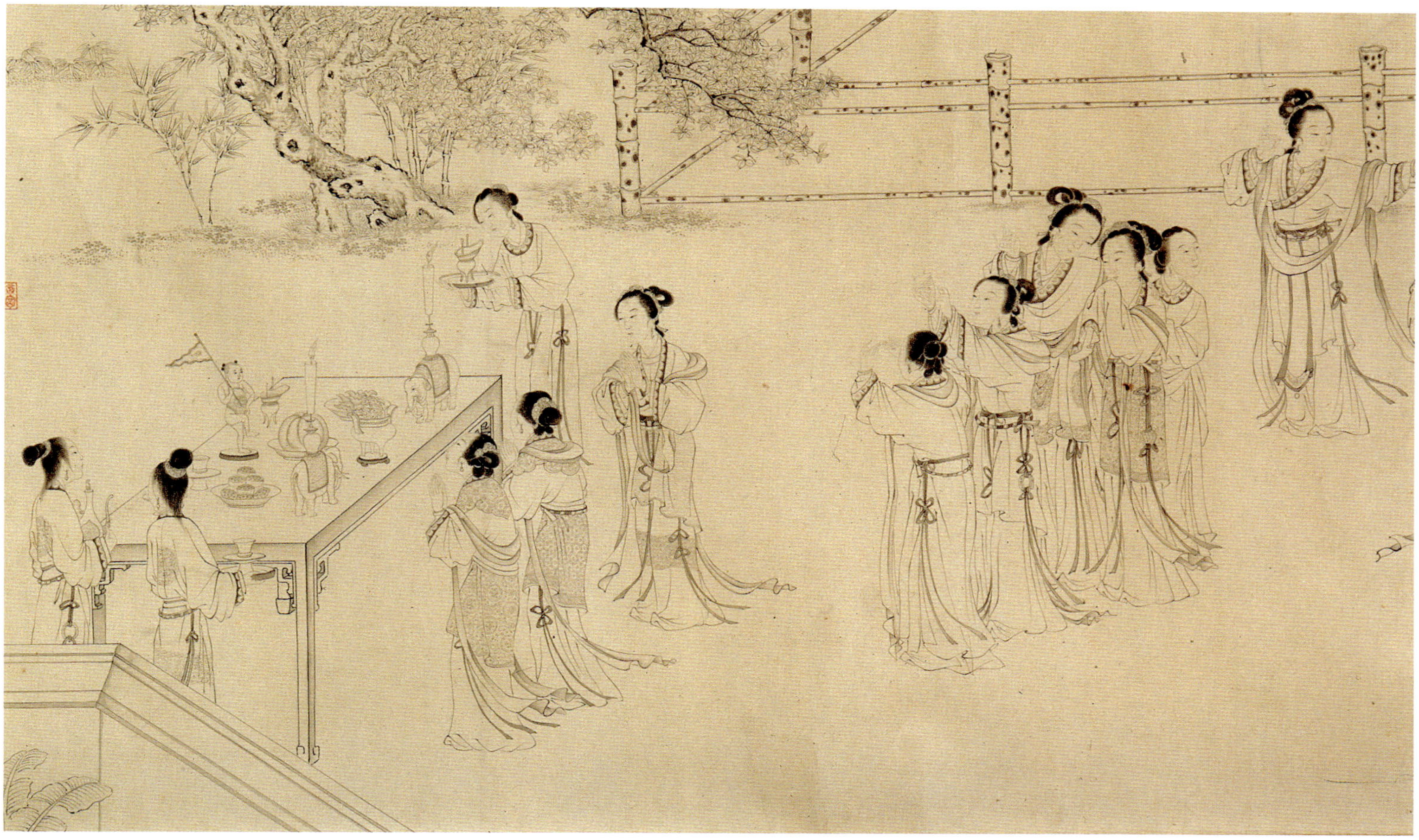

something truly special for the festival. A calligraphy couplet on the screen mentions the Milky Way, invoking the legend of the cowherd and weaving maiden—and additionally alludes to a poem from the ancient classic *Book of Odes (Shijing)* that names the steps of agriculture and sericulture.[10] The embroidered imagery combines scenes of Double Seventh festivities, such as putting offerings on an altar, with references to plowing and weaving. The screen thus serves as a memento of the Double Seventh Festival amusements enjoyed by consorts while reminding them of the virtues and obligations of promoting sericulture in order to serve the emperor and the state.

Women in Court Paintings

Among the most complex and fascinating paintings for investigating the female realm at the early Qing court is a set of twelve almost life-size images of individual women pictured in stunningly furnished garden residences. Here called *Yinzhen's Twelve Ladies* (figs. 7–18), the paintings are also known by other titles depending on whether they are interpreted as imperial portraits of consorts or generic images of beauties.[11] They were commissioned in the first quarter of the eighteenth century, possibly as panels for a screen, by the Yongzheng emperor (r. 1723–35) when he was still a prince and known by his personal name, Yinzhen. (For convenience we will call him Yongzheng here, although at the time of the commission he did not yet have that title.[12]) James Cahill has persuasively argued that, although the paintings are Imperial Workshop (Zaoban chu) productions and are unsigned, they should be largely attributed to Zhang Zhen or his son Zhang Weibang, both leading painters from China's southern Jiangnan region who sometimes worked as court artists in Beijing.[13]

Paintings produced at the Qing court borrowed features from several well-established Chinese genres while also incorporating new traits, such as a penchant for adding auspicious imagery to reinforce a harmonious view of court society.[14] In portraying women, court painters drew on stylistic attributes from a category known as "depictions of gentlewomen" (*shinü tu*), including its subgenres "paintings of beautiful ladies" (*meiren hua*) and "paintings of inner-palace admonitions" (*gongxun tu*). The identity of these twelve women has been debated because the paintings are untitled and have therefore been associated with different archival records. Their identification as consorts is based on several factors, including palace inventory numbers indicating the paintings were once stored in a building devoted to imperial portraits and an archival document describing them as imperial portraits (*yurong*).[15] Another school of thought has associated the paintings with

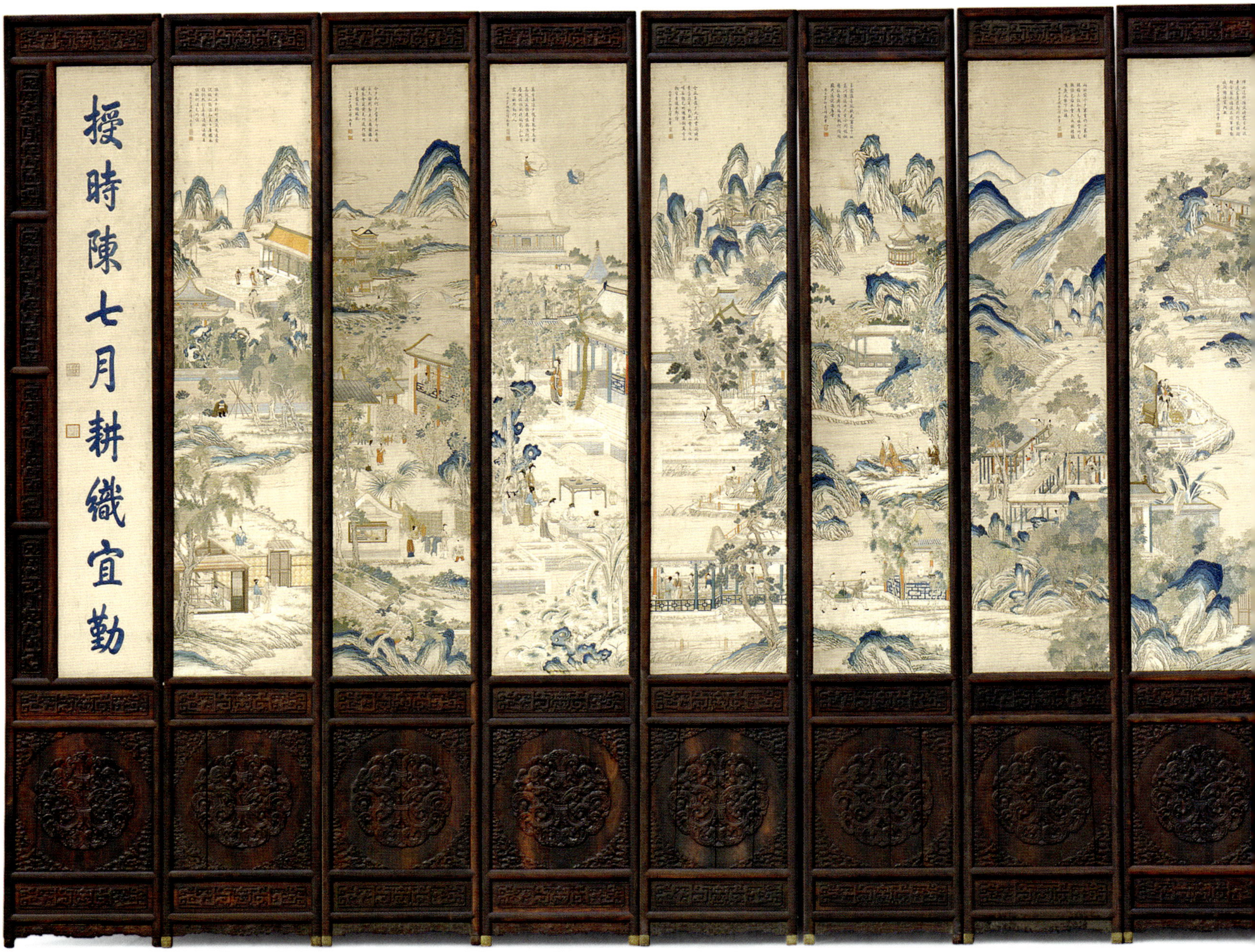
授時陳七月耕織宜勤

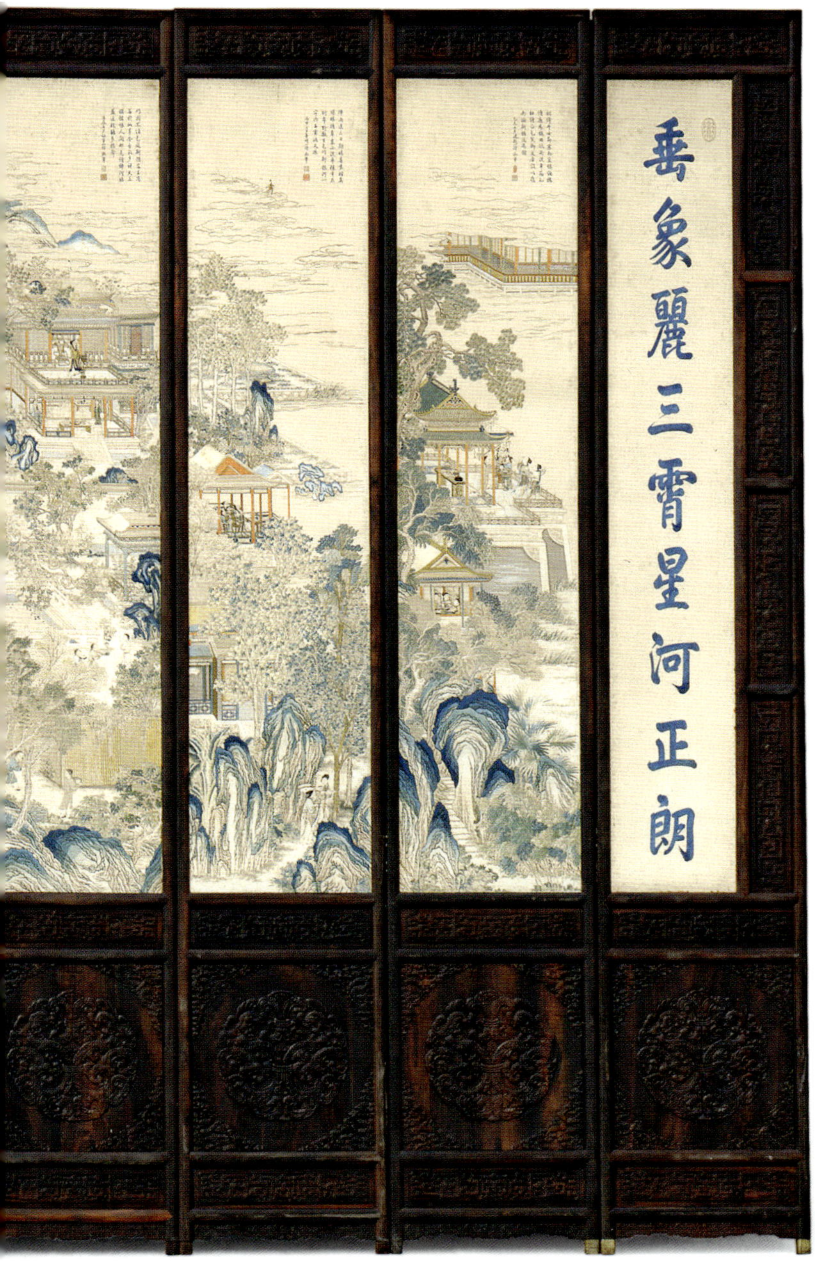

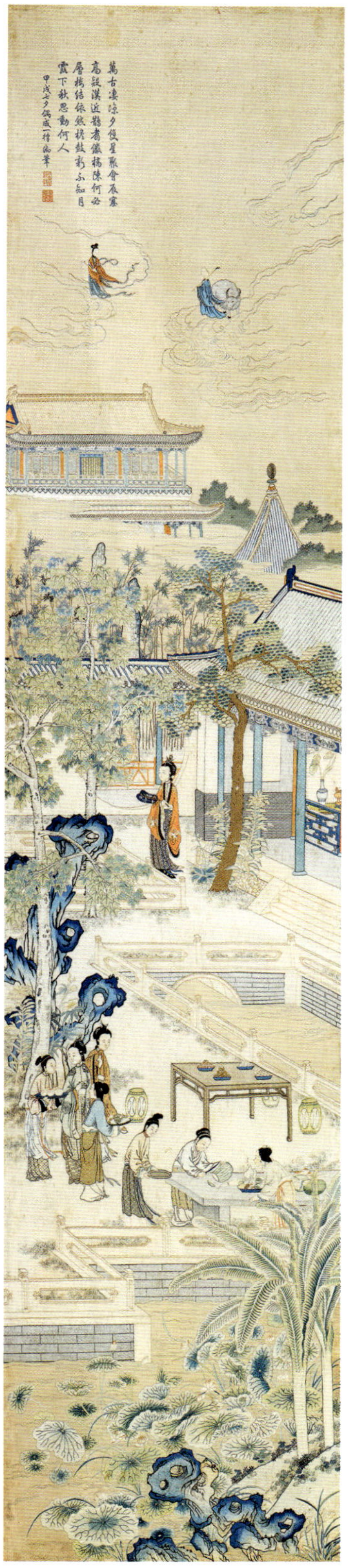

DETAIL

FIGURE 6

Twelve-panel folding screen with calligraphy and scenes of the Double Seventh Festival and tilling and weaving. Imperial Silk Manufactory, Suzhou (embroidery), Qianlong period, about 1777, embroidery, polychrome silk threads on silk, *zitan* wood frame, $156\frac{11}{16} \times 295\frac{15}{16}$ in. (398 × 751.6 cm), Gu210710.

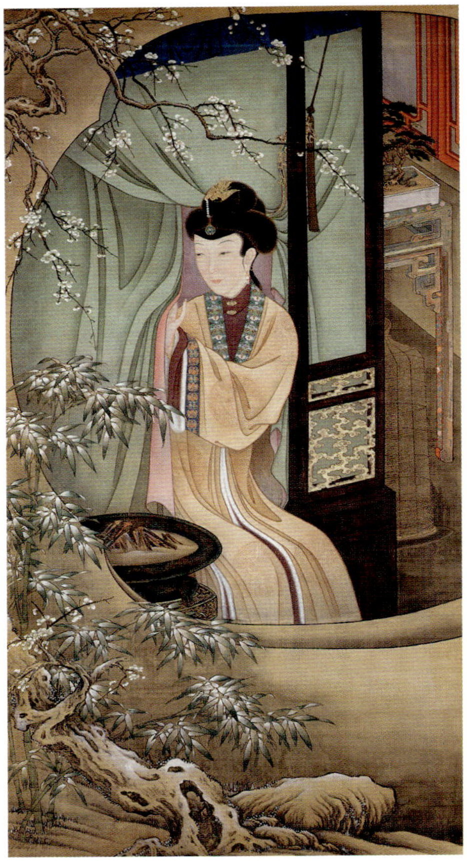

FIGURE 7 LOOKING AT PLUM BLOSSOMS

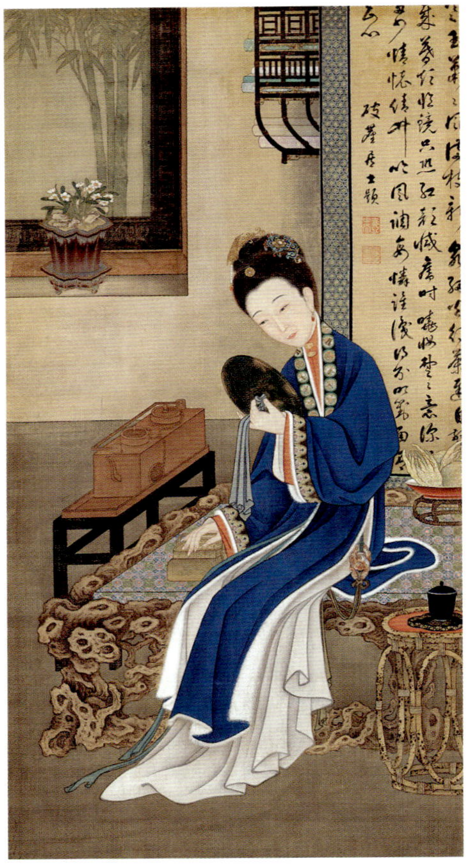

FIGURE 8 LOOKING IN A MIRROR

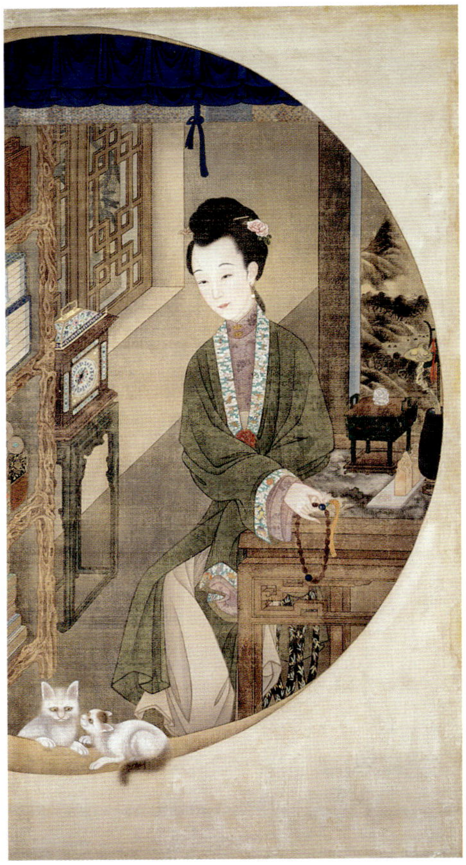

FIGURE 9 WATCHING CATS

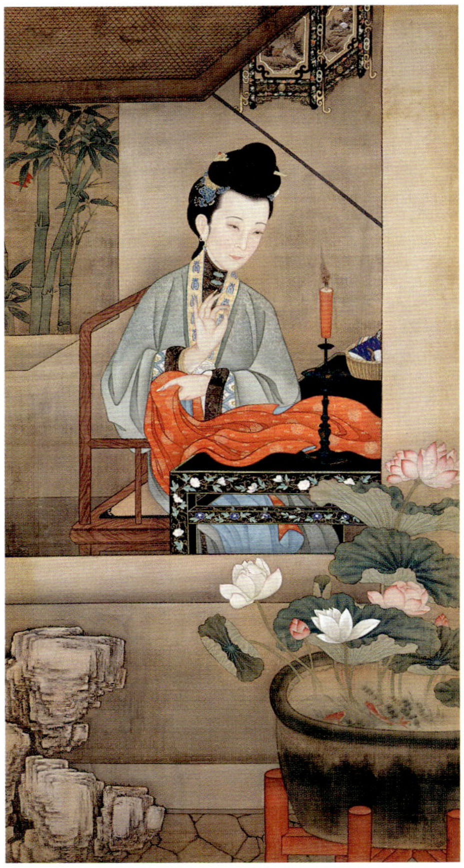

FIGURE 13 SEWING BY CANDLELIGHT

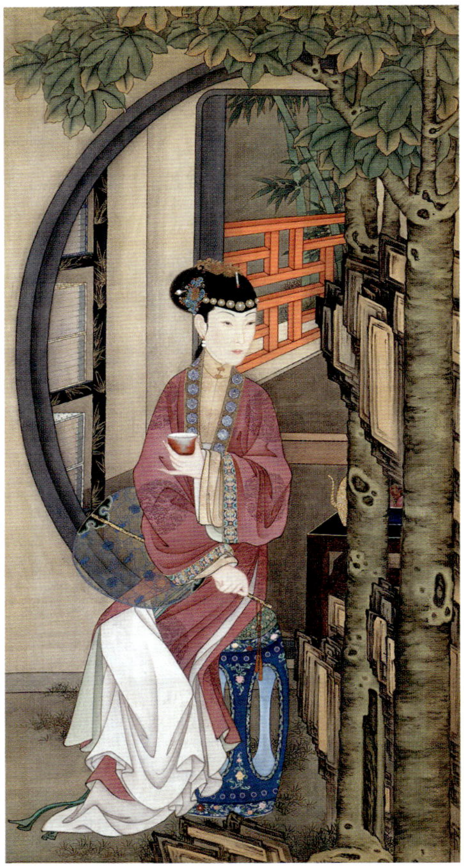

FIGURE 14 DRINKING TEA

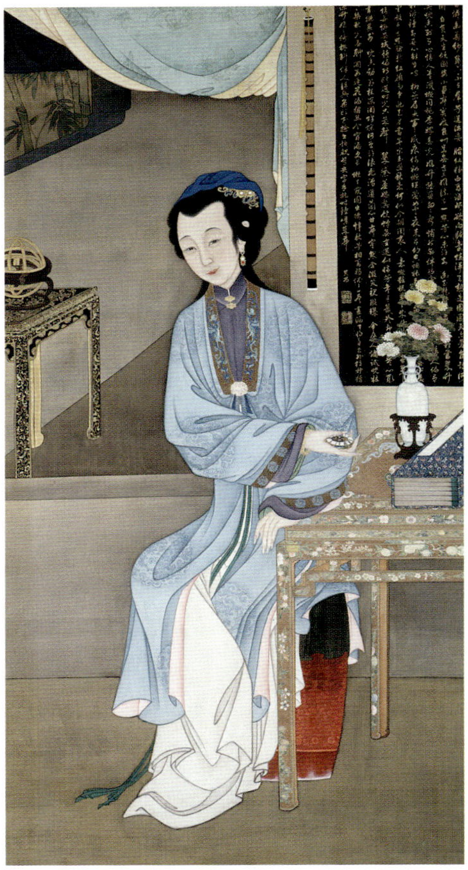

FIGURE 15 HOLDING A WATCH

FIGURES 7–18

Yinzhen's Twelve Ladies. Court painters, Beijing, possibly including Zhang Zhen (active late 17th–early 18th century) or his son Zhang Weibang (about 1725–about 1775), Kangxi period, 1709–23, hanging scrolls, ink and color on silk, cat. 2–5.

Yinzhen was the personal name of the future Yongzheng emperor. The original order of the paintings is unknown. They are grouped here by season: winter (figs. 7–9), spring (figs. 10–12), summer (figs. 13–15), and autumn (figs. 16–18).

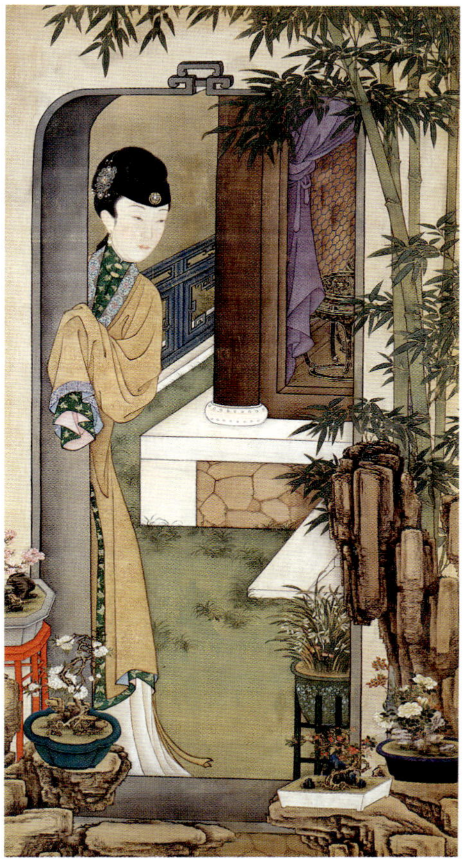

FIGURE 10 LEANING IN THE DOORWAY

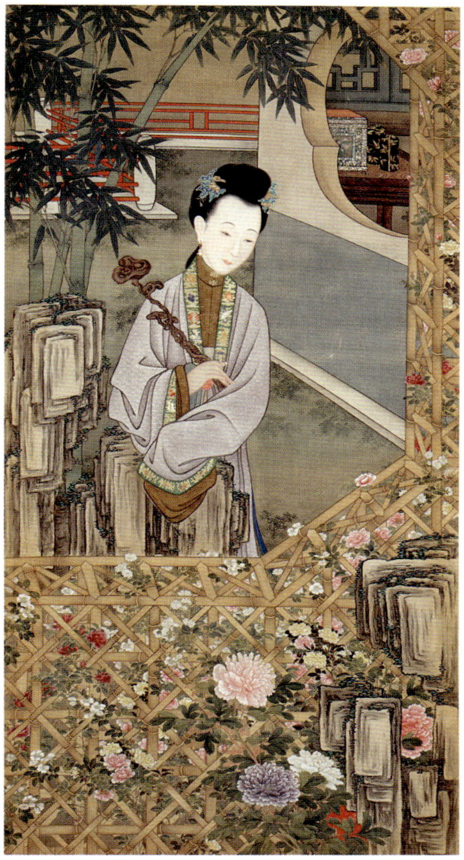

FIGURE 11 HOLDING A SCEPTER

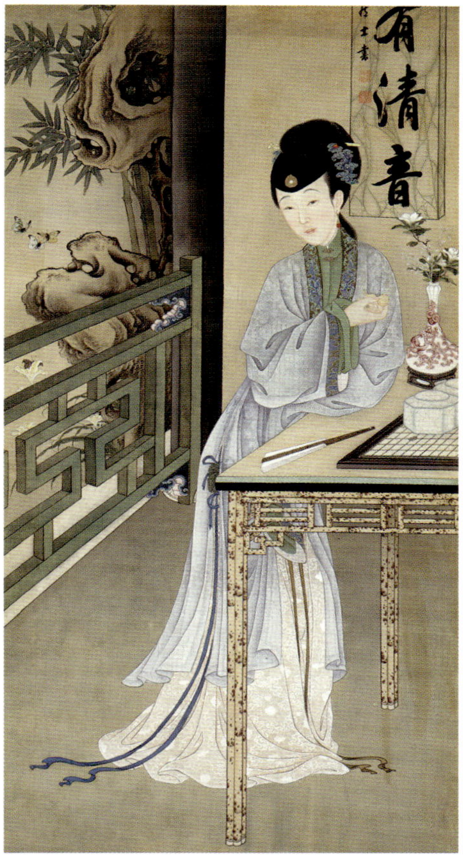

FIGURE 12 FLITTING BUTTERFLIES

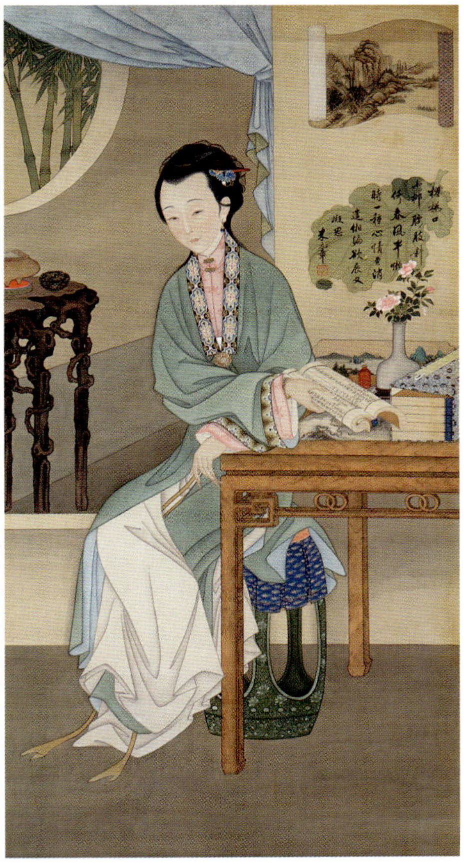

FIGURE 16 READING

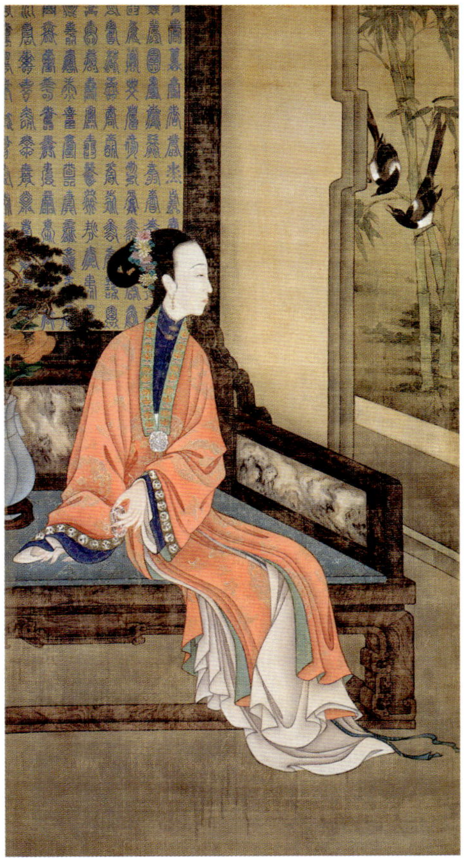

FIGURE 17 LISTENING TO MAGPIES

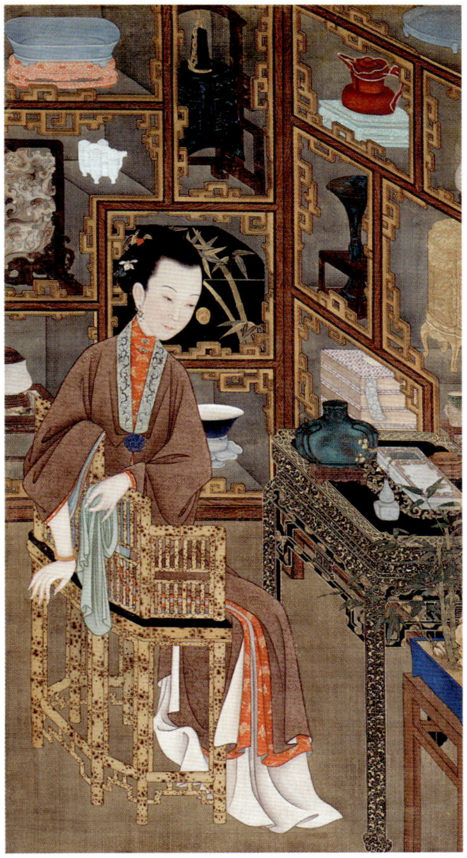

FIGURE 18 SURROUNDED BY ANTIQUITIES

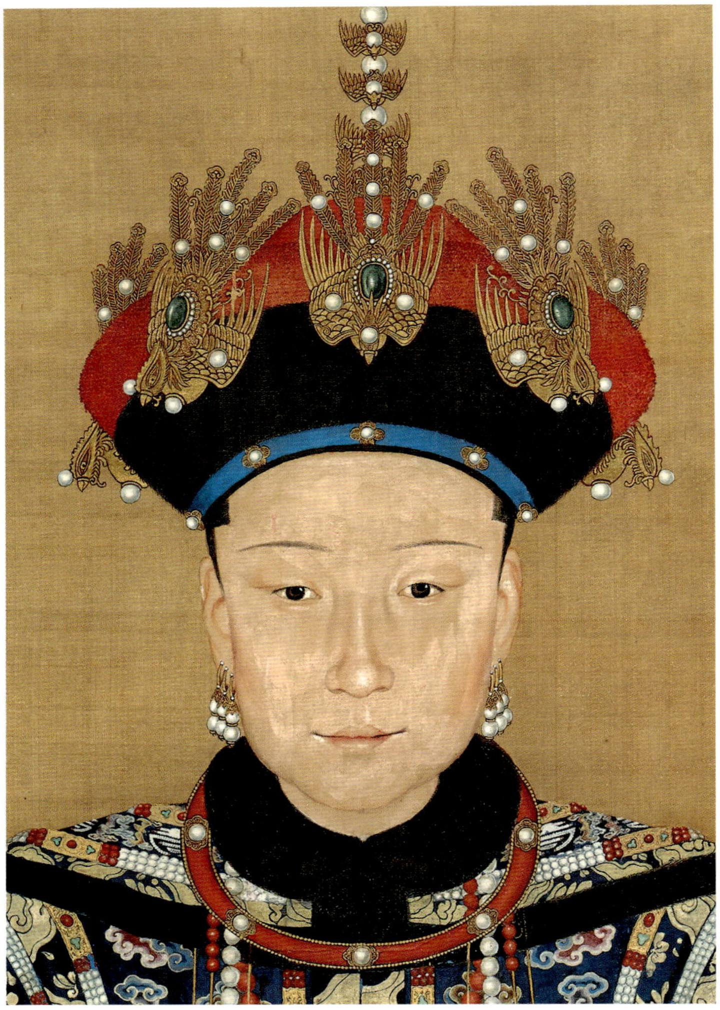

FIGURE 19

Empress Xiaoxian (detail). Ignatius Sichelbarth (Ai Qimeng; Bohemia, 1708–1780), Yi Lantai (active about 1748–86), and possibly Wang Ruxue (active 18th century), Qianlong period, 1777 with repainting possibly in 19th century, hanging scroll, ink and color on silk, Peabody Essex Museum, cat. 12.

FIGURE 20

Pair of triple earrings. Probably Imperial Workshop, Beijing, 18th century, pearls and gold alloy, 2 in. (5 cm) each, Gu11706.

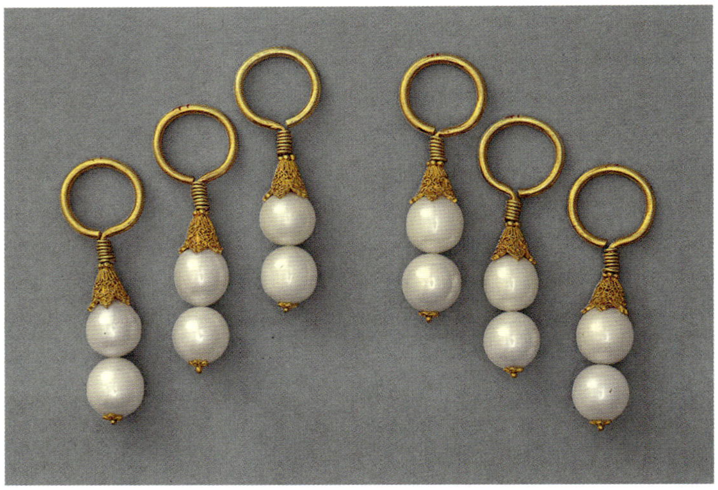

an alternative document containing the word *meiren*, denoting a sexually alluring beauty, which led to the misidentification of the ladies as generic beauties.[16] The best way to understand these paintings is to see them as portraits of real consorts that were selectively enhanced with traits borrowed from "paintings of beauties" in order to bestow upon Yongzheng's wives a mantle of seductive charm.

Yongzheng felt close enough to the women in the works to embed his own calligraphy and seals in a few of the paintings, which he disguised to look like artworks decorating the women's rooms. Handwriting and seals were powerful signs of personal identity in China, and they serve here to symbolically interject Yongzheng's presence into the lady's residences—another element that supports the argument that these are portraits of women with whom he consorted and not just fantasy images. Records are silent on who the women are, but judging from facial types, at least three consorts are likely portrayed, including Lady Ula Nara (1679–1731), who was the mother of Yongzheng's first son and became Empress Xiaojing.[17]

Despite the fact that the paintings depict consorts, they incorporate references to Chinese courtesan culture, notably in dress. Modern scholars tend to discuss female appearance in the Qing imperium as distinctively "Manchu" or "Chinese," viewing these qualities as mutually exclusive. Yet when the concept of "being Manchu" first arose in the early Qing, it referred to political allegiance and not cultural or racial purity.[18] Defining a visual code for the new concept of "Manchu-ness" was gradual and developed in part by contrasting it with a Chinese "other." Emperors prohibited empresses and other consorts from wearing Han Chinese–style garb—such as garments with wide sleeves—to create clearly visible boundaries between Manchu and Han Chinese cultures and to bolster the separation between rulers and subjects.[19] Yet still in Yongzheng's time, a degree of fluidity in dress seems to have been tolerated as long as it did not undermine Manchu heritage.[20]

Jewelry illustrates one such permeable boundary. In Manchu tradition, empresses (up to the time of Empress Dowager Cixi) always wore three (usually double-pearl-and-gold) earrings in each earlobe as a sign of their ethnicity when pictured for formal occasions (figs. 19 and 20). Yet in more leisurely situations and in private spaces—as *Yinzhen's Twelve Ladies* shows—the custom must have been relaxed, and women were allowed to flirt with some Chinese-style fashions, such as wearing a single earring per ear. Indeed, the emperor encouraged the practice, as court records indicate Yongzheng often ordered pairs of two and not six earrings to be made in the Imperial Workshop for his consorts.[21]

It is often noted that the women in *Yinzhen's Twelve Ladies* wear Han Chinese–style clothing and therefore could not represent consorts, but this reasoning seems flawed. It is true that their long, flowing robes are similar to those worn by "beauties" in many Chinese vernacular paintings of the same period, such as *Beautiful Woman in an Interior, with a Dog* by Leng Mei (about 1670–1742), in which both the pose and the dress of the woman closely resembles that of the lady in *Yinzhen's Twelve Ladies* leaning on a table with a chess (*weiqi*) board (fig. 12).[22] The costumes in both images are indeed associated with the clothing of "graceful Chinese women" but do not in fact represent actual garments. Artists (both at and outside the court) who painted informal images of women typically garbed them in supple, sinuously arrayed silk robes with trailing sashes, a combination of Han Chinese styles from several dynasties whipped into a pleasing and timeless garment. Qing texts refer to it as "ancient garb" (*guzhuang*), using "ancient" (*gu*) to invoke an idealized sense of antiquity as a designation of quality and refinement rather than a specific era. Therefore, the sophisticated robes and headdresses depicted in *Yinzhen's Twelve Ladies* are ahistorical confections that, while redolent of Han Chinese taste, are not actual Chinese garments. Furthermore, many details of decoration, such as designs on collars, have been manipulated to convey auspicious wishes rather than always copying existing textiles, underscoring the fact that we should not be too literal in interpreting the details of dress in these works.

In the same general period that Yongzheng commissioned the twelve images of his consorts, he also had himself painted in a variety of guises, including as a European hunter, a Chinese Daoist master, and a Tibetan monk. He did not actually impersonate these figures, but by mapping a broad spectrum of different personae onto his own identity, he symbolically encompassed the world's diversity within himself as an expression of his supramundane status. Similarly, by imbuing portraits of his consorts with notions of beauty and sexuality borrowed from southern China, he acknowledged that they too embodied alternative identities or forms of femininity. While alarms had been raised in the early Qing to watch for weakness and licentiousness at the court resulting from indulgence in a lifestyle filled with the charms of Jiangnan courtesans, this did not prevent the emperor from fantasizing about—and his artists from painting—imperial women with the charms of the region's courtesans.[23]

Thus, as Yongzheng enjoyed these portraits, he could assume one more alter ego—that of a Chinese scholar-elite consorting with the most refined courtesans of the south. Some modern interpretations give this phenomenon a political reading, seeing it as a "conflation of geography with gender, culture, and social identity" and leading Qing emperors to sometimes personify the Jiangnan region and its elite literary tradition as a sexually available Han woman, a process known as "geogendering."[24] In this interpretation *Yinzhen's Twelve Ladies* takes on a distinctly allegorical meaning, with the women serving as a representation of China under Yongzheng's rule.

A Closer Look

If we step back to remind ourselves that the women actually are consorts, then references to sexuality and fertility in the paintings are especially enlightening and allow us to envision more clearly intimate aspects of the consorts' lives—or at least the importance their husband placed on these topics. Despite the overall refinement of the twelve ladies, a viewer steeped in the Chinese visual code will soon notice that they draw more attention to their physical charms than is normal in paintings of consorts, such as *Yinzhen and Consorts* (see p. 36, fig. 3), in which four consorts stand demurely in a garden waiting for their spouse, who is seated in a pavilion. The attire of the senior consort in that painting (probably Lady Ula Nara), consisting of a Manchu-style apricot-colored robe embellished by court jewelry similar to that seen in formal portraits (three double-pearl earrings in each ear and a torque around her neck), fully accords with court protocol for being seen in public.

By contrast, the consorts in *Yinzhen's Twelve Ladies* are more seductive in their dress, and their faces register more expression than usual: they are seemingly lost in thought, expectantly waiting for someone—someone who, their titillating gestures suggest, might well be an absent lover. Most of the women appear just inside the threshold of a door or window, a stance that draws on a popular convention in seventeenth-century Chinese literature that described available women appearing in the liminal zone separating a publicly shared space from an intimate, private enclosure.[25] Some of the ladies' poses further a provocatively sexual reading: one woman sits on the edge of her curtained bed (figs. 7 and 21); another's sleeve is caught on the back of her chair, tantalizingly exposing her delicate forearm (fig. 18); yet another hugs a garden door, looking out as if to welcome a guest, while coquettishly pointing with her shoulder toward a curtained chamber furnished with two adjacent stools for an intimate tête-à-tête (fig. 10). These erogenous details have supported the theory that the women must be imaginary beauties because their flirtatious deportment seems infelicitous for an imperial consort. Yet, the standards of public decorum would not have applied in the privacy of their residence as they waited for their imperial lover.

Through these artworks we see the imperial wives as Yongzheng saw them; as such, any notion of impropriety dissipates. The sexual charge bears witness to the passion between a husband and his wives—a state generally unacknowledged in Qing and modern accounts of the lives of consorts but, as these paintings attest, likely a real part of their experience. Yongzheng, who commented on every draft of an artwork before it was completed, must have commanded the artists to show his wives in a state of anxious expectation of his conjugal visit. Imperial vanity may have been the motivation, but we can fairly speculate that the sense of anticipation, including its sexual overtones, was genuinely felt by the consorts, all of whom would have prized the opportunity to carry a son and thereby gain status and possibly promotion at court, beyond whatever other pleasures motherhood brought.

Images that hint at physical union and its potential result abound in *Yinzhen's Twelve Ladies*. Butterflies fly wing to wing and penetrate a flower (fig. 12), two amorous cats cavort (fig. 9), and a pair of goldfish swim together (fig. 13). In the painting of the woman gazing into a mirror (fig. 8), the red-glazed bowl beside her contains Buddha's hand fruit, a fragrant citron offered as a sign of good fortune at temples at the Chinese New Year (the narcissus on the windowsill confirms this time frame). However, the fruit also has a hidden meaning. Its shape is suggestive of female genitalia, so Qing painters often appropriated it as sign of sexual availability, a connotation that here suggests intimacy between Yongzheng and his consort.

Their engagement—physical and emotional—is echoed in Yongzheng's poem that appears behind the woman written in his own hand. The verse, written in a female voice, includes a line decrying the loss of her rosy complexion and fading allure, and it is usually interpreted as Yongzheng's harsh judgment on the rapidity with which female beauty diminishes. Yet, this interpretation ignores the following lines: "How many feelings are expressed by the sighing bamboo? Who will appreciate her character, the [one] who knows [her] heart is just opposite." Thus, the poem ends with Yongzheng's acknowledgment that he looks beyond physical beauty to value his consort's character. The line about "sighing" bamboo suggests that Yongzheng adopted the bamboo as a metaphor for himself and may explain its ubiquity in all twelve paintings: bamboo represents Yongzheng's emotional connection to each of the women.

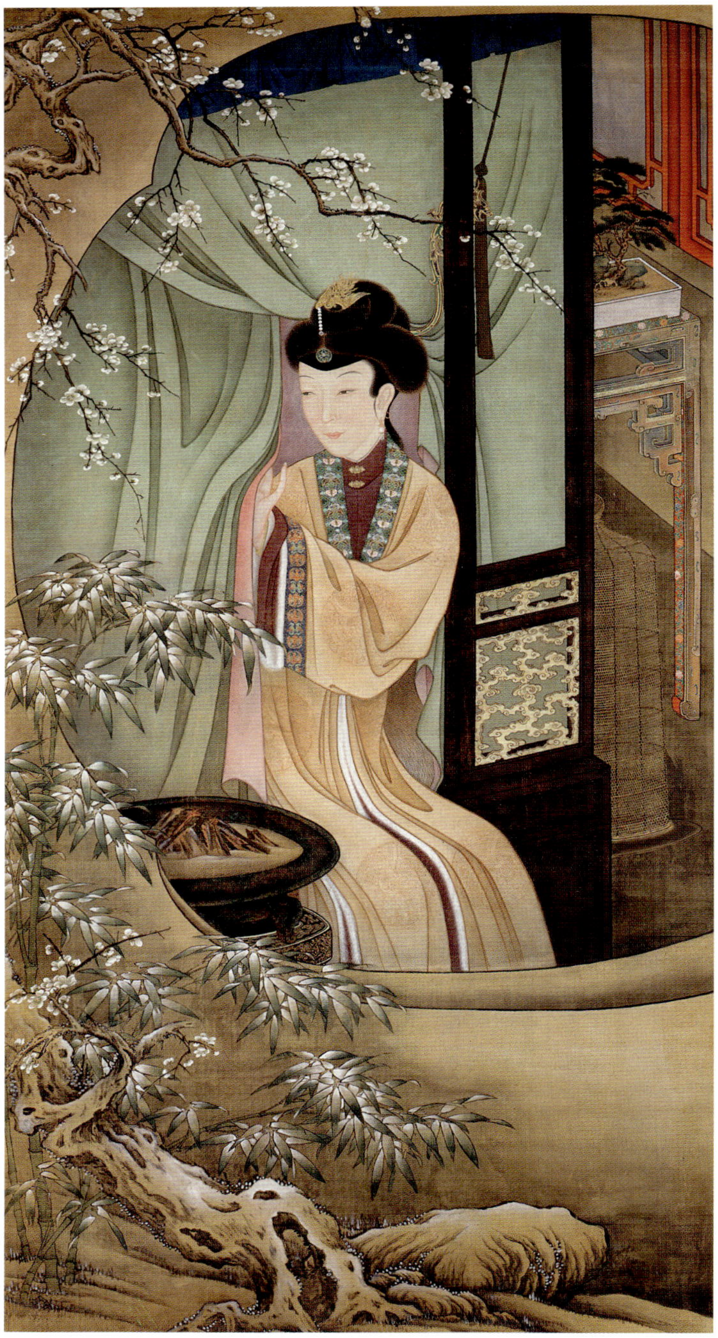

FIGURE 21
Looking at Plum Blossoms from Yinzhen's Twelve Ladies, cat 3.

The image of a woman listening to two magpies (fig. 17) specifically refers to marital relations: The Chinese word for magpie, *xi*, is a homophone with the word for "happiness," hence two magpies convey "double happiness," a Chinese phrase that conjures conjugal joy blessed by sons. The magpie's song was said to "announce the arrival of a visitor," here suggesting the imminent union of the consort and her husband. She fingers an ornament of two interlocking jade rings that symbolizes unbroken continuity for a family and thus for the dynasty. The screen behind her is decorated with a hundred different ways of writing the character for longevity (*shou*), embedding in the scene a wish for a lengthy marriage blessed by long-lived progeny. Another auspicious reference is implanted in the vase with a cypress bough and fruiting persimmon branch, elements that form a rebus for "may all your myriad affairs be peaceful."[26] Furthermore, in Chinese custom a groom wears a cap decorated with cypress branches to symbolize wishes for "many" or "much"—years of life, children, and money.

Other symbols in *Yinzhen's Twelve Ladies* create similar messages. In the painting with a consort waiting to start a chess game with an unseen partner (fig. 12), Yongzheng is symbolically present through the vehicle of the calligraphy plaque written in his hand and signed with his seals. Outside, the butterfly pollinating an open day lily alludes to their union with the hope for the favorable result of a son, as the flower's name sounds like the phrase "may you give birth to a son." Reinforcing this, she fingers a gourd—a symbol of fecundity. The words for "small gourd" and for "butterfly" are both pronounced *die* and are homophones for another word that means "long lived."

Environment

The settings of *Yinzhen's Twelve Ladies* are somewhat ambiguous. Are the garden quarters the women's own or the prince's?[27] Furnishings in all twelve works correspond to the palace milieu: many are identical to ones that appear in paintings of Yongzheng's own chambers, and some perfectly match objects handed down through the imperial collection and are now in the Palace Museum.[28] Yet princes and emperors gave to their women items similar in style and quality to those they personally enjoyed, so that living environments in the palace were in truth more "gender neutral" than specifically feminine or masculine spaces. For example, the staggered shelved cabinet in the image of the lady looking at antiquities (fig. 18) corresponds to a pair of cabinets that were in the Empress Dowager Chongqing's palace (pl. 24). The exquisite antiquities surrounding the woman—jades, bronzes, and porcelain vessels, all set on handsome display stands—resemble luxuries empresses and other consorts were familiar with in their personal spaces. This point is underscored by the pattern on a festive robe (*jifu*) worn by one of Qianlong's consorts (pl. 21). It is decorated with images of porcelain vases on stands, showing that a woman considered such objects to be an integral part of her personal world, one she felt comfortable using to project her identity in her daily existence. It was not exclusively a male prerogative to live among stunning modern and antique collectibles.

Many of the twelve consorts' rooms contain painted and inlaid lacquer tables and stools, a type of furniture traditionally associated with female taste, yet court documents indicate Yongzheng commissioned lacquered furniture for himself. The spotted-bamboo chair in the image of the woman with antiquities (fig. 18) has traditionally been identified as a type of seat favored by women because its delicate frame fit their dainty physique, but research has shown such chairs were also used by men who favored the low-back chair as it could be put under a window ledge. It is almost futile to try to draw a clear divide between male and female furnishings in Qing palace residences, but small details are suggestive of these as female domains. In the painting with the rose and peony trellis (fig. 11), an exclusively female type of dressing case appears on a table in the background (pl. 26). Among the very few objects in the paintings that are primarily male is a snuff bottle on a table in a scene that also contains Yongzheng's calligraphy on the wall (fig. 16), giving the emperor an almost palpable presence, as if the bottle is just another indication that he is in the room with his wife.[29]

The books in several of the *Yinzhen's Twelve Ladies* paintings underscore female literacy, a source of pride and pleasure for the female community. Well-stocked bookshelves appear in many court paintings of women, including those that hover even more ambiguously between generic beauty paintings and images of court women, such as *Lady with a Hairpin* by Jin Tingbiao (fig. 22). While this painting is not a portrait per se, the woman's attention to her toilette as her lady-in-waiting fetches her a book off the shelf speaks to the dual parameters of a consort's existence, one grounded in a desire to be both attractive and educated. The table at the back of the room displays a small statue of Avalokiteshvara (Guanyin), a Buddhist deity to whom women prayed for children, pointing to one more ever-present aspect of the consorts' world.

Some court paintings illustrate another dimension of literacy—the duty of empresses to maintain and promote family and dynastic order through education. Women's role in schooling their young offspring is the subject of several didactic court paintings used to instill Confucian virtues in

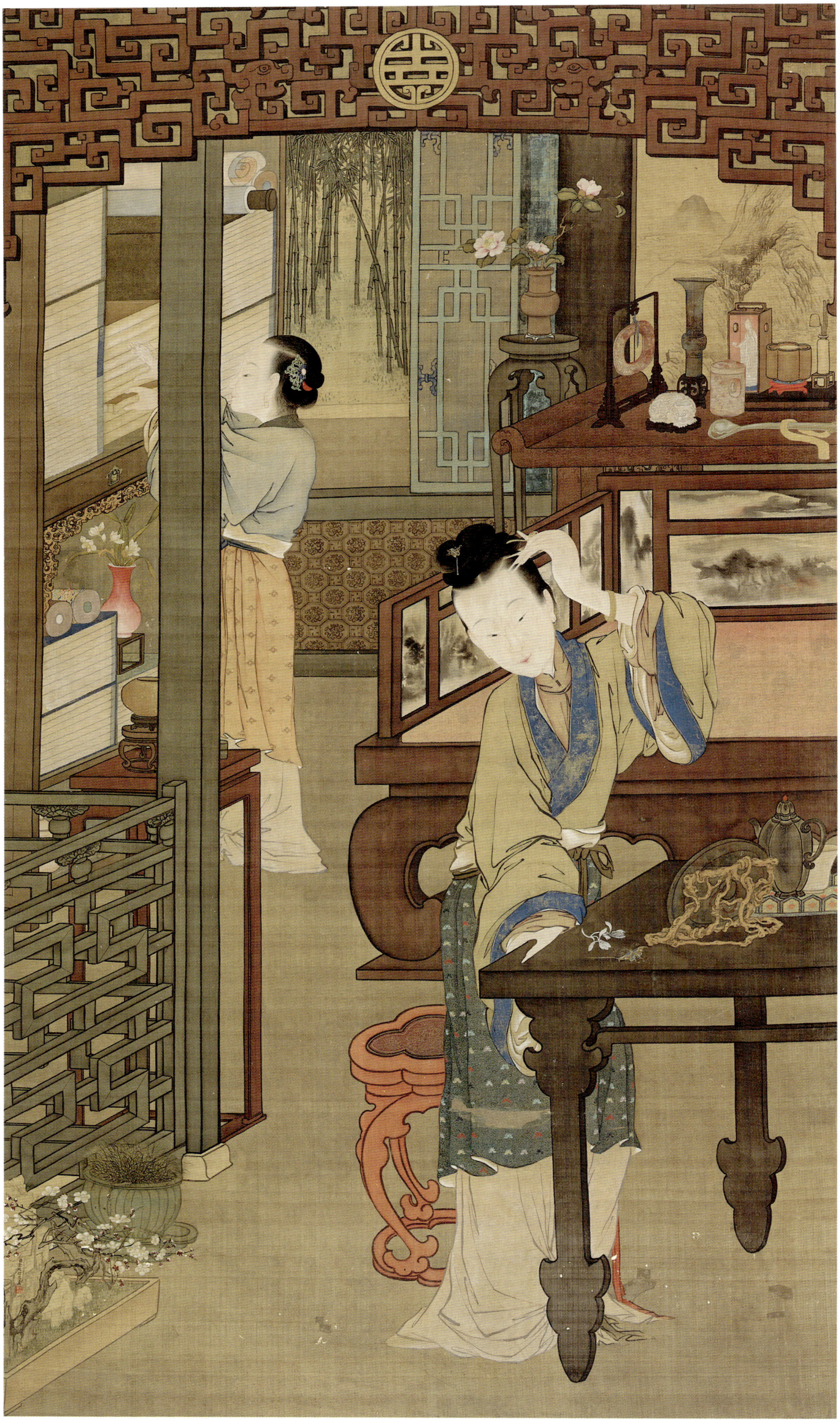

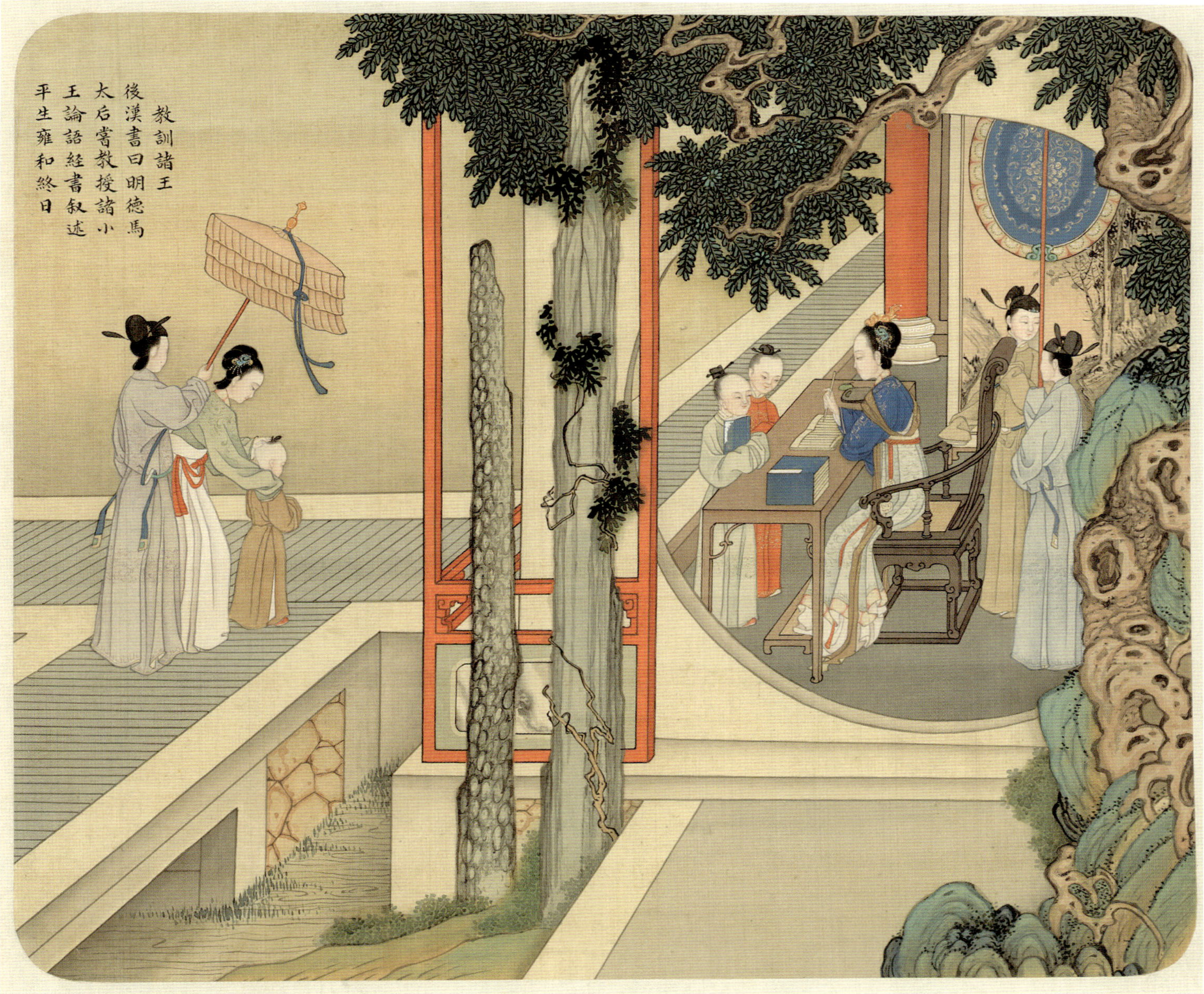

FIGURE 22
Lady with a Hairpin. Jin Tingbiao (d. 1767), Qianlong period, mid-18th century, hanging scroll, ink and color on silk, cat. 7.

FIGURE 23
Empress Mingde Instructing Princes from Virtuous Empresses and Empresses Dowager in Successive Dynasties. Jiao Bingzhen (about 1660–1726), Kangxi or Yongzheng period, early 18th century, album leaf, ink and color on silk, cat. 31.

palace women. Qianlong was particularly insistent that his consorts adhere to these values, and he collected, commissioned, and created paintings that expressed his views of proper female behavior. The famous ancient scroll *Admonitions of the Instructress to Court Ladies*, attributed to the seminal figure painter Gu Kaizhi (about 344–about 406), was a prized possession of the emperor, as was a later ink copy attributed to Li Gonglin (1049–1106). Qianlong copied the latter work in his own hand, moved by both the artistic style and the moralistic content of the scroll (cat. 27). The many female figures in the scroll serve as paradigms for virtuous behavior that Qianlong wished his wives to practice. One scene includes an image of a tutor instructing an imperial son and daughter, offering an ancient model for female education at the court.

Virtuous Empresses and Empresses Dowager in Successive Dynasties, painted by Jiao Bingzhen (fig. 23), illustrates in sumptuous detail the valued role of literate females in educating royal heirs. In one scene, Empress Mingde (a name that means "virtuous and bright") of the Eastern Han Dynasty (25–220 CE), instructs young princes in the Confucian classics. She did not have children of her own but acted as the mother to one of her husband's sons, who appears here in red as the heir apparent. Mingde looked after him as if he were her own and taught him to read and write; this role, along with her frugality and generosity, made her a model for future empresses. In his version of this episode, Jiao included early-eighteenth-century furniture and architectural details to make it easier for contemporary audiences to relate to the tale. Jiao's album reinforces the suggestion in *Yinzhen's Twelve Ladies* (created around the same time) that palace women were educated and used their learning both for personal pleasure and to fulfill their role in educating the imperial princes (regardless of whether they were the birth mother).

Conclusion

Qing dynasty artworks make clear that senior court women led active and stimulating lives, whether studying snowy boughs to inspire poetry, relishing tea, cherishing antiques, sewing, or boating on a lake. All of these pursuits are vividly rendered in many paintings (including *Yinzhen's Twelve Ladies*) and photographs, and some activities—such as making tea and sewing—are even addressed in the Qianlong emperor's eulogy to Empress Xiaoxian, corroborating their importance (see pl. 2). Beyond the amusements of court life, imperial women took on larger roles in rituals and education that endowed their lives with significant purpose. Certainly, the importance of bearing imperial sons—and the corresponding fear of infertility—were unavoidable realities, but these pressures should not erase the possibility for sexuality, emotional connection, and a rich inner life that Qing paintings acknowledge. Such artworks do much to challenge the notion of empresses as victims of a too-constrained lifestyle bereft of joy, intimacy, and love and offer instead a far more nuanced view of life in the Forbidden City.

Notes

1 For the cake recipe enjoyed by Qianlong, see Ho 1998, 80.

2 Elisseeff 2017, 170.

3 Wu Hung 1997, 352.

4 Chen Pao-chen 2011, 336.

5 For more on consorts and prince's wives substituting for the empress, see Rawski 2004, 72.

6 Qianlong ordered that paintings of virtuous behavior be displayed in consorts' residences. For example, *Empress Cao of the Song Respecting the Value of Agriculture and Sericulture* was hung in the Palace of Prolonged Happiness (Yanxi gong). See Chen Pao-chen 2011, 351, for a list of twelve didactic paintings.

7 Stuart 2011, 309.

8 The photograph of Cixi is analyzed in Hogge 2010.

9 Stuart 1998, 63–64.

10 The poem cited is "The Seventh Month" (*Qi Yue*).

11 Other titles include *Yinzhen's Twelve Beauties* and *Yinzhen's Twelve Majesties* (or *Consorts*). See Yan Qianpei 2011 for a comprehensive list of titles in Chinese and English. A pdf is available at http://art.ncu.edu.tw/artConf/main/public/16/[2]_pp.29-74_十二美人圖研究.pdf.

12 Yongzheng's seals on some paintings indicate a date between 1709 and 1723.

13 Cahill 1996, 63–64.

14 W. Cheng 2014.

15 Persuasive arguments they actually are portraits were put forth in Lin Shu 2015d. She notes the paintings were once stored in the Hall of Imperial Longevity (Shouhuang dian), which contained only portraits of Qing noblepersons, and before that were interred within a monumental golden stupa with a portrait sculpture of Yongzheng when he was still a prince, facts suggestive of their status as real people.

16 In 2006 I mistakenly believed it was a misidentification of the subject matter to call them portraits; see my catalogue entry on the *Yinzhen's Twelve Beauties* in Rawski and Rawson 2006, 431. Advocates for the theory that they are generic beauties include Zhu 1986, 45; Wu Hung 1996; and Wu Hung 1997.

17 Yang Xin 2013.

18 Ko 1998, 38.

19 See Rawski 2009, 41, for the Qianlong emperor's prohibition of bannerwomen adopting Han Chinese dress customs.

20 See also Ko 1998, 39: "As long as a few distinguishing traits were kept conspicuous, the court could manipulate Han symbols and appropriate Ming practices."

21 See Yang Zhishui 2014, 826, quoting from records in the archives of the Hall of Mental Cultivation (Yangxin dian).

22 The painting is in the Tianjin Museum. For an illustration, see Cahill 2010, 186.

23 Cahill 1996, 62–63.

24 Kleutghen 2015, 254; Wu Hung 1996, 221.

25 See Xu Zhen (active 1659–1711), *Meiren pu* (Manual of beautiful women; completed about 1659), as discussed in Wu Hung 1997, 327–28.

26 Three pairs of homophones form the rebus: "cypress" sounds like "one hundred" or "myriad," "persimmon" like "affairs," and "vase" like "peace."

27 He Li 2014 describes the paintings as a "juxtaposition between feminine figures and masculine objects."

28 Wu Meifeng discusses the furniture in the paintings as representing Yongzheng's artistic taste; see Wu Meifeng 2007, 146–67. Peng 2006 compares objects in the paintings with those in the National Palace Museum, Taibei. Cheng Zijin 2016 discusses comparisons between objects in the paintings and the Palace Museum collection in Beijing.

29 He Li 2014 describes an "axe" in a container on the table in the painting with the cats (fig. 9) as a singularly masculine object. Actually, it is a halberd (*ji*), which appears in many Chinese decorative arrangements for its meaning as a homophone for a word that means "auspicious." Here it is next to a wish-granting scepter (*ruyi*), furthering the symbolic message of good wishes rather than harboring a masculine connotation.

Empress Dowager Chongqing and the Palace of Longevity and Health

LIN SHU

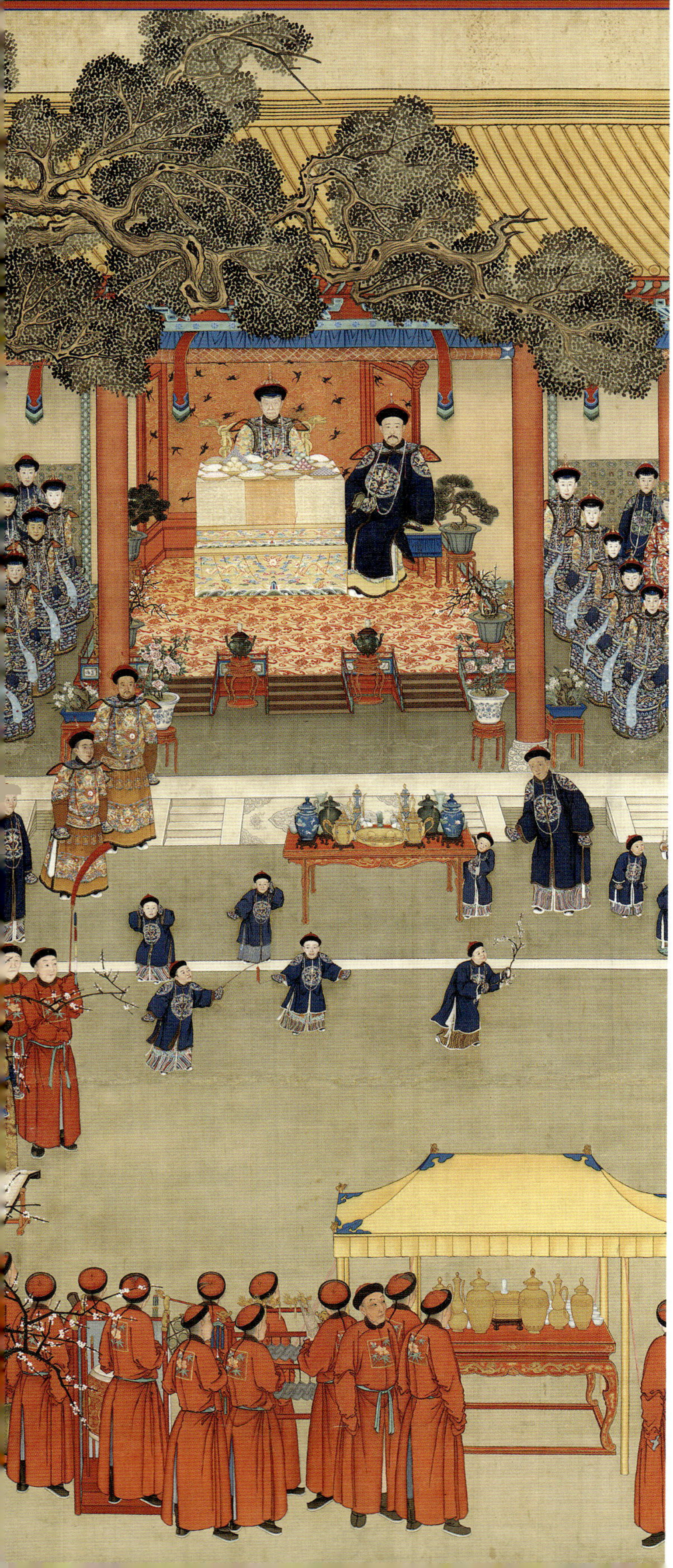

Within the Forbidden City, Qing empresses and other imperial consorts were assigned living quarters in the inner court (*neiting*), which was separated by walls from the outer court (*waichao*), site of the public offices of governmental affairs. While the emperor also lived in the inner court, the residences of imperial women were apart from that of the emperor. Accommodations were assigned according to the rank and status of the women per court regulations.[1]

Empress Dowager Chongqing (Empress Xiaosheng; 1693–1777) started her path to the palace as a low-ranking consort of the Yongzheng emperor (r. 1723–35). As the birth mother of the next emperor, Qianlong (r. 1736–95), she was granted the title of empress dowager—the highest rank among imperial woman—during her lifetime and was posthumously honored as Empress Xiaosheng (fig. 1). Before the Qianlong emperor's reign began, two complexes inside the Forbidden City served as living quarters for Qing empresses dowager: the Palace of Compassion and Tranquility (Cining gong) and the Palace of Tranquility and Longevity (Ningshou gong). The former, built in 1653 on the west side of the Forbidden City (no. 1 on the map on pp. 30–31), had been the home of Empress Xiaozhuang (1613–1688), the mother of the Shunzhi emperor (r. 1644–61) and grandmother of the Kangxi emperor (r. 1662–1722). The latter, located on the east side of the Forbidden City (no. 17 on the map on pp. 30–31), was built in 1689 for Empress Xiaohui (1641–1717), wife of the Shunzhi emperor. Yet the Qianlong emperor decided that neither palace was a suitable residence for his mother, Chongqing. By 1736 the rear hall of the Palace of Compassion and Tranquility had been designated as a space for Buddhist activities (see Luk Yu-ping's essay, pp. 110–27), and five other halls originally built for Xiaozhuang had been demolished. Since some of the late Kangxi emperor's consorts were still living in the Palace of Tranquility and Longevity, the emperor faced a quandary: Qianlong and Chongqing did not deem it appropriate to ask senior consorts to move out of the palace, yet court protocol prohibited the empress dowager from residing in a palace with widowed consorts of earlier generations. This situation made it imperative to build a new residence for Chongqing.

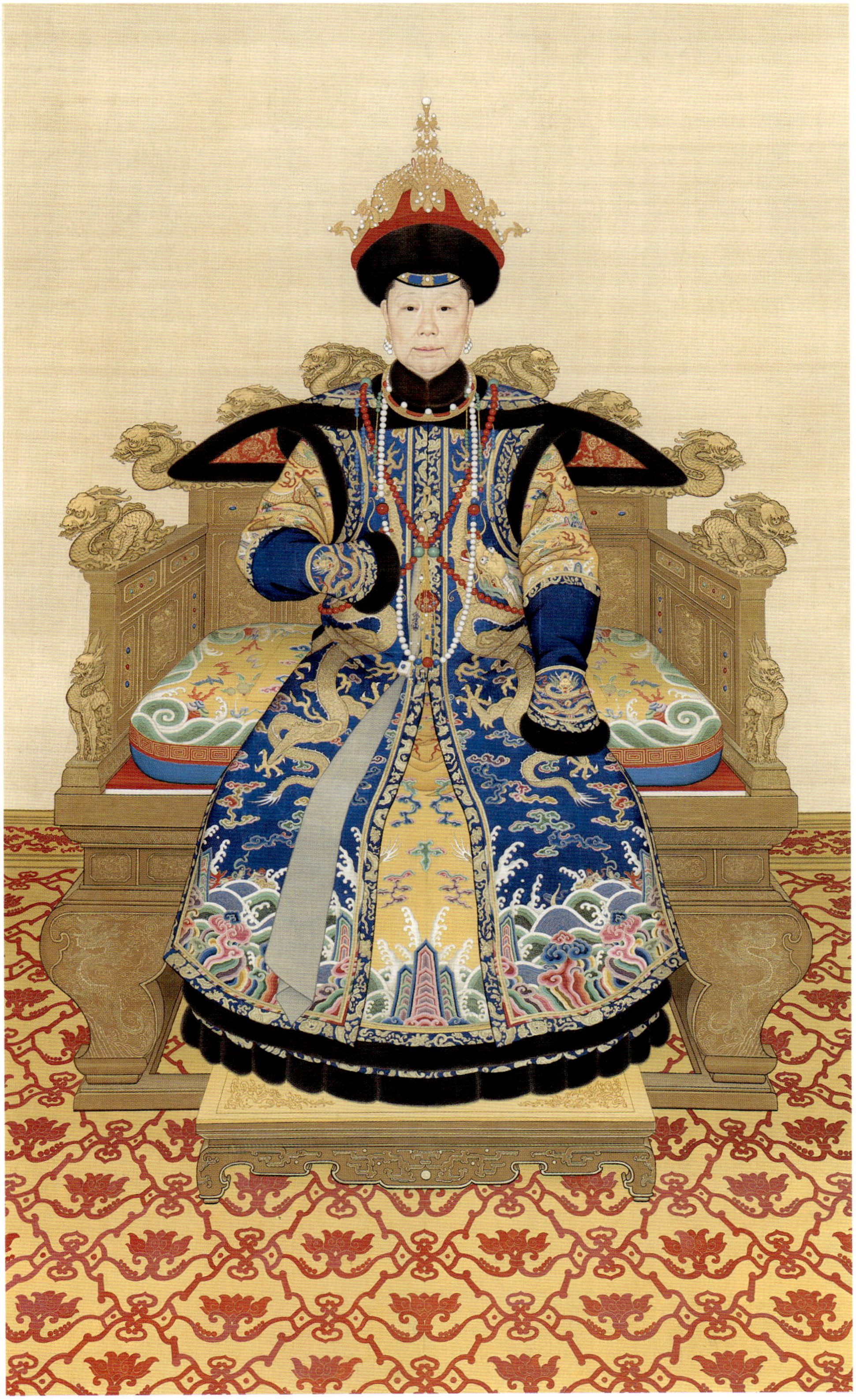

FIGURE 1

Empress Dowager Chongqing at the Age of Seventy. Probably Giuseppe Castiglione (Lang Shining; Italy, 1688–1766) and other court painters, Beijing, Qianlong period, about 1761, hanging scroll, ink and color on silk, cat. 10.

Building an Auspicious Home

Four days after Qianlong's enthronement in 1735 architectural drawings for a new palace were completed and presented to him. Three months later construction started, and soon thereafter a ceremony marked the raising of the principal beam of the main hall, signaling the completion of its timber frame.[2] The complex was completed at considerable cost to the court in the tenth lunar month of 1736. Qianlong gave it an auspicious name: the Palace of Longevity and Health (Shoukang gong; no. 3 on the map on pp. 30–31).[3] Chongqing moved into the palace in late 1736. For the rest of her life, she resided there about two months each year to celebrate such important occasions as the winter solstice, the lunar New Year, and her birthday on the twenty-fifth day of the eleventh lunar month.[4] The rest of the time she either traveled or resided in one of the other Qing palaces.

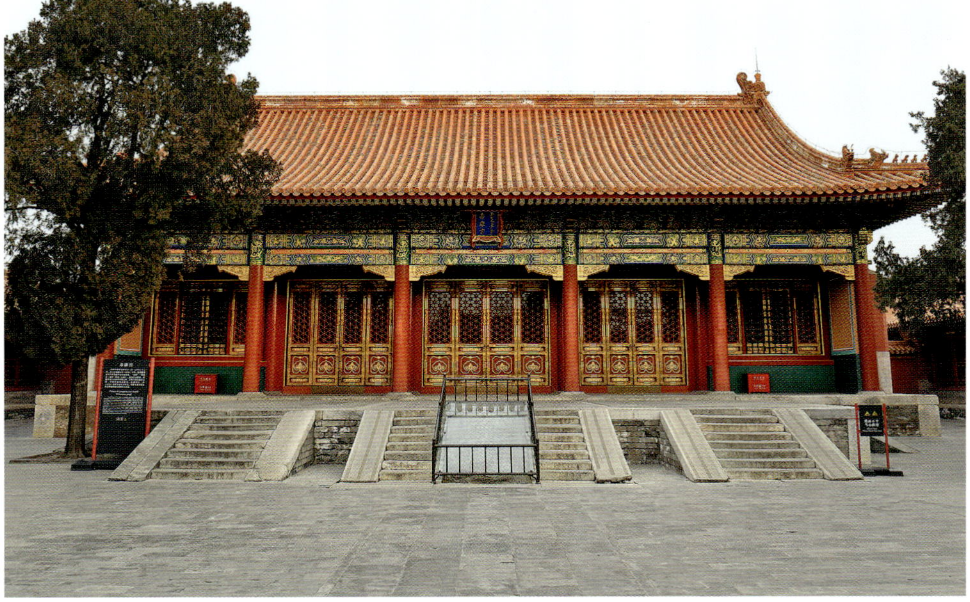

FIGURE 2
Exterior of the Main Hall of the Palace of Longevity and Health.

FIGURE 3
Floor plan of the Palace of Longevity and Health. Adapted from the floor plan by the Exhibition Design Department, Palace Museum.

The Palace of Longevity and Health is located in the western section of the Forbidden City, adjacent to the Palace of Compassion and Tranquility and close to the living quarters of other widowed consorts, such as Three Rear Palaces and Three Lodges (nos. 4 and 5 on the map on pp. 30–31). Scale, building materials, and exterior and interior decoration indicate the status of these buildings' inhabitants, with the most striking contrast being between the shining yellow tiles of the Palace of Longevity and Health (fig. 2) and the dull gray roof tiles of the other structures. Enclosed within red walls, the Palace of Longevity and Health is actually a cluster of structures occupying an area of about 90,804 square feet (8,436 square meters). The main entrance, flanked by guard houses and located in a spacious forecourt at the south end of the complex, is known as the Gate of Longevity and Health. Within the compound stand seventy-five structures with diverse functions.

The Palace

The palace proper consists of three buildings—the Main Hall, the Rear Hall, and the Rearmost Hall—that constituted areas for court rituals, devotional activities, and Chongqing's living quarters and entertainment spaces (fig. 3).[5]

RITUAL SPACE

The central rooms of the Main Hall and the Rear Hall were designated for court rituals, and each was furnished with a throne and a standing screen (fig. 4). The three-bay central room of the Main Hall (A) features a coffered ceiling, a detail that signaled Chongqing's revered status. Here on the lunar New Year and the day after the winter solstice she would receive greetings from the emperor, the empress, and high-ranking consorts; outside the palace, princes and ministers lined up to prostrate themselves.

Taking her place on a throne in the central room of the Rear Hall (B), Chongqing received Qianlong's lower-rank consorts during her birthday celebrations and the occasions mentioned above. And it was here that she accepted the congratulations of these consorts, her grandsons, and her great-grandsons when she was granted the title of empress dowager soon after the palace was erected and on other occasions when she received further honorifics.[6]

DEVOTIONAL SPACE

The Main Hall's two side chambers were reserved for Buddhist activities and ancestral worship.[7] A spirit tablet for Chongqing's late husband, the Yongzheng emperor, was the focus of veneration rites in the West Chamber (C), and the empress dowager would worship Buddhist deities in the East Chamber (D). After Chongqing's death, the latter held the gold stupa commissioned by her son to enshrine her hair (see pl. 37).[8]

LIVING QUARTERS

Chongqing's living quarters were located in the Rear Hall and the Rearmost Hall. The West Warm Chamber in the Rear Hall consists of two rooms connected by a wooden

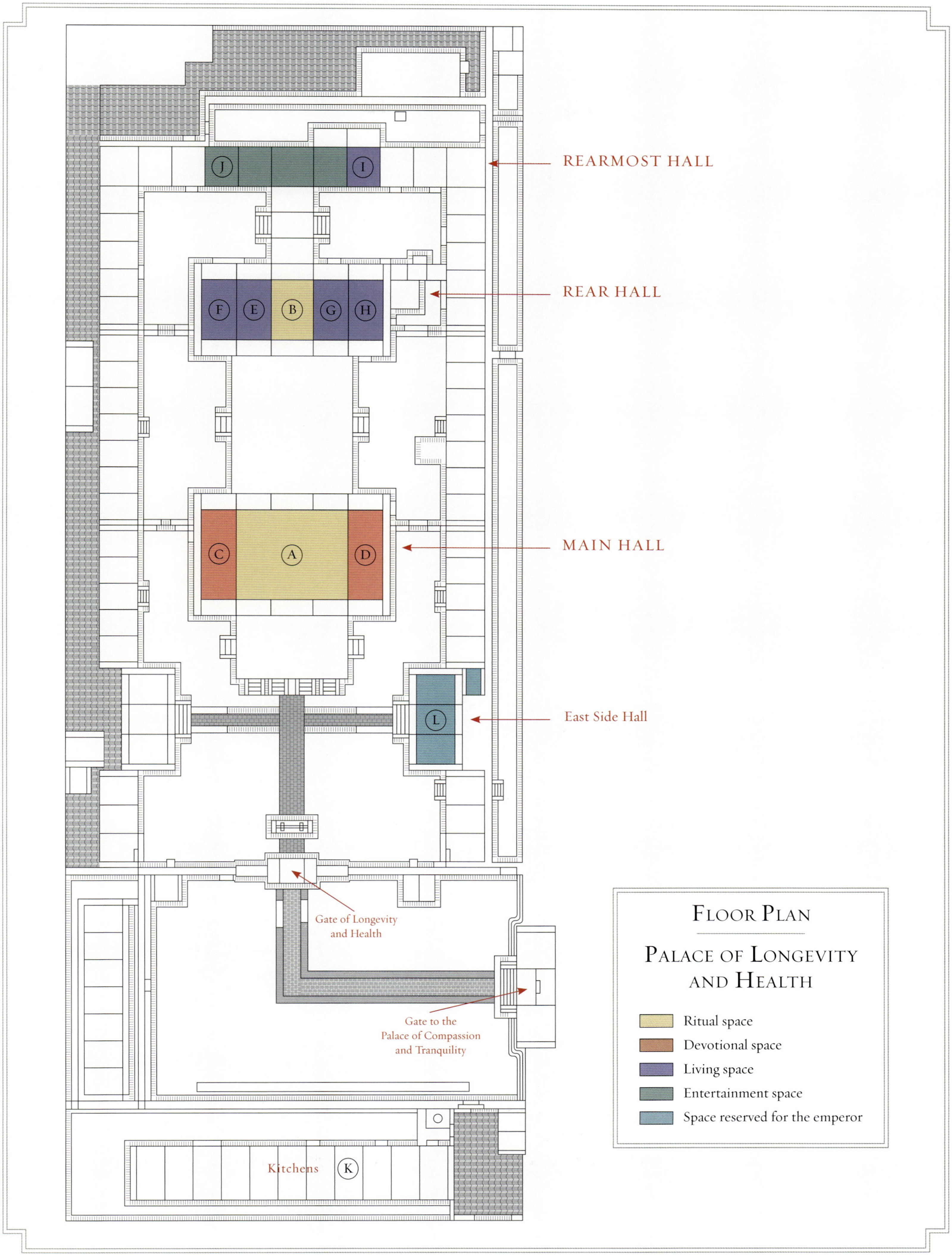
REARMOST HALL
REAR HALL
MAIN HALL
East Side Hall
J
I
F
E
B
G
H
C
A
D
L
Gate of Longevity and Health
Gate to the Palace of Compassion and Tranquility
Kitchens
K
FLOOR PLAN
PALACE OF LONGEVITY AND HEALTH
Ritual space
Devotional space
Living space
Entertainment space
Space reserved for the emperor

FIGURE 4

Ritual space in the Main Hall of the Palace of Longevity and Health.

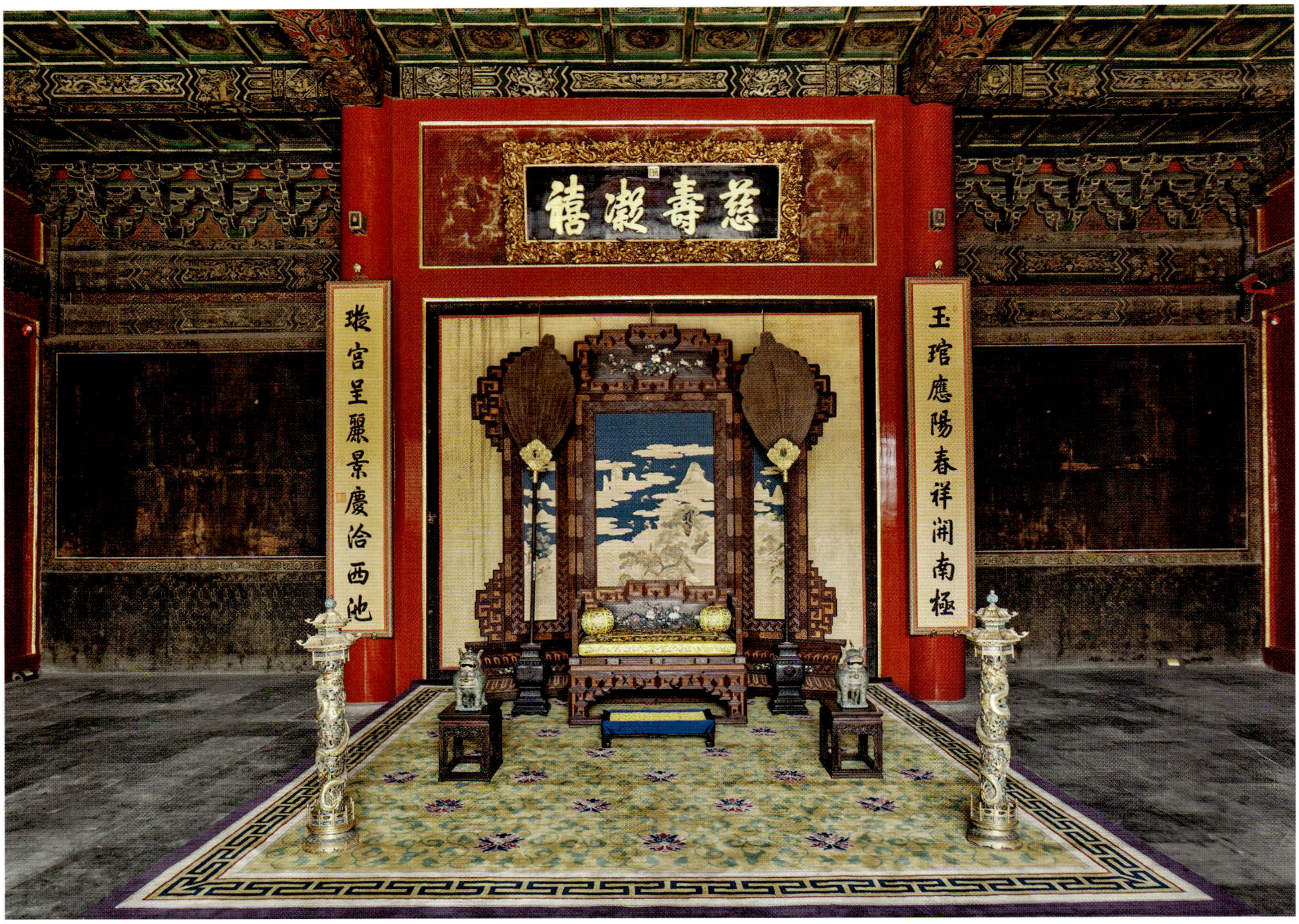

doorway decorated with stylized dragons. In the first room (E) a heated platform couch (*kang*) was located along the south wall near a row of windows, creating a well-lit sitting area where Chongqing could read and receive visitors. The room's north wall is entirely concealed by a pair of *huanghuali* wood cabinets with carved dragons and clouds, behind which stairs lead up to a storage alcove. The second room (F) was more intimate. Another platform couch near the window served as her grooming area, while her bed was placed along the north wall (fig. 5). In order to bring more natural light into these spaces, panes of glass—novel and highly prized items available largely through import at the time in China—were installed in the windows in the south wall of these rooms in 1771.[9]

The East Warm Chamber in the Rear Hall consists of two rooms (G)(H) divided by a wide wooden latticework frame that created a spacious area for the emperor, the empress, and other consorts to pay homage to the empress dowager (fig. 6). Chongqing's seat was set on a long heated platform along the east wall. A door on the north wall provided access to a corridor that led to a lavatory.

The second room of the East Chamber of the Rearmost Hall also served as living space for Chongqing (I). It featured a platform couch near windows on the south wall and a bed along the north wall. Located in the quietest part of the complex, this chamber served as another area for the empress dowager to repose.

ENTERTAINMENT SPACE

The Rearmost Hall functioned mainly as the empress dowager's entertainment space. She was an avid lover of opera, which prompted a 1769 imperial order to convert its West Chamber into a small indoor theater (J), complete with a stage and a "scenic illusion" wall painting (*tongjing hua*) by the court painter Wang Youxue (active about 1733–80s).

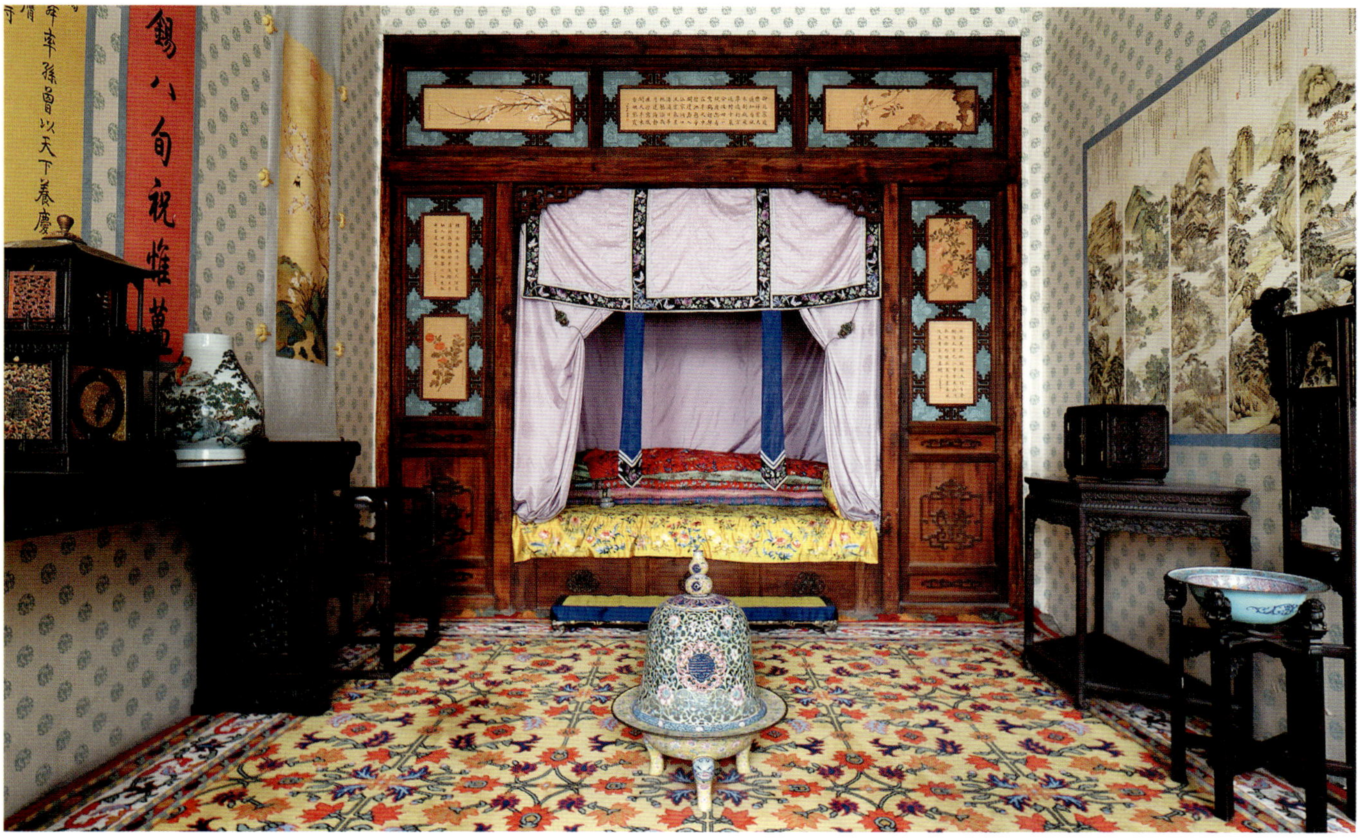

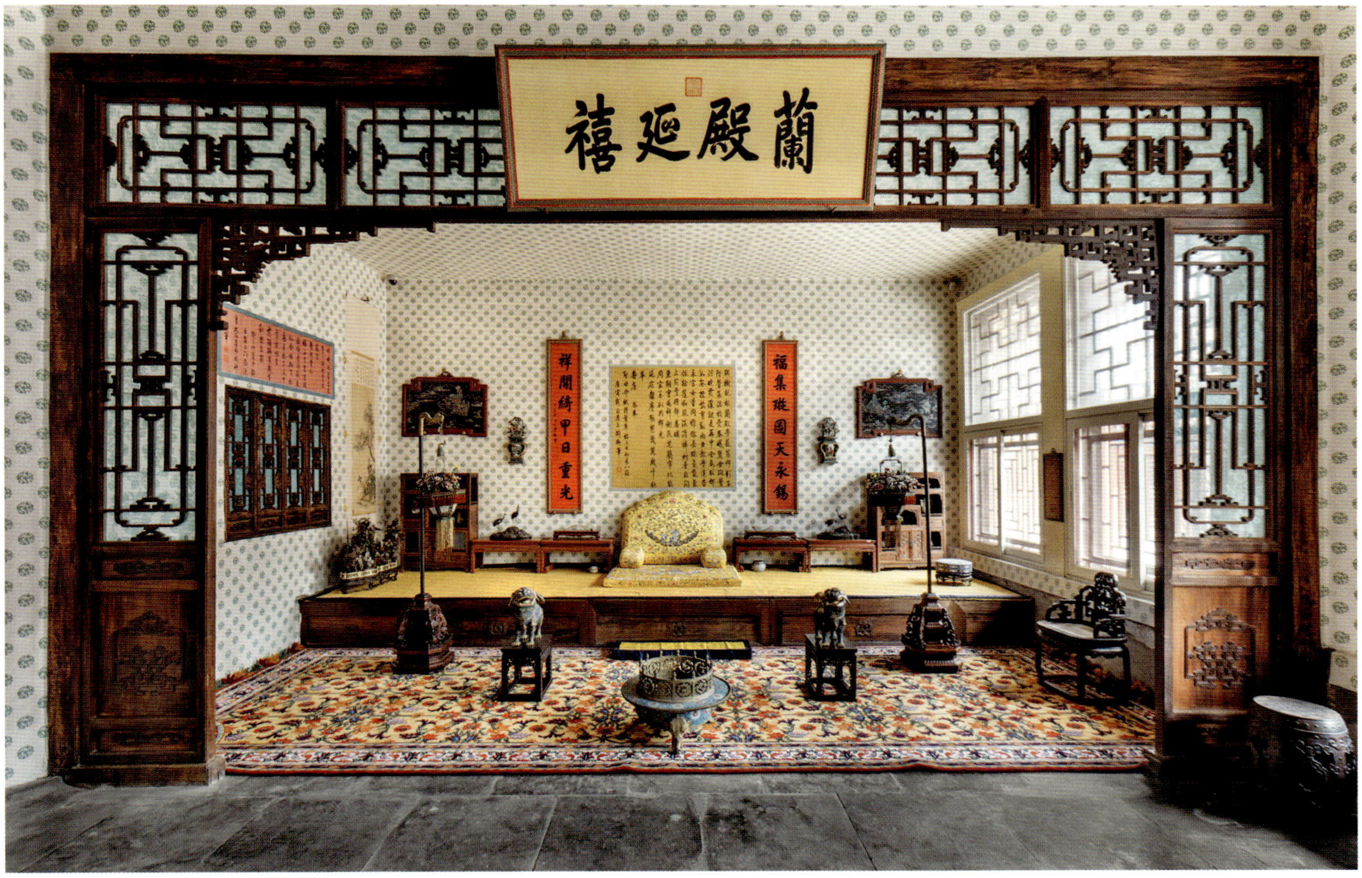

FIGURE 5

Bedroom in the West Warm Chamber of the Rear Hall of the Palace of Longevity and Health.

FIGURE 6

Living space in the East Warm Chamber of the Rear Hall of the Palace of Longevity and Health.

SERVICE AREAS

Chongqing was attended by sixteen palace maids who lived in two long, narrow buildings abutting the west and the east walls of the palace. Other members of the service staff, including some ninety eunuchs, were not allowed to spend their nights in the Palace of Longevity and Health or the residences of other imperial women. The kitchens (K) were located in a row of eleven rooms along the perimeter of the southern forecourt outside the Gate of Longevity and Health, an arrangement intended to keep noise and other disturbances away from the empress dowager's residence.

Mother, Son, and Greeting Rites

Chongqing received her son regularly at the Palace of Longevity and Health. Protocol surrounding the emperor's visits evolved into a special court rite.[10] When the emperor arrived at the palace, he was required to wait in a room in the East Side Hall reserved for this purpose until his arrival was announced to Chongqing by eunuchs (see (L) in fig. 3). When traveling with Chongqing, the emperor greeted her at her temporary residences or on imperial barges. He also often visited her at the Garden of Delightful Spring (Changchun yuan), a palatial residence in northwestern Beijing. When away from his mother, Qianlong regularly sent her letters of greeting.

In 1747, while Qianlong was outside the Forbidden City, Chongqing fell ill. He immediately returned and visited her at the Palace of Longevity and Health. Concerned about his mother's well-being, he stayed at the Studio of Embodied Clarity (Hanqing zhai) in the Garden of the Palace of Compassion and Tranquility, adjacent to the Palace of Longevity and Health. The next day he visited his mother three times and checked her medication. Only when he was assured of her recovery did he return to his own residence at the Hall of Mental Cultivation (Yangxin dian) also inside the Forbidden City. For the next month Qianlong visited his mother almost every day.[11] When she had recovered, Qianlong hand-copied the Buddhist sutra *White-robed Avalokiteshvara Five Mudras Heart Dharani* (*Baiyi dabei wuyinxin tuoluoni jing*), which was then placed on the altar table at the Palace of Compassion and Tranquility to ensure Chongqing's good health.

The relationship between Chongqing and her son was warm. They often discussed the weather, as Chongqing worried about droughts and their effect on agricultural production. After her son returned from court ceremonies to pray for rain, she always consoled him. Important political and military affairs also concerned the empress dowager, and she commented on these topics in her conversations with her son. While Qing imperial women were not supposed to interfere in political matters, on certain occasions Chongqing's words inspired her son's imperial orders. One notable example occurred in 1748 after Qianlong appointed his brother-in-law Fuheng (1720–1770) a grand councilor in charge of military affairs. After receiving an imperial order to suppress rebellious tribes at Jinchuan (present-day Sichuan province), the site of challenging terrain and previous Qing military failures, Fuheng worried his standing would suffer if he did not triumph. Chongqing observed that one goes into battle to serve the state and not to attain glory or fame, and she suggested that Fuheng carry out his orders without being overly concerned about his reputation.[12] Qianlong conveyed Chongqing's insights in the form of an imperial order, and Fuheng successfully quelled the uprising. Upon Fuheng's return to Beijing, Chongqing spoke to her son again: "You have ordered the return of troops from Jinchuan, making it a celebratory occasion for the state. The Grand Councilor Fuheng is a loyal and diligent person and a brave strategist who has achieved great success. My thought is that the court should honor him with the second-rank title of duke. What does the emperor think?" Qianlong followed her suggestion and bestowed upon Fuheng the title "Duke of Loyalty and Bravery."[13] Chongqing was credited by Qianlong for the military success at Jinchuan and likewise received an honorific title.[14]

Birthday Celebrations

The grandest festivities held at the Palace of Longevity and Health were Chongqing's sixtieth, seventieth, and eightieth birthdays, occasions when she received honorific titles and her son composed poems and commissioned paintings and calligraphy pieces in her honor. The whole country rejoiced during these celebrations. She received gifts as grand as the 108-volume Kanjur Sutra (pl. 41) and as small as toothbrushes and tongue scrapers from well-wishers within the palace and beyond. For her sixtieth birthday, she received gifts for five consecutive days; for her seventieth birthday, eleven days; and for her eightieth, thirty-three days.

Both the Kangxi and Qianlong emperors had commissioned works to commemorate their own birthdays, but the paintings marking Chongqing's anniversaries were unprecedented in number.[15] These included a set of handscrolls depicting her sixtieth birthday (pl. 8), a magnificent album for her seventieth birthday, and a large painting originally mounted on a wall (*tieluo*) for her eightieth birthday (fig. 7; pl. 7). The paintings commissioned for her sixtieth and seventieth birthdays were such ambitious undertakings that each took ten years to complete, meaning that the sixtieth-birthday scrolls

FIGURE 7
Celebrating Empress Dowager Chongqing's eightieth birthday (detail). Yao Wenhan (active 1740s–70s), Zhou Ben (active 1760s–70s), and Yi Lantai (active 1748–86), Qianlong period, 1771–1772, painting originally mounted on a wall (*tieluo*), ink and color on silk, pl. 7.

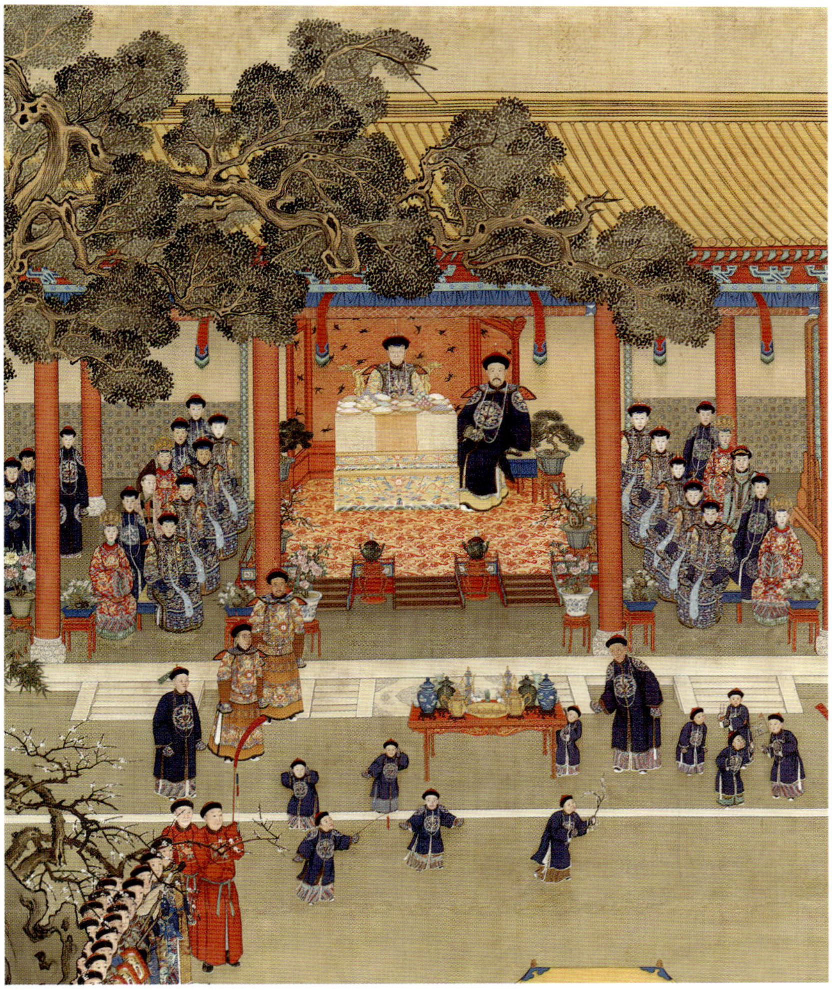

were presented as the emperor's principal gift for Chongqing's seventieth birthday, and the seventieth-birthday album became her chief eightieth-birthday gift. Not only did Qianlong order the best court painters to create these works, but he also gave the artists detailed instructions on format and content.[16]

The Art Collection

Thanks to all the lavish gifts Chongqing received, the Palace of Longevity and Health became a major repository of imperial treasures.[17] Its interiors were furnished with a dazzling array of sumptuous objects, and an even larger and more diverse assortment was kept in storage. An inventory made after the empress dowager's death recorded objects that had entered the collection from 1735 to 1777. Two of the eight ledgers survive, detailing 623 jade objects, 1,592 wish-granting scepters (*ruyi*), 30 books, and 167 paintings and calligraphy pieces (exclusive of those distributed as mementos following Chongqing's death). An additional 2,517 ceramic works and 246 pieces of lacquerware, such as boxes for food, that had once been in the Palace of Longevity and Health were returned to imperial stores for future use after she died.[18]

Reflecting the empress dowager's status, this collection consisted of the finest art objects, as well as quotidian objects of the best craftsmanship. Among the art—which included ancient bronzes, jades, painting, and calligraphy—was one of the most important examples of early Chinese calligraphy, "Letter on recovery from illness" (*Pingfu tie*) by Lu Ji (fig. 8).[19] Other important items included works attributed to such renowned artists as Su Shi (1037–1101), Wang Zhenpeng (active 1280–1329), Zhao Mengfu (1254–1322), and Dong Qichang (1555–1636).[20]

The objects in Chongqing's collection came from three main sources: items supplied by the Imperial Household Department (Neiwu fu); gifts from the emperor and others on special occasions; and tributes from government officials. For example, in 1736, a provincial officer named Li Bingzhi presented Chongqing with the magnificent cabinets of *huanghuali* wood mentioned above. The largest of their kind in the Forbidden City, these cabinets were placed in the Rear Hall of the Palace of Longevity and Health. For this gift Li was rewarded by the emperor with four bolts of silk satin and ten pieces of sable fur.[21] At one time these cabinets held a group of three wish-granting scepters (*ruyi*) inscribed with Qianlong's poems on the three star gods—deities of good fortune, wealth, and longevity (fig. 9); these items were a gift to the empress dowager from Xiong Xuepeng, the provincial governor of Zhejiang. The story of another official reveals the potential effect of such presents. Luo Xuedan was a former county magistrate in Sichuan who had been demoted. He created ten albums each with 1,000 gold characters for longevity (*shou*) in various scripts, and presented them to Chongqing while she was on a southern tour with her son.[22] Thanks to this special gift, Luo was soon reestablished in his government career.

A notable feature of Chongqing's collection is the high concentration of works by her son. The palace inventory shows 210 paintings and calligraphy pieces by Qianlong, including a painting of the God of Longevity, a birthday gift to his mother (fig. 10). Many works were inscribed by the emperor with his personal name and the prefix *chen*, meaning "your servant" or "your minister"—a title used by officials presenting works to the emperor and here used by the emperor to show his respect for his mother.

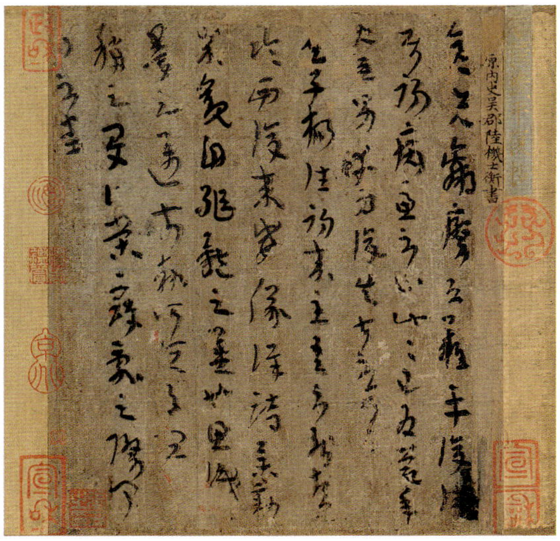

FIGURE 8
"Letter on recovery from illness." Lu Ji (261–303), Western Jin dynasty (265–316), late 3rd or early 4th century, handscroll, ink on paper, 9⅜ × 8⅛ in. (23.7 × 20.6 cm), Xin 44430.

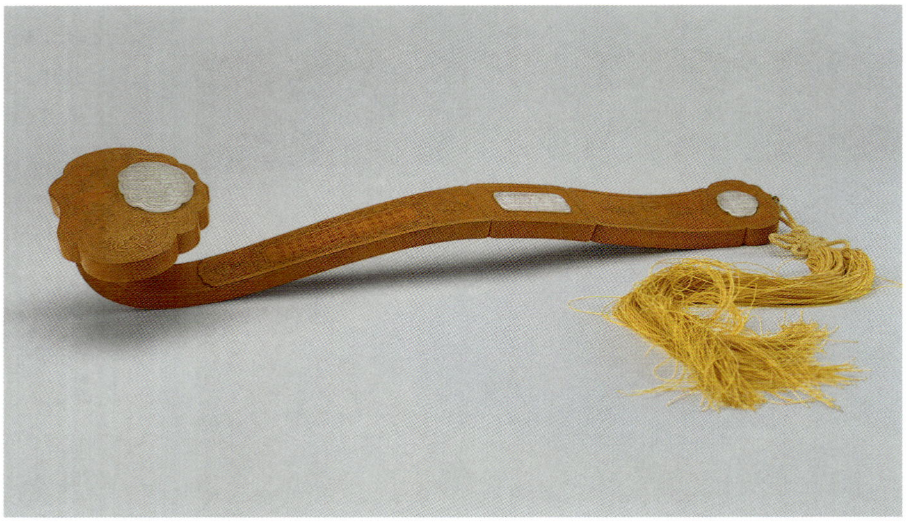

FIGURE 9
Wish-granting scepter (*ruyi*) with image of the God of Wealth and transcription of a poem by the Qianlong emperor. Qianlong period, mid-18th century, bamboo, jade (nephrite), and silk tassels, cat. 155.

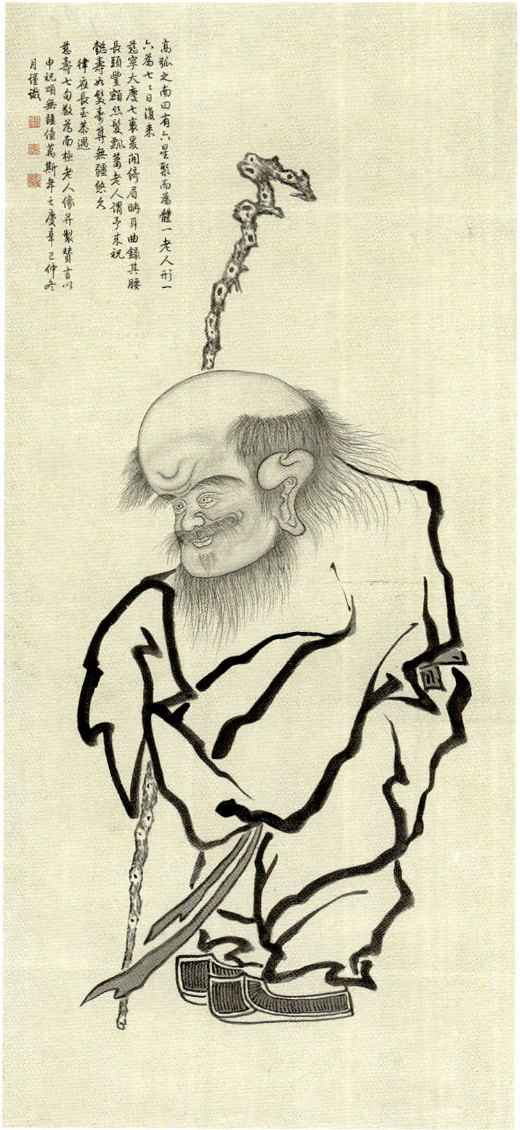

FIGURE 10
God of Longevity inscribed with a poem. The Qianlong emperor (1711–1799), Qianlong period, 1761, hanging scroll, ink on paper, 36 × 16½ in. (91.6 × 42 cm), Gu237288.

Conclusion

For forty-two years Empress Dowager Chongqing resided in the Palace of Longevity and Health, enjoying the company of imperial family members—most notably, her son, the Qianlong emperor. After her death, it remained the home of the primary wives of deceased emperors or the birth mothers of reigning monarchs. All aspects of the palace—its architecture, interior decoration, art collection, and staffing—testify to Chongqing's revered position and her son's filial attention. The construction of the palace was a project of great importance, one that Qianlong prioritized immediately after his accession to the throne. It was motivated in part by the notion of ritual propriety—the desire to openly display filial piety, a fundamental Confucian (and Han Chinese) virtue—and in part to demonstrate rulership in accord with ancient Chinese practice to strengthen the emperor's position as the ultimate sovereign.[23] While arising from the power of her son, Chongqing's palace—the lavishness of its decor and the richness of its art—as well as the care she received from her son illustrate the vitality and importance of key women at the Qing court.

Chongqing's exalted status was likely a source of pride for an emperor who believed that his filial conduct opened a new chapter in history. He wrote: "[I] reached sixty while [my] mother has lived to eighty years, who has ever seen a precedent in history?"[24] Chongqing's last recorded words convey a similar sentiment: "I have already reached the ripe old age of eighty-six. I have been mothering the state and enjoying the respectful care [of the emperor] for forty-two years. Thanks to the accolades [bestowed upon me], I received three honorific titles. Three grand celebrations were held for my birthdays. Now the great state is unified, and I enjoy a family of five generations. Looking back in history, this is indeed a rare circumstance. As I revel in many blessings and good fortune in old age, I have no more regrets."[25]

Translated by Doris Sung and Daisy Yiyou Wang

Notes

1 Qing imperial women of high rank, such as Empresses Dowager Chongqing and Cixi, had their own residences in imperial palaces outside the Forbidden City.

2 Haiwang 1735.

3 Haiwang 1737.

4 The traditional Chinese calendar is based on the movement of the moon and is about twenty to fifty days behind the Gregorian calendar. It was used for celebrating birthdays and determining dates of important festivals.

5 Records show the palace has undergone minor renovations over the years—an indoor opera stage was added to the Rearmost Hall, for example—but its overall structure and interior decoration are basically consistent with its original form. A reconstruction of the Palace of Longevity and Health was completed in 2015 by a team led by the author.

6 E'ertai and Zhang Tingyu (1769) 1987, *juan* 5.

7 "Warm chambers" (*nuan'ge*) were the innermost rooms in a Qing palace, usually separated by walls from the central room. Away from the main entrance to the palace, they are relatively warmer than the other rooms in the palace, hence the name.

8 ZGDYLSDAG 2005, 7:103.

9 ZGDYLSDAG 2005, 34:412.

10 "Dianli yi" [Court rites 1] in E'ertai and Zhang Tingyu (1769) 1987, *juan* 5.

11 See "Records on the tenth day of the eleventh lunar month of the twelfth year of the Qianlong reign" [1747], in ZGDYLSDAG 2002.

12 "Records on the *yisi* day of the twelfth lunar month of the thirteenth year of the Qianlong reign" [1748], in *Qing Gaozong shilu*, 331:5.

13 "Records on the *dingmao* day of the first lunar month of the fourteenth year of the Qianlong reign" [1749], in *Qing Gaozong shilu*, 333:11.

14 "Records on the *bingshen* day of the second lunar month of the fourteenth year of the Qianlong reign" [1749], in *Qing Gaozong shilu*, 335:10.

15 The earliest examples of paintings depicting an imperial birthday celebration in the Palace Museum collection are two handscrolls made for the Kangxi emperor.

16 See Lin Shu 2015a.

17 E'ertai and Zhang Tingyu (1769) 1987, *juan* 17.

18 Zongguan neiwu fu 1777a; Zongguan neiwu fu 1777b.

19 It is unclear how "Letter on recovery from illness" (*Pingfu tie*) entered the collection, but after Chongqing's death, her grandson Yongxing (1752–1823) received it as a memento as evidenced by a postscript added to the piece. It is worth noting that no seals of Chongqing have been found on artworks once held in the Palace of Longevity and Health, which suggests she did not follow Qianlong's practice of putting his many seals on paintings and calligraphy works in the imperial collection.

20 "Shoukang gong dengchu shuji guazhou shoujuan ceye shumu qingce."

21 ZGDYLSDAG 2005, 7:204.

22 "Records on the *bingzi* day of the second lunar month of the twenty-second year of the Qianlong reign" [1757], in *Qing Gaozong shilu*, 532:24.

23 "Records on the *guisi* day of the ninth lunar month of the first year of the Qianlong reign" [1736], in *Qing Gaozong shilu*, 481:25; "Records on the *guimao* day of the first lunar month of the twentieth year of the Qianlong reign" [1755], in *Qing Gaozong shilu*, 1027:47; "Records on the *gengzi* day of the seventh lunar month of the fifty-seventh year of the Qianlong reign" [1792], in *Qing Gaozong shilu*, 1408:5.

24 See the poem entitled "Dongzhi yue nianwuri shengmu huangtaihou baxun daqing Cining gong xingli xicheng zhangshen" [Feeling joyful when greeting the empress dowager at the celebration of her eightieth birthday at the Palace of Compassion and Tranquility on the twenty-fifth day of the lunar month of the winter solstice], in *Qing Gaozong yuzhi shiwen quanji*, *juan* 100.

25 "Records on the *gengyin* day of the first lunar month of the forty-second year of the Qianlong reign" [1777], in *Qing Gaozong shilu*, 1025.

THREE

Deciphering Portraits of Qing Empresses

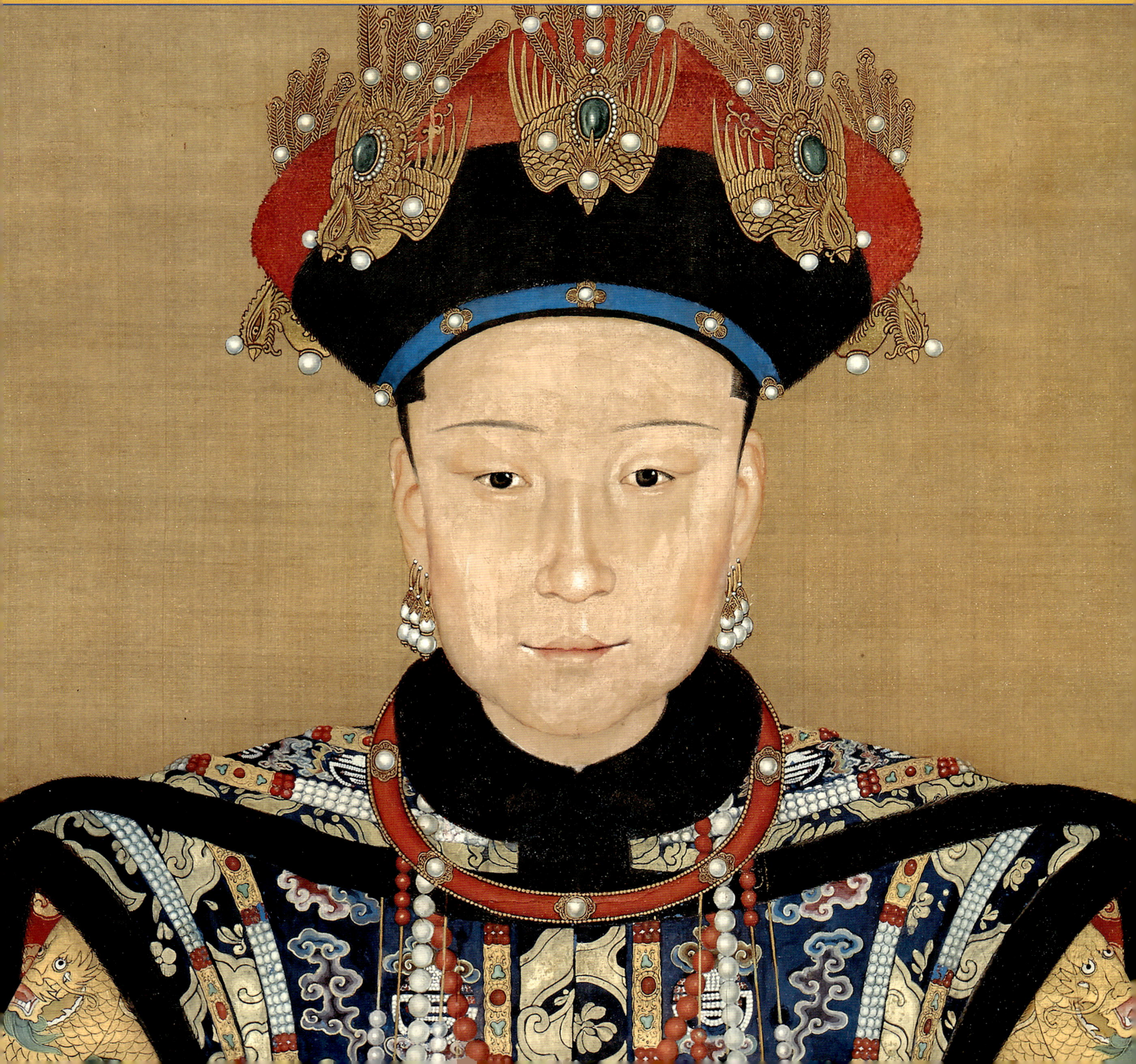

DAISY YIYOU WANG

Portraits of dead empresses painted in water-colors on faded silks recall the candid grace of the Italian Primitives—portraits so pale, so colorless, as to seem like fleeting reflections of persons, yet showing a perfection of modeling attained with absolute simplicity, and with a look of concentration in the eye that makes you feel the likeness and enables you for one strange moment to live face to face with these princesses of the past who have slept for centuries in this splendid mausoleum. All these paintings were sacred, never seen or even suspected to exist by Europeans.[1]

ENCOUNTERING PORTRAITS of Qing empresses for the first time in 1900, Frenchman Pierre Loti (1850–1923) was deeply impressed by their refinement and spiritual power despite having little understanding of why and how they were created. Due to the current scholarly focus given to images of the emperors, these portraits of Qing imperial women for ancestral veneration remain little known today.

Two life-size portraits of Qing empresses in the collection of the Peabody Essex Museum offer us new insights. Titles identify the subject of each work: Empress Xiaoxian (1712–1748; opposite and fig. 1), wife of the Qianlong emperor (r. 1736–95); and Empress Xiaomu (d. 1808; fig. 5), the first and primary wife of the Daoguang emperor (r. 1821–50). Between 2012 and 2014 these portraits were conserved to address condition issues. This project provided an opportunity to pursue further research on these two important but little-understood portraits. Working together, scholars at the Palace Museum, Beijing, and the Peabody Essex Museum studied these paintings and compared them with portraits in the Palace Museum's collection. Qing imperial edicts, workshop records, and collection inventories were examined to reveal how these paintings were produced and used in their original context.[2] The Qing court produced the largest group of surviving portraits of empresses in China as well as a rich body of archival documents, allowing this investigation to shed new light on Qing imperial portraiture through the lenses of court ritual, gender, and costume history.

Imperial Portraits and Ancestral Rites

These paintings were once part of an imperial portrait collection used for ancestor worship at the Hall of Imperial Longevity (Shouhuang dian), located in the Prospect Hill (Jingshan) area in Beijing. This hall functioned in the early Qing period as a temporary resting place for deceased emperors and empresses in the time between the sealing of their coffins and their burial in mausoleums outside Beijing. The earliest record concerning the veneration of a portrait there dates to 1723, when the newly enthroned Yongzheng emperor (r. 1723–35) placed a painting of his recently

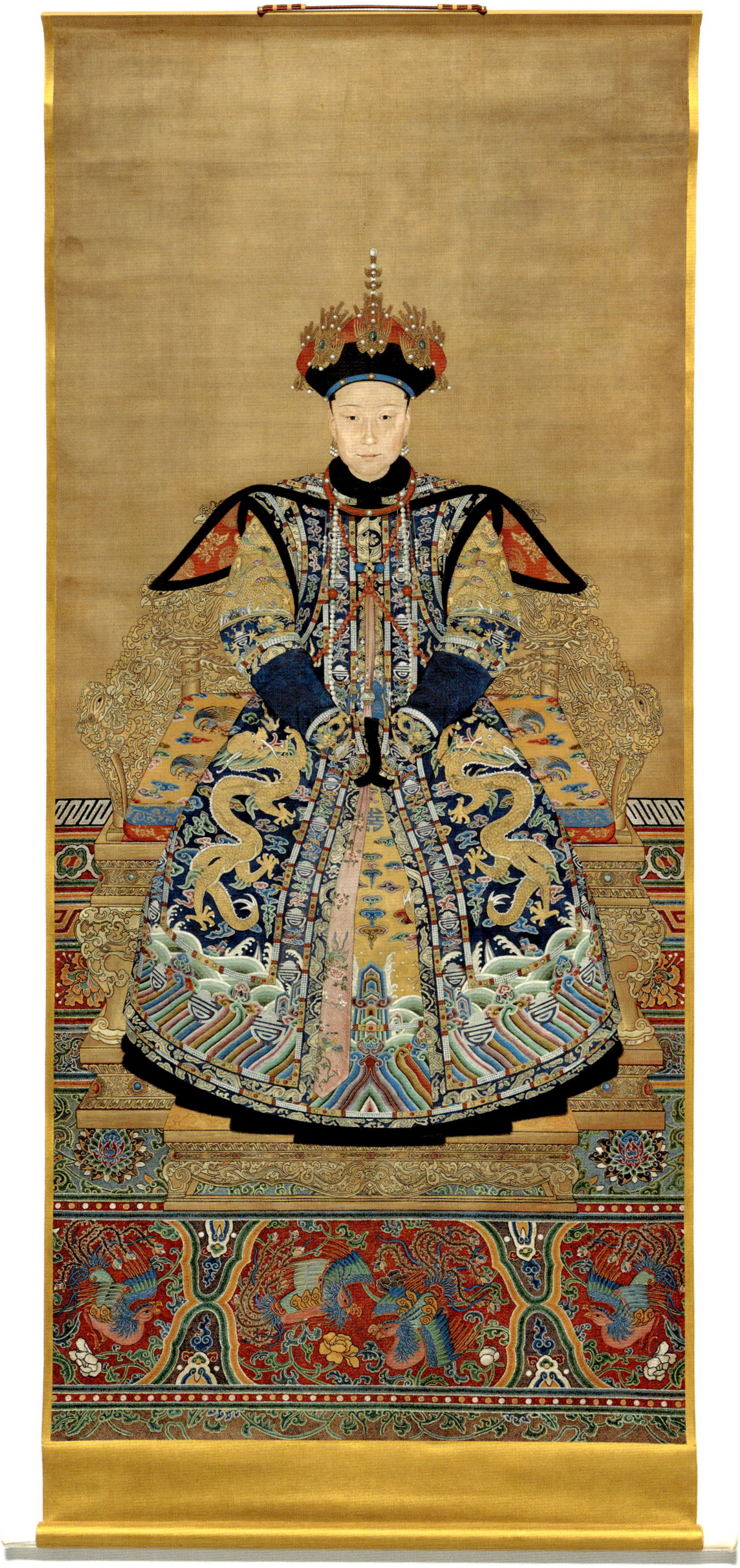

FIGURE 1

Empress Xiaoxian. Ignatius Sichelbarth (Ai Qimeng; Bohemia, 1708–1780), Yi Lantai (active about 1748–86), and possibly Wang Ruxue (active 18th century), Qianlong period, 1777, with repainting possibly in 19th century, hanging scroll, ink and color on silk, Peabody Essex Museum, cat. 12.

deceased father, the Kangxi emperor (r. 1662–1722), in the hall. Yongzheng visited the portrait regularly, especially on notable occasions such as the anniversaries of his father's birth and death and the lunar New Year. After a three-year mourning period, the emperor ordered the rites that had developed around the portrait be continued throughout his lifetime. Aware that this practice departed from Qing precedent, Yongzheng, citing his sincere admiration and longing for his father, declared it a special personal case and cautioned that his successors should not follow suit.[3] Yongzheng is also known to have paid his respect to the portrait of his mother, Empress Xiaogong (1660–1723), on her death anniversary—the earliest known case of the portrait of a Qing empress being worshipped in the Hall of Imperial Longevity.[4] It is not clear, however, what the style and format of that portrait was, who painted that portrait, what specific rites were performed around it, or how frequently the emperor visited it.[5]

Despite Yongzheng's injunction, his son, the Qianlong emperor, in the first year of his reign, placed a portrait of Yongzheng for veneration in the Hall of Imperial Longevity next to that of Kangxi. In 1748 or 1749 Qianlong initiated an ambitious project to expand and relocate the hall. From this point on, it no longer served a funerary purpose but became an imperial family altar where sacrifices to ancestors took place in front of portraits.[6] In 1750 a new complex rose on a spot north of the Forbidden City, a location that alluded to the Qing rulers' Manchu ancestry in northeastern China. The alignment of this complex with the central north-south axis of the Forbidden City was understood to connect the realm of the dead to that of the living and was based on the belief that revering ancestors brought the living prosperity and good fortune.[7] The main building boasted a nine-bay structure with a double-eaved roof and splendid decoration that signified its supreme status in Qing imperial architecture. It was modeled on the Temple of the Ancestors (Tai miao), an edifice that served as the most important Qing site for sacrifices to imperial ancestors at the state level.[8] There, the deceased emperors and empresses were represented not by portraits but by spirit tablets (*shenwei*, *shenpai*, or *shenzhu*), wooden plaques bearing the names and titles of ancestors but no imperial likenesses. Both the Temple of the Ancestors and the Hall of Imperial Longevity held spirit tablets, but only the latter was a site for activities involving the worship of imperial portraits.[9]

Around the time the new hall was completed, Qianlong began to systematically commission portraits for veneration, establishing detailed rules on their use as well as on schedules, participants, procedures, offerings, and staffing for ritual activities at the hall. He observed that in previous dynasties imperial portraits had been placed in various temples and imperial palaces and lacked a central repository. In his time, the portraits of early Qing rulers Nurhaci (r. 1616–26), Hong Taiji (r. 1626–43), and Shunzhi (r. 1644–61), as well as those of deceased empresses, were stored in the Pavilion of Practicing Benevolence (Tiren ge) inside the Forbidden City; these portraits had not been properly venerated.[10] This prompted the emperor's decision to commission, gather, and worship the portraits of his ancestors in the newly built Hall of Imperial Longevity and his direction to the Secretary of the Grand Secretariat and staff in the Imperial Household Department (Neiwu fu) to assess related ritual matters in detail.[11] In 1750 new portraits of his ancestors, including five emperors and five empresses, were painted on his order.[12]

On the day marking its completion in the fifth lunar month of 1750, portraits of the Kangxi and Yongzheng emperors were put on display in the Hall of Imperial Longevity, and Qianlong conducted a veneration ceremony.[13] He also ordered that on the eve of the lunar New Year portraits of deceased Qing emperors and empresses—likely eleven in total—be hung together in the hall.[14] He stipulated that on New Year's Day altar tables be placed in front of these portraits with offerings of food, wine, and incense and that ritual music be performed when he conducted the grand sacrifices there. The next day, before the portraits were taken down and returned to storage, his sons took their turn paying homage to them.

Shortly after the death of his mother, Empress Dowager Chongqing (Empress Xiaosheng, 1693–1777), Qianlong realized there was no dedicated space to store and display portraits of his mother and other deceased empresses. Some portraits of Qing empresses had been stored in the inner court of the Forbidden City.[15] In the Palace of Eternal Spring (Changchun gong), the residence of his late wife Empress Xiaoxian, there existed a hall of portraiture (*yingtang*) holding pictures of Xiaoxian and other deceased consorts of his. Qianlong commemorated these women on their death anniversaries and at the end of every year.[16] He ended this practice and decreed that portraits of empresses thereafter be placed in the Hall of Imperial Longevity, making it the main repository for a wide range of portraits of imperial wives as well as the emperors, including paintings for veneration and other purposes.

As these developments show, during the Qianlong reign imperial ancestral rites reached an unprecedented level of grandeur. In addition to the Hall of Imperial Longevity, the emperor renovated two other major sites for the worship of imperial forebears: the above-mentioned Temple of the Ancestors and the Hall of the Ancestors (Fengxian dian) inside the Forbidden City. His reign also produced the most comprehensive regulations on the subject in China's dynastic history. For example, the fifty-volume *Comprehensive Canon on Rituals of the Great Qing* (*Da Qing tongli*), compiled in 1759, established ancestral veneration as one of the most important among five categories of Qing court rites.[17]

From the mid-eighteenth century onward, ancestral rituals became a matter of primary political and personal importance to Qing emperors who ruled over a multiethnic population with a Han Chinese majority. While the Qing court still performed traditional Manchu shamanic rites related to the foundation myths of the Qing ruling house, ancestor worship practiced by the Chinese population gained growing prominence at the court, as Evelyn S. Rawski has observed.[18] As the Qing dynasty entered a phase of expansion and relative prosperity in the mid-eighteenth century, the attention paid to ancestor rites reflected a need to construct a coherent and distinctive dynastic history out of what Mark Elliott has called a "fragmented and humble past" in order to validate and burnish the pedigree of the ruling Manchu line.[19] By setting rules and precedents regarding ancestor veneration for his successors to follow, Qianlong was both forward looking and self-serving, as these efforts secured him a prestigious place in Qing court ancestral rites ever after.

Two core concepts of Confucianism underlaid Qianlong's efforts to connect the Manchu rulership to the values of its Han Chinese subjects and to link family rites to state affairs. One was filial piety (*xiao*), the attitude of devotion and care toward one's parents and elder family members. Ancestor veneration extends filial piety into the world of the deceased in order to ensure good fortune for the living. The other key concept was ritual or proper conduct (*li*).[20] In the context of the imperial court, this translated into rites, such as sacrifices to ancestors and heaven, performed to regulate human conduct and maintain the order of the cosmos. Because the emperor was the head of both his family and the state, his ritual activities honoring his forebears were key to the sociopolitical stability of the state at large.

Ancestral rites drawn from more than 2,000 years of tradition and precedent set by Han Chinese and non-Han rulers offered Qing emperors ready means to legitimatize their place in China's dynastic history.[21] Qianlong, in particular, selectively adopted established practices for his own ends. One possible inspiration for rebuilding the Hall of Imperial Longevity and commissioning portraits for ancestor worship was the proliferation of ancestral shrines in the Liao (907–1125) and the Northern Song (960–1127) dynasties as sites for the performance of elaborate rituals and the veneration of painted images and sculptures of emperors and empresses. The emperor Shenzong (r. 1067–85), for example, expanded the Jingling Palace in order to house portraits of deceased imperial persons and to provide a central place for portraits previously scattered in various Daoist and Buddhist temples.[22]

Deciphering the Portraits

Unlike state portraits of eighteenth-century European kings and queens, copies of which were distributed to government offices and embassies, Qing imperial portraiture was not intended for public circulation or viewing.[23] In particular, the paintings created for ancestor worship at the Hall of Imperial Longevity were strictly reserved for members of the imperial clan. However, in 1900 the French naval officer Pierre Loti became an unintended early viewer of the imperial portraiture when he traveled to China as part of an international expedition responding to the antiforeign Boxer Uprising. Not knowing their exact function or the identity of their subjects, Loti observed the immediacy and communicative power of these images of Qing imperial women, as the quote from him at the beginning of the chapter shows.

No known records document the response empresses' portraits provoked, but a 1723 incident gives us a sense of the emotional impact similar paintings could have. Records relate that the Yongzheng emperor could not stop crying as he knelt to view a portrait of his father, the Kangxi emperor, by the court official Mangguri (1672–1736), who had vividly captured Kangxi's likeness from memory.[24]

Such instances underscore the compelling presence imperial ancestral portraits for the Hall of Imperial Longevity were intended to have. These life-size, full-body paintings—called sacred likenesses (*shengrong*) or spirit vehicles (*shenyu*)—encouraged in worshippers a personal, emotional experience. A critical element of these portraits was verisimilitude (*zhen*), as the faithful depiction of the likeness and the heaven-endowed essence or spirit of the subject was, as Jan Stuart and Evelyn S. Rawski have noted, essential to the efficacy of sacrifices to ancestors.[25] While the faces of the empresses lack expression and appear somewhat stylized, they often capture the distinctive physiognomic traits of their subjects around the time of their death. The ancestral portrait of Empress Dowager Cixi (Empress Xiaoqin; 1835–1908) created around 1908 for the hall, for example, shows lines on her forehead and wrinkles around her eyes and mouth (fig. 2). Such a candid rendering contrasts with the photographic print created about four years earlier and given by Cixi to the American diplomat Edwin Conger (1843–1907) and his wife, Sarah Pike Conger (1843–1932). In that image, the photographer manipulated the glass-plate negative and retouched the print at Cixi's behest to erase signs of aging and create an illusion of a youthful and beautiful appearance (fig. 3).[26]

The techniques employed to portray the empresses in the ancestral portraits vary a great deal. While the faces in most of the nineteenth-century portraits appear flat, those painted in the eighteenth century were rendered in a more

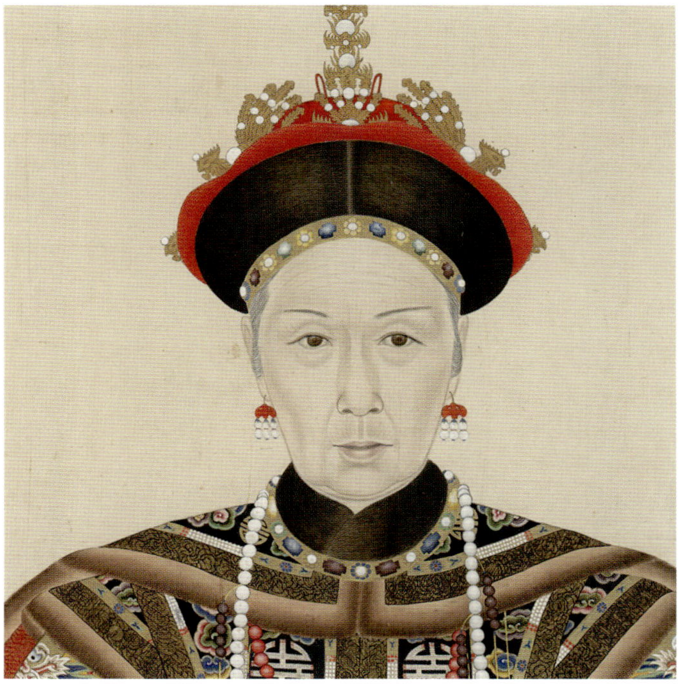

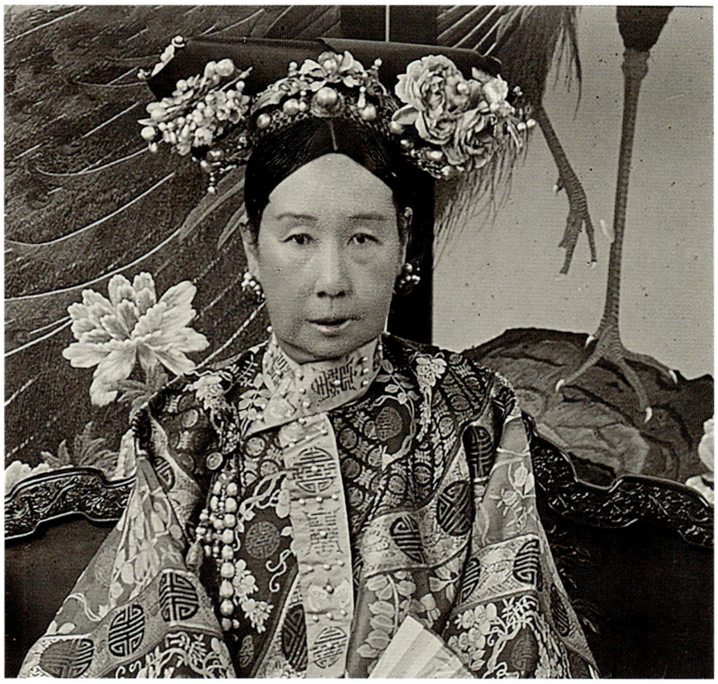

FIGURE 2
Empress Xiaoqin [Empress Dowager Cixi] (detail). Court painters, Beijing, Guangxu period, about 1908, hanging scroll, ink and color on silk, cat. 19.

FIGURE 3
Her Imperial Majesty, the Empress Dowager of China (detail). Photographed by Yu Xunling (1874–1943), Guangxu period, about 1903, hand-colored silver gelatin print, Museum of Fine Arts, Boston, cat. 190.

naturalistic manner thanks to the introduction of European painting methods to the Qing court. Take the portrait of Empress Xiaoxian painted by the Jesuit court painter Ignatius Sichelbarth as an example: modeling helps articulate the structure of her face, and white pigment applied to her eyes draws attention to her irises and facilitates eye-to-eye contact (fig. 4).[27] As James Cahill has observed, Western-inspired pictorial elements such as chiaroscuro were adopted by Qing court painters not merely for their novelty but because such illusionistic techniques allowed viewers to more deeply engage with the portraits.[28]

How the empresses' faces were portrayed in these portraits changed over time, reflecting evolving notions of beauty and propriety and conveying a sense of historical accuracy. While faces of empresses often appear flesh toned in eighteenth-century portraits, the portrait of Empress Xiaomu created in the mid-nineteenth century depicts her with a distinctly paler countenance to suggest the thick, opaque white makeup she wore (fig. 5). This effect was achieved in part by applying white pigment to the reverse of the painting to enhance the pallor of her face.[29] Further, Xiaomu's lower lip is partially covered by a red dot, suggesting the application of rouge, a common feature in nineteenth-century empresses' portraits but not one found in comparable examples painted a century earlier.

Another way to enhance the ritual effectiveness of portraits was to visually and spatially connect worshippers to the painted figure. This was achieved by placing the subject at the center of a symmetrical setting with face and body depicted frontally, an arrangement that conveyed the elevated status of the sitter and the solemnity of the setting. Such an orientation and composition likely mirrored an empress's place in actual rituals during her lifetime and harmonized with the majesty of the symmetrically arranged Hall of Imperial Longevity. Worshippers would position themselves directly in front of such a painting—or rather, below it, as portraits were hung in an elevated position so that the venerated figure "looked" down on standing or kneeling worshippers (fig. 6).

Costume played a significant role in defining the status and identity of the subjects in these ancestral portraits as well as identifying the occasions depicted therein. In contrast to the individualized faces of figures, clothing in these portraits exhibits a high degree of uniformity, following the court codes regulating what should be worn in real life. All portraits featured the sitter in court attire (*chaofu*), which consisted of a long dark blue vest worn over a yellow robe and a skirt beneath the robe (see fig. 1). The form-fitting robe featured projecting epaulets, tapering sleeves, and horse-hoof-shaped cuffs—a vestige of the Manchus' seminomadic origins. A detachable cape-like collar with pointed tips completed the ensemble.

In addition to these vestments, all empresses wore elaborate court jewelry. In the portrait of Empress Xiaoxian, for instance, her hat is adorned with pearls, tiger's-eye stones, and seven gold phoenixes, the mythical bird that symbolized the power of the empress (fig. 7; see figs. 1 and 4). The phoenix motif also appears in the throne, the throne cushion, and the carpet in her portrait. She is pictured wearing a gold headband decorated with lapis lazuli and pearls as well as three court necklaces: a string of pearls around her neck and two strings of red coral beads crossing her torso. Other notable adornments are the three earrings Xiaoxian wears in each ear, made with the finest pearls from the Manchu homeland in northeast China, to signify her exalted status. Additional ornaments include a metal torque around her neck with inset red coral and pearls; a long, pointed ceremonial sash; and pendants and pouches hanging from a button on her vest.

Such opulent court attire was reserved for imperial women of the highest rank—the empress and the empress dowager—on the most formal occasions. This was no individual fashion statement but a uniform strictly regulated by court codes from the mid-eighteenth century on in such works as *Illustrated Precedents for the Ritual Paraphernalia of the Qing Imperial Court* (*Huangchao liqi tushi*), completed in 1759, and the *Administrative Code of the Great Qing Dynasty* (*Da Qing huidian*) completed in 1764 (fig. 8).[30] While the basic components and style of court apparel depicted in these portraits conformed to these regulations and remained largely unchanged throughout the Qing dynasty, certain decorative elements and features evolved over time. Given the importance of verisimilitude and historical accuracy in these portraits, painters were highly conscious of subtle sartorial changes. In addition to consulting

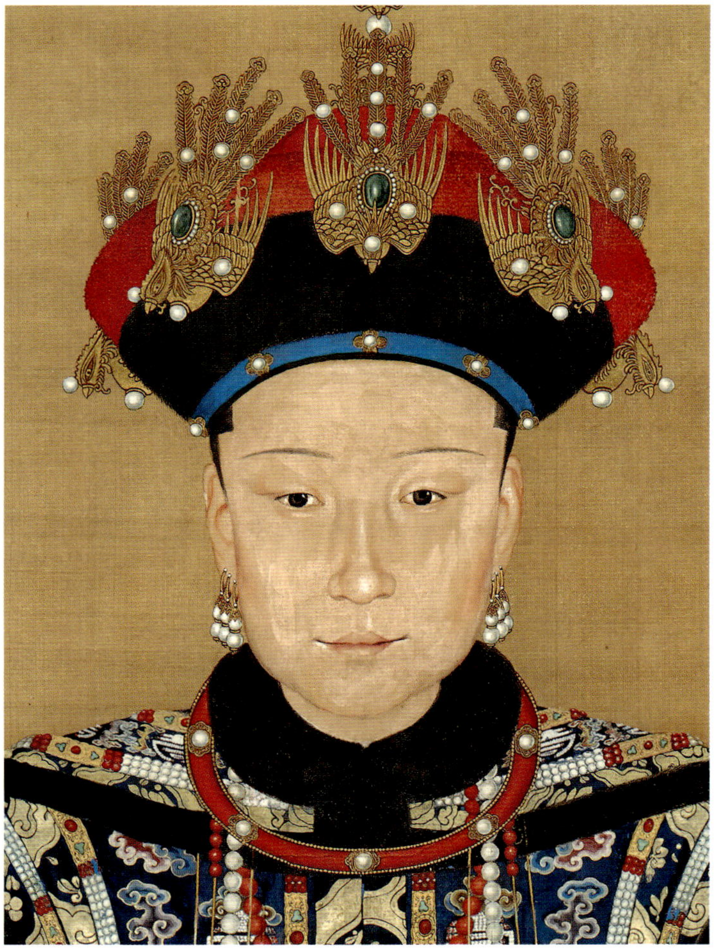

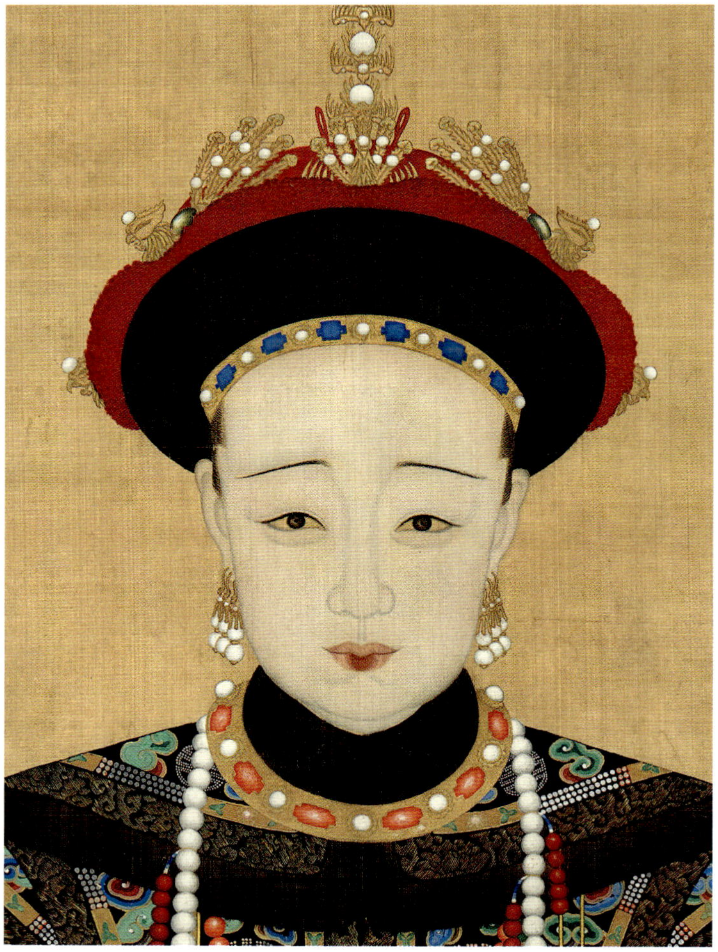

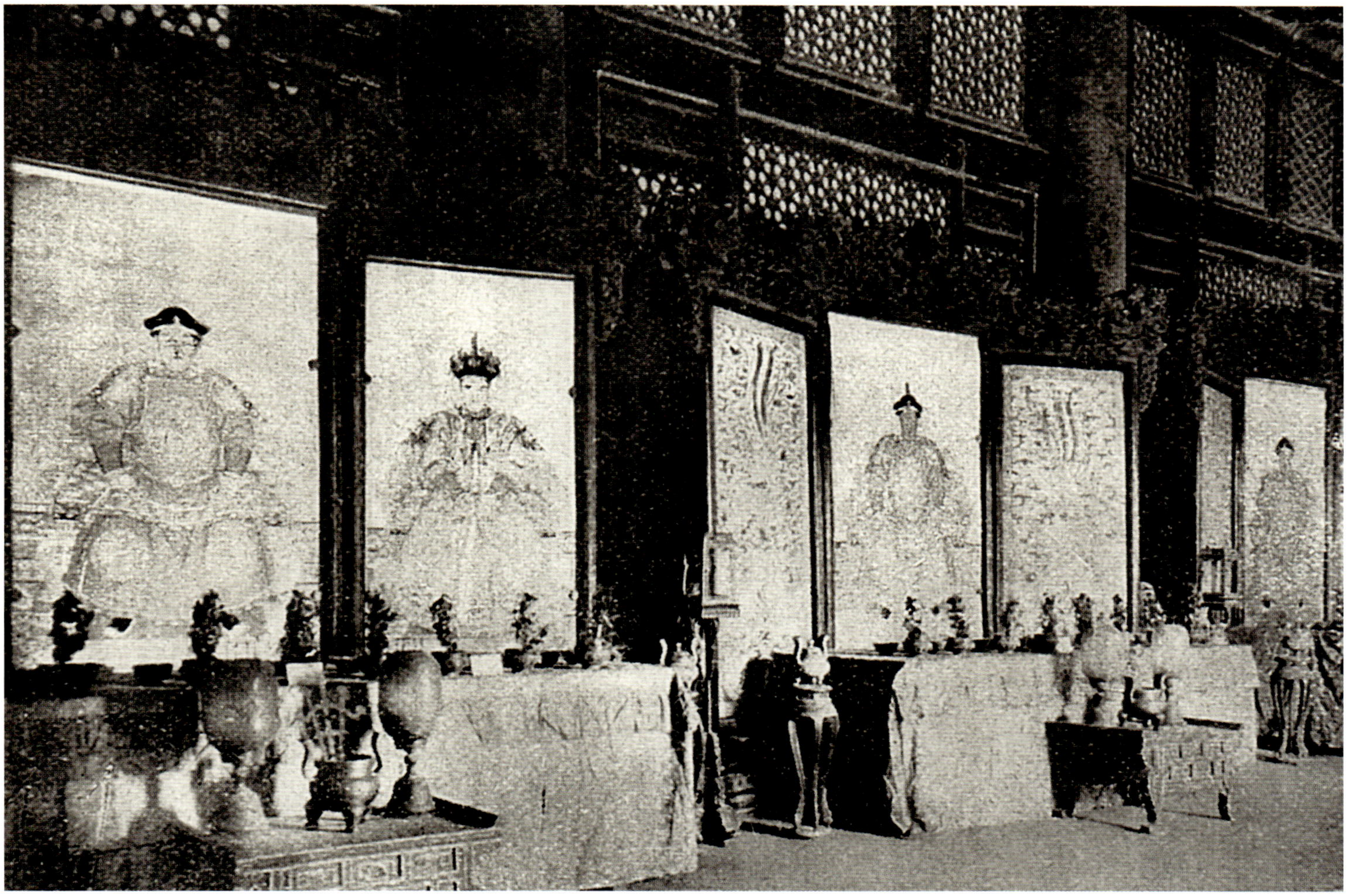

FIGURE 4
Empress Xiaoxian (detail of fig. 1), cat. 12.

FIGURE 5
Empress Xiaomu (detail). Court painters, Beijing, Daoguang period, 1850, hanging scroll, ink and color on silk, Peabody Essex Museum, cat. 13.

FIGURE 6
Interior of the Hall of Imperial Longevity. 1930 or earlier, from *Palace Museum Weekly* 22 (1930): 13.

FIGURE 7
Court hat with phoenixes. Probably Imperial Workshop, Beijing, 18th or 19th century, sable, velvet, silk floss, pearls, tiger's eye stone, lapis lazuli, glass, birch bark and metal with gilding, and kingfisher feather, cat. 70.

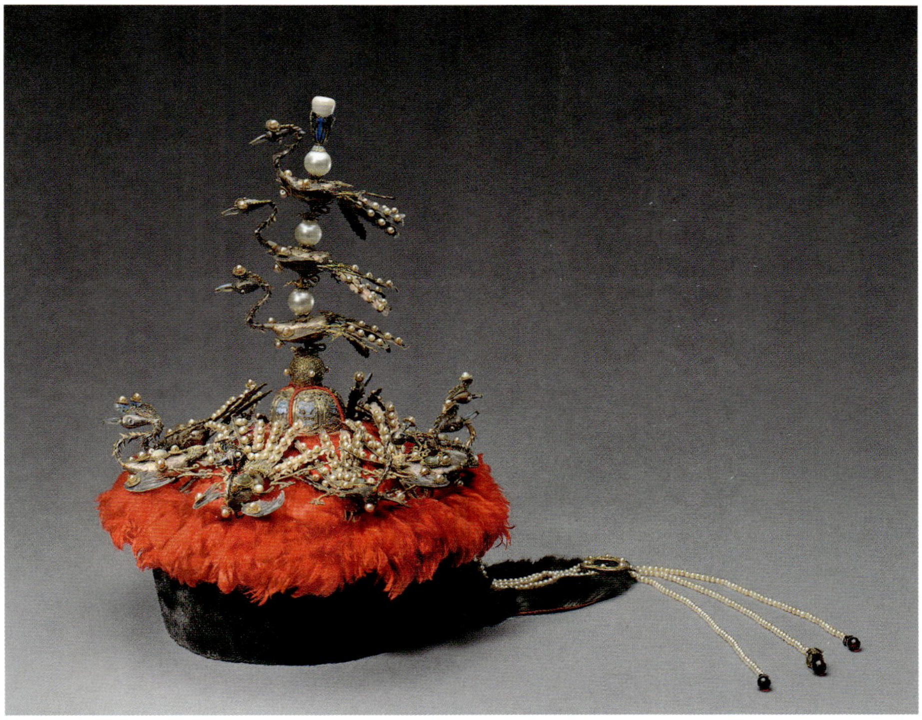

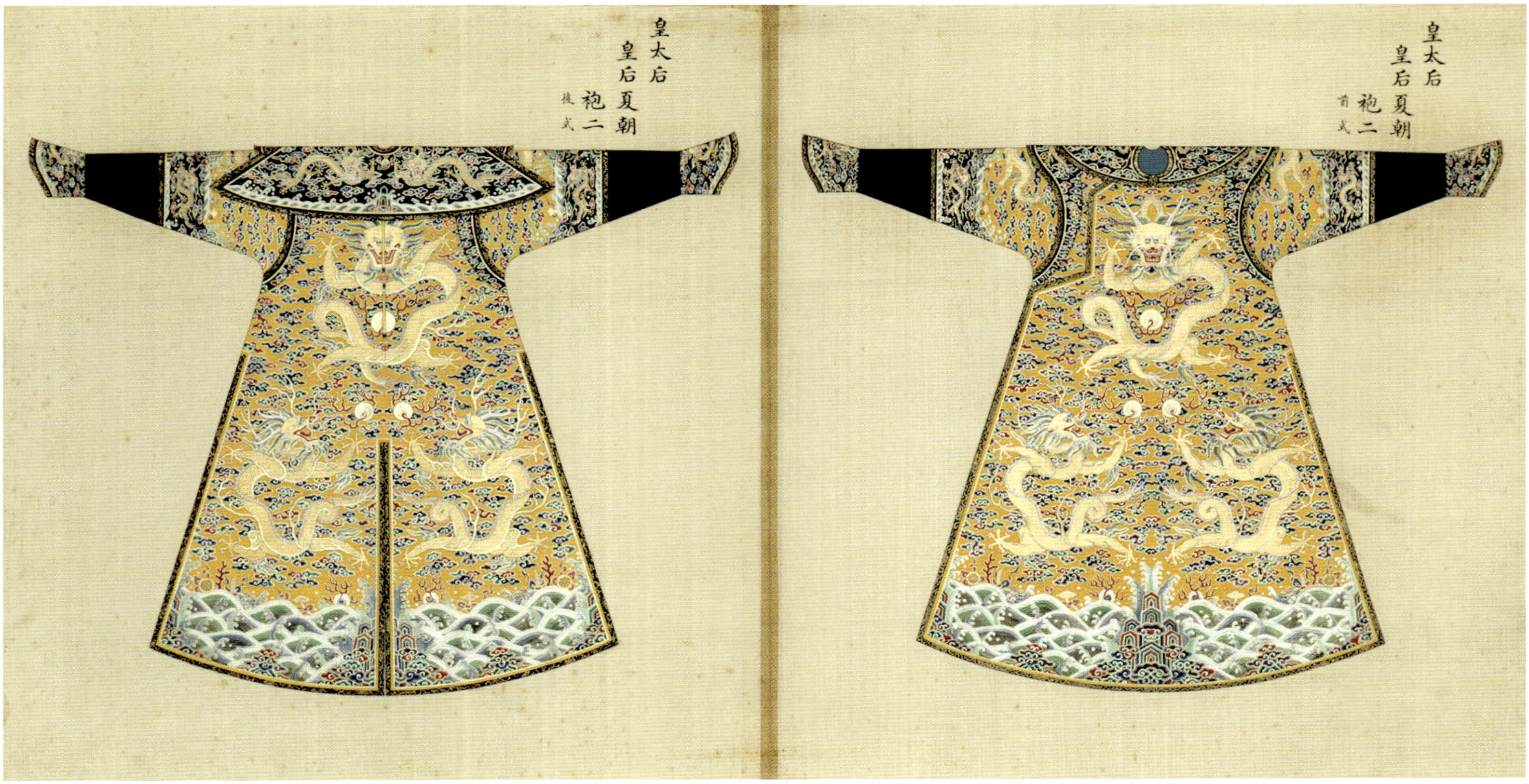

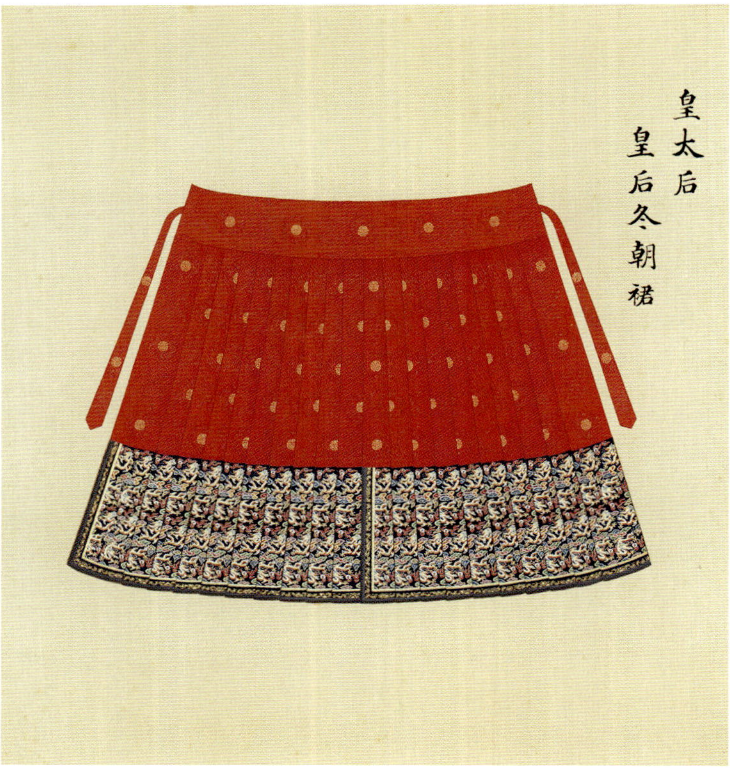

FIGURE 8

Summer court robe (top) and winter court skirt (bottom) for empress dowager and empress from Illustrated Precedents for the Ritual Paraphernalia of the Qing Imperial Court. Leng Jian (active 18th century), Huang Men (active 18th century), and other court painters, Beijing, Qianlong period, probably 1772, album leaves, ink and color on silk, 16 × 31½ in. (41 × 80 cm), Gu6116-41/92.

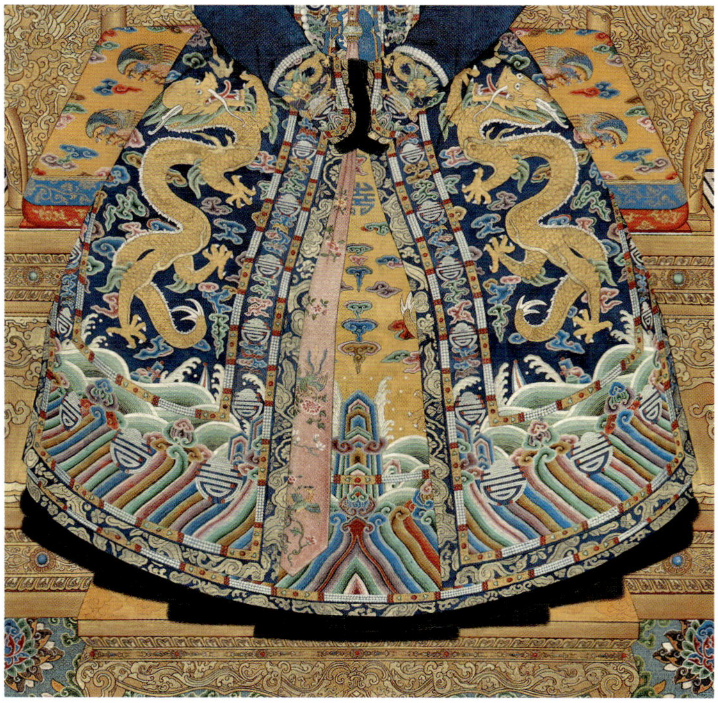

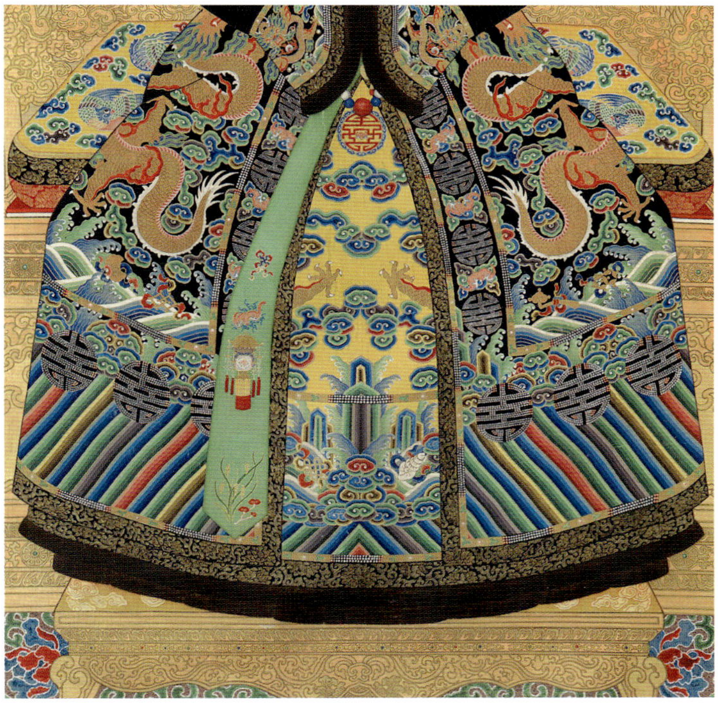

FIGURE 9
Pink ceremonial sash in the portrait of Empress Xiaoxian (detail of fig. 1), cat. 12.

FIGURE 10
Green ceremonial sash in the portrait of Empress Xiaomu (detail; see fig. 5), cat. 13.

these codes—and heeding specific imperial instructions—painters might have studied portraits of a subject and referenced actual objects from the subject's time to accurately capture appropriate sartorial features. In Xiaoxian's portrait, for example, she wears a pink ceremonial sash emblazoned with peonies and a pair of phoenixes that did not conform to the rule in *Illustrated Precedents* stipulating that the empress should wear a green sash ornamented with a lantern and grains (emblems of prosperity and harvest) such as the one in Empress Xiaomu's portrait—and indeed in all portraits of empresses after Xiaoxian's generation (figs. 9 and 10). This apparent lapse in decorum can be explained by the fact that Xiaoxian died in 1748, more than ten years before *Illustrated Precedents* was compiled. When creating her portrait in 1777, the painters likely based the pink sash on one in use during her time that does not survive.[31]

Further examination of Xiaoxian's portrait reveals another puzzle. All empresses before her were portrayed wearing summer garments, while all empresses after her wear winter attire. At some point in the life of Xiaoxian's portrait, parts of the vest and robe were covered with a layer of yellow or blue pigment on which new designs quite different from the original were imposed. Broad black borders representing sable fur trim were added, making her summer outfit into a winter ensemble (see fig. 1). In design and decoration the repainted garment resembles a Qianlong-period winter court robe and vest with lavishly embroidered and beaded decoration, suggesting it might have served as a model for the painted alterations (fig. 11). When and why did the repainting happen? One possible explanation is that these changes to Xiaoxian's portrait, originally created in 1777, were likely made in the nineteenth century to honor Qianlong's decision to designate the lunar New Year as the most important occasion for the veneration of the portraits of deceased empresses at the Hall of Imperial Longevity. If that was the case, winter attire, which was often more elaborately decorated than summer attire, would be more appropriate for the season when the portrait was displayed.

Painting the Empresses

After Empress Dowager Chongqing died in 1777, her son, Qianlong, commissioned a portrait of her for the Hall of Imperial Longevity (fig. 12). Three court painters who had worked together on a portrait commemorating the empress dowager's eightieth birthday six years earlier (fig. 13) were assigned to this project: Ignatius Sichelbarth, Yi Lantai, and Wang Ruxue.[32] That same year, Qianlong ordered that a portrait of his late wife Empress Xiaoxian be painted by

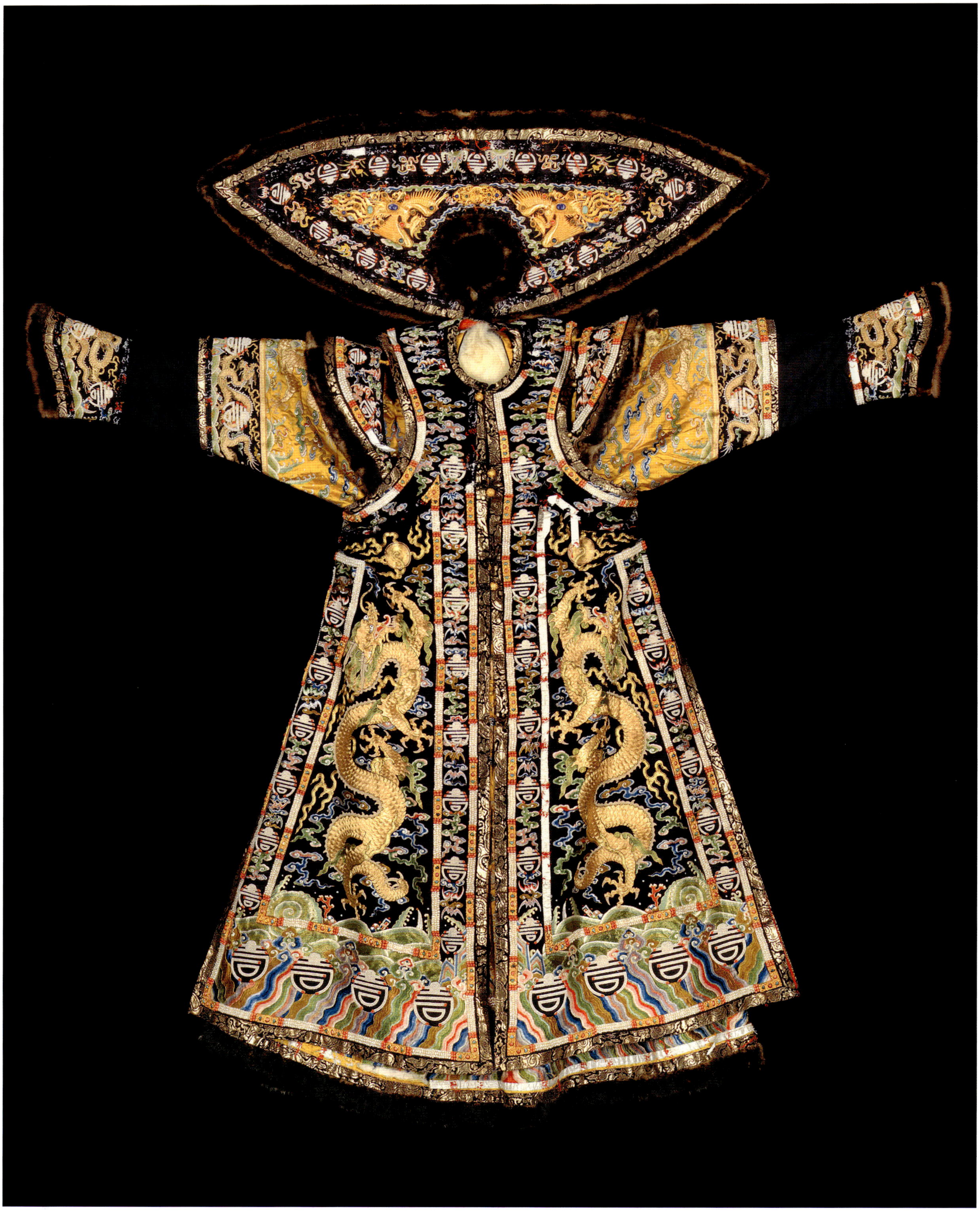

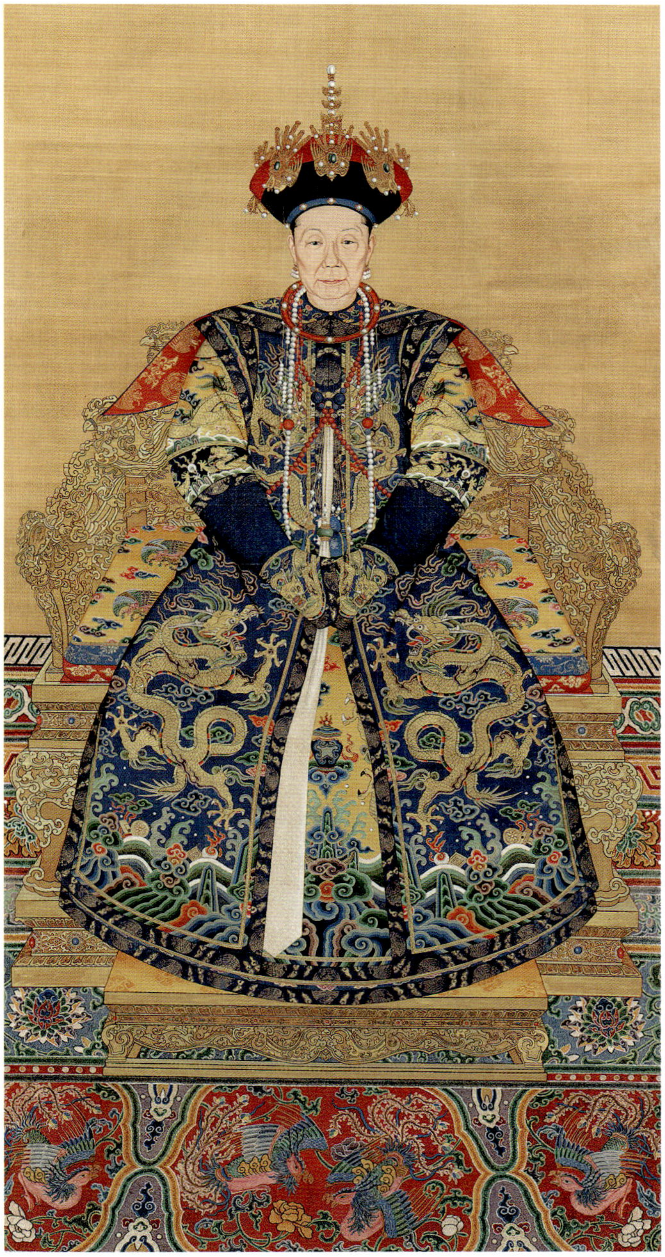

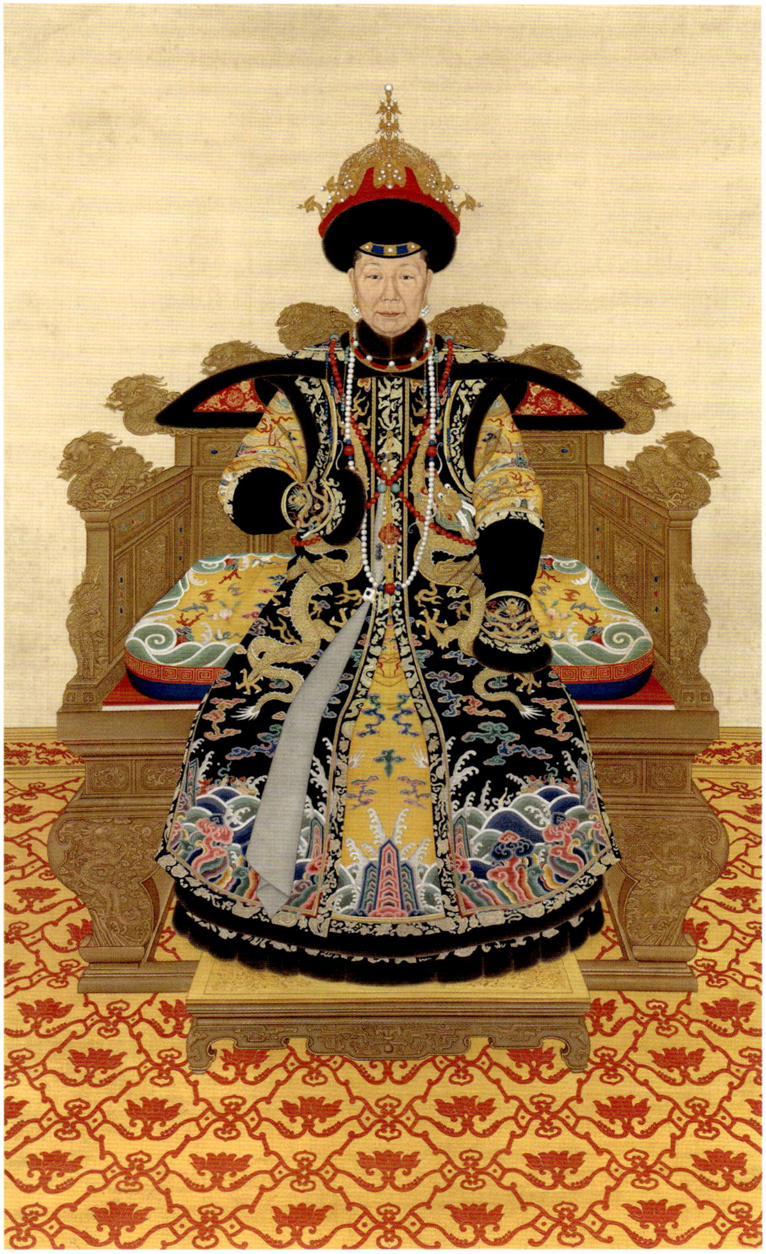

FIGURE 11
Court vest with dragons and clouds over court robe. Imperial Silk Manufactory, Suzhou (embroidery), and Imperial Workshop, Beijing (tailoring), Qianlong period, 1736–95, embroidery, polychrome and metallic-wrapped silk threads, coral beads, seed pearls, and gold plaques on silk satin with fur, Gu45201, Gu45200.

FIGURE 12
Empress Dowager Chongqing. Ignatius Sichelbarth (Ai Qimeng; Bohemia, 1708–1780), Yi Lantai (active about 1748–86), and Wang Ruxue (active 18th century), Qianlong period, 1777, hanging scroll, ink and color on silk, $97\frac{15}{16}$ × 46 in. (248.7 × 116.8 cm), Gu6455.

FIGURE 13
Empress Dowager Chongqing at the Age of Eighty. Ignatius Sichelbarth (Ai Qimeng; Bohemia, 1708–1780), Yi Lantai (active about 1748–86), and Wang Ruxue (active 18th century), Qianlong period, 1771, hanging scroll, ink and color on silk, cat. 11.

Sichelbarth, Yi Lantai, and likely Wang Ruxue after his mother's portrait was completed, specifying that it should have the same dimensions as the painting of his mother.[33] These details explain the nearly identical format and similar style of the two portraits in the collections of the Palace Museum and the Peabody Essex Museum (figs. 1 and 12).

All portraits of Qing empresses created for worship at the Hall of Imperial Longevity were commissioned by emperors. From the early eighteenth century on, the portrait of an emperor was made soon after his death. The creation of an empress's portrait followed a less predictable timetable. The portrait of Empress Dowager Chongqing mentioned above was commissioned less than two weeks after her death in 1777. By contrast, almost thirty years passed before painters created the portrait of her daughter-in-law, Empress Xiaoxian, who died at the age of thirty-six in 1748. This discrepancy in timing has to do with several factors. According to Qing court convention, a deceased emperor's portrait could be worshipped at the Hall of Imperial Longevity before his wife passed away, but the portrait of a deceased empress could not be venerated until her husband had died. Empress Dowager Chongqing died some forty years after her husband, the Yongzheng emperor. Since his portrait had been on display all those years, hers could be placed next to his soon after her death. But Empress Xiaoxian died when her husband and mother-in-law—the most senior imperial woman—were still alive, meaning that, beloved as she was by Qianlong, her portrait could not be venerated at the hall during his lifetime. Probably in deference to Chongqing's seniority in rank and generation, Xiaoxian's portrait was not created until her mother-in-law had passed away in 1777, and it was not displayed until Qianlong died some twenty years after that.

According to court records, the face of Empress Dowager Chongqing in the 1777 portrait was done by Sichelbarth, while the costume, furniture, and furnishing were completed by Yi Lantai and Wang Ruxue, evincing the division of labor common in creating similar Qing imperial ancestral portraits.[34] It is noteworthy that they painted this posthumous work not in buildings designated for use by the Imperial Workshop (Zaoban chu) but at Chongqing's residence, the Palace of Longevity and Health (Shoukang gong) inside the Forbidden City. It is tantalizing to think that court painters, all of them male before the time of Empress Dowager Cixi, might have seen their imperial subjects while they were still alive or shortly after they died, but no known written records support this hypothesis. If it did occur, the lack of evidence might be explained by the decorum associated with the gender and exalted status of the empresses, who were to be seen only by men in the imperial family, high-ranking court officials, and eunuchs. Or perhaps it was due to the general absence of imperial women in official documents, which were written by those who did not deem it necessary to record details regarding the process of making such portraits.

In order to create accurate facial likenesses of deceased empresses, court painters often referred to existing portraiture. For example, in the above-mentioned posthumous portrait of Chongqing, Sichelbarth probably drew on the painting he had done for her eightieth birthday given the similarities between the faces in the two works (figs. 12 and 13). Painters often lifted details from existing portraits, a practice that helps explain the consistent treatment of costumes, furniture, and other accoutrements in nineteenth-century portraits of empresses.[35] The painter who created the face in the full-body portrait of the long-deceased Empress Xiaozhuang (1613–1688; fig. 14) likely worked from a bust-length sketch in which her carefully delineated face was imbued with a strong sense of individuality (fig. 15).

A newly discovered sketch created around 1908 reveals the method of creating Qing imperial ancestral portraits.[36] In preparation for the final painting of Empress Dowager Cixi, her figure, her costume, the throne, and the carpet, as well as the decorations on them, were outlined in ink on the sketch. Chinese characters for colors (some in simplified form) and sparsely applied pigments in certain areas provided a guide for the coloring of the final painting. This color-coded sketch—not unlike a paint-by-numbers kit—does not completely match the finished portrait, suggesting that the painter(s) might have followed an imperial order to make certain adjustments or took the liberty of changing certain colors during its execution (figs. 16 and 17).

The finest materials were used to create these portraits. After outlines were inked, a vibrant palette of pigments and gold of various tones were applied. Great care was taken to mount the painting as a scroll that could be hung from a cord. For instance, the image of Empress Xiaoxian was painted on a single piece of plain-weave silk (see fig. 1). It was surrounded on three sides by yellow silk satin borders and supported on the back by paper and yellow silk tabby. Other components included a top stave, a bottom dowel, and two roller ends of ivory—a precious material often used for portraits of the most important imperial figures. [37]

Despite all the effort that went into producing these portraits, they were not considered artworks by their painters or worshippers; rather, they were understood as ritual objects imbued with sacred power that served as vessels for the spirits of ancestors. For this reason, none of these portraits bear the inscriptions, signatures, or seal marks of the artists who painted them or the emperors who commissioned them. Emperors refrained from placing their marks on these

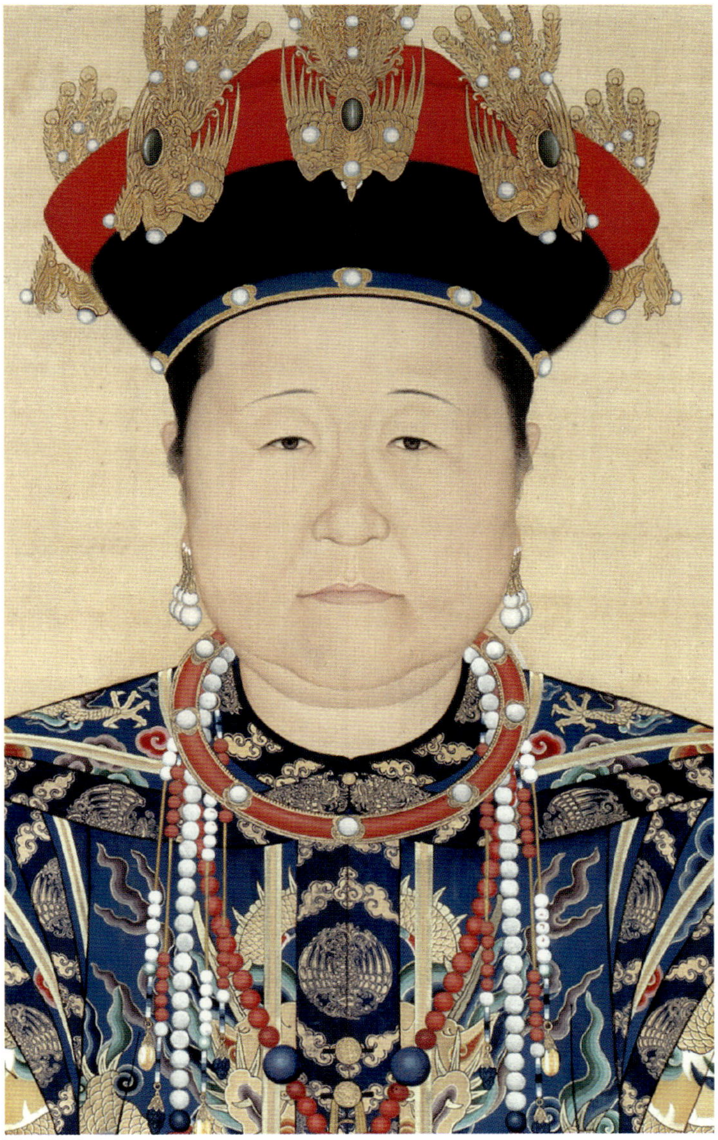

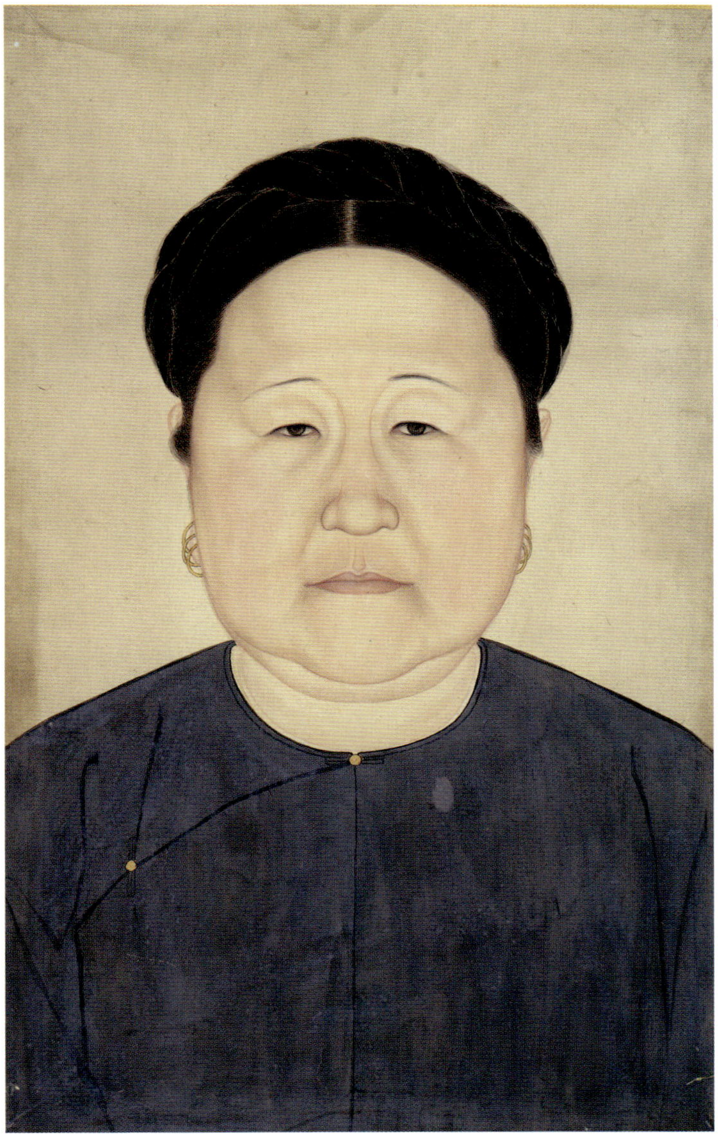

FIGURE 14
Empress Xiaozhuang (detail). Court painters, Beijing, probably Qianlong period, about 1750, hanging scroll, ink and color on silk, 100⅝ × 46 in. (255.5 × 116.8 cm), Gu6378.

FIGURE 15
Empress Xiaozhuang (detail).Court painters, Beijing, probably Qianlong period, about 1750, bust-length sketch, ink and color on paper, 22 1/16 × 13 15/16 in. (56 × 35.4 cm), Gu6381.

portraits out of respect for their ancestors, and the role of the painters was considered inconsequential. The situation was different in portraits not intended for ancestor worship at the Hall of Imperial Longevity, as in the painting depicting the Qianlong emperor, Empress Xiaoxian, and his other consorts (fig. 18). That painting's first section, commemorating his birthday in the year of his inauguration, bears Qianlong's seal marks and inscriptions.[38]

The Empresses on Display

The display of ancestral portraits at the Hall of Imperial Longevity visualized the place of empresses in the Qing imperial family. The selection of which imperial women would be venerated during the New Year rites mirrored the patriarchal and patrilineal structure of the ruling clan and was tied to a woman's membership in the imperial lineage rather than her natal family.[39] Women in the patrilineal line—particularly mothers—were endowed with certain privileges, including

FIGURE 16
Empress Dowager Cixi. Court painters, Beijing, Guangxu period, about 1908, sketch, ink and color on paper, Shu3388.

FIGURE 17
Empress Xiaoqin [Empress Dowager Cixi] (detail; see fig. 2), cat. 19.

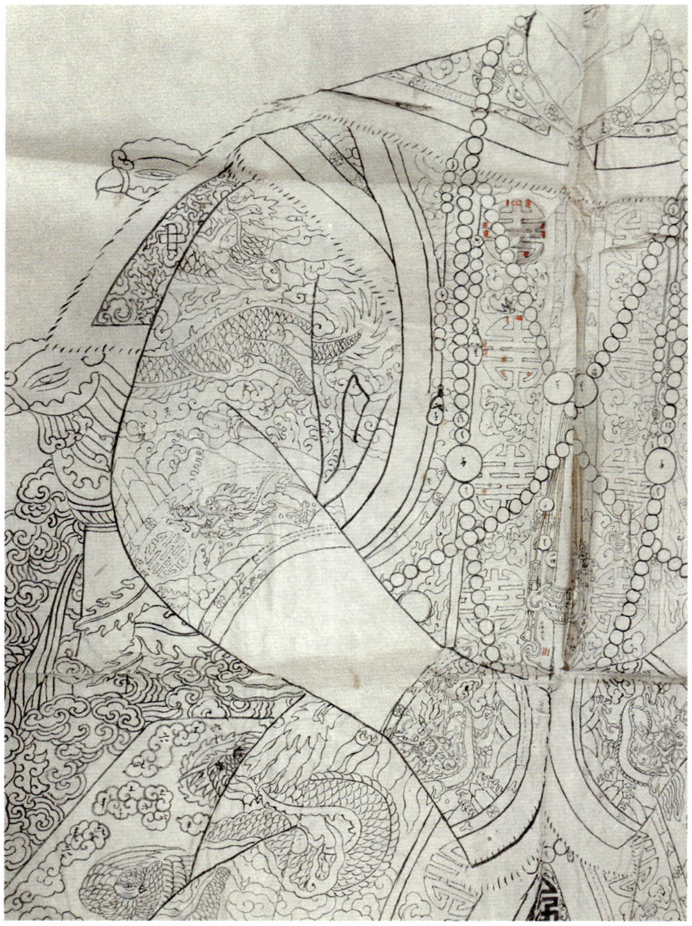

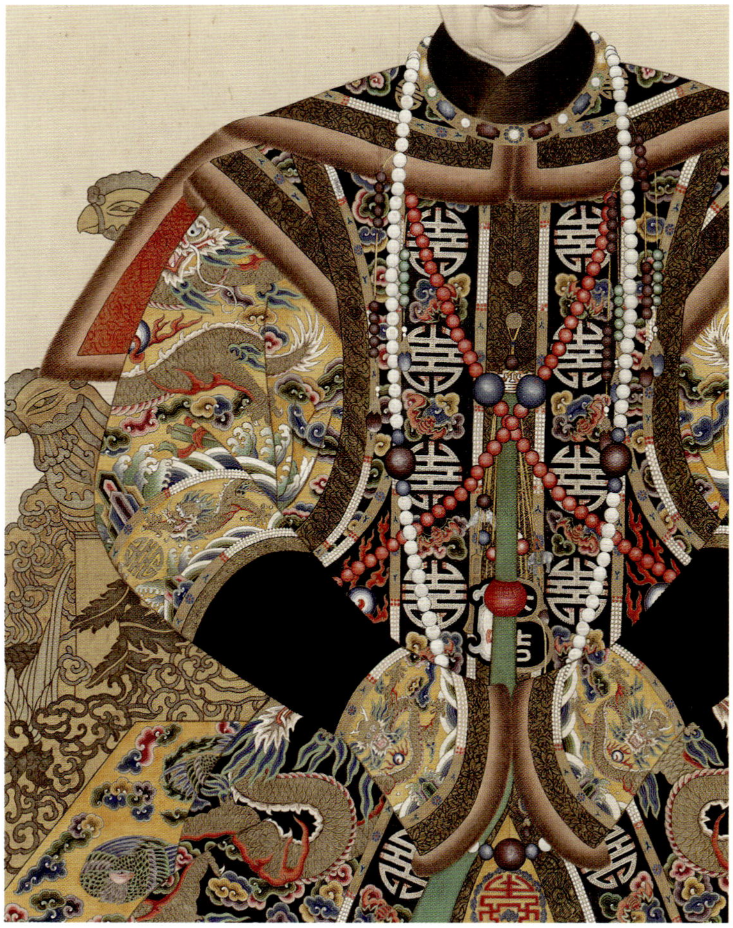

respect and devotion from their sons, as Bret Hinsch has noted.[40] During the Guangxu reign (1875–1908) portraits of seventeen Qing empresses joined those of ten emperors for veneration at the hall, a clear acknowledgment of the value of women in maintaining the well-being of the family and the state.[41] Drawing on cosmology and political philosophy that can be traced back to the Han dynasty (206 BCE–220 CE), Qing emperors maintained that the union of man and woman formed a family, which constituted the bedrock of all human relationships and the cornerstone of the state. The empress had a key role to play in the affairs of the imperial family, which formed the foundation of the state affairs overseen by the emperor. Cosmologically, she represented the yin, or female force, and complemented the emperor's yang, or male energy.[42] The interaction of these two interdependent elements was understood to have given birth to the cosmos and produced the social order. As Susan Mann has stated, these "complementary-yet-hierarchical" gender relations were part of the state ideology sustaining social norms and household-based political economy, with males and females performing paired tasks in endeavors such as farming and weaving.[43]

The Hall of Imperial Longevity was not an official state altar but rather a site for members of the Qing imperial family to venerate their forebears. In contrast with the Temple of the Ancestors and the Hall of the Ancestors, where all deceased Qing empresses were represented by spirit tablets, the emperors' decisions about which empresses' portraits would be included at the hall appeared somewhat inconsistent due to their personal preferences and the empresses' role and influence in the Qing imperial family and dynastic history. Notably absent from the New Year rites at the Hall of Imperial Longevity during the Guangxu period were Xiaoci (1575–1603), the very first Qing empress and wife of the founder of the dynasty, Nurhaci; and Empress Xiaoduan (1599–1649), the primary wife of the second emperor, Hong Taiji. Xiaozhuang, a consort of Hong Taiji, was the earliest Qing empress included in the hall. Her rank was actually lower than that of Xiaoduan, but Xiaozhuang's critical role in the Qing imperial family—spouse of an emperor, mother

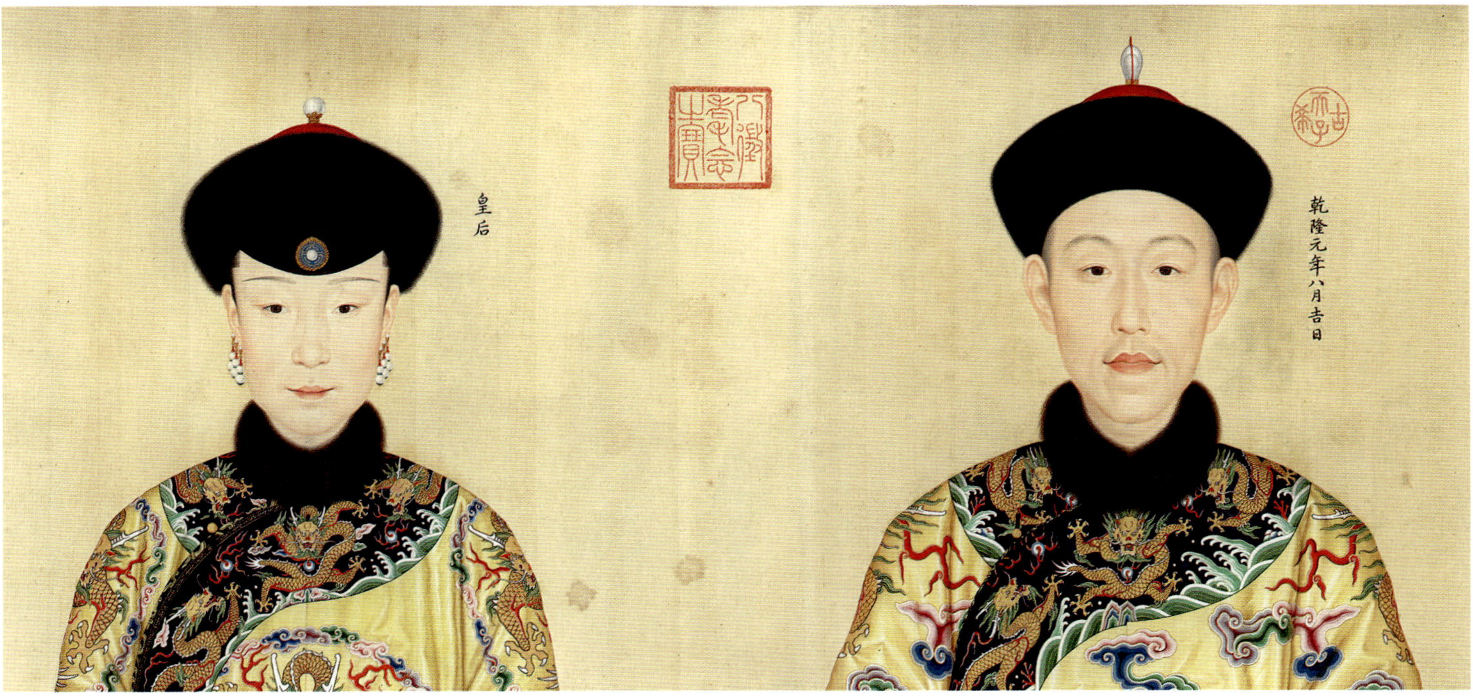

and grandmother of two emperors, a key political figure after the court moved to Beijing in 1644—earned her a privileged position as the most senior matriarch of the imperial clan in the hall. Xiaoding (1868–1913), who died shortly after the fall of the dynasty, was the last empress whose portrait entered the hall.

The omission of certain empresses from the Hall of Imperial Longevity can also be explained by the rule that portraits of no more than two empresses could accompany that of their husband: the first and primary wife of the emperor and the birth mother of the succeeding emperor (often granted the title of empress posthumously). Empress Dowager Ci'an (Empress Xiaozhen; 1837–1881), who was made empress during her lifetime, never received the honor of having her portrait worshipped at the hall because she was neither the first wife of the Xianfeng emperor (r. 1851–61) nor the birth mother of the next emperor, Tongzhi (r. 1862–74).[44] Cixi, however, though junior to Ci'an in rank, was represented by an ancestral portrait in the hall because she gave birth to the future Tongzhi emperor. The absence of Ci'an's portrait at the hall hinted at her influence at court being overshadowed by Cixi (see Ying-chen Peng's essay, pp. 128–41). The Tongzhi and Guangxu (r. 1875–1908) emperors were accompanied only by a portrait of each one's primary wife because none of their other consorts bore an heir and thus were not posthumously granted the title of empress.

Within the Hall of Imperial Longevity, portraits were displayed according to a strict hierarchy based on the subject's generational seniority, gender, and rank. In the Guangxu period the hall was divided by wooden panels into two sections

FIGURE 18
The Qianlong emperor and Empress Xiaoxian, detail from Portraits of the Qianlong Emperor and His Twelve Consorts. Giuseppe Castiglione (Lang Shining; Italy, 1688–1766) and other court painters, Beijing, Qianlong period, 1736–about 1770s, handscroll, ink and color on silk, $20\frac{13}{16} \times 270\frac{15}{16}$ in. (53 × 688.3 cm), Cleveland Museum of Art, John L. Severance Fund, 1969.31.

FIGURE 19
Chart indicating the placement of portraits in the Hall of Imperial Longevity for the lunar New Year veneration rites during the Guangxu period, 1875–1908; from *Da Qing wuchao huidian: Guangxu huidian tu, juan* 9, courtesy of Li Shi.

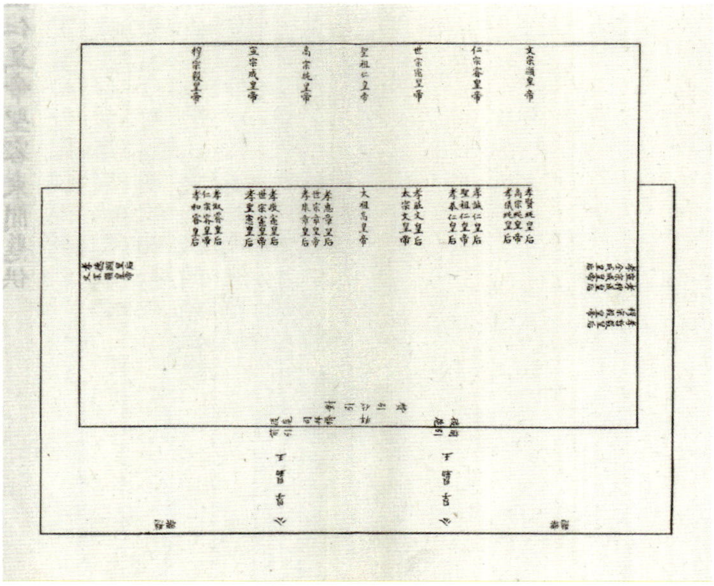

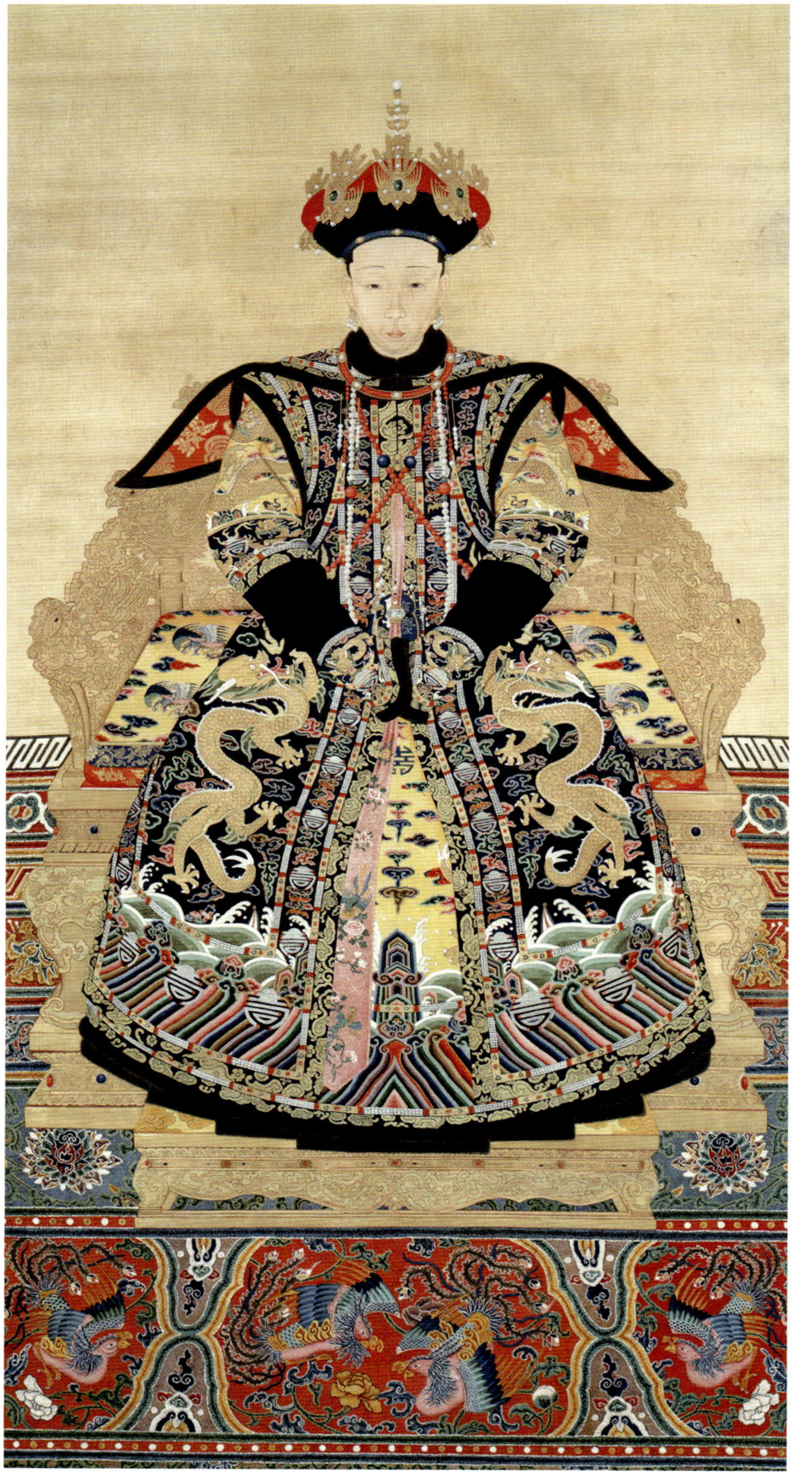

(fig. 19).[45] The rear area contained seven chambers, each devoted to a deceased Qing emperor, and each permanently displaying portraits of the emperor.[46] The front portion of the hall was reserved for the grandest veneration rites, occurring on New Year's Eve and New Year's Day, when full-body, life-size portraits of deceased emperors and empresses were put on view. This was the main occasion for the worship of portraits of Qing empresses at the hall.

The portraits were displayed on standing screens of similar size, each divided into three sections with the central panel flanked by two smaller, shorter ones (see fig. 6). A single portrait was hung from the top of each panel, covering the entire surface within the screen's wooden frame.[47] When the paintings were displayed together on one screen, the edge of the carpet in each would align, forming a kind of horizon that visually and spatially unified the works of different scales and heights (fig. 20). The uniformity of the setting and method of display determined the consistent size, format, and overall composition of the empresses' portraits.

In Qing imperial spaces the center was regarded the most important position, with the significance of other positions determined by their distance from and orientation to the center: the shorter the distance, the more important the position; when two positions were equidistant from the center, the one to the proper left of center was more important. The display of imperial portraits for the New Year rites adhered to these

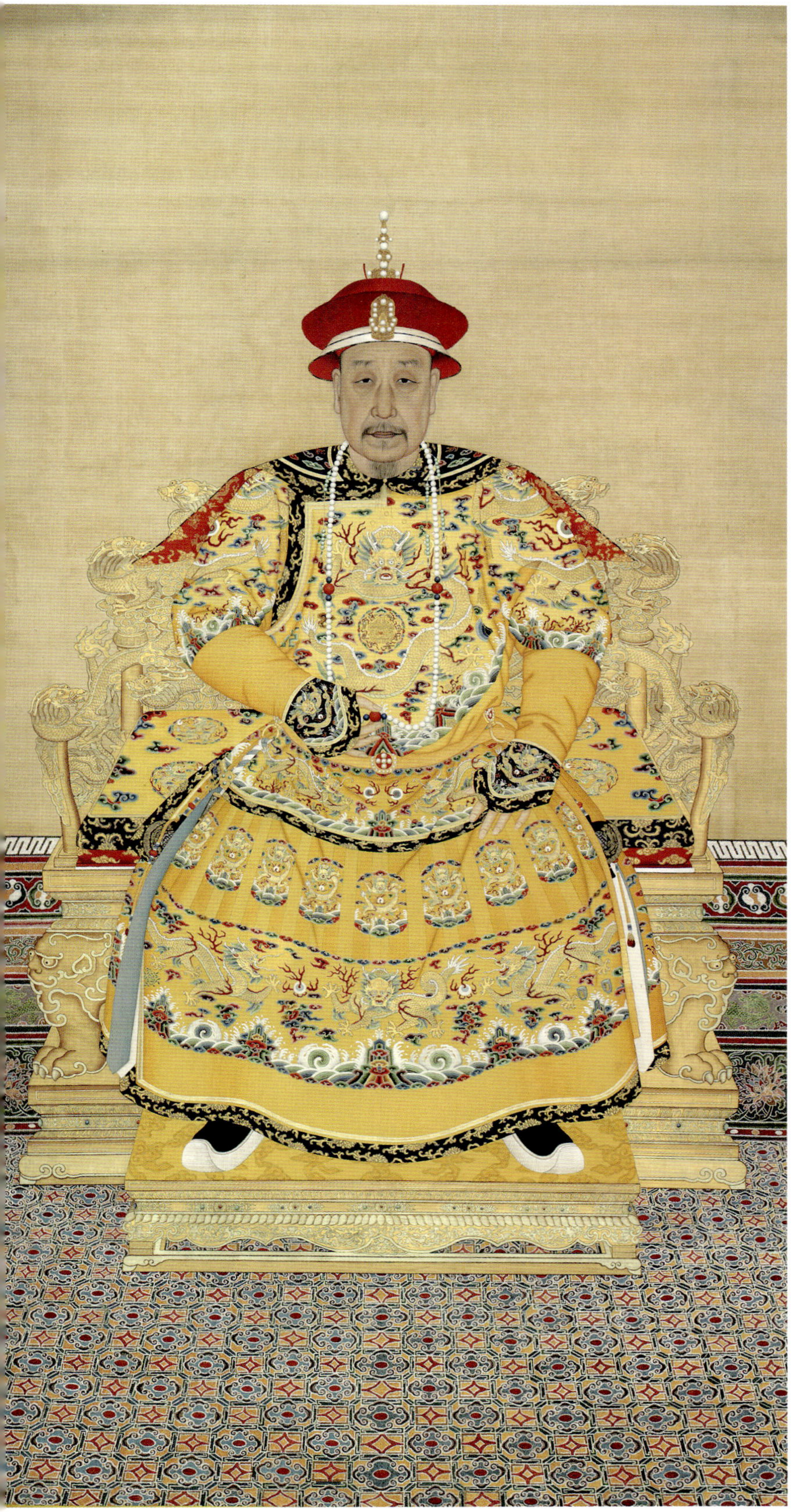

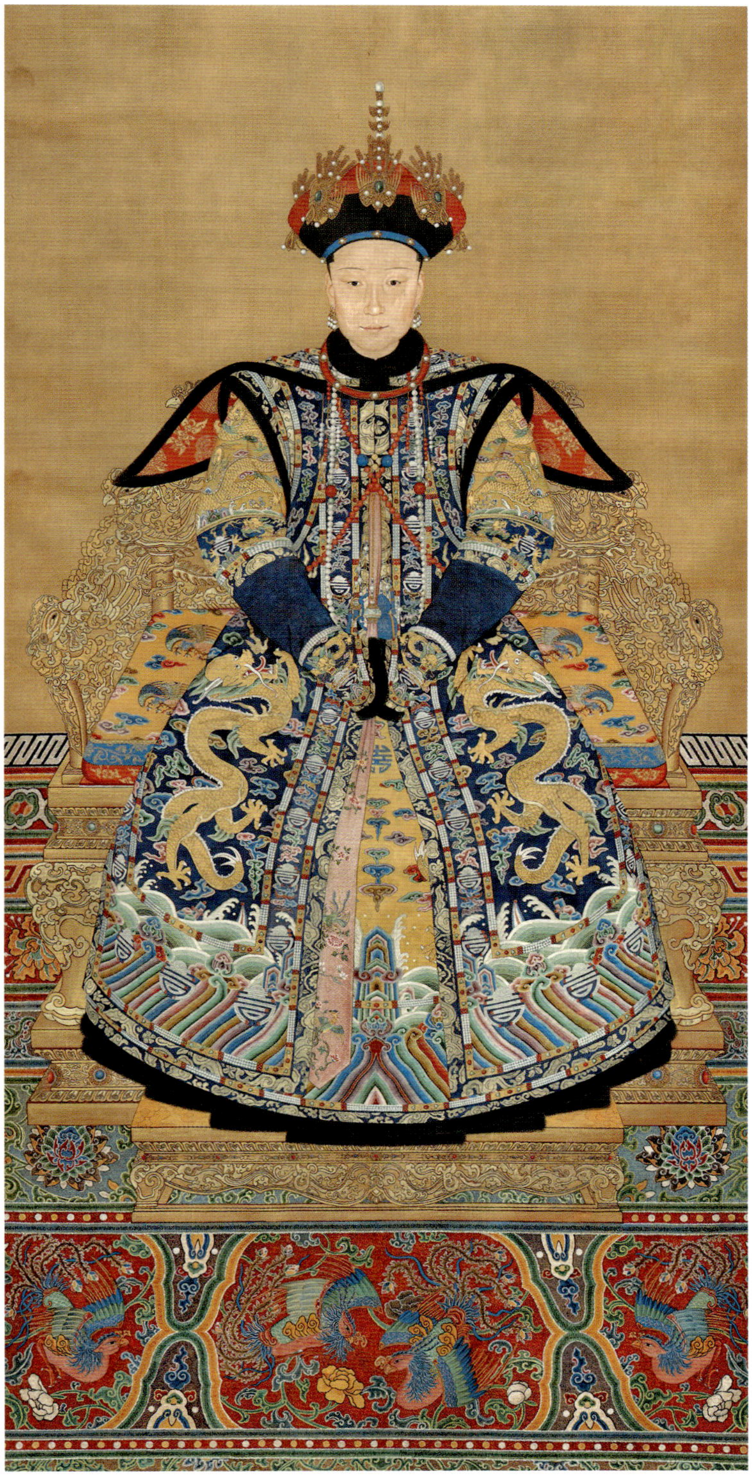

FIGURE 20

Reconstruction of the display of portraits in the Hall of Imperial Longevity (left to right):

Empress Xiaoyi. Court painters, Beijing, probably 19th century, hanging scroll, ink and color on silk, 96 7/8 × 45 5/8 in. (246 × 116 cm), Gu6522.

The Qianlong emperor. Court painters, Beijing, Jiaqing period, about 1799, hanging scroll, ink and color on silk, 101 1/8 × 59 1/2 in. (257 × 151.2 cm), Gu6459.

Empress Xiaoxian (see fig. 1), cat. 12.

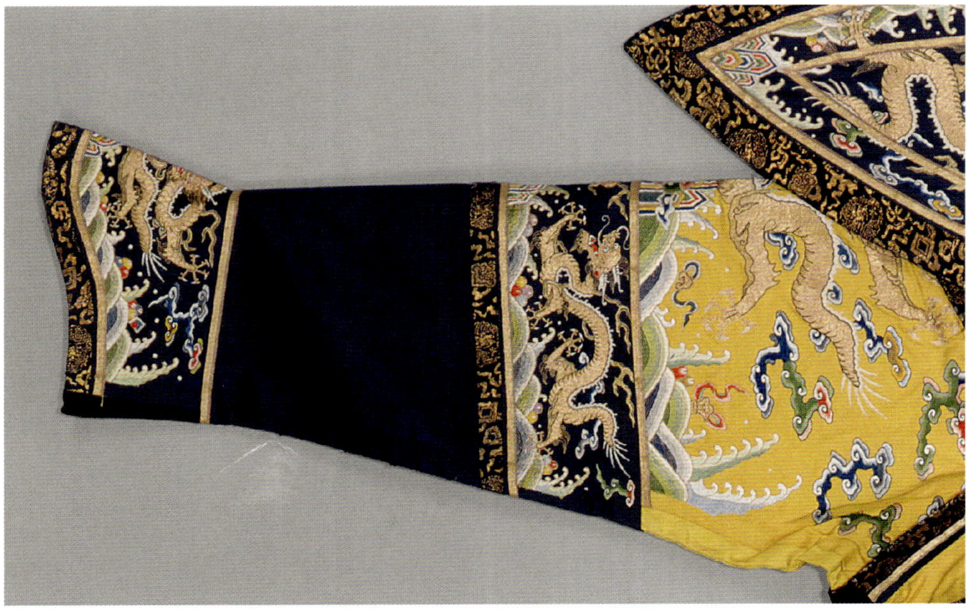

FIGURE 21
Sleeve band of an empress's court robe with dragons and clouds. Imperial Silk Manufactory, Suzhou (embroidery), and Imperial Workshop, Beijing (tailoring), Yongzheng period, 1723–35, embroidery, polychrome and metallic-wrapped silk threads on silk gauze, cat. 44.

FIGURE 22
Empress Xiaoqin [Empress Dowager Cixi] (detail; see fig. 2), cat. 19.

rules.[48] The portrait of Nurhaci, the founder of the dynasty and most senior patriarch in the imperial lineage, occupied the screen at the center of the hall. Subsequent screens, each representing a generation, were placed to either side of the central screen based on seniority. Space constraints in the hall during the Guangxu period required that portraits of the three most recent generations be placed on screens on the east and west sides of the hall, flanking the portraits of the earlier generations mounted on south-facing screens.

The status of two empresses of the same generation was likewise reflected by the position of their portraits (fig. 20). For example, on Qianlong's left, the more important position, sat his first and primary wife, Empress Xiaoxian; on the back of her portrait is written the Chinese character for "left" as an instruction to staff responsible for hanging it. On Qianlong's right was Empress Xiaoyi (1727–1775), whose status—dependent as it was on her role as the birth mother of the next emperor—was lower than Xiaoxian's.

Such a display also heightened gendered treatments in the portraits. As the head of the patriarchal imperial household, an emperor was represented by a portrait placed in the central panel and significantly larger than that of an empress on a side panel. The portrayal of his face and body was also larger than that of an empress. As a rule, an empress's feet and hands were hidden to make her appear more demure, while the emperor struck an open pose as suggested by his boots, and his right hand fingers a court necklace. The bright yellow of the emperor's robe dominates his portraits; it was a color associated with imperial power and was reserved for the emperor, the empress dowager, the empresses, and the second-rank imperial consort. The empress likewise wore a yellow court robe, but it was covered by a long dark vest in blue, a color that made her portrait appear more subdued than his.

One feature distinguishing an empress's court robe from an emperor's was the band encircling its sleeves.[49] This band was usually made from a strip of deep-blue silk with dragons, which differed in color and decoration from the surrounding material (fig. 21). In her portrait, however, Empress Dowager Cixi wears a yellow sleeve band decorated with dragons, waves, and clouds, a striking deviation from convention followed in all other portraits of empresses for worship at the Hall of Imperial Longevity (fig. 22). As her sleeve band is barely discernable from the upper part of the sleeve, Cixi's attire more closely resembles that of an emperor. A title on the sketch for this portrait, "Portrait of the Emperor"—probably inscribed around the time the sketch was made—confirms such an attempt to subvert gendered dress rules and to visualize Cixi, the dynasty's de facto ruler for nearly five decades, as on a par with male rulers. Trumping these gender- or rank-based hierarchies was generational seniority. The portrait of Empress Xiaozhuang, for example, occupied a position senior to that of her son the Shunzhi emperor and her daughter-in-law Empress Xiaohui (1641–1717).

Court records suggest that formal worshippers of the imperial portraits at the Hall of Imperial Longevity during the New Year rites were an all-male group that included the emperor, princes, and other members of the Qing imperial clan. While these records do not specify empresses' participation in such rituals, we know that a number of them did visit the hall. Empress Dowager Chongqing did so with Qianlong at the end of 1750, and Empress Dowager Cixi, accompanied by court military officials, visited it in 1872, about one month

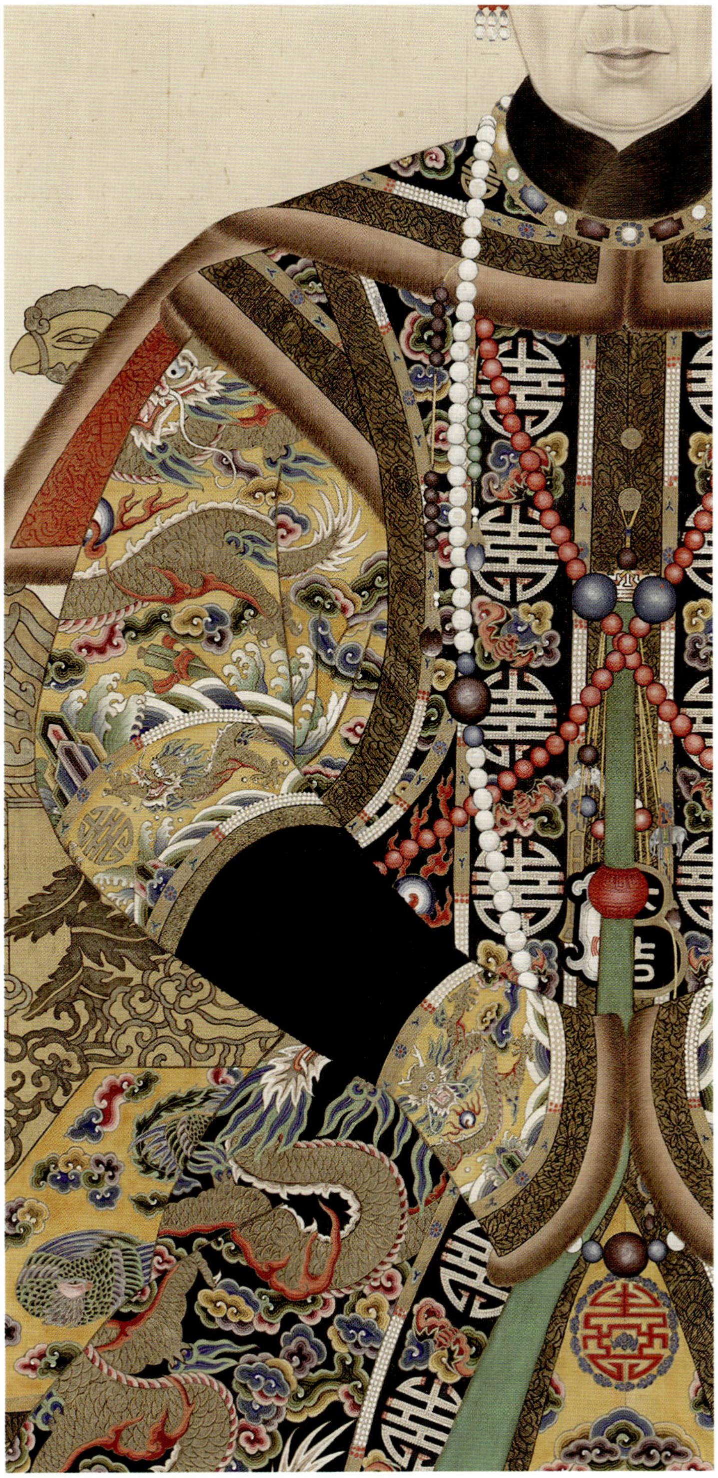

after the wedding of her son, the Tongzhi emperor.[50] It is not clear what the specific purposes of their visits were or whether they venerated the portraits there. But in 1872, after their wedding, the Tongzhi emperor and his wife Empress Xiaozhe (1854–1875) lit incense, knelt, and prostrated themselves before portraits in the hall as part of their marriage rites (see Ren Wanping's essay, pp. 51–59).[51] These visits by high-status imperial women seem to represent a break with the Qing tradition barring them from conducting or participating in rites at the Hall of the Ancestors or the Temple of the Ancestors (despite the fact that female ancestors of the imperial family were enshrined at both sites).[52] Perhaps the Hall of Imperial Longevity, as a familial altar outside the Forbidden City, presented certain empresses with a more personal and private setting in which to pay homage to their forebears.[53]

Due to the sacred nature of her image and a concern for decorum, people outside the Qing court had virtually no opportunity to see an empress in person or view her portrait. This is evident in paintings of empresses' travels outside the Forbidden City. For example, the Qianlong emperor was often depicted in such paintings engaging in various activities in public settings, while his mother, Empress Dowager Chongqing, was portrayed riding inside a palanquin or a houseboat, with no hint of bodily presence. Thus, until the advent of the mass media and the popularization of photographic images in China in the early twentieth century, imperial women were almost entirely invisible to the populace outside the court—a fact that made the display of Cixi's colossal portrait, viewed by thousands of visitors from all over the world at the 1904 St. Louis Exposition, such a radical break from Qing court convention regarding female portraiture (see pl. 46).

The portraits of Qing empresses for veneration at the Hall of Imperial Longevity reflected their place in their family and Qing society. The production, display, and worship of these portraits embodied not only the hierarchical and patriarchal structure of the Qing court, but also—as the Qianlong emperor put it—their indispensable role in "harmonizing the family system."[54]

Notes

1 Loti 1902, 121–22. At this time, a wide variety of portraits of Qing imperial women were stored in the Hall of Imperial Longevity. Loti's description suggests he had encountered formal portraits of empresses and likely other high-status imperial women in frontal view.

2 The author is grateful to Li Shi and Lin Shu of the Palace Museum, whose research has helped illuminate the production of these two portraits in the collection of the Peabody Essex Museum. See Li Shi 2017 and Lin Shu 2015b.

3 *Qinding da Qing huidian: Jiaqing chao, juan* 369 and 891.

4 Court records contradict the statement that the Qianlong emperor was the first to sacrifice before the imperial portraits in the Hall of Imperial Longevity. See Rawski 2009, 269.

5 *Qinding da Qing huidian: Jiaqing chao, juan* 891.

6 After the Hall of Imperial Longevity was rebuilt in 1750, funerary functions were observed at the Hall of Observing Virtues (Guande dian) in the Prospect Hill area.

7 See Stuart and Rawski 2001, 36–38. The author is indebted to their pioneering scholarship in the field of commemorative portraits and their invaluable guidance when this manuscript was being prepared.

8 *Qinding da Qing huidian: Jiaqing chao, juan* 662.

9 *Qing Gaozong shilu, juan* 663. For a discussion on the difference between imperial portraits and spirit tablets, see Xu Jin 2015; and Rawski 2009, 285–87. For the function of the Temple of the Ancestors and the Hall of the Ancestors, see Rawski 1988, 232–34.

10 Other places storing and displaying imperial portraits in the Qing dynasty included the Phoenix Tower (Fenghuang lou) in Shenyang; the Hall of Mental Cultivation (Yangxin dian) and certain palaces inside the Forbidden City; the Palace of Harmony and Peace (Yonghe gong); the Palace of Peace and Blessing (Anyou gong) in the Garden of Perfect Brightness in Beijing; and the Temple of Eternal Blessing (Yongyou si) in Chengde. See Xu Jin 2015.

11 *Qinding da Qing huidian: Jiaqing chao, juan* 891.

12 Neiwu fu 1750a; Neiwu fu 1750b.

13 ZGDYLSDAG 2002, 9:152.

14 *Qinding da Qing huidian: Jiaqing chao, juan* 891. According to records from the Jiaqing period, an altar table was placed in front of each portrait. The mention of eleven tables here suggests that during the Qianlong reign eleven portraits were on view: Nurhaci, Hong Taiji, Empress Xiaozhuang, the Shunzhi emperor, Empress Xiaohui, Empress Xiaokang (1640–1663), the Kangxi emperor, Empress Xiaocheng, Empress Xiaogong, the Yongzheng emperor, and Empress Xiaojing. See *Qinding da Qing huidian: Jiaqing chao, juan* 74.

15 Zhuang qinwang Yunlu et al. 1738.

16 *Qing Gaozong shilu, juan* 1027.

17 Liu Lu 2004, 138.

18 Rawski 2009, 269.

19 The shaping of the myth and history of Manchu origins was part of the effort to construct a unified image of Qing rule during this period. For the importance of lineage to Qing rulers, see Elliott 2001, 42–47, 65–67.

20 Stuart and Rawski 2001, 38.

21 Wang Yanyun 2008; Zhang Peng 2016.

22 Liu Xingliang 2012; see also Stuart and Rawski 2001, 38–40.

23 Storey 2017, 229.

24 *Qinding da Qing huidian: Yongzheng chao, juan* 97; *Qinding da Qing huidian: Jiaqing chao, juan* 891. For more on portraits of the Kangxi emperor, see Zhang Qiong 2004 and Wang Qi 2004.

25 Stuart and Rawski 2001, 10.

26 Hogge 2011.

27 For a discussion of the relationship between the viewer and the portrait, see Stuart and Rawski 2001, 84–85.

28 Cahill 2010, 19.

29 The author thanks Jing Gao and Hsin-Chen Tsai of the Asian Conservation Studio, Museum of Fine Arts, Boston, for providing information gathered in the process of conserving the portrait of Empress Xiaomu.

30 Liu Lu 2004, 130–44.

31 For a discussion of the relationship between Qing imperial costume and portraits, see Zhang Qiong 2004, 60–74. I thank Ren Wanping and Yan Yong for sharing their knowledge of Qing imperial ceremonial sashes.

32 ZGDYLSDAG 2005, 40:375.

33 ZGDYLSDAG 2005, 40:263–64. According to this record, the portrait of Empress Xiaoxian was painted at the Palace of Shared Fortune (Xianfu gong) inside the Forbidden City. This record also corrects an earlier attribution of this portrait to the Jesuit court painter Giuseppe Castiglione (Lang Shining; Italy, 1688–1766).

34 ZGDYLSDAG 2005, 40:375.

35 For examples revealing the process of creating nineteenth-century imperial portraits for the Hall of Imperial Longevity, see Li Shi 2017, 45.

36 The author is grateful to Zhang Rong of the Palace Museum, who discovered the sketch and made it available for study.

37 See Li Shi 2017, 46.

38 This painting was once stored in the Hall of Imperial Longevity. See Zhu Saihong 2013, 89.

39 Rawski 2009, 156.

40 Hinsch 2011, 11–13.

41 In contrast to the side-by-side display of Qing emperors and empresses during the New Year rites, images of the Song dynasty (960–1279) empresses and empresses dowager were not paired with those of emperors before the 1080s. Later, the portraits of women were lodged in halls separate from those containing portraits of men. See Stuart and Rawski 2001, 39.

42 Liu Lu 1997, 54.

43 Mann 2011, 28–31.

44 Unlike contemporaneous Western European monarchs or the Han Chinese rulers of the Ming dynasty (1368–1644), Qing emperors did not limit succession to the eldest son of their first wife, making possible the upward mobility of lower-status consorts, as was the case with Empress Dowager Cixi. Rawski 2009, 132; Rawski 1991, 186–87.

45 *Qinding da Qing huidian: Guangxu chao, juan* 1180.

46 While no separate rear chambers were designated for the empresses, portraits—likely bust length—of four empresses in panel format were on display in the rear area with their husband's portraits in 1863. See Zhu Saihong 2013, 80, 82.

47 This type of display explains the unusual format of the portraits: in order to fit into the frame, the image proper begins from the top stave of the scroll without an upper silk border, a device commonly found in hanging scrolls intended to be displayed without the wooden frame of the screen.

48 The display of spirit tablets for ancestors at the Temple of the Ancestors followed similar rules; see Rawski 1988, 232–33.

49 In the *Illustrated Precedents for the Ritual Paraphernalia of the Qing Imperial Court* (*Huangchao liqi tushi;* see fig. 8), the sleeve band of an empress's court robe was painted blue, but the accompanying text did not specify its color.

50 ZGDYLSDAG 2002, 9:410; Xianghuangqi hujunying 1872. According to Stuart and Rawski, domestic rituals were performed by women as well as men at the Hall of Imperial Longevity. I have not found substantial archival records to show women's regular activities at the hall except for the cases mentioned above. See Stuart and Rawski 2001, 45.

51 *Tongzhi dahun dianli hongdang*.

52 Wang Baizhong 2007, 105; Rawski 2009, 298.

53 There was a precedent for the Qing empresses' visits to the Hall of Imperial Longevity: During the Liao dynasty (907–1125) an empress dowager, along with the emperor and the empress, led ministers to pay respect in the Hall of Imperial Portraiture on the winter solstice, lighting incense and offering wine to the ancestors. See Zhang Guoqing 1993, 85–89. Another earlier example occurred during the Southern Song dynasty (1127–1279), when palace ladies, led by the empress, participated in imperial ancestral veneration rites on the death anniversaries of imperial forebears at the Jingling Palace in Hangzhou. See Stuart and Rawski 2001, 39.

54 *Qinding da Qing huidian: Jiaqing chao, juan* 891.

FOUR

Qing Empresses as Religious Patrons and Practitioners

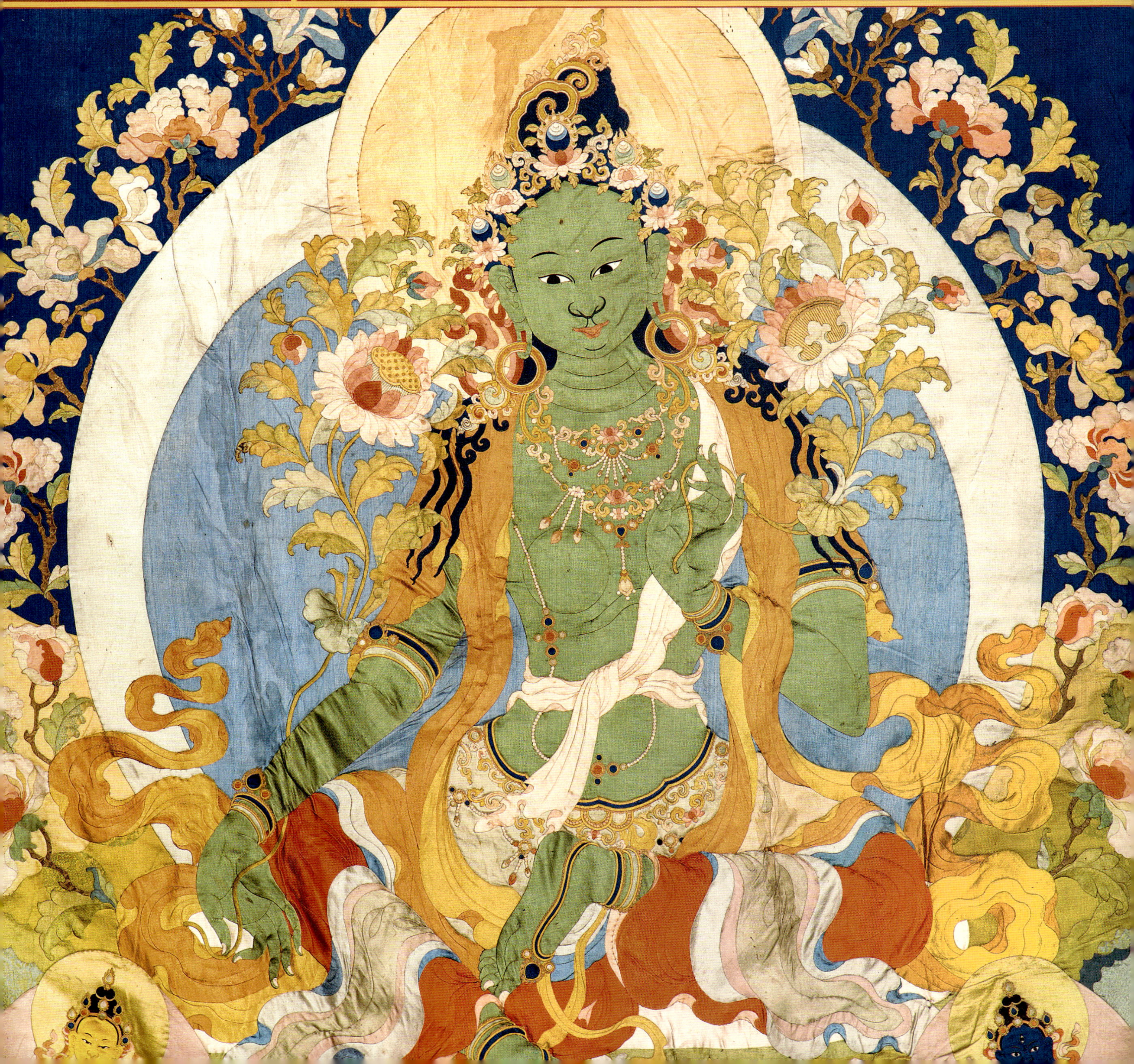

LUK YU-PING

THE RELIGIOUS LANDSCAPE OF THE QING COURT was a complex interweaving of different belief systems: the traditions and interests of the Manchus were combined with those of their conquered Chinese, Mongol, and Tibetan subjects.[1] Qing empresses played a more active role in this sphere than is commonly understood, one that allowed them to express their agency, forge networks, and fashion their own identities. While women have played similar roles in the religious life of court cultures throughout history, the significance of Qing empresses as religious practitioners and patrons has largely been overlooked.[2]

Shamanism

By the eleventh century, the people who became the Manchus practiced shamanism, a belief system widespread among the peoples of northeast Asia that understood the world under heaven to be animated by nature deities and ancestral spirits.[3] Female and male shamans were able to access the spirit realm through ritual performances for purposes such as healing and divination.[4] When the Manchus emerged as a ruling dynasty during the early decades of the seventeenth century, this practice was institutionalized and became a part of their court ceremony. Shamanic rituals were performed in the residence of the emperor Hong Taiji (r. 1626–43) and Empress Xiaoduan (1599–1649), the Palace of Pure Tranquility (Qingning gong), at Mukden (present-day Shenyang), the Manchu capital before 1644.[5] After the Manchus conquered Beijing, they remodeled the Palace of Earthly Tranquility (Kunning gong), located along the central axis of the Forbidden City, according to a plan based on the Palace of Pure Tranquility, and it then became the principal site for courtly shamanic rituals inside the palace complex (fig. 1).[6] The choice of this palace as a locus of religious life is especially notable since it was initially established as the empress's abode during the Ming dynasty (1368–1644).[7] It retained those associations throughout the Qing dynasty, even after the empresses stopped living there during the reign of the Yongzheng emperor (1723–35).[8]

The performance of shamanic rituals at the Palace of Earthly Tranquility suggests a symbolic connection of Manchu empresses with shamanism and its access to spiritual powers. Early in the Manchu reign, according to the *Manchu Rites for Sacrifices to the Spirits and to Heaven* (*Manzhou jishen jitian dianli*; 1756), the ruler's primary consort (*neiting zhengwei*, or the "central position of the inner court") and the wives of princes performed as shamans.[9] By the time the capital was established in Beijing in 1644, consorts no longer served as palace shamans—a shift that suggests the emergence of a new understanding of their roles. Shamans were thereafter selected from the wives of important officials of the Aisin Gioro lineage, the imperial clan of Manchu emperors.[10] Nevertheless, empresses continued to attend shamanic rituals held at the Palace of Earthly Tranquility during the Qing dynasty.[11] These rituals were directed at a pantheon of different deities: in addition to the spirits of the natural world

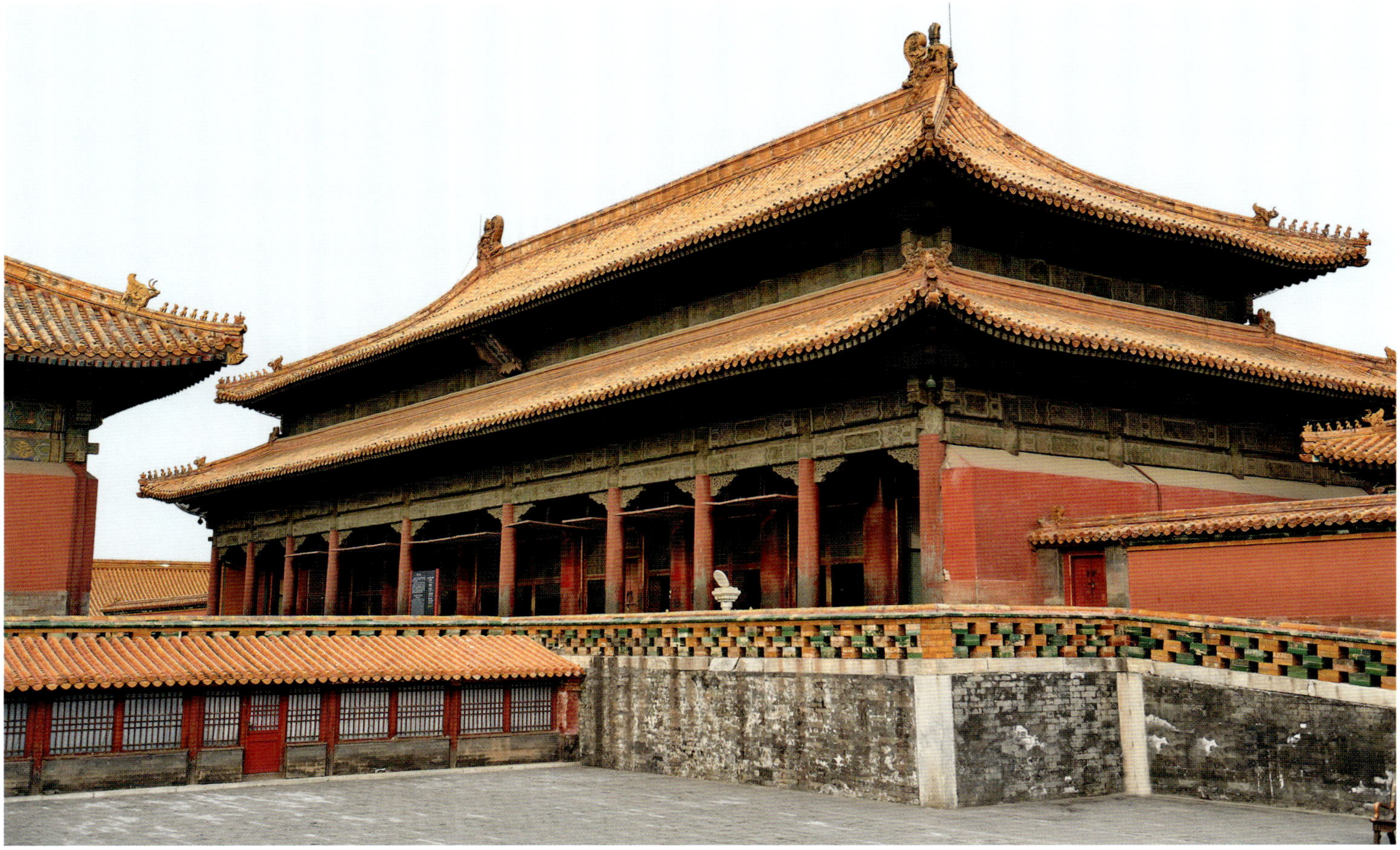

and ancestral deities the Manchus traditionally worshipped, Guandi (the deified Chinese general of the Three Kingdoms period, 220–80), deities of the Mongols, the Buddha, and bodhisattvas were also venerated.[12]

State and Domestic Rituals

Qing rulers maintained shamanism as a part of their Manchu identity, but they were also quick to adopt Han Chinese state rituals as a way to appeal to the subjects of the conquered Ming dynasty.[13] These rituals were closely connected to the Confucian outlook of the educated Chinese elite, for whom ritual was key to the internalization and performance of moral ideals.[14] These rituals had religious dimensions, including belief in a divine heaven from which the sovereign received the mandate to rule, and they were also clearly gendered.[15]

State rituals, such as sacrifices to heaven and earth and prayers for a good harvest, were conducted by the emperor, princes, and male officials on behalf of their subjects.[16] Women were occasionally known to perform prayers for rain at temples or altars at the imperial villas during prolonged periods of drought.[17] However, on the whole, they did not participate in state rituals, except for those connected with silk production.[18] This ritual of sericulture, which was the duty and prerogative of the Qing empress, involved sacrifices to the deity of silkworms and was equivalent to the agriculture ritual performed by the emperor.[19] As Susan Mann has noted, the performance of these sacraments made "the emperor and empress archetypal father and mother of the realm who serve as examples for the people."[20] Practiced in China from around the second century BCE to the early twelfth century, the sericulture ritual was revived during the Jiajing reign (1522–66) of the Ming dynasty but was suspended again thereafter (for more on sericulture, see Jan Stuart's essay, pp. 60–77).[21] The Qianlong emperor (r. 1736–95) reinstated this ritual and ordered a new altar built for it in the northeast corner of Beihai Lake, outside the Forbidden City but still within the imperial walls.[22] In 1744 the ritual was performed for the first time during the Qing dynasty by Empress Xiaoxian (1712–1748), and it continued to be performed in the third lunar month of every year until the nineteenth century.[23] The ceremony conducted by Xiaoxian is recorded in a set of four scroll paintings dated to around 1751 and produced by a team of court artists, including the Italian Jesuit painter Giuseppe Castiglione (Lang Shining; 1688–1766).[24] It shows the empress flanked by other consorts and wives of officials at each stage of the ceremony and accompanied by a large entourage in procession between the palace and the altar.

FIGURE 1
The Palace of Earthly Tranquility.

FIGURE 2
The plaque over the entrance to the Main Hall of the Palace of Compassion and Tranquility.

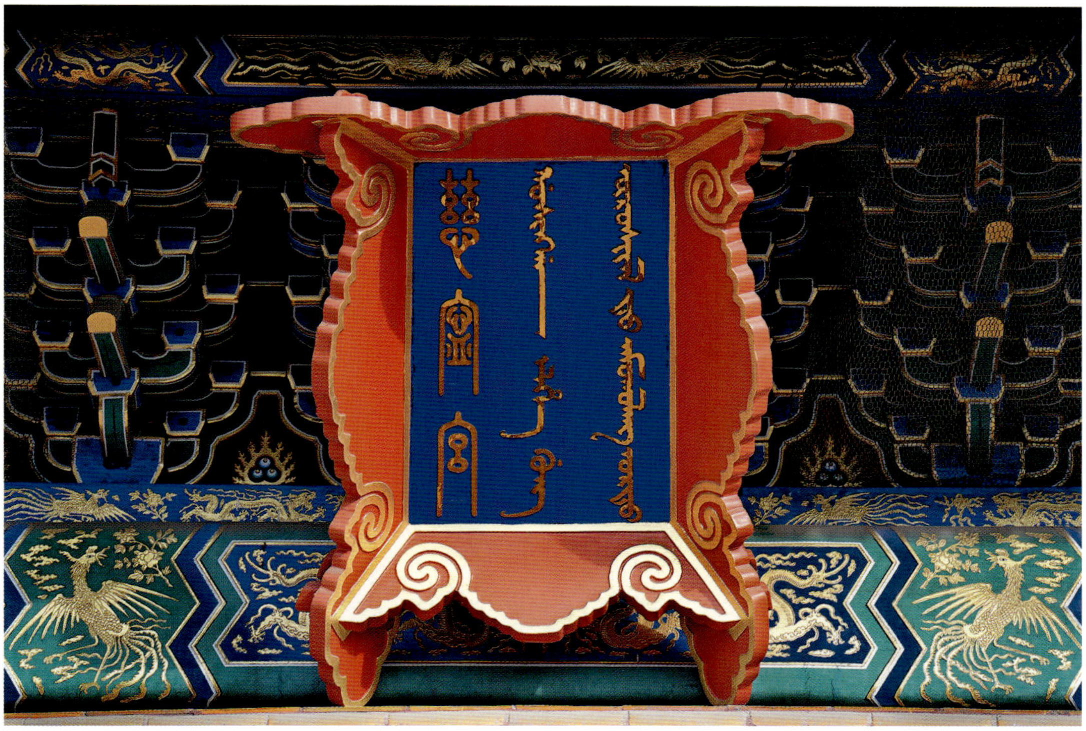

Apart from the ritual of sericulture, empresses did not participate in state rituals, yet their lives—together with those of the rest of the Qing imperial household—were regulated by a busy calendar of domestic rituals and festivals that took place throughout the year, many of which they shared with their Chinese subjects.[25] These included seasonal festivals, such as the lunar New Year, and those with more direct religious associations, such as the bathing of images of the Buddha on the Buddha's birthday and the offering of sacrifices to the Kitchen God—ceremonies in which the emperor and empress both participated.

Empress Xiaozhuang and the Great Buddha Hall

Another key religious dimension of the Manchu reign was its patronage of Tibetan Buddhism, which encompasses mystical concepts and practices that distinguish it from other traditions practiced in China. While this support for Tibetan Buddhism was often undeniably personal, it was also politically and strategically important as it enabled the Manchus to propagate the notion of a multiethnic Qing Buddhist empire that extended control over Tibet as well as the Mongols who had reconverted to Tibetan Buddhism by the seventeenth century.[26] By 1616 the Manchu chieftain Nurhaci (r. 1616–26) had established official relations with Tibetan religious hierarchs.[27] The Shunzhi emperor (r. 1644–61) subsequently met with the fifth Dalai Lama (1617–1682) in Beijing in 1653, and the Qing court therewith established support for the dGe lugs pa (Yellow Hat) order of Tibetan Buddhism favored by the Mongols.[28] Much less recognized, however, is the crucial role that empresses played in the support for Tibetan Buddhism and its integration into the fabric of court life, particularly at the beginning of the Qing dynasty.

While the Palace of Earthly Tranquility was the site of shamanic rituals in the Forbidden City, it was the residence of Empress Xiaozhuang (1613–1688)—the Palace of Compassion and Tranquility (Cining gong), on the west side of the Forbidden City—that was the focal point of Tibetan Buddhist worship during the early Qing dynasty (fig. 2). The Palace of Compassion and Tranquility was initially built during the Ming Jiajing era as the home of an empress dowager.[29] After renovations during the early Qing period, it became the residence of Xiaozhuang from 1653 to her death in 1688.[30] The palace's central front hall was used for rituals such as birthday celebrations, while a larger rear hall was, by 1679, used for Buddhist worship.[31] This hall was called the Great Buddha Hall (Da fotang) by the time of the Qianlong

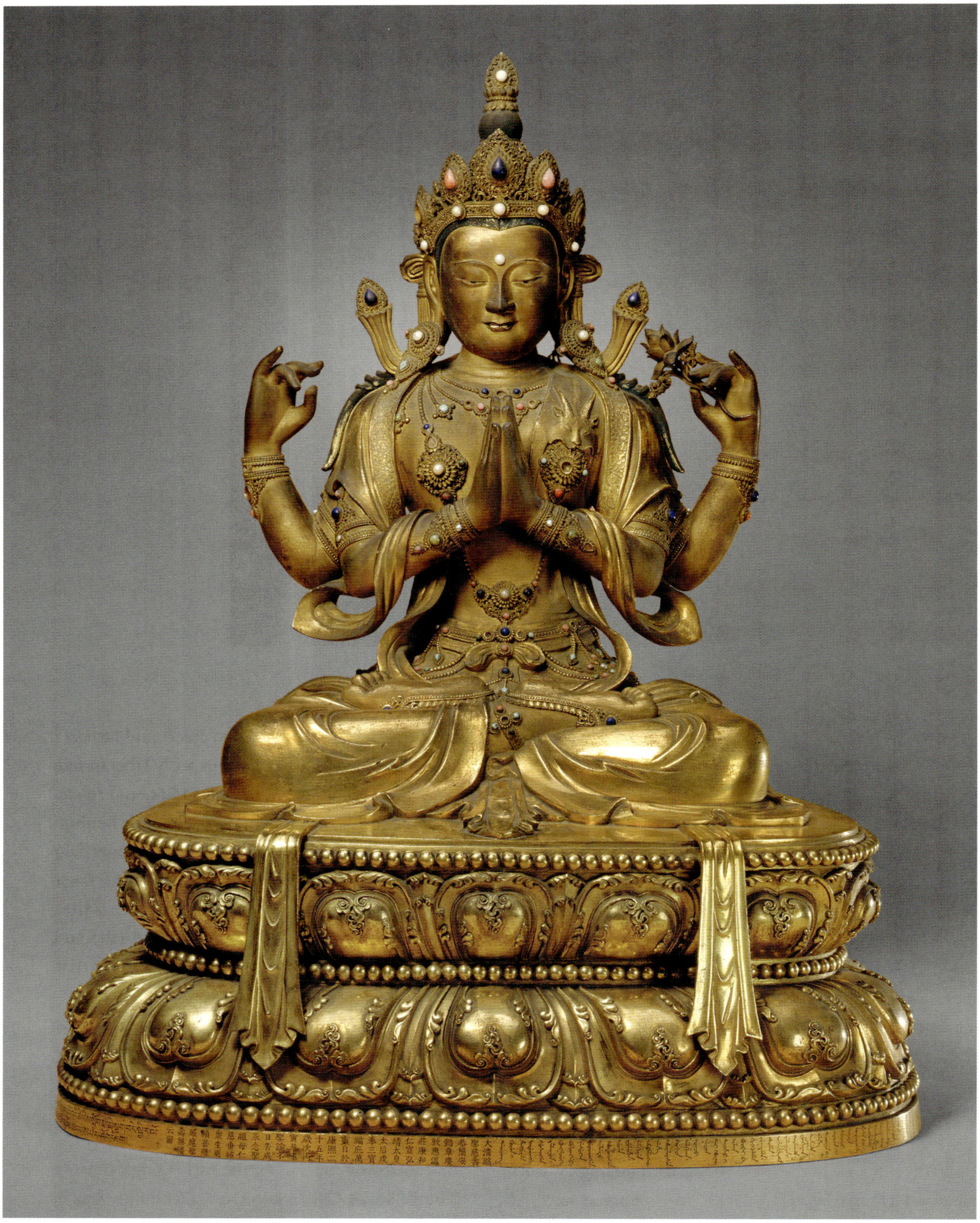

FIGURE 3
Four-armed bodhisattva Avalokiteshvara (Guanyin). Kangxi period, 1686, bronze with gilding, pearls, coral, turquoise, and lapis lazuli, H: 28¾ in. (73 cm), Gu202374.

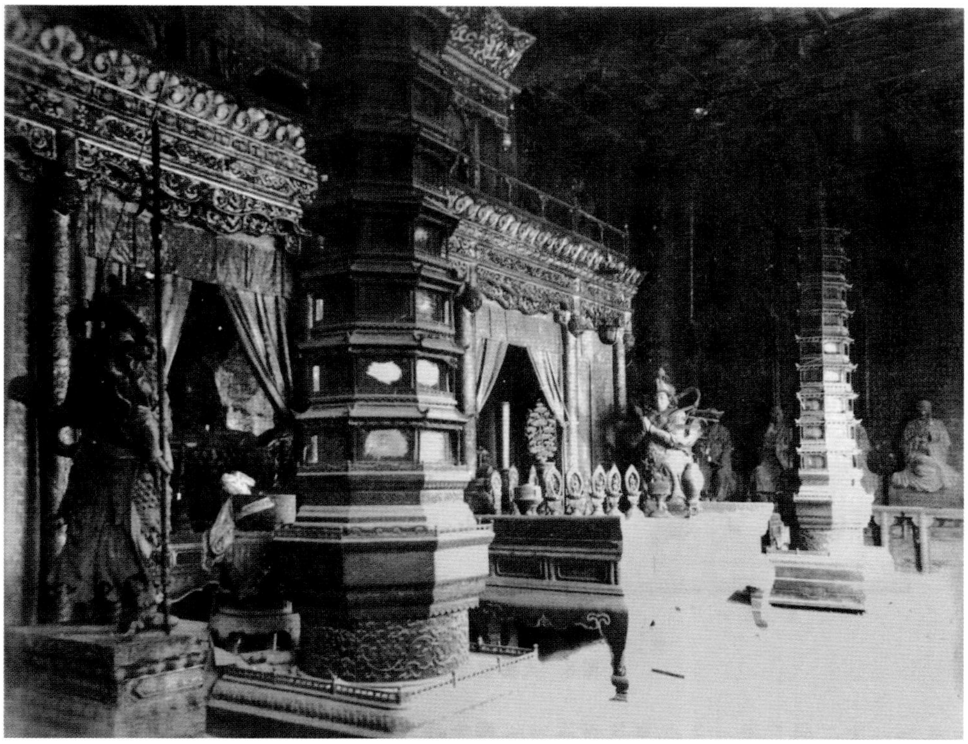

FIGURE 4
Interior of the Great Buddha Hall of the Palace of Compassion and Tranquility, 1973; from Wang Jiapeng 2014, 455.

reign (1736–95).[32] As the palace took on more religious functions, Xiaozhuang moved into one of the side buildings.[33]

The Great Buddha Hall and Xiaozhuang's patronage are important for understanding the development of Tibetan Buddhism at the Qing court. Although Nurhaci and the Shunzhi emperor showed support to Tibetan hierarchs, there is little to indicate that they were personally interested in Tibetan Buddhism beyond the political advantages it offered.[34] On the other hand, Empress Xiaozhuang was a Khorchin Mongol by birth and would have been brought up as a follower of the dGe lugs pa order, which had spread among the Khorchin by the late sixteenth century.[35] Xiaozhuang's religious devotion must have had some influence on her grandson, the Kangxi emperor (r. 1662–1722), who showed greater interest in Tibetan Buddhism than did his forebears and, in 1697, established an office to manage Tibetan Buddhist affairs at the Hall of Central Uprightness (Zhongzheng dian) in the Forbidden City.[36] Prior to the Kangxi emperor's establishment of this office, the Palace of Compassion and Tranquility, under Empress Xiaozhuang, was the center of Tibetan Buddhism at the Forbidden City. Lamas and monks were frequently employed to perform Buddhist rituals for Xiaozhuang at the Great Buddha Hall and in the garden area to the south of the palace.[37] She took a personal interest in the care of the Great Buddha Hall, including ordering small repairs and the replenishing of ritual objects.[38]

After Xiaozhuang's death, the Palace of Compassion and Tranquility became a permanent site of Buddhist worship, and no consorts would live there again. Her arrangement of Buddhist sculptures in the Great Buddha Hall was left unchanged, even when the hall was expanded and renovated and other objects were added during the Qianlong era.[39] This remained the case until 1973, when almost all the Buddhist objects from the Great Buddha Hall were transferred to Luoyang, Henan province.[40] A gilt-bronze statue of the four-armed Avalokiteshvara—or Guanyin, as the deity is known in China—is one of the few objects original to Xiaozhuang's Great Buddha Hall that remain at the Palace Museum (fig. 3). An inscription on its lotus pedestal, written in the four official languages of the Qing court (Tibetan, Mongolian, Manchu, and Chinese), states that the statue was produced in 1686 and commissioned by the Kangxi emperor at the request of Xiaozhuang, who is referred to by her official title with an impressive twenty honorifics.[41]

Based on records from the Qianlong reign and the 1973 move, we know that the central altar in the Great Buddha Hall established by Xiaozhuang housed lacquered sculptures of the buddhas of the past, present, and future.[42] During the Qianlong reign these were dressed in golden robes and lavishly decorated with pearls and coral.[43] Placed before them were the figures of Weituo, a bodhisattva and guardian of the principles of Buddhism, and Tuota, one of the four Heavenly Kings, while sculptures of the eighteen *luohan* (or arhats, the enlightened disciples of the Buddha) stood to each side of the buddhas (fig. 4). Interestingly, these sculptures were not made during the Qing dynasty but have been dated to the Yuan and

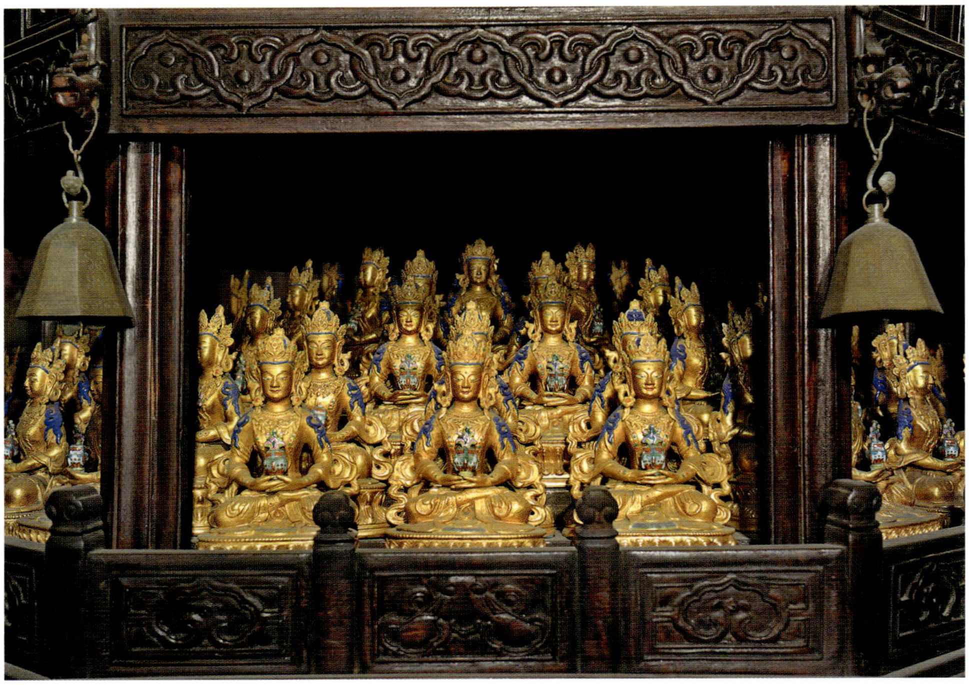

FIGURE 5
Ceramic Amitayus Buddhas placed in a pagoda inside the Hall of Universal Harmony (Xianruo guan) in the Garden of the Palace of Compassion and Tranquility.

FIGURE 6
Entrance to the Hall of Universal Harmony.

early Ming periods (1271–about 1450).[44] Printed material found inside the sculptures suggest that they came from a temple in Beijing outside the Forbidden City. It is not clear when they were moved to the Great Buddha Hall, but it is possible the sculptures were inherited from an earlier resident of the Palace of Compassion and Tranquility: Empress Dowager Li (1544–1614), the mother of the Wanli emperor (r. 1573–1620) of the Ming dynasty and a devoted Buddhist patron.[45] If true, this group of sculptures suggests that Xiaozhuang venerated and preserved religious material inherited from the Ming court, and it raises the interesting possibility that Qing empresses looked to the previous dynasty for imperial models of piety and patronage.

Moreover, the arrangement of elements in the Great Buddha Hall in Xiaozhuang's time reveals a complex interrelationship between Tibetan and Chinese Buddhism that may be part of a broader process of the Manchus' adaptation in their role as the new rulers of China. While Tibetan Buddhist rituals were primarily performed at the Palace of Compassion and Tranquility, the sculptures now in Luoyang are not in the distinctive Indo-Himalayan style derived from Nepal and central Tibet. Further, the sculptures of buddhas flanked by *luohan* is an arrangement commonly found in the main halls of Chinese Buddhist temples and not in Tibetan Buddhist sanctuaries. The coexistence of these strains of Buddhism under Xiaozhuang is clearly evident in the management of the Great Buddha Hall, where responsibility was shared between Chinese eunuch-monks and Tibetan eunuch-lamas.[46] This arrangement would continue until 1778, when management of the Palace of Compassion and Tranquility was wholly taken over by eunuch-lamas.[47]

After Xiaozhuang's death, the garden to the south of the Palace of Compassion and Tranquility, already a site for Buddhist ceremonies, took on further religious significance when it underwent extensive renovations during the Qianlong reign.[48] Buildings were transformed into spaces devoted to Buddhist worship and the storage of Buddhist objects (figs. 5 and 6). This project catered to the religious piety of Qianlong's mother, Empress Dowager Chongqing (1693–1777), whose residence—the Palace of Longevity and Health (Shoukang gong), completed in 1736—was located next to the garden (see Lin Shu's essay, pp. 78–87).[49] Together these spaces formed a larger complex in the western part of the Forbidden City that closely connected Tibetan Buddhist practices with empresses dowager and other retired consorts who lived in the vicinity.[50] It also became a place where Buddhist prayers for deceased emperors, empresses, and other consorts were performed.[51]

Transcribing and Translating Buddhist Sutras

By the time of the Qing dynasty, copying and translating sutras were long-established practices in Buddhism through which followers could accumulate merit. Empress Xiaozhuang was known to have personally copied sutras in Mongolian, her native language, both alone and with other consorts and palace women.[52] In addition, she had lamas and scribes copy sutras, and she commissioned translations of sutras into Mongolian,

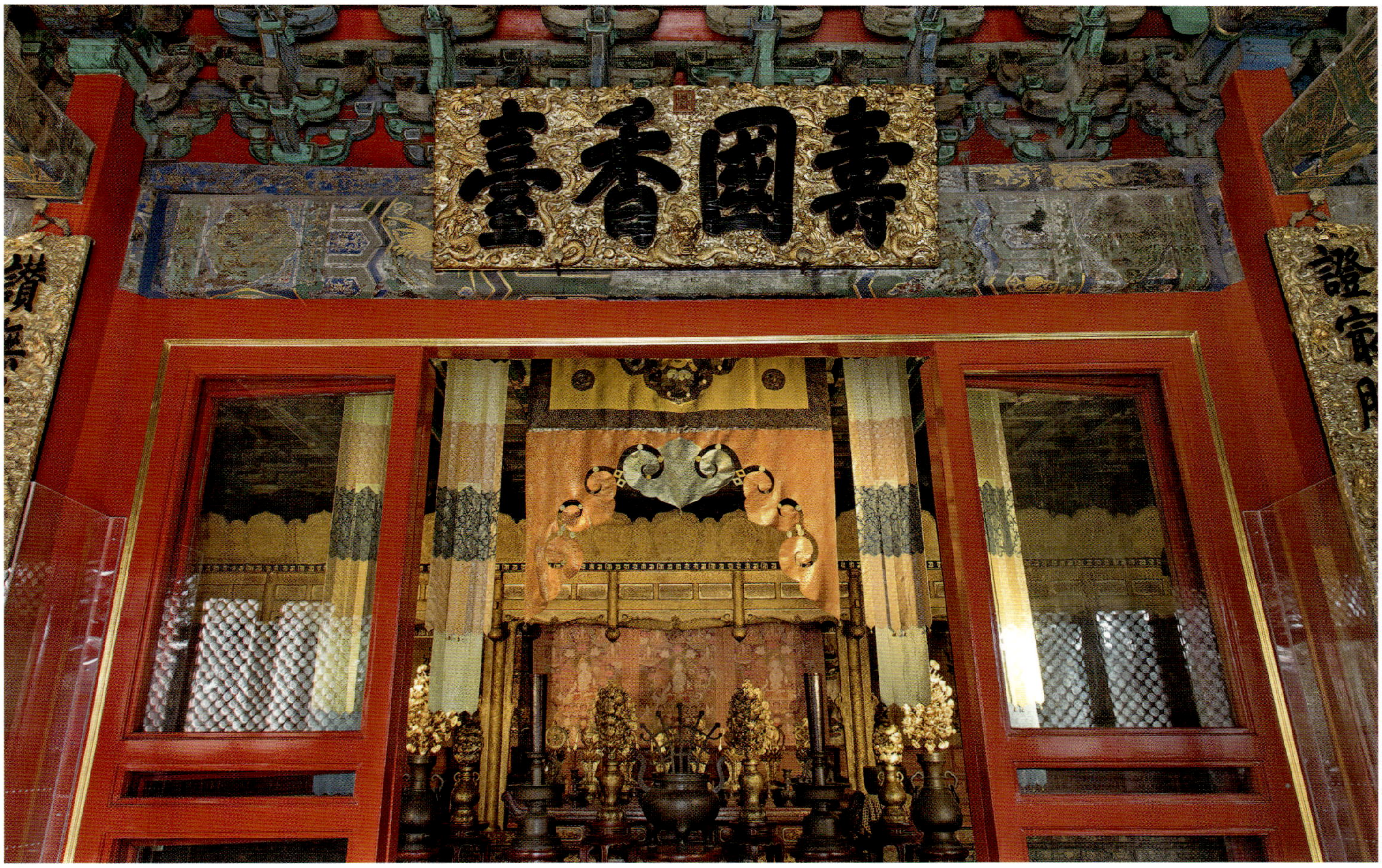

usually based on existing versions.[53] One of these, the *Diamond Sutra*, was a joint commission of Xiaozhuang and her son, the Shunzhi emperor, and was the first Mongolian Buddhist sutra produced by the Qing imperial court.[54]

The most spectacular sutra associated with Xiaozhuang is a Tibetan Kanjur compiled from 1667 to 1669.[55] The Kanjur (consisting of words ascribed to the Buddha) together with the Tanjur (commentaries and treatises) formed the Tibetan Buddhist canon. According to a preface written by the Kangxi emperor, the 1667–69 Kanjur was based on a Ming imperial edition that was discovered in the palace archives.[56] Consisting of more than 50,000 leaves, the text is handwritten in gold on indigo paper, protected by two panels decorated with images of Buddhist deities encircled by precious gems and further covered by two outer red lacquered panels with gold decoration. A team of 125 makers was employed for two years on this project.[57] It was financially supported by the thirteen-year-old Kangxi emperor, but its most potent backer was his grandmother, Xiaozhuang, who was in turn supported by her Mongolian relatives of the Khorchin, Sunit, and Bairin tribes, many of whom were Manchu princesses married to the Mongols.[58]

The web of powerful connections and the ostentatious show of resources that brought the Kanjur into being suggest its existence cannot be explained by personal spiritual aims alone. Indeed, the project was launched at a critical time for Kangxi. Shortly before the Kanjur was commissioned, Xiaozhuang agreed that the young emperor could govern directly without regents. This decision was made with some urgency, as Oboi (about 1610–1669), one of Kangxi's four regents, had expanded his power clique at court and threatened to gain absolute power.[59] The commissioning of a large-scale and luxurious Kanjur at that moment may thus be interpreted as the material manifestation of the networks Xiaozhuang drew on in support of her grandson. Significantly, this was—as Lin Shi-Hsuan has described it—a demonstration of support from Manchu-Mongol alliances, sealed by marriage, that had been critical to the formation of the Qing empire.[60] Moreover, the Kanjur was produced under Kangxi's name, thus claiming for the young emperor the role of protector of the Buddha's teachings and universal ruler of the Qing empire. Its basis in an earlier Ming-dynasty imperial edition further bolsters the legitimacy of the Kangxi emperor as inheritor of the Mandate of Heaven in China. When it was completed in 1669, the Kanjur was brought to the Palace of Compassion and Tranquility, where it was consecrated at a ceremony lasting five days.[61] Two months after the Kanjur was completed and after

FIGURE 7
Green Tara. Qianlong period, 1736–95, appliqué and embroidery on silk, 68⅞ × 45¼ in. (175 cm × 115 cm), Palace of Harmony and Peace, Beijing.

carefully biding his time, Kangxi had Oboi arrested and took control of the state under the guidance of Xiaozhuang.

The production of the 1667–69 Kanjur suggests that Xiaozhuang was keenly aware of the political implications of religious patronage and the interconnectedness of Tibetan Buddhism with the wider ambitions of the Qing dynasty. The Tibetan Kanjur commissioned by Xiaozhuang was the first Kanjur produced by the Qing imperial court, setting a precedent for a series of large-scale imperial commissions of Buddhist texts in the four official languages of the Qing dynasty that were woodblock-printed and circulated to major monasteries.[62] It was also the model for a second handwritten copy of the Tibetan Kanjur completed in 1770 under the order of the Qianlong emperor (pl. 41).[63] The Qianlong edition is similar in format and decoration to the earlier version but with some notable changes: an additional text, the *Surangama Sutra*, was included, and the imperial preface was written in all four official languages rather than only Manchu and Tibetan.[64] According to this preface, Qianlong ordered the Kanjur in anticipation of the eightieth birthday of his mother, Chongqing, the following year.[65] The commission is presented as an act of filial piety, one echoing that of Kangxi, who had heeded Xiaozhuang's request in producing the earlier scriptures. The difference here, however, is that Chongqing is shown as a passive recipient of Qianlong's Kanjur, one who becomes the justification for Qianlong's commission. Harold Kahn has aptly described Qianlong's acts of devotion to his mother as demonstrating the "politics of filiality," which became an integral part of how the ethics of Qing rule were manifested during the Qianlong reign.[66]

Patronage outside the palace

After Xiaozhuang, less is recorded of the religious activities of Qing empresses until Empress Dowager Cixi (Empress Xiaoqin; 1835–1908) arrives on the scene. This is not surprising given the political significance of these two women.[67] For other Qing empresses it is often difficult to untangle their agency from acts performed in their honor.[68] Qianlong's mother, Chongqing, is a good example. She received many gifts for her birthdays, such as the Kanjur and the Buddhist sculptures that filled the buildings in the Garden of the Palace of Compassion and Tranquility (Cining gong huayuan). We can only assume, however, that these gifts catered to her tastes or that they resulted from informal requests of the emperor.[69] The gift of cloisonné ritual implements to the abbot of the Chan Buddhist Pool and Zhe Tree Monastery (Tanzhe si) in the Western Hills of Beijing in 1764, offered together with gifts from Qianlong, is a rare example in which Chongqing is clearly identified as a donor.[70]

It is likely that Chongqing did patronize other sites, namely the Palace of Harmony and Peace (Yonghe gong), commonly known as the Lama Temple, located in the northeastern part of the Inner City of Beijing. This complex was once the princely residence of the future Yongzheng and Qianlong emperors before it was converted into a temple in 1744. The site was personally significant to Chongqing because it was there that she gave birth to the future Qianlong emperor. An embroidered hanging depicting the Buddhist goddess Green Tara and other deities in the temple's collection is believed, though not proven, to have been made by Chongqing with other palace women (fig. 7).[71]

Susan Naquin has observed that "records about the generosity of [Qing] empresses towards temples that lay beyond the imperial sphere are rather few."[72] Some concrete examples do exist: for example, Empress Xiaohui (1641–1718), a consort of the Shunzhi emperor, provided monetary support to the Pool and Zhe Tree Monastery.[73] She also funded the rebuilding of another monastery in western Beijing in 1703 and ensured it received an income from the imperial household.[74] On the whole, however, Qing empresses directly patronized fewer religious institutions outside their imperial residences than their Ming predecessors had. Naquin has suggested that this may be due to the "plenitude of . . . private places of worship within this enlarged domain" of the palace and imperial villas, which made it "less necessary for them to be involved outside it." The court's control over the possessions of imperial women may also have limited their ability to tap into palace funds to support external sites.[75]

Another notable difference was that Qing empresses were able to take advantage of opportunities to travel to external sites, an option not open to Ming empresses, except when visiting imperial mausoleums.[76] This meant that Qing empresses could offer support through their physical presence rather than through intermediaries and could focus their attention on a few select sites. For example, in 1683, the

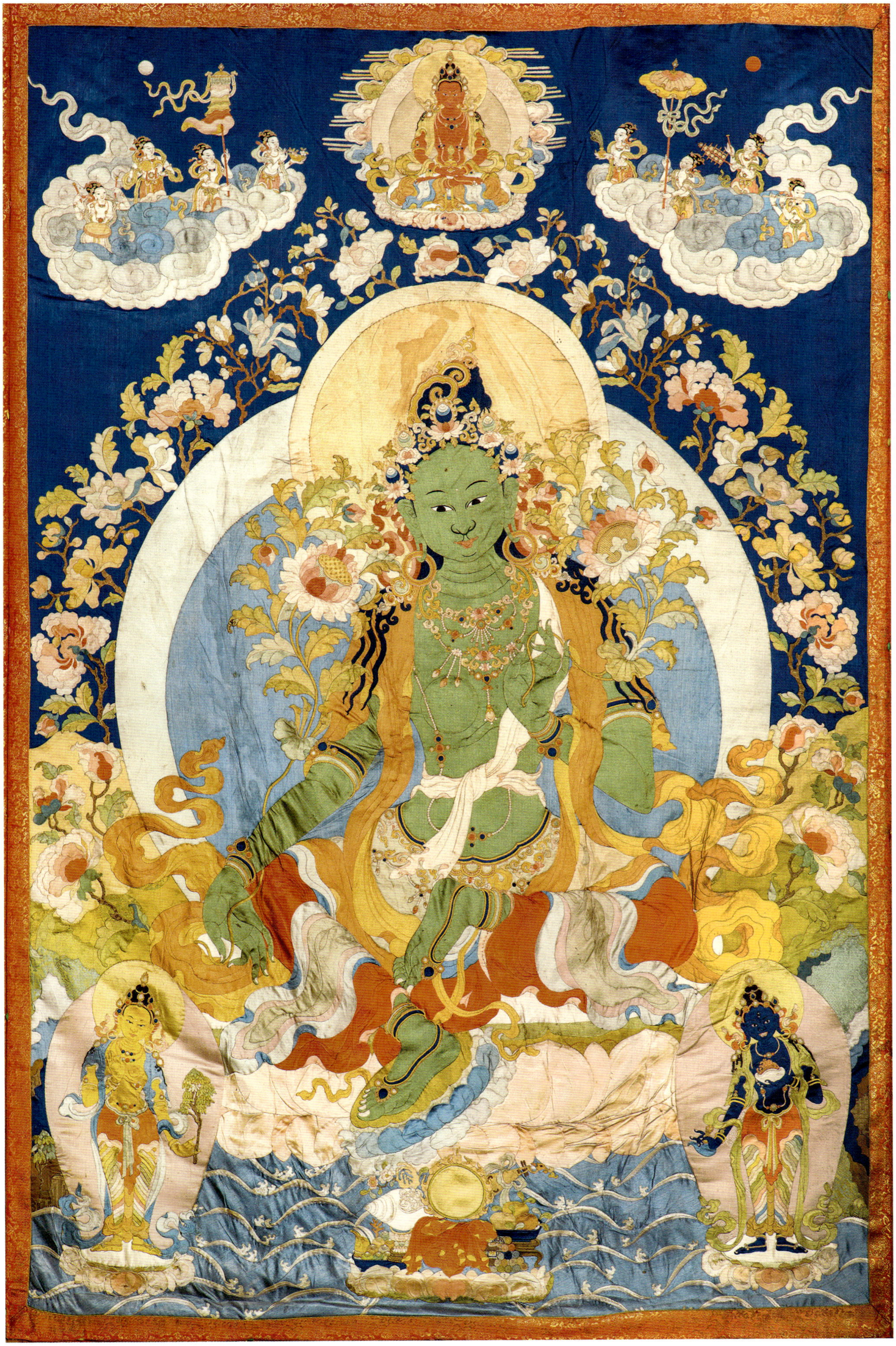

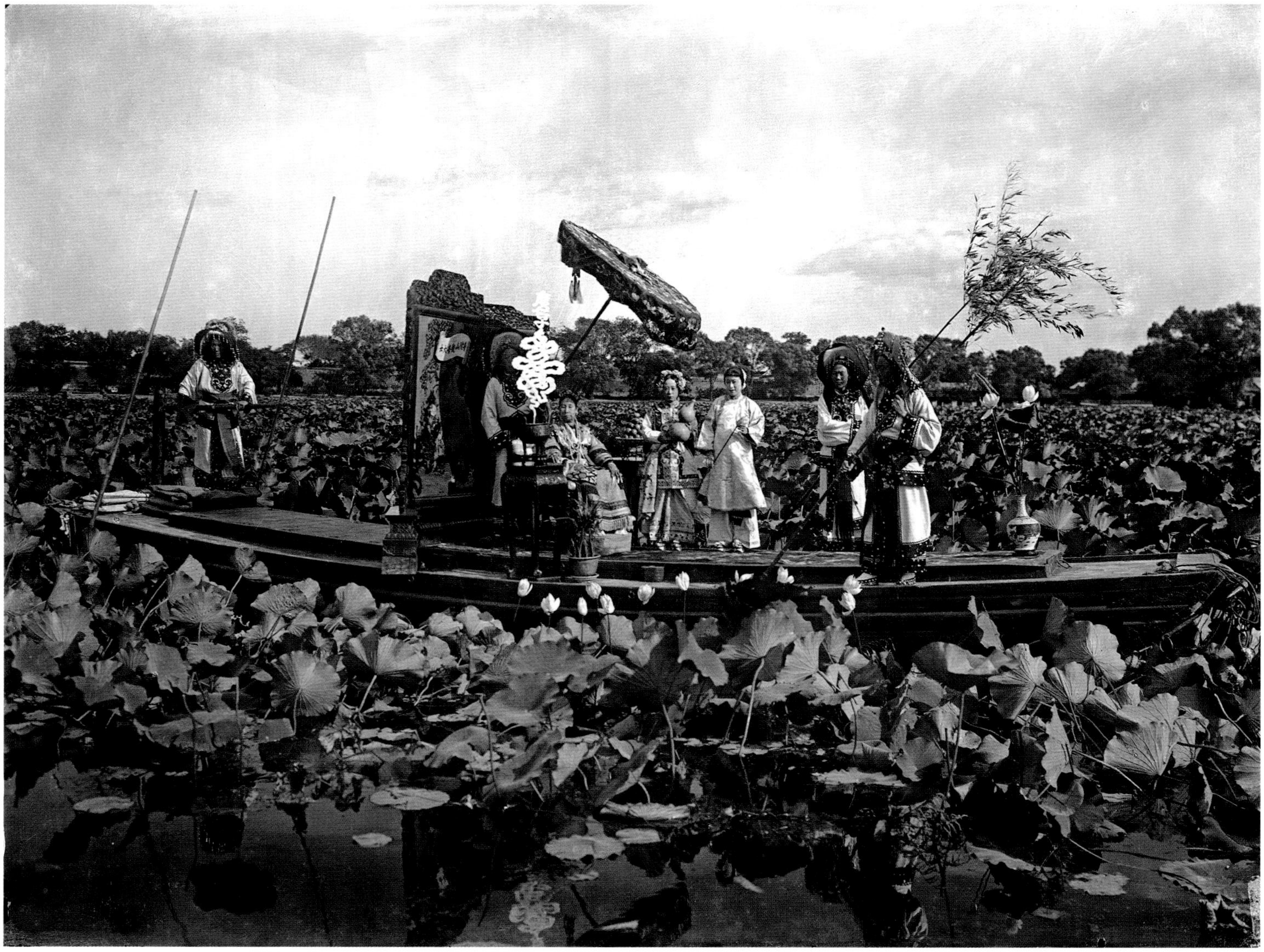

FIGURE 8
Empress Dowager Cixi and Attendants on the Imperial Barge on the Zhonghai [Middle Sea], Beijing. Photographed by Yu Xunling (1874–1943), Guangxu period, 1903–05, print from glass-plate negative, 9½ × 7 in. (24.1 × 17.8 cm), Freer Gallery of Art and Arthur M. Sackler Gallery Archives. FSA A.13 SC-GR-243. Smithsonian Institution, Washington, DC, purchase.

seventy-year-old Empress Xiaozhuang embarked on a journey to Mount Wutai (Wutai shan) in Shanxi province with the Kangxi emperor.[77] Mount Wutai was believed to have special significance as the dwelling place of Manjusri, the bodhisattva that Manchu rulers personally identified with.[78] Empress Xiaohui also accompanied Kangxi on his visits to the Pool and Zhe Tree Monastery, which she supported.[79] An imperial traveling palace was established there, which included a hall known as the Empress Dowager Hall (Taihou dian).[80] Qianlong traveled to Mount Wutai six times, the first three times with Chongqing (in 1746, 1750, and 1761).[81] During the nineteenth century, Empress Xiaohe (1776–1850), consort of the Jiaqing emperor (r. 1796–1820), is said to have personally attended a reopening of a temple at Mount Yaji (Yaji shan), east of Beijing.[82] Empress Dowager Cixi apparently also visited this site as well as Mount Miaofeng (Miaofeng shan), northwest of Beijing.[83] Both Mount Yaji and Mount Miaofeng are Daoist pilgrimage sites. In addition, Cixi regularly spent time at the Ten Thousand Longevities Monastery (Wanshou si) en route to her summer villa, the Garden of Nurturing Harmony (Yihe yuan), which was being constructed during the 1880s. This monastery was founded by Ming Empress Dowager Li and was renovated by the Qianlong emperor for Chongqing around 1751. It seems likely that Cixi was aware of this major female religious patron from the previous dynasty, as were Qianlong and Chongqing.

Daoism

During the nineteenth century, another long-established system of belief, Daoism, became important for Qing empresses—though imperial patronage of Daoism can in fact be traced back to the Northern Wei dynasty (386–534). Daoism encompasses diverse practices that centered on the Dao, or the "Way," believed to underlie all things in the universe. Devotees engage with these practices for many reasons, including the wish for longevity and protection. Qing rulers continued the Ming practice of holding Daoist rituals at the Hall of Imperial Peace (Qin'an dian) located in the imperial garden of the Forbidden City.[84] The Yongzheng emperor became particularly interested in Daoism after its rituals were believed to have cured him of illness.[85]

Daoism had thus been a part of the Qing imperial religious landscape since the early part of the dynasty, though there is little evidence that empresses were deeply involved before the nineteenth century. At that point, empresses began to visit Mount Yaji and Mount Miaofeng, sacred sites venerating the Daoist deity Bixia yuanjun (Primordial goddess of azure clouds), believed to be the daughter of the God of Mount Tai (Tai shan), one of the most revered peaks in China.[86] In addition to visiting Mount Yaji, Empress Xiaohe supported the restoration of a temple there dedicated to the goddess.[87] She also sponsored an incense association (*xianghui*) that provided services to pilgrims visiting Mount Miaofeng. Empress Dowager Cixi likewise took an interest in incense associations. Since the pilgrimage route to Mount Miaofeng passed by her residence, the Garden of Nurturing Harmony, Cixi arranged to watch the traveling devotees from an elevated hall there each spring during the 1890s.[88] In addition, she sponsored entertainers who provided services to pilgrims and invited them to give performances in the garden.[89]

Cixi made donations to Daoist temples as well.[90] Notably, she developed a close relationship with Zhang Yuanxuan (d. 1887), abbot of the White Cloud Monastery (Baiyun guan), the headquarters of the Quanzhen (Complete Perfection) sect of Daoism in Beijing. Zhang won Cixi's favor by performing a six-month-long service for a deceased imperial relative.[91] In return, the empress dowager gave the abbot a prestigious gift of a purple robe and jade belt. She also donated money to his monastery that enabled the abbot to stage a mass ordination in 1871 that was attended by Manchu noblemen and court officials, including Cixi's favored eunuch, Liu Chengyin (Liu Suyun; d. 1894).[92] Zhang's successor, Gao Rentong (1841–1907), inherited these elite connections when he became abbot in 1877. He continued to receive patronage from Cixi and Liu to the extent that foreign diplomats and Qing officials saw Gao as a channel for gathering information about the empress dowager.[93] It was through Gao that Cixi received the Daoist title of Guangren zi (Master of broad benevolence).[94] She accepted this as part of her self-identity, as is evident in photographs of the empress dowager in which the title appears in the form of smoke emerging from a censer (fig. 8).[95] The personal significance of Daoism for Cixi is further demonstrated by the fact that even while in exile in Xi'an, where she fled with the Guangxu emperor (r. 1875–1908) in 1900 after the Boxer Uprising, she paid visits to a Daoist site, the Eight Immortals Palace (Baxian gong), which had ties to the White Cloud Monastery.[96]

Cixi was the most eminent figure in a network of Qing elite women who patronized the White Cloud Monastery and Abbot Gao in Beijing. The importance of these connections to the monastery is revealed by a group of paintings commissioned by the abbot in 1890 (fig. 9).[97] They show a newly devised depiction of Bixia yuanjun as a patron and adept of the practices of inner alchemy (*neidan*), a method of cultivating bodily forces to achieve spiritual transcendence that was a feature of Quanzhen practices. Liu Xun has argued that this set of paintings was developed and directed specifically at the spiritual needs and aspirations of the monastery's elite female patrons.[98]

Empress Dowager Cixi and Divine Rulership

Empress Dowager Cixi was an exceptional Qing empress in many ways, as she actively and directly shaped her role as a female monarch within a patriarchal system of rulership. Religion was an important part of her self-fashioning, both as a devotee expressing her personal beliefs and as a ruler navigating the symbolic and political significance of religious performance. Like other sovereigns before her, she assumed multiple roles that aspired to universal legitimacy: apart from her Daoist title Master of Broad Benevolence, she was also addressed as "Holy Mother" (*shengmu*) as part of her official title and as "Venerable Buddha" (*Laofoye*).[99]

Cixi's interest in Buddhism was particularly focused on the bodhisattva Avalokiteshvara (Guanyin)—not the

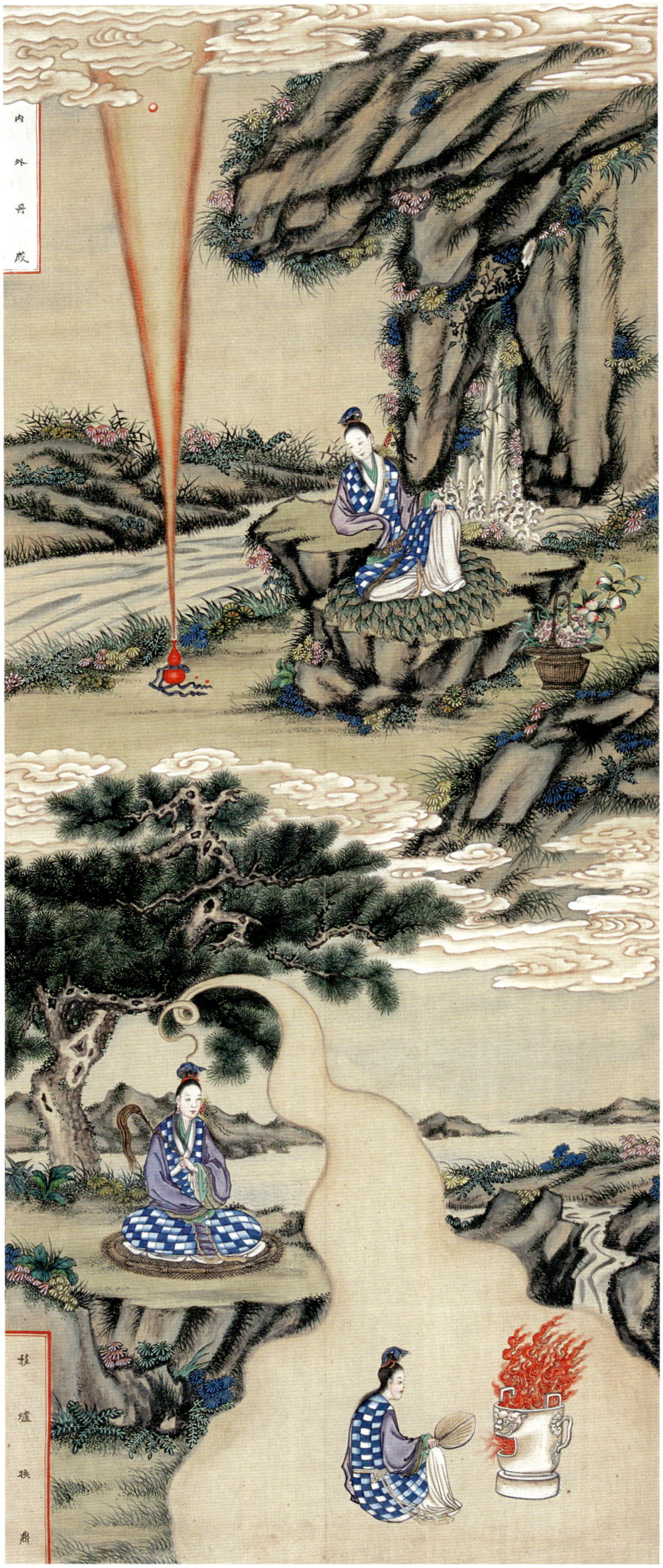
內外丹成
移爐換鼎

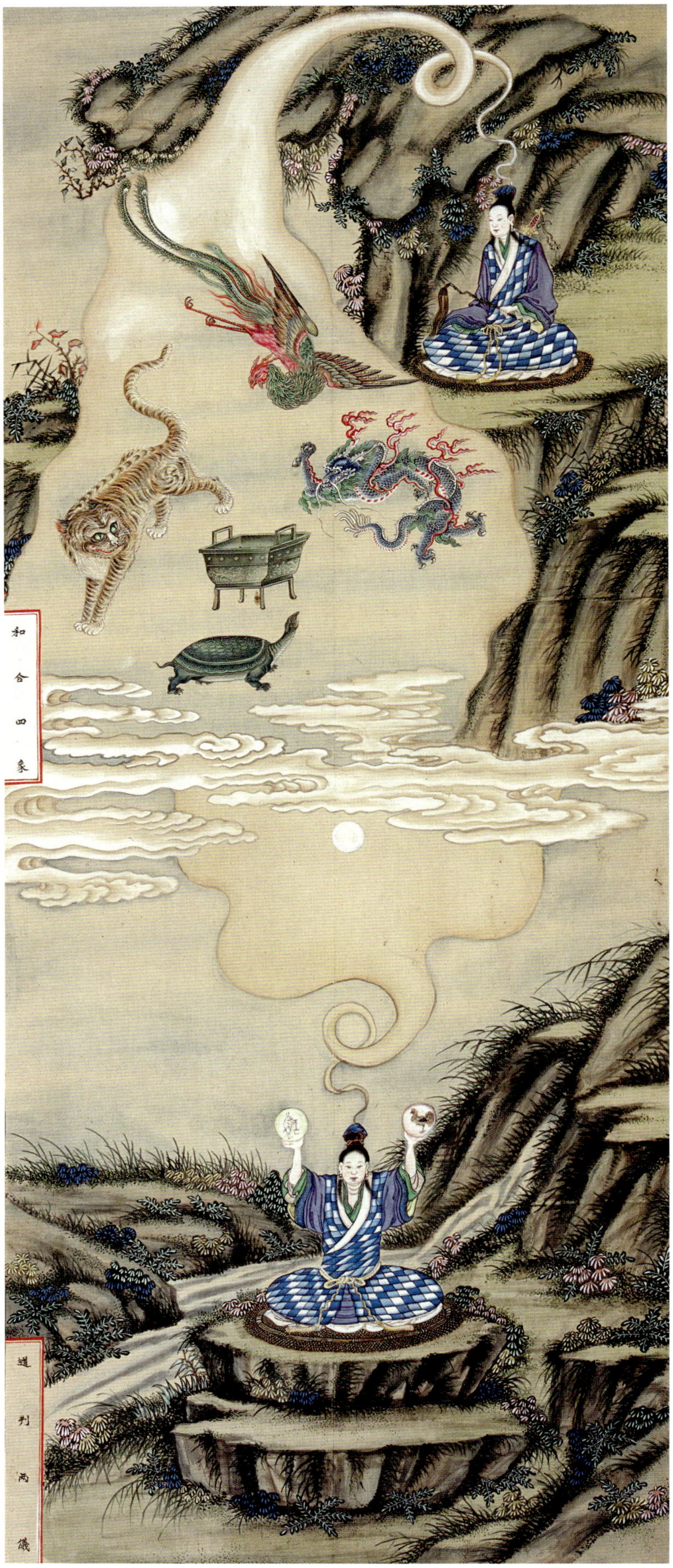
和合四象
道判兩儀

FIGURE 9

Two paintings from Our Lady Divides Her Body, a set of 22 paintings. Guangxu period, 1890, hanging scrolls, ink and color on silk, 71⅝ × 29⅛ in. (182 × 74 cm) each, White Cloud Monastery, Beijing.

FIGURE 10

Empress Dowager Cixi in the guise of the bodhisattva Avalokiteshvara (Guanyin). Guangxu period, 1875–1908, hanging scroll, ink and color on silk, 75¼ × 39⅜ in. (191.2 × 100 cm), Gu6602.

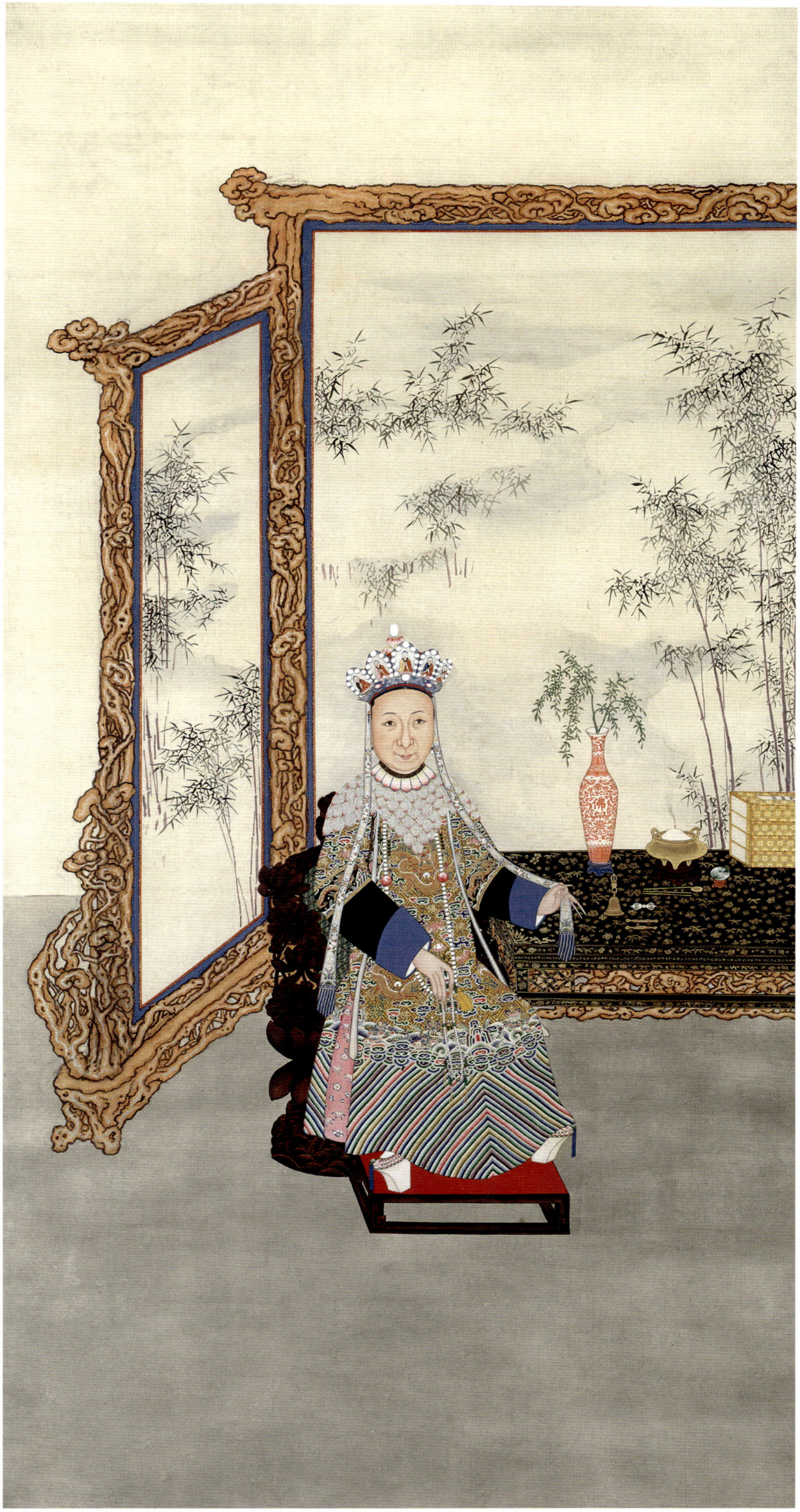

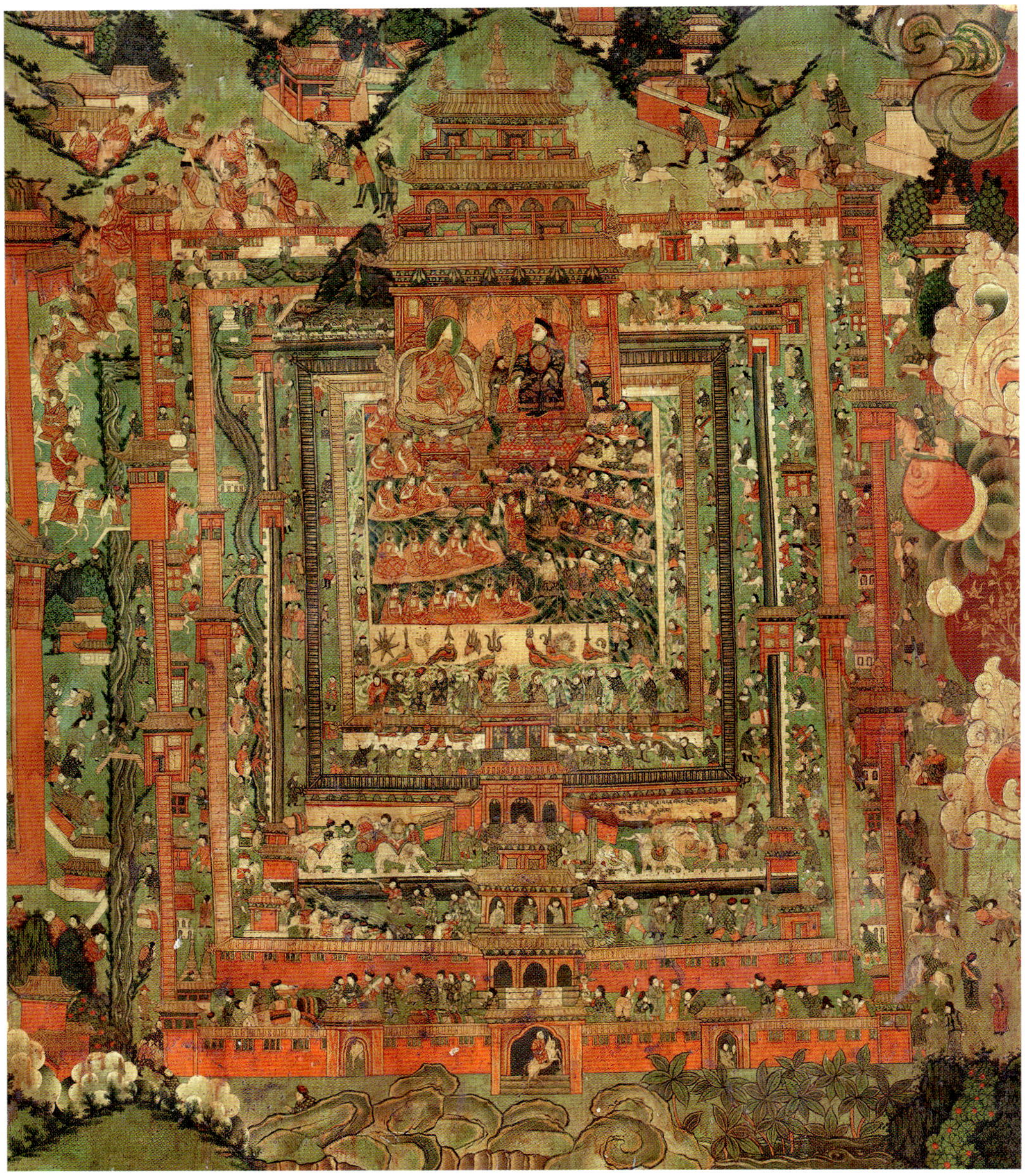

four-armed Tibetan Buddhist manifestation of the deity discussed in relation to Empress Xiaozhuang, but the Chinese-style White-Robed Guanyin.[100] Cixi prayed to the god daily, and she famously presented herself as Guanyin in a series of striking photographs and paintings, among them two hanging scrolls.[101] One shows her within a courtly domestic setting dressed in a festive robe (*jifu*) embellished with Guanyin accessories and Tibetan Buddhist emblems (fig. 10).[102] The other portrays her in an imagined landscape full of auspicious birthday symbols and depicts the popular theme of the boy Sudhana (Shancai) making an offering to Guanyin (pl. 42).[103] Photographs of Cixi as the bodhisattva were carefully staged, and at least one portrait of her as the White-Robed Guanyin was inserted into a sutra that she copied. These varied examples show the creative ways Cixi explored this mode of self-expression.[104] Unlike some other images of her, portraits of Cixi as Guanyin seem to have been created for her own satisfaction rather than for public consumption, even though some were circulated via unofficial channels.[105] These images could be interpreted as Cixi modelling herself on past emperors (and some empresses) who channeled divine power by adopting a deified persona and immortalizing it through paintings and prints.[106] Portraits of the Qianlong emperor as the bodhisattva Manjusri in an assembly of Buddhist deities provide a close precedent.[107] However, more recent research has emphasized the elements of fashion and theatricality in these images of Cixi and suggests she was participating in the custom of dressing up as Guanyin, which was an established way for women to demonstrate their piety during the Qing dynasty.[108]

Two other surviving images of Cixi in a religious context carry an unmistakable political charge. These are wall paintings in the mausoleum of the thirteenth Dalai Lama (1876–1933) in the Potala Palace in Lhasa, completed in 1935, twenty-three years after the fall of the Qing dynasty.[109] The large-scale paintings record scenes from the life of the Dalai Lama and include his visit to Beijing and his meetings with

FIGURE 11

The fifth Dalai Lama meets with the Shunzhi emperor (detail). Shunzhi period, about 1653, mural in the West Main Hall, Potala Palace, Lhasa.

FIGURE 12

The thirteenth Dalai Lama having an audience with the Guangxu emperor and Empress Dowager Cixi. Republican period, 1934–35, mural on the west wall of the upper corridor of the chapel housing the thirteenth Dalai Lama's funerary stupa, Potala Palace, Lhasa.

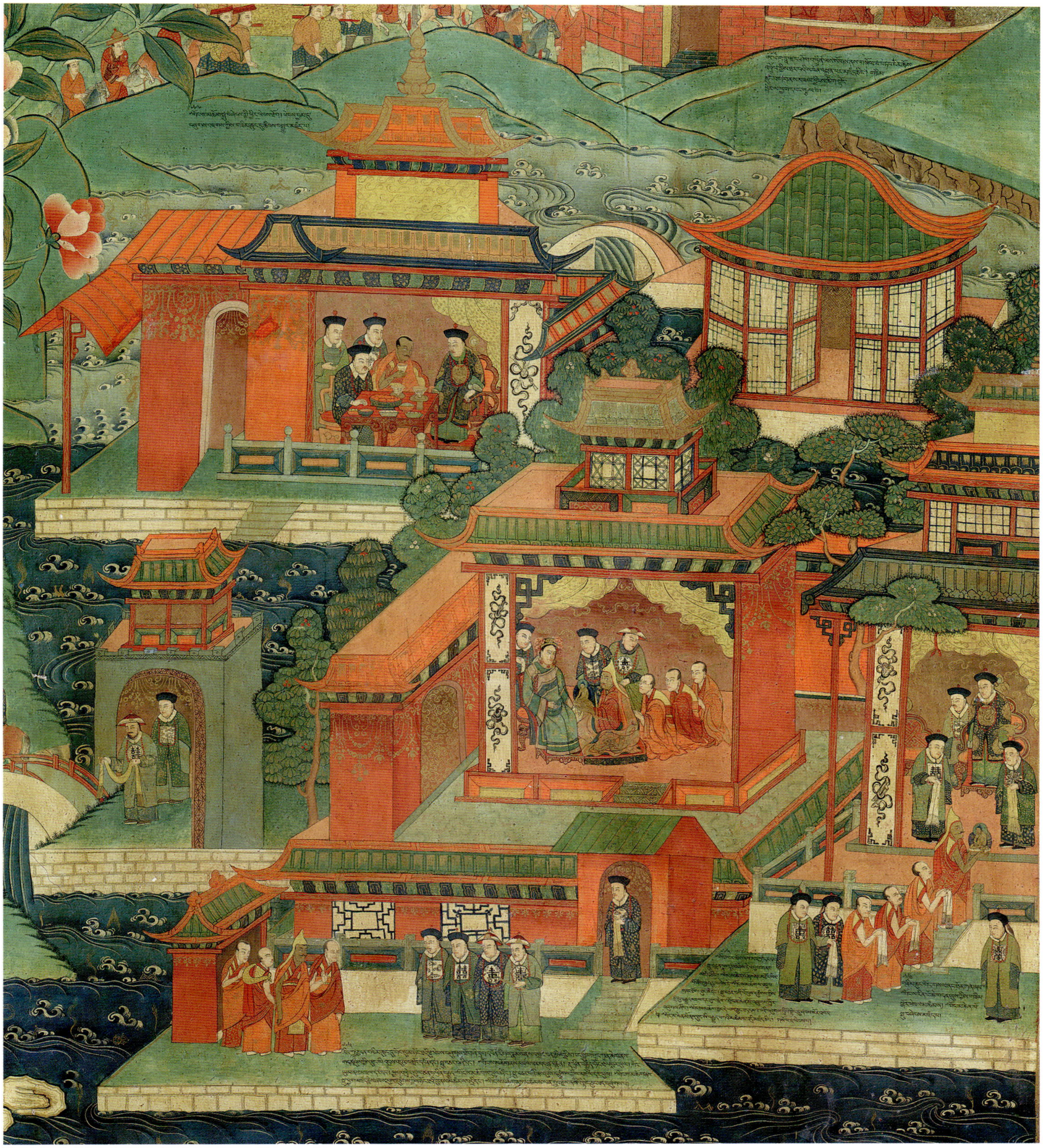

Cixi and the Guangxu emperor while he was in exile from Tibet in 1908. In one scene, the Dalai Lama and Cixi are shown seated side by side in the center of a palace-temple complex; there, he presents her with a jeweled wheel of the law, or dharma wheel, an implement symbolizing the Buddhist scriptures. This composition is modeled on another painting in the Potala Palace depicting the 1693 meeting of the fifth Dalai Lama and the Shunzhi emperor as "rulers atop a worldly palace, and as deities at the center of the celestial palace of the mandala" (fig. 11).[110]

In another scene from the 1935 series, the Dalai Lama is shown kneeling before Cixi and offering her a Buddhist statue, but the relationship between the two here is ambiguous as well since the Dalai Lama is situated in the center of the interior space (fig. 12).[111] These wall paintings clearly attempt to reimagine the events of the twentieth century through the lens of the seventeenth, imbuing the life story and cosmography of the thirteenth Dalai Lama with the spirit of that bygone age. Yet the world of 1908 was a vastly different place: the Qing dynasty was near collapse, and Tibet was under the threat of British and Russian forces. The paintings are nevertheless a clear acknowledgment that at the end of the Qing dynasty, an empress was understood to be the true monarch of China and the inheritor of the role of the divine "universal ruler."

Conclusion

Religion was an integral part of the lives of Qing empresses —as devotees, as political players, and as public figures. Empresses dedicated their attention and energy to religious spaces and activities that they believed would benefit themselves, their families, and the well-being of the dynasty. Judging from surviving sources, some Qing empresses were more active and visible in this sphere than others. Despite the lacunae in available records, it is clear that empresses were not simply passive followers of a preexisting environment determined by emperors. Rather, as most clearly seen in the careers of Xiaozhuang and Cixi, it was possible for empresses to actively shape not only their own religious lives but also the wider religious—and political—environment of the imperial court and the Qing empire.

Notes

1 For a concise introduction to the religious landscape at the Qing court from the Kangxi to Qianlong reigns, see Rawski and Rawson 2006. Also see Rawski 2009, part 3, "Qing Court Rituals."

2 Many publications address the topic of courtly women. See, for example, Ruggles 2000, with essays on Islamic societies; Silleras-Fernandez 2008 on queenship in late medieval Spain; and Luk 2015 on a Ming empress.

3 Rawski 2009, 232. On Qing shamanism, see Rawski 2009, 231–44; Di Cosmo 1999, esp. 361–63; Yan Chongnian 1993; Zou Ailian 1996.

4 Rawski 2009, 233.

5 Rawski 2009, 238. Zhang Guobin 2016.

6 Di Cosmo 1999, 381.

7 Meng Fanren 2010, 279–82.

8 Song Wen 2015, 5–6.

9 *Manzhou jishen jitian dianli*, *juan* 1.12a. On this code, see Di Cosmo 1999; and Zhang Naiwei 1988, *juan* 4, p. 286.

10 Zou Ailian 1996, 99.

11 Song Wen 2015, 32.

12 *Manzhou jishen jitian dianli*, *juan* 1.11a.

13 Rawski 2009, 198.

14 For more on Chinese state and court rituals, see McDermott 1999.

15 Some scholars have discussed Confucian rituals separately from religion. See, for instance, Rawski and Rawson 2006 on the Qing court. On debates over Confucianism as religion, see Chen Yong 2013.

16 On Qing state rituals, see Rawski 2009, chap. 6.

17 Rawski 2009, 226–67; McMahon 2016, 226.

18 Rawski 2009, 226–27; McMahon 2016, 226.

19 The steps of the ceremony are summarized by Li Zhi'an 2013.

20 Mann 1997, 152.

21 Zhao Zhongnan et al. 2010, 1:204–06; Yi Jo-lan 2014.

22 Naquin 2008, 308.

23 Li Zhi'an 2013, 360.

24 This set of paintings is in the National Palace Museum, Taibei. See Tong Wen'e 2006.

25 On these rituals, see Rawski 2009, chap. 8; Liu Housheng 1997, chap. 10 and 11; Wang Peihuan 2014, chap. 7.

26 On Tibetan Buddhism and Manchu rulership, see Rawski 2009, 244–63; Berger 2003.

27 Di Cosmo 1999, 371.

28 Rawski 2009, 252.

29 Wang Jiapeng 2014, 71.

30 Wang Jiapeng 2014, 73; Lin Shu 2015a, 47.

31 Wang Jiapeng 2014, 444; Lin Shu 2015a, 47–48.

32 Wang Jiapeng 2014, 74. On the Great Buddha Hall, also see Wang Zilin 2014; Gu Xinchun 2015.

33 Lin Shu 2015a, 48.

34 Farquhar 1978, 20.

35 Hyer 1981, 5.

36 Rawski 2009, 252–54; Wang Jiapeng 1991.

37 Wang Jiapeng 2014, 450.

38 Wang Jiapeng 2014, 450–01.

39 The removal of Buddhist objects from the Great Buddha Hall resulted from a government decision to use this collection to replenish the White Horse Temple (Baima si), the first recorded Buddhist temple in China. Its collection was destroyed during the Cultural Revolution (1966–76). See discussions in Wang Jiapeng 2014 and Wang Zilin 2014.

40 On this move, see, for instance, Wang Liping and Feng Jian 2016; Gu Xinchun 2015. The hall has been used as a sculpture gallery since 2015.

41 Wang Zilin 2014, 75.

42 Wang Zilin 2014, 78–81; Wang Jiapeng 2014, 454–58.

43 Wang Jiapeng 2014, 458.

44 Wang Jiapeng 2014, 459–62, dates them to the early Ming. Gu Xinchun 2012 dates them to Yuan–Ming periods.

45 The temple is the Da Nengren si, which no longer exists. Wang Zilin 2014, 82–83; Gu Xinchun 2012. On Empress Li as a religious patron, see Naquin 2008, 156–61.

46 Wang Jiapeng 2014, 451–52.

47 Wang Jiapeng 2014, 451–52.

48 Wen Ming 2015.

49 Lin Shu 2015a.

50 On the arrangement of the site, see Meng Fanren 2010, 332–34.

51 Wen Ming 2015, 27–31.

52 Chun Hua 2011, 58.

53 Chun Hua 2011, 58–59.

54 Chun Hua 2011, 58.

55 On this Kanjur, see Feng and Lu 2015; Weng Lianxi 2013; Li Baowen 2011; Lin Shih-Hsuan 2011; and Wang Qiuju 2017. The earliest record of this is found in the imperial catalogue *Midian zhulin* (Pearl Forest of the Secret Hall, 1744), *juan* 24.

56 This refers to a handwritten Ming imperial Tibetan Kanjur from the Ming Jingtai reign (1450–57); see Weng Lianxi 2013, 2.

57 Li Baowen 2011, 10.

58 Li Baowen 2011; Lin Shih-Hsuan 2011.

59 On the conflict between Kangxi and Oboi, see Peterson 2002, 126–34.

60 Lin Shih-Hsuan 2011.

61 Li Baowen 2011, 14–16.

62 Naquin 2008, 344.

63 Weng Lianxi 2013. With thanks to Shu Yue for finding a copy of this article for me.

64 The Qianlong emperor believed the sutra to be authentic, something that had previously been disputed. Weng Lianxi 2013, 3–4; Berger 2003, 88.

65 Gugong bowuyuan 2015b, 108; Gugong bowuyuan 2015a, 164–69, no. 11

66 Kahn 1967.

67 The two empresses have been compared to each other. See, for instance, Shang Hongkui 1982.

68 Susan Naquin has expressed this view regarding Chongqing; see Naquin 2008, 347.

69 Zhao Erxun 1960, *juan* 214. In one episode, Chongqing called Qianlong's attention to a temple in the capital that needed renovating, and he immediately followed her suggestion. The record goes on to say Qianlong was not pleased by her meddling.

70 Naquin 2008, 347n148.

71 Huang Chongwen 2014. It was displayed in the Hall of Eternal Protection (Yongyou dian), the private chamber of Yongzheng and where his coffin was kept before it was interred. On the function of this hall, see Greenwood 2013.

72 Naquin 2008, 346.

73 Naquin 2008, 347.

74 Naquin 2008, 347; Yu Minzhong (about 1785) 1983, *juan* 99, p. 1644.

75 Naquin 2008, 346; Rawski 2009, 142–44, 158–59.

76 Xiaohui was also a companion to Kangxi on his third southern inspection tour in 1699. The Qianlong emperor traveled extensively with his mother, Empress Dowager Chongqing, including her on four of his southern inspection tours. See Lin Shih-Hsuan 2011, 120; Kahn 1967, 198.

77 On this journey, see, for instance, Chang Jianhua 2016a and 2016b.

78 Rawski and Rawson 2006, 131; also see Berger 2003.

79 Naquin 2008, 347.

80 Jin Lei 2008, 54–63.

81 Kahn 1967, 198.

82 Naquin 2008, 347, 561.

83 Naquin 2008, 561.

84 Guan Jing 2015.

85 Guan Jing 2015, 86.

86 On this goddess, see Little et al. 2000, 278–79.

87 Naquin 1992, 354.

88 Naquin 1992, 344; Wu Xiaoqun 2005.

89 Wu Xiaoqun 2005, 41.

90 Naquin 2008, 348.

91 Liu Xun 2004, 74.

92 Liu Xun 2004, 74.

93 Yin Zhihua 2010, 47.

94 Hogge 2011; Xin 1992, 191.

95 Hogge 2010; Peng 2012.

96 Pan Cunjuan 2012.

97 Liu Xun 2004.

98 Liu Xun 2004.

99 Naquin 2008, 348.

100 Li Yuhang 2012, 111.

101 On these images, see Rojas 2008; Li Yuhang 2011, 2012; Pang 2005; Peng 2012; Peng 2014; Wang Cheng-hua 2012b; and Hogge 2011.

102 Li Yuhang 2011, 186–88.

103 Li Yuhang 2011, 189–92.

104 Peng 2014, 13

105 Wang Cheng-hua 2012b, 257.

106 On Ming empresses, see Luk 2016.

107 On these paintings, see, for instance, Berger 2003, 55, 58–61; and Rawski and Rawson 2006, no. 47.

108 Li Yuhang 2011; Li Yuhang 2012; Peng 2014.

109 On these mural paintings, see Jagou 2009; and Chou 2014.

110 Chou 2014, 436; see also Berger 2003, 21.

111 A meeting between the Dalai Lama and the Guangxu emperor at a banquet is shown separately in a building further back and to the left of the painting. This unusual arrangement is in fact based on events that took place during the Dalai Lama's visit. On arrangements for the visit, see Jagou 2009.

FIVE

Empresses and Qing Court Politics

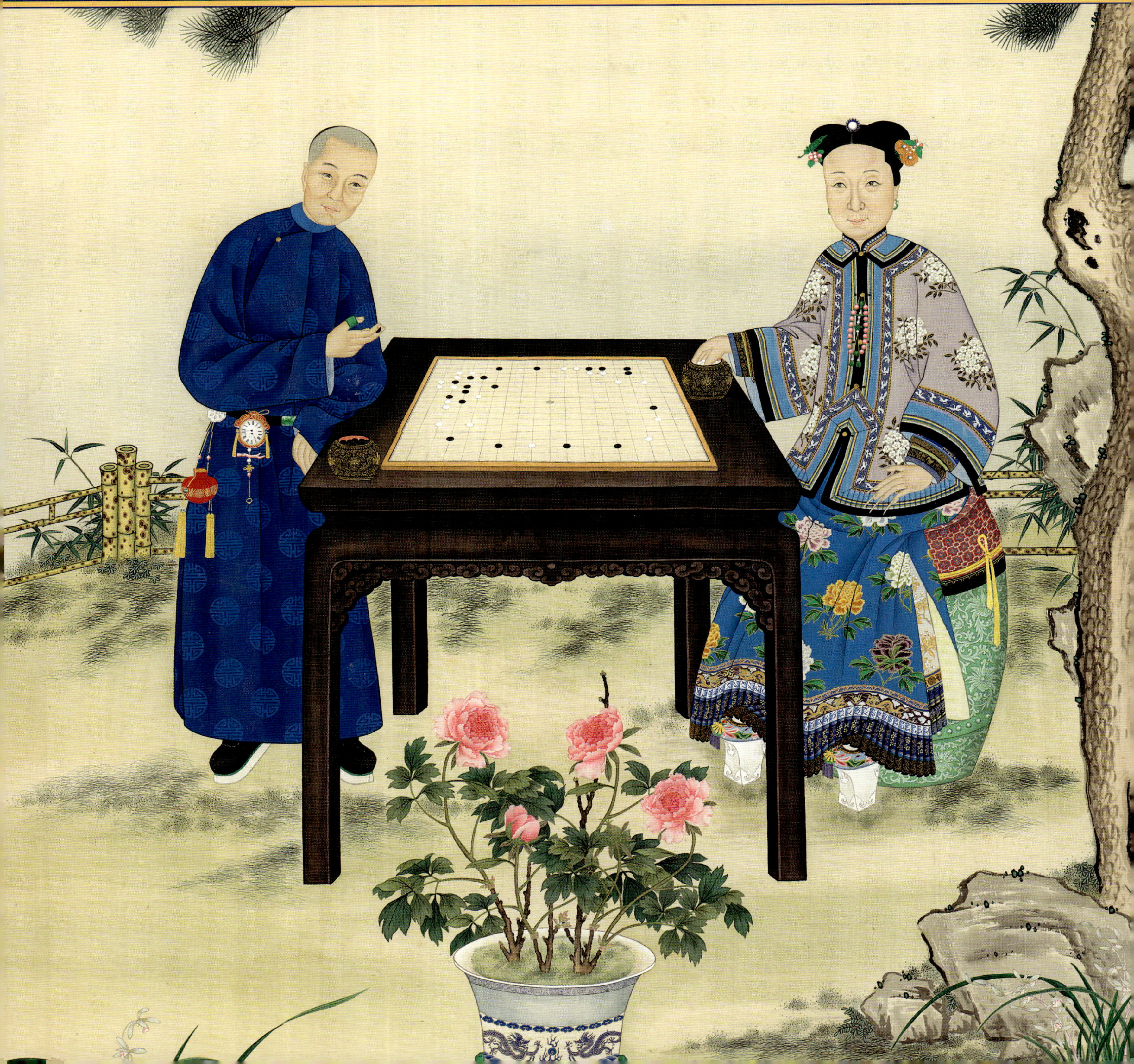

YING-CHEN PENG

BEFORE THE QING DYNASTY, Chinese empresses were simultaneously respected and carefully watched—venerated for giving birth to and raising successors to the throne while monitored by the establishment to prevent them from intervening in court politics. Such a complex attitude was based on the male desire for female fecundity and fear of the potential power that it germinated, resulting in a long tradition of regulating women in the inner court. Whenever an imperial woman asserted power beyond the domestic domain, the patriarchal system responded by further tightening its scrutiny.[1] Compared to the anxiety experienced by their Han Chinese counterparts, steppe states such as the Mongol-Yuan dynasty (1279–1368) took a more flexible stance on women's involvement in politics: life on horseback required mature leadership to navigate through the uncertain and harsh environment of the steppe, and an experienced woman in the ruling clan could merit as much respect as her male counterparts.[2] This status extended to property rights, as a widow in the steppe states could inherit the assets of her deceased spouse, although her in-laws could keep the property by pursuing the widow's levirate—that is, the arrangement of remarrying her to her late husband's younger brother.[3]

By the time the Manchus—another ethnic group rising from the steppe—established the Qing dynasty, they had been in contact with Han Chinese culture for centuries.[4] Manchu rulers cherished filial piety, one of the virtues valued by the Han Chinese, for it was deemed the cornerstone of the social order. Its significance in the Qing dynasty is best illustrated by the fact that the posthumous title of every Qing empress began with the character for "filial piety" (*xiao*), which had been a convention of the Han Chinese Ming dynasty (1368–1644) that the Manchus overthrew. The influence of this principle was multifaceted. By equating the emperor with a devoted son, the Qing acknowledged an understanding of and respect for Han Chinese values, which helped mitigate tensions between the ruling Manchus and the Han Chinese cultural elites, who questioned the legitimacy and capability of the former.[5] Filial piety could also potentially alleviate the rigid protocol that restrained an imperial woman's talent and ambition. In other words, theoretically and under certain conditions, it allowed the empress dowager to assert political authority in the name of her son.

The three Qing empresses discussed in the following pages illustrate the complex relationship between filial piety and women's participation in court politics. Each lived a long life and received the title of empress dowager under similar circumstances, but their engagement with politics differed. The first, Empress Xiaozhuang (1613–1688), prepared her grandson to be the Kangxi emperor (r. 1662–1722), who inaugurated the heyday of the Qing dynasty; thus was she eulogized as the model for succeeding Qing empresses. Kangxi's grandson, the Qianlong emperor (r. 1736–95), was also renowned for being a dutiful son, but his birth mother, Empress Dowager Chongqing (Empress Xiaosheng; 1693–1777), did not wield much political agency.

Rather, Qianlong's use of her name and image transformed Chongqing into a symbol of *his* filial piety. In contrast to Chongqing's quieter presence, Empress Dowager Cixi (Empress Xiaoqin; 1835–1908) was the maverick of Qing imperial women. Her strategic manipulation of two child emperors' filial piety was key to a four-decade female regency and de facto rulership.

The Model

In 1625 a twelve-year-old scion of the royal Mongol Borjigit lineage, Borjigit Bumbutai, became a consort of the Manchu emperor Hong Taiji (r. 1626–43), the ruler of the Later Jin dynasty who subsequently renamed it Qing in 1636.[6] Later granted the title Empress Xiaozhuang, at that time she was one among many Mongol consorts in the Manchu inner court, where a variety of seminomadic traditions, such as levirate marriage, were still practiced.[7] She bore Hong Taiji a son and three daughters, but she was never his favorite. Hong Taiji died in 1643 without appointing a successor. The ensuing power struggle among the ruling clans led to the enthronement of Xiaozhuang's five-year-old son as the Shunzhi emperor (r. 1644–61), an unusual repudiation of the Manchu tradition of adult leadership. Shunzhi's elevation to the throne ensured the continuing rule of Hong Taiji's bloodline and simultaneously created opportunities for powerful clan members to assert political power through their regency.[8] As the birth mother of Shunzhi, Xiaozhuang was honored with the title of empress dowager, yet her political influence during the Shunzhi reign was murky. At first she worked closely with the regent, her brother-in-law Dorgon (1612–1650), but eventually her concerns turned to the continued alliance between the Mongols and Manchus through intermarriage. However, her attempts to recruit a daughter-in-law from her own clan were met with furious resistance from her son, the emperor and groom. His subsequent divorce from two empresses, Xiaozhuang's niece and grandniece, further strained their relationship.[9]

Shunzhi died at the age of twenty-two and left the Qing dynasty with another underage ruler, Xiaozhuang's grandson, the six-year-old Kangxi emperor. Having outlived her husband and son, Xiaozhuang became the dominant figure in the imperial family. Her mentorship encouraged the Kangxi emperor to become an erudite ruler who maintained Manchu tradition while also recognizing the value of Han Chinese culture[10]—as when Kangxi stated, "We rule the empire with filial piety."[11] The intimate relationship between the grandmother and the grandson was recorded extensively in official court publications; one account tells of how Kangxi, accompanying Xiaozhuang on a pilgrimage to Mount Wutai (Wutai shan), a mecca for Tibetan Buddhism, would help carry his grandmother's palanquin when the path was wet and slippery.[12] While such an action unquestionably underlined their close bond, it also publicized Kangxi's image as a devoted grandson to assuage any doubt about the Manchu ruler's understanding of and sympathy for the Han Chinese tradition and, by extension, his capacity to rule an empire whose majority population was Han Chinese.

In addition to overseeing Kangxi's upbringing, Xiaozhuang actively supported the young emperor and his empire. She donated her personal savings to famine-relief efforts and rewarded Manchu soldiers who fought in the Revolt of the Three Feudatories (1673–81), a civil war that ultimately resulted in consolidation of the Qing regime.[13] Another example of her involvement with Kangxi's career is the splendid Kanjur Sutra, consisting of more than 50,000 sutra leaves in gold ink on indigo paper and preserved in covers decorated with inlaid jewels. This expensive commission originated with Xiaozhuang in 1667 and received Kangxi's full support, despite the objections of court officials for its extravagance. While this commission clearly reflected the empress dowager's religious piety, the political motivation behind the creation of the sutra cannot be overlooked. The project was initiated during the civil war, and it succeeded in unifying the Manchus and the Mongols, who were practicing Tibetan Buddhists, against the Han Chinese rebels.[14] When Xiaozhuang died in 1688, the bereaved Kangxi wailed for the loss of his beloved grandmother and unconditional supporter. Her death also marked the diminishing influence of Mongol consorts and intensified patriarchal control over imperial women at the Qing court.[15]

The Symbol

In the eighteenth and early nineteenth centuries, succession to the Qing throne was uneventful, as five consecutive emperors ascended the throne at a mature age. With Han Chinese protocol permeating the inner court, the presence of imperial women in politics decreased significantly, a trend represented by the Qianlong emperor's birth mother, Empress Dowager Chongqing. In 1704 Lady Niohuru, a lowly consort, was married to Yinzhen, who subsequently became the Yongzheng emperor (r. 1723–35). She received the title of Empress Dowager Chongqing after her son became the emperor in 1735, but her agency was carefully proscribed during his reign. Unlike his grandfather, Qianlong took precautions against women's involvement in matters beyond the inner court. His displays of devotion to his mother, public and gaudy though they were, were designed to reflect merit on him and his reign without empowering his mother (although he did follow her advice on certain occasions; see Lin Shu's essay, pp. 78–87). He did comply with Chongqing's request to repair a temple but soon after summoned her eunuchs, warning them to dissuade the empress dowager from pursuing such ideas in the future, because, as he claimed, Empress Xiaozhuang had never asked the Kangxi emperor to build or repair temples.[16] With such a tenacious ruler in control, Chongqing's engagement with court politics was doomed to be limited.

And yet Qianlong made much of his close relationship with Chongqing. In addition to annual trips to pay homage at the Qing emperors' mausoleums and autumn hunting events, Qianlong took his mother on numerous inspection tours. When she became too weak to travel, the emperor suspended all such tours and did not recommence them until he had observed three years of mourning following her death in 1777.[17] While Chongqing no doubt enjoyed these journeys, few records document her activities or suggest that she played any formal or official role while traveling with the emperor. The fact that they traveled together effectively promoted Qianlong's image as a devoted son to his subjects, which further strengthened the legitimacy of Manchu rule.

The elaborate celebration of Chongqing's decennial birthdays was another aspect of Qianlong's campaign to be seen as a dutiful son. In 1750 he announced a major expansion of the imperial precinct in western Beijing for his mother's upcoming sixtieth birthday. A piece of land to the west of the Garden of Perfect Brightness (Yuanming yuan) was chosen as the site of the Garden of Clear Ripples (Qingyi yuan), where the Temple of Recompense and Longevity (Dabaoen yanshou si) would be built and dedicated to Chongqing.[18] Why was it necessary to build the temple in a new garden? After all, Qianlong had previously dedicated the nearby Garden of Delightful Spring (Changchun yuan) to his mother in 1738 and could have erected the temple there.[19] In reality, this display of devotion was a cover for his enthusiasm for garden construction and the need to secure a water supply for the ever more populous capital.[20] This hidden agenda is proven by the fact that the Pavilion of Buddhist Fragrance (Foxiang ge), a nine-story pagoda holding sculptures of Buddhist deities that was the highlight of the temple, was still under construction when the empress dowager's birthday celebration took place in 1751. Had this been the true priority, it certainly would have been completed by its stated deadline.

Qianlong also promoted his filial piety by utilizing Chongqing's images in paintings marking her eightieth birthday (see pl. 7). These carefully crafted commemorative works both feature frontal views of the empress dowager.

FIGURE 1
Celebratory Banquet at the Palace of Compassion and Tranquility for Empress Dowager Chongqing's Seventieth Birthday (detail) from Scenes of Bliss and Celebration. Jin Tingbiao (d. 1767) and other court painters, Beijing, Qianlong period, 1761–71, album leaf, ink and color on silk, cat. 34.

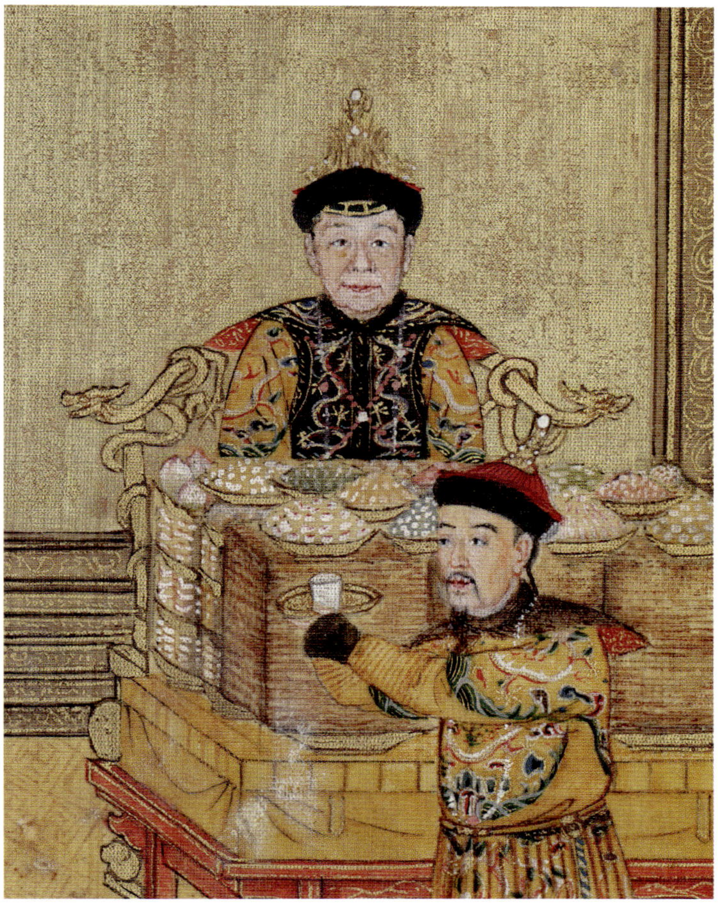

Frontality—along with symmetry, stasis, and compositional centrality—had been the norm for ancestor portraits in China since the Ming dynasty, and it was an important device for reinforcing the solemn majesty of the subject, thereby transforming the sitter from a living person into an eternal icon.[21] *Celebratory Banquet at the Palace of Compassion and Tranquility* [Cining gong] *for Empress Dowager Chongqing's Seventieth Birthday* from the album *Scenes of Bliss and Celebration* (fig. 1) presents a formal birthday banquet at Chongqing's palace in the Forbidden City and shows her positioned higher than Qianlong—a surprising compositional choice given the convention of making the emperor the most prominent figure in a painting. Similarly, *Celebrating Empress Dowager Chongqing's Eightieth Birthday* (pl. 7) portrays Chongqing in the same manner while documenting a more intimate moment at the event.[22] Note that Chongqing is the only figure portrayed frontally in those paintings, an arrangement that emphasizes her place at the center of the event. Nevertheless, the viewer's gaze is soon redirected to the image of Qianlong and the surrounding activities, underscoring the emperor as the mastermind of the celebration. In other words, the image of Chongqing served as a symbol of her son's filial deeds for the future generations to remember.

The Maverick

A century of Qing prosperity ended in the mid-nineteenth century with a string of domestic and international crises that challenged the existence of the regime and the values that anchored it. The empire was shaken by the prolonged Taiping Rebellion (1851–64) in southern China and the Second Opium War (1857–60), which forced the imperial family to flee Beijing. It was against this backdrop that Empress Dowager Cixi, the most controversial of all Qing imperial women, overturned the system that had suppressed the political involvement of imperial women. Entering the inner court as a low-ranking consort of the Xianfeng emperor (r. 1851–61), Cixi gave birth to his only male heir and soon advanced to a rank second only to that of Xianfeng's primary wife, Empress Dowager Ci'an (Empress Xiaozhen; 1837–1881). In 1861 Cixi's son ascended to the throne at the age of six as the Tongzhi emperor (r. 1862–74), and she assumed the title of empress dowager.[23] Despite the auspicious meaning of her title—"benevolent and happy"—her time as empress dowager was neither. Her appointment was announced a day after Ci'an's, prompting recent scholars to suggest that Cixi claimed the title for herself using Tongzhi's filial piety as a cover.[24] Forming an alliance with Ci'an and Xianfeng's younger brother, Prince Gong (Yixin; 1833–1898), Cixi plotted a coup immediately after the imperial family returned to Beijing from exile, killing Xianfeng's advisers who opposed her participation in politics and establishing a regency of two empresses dowager and one prince.[25]

Ci'an's role in most political events was nominal; regency meant little to her, as her priority was the domestic domain.[26] She seldom held audiences alone or expressed concrete opinions about state affairs and instead spent most of her time in the inner court. A rare account of Ci'an's regency comes from her brief 1880 audience with the Admiral of Hunan, Bao Chao (1828–1886), which she held on behalf of Cixi, who was ill. Unable to ask any questions related to politics, she merely inquired about the length of his trip and greeted his family.[27] Ci'an's motherly image overrode any active role she might have played as a regent. It is vividly reflected in her portraits, on which Tongzhi wrote the inscriptions "May the sun forever shine in women's residences" (*Xuanwei riyong*; see pl. 51) and "May the mother's benevolence be as lasting as the evergreen bamboos" (*Cizhu yanqing*; see fig. 2), both popular phrases for a mother's birthday.

By contrast, images of Cixi rarely revealed any nurturing qualities. Two portraits of the empresses dowager early in their regency best illustrate their distinct personas (figs. 2 and 3). Both are garden scenes featuring a seated woman—a conventional schema of Qing court portraiture. Both women wear dark informal robes decorated with roundels of the longevity character (*shou*) appropriate for widows. Cixi's portrait, however, departs from tradition by including on the table at her left an open book, a symbol of erudition that was a common prop in portraits of Qing emperors, one that revealed her aspiration for power.[28] The Kangxi emperor was, for example, depicted in a portrait with an open book before him (fig. 4). This motif was uncommon in paintings of Qing imperial women, as the Manchus did not generally encourage their daughters to become learned scholars (for an example of an imperial woman teaching young princes, see p. 75, fig. 23).[29]

As time passed and Cixi's power increased, her relationship with Tongzhi grew fraught. Her dissatisfaction with the emperor's educational progress as recorded by his mentor bespoke the anxiety of a "tiger mother" about her son's ability to rule.[30] Tensions only intensified as Tongzhi entered adulthood. In 1872 he disregarded Cixi's wishes and selected an empress preferred by Ci'an.[31] That drama was followed the next year by a power struggle when Tongzhi reached his majority and began to rule without regents.

Empress Dowager Cixi playing Chinese chess (*weiqi*) visualized this conflict (fig. 5). For many years the identity of the man in this painting was open to conjecture due to the lack of textual records; some scholars assumed he was Cixi's top eunuch, Li Lianying (1848–1911), while others suspected he might be Cixi's younger brother. However, as Wang Cheng-hua has pointed out, the game of chess was a highly politicized subject in imperial portraiture, and the eunuch and Cixi's brother were not important enough to be shown competing with the empress dowager. Only the most powerful of men during Cixi's regency would have been shown in this work. The small mouth and high cheekbones of the man here resemble the image of the emperor in other portraits, confirming that this painting is a rare depiction of imperial mother and son.[32] The two figures are shown playing Chinese chess in a garden, each occupying one side of a table, a pine tree on Cixi's side giving her a stronger visual emphasis. The peony blossoms in the center of the composition symbolize their prosperous joint rulership, while the chess pieces signify competition. Cixi, holding the white pieces that control the game, waits for Tongzhi's next move.[33] Such a depiction of rivalry between mother and son was unprecedented in Chinese portraiture and stands in vivid contrast to the serenity in Ci'an's portraits.

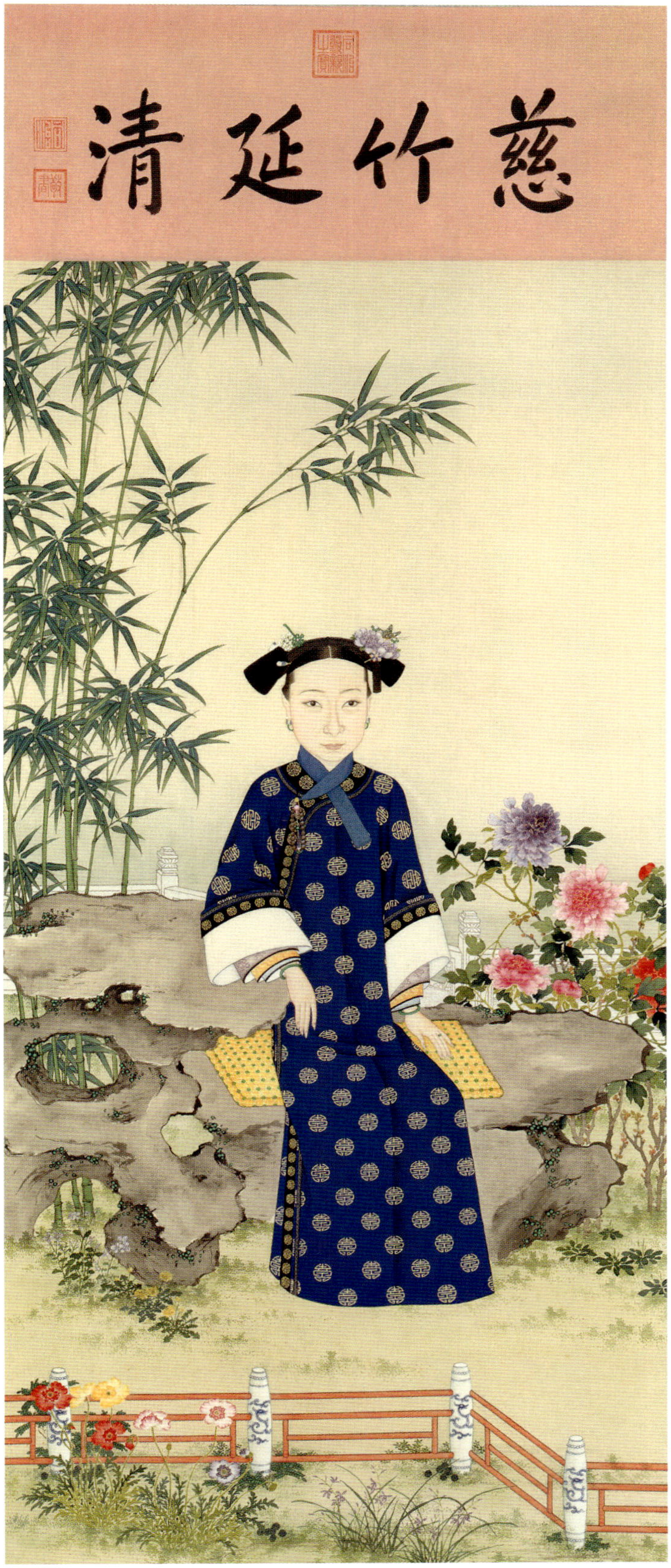

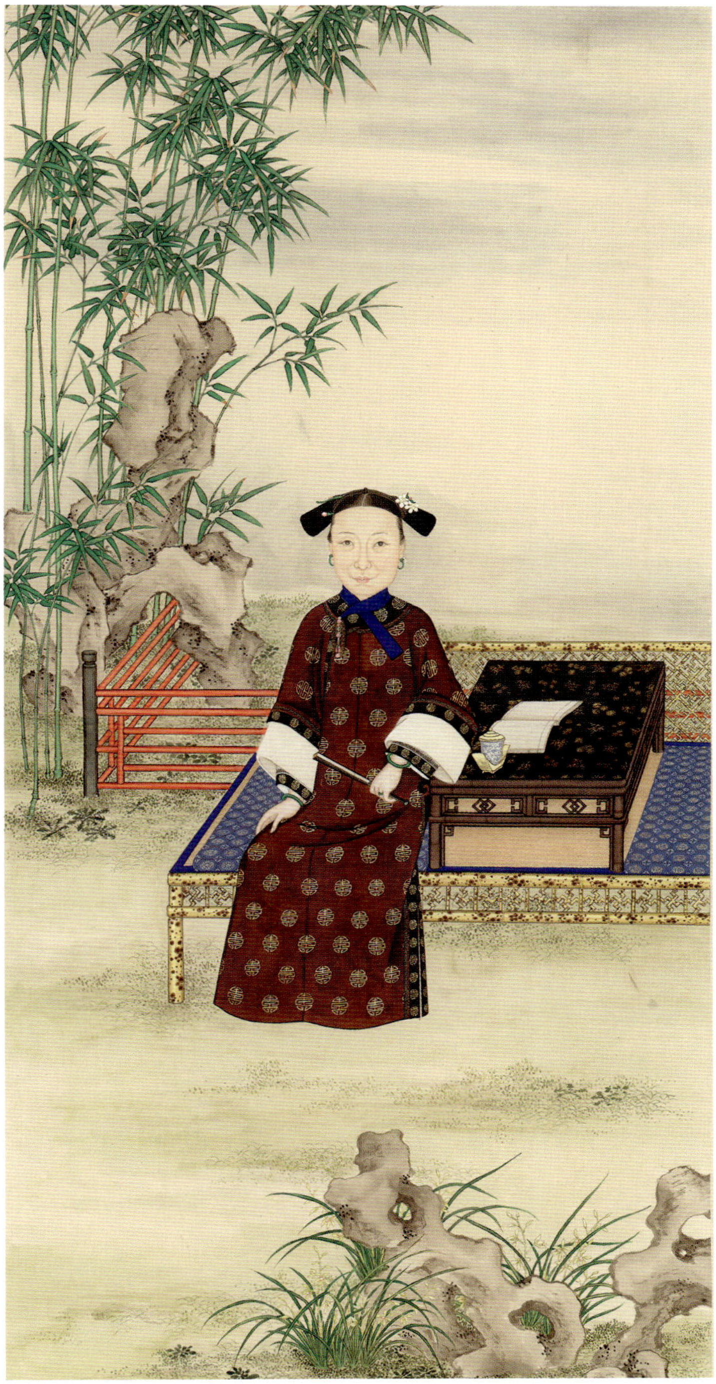

FIGURE 2

Empress Dowager Ci'an in a garden with rocks, bamboo, and peonies. Court painters, Beijing, Tongzhi period, about 1872–73, hanging scroll, ink and color on paper, cat. 15.

FIGURE 3

Empress Dowager Cixi in a garden with rocks and bamboo. Court painters, Beijing, Tongzhi or Guangxu period, probably 1870s, hanging scroll, ink and color on paper, cat. 17.

FIGURE 4
The Kangxi Emperor Reading. Kangxi period, 1662–1722, hanging scroll, ink and color on silk, 53 15/16 × 41 3/4 in. (137 × 106 cm), Gu6411.

FIGURE 5
Empress Dowager Cixi playing Chinese chess (*weiqi*). Court painters, Beijing, Tongzhi or Guangxu period, 1862–1908, hanging scroll, ink and color on silk, cat. 18.

FIGURE 6
Panorama of the Garden of Nurturing Harmony. Guangxu or Republican period, probably early 20th century, painting originally mounted on a wall (*tieluo*), ink and color on paper, Peabody Essex Museum, cat. 43.

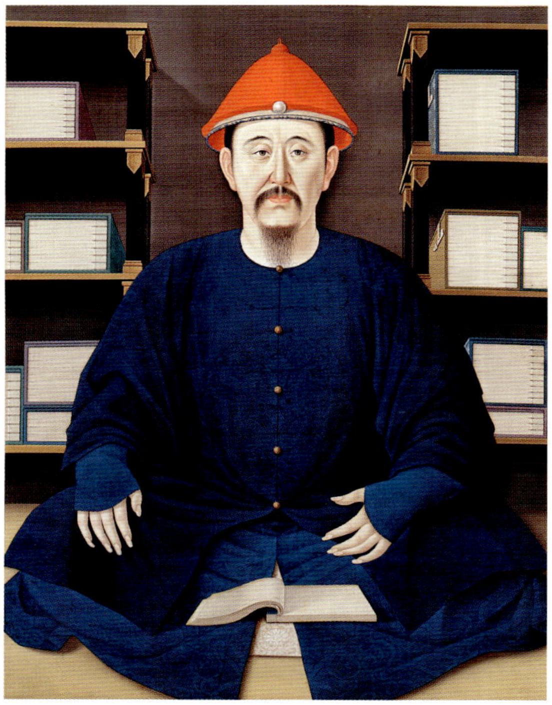

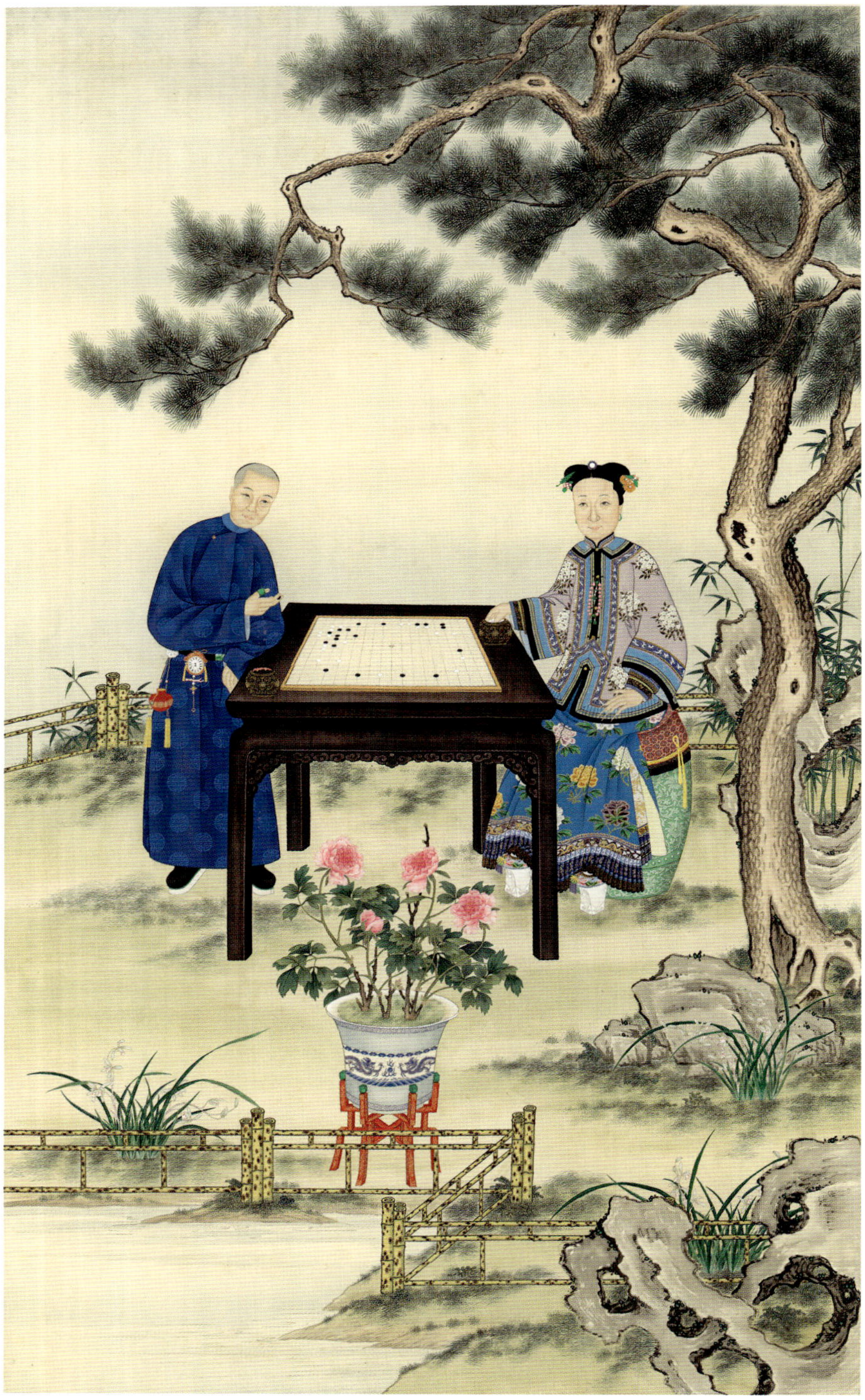

As if to ease the tension with his mother, Tongzhi announced the reconstruction of the Garden of Beautiful Spring (Qichun yuan), which had been destroyed in the Second Opium War, as the Garden of Myriad Springs (Wanchun yuan) on Cixi's retirement from the regency and dedicated it to the two empresses dowager in the autumn of 1873.[34] Following Qianlong's precedent, the project was largely motivated by Tongzhi's interest in garden design, yet it was also an act of filial piety—and a nuanced tactic to keep Cixi at a distance.[35] However, unlike Chongqing's passive acceptance of her son's gift of a garden, Cixi turned it to her own purposes, participating enthusiastically in the design of a palace compound much larger and more luxuriously decorated than that of her superior, Ci'an.[36] To ensure that the interior of the palace would be decorated with bright colors and auspicious symbols of flowers and birds, she commissioned the imperial kiln to produce a vast range of porcelain pieces.[37] Especially noteworthy on such vessels is the inscription "Daya zhai" (Studio of Utmost Grace) and oval seal in red (see pl. 55). These often appeared on Cixi's paintings, and on the porcelain they became her mark of ownership. This was an explicit transgression of Qing convention, as

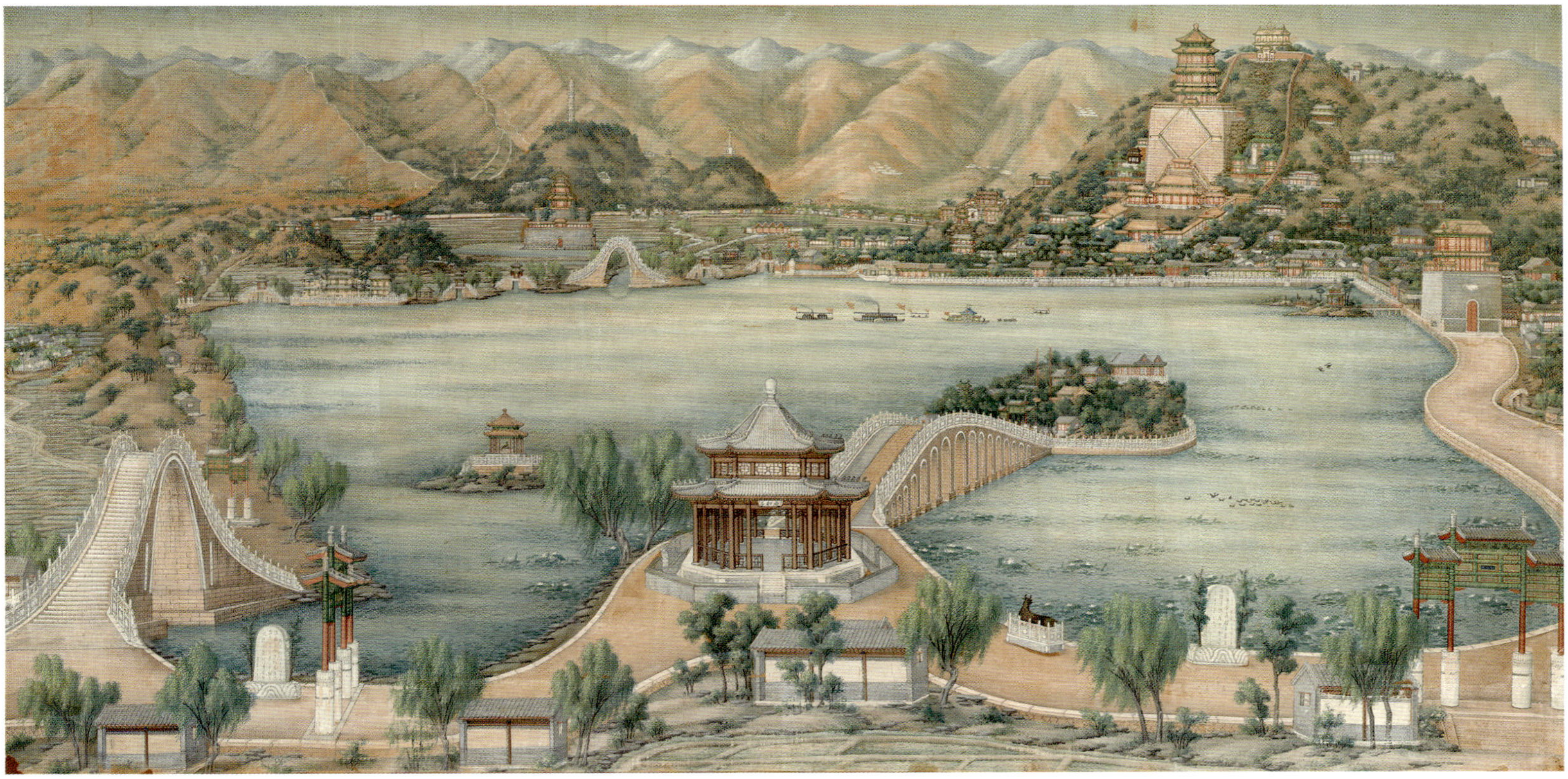

commissioning porcelain was a privilege reserved for the emperor, one that had been tinged with political significance during Qianlong's time.[38] However, all of the grand plans for the Garden of Myriad Springs collapsed within a year. Mounting expenditures and scandals involving the purchase of wood forced Tongzhi to abandon the project in the autumn of 1874, and in early 1875, the eighteen-year-old emperor died of smallpox. In the end, the Daya zhai ware was the only part of the project to be realized, as the imperial kiln was already in the process of firing the pieces when the project was cancelled.

While she grieved the loss of her son, Cixi had no intention of remaining in retirement. She named her four-year-old nephew as Tongzhi's successor, the Guangxu emperor (r. 1875–1908), and reactivated the empresses dowager's regency without objection from officials, an indicator of her enduring power. Ci'an's death in 1881 made Cixi the sole matriarch of the Qing empire. While Guangxu was a dutiful protégé, Cixi no longer required his filial piety to justify her power. More than a decade of regency and the installation of her supporters at the court made this formidable woman an indispensable presence in late Qing politics—a fact reflected in her portraits. Authority, be it religious or political, became the key concept in these pictures. Cixi's devotion to the bodhisattva Avalokiteshvara (Guanyin) prompted her interest in embodying the deity on various occasions (see Luk Yu-ping's essay, pp. 110–27).[39] While genuine piety was undoubtedly at play here, her interest in theatrical performance transformed these images into a mixture of secular and religious dominion. In *Empress Dowager Cixi in the Guise of the Bodhisattva Avalokiteshvara (Guanyin)* (pl. 42), Cixi wears a robe decorated with golden bamboo and a five-Buddha headdress—not the standard appearance of Guanyin in religious paintings. The theatrically attired empress dowager is surrounded by peaches and butterflies, the character for longevity, and she is accompanied by a boy whose facial features resembled those of her top eunuch, Li Lianying.[40]

The matriarch's authority began to worry Qing officials, however. The abandoned renovation of the Garden of Perfect Brightness inspired their plan to distract her from politics. They proposed resuming the imperial navy's annual exercises on Kunming Lake in the Garden of Clear Ripples and repairing the surrounding buildings in 1886.[41] This sparked Cixi's unfulfilled desire to construct a garden of her own, with the precedent of the Garden of Clear Ripples, given as a gift to Empress Dowager Chongqing on her sixtieth birthday, further legitimizing the project. The reconstruction of this garden began soon afterward; an edict was announced by Guangxu in 1886 to officially rename it the Garden of Nurturing Harmony (Yihe yuan) in commemoration of Cixi's retirement from her second regency (fig. 6).[42]

Cixi's relationship with Guangxu was complex. She appointed the renowned scholars Weng Tonghe (1830–1904) and Li Hongzao (1820–1897) as his mentors; these men had played a similar role for Tongzhi and encouraged the young emperor to rule with compassion and ambition. And yet Cixi also forced Guangxu to marry her niece in order to establish a tie between her Yehe Nara clan and the royal Aisin Gioro clan. Guangxu's obedience to Cixi did not survive long after his marriage and assumption of direct rule in 1889. Stung by the humiliating defeat in the Sino-Japanese War in 1895, Guangxu realized the urgent need for political change. Under the influence of radical advisers, Guangxu announced wholesale reforms in 1898. Conservative officials and moderates concerned about the impact of these policies rallied around Cixi in the hopes of having them rescinded. The ensuing political storm ended with Cixi's return to the Forbidden City from the Garden of Nurturing Harmony, her ordering the house arrest of Guangxu, and the initiation of her third regency in 1898. This sequence of events fundamentally overturned the traditional connection between filial piety and the regency of an empress dowager.[43] This time, Cixi's regency was anything but placid due to mounting antiforeign sentiment in China that erupted into the Boxer Uprising of 1900. After several foreign-born citizens were killed in China, eight nations responded by sending troops to Beijing, forcing the Qing court to flee to Xi'an in central China, where it remained for two years. With Cixi's role in the quelling of Guangxu's radical reform still fresh, her international reputation plunged, as exemplified by a horrifying caricature on the cover of the French tabloid *Le Rire* (fig. 7).

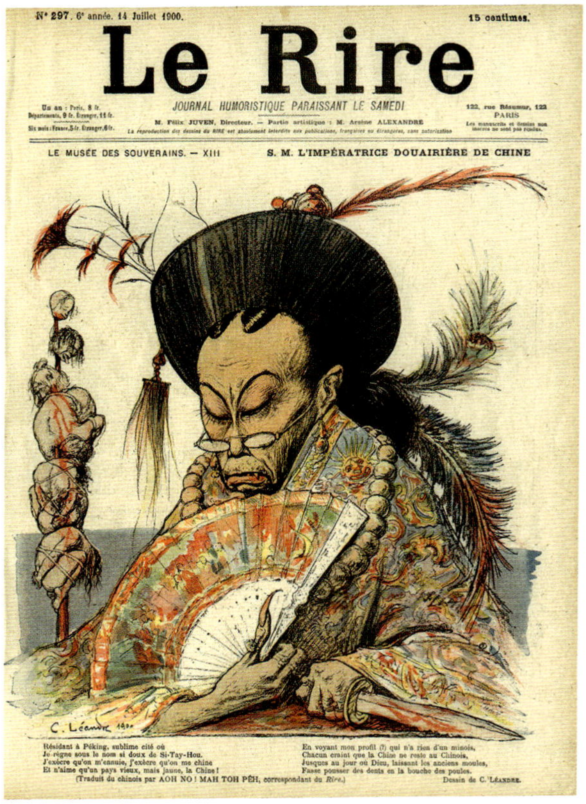

FIGURE 7
Caricature of Empress Dowager Cixi by Charles Lucien Léandre (France, 1862–1934) on the cover of *Le Rire* 6, no. 297 (July 14, 1900). Image courtesy of Freer Gallery of Art and Arthur M. Sackler Gallery Archives, Smithsonian Institution, Washington, DC.

Such smear campaigns did not scare away all the female members of the foreign delegations in Beijing. Sarah Conger (1843–1932), the wife of the US ambassador to China, was particularly curious about this formidable woman and soon cultivated a close relationship with her, as documented in a photograph from just after the turn of the twentieth century (see p. 47, fig. 12). It shows Cixi surrounded by a group of Western women, with Conger, standing to Cixi's left, the only one in physical contact with the empress dowager. In 1903 Conger proposed that Cixi sit for an oil portrait to be displayed the following year at the world's fair in St. Louis, recommending the painter Katharine A. Carl for the commission.[44] According to Cixi's lady-in-waiting Yu Deling (1885–1944), the proposal seemed odd to Cixi, as in China there was no such tradition of displaying the ruler's portrait in public; in fact, any exhibition of the image of a woman with high social standing was considered unethical.[45] Nonetheless, Cixi agreed, very likely because she was aware the portrait would help improve her reputation and that of the Qing dynasty abroad.

Carl's account of her almost yearlong stay in China opens a window on life behind the tall red walls of the imperial precincts.[46] One incident in Carl's memoir captures the power

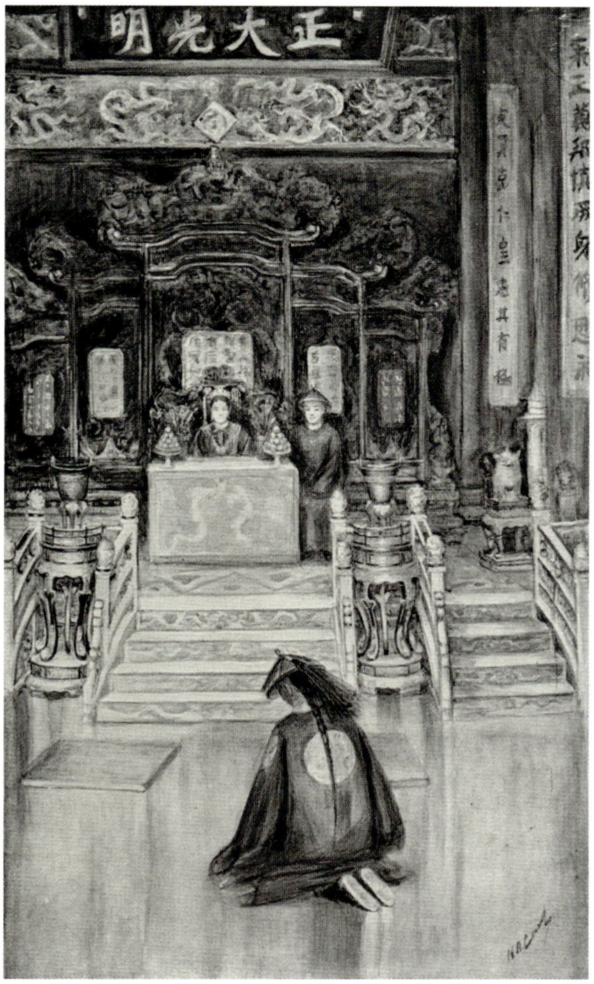

FIGURE 8
Empress Dowager Cixi holding an audience in the Palace of Heavenly Purity of the Forbidden City by Katharine A. Carl (United States, 1865–1938). About 1904; from Carl 1905, 146.

dynamic at court: upon the invitation of the empress dowager, the painter entered the prestigious Palace of Heavenly Purity (Qianqing gong) in the Forbidden City to observe the audience Cixi and Guangxu held jointly with court officials (fig. 8).[47] Cixi sat on a large throne in the center of the room, while the pale and quiet Guangxu was seated on a smaller throne. No screen or device of any type separated the reporting male officials from the matriarch, underscoring Cixi's flouting of Confucian norms, which forbade women from revealing themselves to men other than relatives. Whether a performance arranged for a foreign guest or a routine occurance, in this account she was the embodiment of subversive female agency.

In the course of determining her posture for the portrait and choosing accoutrements for it, Cixi became fascinated by photography.[48] Impressed with the convenience and striking realism of the medium, the empress dowager had the photographer Yu Xunling (1874–1943) take a wide variety of pictures: formal portraits that she gave away (fig. 9), images for her own pleasure (fig. 10), and studies for Carl's portrait. In these studies Cixi is shown with a kerchief and a spittoon by her side, indicating the informality of the photo sessions.[49] The finished oil portrait shares a nearly identical composition with the studies (pl. 46): a frontal view of Cixi with her hands hidden beneath her sleeves, a signature posture in formal portraits since the Ming dynasty. Yet the sharp persona and individuality one observes in the photo portraits is all but missing from the painting,[50] where Cixi appears flat and stiff, her face masked with a benevolent and youthful mien deemed necessary for the improvement of her reputation. Such artificiality was rooted in a rigid conformity with tradition—seen not just in Cixi's pose but also in the presence in the picture of nine phoenixes, the mythical creature symbolizing the power of the empress. This blend of elements reveals Cixi's attitude toward oil painting and Western civilization at large: Occidental practices and ideas were welcome to supplement and aid China's progress, but the core of Chinese and Manchu tradition and values would not be challenged.

Conclusion

The principle of filial piety variously aided, shaped, and limited the involvement of imperial women in court politics over the three centuries of the Qing dynasty. The achievement of Xiaozhuang as an empress and politician, assisting two young emperors to establish and stabilize Qing rule and prepare the dynasty for an ensuing golden age, was praised in *Draft History of the Qing* (*Qingshi gao*). However, this tribute acknowledges that her engagement with politics had been informal and was

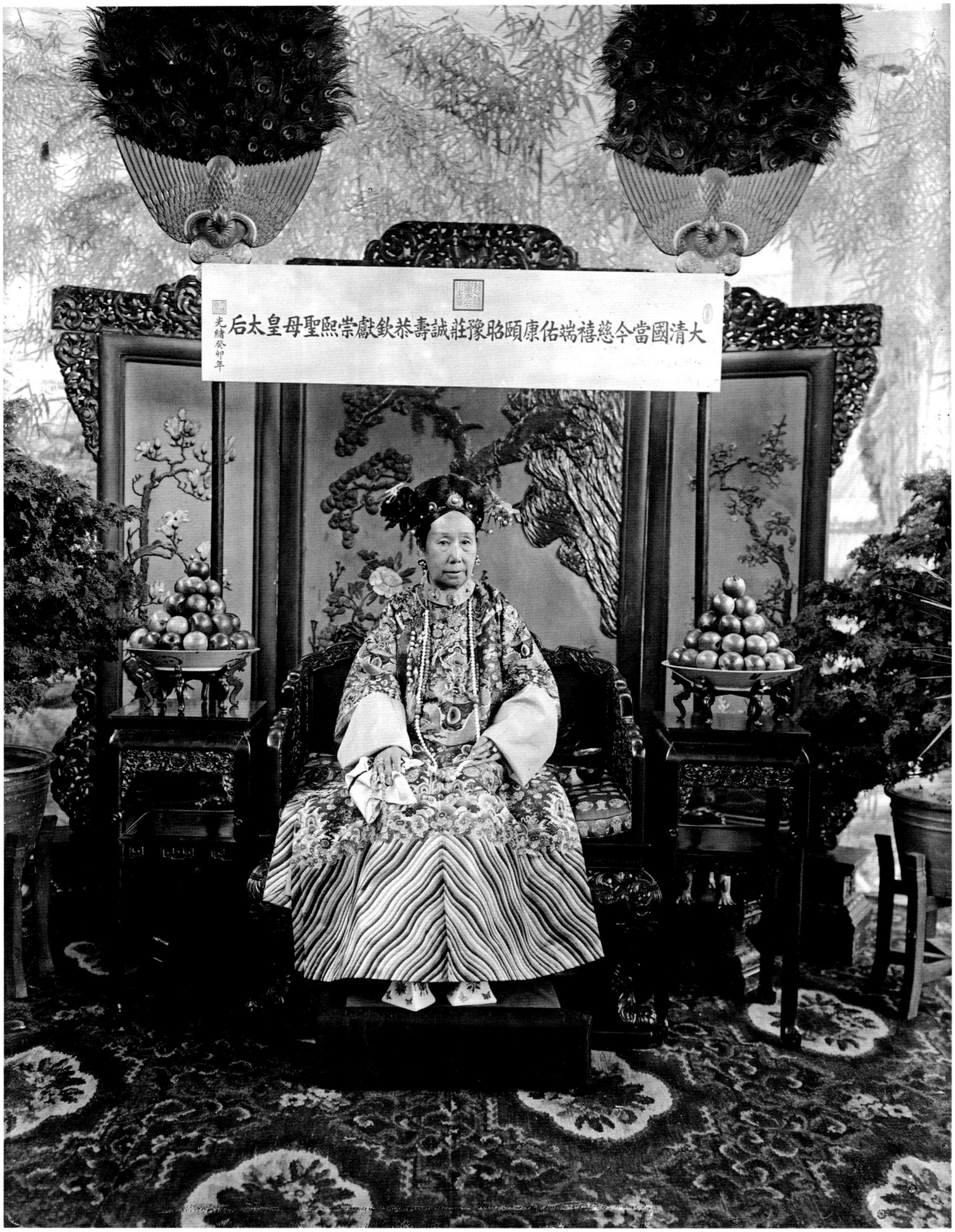

FIGURE 9
Empress Dowager Cixi. Photographed by Yu Xunling (1874–1943), Guangxu period, 1903–05, print from glass-plate negative, 9½ × 7 in. (24.1 × 17.8 cm), Freer Gallery of Art and Arthur M. Sackler Gallery Archives, FSA A.13 SC-GR-262, Smithsonian Institution, Washington, DC, purchase.

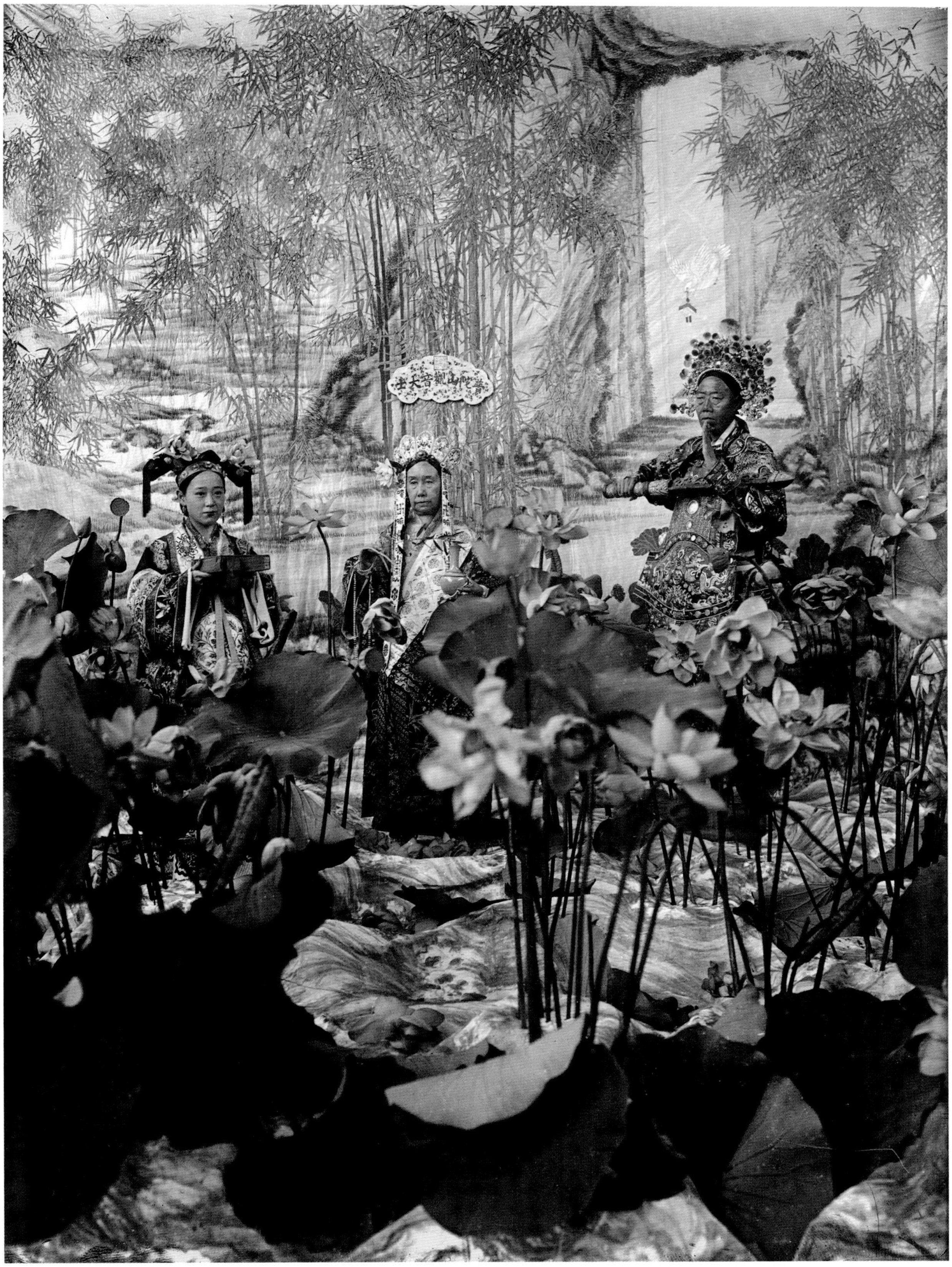

FIGURE 10

Empress Dowager Cixi in the guise of the bodhisattva Avalokiteshvara (Guanyin). Photographed by Yu Xunling (1874–1943), Guangxu period, 1903, print from glass-plate negative, 9½ × 7 in. (24.1 × 17.8 cm), Freer Gallery of Art and Arthur M. Sackler Gallery Archives, FSA A.13 SC-GR-246, Smithsonian Institution, Washington, DC, purchase.

tied to the Kangxi emperor's filial deeds. Chongqing's potential was suppressed due to the Qianlong emperor's political maneuvers, which fixed her as a mere symbol of his virtue as a devoted son. By contrast, Cixi's effective rulership, while springing from and facilitated by similar notions of filial piety, eventually grew so powerful as to detach itself from the actions of her son and nephew and consequently drew sharp criticism that associated her ambition with the fall of the Qing empire.[51] Such a stance reflected the lingering male anxiety over women's participation in politics. Yet that disquiet with the role of women at court would soon be swept aside. Not long after Cixi died in 1908, China's last dynasty would be replaced by the Republic of China. In the next decades, women in China would step out of the inner quarters and participate in politics as individuals rather than as annexes to men who wielded authority in the name of filial piety.

Notes

1 The regency of Empress Liu (968–1033) of the Northern Song exemplified male officials' anxiety and imperial women's awareness of keeping a low profile to secure their political power. Ruling on behalf of her adopted son, the Renzong emperor (r. 1022–1063), Liu took scrupulous precautions to avoid being compared with Empress Wu (624–705), whose enthronement interrupted the continuation of the Tang dynasty for fourteen years. For her expression of power in art, see Lee 2010, 23–69.

2 Holmgren 1991, 86.

3 Rawski 2009, 113–14.

4 One example of this cultural exchange was costume. The Manchus used fabrics decorated with various patterns, most of which they traded with or looted from their Han Chinese neighbors. Yi Min-hwan (1573–1649) 1978, 43.

5 Duindam 2016, 37–38.

6 Like their Han Chinese counterparts, the Manchus also adopted polygamy. A Manchu man could marry multiple wives, but the primary wife was almost always Manchu or Mongol. Elliott 2001, 254–55.

7 For instance, the levirate, a symbol of barbarism in Han Chinese eyes, was not forbidden until 1631 and 1636, with the exception of the marriages of Hong Taiji's half-sister and daughter. Rawski 2009, 114.

8 Among the most powerful candidates for the throne were Hong Taiji's brother Dorgon and his eldest son, Hooge (1609–1648). The former received endorsements from a majority of the Deliberative Council of Princes and Ministers, the most authoritative advisory body for Qing emperors at the time. However, Dorgon declined and insisted on sending one of Hong Taiji's sons to the throne. The decision to install the child Shunzhi emperor and appoint Dorgon as one of two regents was thereby the result of accommodating the wishes of Dorgon and other powerful Manchu aristocrats. Dennerline 2002, 73–78.

9 This tension is reflected in the lengthy descriptions of Shunzhi's dispute with officials over the divorces, accounts that contrast with the brief record of his interactions with Empress Xiaozhuang in *Draft of Qing History* (*Qingshi gao*), which mentioned only the promotion of her father in 1654 and his gift of thirty poems to celebrate Xiaozhuang's birthday in 1657. Zhao Erxun 1960, 948.

10 According to *Draft of Qing History*, Xiaozhuang would remind Kangxi not to ignore the Manchu military tradition, but she also admired the Manchu translation of Confucian classics that Kangxi presented to her. Zhao Erxun 1960, 948.

11 S. Wu 1979, 52.

12 Zhao Erxun 1960, 948.

13 Zhao Erxun 1960, 948.

14 For a discussion of Xiaozhuang's views of religion and politics, see Lin Shih-Hsuan 2011.

15 After the Kangxi reign, only two empresses came from Mongol lineage: Empress Xiaojing (1812–1855) of the Daoguang emperor (r. 1821–50) and Empress Xiaozhe (1854–1875) of the Tongzhi emperor. It should be noted that while the Qing imperial harem generally had more flexibility than the Ming, virtuous Han Chinese women would serve as role models for Qing imperial women. Sometimes stories of the virtuous women were painted to decorate the palaces in the inner court. Zhu 2008, 55.

16 Zhao Erxun 1960, 949–50.

17 Zhao Erxun 1960, 62.

18 *Gaozong shilu* 1968, 163.

19 Zhao Erxun 1960, 42.

20 Qinghua 2000, 32–34; Peng 2017, 197–98.

21 Stuart and Rawski 2001, 83–84.

22 This large painting was recently identified in Lin Shu 2015a, 54–66.

23 Although both empresses received the title of empress dowager, the fact that Ci'an was Xianfeng's primary wife while Cixi was a lower-ranking consort made the former superior to the latter in terms of the hierarchy in the inner court.

24 Xu Che 1994, 107–08.

25 The execution of Xianfeng's advisers was deemed necessary by Cixi, for they represented a political force strongly opposed to her regency. Moreover, she could fill the vacancy with officials loyal to the new regents, which was critical to the solidification of her early regency. Xu Che 1994, 147–51.

26 Xu Che 1994, 286–88.

27 Wu Xiangxiang 1969, 6.

28 Wang Cheng-hua 2012b, 248–49.

29 Manchus generally adopted the practice of their Han Chinese counterparts in women's education. Girls were taught to read at young ages, and then they were introduced to the *Four Books for Women* (*Nü sishu*), readings intended to prepare them for marriage. This emphasis on education can be observed in the works of female Manchu poets, too. Idema 2017, 21–22.

30 Zhao Zhongfu 1970, 528, 531, 589, 606.

31 Although it might seem unremarkable for a young man (and an emperor!) to challenge the authority of his mother, Cixi's strong personality and political authority made Tongzhi's resistance noteworthy. His decision soon backfired as Cixi limited the amount of time he spent with his empress on the grounds it would "impede his political responsibility." Xu Che 1994, 233–34.

32 Wang Cheng-hua 2012b, 249–50.

33 Wang Cheng-hua 2012b, 251.

34 ZGDYLSDAG 1991, 628. This unfinished reconstruction project was detailed in Liu Dunzhen 1933, 287–390.

35 For an analysis of Tongzhi's political agenda, see Mokros 2012.

36 For more on the design and decoration of this palace, see Peng 2002, 57–70.

37 Although the reconstruction project was called off, the porcelain commission was completed. Most of the Daya zhai porcelains are in the collections of the Palace Museum. For the publication of most types of the Daya zhai ware, see Gugong bowuyuan 2007; Gugong bowuyuan and Shoudu bowuguan 2013.

38 Hsieh 2003, 7–8.

39 Li Yuhang 2012, 117.

40 Li Yuhang 2011, 192.

41 *Neiwufu dang'an* [Archives of the Imperial Household Department], vol. 4602, cited in Ye Zhiru and Tang Yinian 1986, 111.

42 *Dezong shilu* 1963, 47:37–38.

43 Xu Che 1994, 352–55.

44 Conger 1909, 247–48.

45 Yu Deling served as Cixi's lady-in-waiting between 1902 and 1904 and is more famously known as Princess Der Ling. Her many publications in English helped push the interest in late Qing court life in early twentieth-century United States. Der Ling 1911, 199–201.

46 According to the recollection of Yu Deling, she and her sister chaperoned the painter to prevent Carl from receiving any information about the Qing court beyond that which Cixi authorized. Der Ling 1911, 207–09.

47 Carl 1905, 142–48.

48 Yu Deling claimed that she explained the process of sitting for an oil portrait and introduced photo portraiture to Cixi. The viability of her statement is questionable because quite a number of high officials and Manchu aristocrats close to Cixi, such as Prince Gong and Prince Chun, had photo portraits taken before Yu Deling began her short career in the inner court, making it unlikely that Cixi was unaware of this form of portraiture. Der Ling 1911, 214–17.

49 Peng 2013, 161.

50 Wang Cheng-hua 2012a, 142–44.

51 Zhao Erxun 1960, 951.

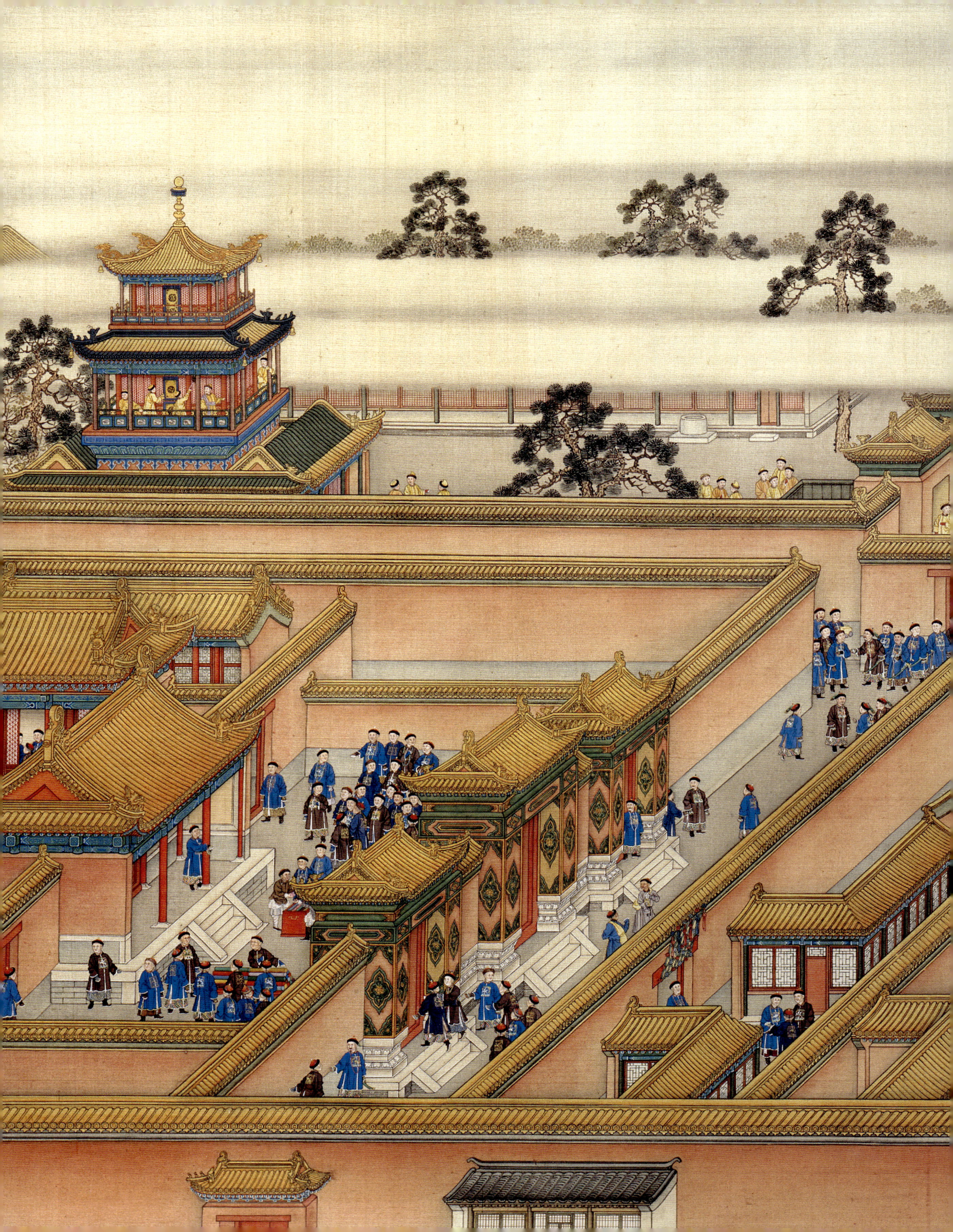

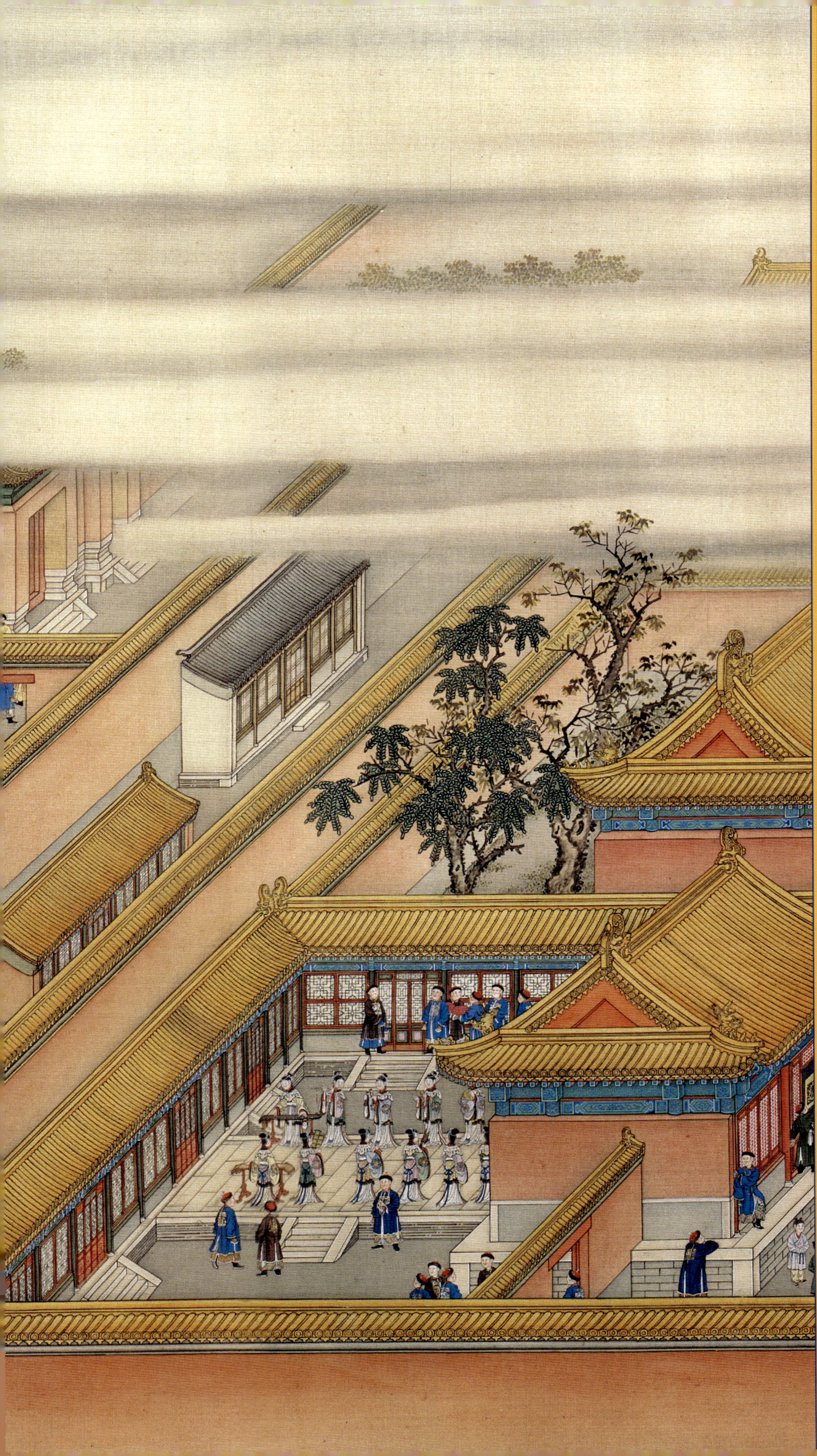

PLATES

PLATE 1

清乾隆　孝賢純皇后吉服半身像油畫屏

Empress Xiaoxian

Probably Giuseppe Castiglione (Lang Shining; Italy, 1688–1766) and other court painters, Beijing
Qianlong period, about 1736
Panel, oil on paper; frame: wood covered with silk brocade
Cat. 37

Here, Empress Xiaoxian, the beloved wife of the Qianlong emperor, is shown wearing the winter dress and hat of the Qing court in a bust-length portrait. It is not clear whether this portrait was made to be displayed or as a study for another portrait. In style and pose it contrasts with portraits intended for display in the Hall of Imperial Longevity (Shouhuang dian), where family rituals venerating ancestors were conducted. Such a formal portrait would have depicted her full figure, seated on a throne, and wearing all of the regalia of the court—including a court robe and vest, a phoenix headdress, and three necklaces (see Daisy Yiyou Wang's essay, pp. 88–109).[1]

The three-dimensional modeling of the face, the naturalistic folds of the robe as it drops from the empress's shoulders, and the use of oil pigments on paper all evince the European painting techniques and media found in palace art produced during the eighteenth century. At that time a group of Jesuits—including Jean Denis Attiret (France, 1702–1768); Ignatius Sichelbarth (Bohemia, 1708–1780); and Giuseppe Castiglione, who served three emperors from 1715 to 1765—worked alongside artists trained in Chinese techniques under Qianlong's supervision in the Wish-Fulfilling Studio (Ruyi guan), part of the imperial painting academy.[2] Instituted at the beginning of his reign, the studio enabled the emperor to carry out many pathbreaking artistic projects, from the construction of a European-style manor in the Garden of Perfect Brightness (Yuanming yuan) to Castiglione's painting of the young ruler with his imperial consorts (now held by the Cleveland Museum of Art; see p. 103, fig. 18), to which this painting bears a close resemblance. (ESR)

1 Nie Chongzheng 2008.
2 On the Wish-Fulfilling Studio and its painters, see Ho and Bronson 2004, 222–23.

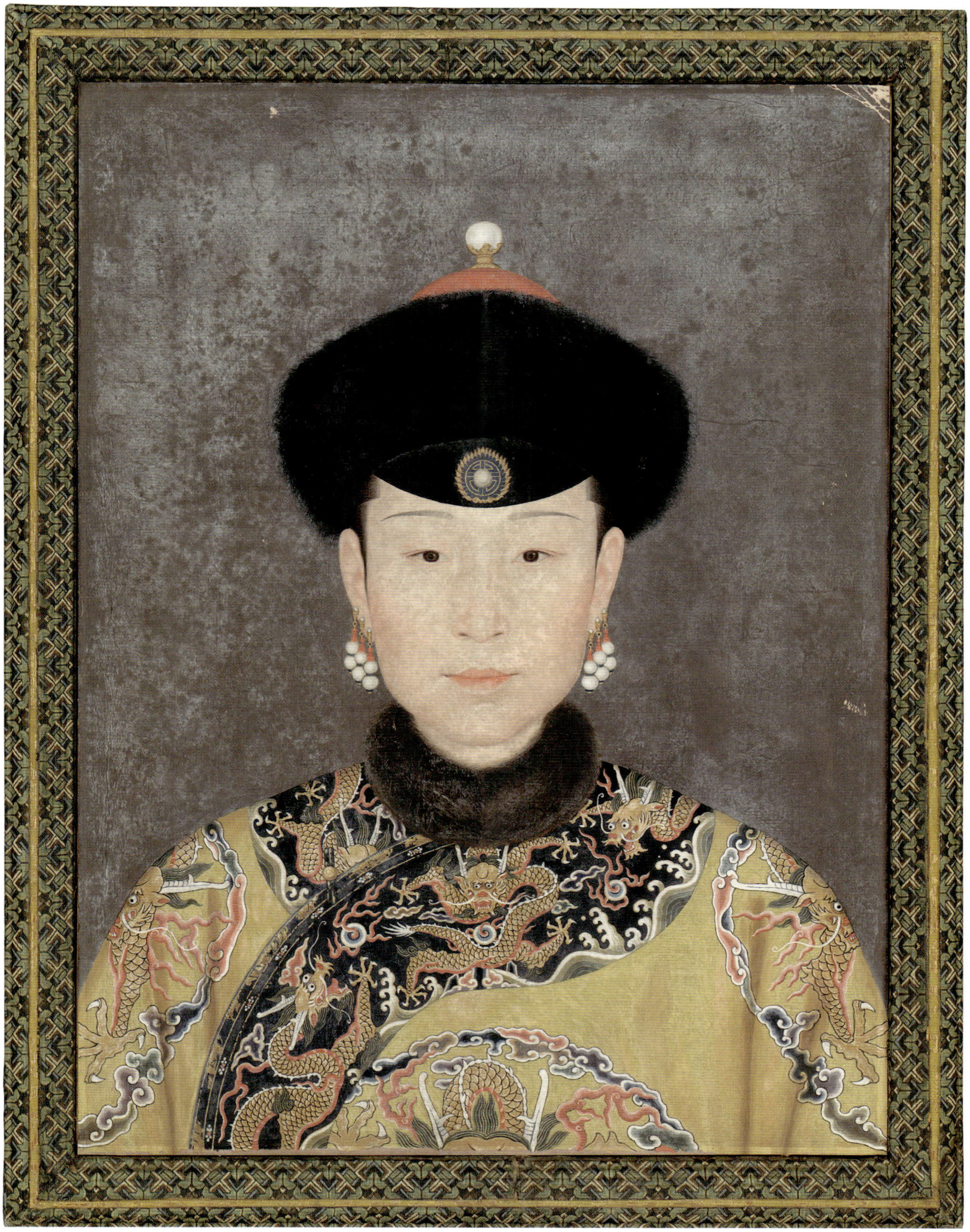

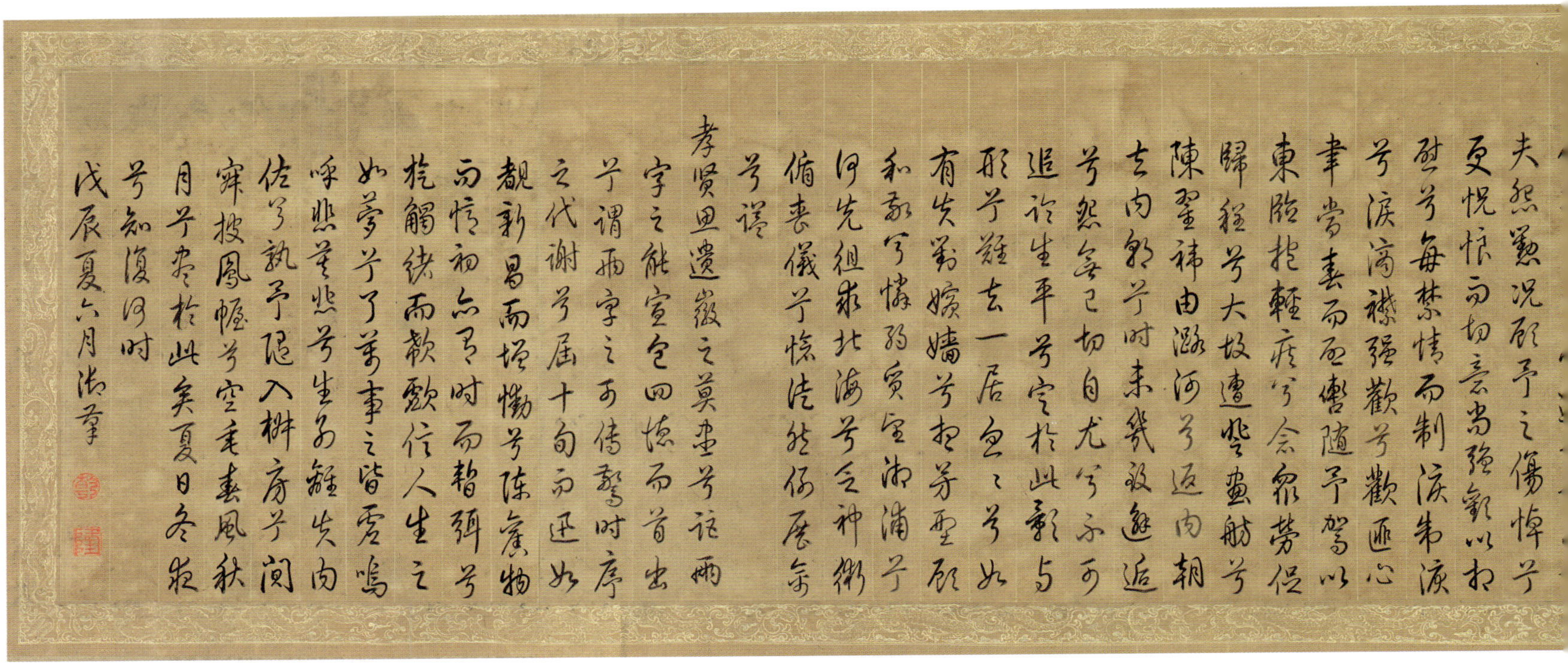

PLATE 2

清乾隆　御筆述悲賦卷

Expressing My Grief

The Qianlong emperor (1711–1799)
Qianlong period, 1748
Handscroll, ink on paper
Cat. 26

This poem—notable for its emotional intensity, literary grandeur, and prosodic splendor—was written by the Qianlong emperor to express his deep sorrow over the death of his beloved wife Empress Xiaoxian. More than a dutiful spouse, Xiaoxian was Qianlong's childhood sweetheart, a soul mate with whom he shared his thoughts and feelings and who had stayed by his bedside for months when he was seriously ill. She was a caring and thoughtful daughter-in-law and a wise, diligent manager of imperial family affairs who garnered respect and gratitude from all, from imperial consorts to maidservants.

In 1748 Xiaoxian, heartbroken by the recent loss of her two-year-old son, fell ill while touring eastern China with her husband. After resting for a few days, she said she felt better and urged the entourage to continue the journey so that she would not burden her fellow travelers. Yet one night soon thereafter, while traveling on a boat, she died. Qianlong never again formed a similarly close attachment with any of the other consorts, although they did bear him twenty-seven children.

In his first three months of mourning, Qianlong visited Xiaoxian in her coffin more than fifty times to perform commemorative rites.[1] One day he entered her residence and, holding her bed curtain, felt a profound emptiness and grief. He lamented, "I can well believe that life is a dream, / And that all things are but empty."

For this poem Qianlong chose to use a rare brown paper that had probably been made in the eleventh century and was usually reserved for Buddhist sutra writing or the frontispieces of prized paintings and calligraphy—a clear indication of the importance and sacredness of this work to the emperor. Qianlong composed more than 100 elegies to Xiaoxian, and he viewed this work again in the final years of his life. Considered a significant literary and calligraphic work, the elegy was recorded in *The Precious Collection of the Stone Moat (Shiqu baoji)*, a catalogue documenting important paintings and calligraphy in the Qing imperial collection.[2] (DYW)

During her funeral service,
　　I grieved to no avail.
In line with established custom,
　　She will be known posthumously as
　　　　The Filial and Virtuous.
In view of her unbounded goodness,
　　How might two words suffice?
Yet as her embodiment of the Four Virtues
　　was exemplary,

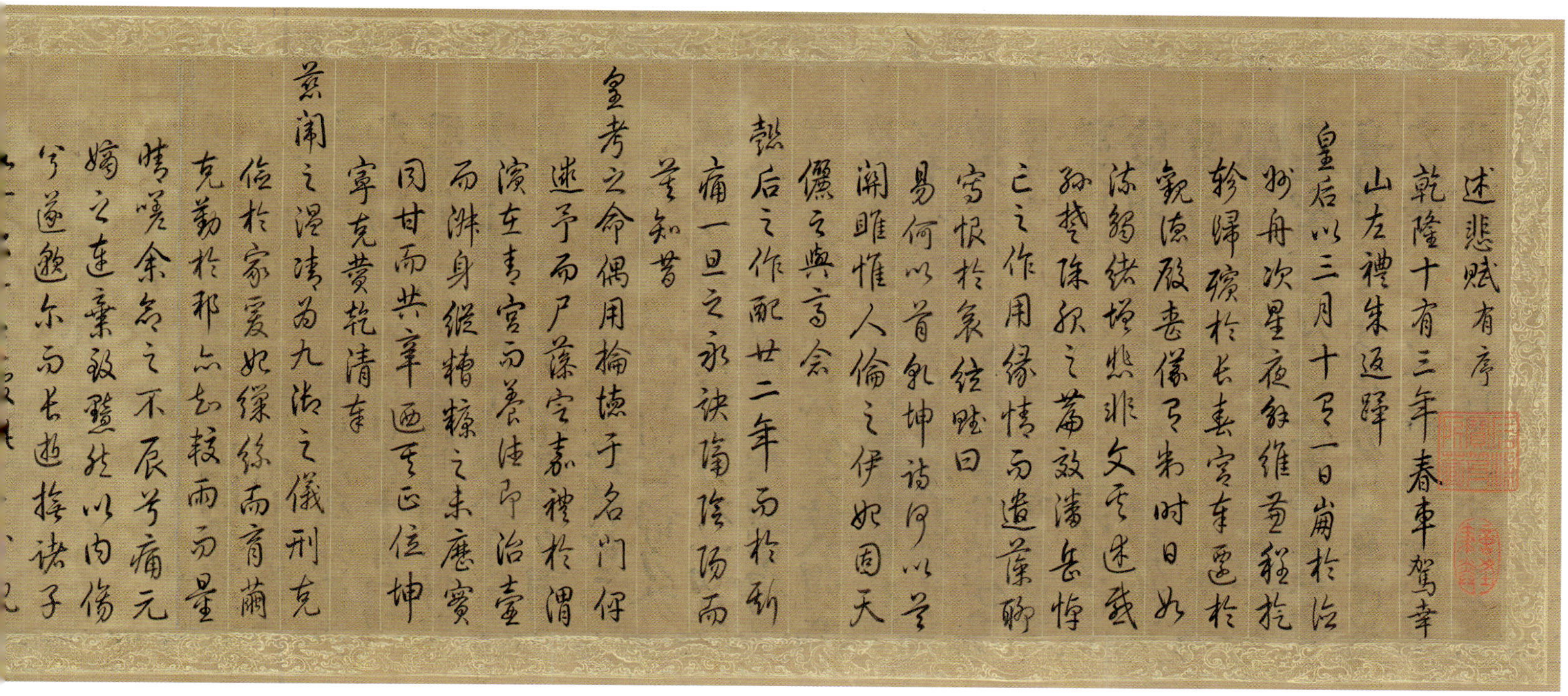

Let these two words convey her nobility
of spirit.
I am startled by the passage of time;
A hundred days have rapidly elapsed.
Seeing the new
Intensifies my sorrow,
While displaying the old
Reminds me of the beginning.
There are times when I find a brief respite,
Yet, before long, my feelings are affected
And I break down once more.
I can well believe that life is a dream,
And that all things are but empty.
Alas! Sorrow laced with sorrow;
To be separated in life!
Having lost my wife,
Who will follow me now?
When entering her bedroom,
I inhale sadness.
I climb behind her phoenix bed-curtains,
Yet they hang to no avail.
The romance of the spring breeze and
autumn moon
All ends here.
Summer days and winter nights spent
with her
Will never come again.

Written by the Imperial Hand this sixth lunar month in 1748.

Translated by Alister Inglis

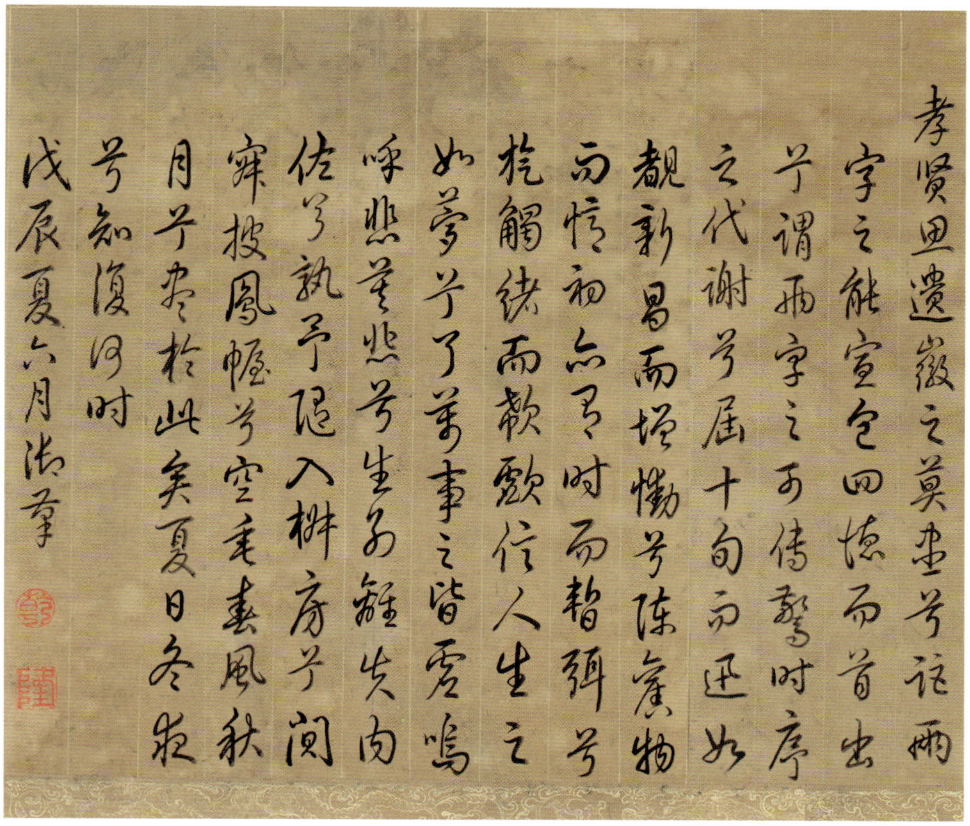

DETAIL, WITH THE QIANLONG EMPEROR'S SIGNATURE

1 ZGDYLSDAG 2002, 7:54–183.
2 *Qinding shiqu baoji xubian.*

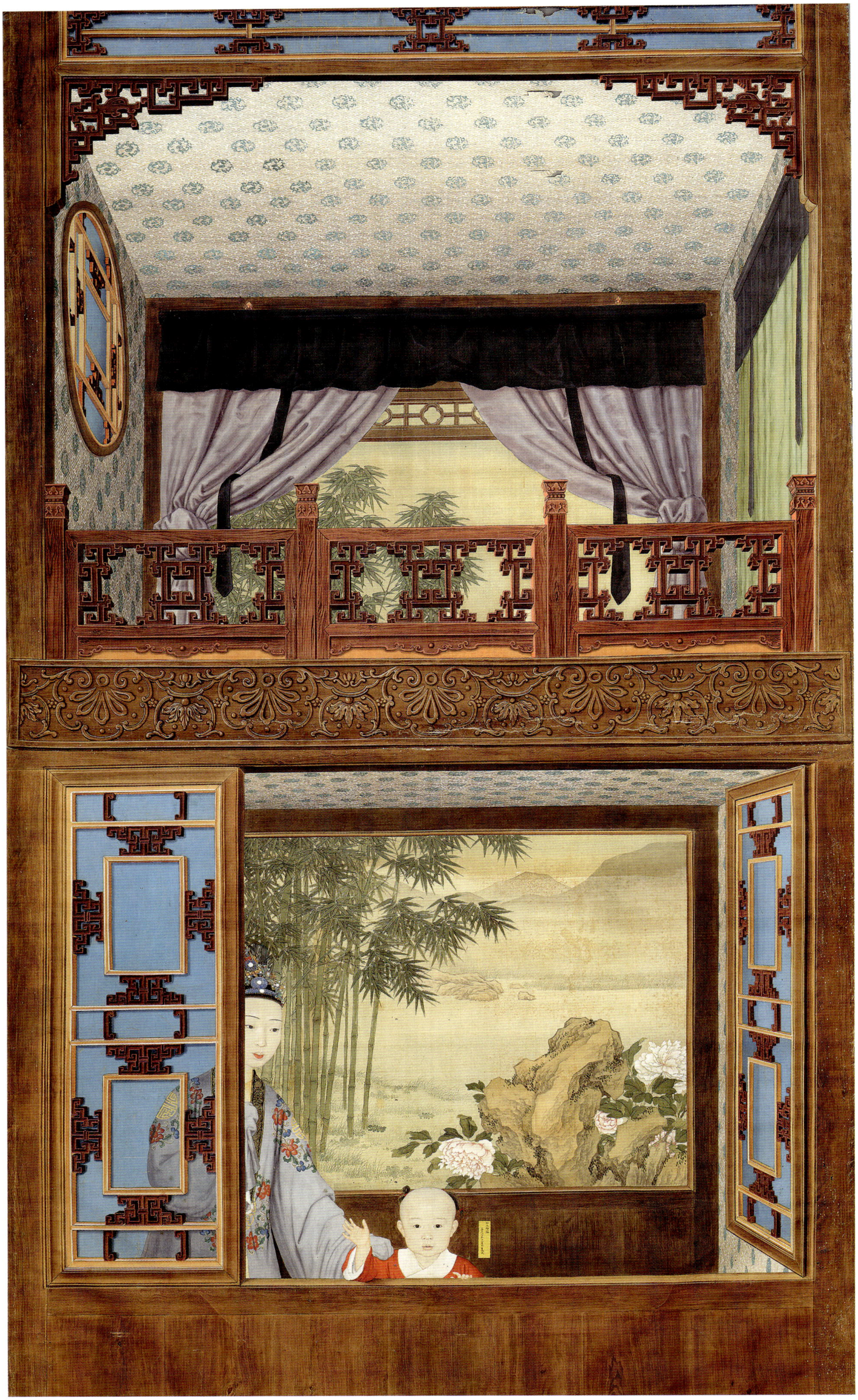

PLATE 3

清乾隆　乾隆帝妃與嘉慶帝幼年像貼落

Consort of the Qianlong emperor and the future Jiaqing emperor in his boyhood

Probably Giuseppe Castiglione (Lang Shining; Italy, 1688–1766) and other court painters, Beijing
Qianlong period, probably 1760s
Painting originally mounted on a wall (*tieluo*), ink and color on silk
Cat. 41

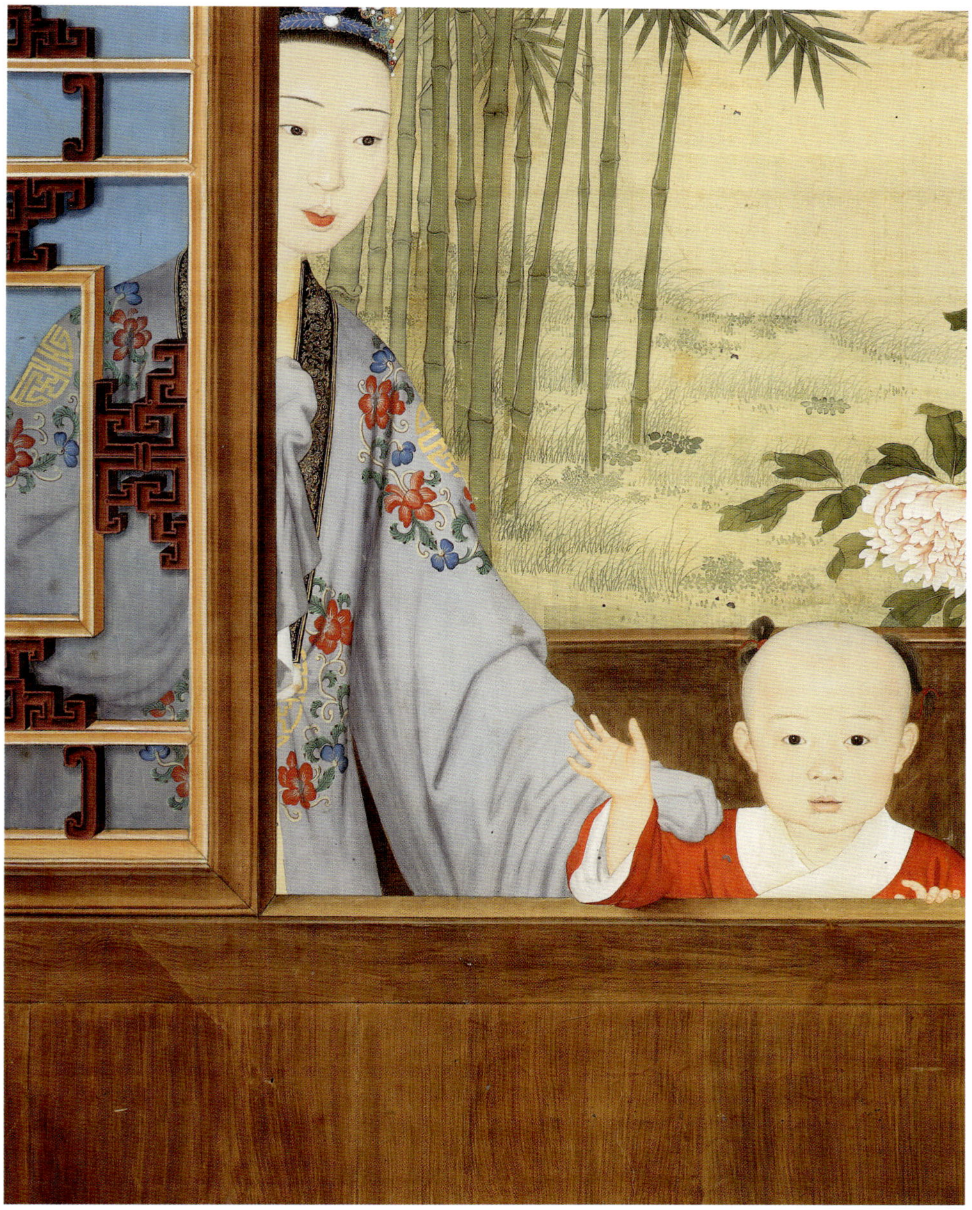

DETAIL

A boy barely tall enough to peek over the partition wall waves and looks directly at us in this painting. Beside him is an imperial consort who pats him gently on the shoulder while standing modestly behind a latticed screen window as if to avoid our gaze. A retrospectively affixed yellow tag on the painting tells us that the boy is the young prince Yongyan, who became the Jiaqing emperor. The woman is most likely Jiaqing's mother, the third-rank consort Ling (Ling *fei*; 1727–1775), wife of the Qianlong emperor.

This work is an example of a "scenic illusion painting" (*tongjing hua*), a genre produced by court artists in the eighteenth century using both Chinese and Western techniques and favored by Qianlong.[1] Images in these monumental wall-mounted paintings merged with the architectural surroundings in which they were installed and for which they were designed, creating seamless pictorial illusions of great depth and detail. This painting was originally mounted in the Studio for Contemplating the Future (Siyong zhai) in the Garden of Eternal Spring (Changchun yuan), a compound east of the Garden of Perfect Brightness (Yuanming yuan) frequented by Qianlong. As it was designed for the emperor's private use, the primary viewer of the painting would have been the emperor himself, and the boy in the painting, therefore, would have been waving to his father.[2]

Numerous court paintings depicting princes and their parents enjoying family life were produced during the Qianlong period.[3] This painting is unusual, however, as it portrays only one particular prince presumably with his mother, which points to Qianlong's fondness for Yongyan and Ling.[4] Although the emperor's intent in commissioning this work is open to debate, the painting acknowledges the significant role of the imperial mother in caring for and educating the future emperor. (DS)

1 "Scenic illusion painting" is a connotative translation devised by Kristina Kleutghen; see Kleutghen 2015, 3–6.

2 On the Studio for Contemplating the Future, see Kleutghen 2015, 124–32.

3 See, for example, two paintings in the Palace Museum by Castiglione and other court artists: *Qianlong Enjoying Himself at Spring Festival* (about 1736–37, Gu6506) and *Qianlong Enjoying Himself in Snowy Weather* (1738, Gu13904).

4 Consort Ling was posthumously given the title Empress Xiaoyi. The identity of the woman in this painting is still debated.

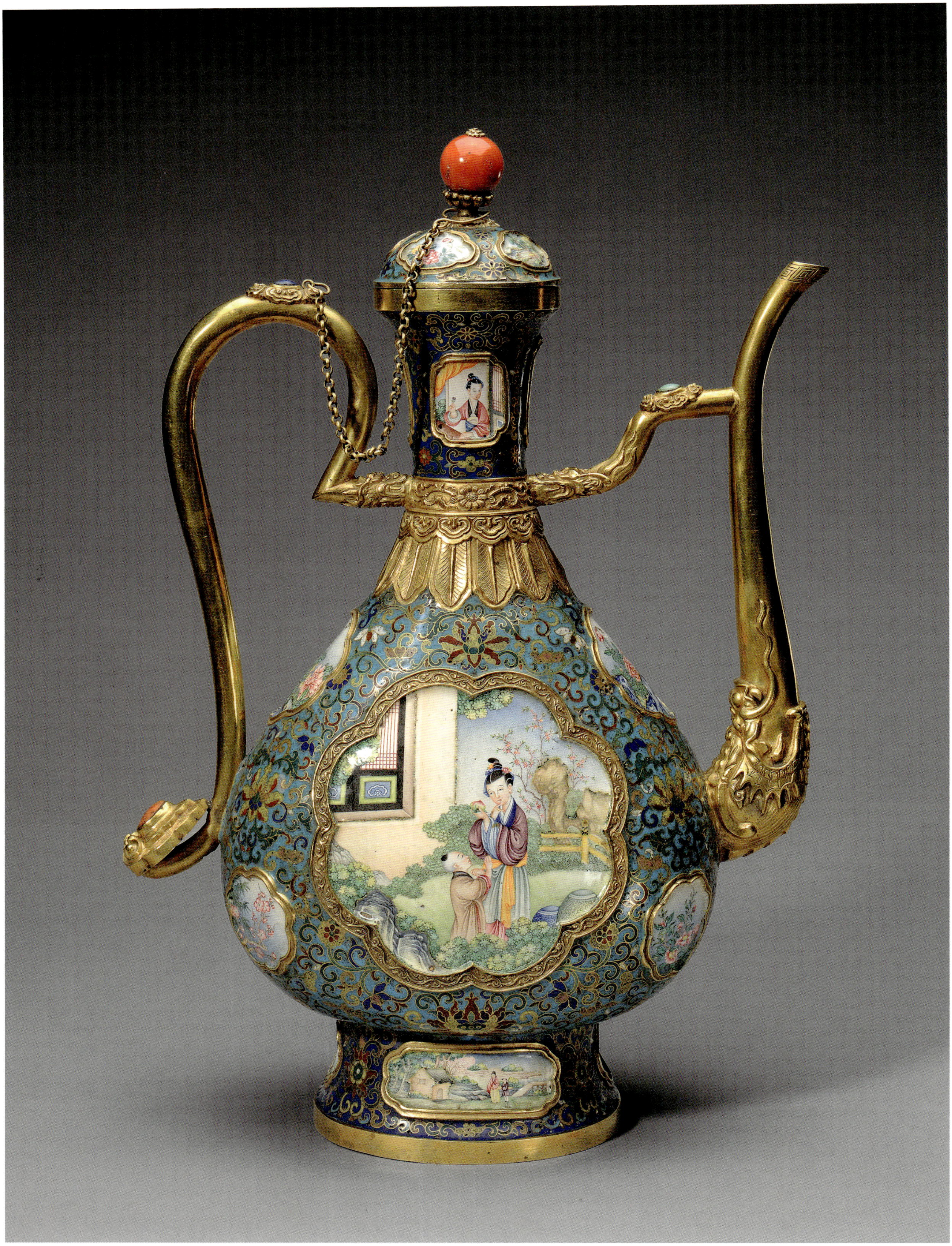

PLATE 4

清乾隆 金胎掐絲嵌畫琺瑯開光庭院母子圖執壺

Ewer with lady and boy in garden on two sides

Imperial Workshop, probably Beijing
Qianlong period, probably 1760s or 1770s
Cloisonné and painted enamel, copper and gold alloy with polychrome enamels and gilding, coral, turquoise, and lapis lazuli
Cat. 163

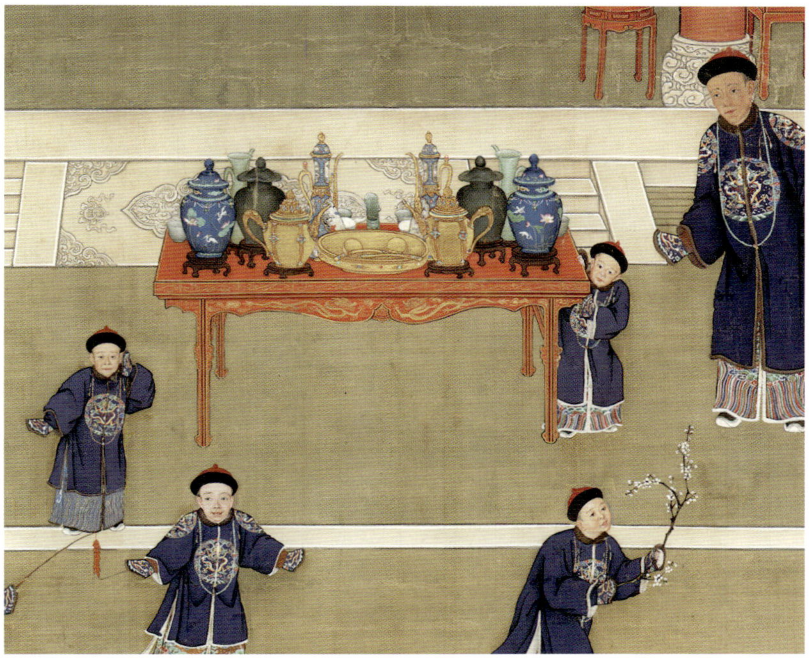

FIGURE 1

Celebrating Empress Dowager Chongqing's eightieth birthday (detail of pl. 7)

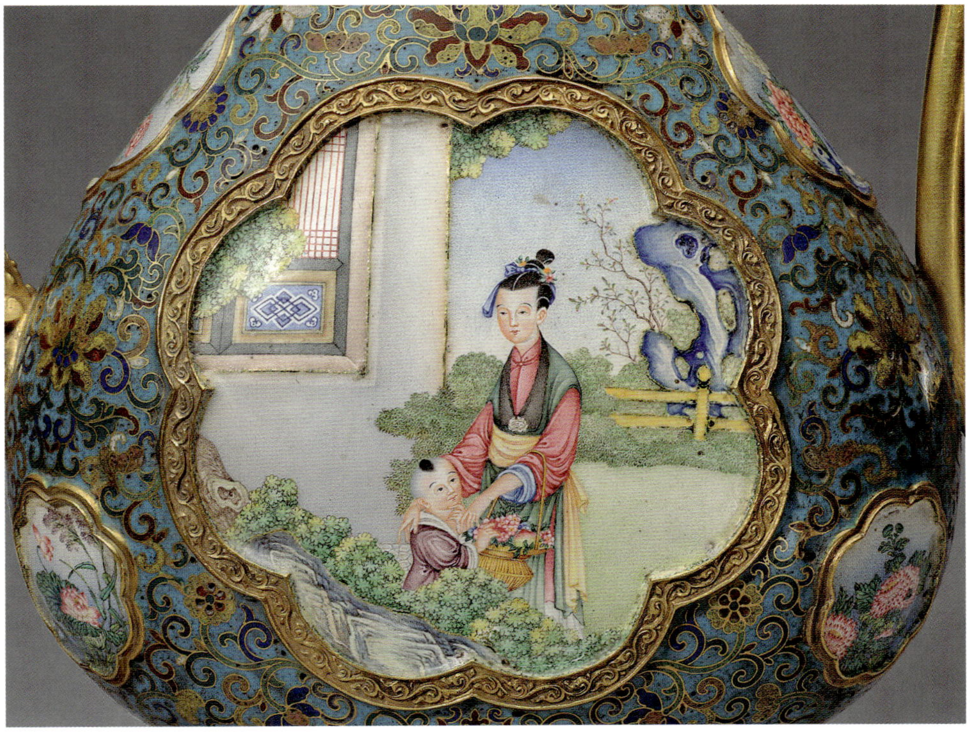

DETAIL, REVERSE

This wine ewer represents the apex of enamel decoration at the Qing court. The paintings in the two lobed cartouches were created with enamel pigments on metal, a technique introduced to China from Europe in the late seventeenth century. The cartouches are surrounded by cloisonné decoration, which involves filling small cells created by wires with colored enamel paste. The combination of the two methods was an innovation of the Qianlong period, when court art was characterized by a taste for sumptuous and complex surface textures and technical perfection.[1] A lid with a coral finial is attached by a chain to a handle in the shape of a wish-granting scepter (*ruyi*), and the spout emerges from the mouth of a dragon. While gilt details give the ewer a glittering appearance, the use of gold for the body under the enamel reveals the true lavishness of this vessel.

The paintings within the cartouches show a lady and a boy in a garden, a motif associated with fertility, motherly activities, and virtues widely depicted—and promoted—in Qing court art and popular visual culture. Ewers of this type bearing similar imagery appear in the painting of Empress Dowager Chongqing's eightieth birthday, where they are the tallest objects on a table laden with ladles, pots, jars, and cups (fig. 1). Although some scholars have proposed that gold-core enamelware was reserved solely for Qing emperors, its presence in the birthday painting suggests that high-ranking imperial women used it as well.[2] Furthermore, this particular ewer was once in the inventory of the Palace of Eternal Longevity (Yongshou gong), where high-status imperial women—including Chongqing—resided.[3] (DYW)

1 Quette 2011a, 14–15; Zhang Rong 2011, 163–67; Li Jiufang 2002, 107; Gugong bowuyuan 2011, 10–11, 157–59, 230.
2 Li Jiufang 2002, 215.
3 My thanks to Lin Shu for providing information about the Palace Museum reference number for this object, which indicates its location during the 1924–30 survey of the palace collection.

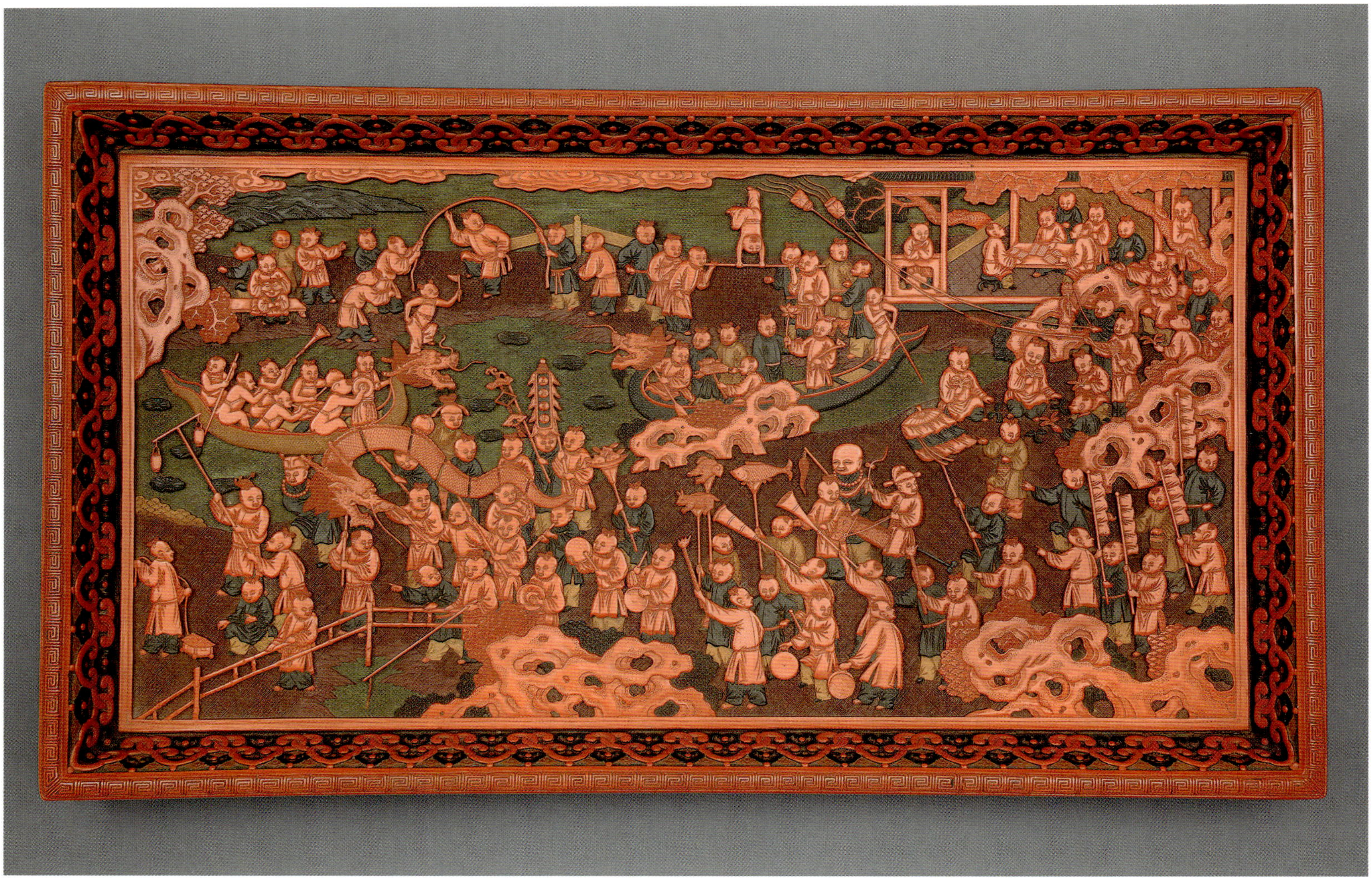

PLATE 5

清乾隆　剔彩百子晬盤

Tray with boys at play

Workshop, Suzhou
Qianlong period, 1742–43
Carved polychrome lacquer on wood core
Cat. 140

According to a Chinese folk custom, when a boy reached one year of age, he was asked to pick an object from a tray filled with books, abacuses, inksticks, brushes, and bows and arrows. The object he picked was considered a prediction of his future achievement. This practice, called the "first-year assessment" (*shizui*), was incorporated into Qing court culture, where it became a key early rite of passage.

This exquisite lacquer tray was made by a workshop in Suzhou and was most likely intended for use at the first-year assessments of young princes.[1] Decorated with children engaging in festive activities—such as racing dragon boats, performing the dragon dance, playing musical instruments, flying kites, and riding a hobbyhorse—this tray features an image of approximately 100 boys (*baizi tu*), a traditional motif that symbolizes the wish for an abundance of male heirs. These lively activities are juxtaposed with a portrayal of youngsters reading in a pavilion in the upper right corner, extolling the importance of cultivating the mind as well as the body.

Auspicious symbols appear throughout: a fish lantern conveys the notion of "overflowing abundance"; a boy riding a horse signifies success and reasserts the seminomadic roots and military prowess of the Manchu; and a wish-granting scepter (*ruyi*) combined with a stone chime (*qing*, a homophone of the Chinese word for happiness and celebration) form a rebus that means "fulfilling one's wish with happiness"—a prime example of the practice, prominent in imperial wares, of combining homophonic and visual icons to form auspicious meanings.

The lively expressions of the boys and meticulous details of the scene are revealed through the painstaking carving of the multilayered polychrome lacquer. This tray represents the height of craftsmanship and creativity in lacquerware production during the Qianlong period. It illustrates the importance of male heirs for the continuation of the imperial lineage—and the expectations placed on empresses and consorts to produce princes who might one day become emperor. (DS)

1 Zhang Rong 2012, 2:209.

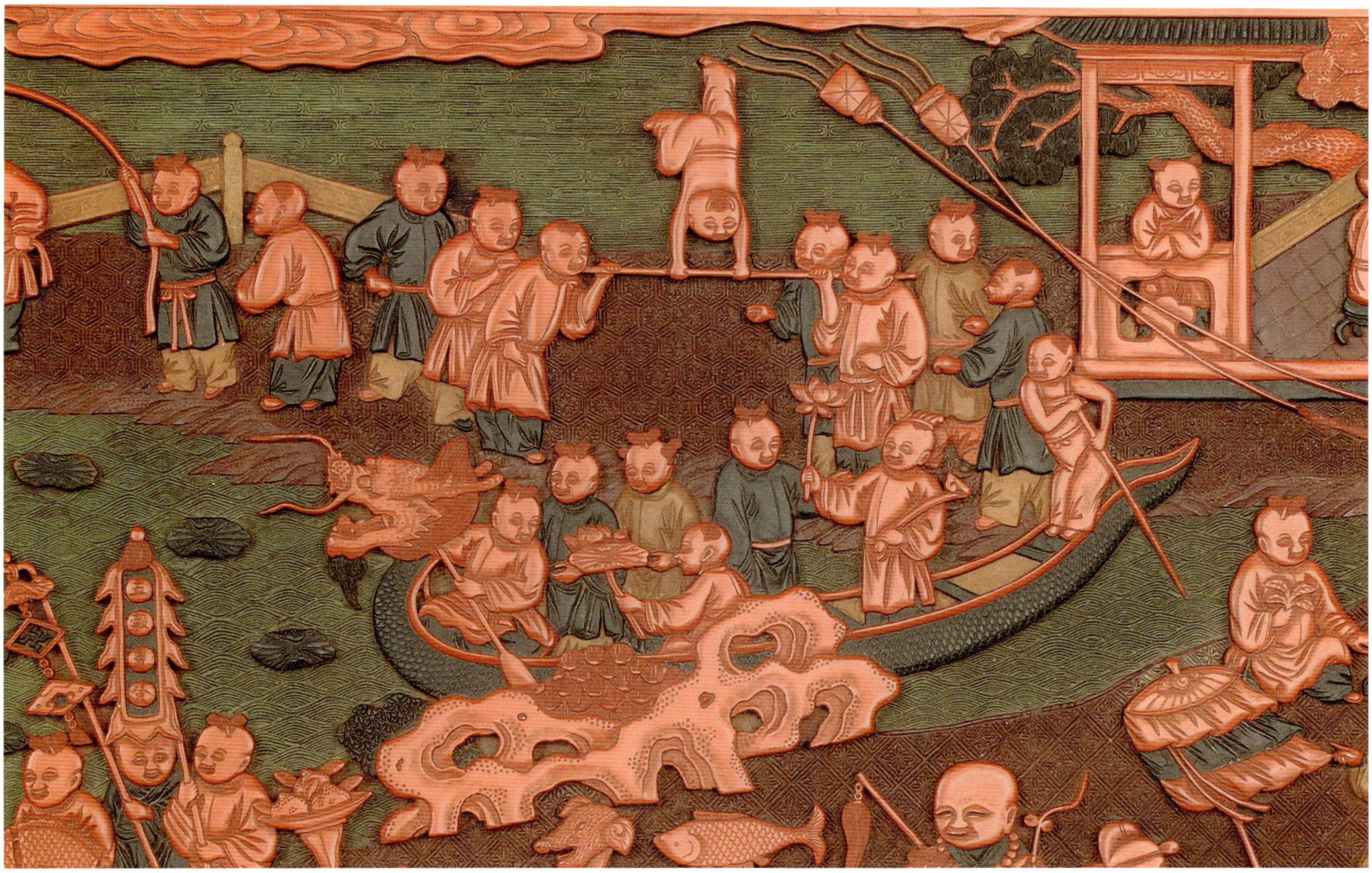

DETAIL

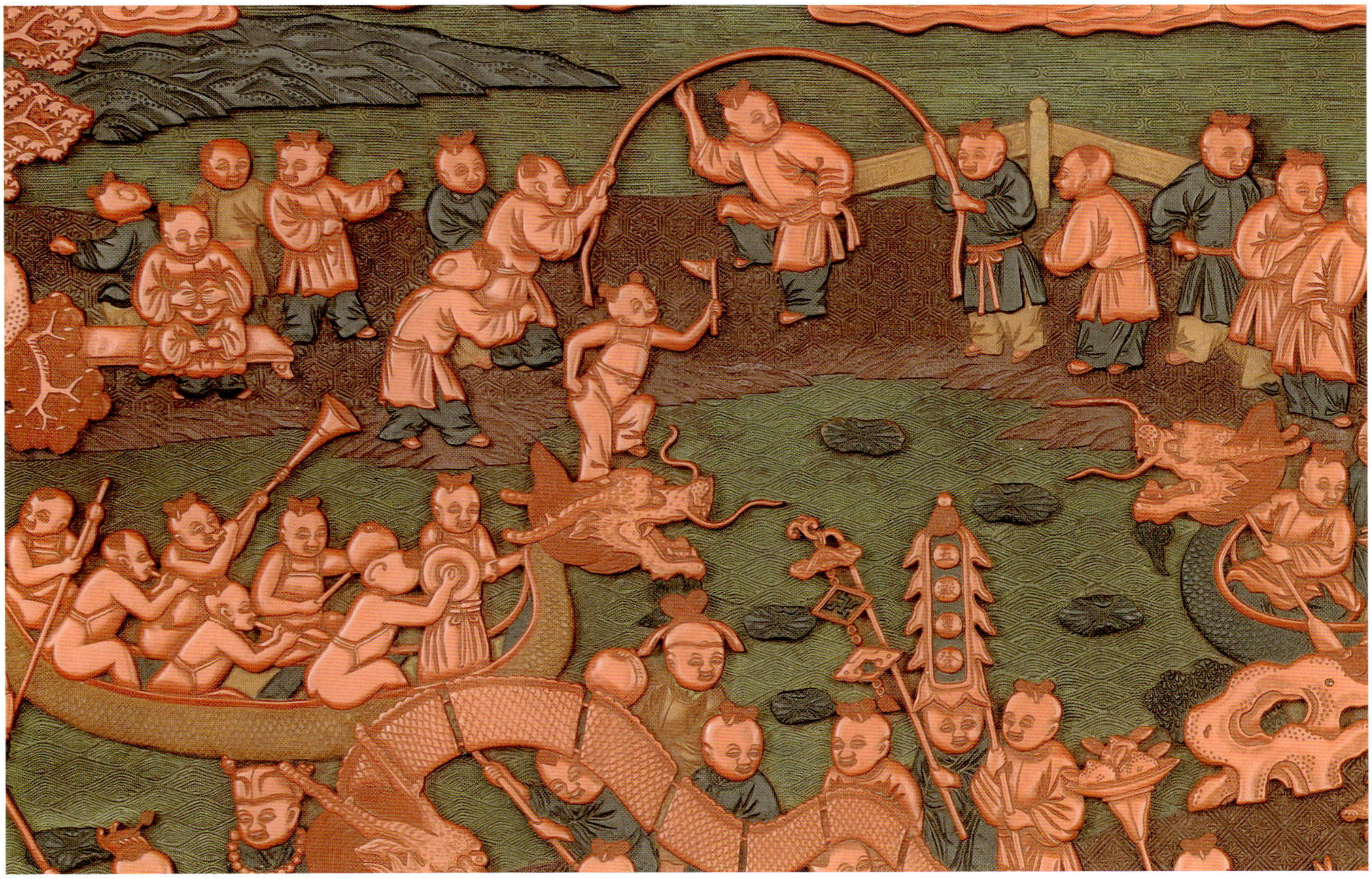

DETAIL

PLATE 6

清乾隆　鬥彩嬰戲圖玉壺春瓶

Vase with boys at play

Imperial Porcelain Factory, Jingdezhen
Qianlong period, 1736–95
Porcelain in joined-colors (*doucai*) technique, cobalt under colorless glaze and polychrome enamels over the glaze, with gold
Cat. 128

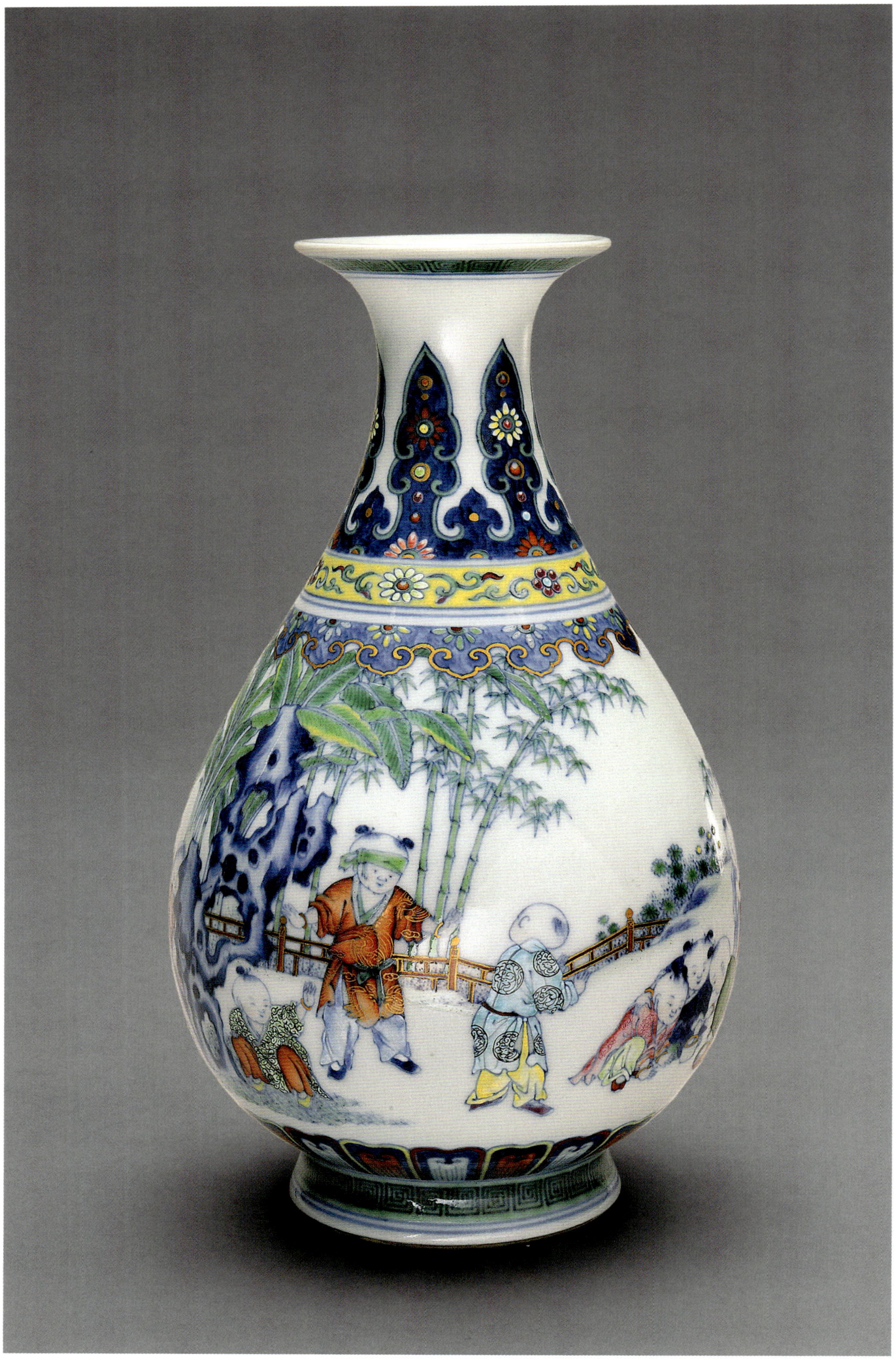

Joyous images of youths playing hide-and-seek, catching crickets, and swinging on a bamboo bar in a garden grace this elegantly shaped vase. The theme of boys at play was common in Chinese decorative arts and vernacular paintings illustrating scenes of everyday life. During the Ming (1368–1644) and Qing dynasties, imperial potters adopted this subject for court porcelains. In so doing, they broadened the types of activities depicted on their wares and created more complex compositions. The multitudes-of-boys motif expressed the value placed on male heirs and carries the wish for an exuberant and prosperous society.

This pear-shaped form is known as a "jade bottle for spring" (*yuhuchun ping*) and originally functioned as a container for wine; later adapted for imperial wares, it became a decorative vessel or a vase. This is an excellent example of the *doucai*, or "joined-colors," technique: outlines of the figures and landscape are drawn in cobalt blue, and a colorless glaze is applied. After firing, colors are applied on top of the glaze, and the vase is fired again. The overglaze pigments produce bright colors that complement the underglaze blue outlines, giving the picture a distinctive vividness. The *doucai* technique matured during the Chenghua period (1465–87) of the Ming dynasty and continued to flourish in the Qing, when it attained brilliant colors and more elaborate designs. The addition of gold paint to highlight the stylized pattern of the head of a wish-granting scepter (*ruyi*) on the shoulder of the vessel further adds to its opulence. Such a vessel might have been found in the room of an empress or other consort, where it would have conveyed the wish for the blessing of a male heir. (DS)

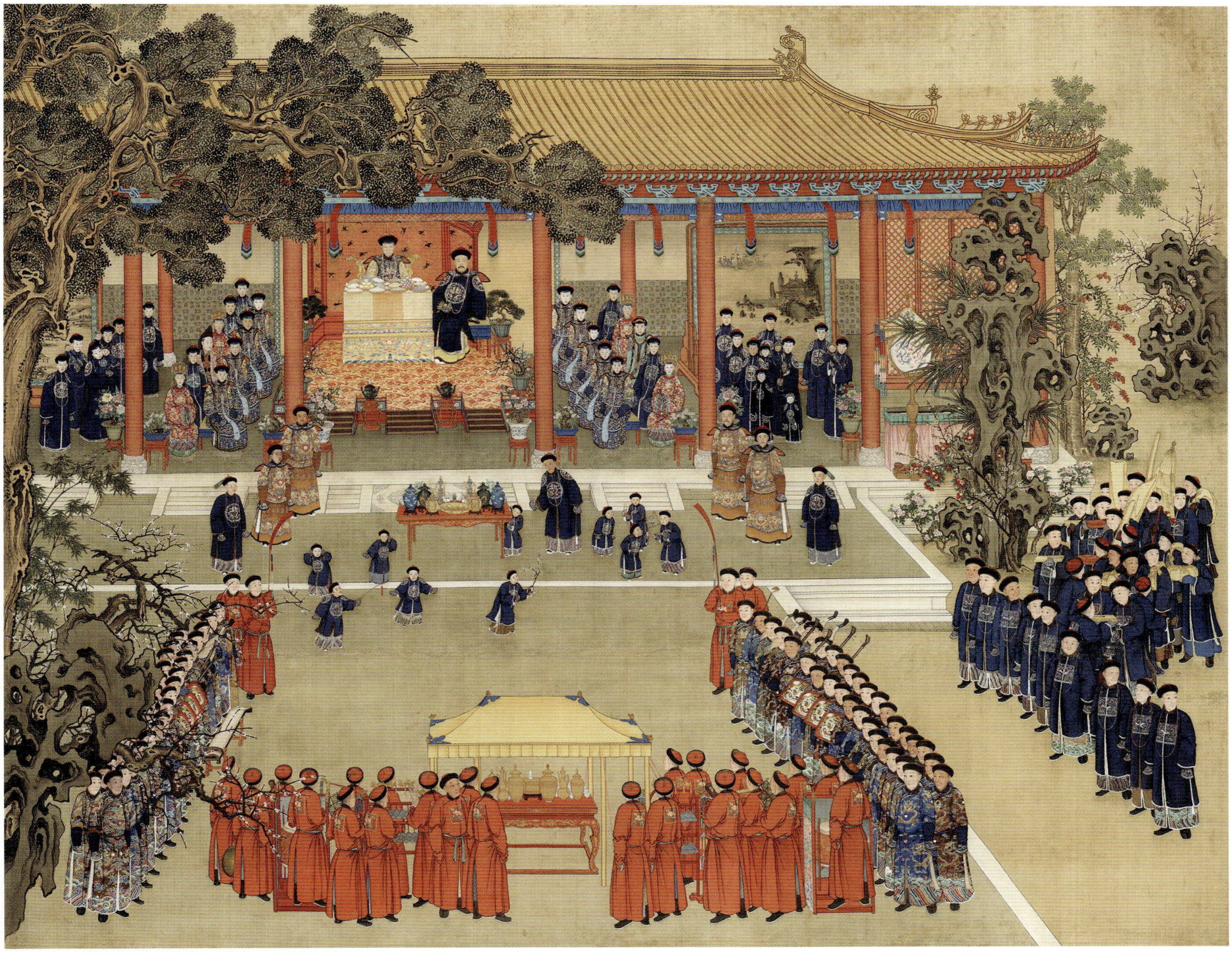

PLATE 7

清乾隆　崇慶皇太后八旬萬壽圖貼落

Celebrating Empress Dowager Chongqing's eightieth birthday

Yao Wenhan (active 1740s–70s), Zhou Ben (active 1760s–70s), and Yi Lantai (active 1748–86)
Qianlong period, 1771–72
Painting originally mounted on a wall (*tieluo*), ink and color on silk
86¼ × 112⅛ in. (219 × 285 cm)
Gu6541

This painting documents Empress Dowager Chongqing's eightieth birthday festivities. They took place at the Palace of Compassion and Tranquility (Cining gong) in the Forbidden City in the winter of 1771. The event was notable not only for her revered status as the most senior imperial woman, but also because so few Chinese people at that time attained such an advanced age.

Chongqing is shown seated at a banquet table on a raised platform. Sitting to her left is her son, the Qianlong emperor, whose body turns toward her in a gesture of respect.[1] She is flanked by her son's many consorts as well as wives of high-ranking officials. At the banquet the Qianlong emperor and other male descendants had performed a dance—accompanied by musicians, dressed in red—to wish Chongqing happiness and good health. Tables are covered with food, wine, and tea in exquisite vessels. The scene is enlivened by Chongqing's great- and great-great-grandsons playing before her. The painting thus illustrates the ideal of a traditional family in China: multiple generations living together harmoniously amid sincere expressions of filial piety, a virtue considered the foundation of a stable family and society.

This large painting was mounted on a wall in the Palace of Longevity and Health (Shoukang gong), Chongqing's residence, and then in the Palace of Longevity and Peace (Shou'an gong), the site of the empress dowager's birthday festivities. Conserved in 2014 and 2015, this painting fills a gap in pictorial representations of Chongqing's birthday celebrations, complementing the set of four handscrolls depicting her sixtieth birthday (pl. 8) and the eight-leaf album documenting her seventieth (see p. 131, fig. 1). (LS; trans. DYW)

1 The Qianlong emperor enjoyed the highest status among all guests represented in this painting. His face is depicted frontally to show such a status while his body is shown in three-quarter view.

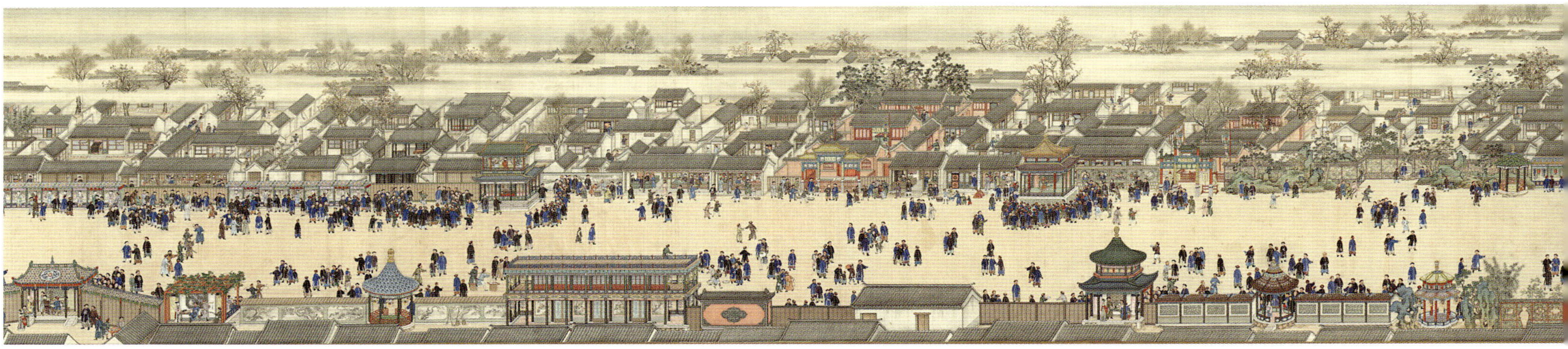

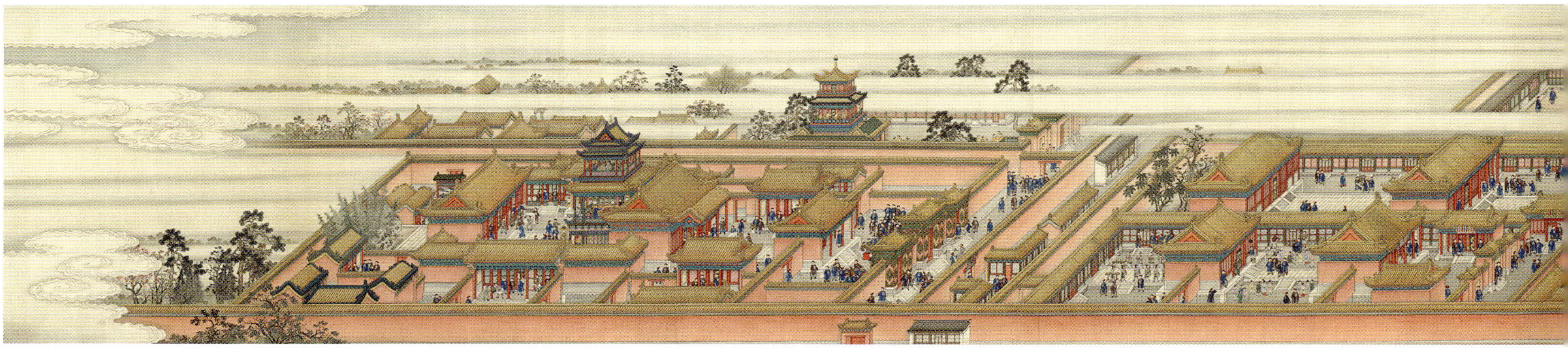

DETAILS

PLATE 8

清乾隆　崇慶皇太后萬壽圖
第四卷蘭殿延禧

Splendid Palaces Filled with Joy, *scroll four of* Celebrating Empress Dowager Chongqing's Birthday

Ding Guanpeng (active 1726–1770), Zhang Gao (active 18th century), Zhang Tingyan (1735–1794), Wu Weiqian (active 18th century), Chen Zhaolong (active 18th century), and other court painters, Beijing and Suzhou
Qianlong period, 1751–61
Handscroll, ink and color on silk
Cat. 28

This is one of four paintings the Qianlong emperor commissioned to commemorate Empress Dowager Chongqing's sixtieth birthday in 1751. The handscroll depicts his mother's return to the Forbidden City following a stay at her palatial retreat in northwestern Beijing, the Garden of Delightful Spring (Changchun yuan). Her routes to and within the Forbidden City are decked out for the festivities. The main street is lined with "pop-up" buildings and decorated with flowers and lanterns. Performances on floats and stages entertain Chongqing, an opera lover (details A and B).

Many of these attractions were sponsored by government departments, including the Grand Council (Junji chu), signaling the importance of these celebrations to the state. Noblemen and officials wearing court attire line up to welcome her (detail C). Those closest to the Forbidden City were of the highest rank.[1] For example, her nephews Prince He (1712–1770) and Prince Guo (1733–1765) were waiting for her outside the West Gate of Glory (Xihua men). Court ritual banners and other paraphernalia are carried in the procession to accompany Chongqing's imperial yellow palanquin.

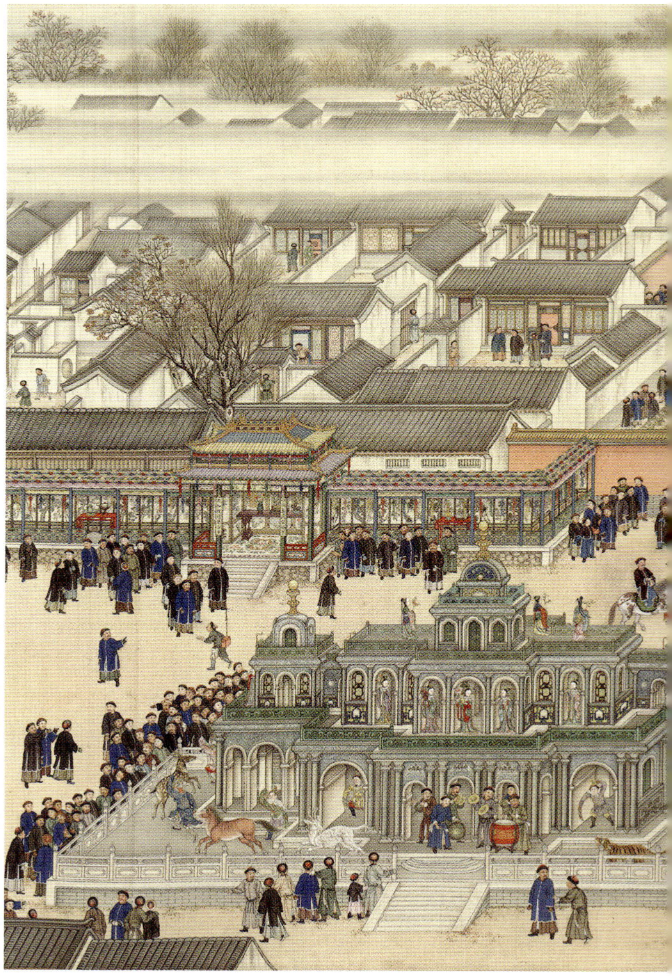

DETAIL A, WITH WESTERN-STYLE STRUCTURE

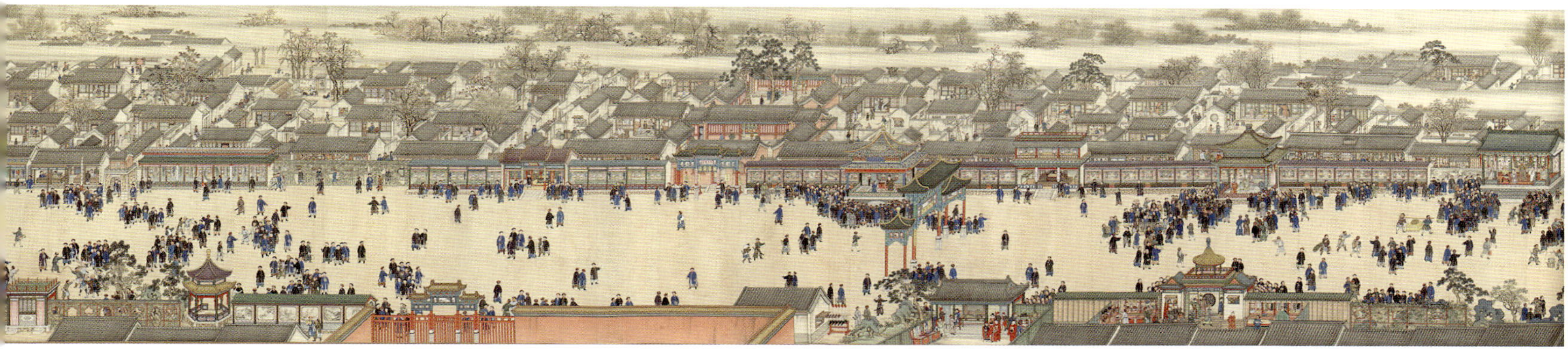

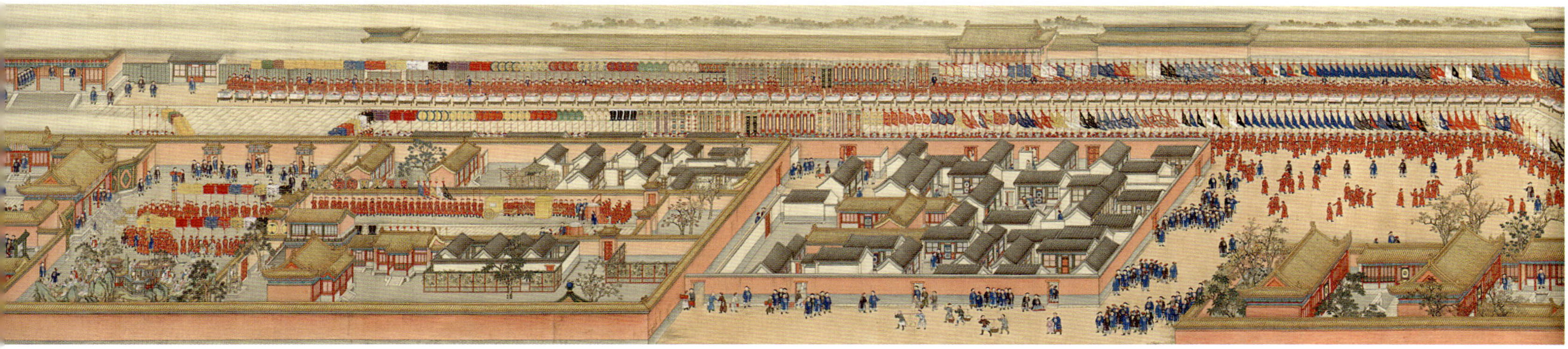

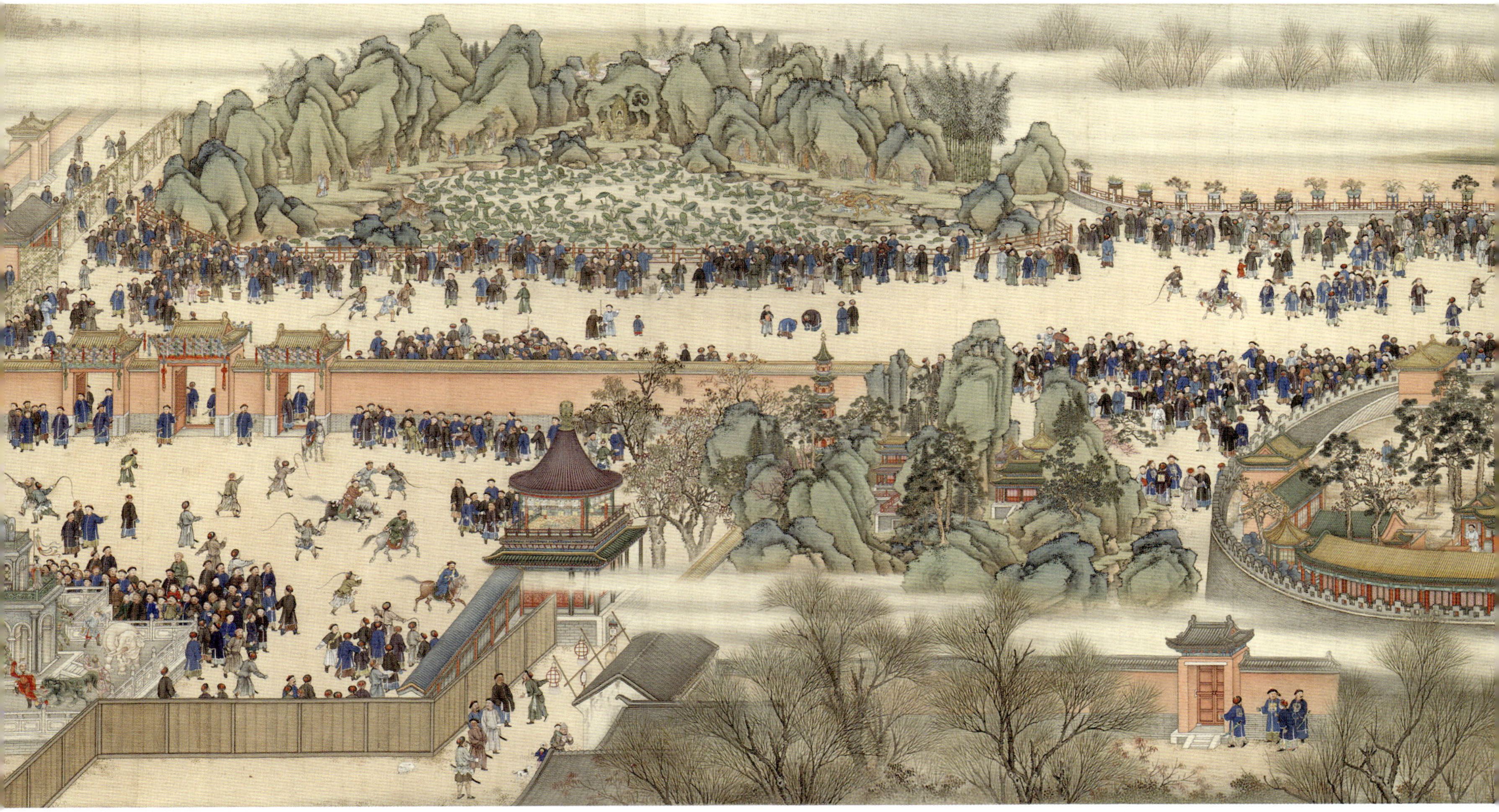

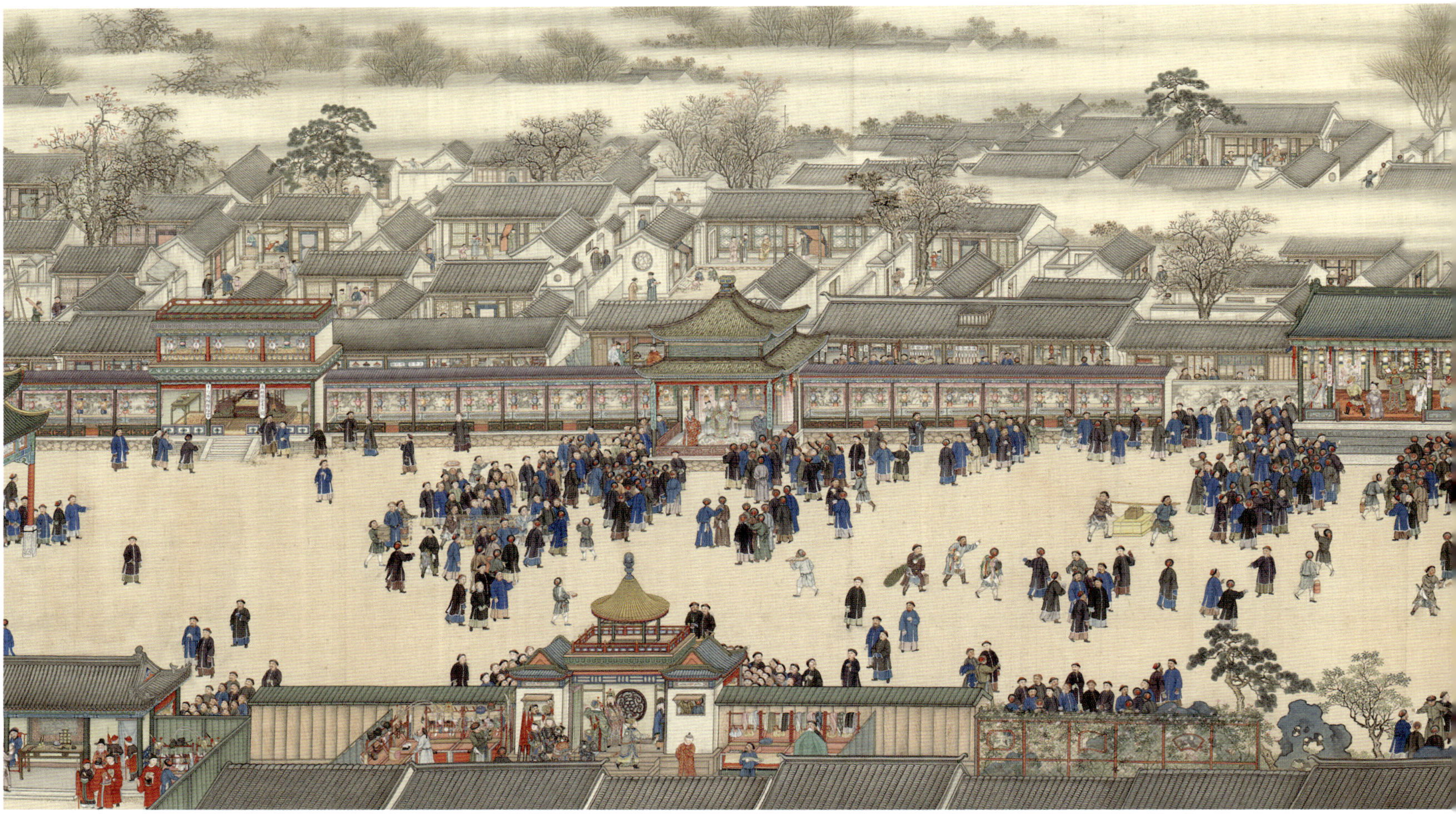

DETAIL B

Within the Forbidden City, the Palace of Longevity and Peace (Shou'an gong), seen at left with its multistory theater, was specially renovated for this occasion (detail D). Palace staff can be seen busily cleaning everywhere—even at the Pavilion of Raining Flowers (Yuhua ge) in the distance.

Indeed, the paintings themselves reflect the importance of the empress dowager's birthday. The scope of the four handscrolls, measuring more than 360 feet (110 meters) in total length, and their refined, detailed style evidence the effort of the twenty-nine painters in Beijing and Suzhou who spent nearly ten years on the commission. Qianlong presented the paintings to Chongqing as the first gift for her seventieth birthday in 1761, inscribing the title on the frontispiece and impressing his seal marks to express respect for his mother.[2] (LS; trans. DYW)

1 Fuheng et al. 1760.

2 ZGDYLSDAG 2005, 21:671; E'ertai and Zhang Tingyu (1769) 1987, 18:425.

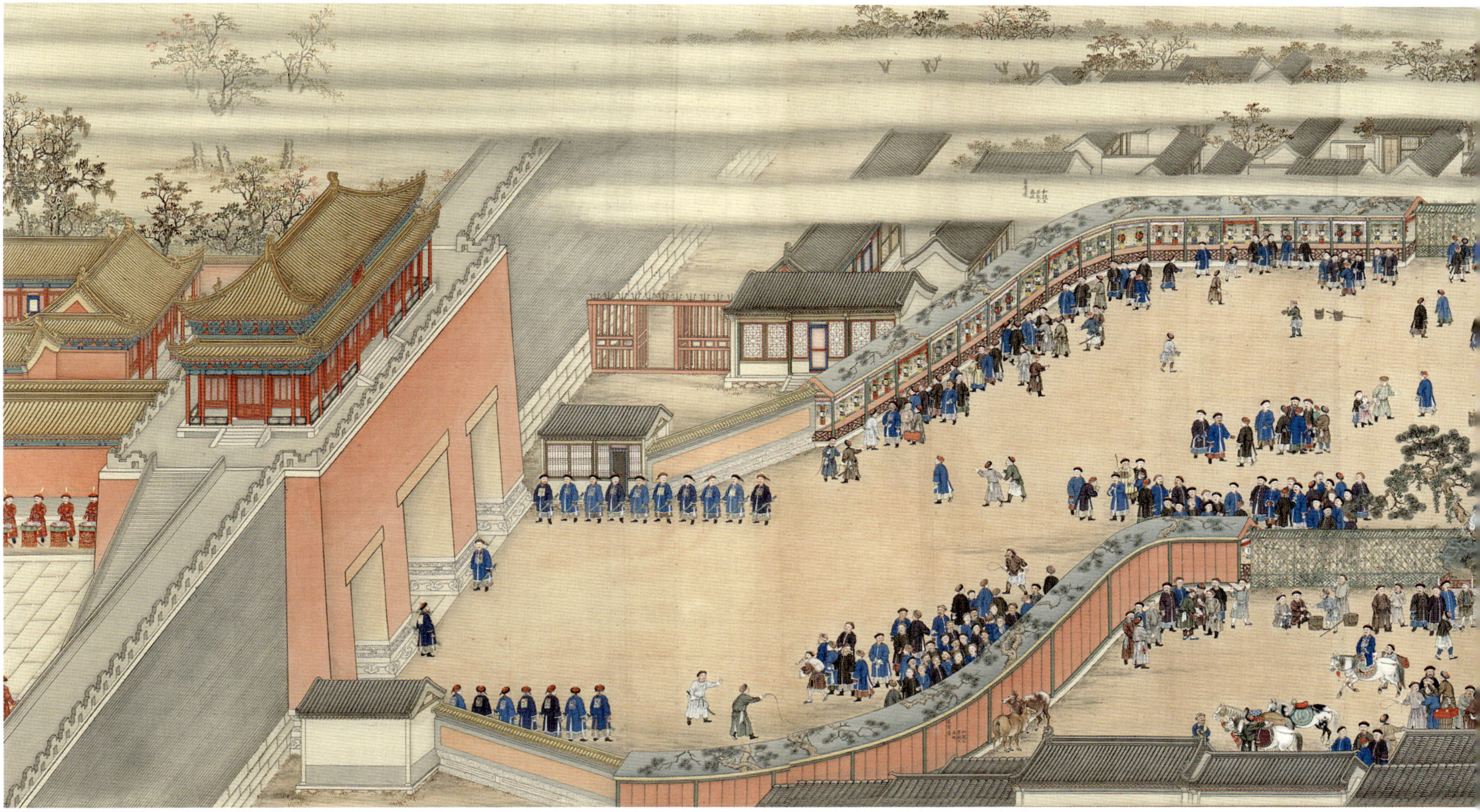

DETAIL C

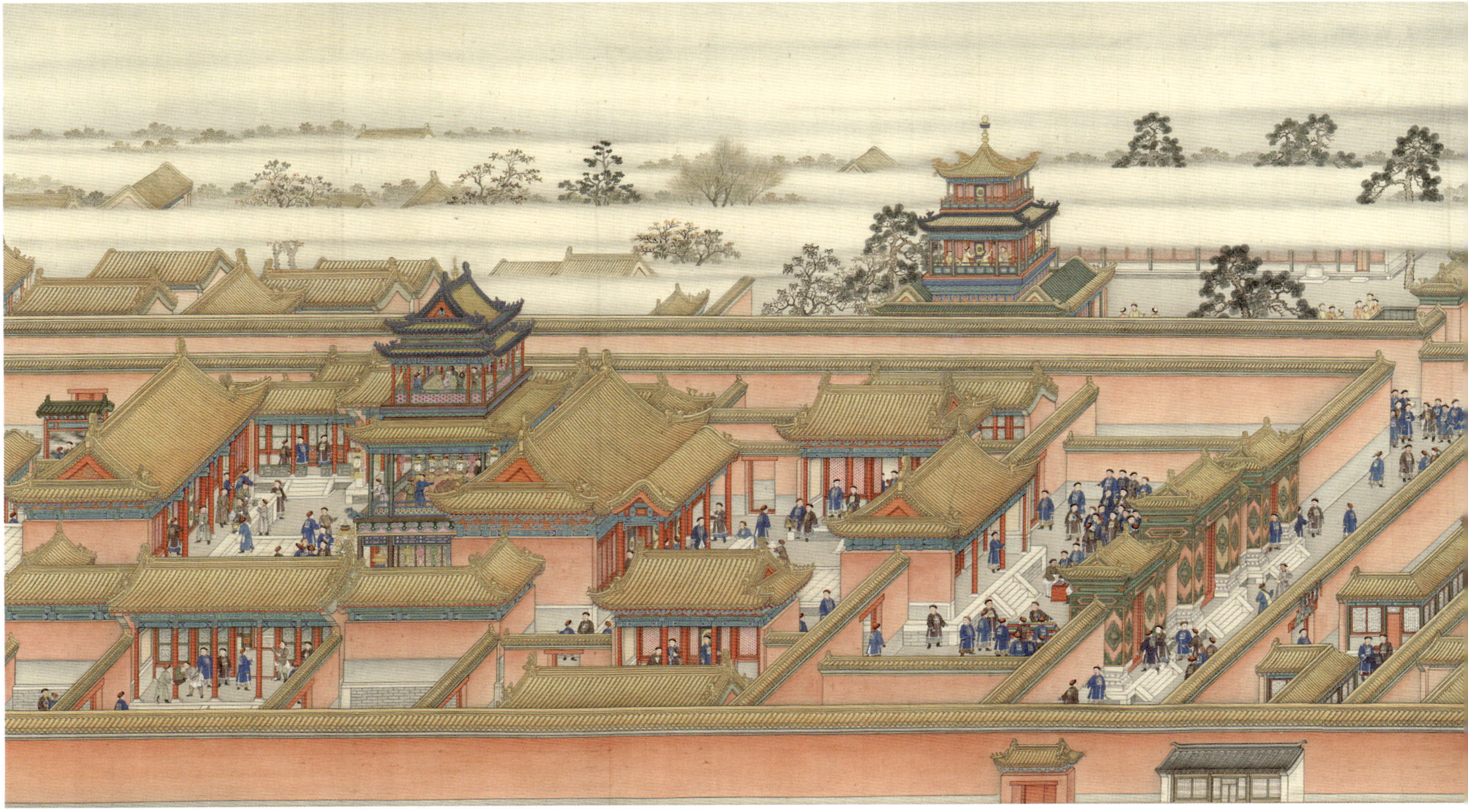

DETAIL D

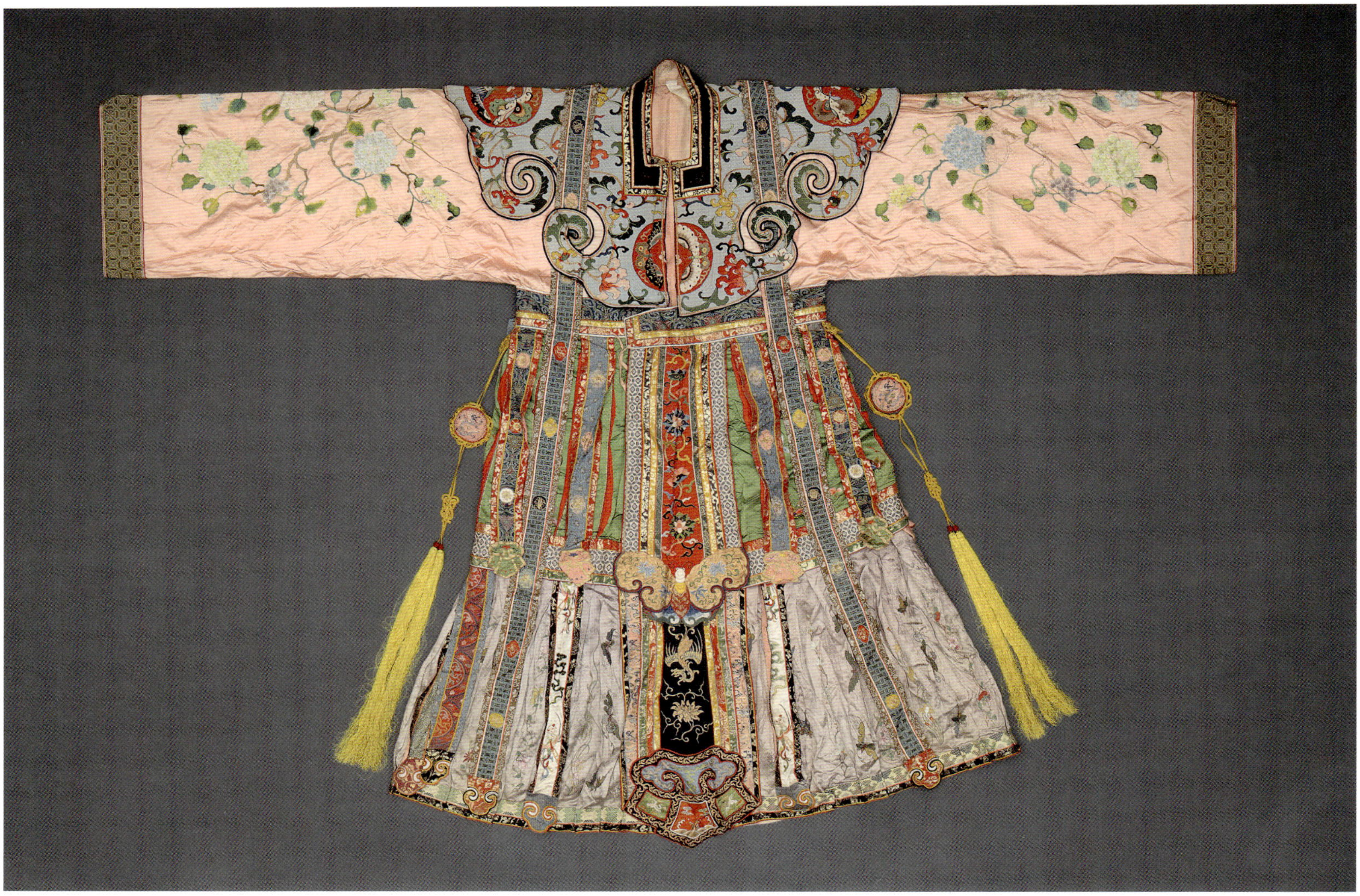

PLATE 9

清乾隆　粉色緞繡折枝花紋宮衣

Theatrical robe with flowers and butterflies

Imperial Silk Manufactory, Suzhou (embroidery)
Qianlong period, 1736–95
Silk tapestry (*kesi*), embroidery, and painting, polychrome silk and metallic-wrapped threads and pigments on silk satin
Cat. 67

This robe is called a palace dress (*gongyi*) or a dance dress (*wuyi*) and was worn in Qing court opera by actors playing such roles as imperial consorts, princesses, noblewomen, goddesses, and female immortals. Such costumes were considered the most suitable means to convey the charm of these female characters, which were played by men. The main actor in the opera *The Drunken Consort* (*Guifei zuijiu*)—playing Yang Yuhuan, a favored consort of Emperor Xuanzong (r. 713–56) of the Tang dynasty—wore this type of costume to communicate her beauty and talent for dance.

The sumptuous robe combines exquisite embroidery with silk tapestry (*kesi*) and painted decoration. Four roundels, each featuring a pair of butterflies symbolizing romance and marital happiness, adorn the collar. The lavishly decorated sashes and pleated skirt responded to and enhanced the movement of the wearer. Its style, palette, and decoration suggest it was used in Kun opera (*Kunqu*), which originated in southern cities such as Suzhou. This robe retains certain sartorial features, such as a rectangular neckline and wide sleeves, of Han Chinese female attire.

Qing imperial women were important and enthusiastic patrons of court theater, and emperors indulged this interest (sometimes in the name of fulfilling their filial obligations) by arranging theatrical entertainments for their mothers, especially as part of birthday celebrations.[1] Empresses Dowager Chongqing and Cixi were especially well known for their love of drama, and Cixi played a major role in reviving court opera after a period of decline. In 1898 she commissioned and participated in an adaption of the *Music of a Grand Age* (*Zhaodai xiaoshao*), an ambitious series of plays about a family of brave and talented women who break away from traditional domestic roles to act as warriors at a time of crisis—a plot paralleling Cixi's own political career. (SZH; translated by DYW)

1 L. Chen 2012, 21–46.

PLATE 10

清乾隆　方竹刻乾隆御題鑲黃玉鳩首杖

Walking stick with bird-shaped finial

Workshop, probably Suzhou
Qianlong period, 1770s or 1780s
Bamboo with jade (nephrite) and metal fitting
Cat. 154

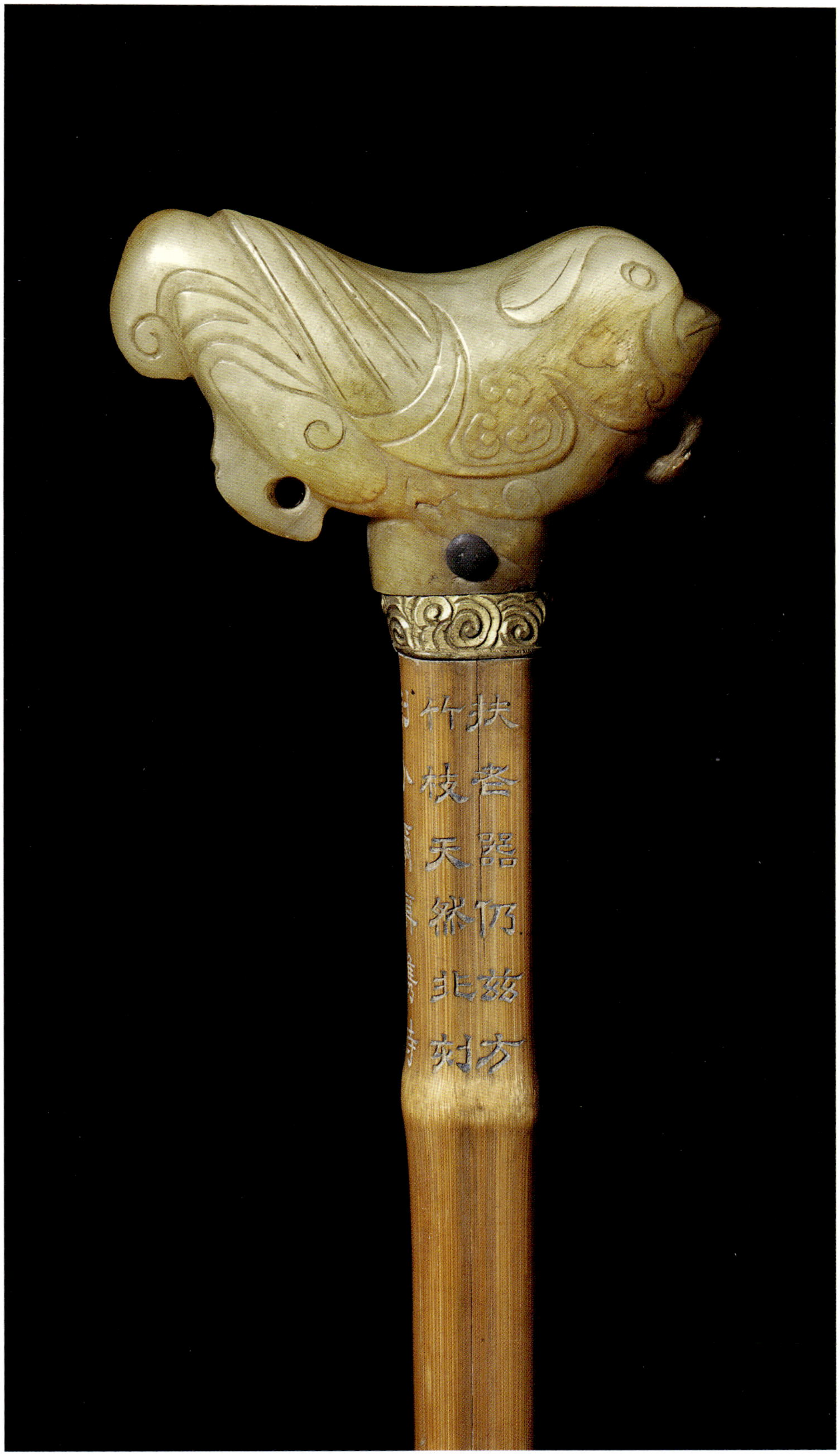

This walking stick illustrates the close relationship between Empress Dowager Chongqing and her only child, the Qianlong emperor. Whenever possible, Qianlong's day opened with a visit to his mother. When official duty kept him away, according to a poem he wrote in 1775, a walking stick such as this one would act on his behalf, accompanying and supporting his beloved mother.[1]

In ancient China, the turtledove symbolized longevity for its reputed power to prevent choking, likely a main cause of death for seniors. A poem by Qianlong inscribed on this walking stick indicates the handle is a jade bird that was worked more than 1,500 years ago. Its curvilinear form and cool, smooth surface made for an ideal grip. The angular profile of the staff, strikingly different from the usual round shape of bamboo, adds to its rarity. In 1785 Qianlong gave walking sticks like this one to nearly 4,000 elders at a banquet to demonstrate his respect for seniors, a prime Confucian virtue.

Chongqing enjoyed extraordinary health and remained physically vigorous until the end of her life. Even in her eighties, she continued touring the country with her son and even climbed to the top of a nine-story pagoda. When she died at the age of eighty-six, she was the longest living empress in Chinese history. A walking stick similar to this one was among the commemorative objects Qianlong placed at his mother's burial site in 1777.[2] (DYW)

1 See *Wenyuan ge siku quanshu*.
2 ZGDYLSDAG 2005, 40:413.

PLATE 11

清乾隆　明黃色彩雲蝠團壽紋妝花緞女棉袍

Festive robe with bats, clouds, and the character for longevity

Probably Imperial Silk Manufactory, Nanjing (weaving), and Imperial Workshop, Beijing (tailoring)
Qianlong period, 1785 or earlier
Patterned silk satin and embroidery, polychrome silk and metallic-wrapped threads on silk fabric
Cat. 54

At the Qing court, festive robes (*jifu*) served as special attire for important occasions, such as birthdays and festivals. While this robe resembles the emperor's robe in cut and color, two features indicate the gender of its user as female: First, it opens on the sides, whereas the emperor's robe has a long central opening at the front and back—a design conforming to Qing notions of decorum. Second, a dark blue band with dragons and clouds has been inserted between the patterned yellow fabric and the plain blue sleeve.

According to Qing sartorial codes, the use of bright yellow indicates that only the most senior imperial women—the empress dowager, empress, and imperial noble consort—were entitled to wear this garment. While these codes specified just three types of festive robe with dragons and clouds for these women, surviving examples show a wide variety of colors and patterns that reflected the wearer's taste and the nature of the occasion on which they were worn. On this robe the more conventional dragon pattern has been replaced by numerous red bats and medallions with the character for longevity (*shou*). The waves and mountains near the hem, together with the bats and the *shou* character, form the rebus "May your good fortune be as vast as the Eastern Sea and your life as everlasting as the Southern Mountain." This message would have been even more vivid as the movement of the wearer animated the designs of the flying bats and undulating waves. These emblems strongly suggest it was worn on the birthday of an imperial woman.

The robe's vibrant palette and exquisite patterns represent the pinnacle of textile production in eighteenth-century China. The fabric was probably made in the Imperial Silk Manufactory in Nanjing, a city known for its advanced weaving technologies, and it was later tailored by the Imperial Workshop (Zaoban chu) in Beijing. Two tags of yellow paper show it was inventoried in the fifth month of 1785 as the property of the Qing court. (YZT; trans. DYW)

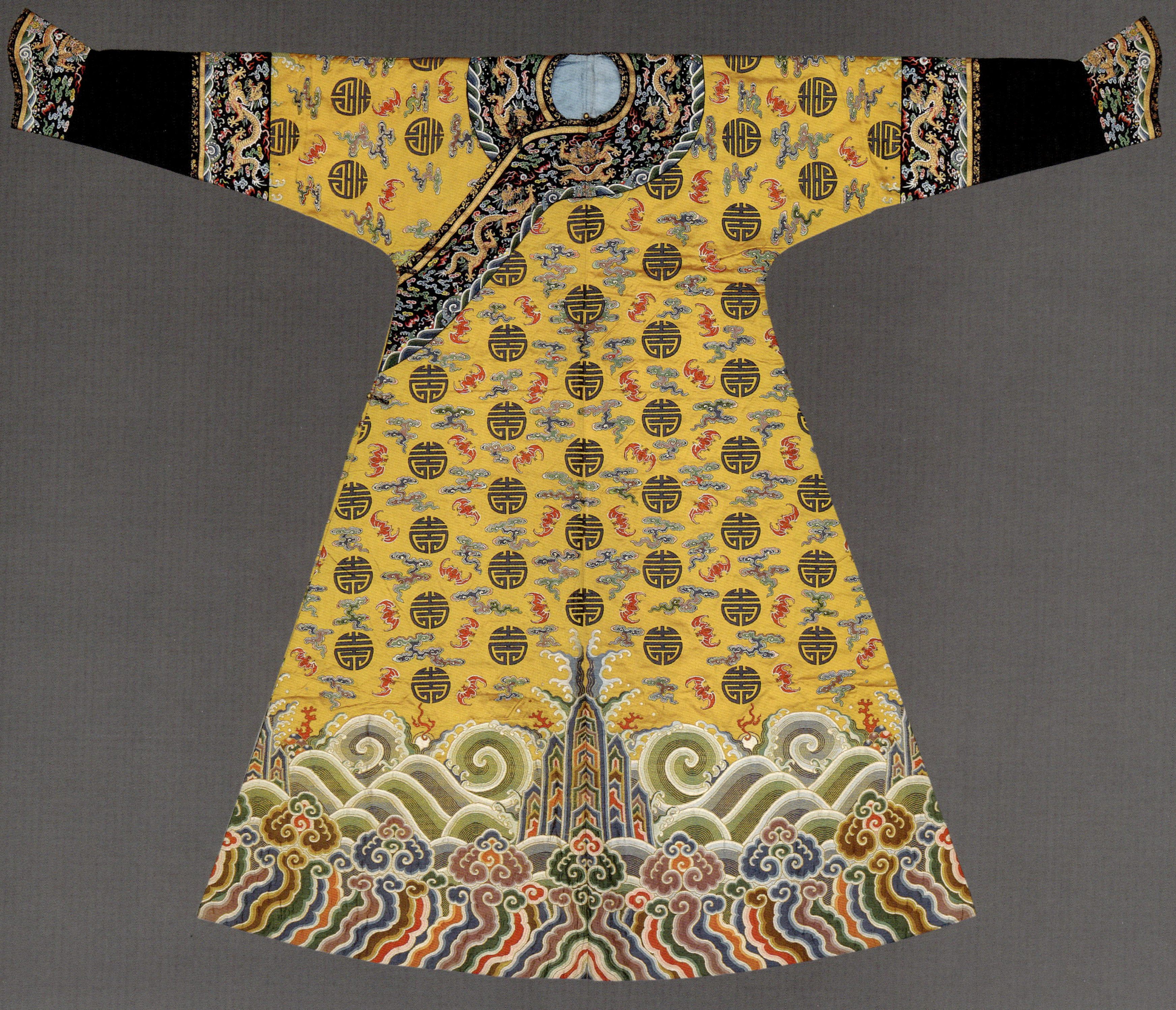

PLATE 12

清同治　金鑲木柄金提爐

Portable censer with phoenixes, gourds, and the character for double happiness

Imperial Workshop, Beijing
Tongzhi period, 1872 or earlier
Gold alloy with *zitan* wood and silk tassel
Cat. 160

PLATE 13

清乾隆　皇朝禮器圖式冊之皇后儀駕提爐頁

Ritual Censer for the Empress *from* Illustrated Precedents for the Ritual Paraphernalia of the Qing Imperial Court

Leng Jian (active 18th century), Huang Men (active 18th century), and other court painters, Beijing
Qianlong period, probably 1772
Album leaf, ink and color on silk
Cat. 35

This ritual censer consists of two parts: a carved wooden handle whose ends are fitted with a gold phoenix head and a wish-granting scepter (*ruyi*), and a lidded container for incense with chains and a flower-shaped disc. All of the components are made of gold. The two parts are connected by a hook beneath the phoenix head. Inscriptions reveal the purity of the gold to be about 80 percent. Auspicious symbols abound. Dragons and phoenixes, the double-happiness symbol, and the gourd all refer to weddings and fertility. The feet of the incense container are shaped like elephants, emblems of peace and prosperity. The style and symbolism of the decoration suggest it was produced for the 1872 wedding of the Tongzhi emperor and Empress Xiaozhe.

Censers—along with gold basins, incense boxes, spittoons, and vases—were among the most important ritual paraphernalia for emperors and empresses. Imperial guards carried censers in processions, as fragrance from the incense arose from the openings in the lid and the dangling bells attached to the disc chimed. During ceremonies, the censer and other ritual objects would be placed on a red lacquer stand near the thrones upon which the emperor and empress were seated (pl. 13).

According to *Illustrated Precedents for the Ritual Paraphernalia of the Qing Imperial Court* (*Huangchao liqi tushi*), the handle of the empress's and empress dowager's censer featured a phoenix, the mythical bird associated with high-status imperial women. (A dragon head adorned the handle of the emperor's censer.) This censer's connection with imperial women is reinforced by a record indicating that it was in the collection of the Palace of Great Benevolence (Jingren gong), a residential complex for imperial consorts in the eastern part of the Forbidden City. After the death of its last occupant, Consort Zhen (Zhen *fei*; 1876–1900) of the Guangxu emperor, the palace served as a repository of items for imperial women.
(HY and LL; trans. DYW)

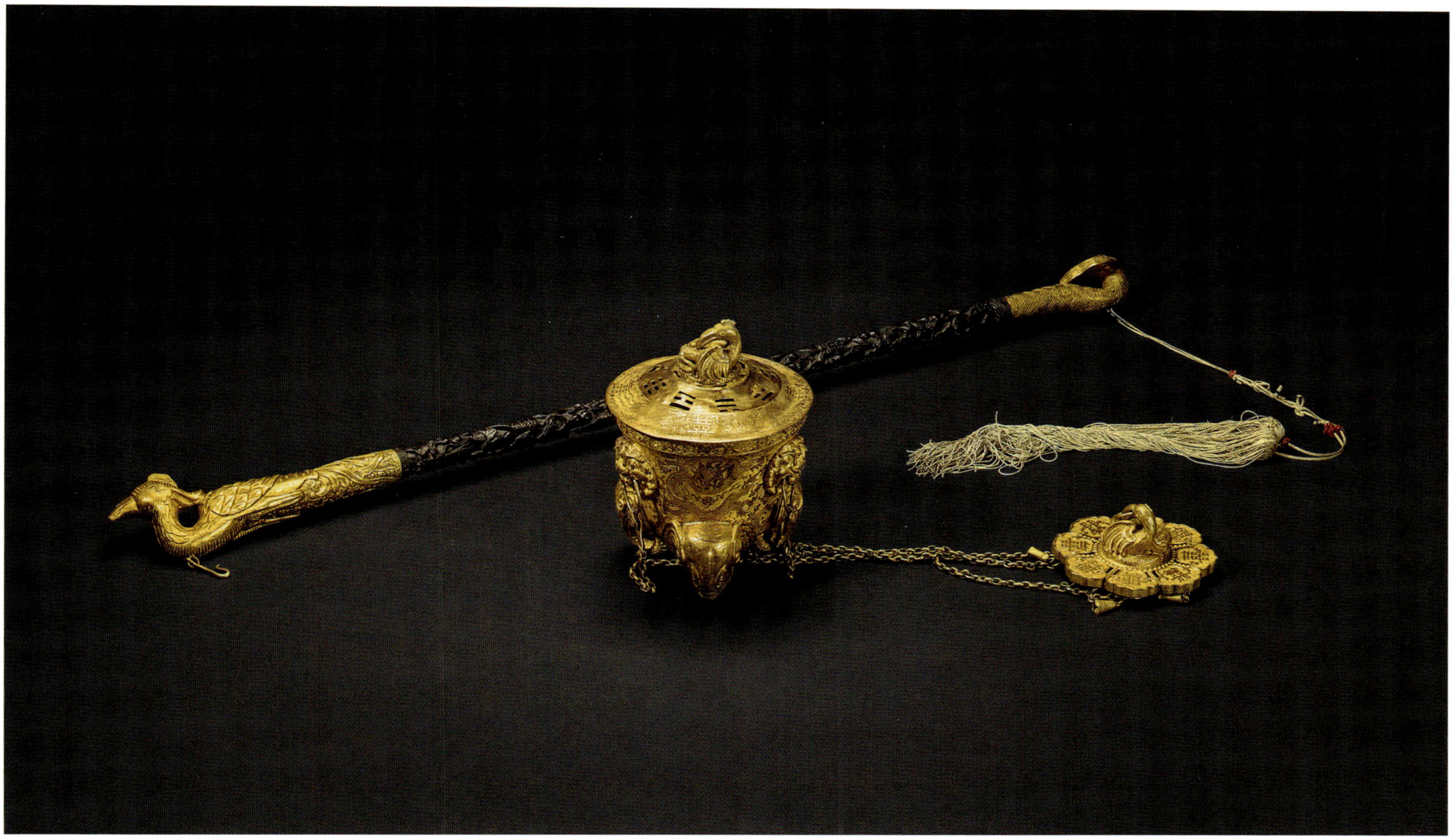

PLATE 12

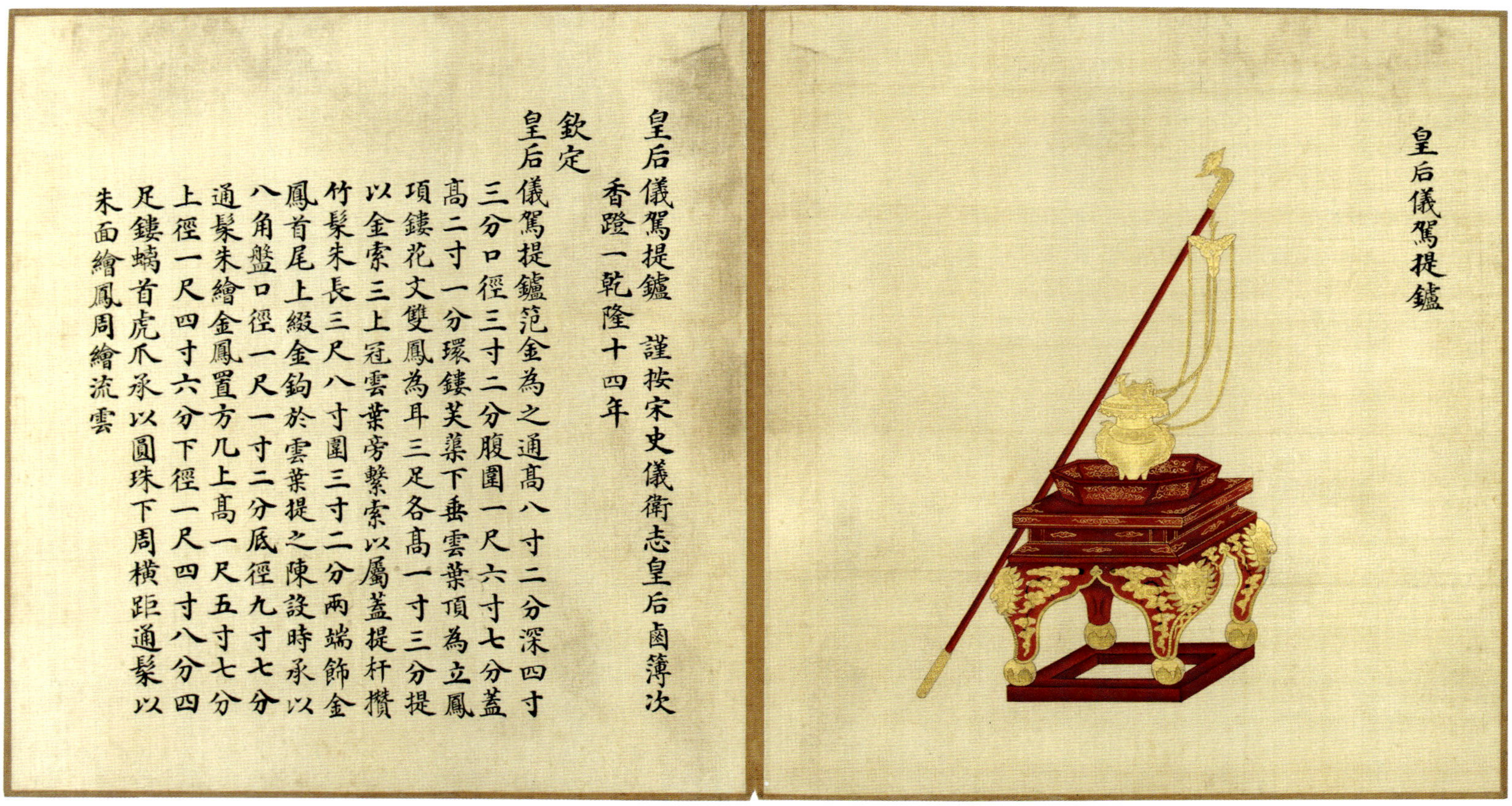

PLATE 13

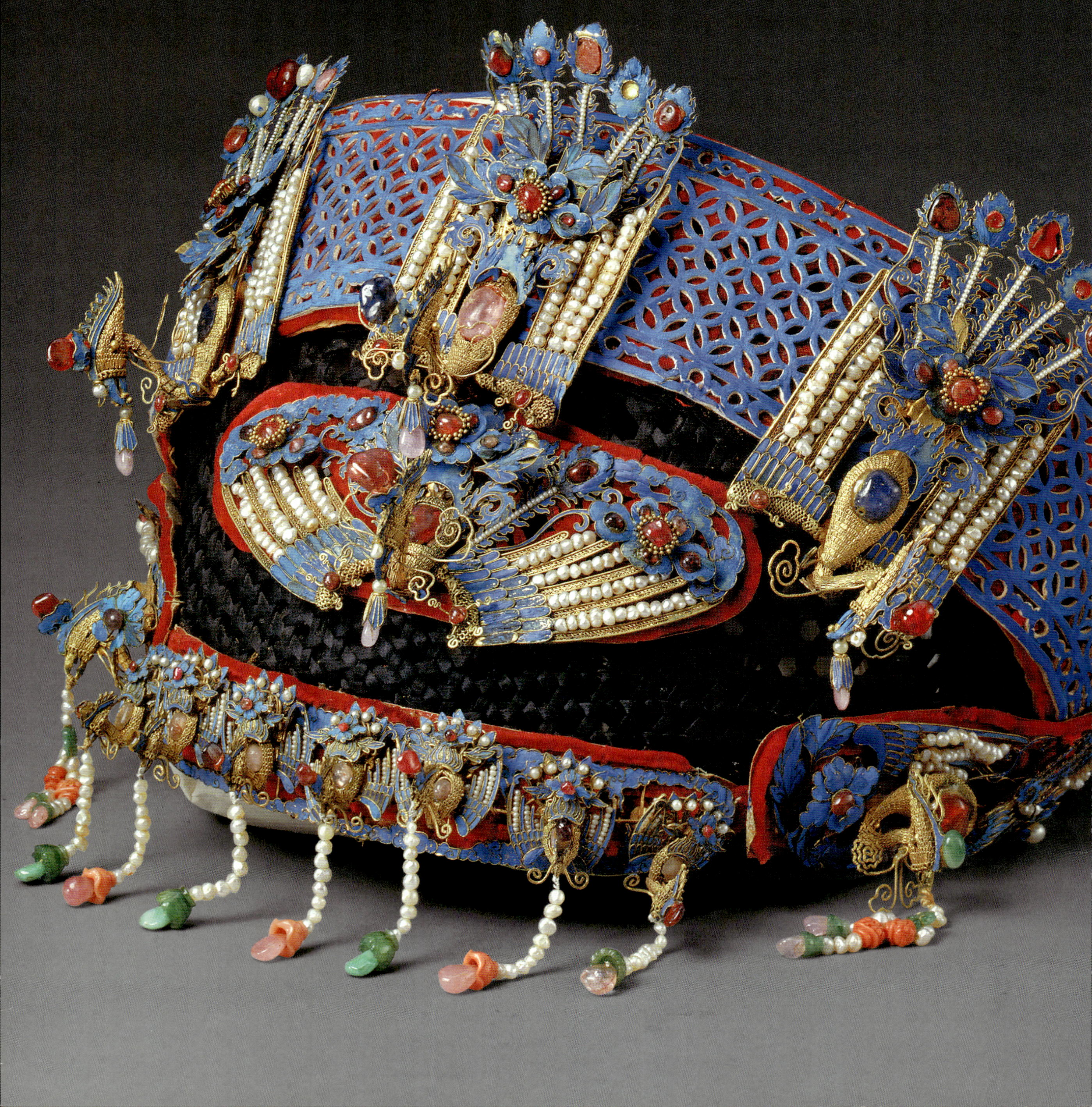

PLATE 14

清晚期　銀鍍金點翠嵌珠石牡丹鳳紋鈿子

Festive headdress with phoenixes and peonies

Probably Imperial Workshop, Beijing
Tongzhi or Guangxu period, probably 1872 or 1888–89
Silver with gilding, kingfisher feather, pearls, coral, jadeite, ruby, sapphire, tourmaline, turquoise, lapis lazuli, and glass; frame: metal wires with silk satin, velvet, and cardboard
Cat. 71

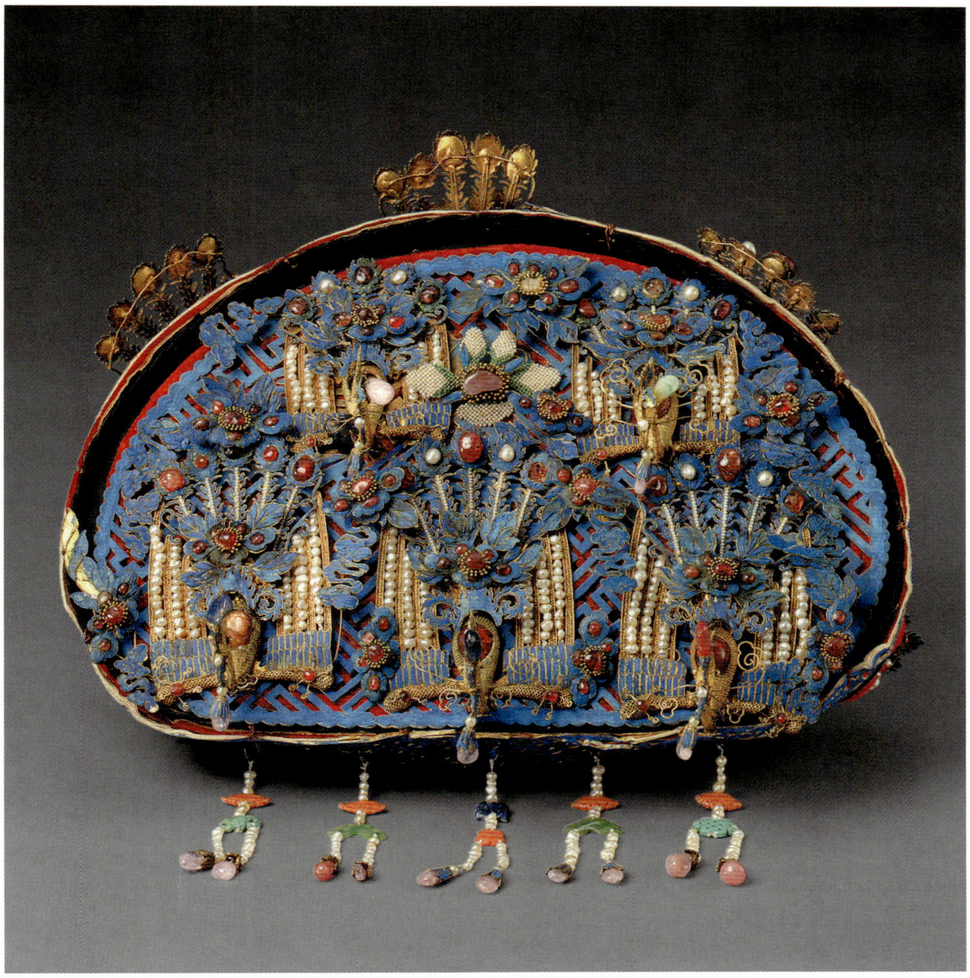

DETAIL, TOP

The distinctive headdress known as a *dianzi* was worn by Qing Manchu women on festive occasions. It consists of a frame of metal wires covered with silken threads to which ornaments are attached. The woman depicted on the far right of the painting *Yinzhen and Consorts* (p. 36, fig. 3) shows how the *dianzi* was worn like a beret.[1]

This *dianzi* is richly decorated with accessories mounted on pieces of velvet-covered cardboard affixed to the frame. Phoenixes shaped with gilt-metal filigree are featured on the front and back of the headdress. These are embellished with a variety of precious materials, including turquoise-colored kingfisher feather, gemstones, and pearls. Beads hang from the mouths of these mythical creatures, displaying auspicious motifs, such as bats, fishes, and the character for "double happiness."

Phoenixes were generally reserved for formal *dianzi* rather than routine headdresses—although since official Qing sumptuary laws do not mention them, some flexibility existed with regard to how they were decorated, who wore them, and on which occasions.[2] One late Qing writer noted that *dianzi* with phoenixes were meant to be worn by newly married women.[3] Indeed, the auspicious symbols on this headdress suggest that it was made for a wedding. It is likely this *dianzi* was meant for the consort of the Guangxu emperor, and it would have been among the imperial wedding gifts that she received. (LYP)

1 Chen Huixia 2016, 64. The other women in the painting appear to wear braided hair rather than *dianzi*. Compare this headdress to the one worn by Lady Wanyan, wife of Prince Hongming (1705–1767), in her portrait in the Arthur M. Sackler Gallery; see Stuart and Rawski 2001, p. 18, no. 2.

2 On the *dianzi*, see Li Zhi'an 2012; Yang Zhishui 2014, 3:782–92; Chen Huixia 2016, 58–69; and Luk 2018.

3 Chong Yi 1982, 33–34.

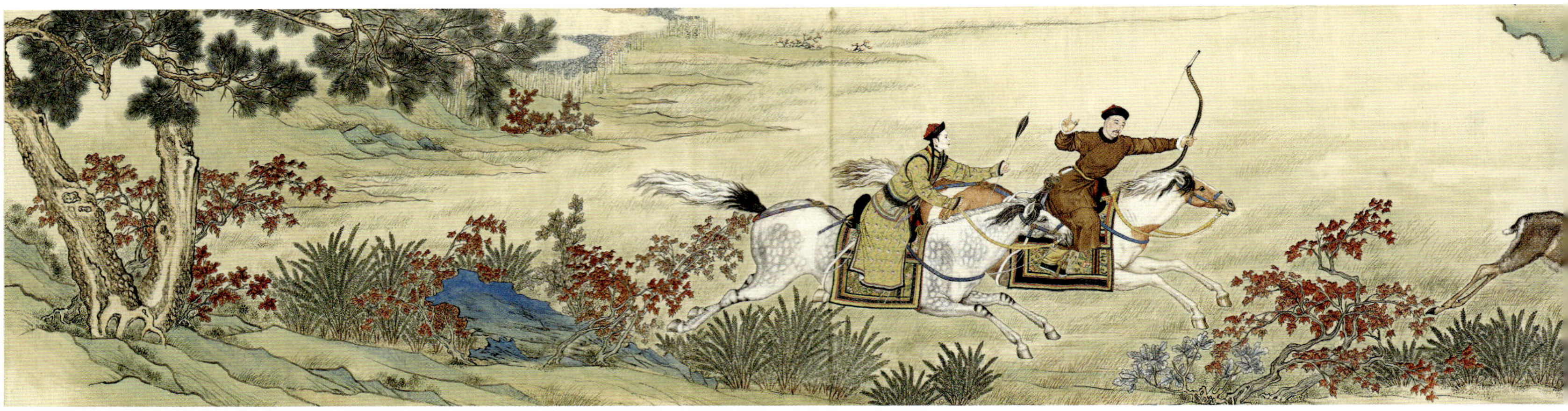

PLATE 15

清乾隆　乾隆帝及妃威弧獲鹿圖卷

The Qianlong Emperor and Imperial Woman Hunting a Deer

Court painters, probably at the Wish-Fulfilling Studio (Ruyi guan), Beijing; frontispiece by the Qianlong emperor (1711–1799)
Qianlong period, probably 1760–79
Handscroll, ink and color on paper
Cat. 29

This scroll depicts the autumn hunt at Mulan, a Qing imperial hunting enclosure in present-day Hebei province, where emperors brought their sons, grandsons, and imperial women to shoot deer.[1] The Qianlong emperor and a female companion are depicted astride galloping horses joined in the thrill of the hunt. He has just fired a fatal shot into a deer, while the woman actively supports him, handing over a fresh arrow. The painting is not recorded in court archives, but its high degree of realism (especially in the horses and figures), vibrant palette and precise brushstrokes in the landscape details, and well-staged, action-filled composition reflect a sophistication that may be credited to a team combining European-born Jesuit artists with Chinese painters working at the court's Wish-Fulfilling Studio (Ruyi guan).[2]

The handsome horsewoman of fair complexion is rendered with convincing specificity, yet her identity and ethnicity have not been established beyond doubt. Scholars at the Palace Museum argue that she is most likely Qianlong's Uyghur consort Rong *fei* (Consort Rong; 1734–1788), citing features such as her twin braids, the floral design on her robe, and the pendant hanging from a red silk cord as Uyghur in style. Other features—the cut of her vest and robe, the hat with red silk streamers, and three pierced earrings in her earlobe—suggest Manchu traditions, leaving open the possibility that she could be another consort or perhaps Qianlong's favored daughter wearing imported Uyghur fabric.[3]

Consort Rong was a Uyghur who entered the imperial harem in 1760 after her family helped the Qing court suppress a Muslim uprising.[4] She rose to become a consort of the third rank. Qianlong's respect and fondness for her was revealed when he provided her with a Muslim chef and created a special place of worship for her with walls carved with text from the Qu'ran. It was named the Temple of Foreign Lands (Fangwai guan), located in the Garden of Perfect Brightness (Yuanming yuan), a favored imperial palace in the suburbs of Beijing.

The emperor must have felt some kind of emotional connection to this enigmatic scroll. It is small for a court painting, suggesting it was commissioned for viewing in an intimate setting. Further, in an unusual request, the emperor asked his sixth son, Yongrong (1744–1790), to paint a landscape on the plain lining of the scroll's silk storage bag. Qianlong showed favor for his son's work by impressing his seal on the landscape. Regardless of her identity, the woman embodies Qianlong's conviction that imperial females should possess the physical stamina and horsemanship to support the emperor during a hunt, a way of expressing Manchu pride and demonstrating the vigor necessary to rule. (WJX and JS, trans. DS)

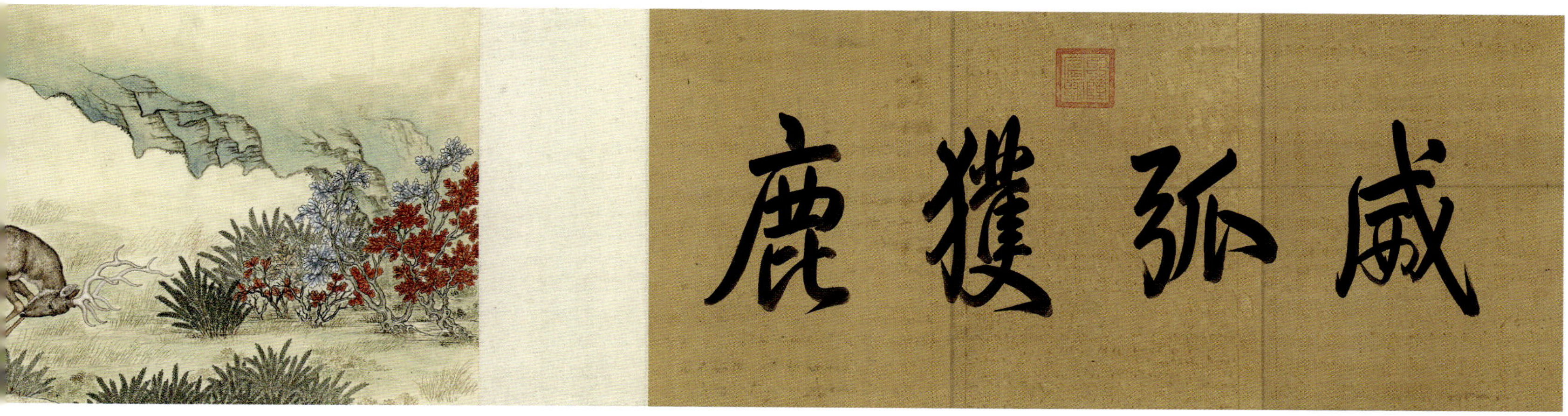

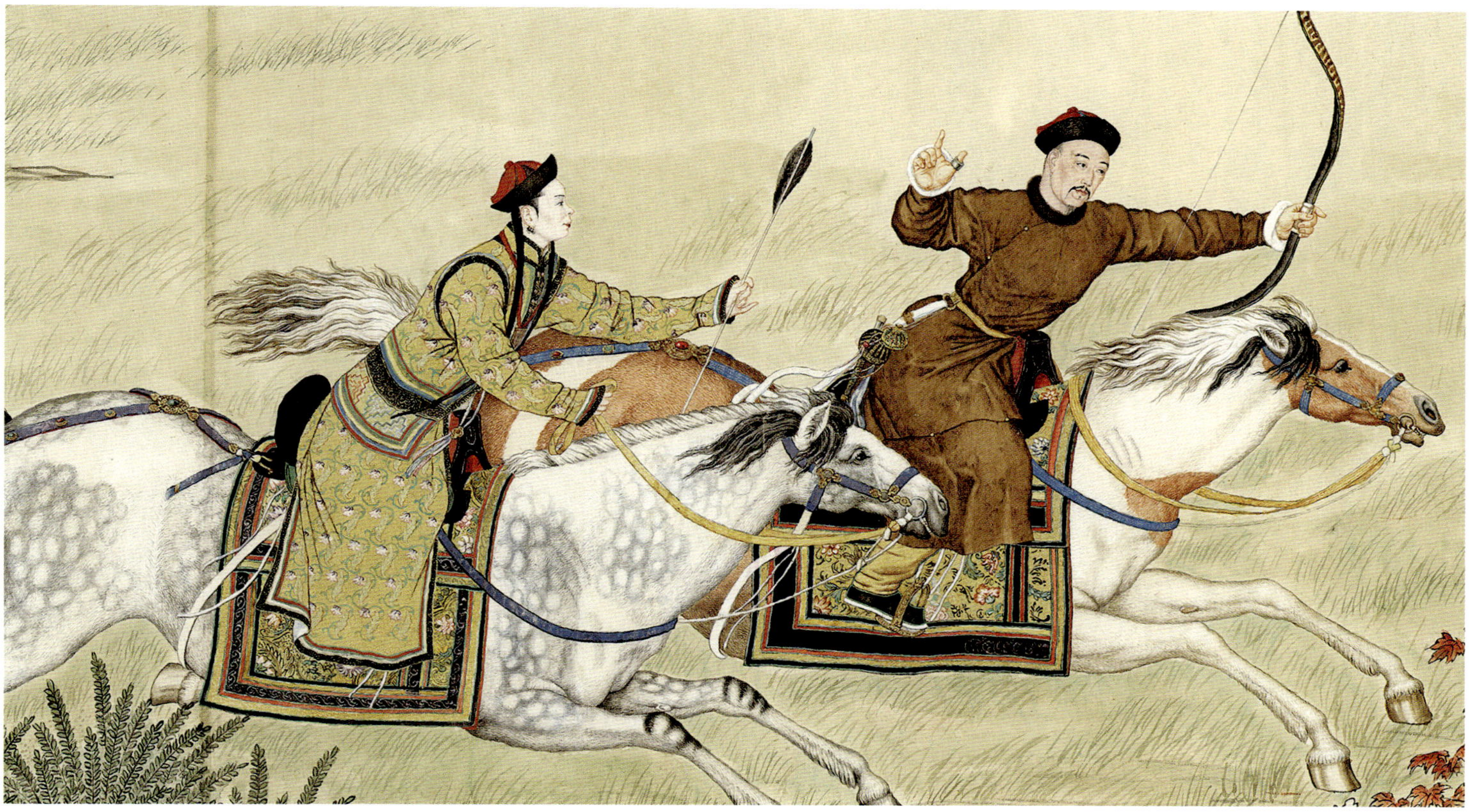

DETAIL

1 Qing archives are silent on the subject of this painting and the circumstances of its commission. The setting of autumn deer hunting corresponds with the imperial hunting rites held at Mulan.

2 See Yang Boda 1984, 7.

3 Evelyn S. Rawski identifies the female rider as Qianlong's tenth daughter, who "dressed in men's clothing, practiced archery, and did hunt alongside the emperor"; see Rawski 2004, 184. Yang Boda, citing Wu Fei's opinion that the woman is Qianlong's daughter, strongly disagrees and argues that the woman is Consort Rong. Yang compares her face to another painting, *Portrait of a Qing Lady in Martial Attire*, that he believes to represent Consort Rong, but the subject of this painting is not universally agreed upon. It is illustrated in Yang Boda 1984, 8.

4 Rawski and Rawson 2006, 159, mentions the uprising briefly.

PLATE 16

清康熙　黃色緞鎖繡花卉鳳凰紋厚底靴

Pair of boots with phoenixes, peonies, and lotuses

Workshop, probably Jiangsu or Zhejiang province
Kangxi period, 1662–1722
Embroidery, polychrome and metallic-wrapped silk threads on silk satin; soles: wood core covered with cotton, leather trim, felted paper
Cat. 75

PLATE 17

清光緒　黃色緞堆綾嵌料石虎頭紋花盆底袷鞋

Pair of platform shoes with tiger heads, the character for longevity, and bats

Guangxu period, 1875–1908
Appliqué, silk satin; platforms: wood core covered with cotton and glass beads
Cat. 80

PLATE 18

清康熙　杏黃色緞打籽繡鳳紋尖底鞋

Pair of shoes with phoenixes

Workshop, probably Jiangsu or Zhejiang province
Kangxi period, 1662–1722
Embroidery, braided and metallic-wrapped threads on silk satin with seed pearls; soles: wood core covered with cotton, leather trim
Cat. 78

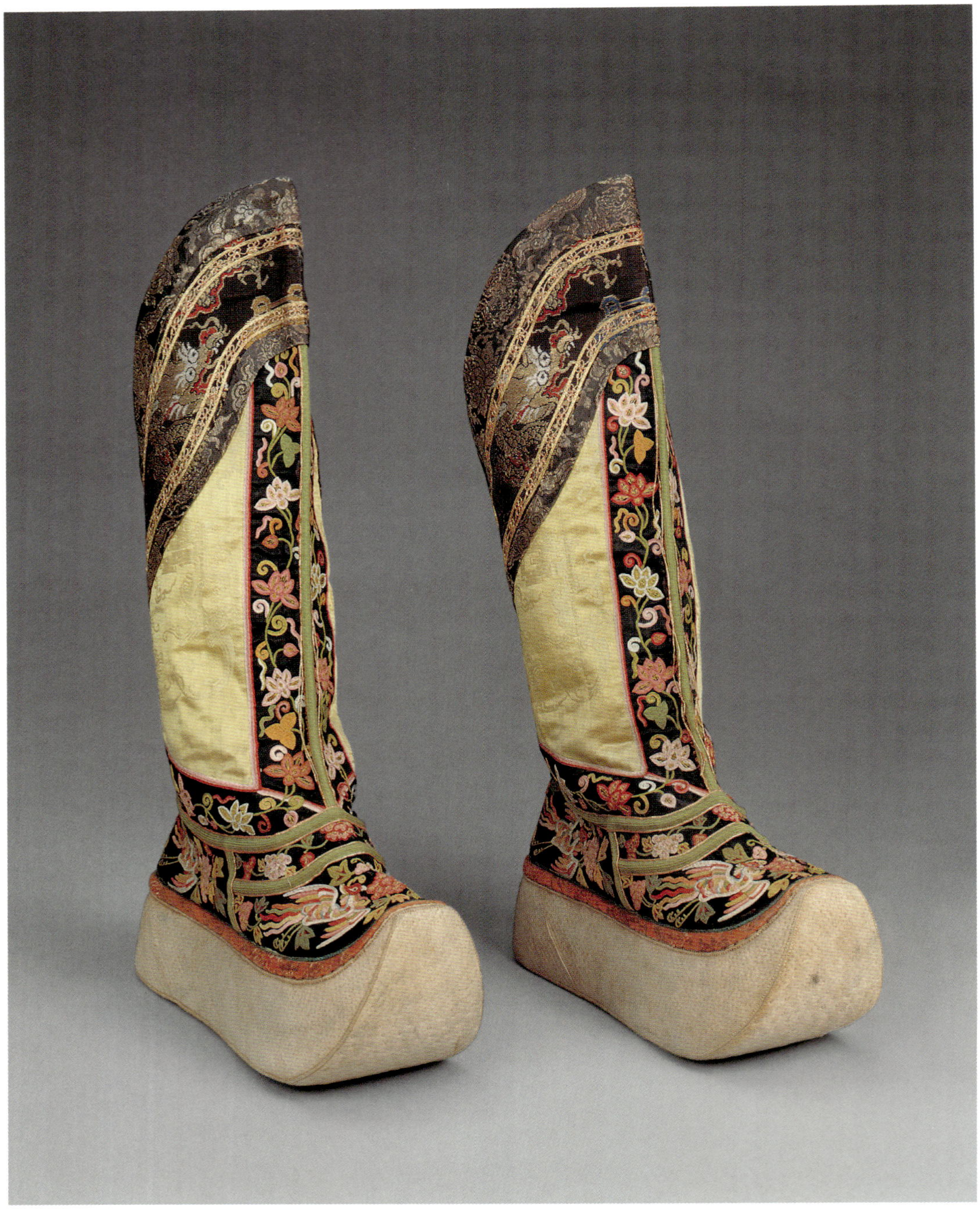

PLATE 16

These shoes for court ladies deftly combine Manchu cultural traditions and Chinese-style embellishment.[1] In contrast to the tiny footwear of Han Chinese women, who bound their feet, Qing court shoes allowed Manchu ladies greater physical mobility and personal freedom, even to the point of riding on horseback and participating in hunts (see pl. 15). Boots, worn by both men and women, were a practical way to keep warm while spending long periods outdoors engaged in sometimes strenuous activities.

Despite their feminine appearance, the pair of boots with phoenixes (pl. 16) resembles footwear long favored by Manchu men.[2] The stiff, thick soles, consisting of layers of felted paper sewn together over a leather base, provided support that enabled the wearer to stand in the stirrups when riding on horseback. These women's boots have silk damask uppers of yellow (the imperial color), with major stress points—the ankles and the upper edges—reinforced with strips of blue silk and ornamented with stitching. The result was surely much admired for its refined and aesthetically pleasing form. This pair of boots was likely made to be worn with court attire (*chaofu*).

While boots and flat-soled shoes continued to be worn after the ascent of the Qing dynasty in 1644, increased contact with Chinese culture and the bound feet of Han Chinese women gradually influenced the sartorial choices of Manchu women. While women of the court were forbidden to bind their feet, platform shoes (pl. 17) allowed them to approximate the "lotus gait" of ladies of earlier dynasties that so titillated men. Photographs of Empress Dowager Cixi show her walking in "horse-hoof" shoes

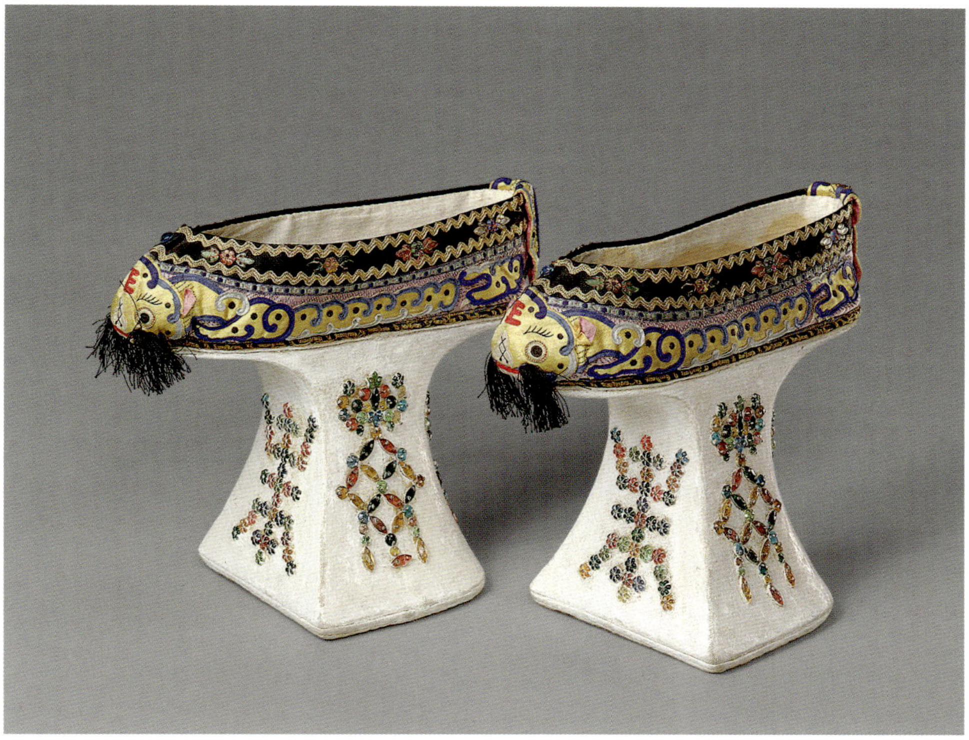

PLATE 17

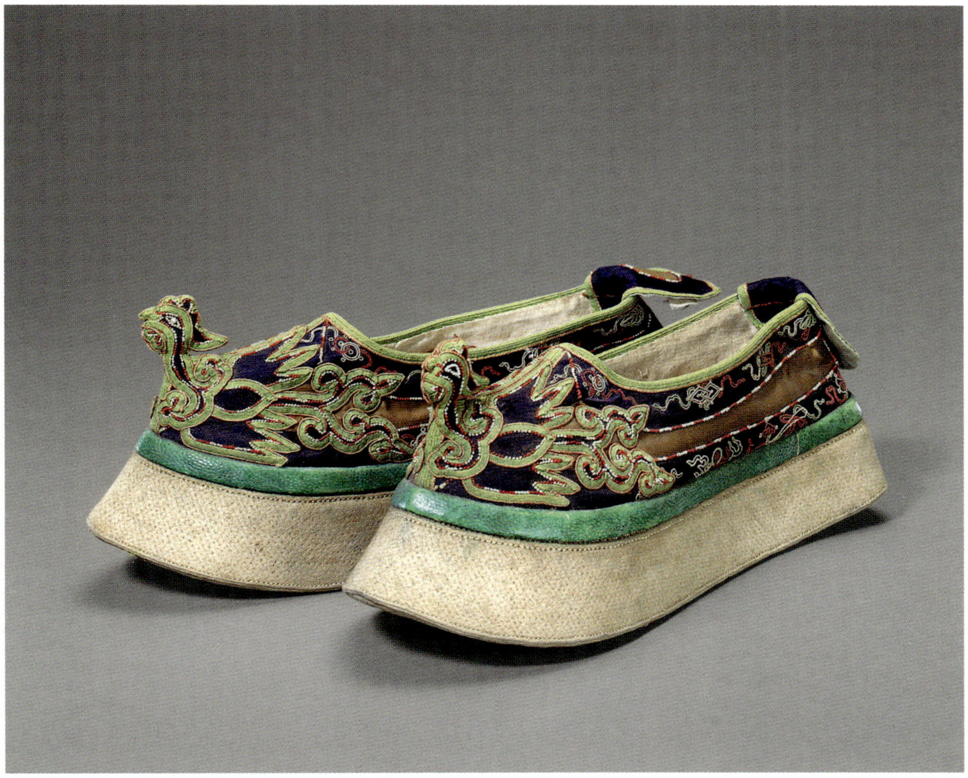

PLATE 18

like these, which, according to Dorothy Ko, were modeled on "a style of . . . unisex shoes" from the Ming dynasty (1368–1644).[3] The sole, which could be four to five inches high, was constructed by wrapping a wooden frame with white cotton cloth. The elaborate bead work featuring the character for longevity (*shou*) and other auspicious motifs was inspired by a rich Chinese design tradition. The tiger heads adorning this pair of shoes are also found on footwear made for children.

Thrusting out from the tip of each of the thick-soled shoes is a phoenix head, an imperial symbol, suggesting that they might have been made for an empress (pl. 18). Embroidering the uppers of shoes was a domestic activity in which court ladies as well as the specialist sewing women in palace service might have engaged. In the famous eighteenth-century novel *Story of the Stone* (*Hongloumeng*), the young ladies of an elite household are described embroidering pieces for their favorite male cousins or brothers. (ESR)

1 See Garrett 1994, 24–25, 45, 59–61; and Garrett 1997, 131–54.

2 See fig. 63, "Emperor's ceremonial boots," in Ho and Bronson 2004, 63.

3 Ko 2004. See fig. 65, "Dowager Empress Cixi," in Ho and Bronson 2004, 67, which shows Cixi sitting on a throne with her full title emblazoned across the top of the photo. Her feet, shod in platform shoes very much like the ones in pl. 17, rest on a footstool in clear view, contravening earlier taboos on showing women's feet in full-length seated portraits.

PLATE 19

清康熙　駝色緞繡平金百鳥朝鳳紋綿襪

Pair of socks with phoenixes and other birds

Workshop, probably Jiangsu or Zhejiang province
Kangxi period, 1662–1722
Embroidery, polychrome, metallic-wrapped, and peacock-filament-wrapped threads on silk satin with silk damask and silk lining
Cat. 82

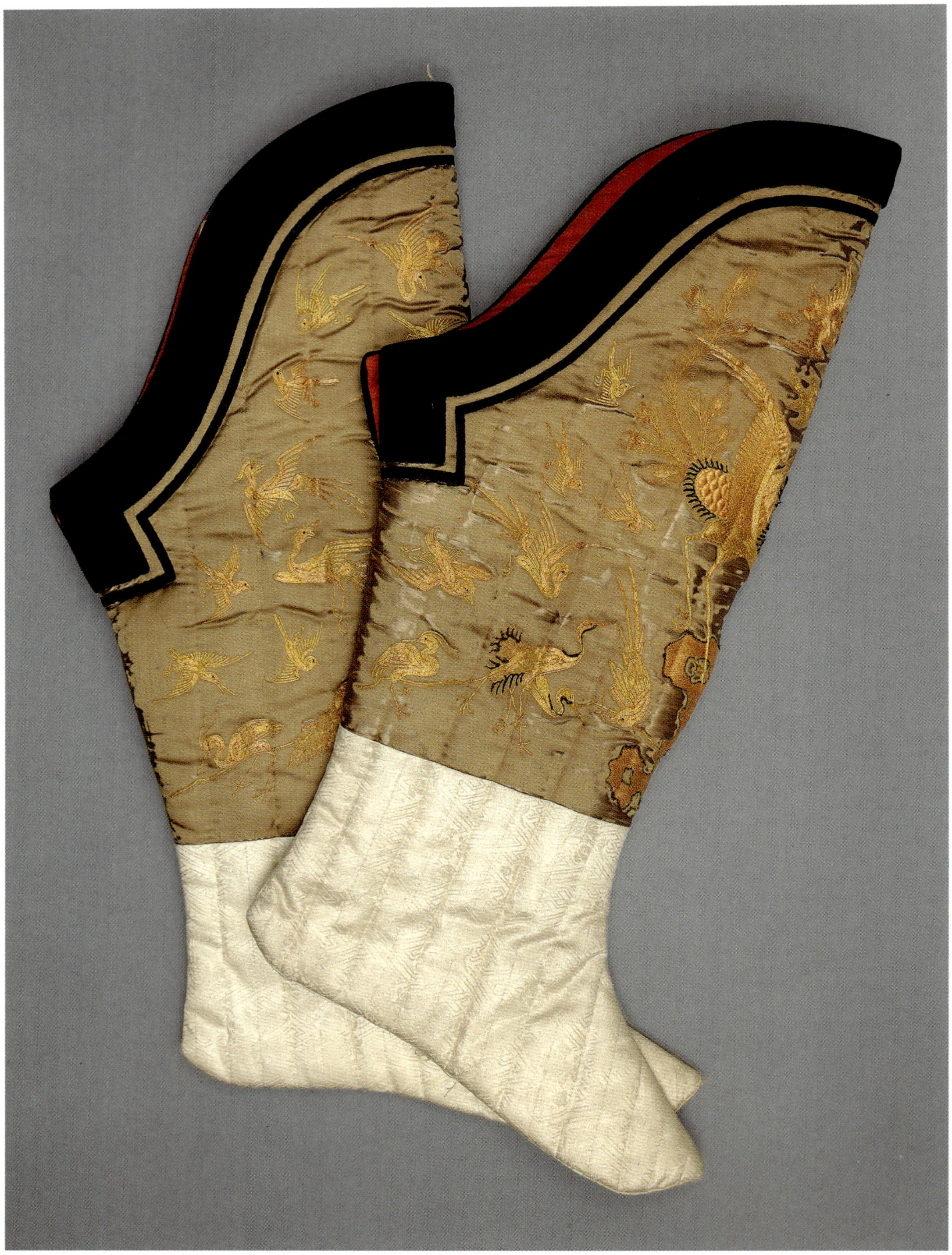

Sartorial regulations dictated the type, designs, and quantities of garments allotted to each consort according to her rank in the eight-level system of emperor's wives. Consorts were granted two lengths of socks: one worn above the ankle and the other (seen here) worn knee high.[1] Both types could be unlined, lined, or padded to suit the season. Note that the feet are full size as Manchu and Mongol women, unlike Han Chinese females, did not bind their feet. The quilted and padded white silk feet of this pair indicate winter wear.

Sparkling gold and shimmering blue-green threads create an exceptionally sumptuous design over the main body of each sock, with expensive velvet trim outlining the opening. Such exceptional materials and workmanship were appropriate only for a woman of great eminence—an empress dowager, empress, or top-rank consort. The design was created by laying gold-wrapped silk threads on the surface and couching them with other threads. Some areas were highlighted with threads wrapped with iridescent peacock-feather filaments. Despite the outstanding quality of workmanship and materials, the socks would have been completely invisible when worn inside tall boots. Nonetheless, a lady of superior rank was understood to deserve such great luxury, even for a concealed undergarment.

The design also signals the status of the wearer. Across the front of the shin a grand phoenix perches atop a large, pierced rock as smaller birds flit through the air paying homage. The phoenix was considered the "king of birds" with both male and female attributes; in its female incarnation it was an important symbol of the empress and female dignity and authority. (JS)

1 Some authors refer to knee-high socks as "stockings," but this is a matter of semantics.

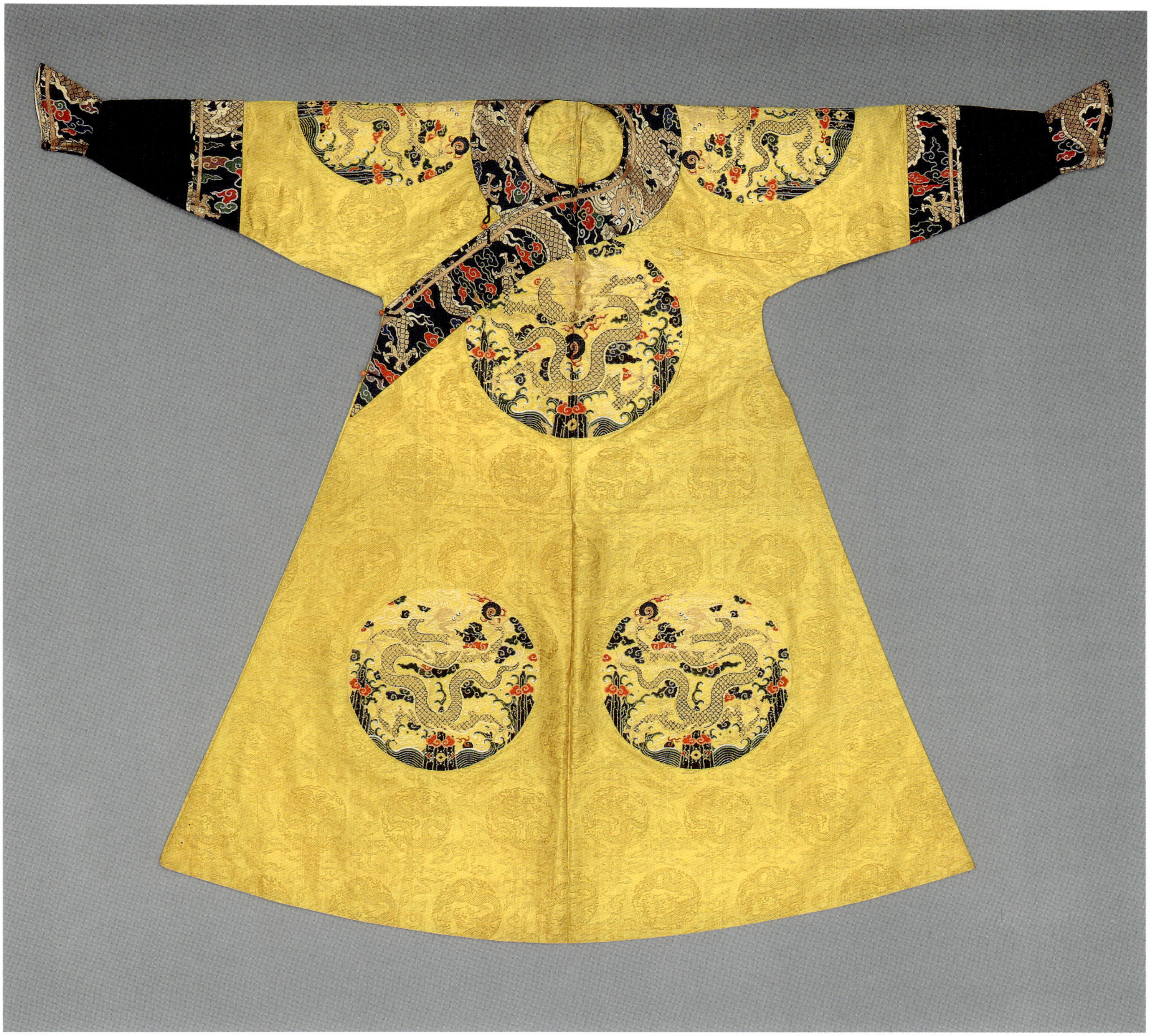

PLATE 20

PLATE 20

清順治　明黃色八團彩雲金龍無水紋妝花紗女單龍袍

Festive robe with eight dragon roundels

Imperial Silk Manufactory, probably Nanjing (weaving)
Shunzhi period, 1644–61
Patterned silk gauze with metallic and polychrome silk threads
Cat. 50

PLATE 21

清乾隆　淺綠色繡博古花卉紋女袍

Festive robe with flowers in vases and butterflies

Imperial Silk Manufactory, Suzhou (weaving and embroidery), and Imperial Workshop, Beijing (tailoring)
Qianlong period, 1736–95
Embroidery, polychrome silk threads on silk satin
Cat. 55

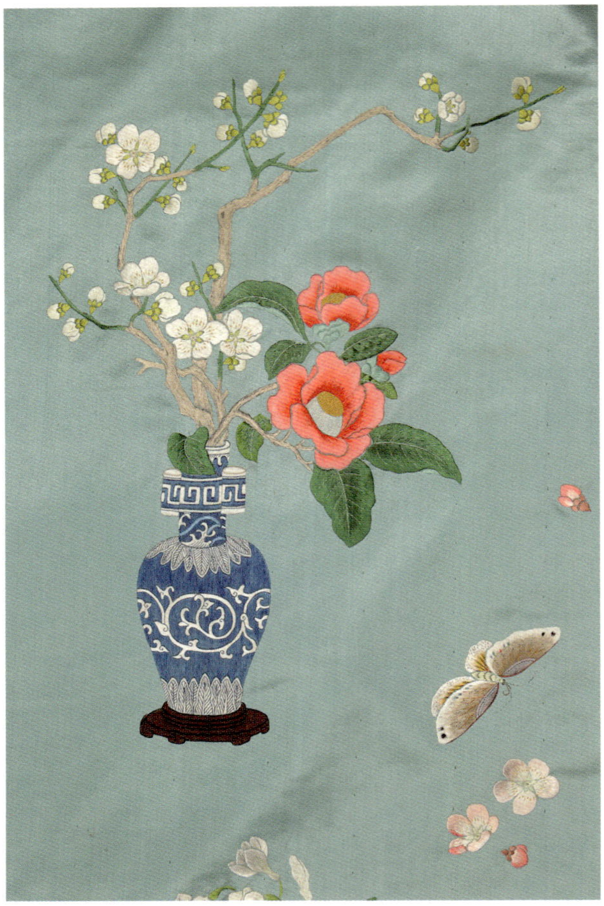

DETAIL

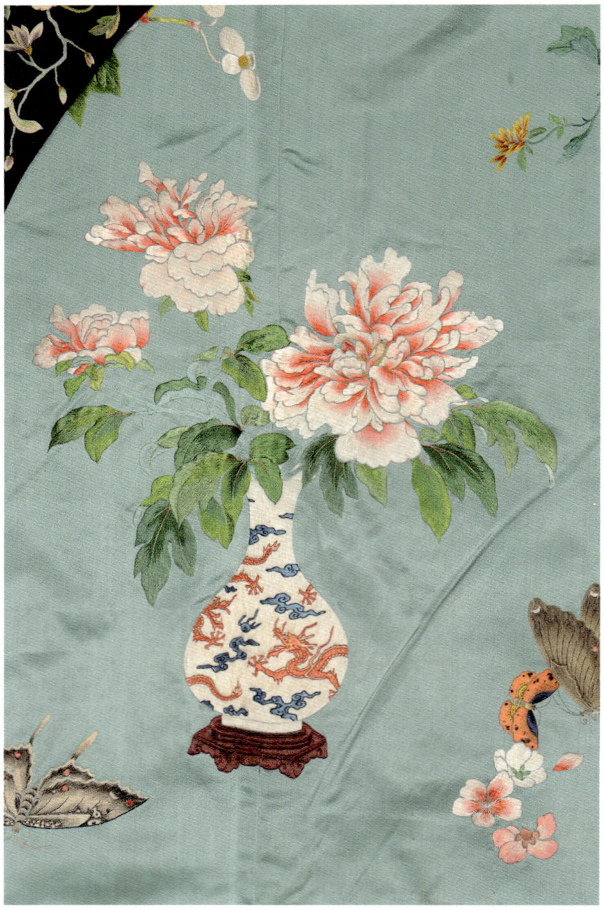

DETAIL

The Qing imperial court had the most stringent and comprehensive regulations on costume in Chinese history. Since the founding of the dynasty, empresses and emperors considered what they wore to be a crucial indicator of a well-maintained social order and a visual reminder of their Manchu ethnicity. A case in point is the early Qing yellow robe for a high-ranking imperial woman (pl. 20). Eight medallions with exquisitely woven dragons, symbols of imperial authority, adorn the shoulders, front, and back of the robe. It features tapered sleeves that end with narrow, horse-hoof-shaped cuffs, articulating the Manchu's seminomadic origins and contrasting sharply with wide sleeves of the loose-fitting Han Chinese garments worn by the majority of the female population in China at the time. The dark blue bands with dragons and clouds encircling the sleeves distinguish it from the emperor's festive robe (*jifu*), and where the emperor's robe had four slits—front, back, and sides—this one, in a nod toward decorum, has only side slits.[1]

The Qianlong emperor issued illustrated codes regulating the costumes of imperial women. Yet even within these strictures, certain costumes for imperial women demonstrate a degree of dynamism and creativity, as seen in the embroidered robe for a consort (pl. 21). It features eight vases holding seasonal flowers, a novel design not recorded in any Qing costume code and one that reflects the imperial taste for ceramics and other art objects. (DYW)

1 Fang Hongjun, Yan Yong, and Wan Jun 2007.

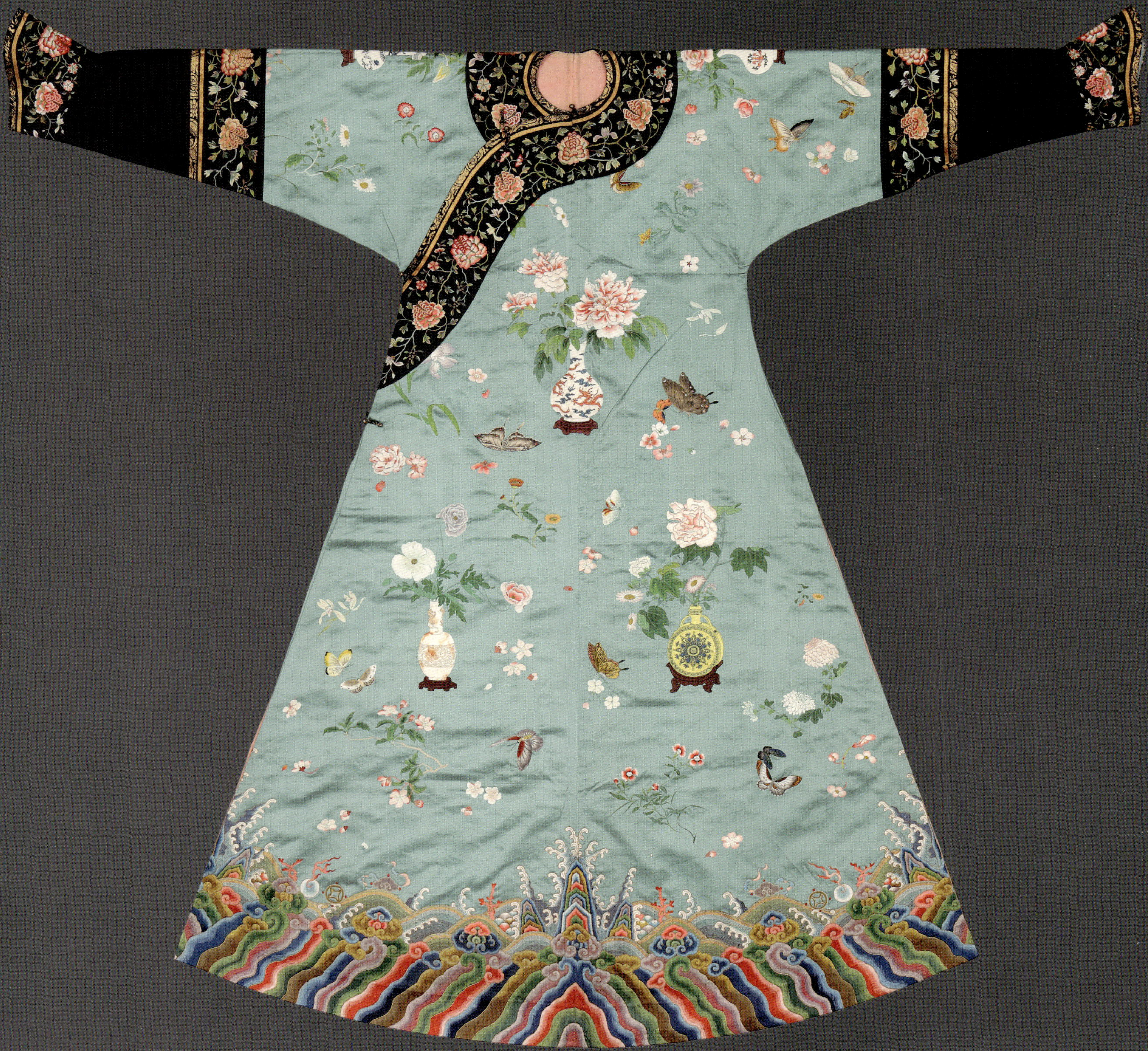

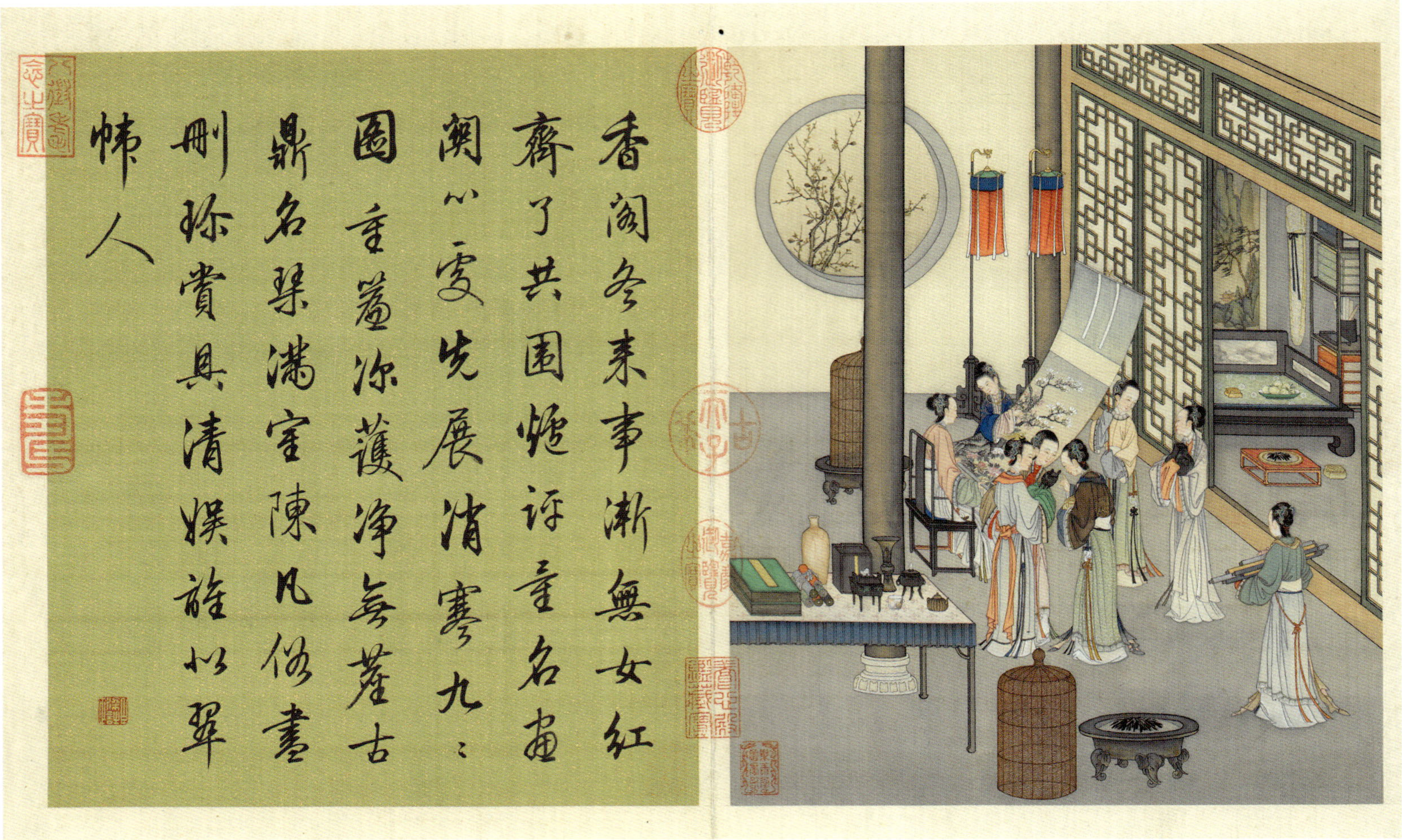

PLATE 22

PLATE 22

清雍正至乾隆　月曼清游冊之十一月圍爐博古頁

Ladies Enjoying Antiquities in the Eleventh Month *from* The Pursuit of Pleasures in the Course of the Seasons

Painting by Chen Mei (1697–1745);
calligraphy by Liang Shizheng (1697–1763)
Painting: Yongzheng period, 1723–35;
calligraphy: Qianlong period, 1738
Album leaf, ink and color on silk
14⅝ × 12½ in. (37 × 31.8 cm)
Gu9224-11-12/12

PLATE 23

清乾隆　象牙雕月曼清游冊之十一月圍爐博古

Ladies Enjoying Antiquities in the Eleventh Month *from* The Pursuit of Pleasures in the Course of the Seasons

Ivory carving by Chen Zuzhang (active 18th century), Gu Pengnian (active 18th century), Chang Cun (active 18th century), Xiao Hanzhen (active 18th century), and Chen Guanquan (active 18th century) at the Wish-Fulfilling Studio (Ruyi guan), Beijing; calligraphy after the Qianlong emperor
Qianlong period, 1741
Ivory with pigments, gold, stone, mother-of-pearl, seed pearls, kingfisher feather, and fabric; frame and cover: wood and glass
15⅜ × 13 × 1¼ in. (39.1 × 32.9 × 3.2 cm)
Gu12474

When the Qianlong emperor was still a prince, he commissioned the court painter Chen Mei to paint twelve lyrical scenes of ladies pursuing seasonal pastimes. The women appear intelligent and lively, reflecting Qianlong's enjoyment of cultivated, engaging female companions. Some of their activities, like viewing antiquities or composing poetry, are gender neutral; others, such as sewing, are specific to women. Chen Mei worked in a hybrid style that integrates features of traditional Chinese painting with European methods such as shading to create volumetric forms and linear perspective to render the illusion of depth. His compositions pull the viewer deep into elegant garden settings that resemble the residences of imperial consorts.

The scene *Ladies Enjoying Antiquities in the Eleventh Month* is the only one of the twelve set entirely indoors. Braziers and hand and foot warmers suggest that the chilly evening air keeps the women indoors to scrutinize paintings, books, ceramics, and bronzes by lantern light. A well-stocked bookshelf and

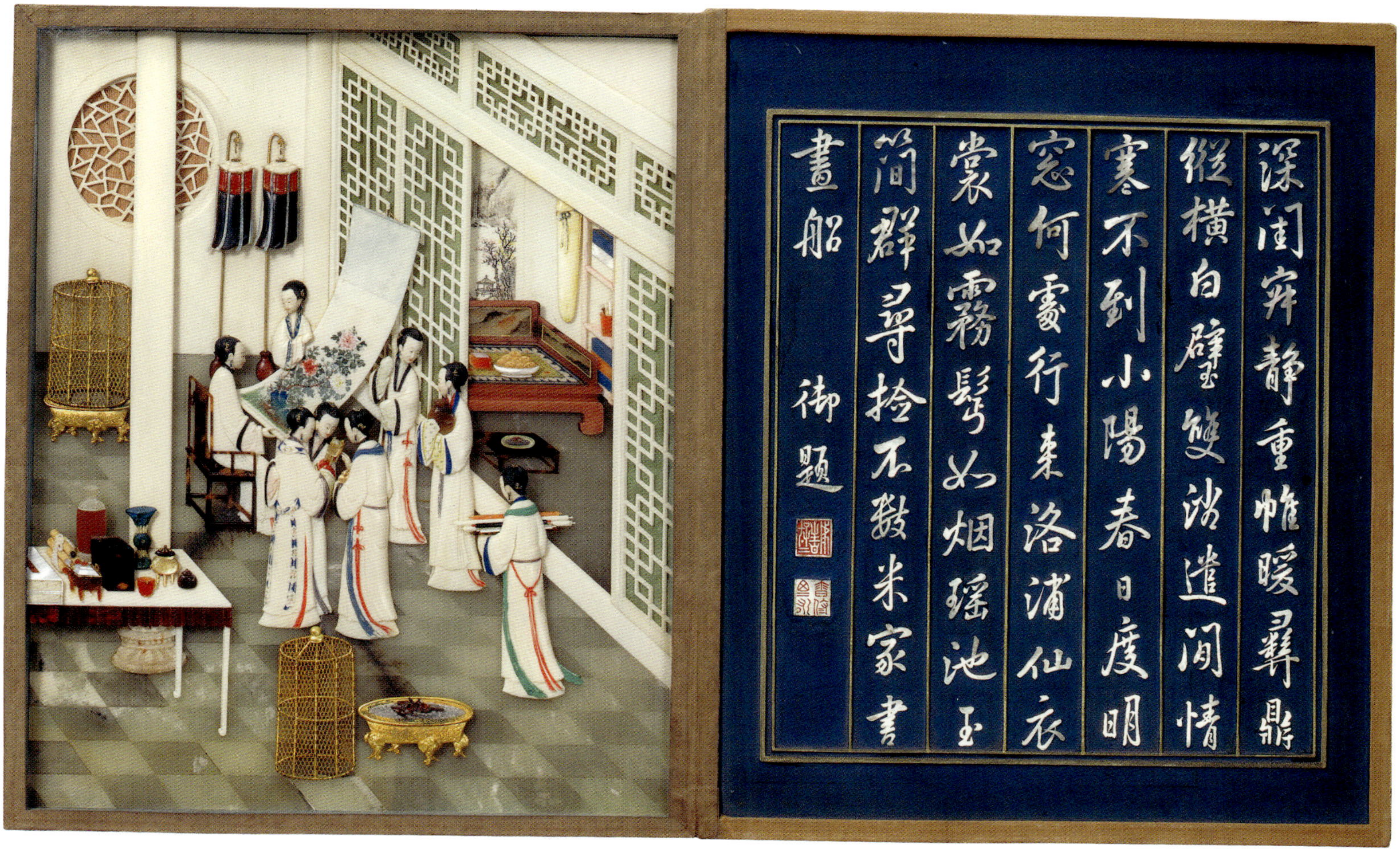

PLATE 23

a wrapped zither hanging on the wall of the inner chamber reinforce the erudition of these women.

This work recalls gatherings of elite male connoisseurs viewing art, a tradition that was often depicted in paintings. In a twist, auspicious wishes are incorporated into the scene, a feature typical of paintings of women created in the Qing court workshop. These good wishes are cleverly embedded in the hanging scroll the women review: the magnolia and crab apple trees and peony flowers create a rebus meaning "may your noble house be blessed with wealth and honor." The round window in the background alludes to the moon and its literary association with femininity. Most of the other paintings in this album either depict the moon in the sky or cleverly suggest it through the architectural feature of a round window or doorway called a "moon gate."

Qianlong must have deeply enjoyed Chen Mei's album. In 1738 he ordered the official Liang Shizheng to write a poem for each scene. The emperor impressed sixty seal marks on the album, suggesting he viewed it several dozen times; some of the seals were only used during his old age, indicating a lifelong appreciation of this work. This admiration was made manifest in 1741 when Qianlong commanded the Imperial Workshop (Zaoban chu) to replicate the paintings as high-relief carvings in ivory approximately the same size as the originals. Five experts from Guangdong, renowned for its ivory carving, were assigned to the Imperial Workshop to execute the figures, architecture, trees, and flowers. Other specialists inset semiprecious stones and other fine materials for the ground, rocks, water, sky, domestic furnishings, and decorative elements. Judicious touches of polychrome complete the costumes and provide the black for the women's hair. The ivory panels closely follow Chen's paintings, but the carvers astutely took latitude in reinterpreting some details to suit their medium. Qianlong composed poems to accompany the ivory panels and had his calligraphy executed in mother-of-pearl on matching leaves.[1]

The conversion of two-dimensional paintings into three-dimensional artworks would have appealed to Qianlong on several levels. The workers' technical success in translating flat paintings into high-relief carvings demonstrated almost unimaginable skill, pointing to Qianlong's exacting standards and total command over art production at the court. From the large number of three-dimensional works—including porcelain vessels decorated to resemble scroll paintings—that he commissioned, it seems the emperor enjoyed the sensory stimulation of holding and touching works of art, an experience that viewing paintings does not provide. Perhaps crossing the boundary from one material to another also reflected his philosophic musings about multivalence and the nature of nonduality, as he liked to question what is illusion and what is reality. (JS)

1 ZGDYLSDAG 2005, 10:377.

PLATE 24

清雍正至乾隆　黑(紫)漆描金
山水圖多寶格櫃

One of a pair of "precious treasures" display cabinets

Yongzheng or Qianlong period, 1723–95
Lacquer with gold on wood core, metal with gilding, and ivory
Cat. 119

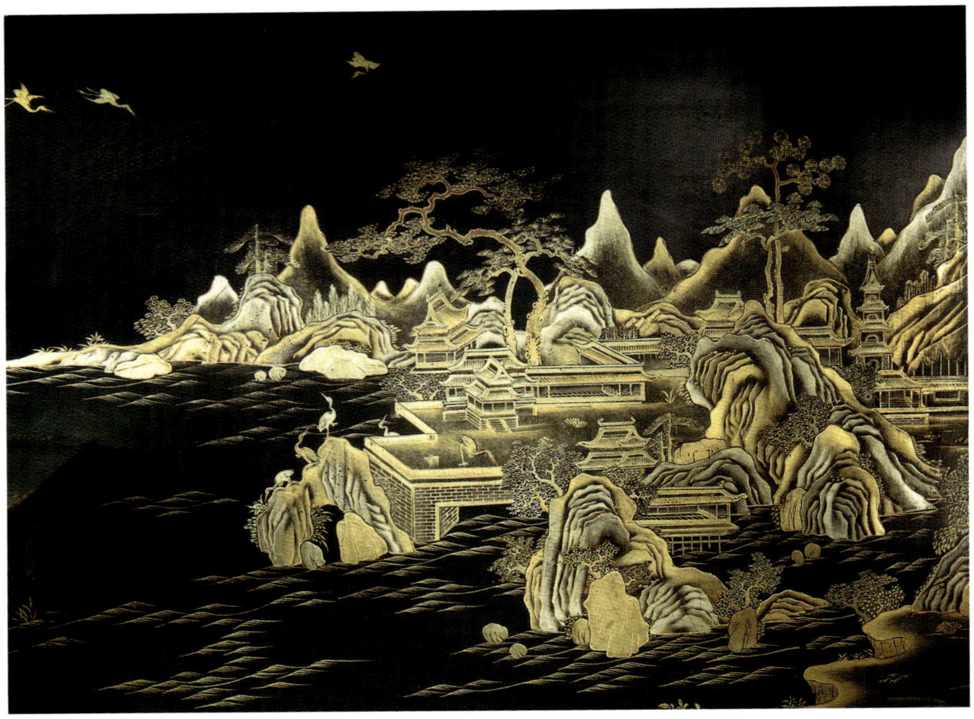

DETAIL, SCENE WITH CRANES EXPRESSING A WISH FOR LONGEVITY

"Precious treasures" cabinets represented the height of artistic novelty in early-to-mid-eighteenth-century palace furniture, when staggered-shelf cabinets were gaining in popularity.[1] Their genesis resulted from a convergence of influences. As combined storage and display units, the cabinets drew upon Ming dynasty (1368–1644) compartmented boxes, multidrawer chests, and open-shelved cabinets as models as well as knowledge at the early Qing court of low-to-the-ground Japanese display units with asymmetrical shelves.[2] Western influence seems strong, too: Jesuits at the Qing court brought the emperors news of *wunderkammer*, or "cabinets of curiosities," popular in Europe since the mid-sixteenth century for their dense displays of disparate objects.[3]

This pair of cabinets was a gift from the Qianlong emperor to his mother, Empress Dowager Chongqing, but they likely were made earlier.[4] A painting of Qianlong's father before he became the Yongzheng emperor (and husband of Chongqing) pictures him next to a similar cabinet filled with books, scrolls, and art objects dating from antiquity to contemporary times.[5] Research into the objects in Chongqing's quarters indicates there was no strict "gender divide" in room furnishings and decorations, and she would have used the cabinet in a similar manner.[6]

The decorative edges of the shelves and the ivory-capped railings framed the displayed objects, setting each apart for individual appreciation. Chinese artists painted flowers, auspicious bats, and landscapes on the cabinets in gold, drawing on the popularity of Japanese black-and-gold lacquer at the early Qing court. The cabinets' side apertures and miniature rails parallel architectural features of the empress dowager's residence, the Palace of Longevity and Health (Shoukang gong), with its fancifully shaped lattice windows and garden fences. Once objects were set on the shelves, Chongqing's treasure cabinets became a world in miniature: their architectonic form and landscape scenes represented the terrestrial world; the art collection on the shelves captured a full sweep of history; and the concept of dense, compartmentalized displays reflected influences from around the world. Thus, taken together, the "fine things" in an empress's residence underscored the same messages as those in an emperor's: the glory and expansiveness of Qing rule. (JS)

1 Staggered-shelf furniture (*duobaoge*; also called *boguge*) first appeared in the Kangxi period (1661–1722). Ding Wenfu asserts that the Japanese-style gold decoration was most popular in the Yongzheng period, suggesting a probable date for these cabinets. See Ding Wenfu 2012, 69.

2 See Chen Huixia 2010.

3 Nicole Ter-chuang Chiang compares Qing and European *wunderkammer* in Chiang 2013.

4 Lin Shu, Palace Museum, in discussion with the author, December 15, 2017.

5 *Yinzhen's Amusements: Reading by a Burner* (Palace Museum, Beijing) can be viewed online at www.npm.gov.tw/exh98/yongzheng/pics/cn_img02j.html. See also Tian Jiaqing 1999, 38–41.

6 These cabinets were published in Rawski and Rawson 2006, p. 446, no. 221, as having have been used by Qianlong because the inventory number associating them with the empress dowager's Palace of Longevity and Health was not known at that time.

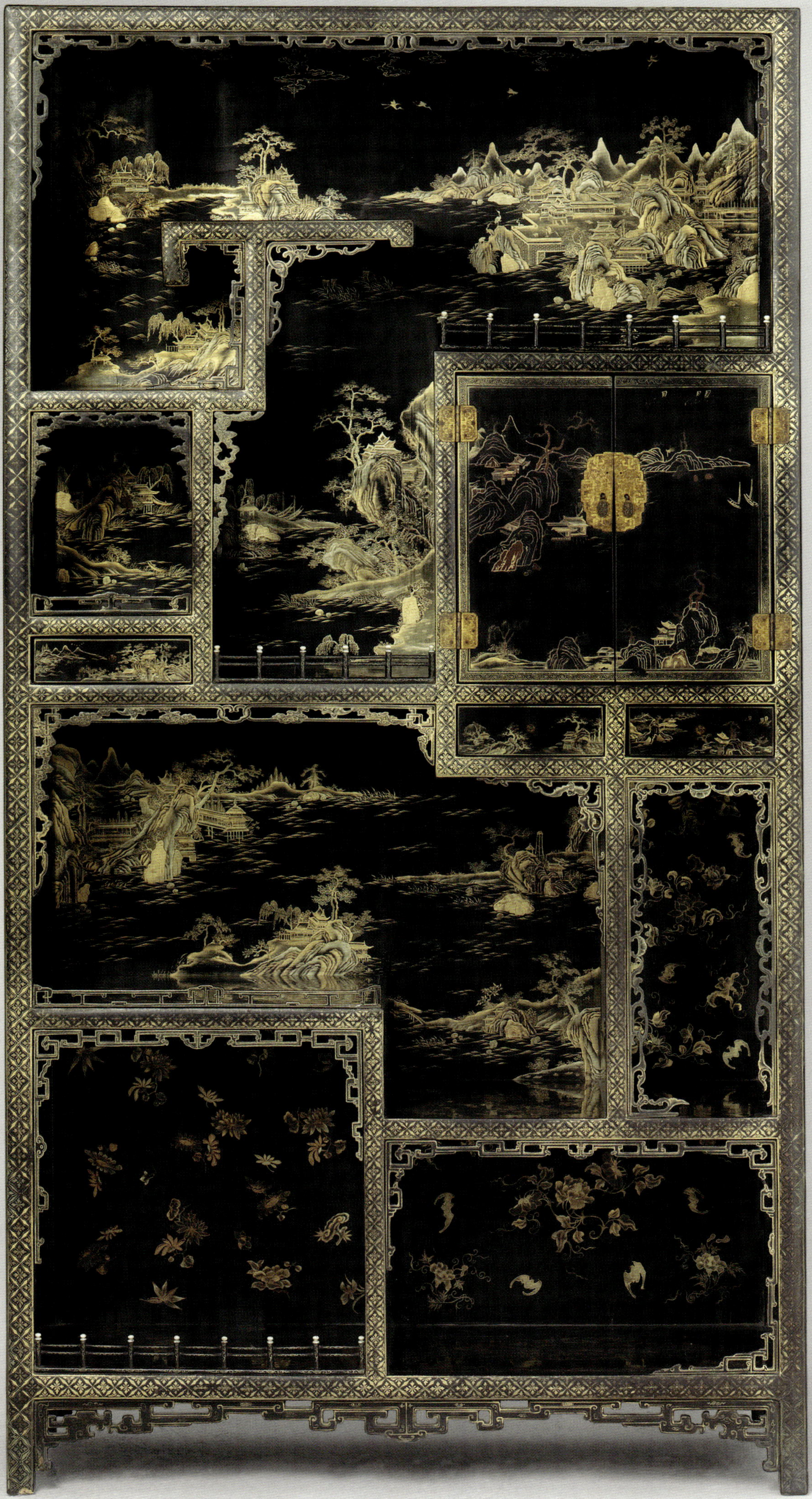

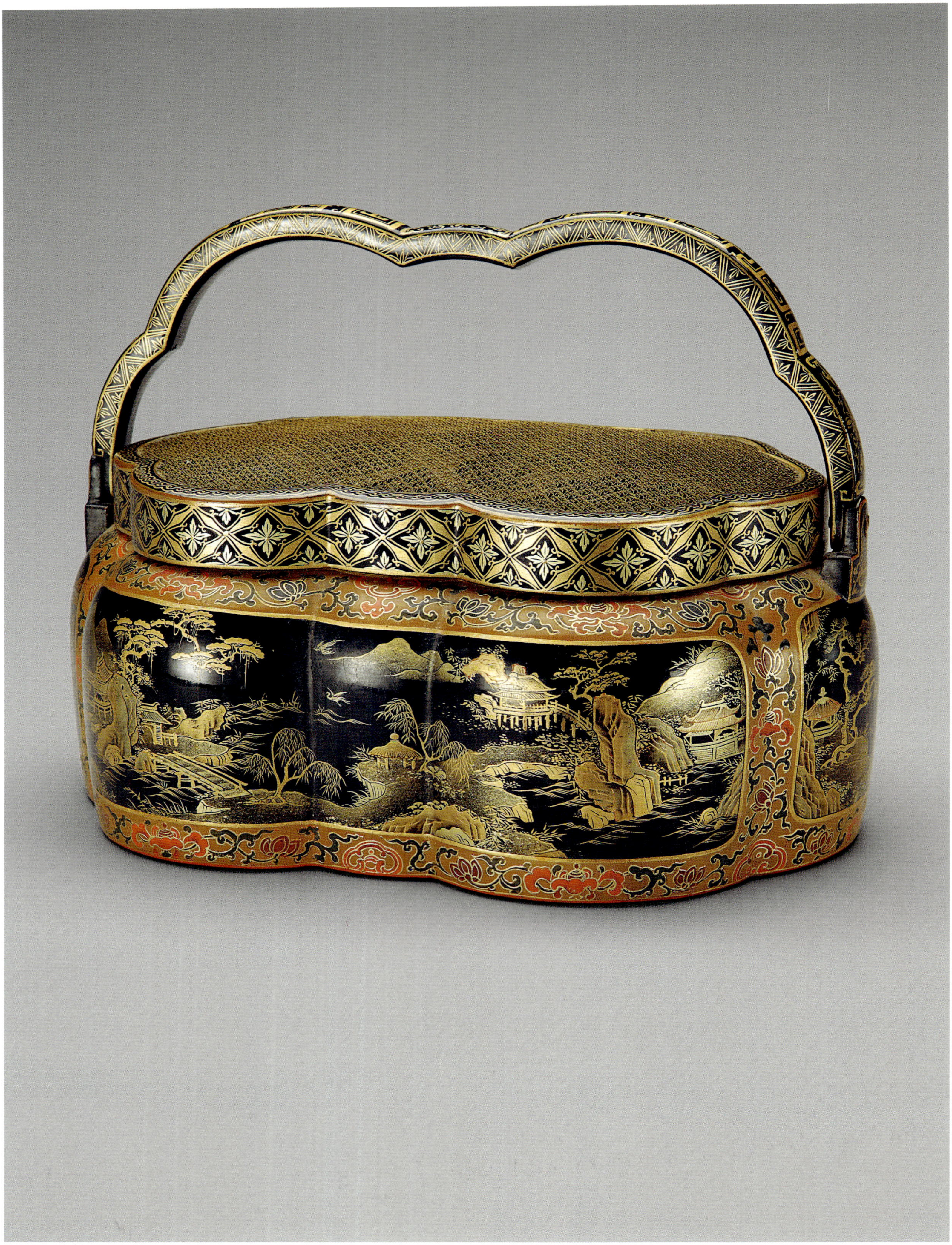

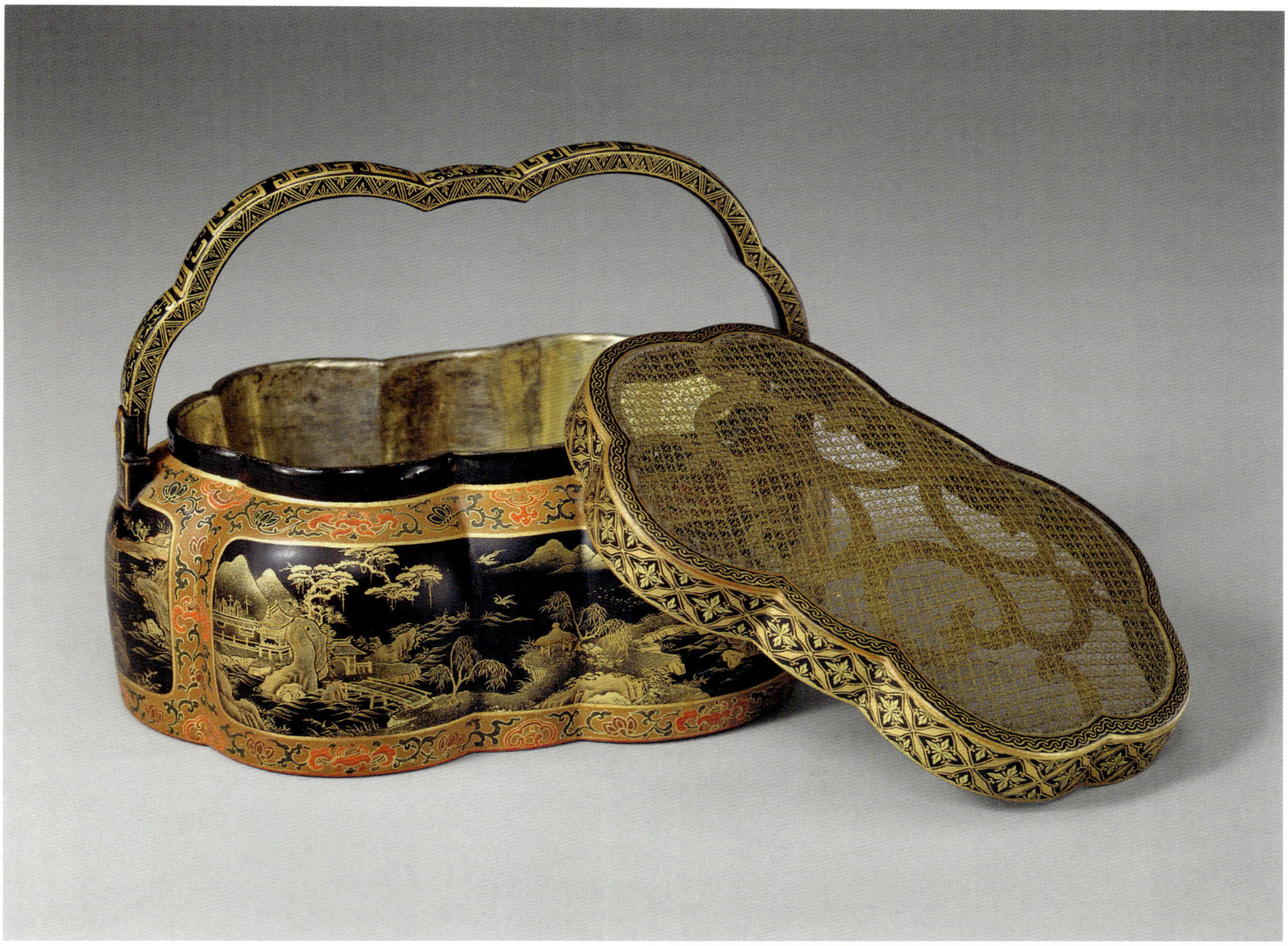

PLATE 25

清乾隆　黑漆描金山水圖手爐

Hand warmer with landscapes

Probably workshop, Suzhou
Qianlong period, 1736–95
Lacquer with gold and pigments on metal core
Cat. 144

A hand warmer provided comfort during cold winters. It typically consisted of a decorated outer box into which was placed an inner metal container to hold hot charcoal. The burning charcoal heated the air in the space between the metal container and the outer box, creating the ideal temperature on the outside for warming hands. As with many functional objects at the court, hand warmers were often embellished with auspicious symbols and lavish designs.

The shape of this hand warmer symbolizes wish fulfillment and longevity. The walls of the box feature four landscape panels, two large and two small. The different shades of gold resemble the effect of modulated ink tones in a brush painting. While many hand warmers found in the imperial collection have an outer box made of copper alloy decorated with painted enamels, this one made of lacquer is highly unusual. The inner container of this warmer shows no trace of ash left from burning charcoal, suggesting it might never actually have been used.

Why would a hand warmer be made of a precious material? Given the rarity of lacquer hand warmers in the palace collection, this may be one of nine lacquer hand warmers Qianlong gave to his mother, Empress Dowager Chongqing, on her sixtieth or seventieth birthday.[1] If it was indeed a birthday gift, the hand warmer would have served as an emblem of Qianlong's concern for his mother's well-being. As this object is a pinnacle of gold-painted lacquerware of the period, it would have demonstrated his utmost respect by giving the empress dowager an uncommon object of supreme craftsmanship that suited her revered position. (DS)

1 E'ertai and Zhang Tingyu (1769) 1987, *juan* 18.

PLATE 26

清乾隆　黑漆描金妝奩盒
(帶鏡子)

Dressing case with mirror stand and handheld mirror

Qianlong period, mid- to late 18th century, with later repairs
Lacquer with gold and polychrome decoration on wood core, *zitan* wood, *suanzhi* wood, mother-of-pearl, bone, metal with gilding; wood-framed mirror with embroidered silk case
Cat. 122

The classical Chinese text *Etiquette and Rites* (*Yili*) lists as one of a noblewoman's four basic duties and virtues the projection of an elegant "wifely appearance" (*furong*). Preparing one's toilette was considered an expression of conjugal devotion, and images of a woman gazing into a mirror had a long history in Chinese art as a metaphor for the transience of female beauty. Alternatively, the same image was used to encourage women to cultivate character over superficial appearance. Such a scene appears in *The Admonitions of the Instructress to Court Ladies* (*Nüshi zhen tu*), a fifth- or sixth-century work in Qianlong's collection that the emperor valued for its didactic messages and visual style. He also acquired and then copied a twelfth-century version of this scroll, likely sharing his work with his harem (see cat. 27).

In this context, the import of a dressing case to a woman is clear. While such items appeared in palace dowries, they were important possessions for women of all ages.[1] This example was used in the Palace of Longevity and Health (Shoukang gong) and was probably made for Empress Dowager Chongqing. Removing the tall cover decorated with auspicious designs in gold reveals the two-tiered construction. The upper level holds a collapsible latticework stand for a traditional bronze mirror, with a support in the shape of a bat (a symbol of good fortune) at the bottom.[2] The exterior of the lower section's doors sparkle with inlaid dyed bone and semiprecious stones that form a floral design. Gold lacquer decoration completely covers the other three sides of the exterior. The doors open to reveal an interior resembling a "precious treasures cabinet" (*duobaoge*; see pl. 24), here intended to hold cosmetics and dressing accoutrements. All of the interior spaces, including the insides of the drawers, are covered with lacquered floral designs. The decorative themes reflect the cosmopolitanism of Qing arts: the flowers on the inside of the doors draw on Japanese-style lacquer decoration; the designs on the drawer with gold painting are inflected by rococo-style European motifs; and the handheld mirror uses reflective glass modeled on European examples. (JS)

1 Records of the Tongzhi emperor's marriage in 1872 reveal he gave his empress a pair of hardwood mirror stands as part of her dowry. See Tongzhi's wedding record in Mao 2007, appendix I, p. 306.

2 Repairs in light-colored wood suggest the case was heavily used. Some gold decorations have later repairs as well.

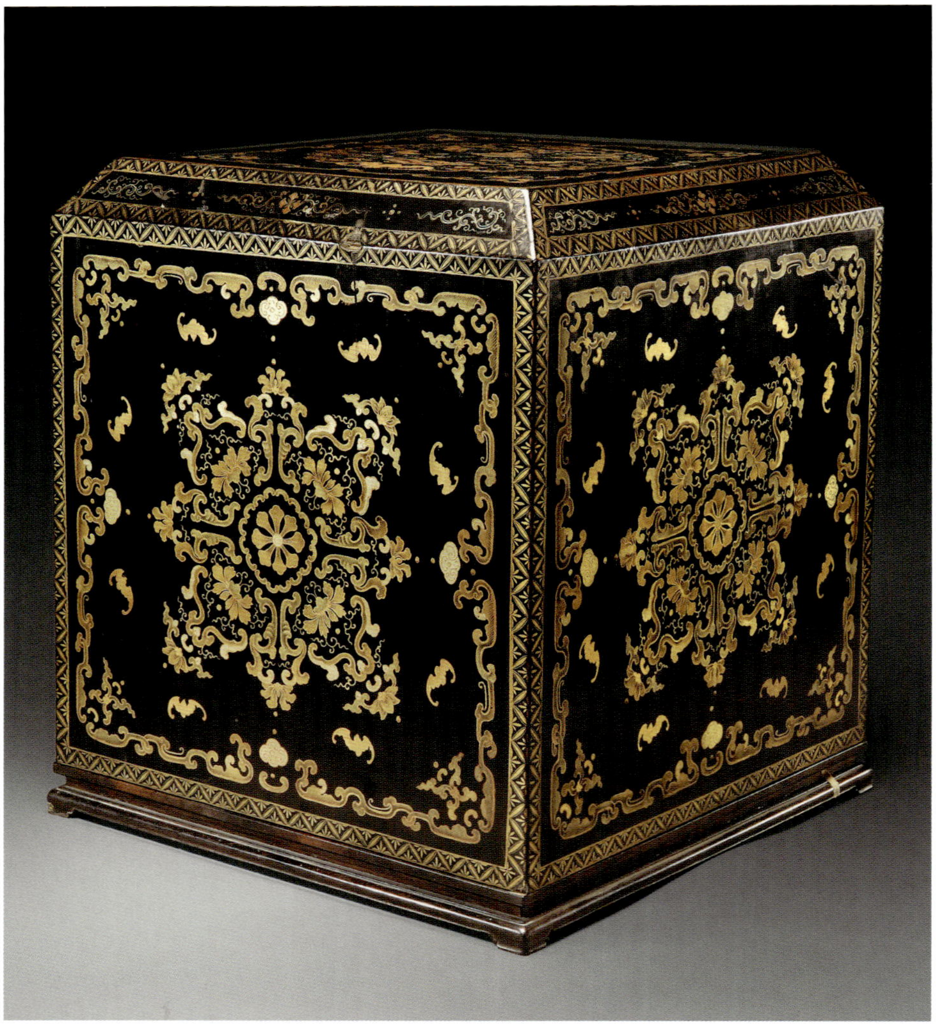

DETAIL, CASE WITH COVER

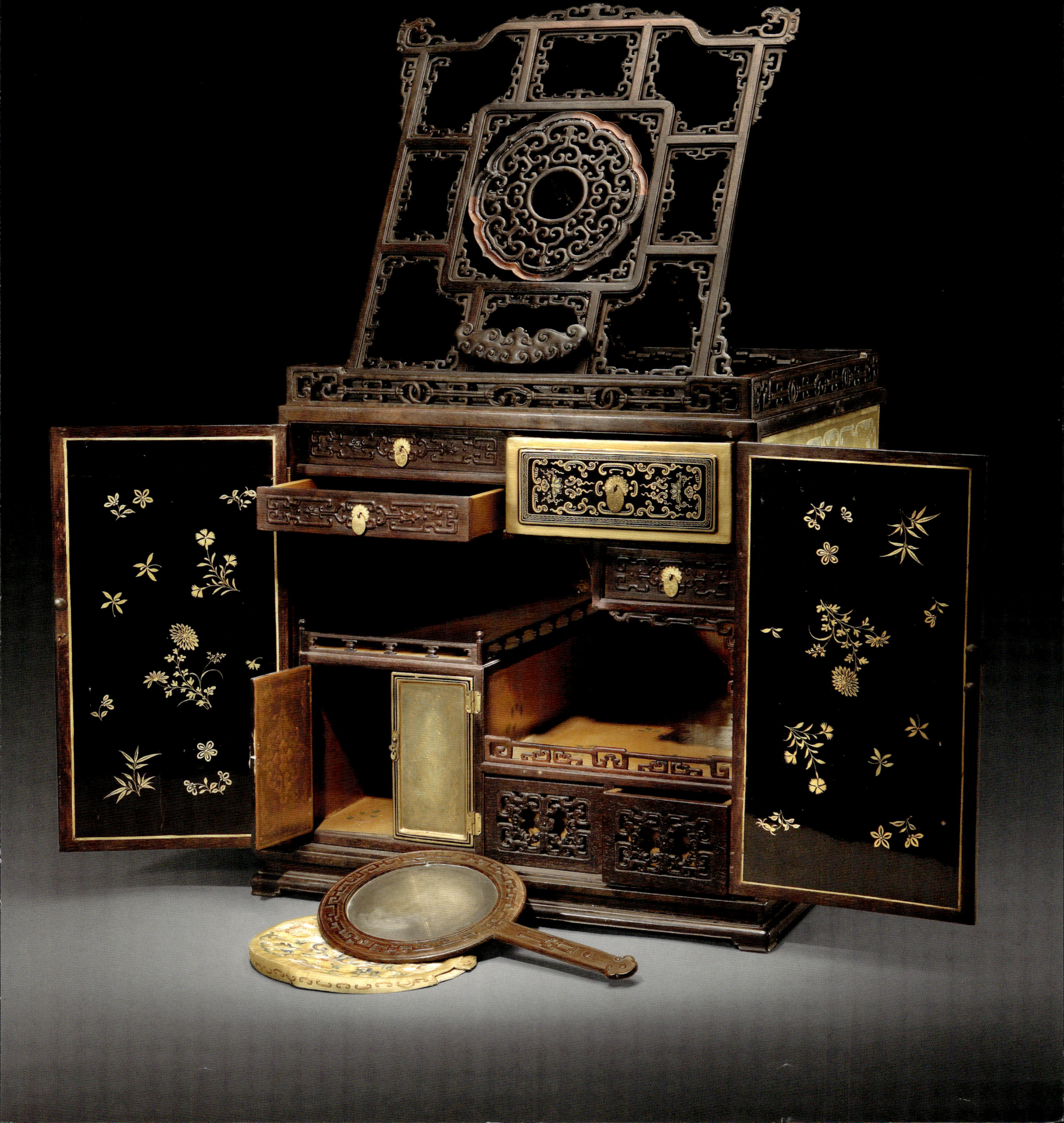

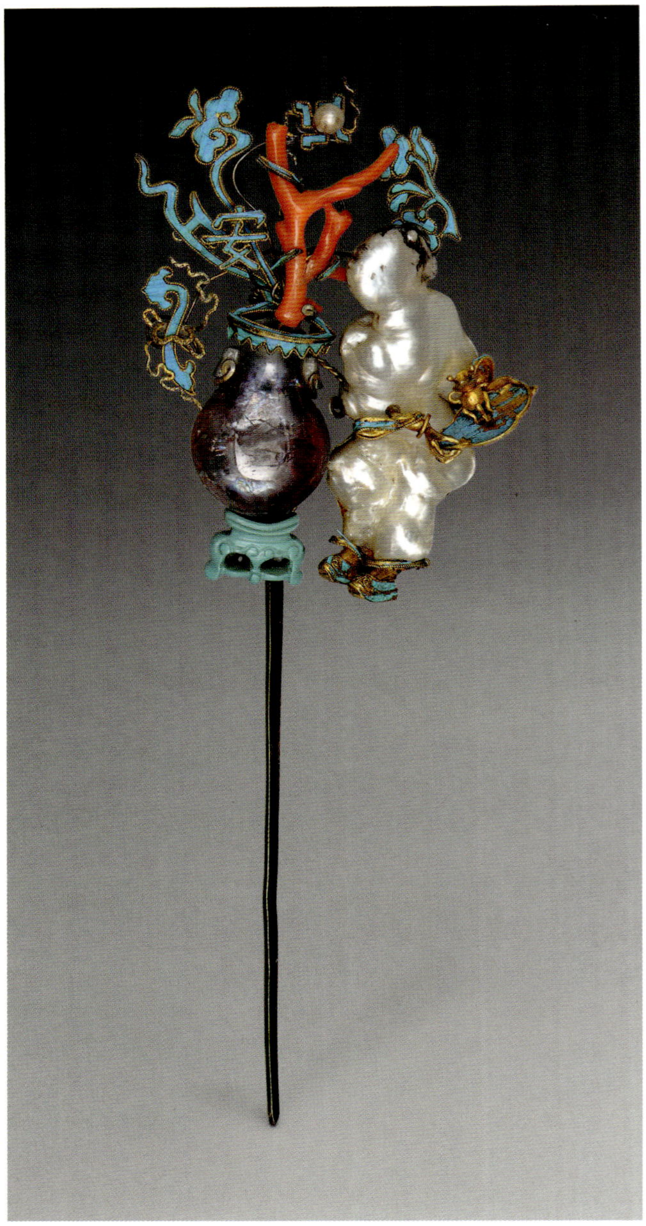

PLATE 27

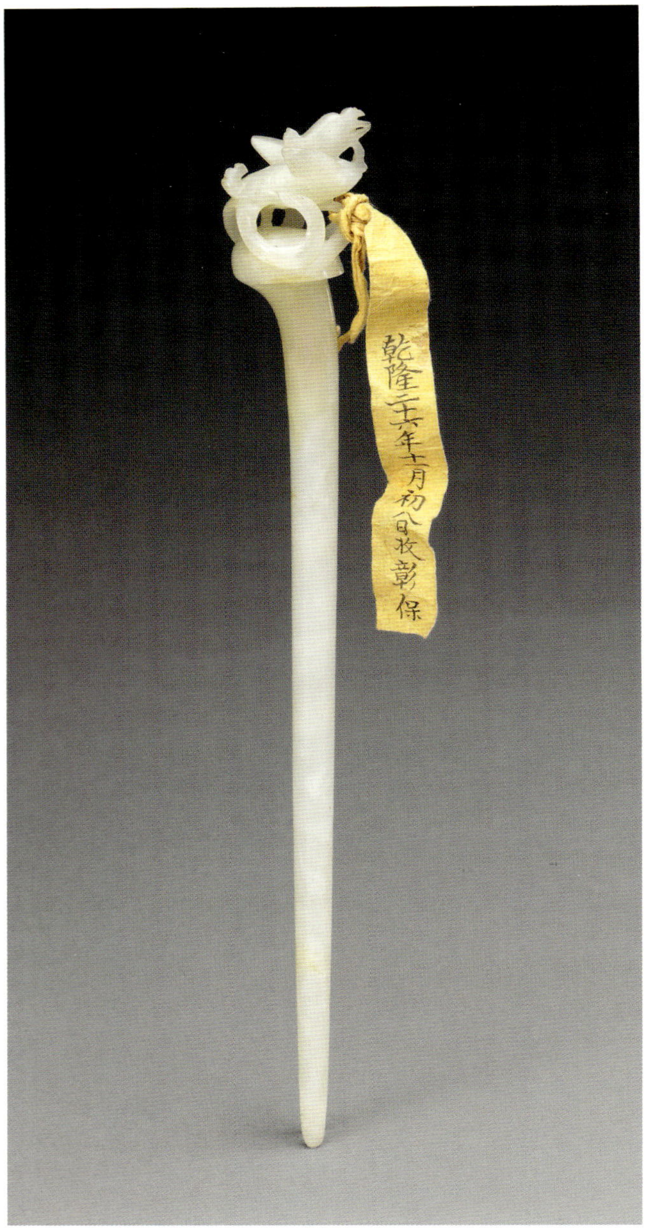

PLATE 28

PLATE 27

清中晚期　銀鍍金鑲珠娃娃瓶式簪

Hairpin with figure and vase

18th or 19th century
Pearls, sapphire, coral, turquoise, kingfisher feather, and silver with gilding
Cat. 105

PLATE 28

明　青玉透雕鳳頭簪

Hairpin with phoenix finial

Ming dynasty, 1368–1644
Jade (nephrite)
Cat. 101

PLATE 29

清道光　銀鍍金嵌寶石玉蟹紋簪

Hairpin with crab and reed

Daoguang period, 1834 or earlier
Jade (nephrite), kingfisher feather, pearls, ruby, and silver with gilding
Cat. 104

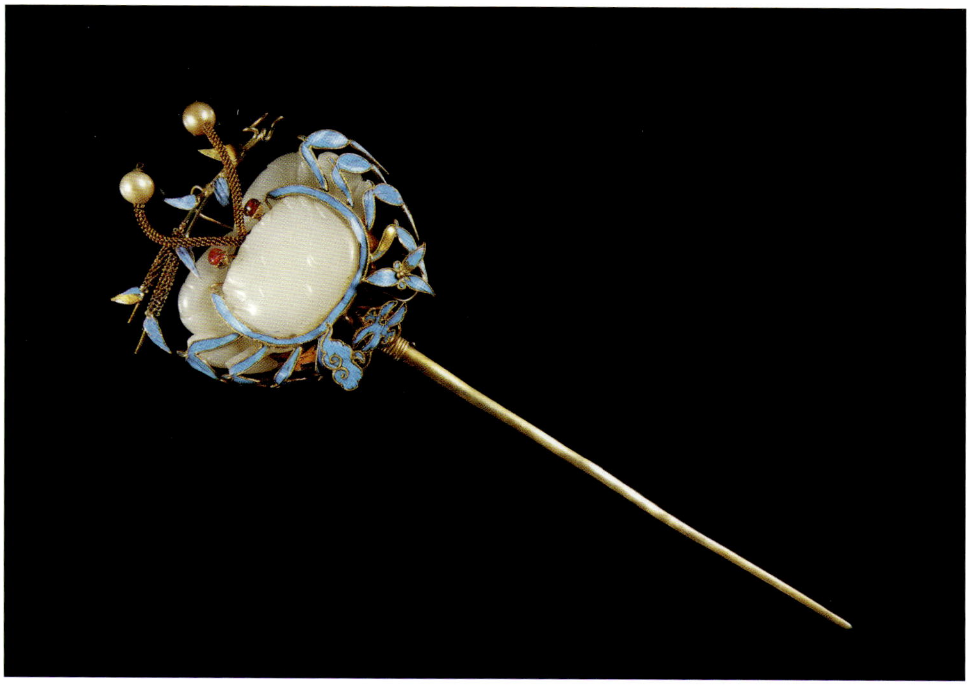

PLATE 29

In the Qing dynasty both Manchu and Han Chinese elite women favored hairpins.[1] They were compatible with a variety of hairdos regardless of the wearer's ethnicity and offered a wide range of possibilities for decoration. Each hairpin for an imperial woman is an ingenious miniature sculpture. To create a sense of movement some hairpins have dangling tassels, while others feature decorative components attached by metal wires that vibrated as the wearer moved (pls. 27 and 29). Precious materials such as gold, pearls, coral, and gemstones were used to create a profusion of contrasting hues and textures. Qing elite women especially favored hair ornaments featuring the iridescent blue kingfisher feather, which was cut into small pieces and glued into cells to form designs.[2] A counterpoint to this taste for the dazzling and extravagant can be found in the simple yet elegant antique white jade hairpin topped by a phoenix (pl. 28).

Hairpins for Qing imperial women are replete with auspicious symbols. In the pin with figure (pl. 27), the vase, the Chinese character, and the wish-granting scepter (*ruyi*) form a rebus for "peace and may your wishes come true," while the irregularly shaped pearl represents a lady holding a gold wine cup on a tray, expressing the wish for promotion of one's official rank. The hairpin with a crab holding a reed (pl. 29) symbolizes success in scholarly examinations, an event that would have led to becoming an official.

Jewelry, including hairpins, was not considered the personal property of Qing empresses or other imperial women. After a consort died, her belongings were managed by the Imperial Household Department (Neiwu fu).[3] Some items might be given to people who had been close to the ladies; some were buried to accompany them into the afterlife; some were inventoried and returned to the palace storehouse, often with a yellow paper or silk tag recording the name of the object, the date, and the name of the inspector (but not the date of manufacture or the name of the user). According to its tag, the white jade hairpin (pl. 28) was inventoried in 1761 but made in the Ming dynasty (1368–1644). Unworn gold and silver court jewelry was weighed and graded based on its purity and melted for future use, and pearls and gemstones were often repurposed.

The Gold and Jade Workshop (Jinyu zuo) and a number of other workshops under the Imperial Household Department handled the manufacture of jewelry for imperial women. A maker's mark on the hairpin with the crab and reed (pl. 29) shows that by the late Qing dynasty jewelers outside the palace also supplied imperial women, blurring the line between court and noncourt jewelry.[4] (DYW)

1 Yang Zhishui 2014, 3:802.
2 McCarthy and Chase 2003, 15–23; Xiaodong Xu and Tong Yu 2017, 42–53.
3 Rawski 2009, 142–44, 158–59.
4 Gugong bowuyuan 2012, 98–99.

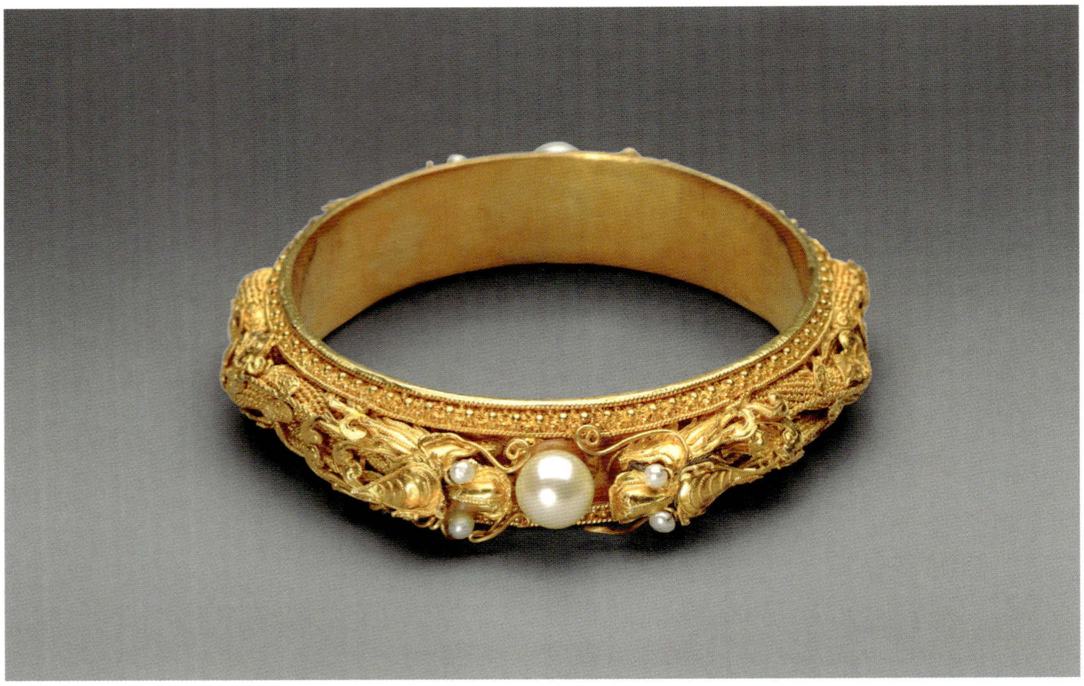

PLATE 30

PLATE 30

清　金鑲四龍戲珠鐲

One of a pair of bracelets with dragons and pearls

Probably 19th century
Gold with pearls
Cat. 94

PLATE 31

清晚期　玳瑁鑲金嵌珠寶桃蝠梅紋鐲

Pair of bracelets with bats, peaches, and flowers

Probably 19th or early 20th century
Tortoiseshell with coral, kingfisher feather, pearls, ruby, jadeite, tourmaline, and silver with gilding
Cat. 96

PLATE 32

清晚期　珊瑚嵌珠萬壽紋鐲

Pair of bracelets with the character for longevity

Probably 19th or early 20th century
Coral with pearls
Cat. 95

Qing empresses and other palace women frequently wore bracelets, usually sporting an identical bangle on each wrist.[1] Elite Han Chinese women of the previous dynasty typically wore a pair of bracelets, drawing attention to the fact that the Qing court modeled much of its jewelry on earlier Chinese traditions. By contrast, the Qing court maintained stricter boundaries between Manchu and Han Chinese practice when it came to clothing. The three pairs of bracelets here suggest that the taste of the imperial harem tended toward flashy jewelry in a wide range of materials, all decorated with auspicious symbols.

The gold bracelet (pl. 30) features four dragons with their faces separated by large pearls and eyes inset with small pearls. The facing-dragons motif, brought from north India by traveling merchants and monks, appeared in bracelet designs in the Tang dynasty (618–907)and remained popular thereafter.[2] The "dragons chasing a pearl" design was understood at the Qing court as an auspicious image of imperial power.

The tortoiseshell bracelets (pl. 31) required considerable skill to artfully combine so many materials. After heating and bending the tortoiseshell into a circle, workers wrapped it with a gold-plated silver band, which they then set with brightly colored gems. The pattern consists of bats

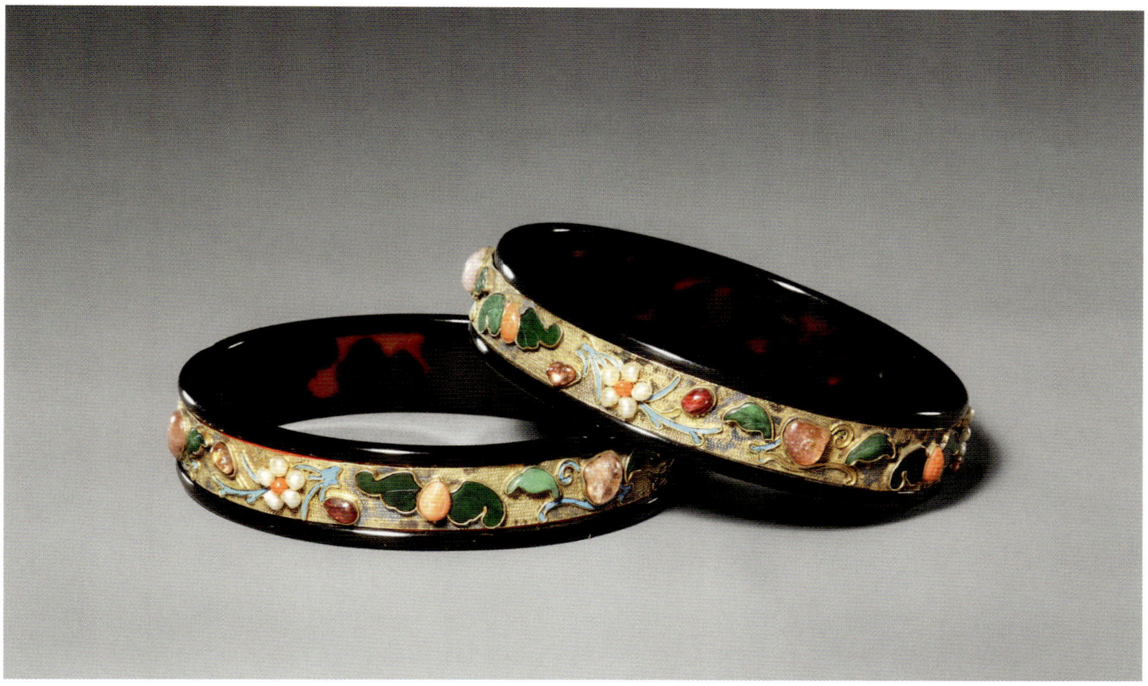

PLATE 31

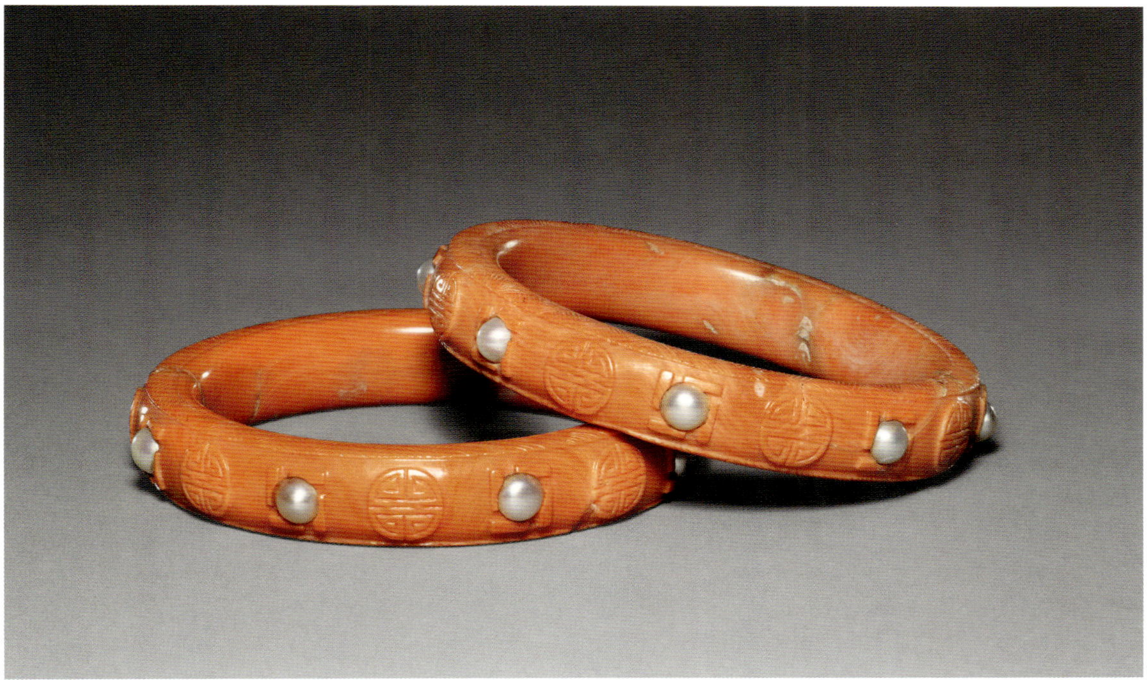

PLATE 32

and peaches (symbols of good fortune and longevity) amid plum blossoms.

The bracelets of coral (pl. 32)—a most precious material—celebrate the theme of longevity, probably having been made for an empress's birthday. The surface is embellished by carvings of the character for long life (*shou*) alternating with pearl-studded swastikas, a symbol borrowed from Buddhism that means "ten thousand," or extended life. According to records of Empress Dowager Cixi's sixtieth birthday, she commissioned pairs of glass bracelets in various colors that closely resemble these coral bracelets, suggesting she particularly liked this look and providing a likely date.[3] (JS)

1 See Wang Chutong 1988; and Yang Zhishui 2014, 3:850–55. Other evidence found in the Qing archives indicates some bracelets were made as single specimens.

2 For a description of the find of 255 gold and silver items discovered in Hejia cun, in the southern part of Xi'an, Shaanxi province, see Hansen 2003.

3 See Wong et al. 2017, 198–99.

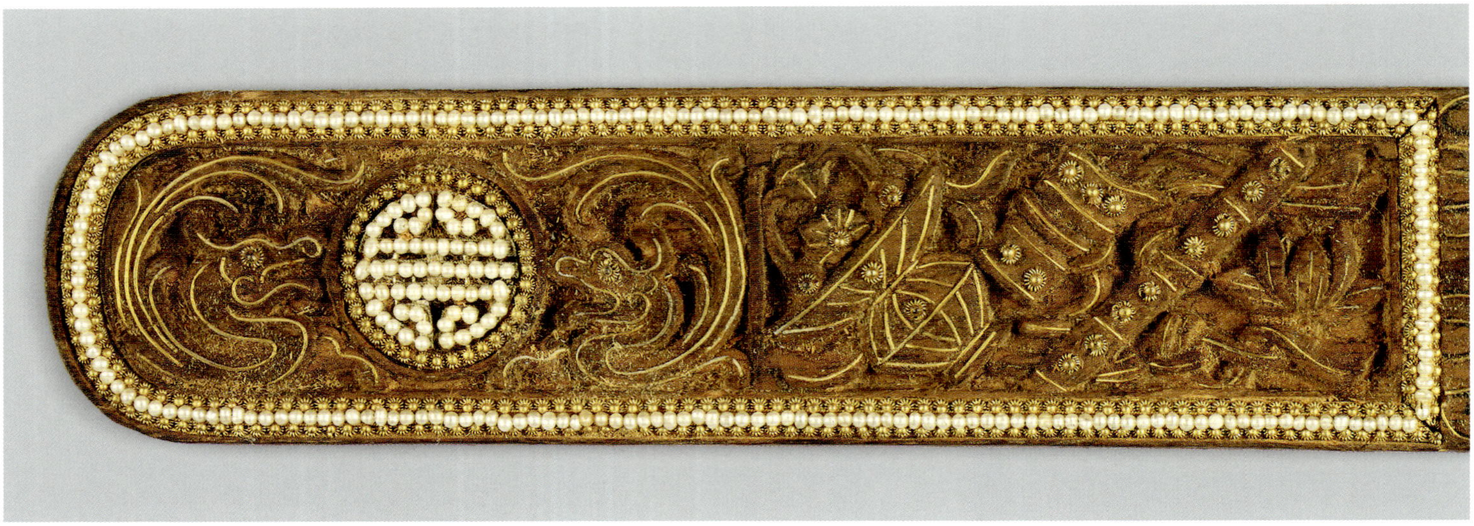

DETAIL

PLATE 33

清晚期　沉香嵌珠夔龍團壽暗八仙紋扁方

Hair ornament with dragons and the character for longevity

Workshop, probably Guangzhou
19th or early 20th century
Agarwood with seed pearls and gold-alloy inlay
Cat. 111

Bar-shaped ornaments like this were essential items for imperial women in the nineteenth and early twentieth centuries. To create a distinctive Manchu hairdo, the wearer wrapped her hair around a long, flat bar and placed it across the top of her head, with the scroll-shaped ornament at the end of the bar on her proper right. Such a hairstyle could accommodate a profusion of flowers and other adornments. As a portrait of Empress Dowager Cixi illustrates (see pl. 46), toward the end of the Qing dynasty, this hairstyle evolved into an even more dramatic form that resembled a large bird spreading its wings and required a framework covered with dark satin or velvet to imitate human hair. This spectacular headdress served to distinguish elite Manchu women from their Han Chinese counterparts.

In contrast to the many court and festive hats worn on formal occasions, this type of hair ornament was worn with the informal garb of everyday life, making it a popular focus for innovative and sumptuous decoration—even though the bar was often almost entirely concealed by hair or fabric. The designs often conveyed auspicious meanings. The item illustrated here boasts two roundels of seed pearls and gold beads forming the character for longevity (*shou*; see detail) and the coin design in the center communicates wishes for wealth.

This bar is carved from agarwood, a rare fragrant heartwood imported from South China or Vietnam as tribute to the Qing court. Its distinctive fruity-floral aroma results from a resin produced when the tree is infected by a fungus or bug. Agarwood was often used to make rosaries, and its medicinal properties were employed to treat stomach ailments.[1] (DYW)

1 Wan Xiufeng 2013.

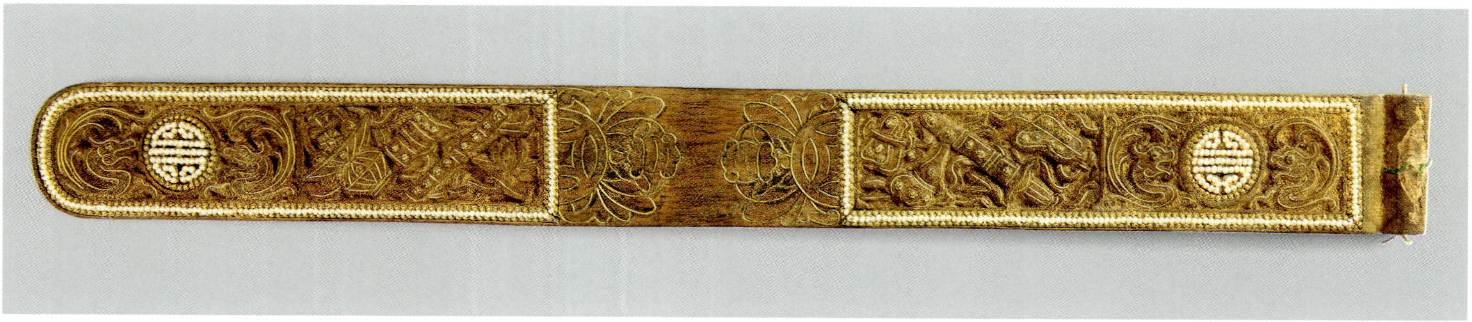

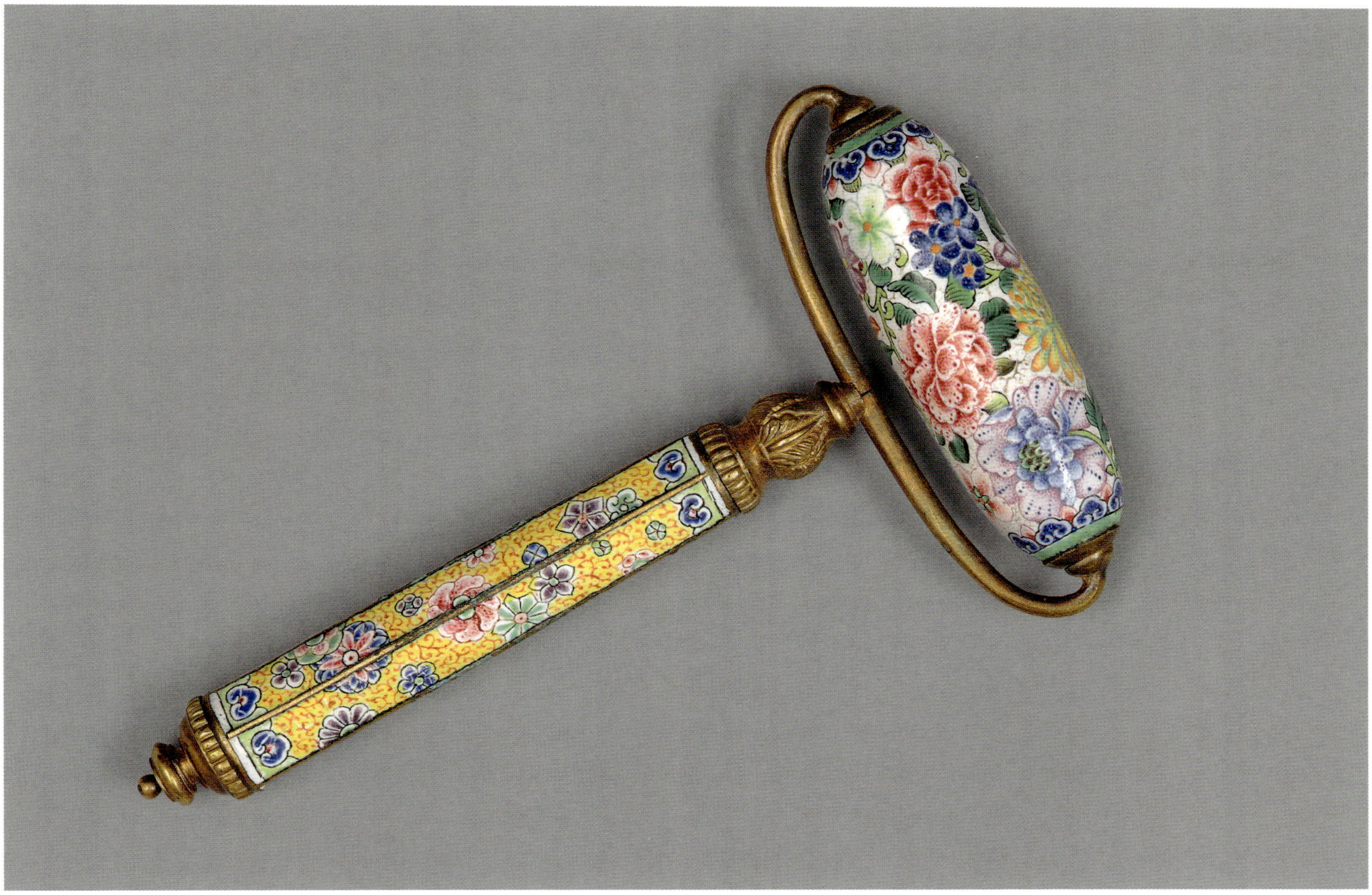

PLATE 34

清中期　畫琺琅花卉紋滾軸
太平車

Massage tool with flowers

18th century
Painted polychrome enamels on copper-alloy core with gilding
Cat. 164

Among the many everyday objects found in the residences of imperial women, massage tools served both decorative and therapeutic purposes.[1] These implements consist of a handle and a cylindrical roller or a few beads fitted on a copper alloy spindle. When used on acupuncture points, they can help improve circulation. Massage has had a long history in Chinese medicine as both a preventive and curative treatment. This roller-type massage tool was also used in the beauty rituals of empresses. Empress Dowager Cixi was known to have suffered from skin ailments and facial muscle spasms. One way for her to address the symptoms was to message her face with a massage tool made of semiprecious stones. Along with other treatments—such as ingesting finely ground pearls and washing her face with a mix of herbal powders—Cixi's skin condition reportedly improved.[2]

Humble though its purpose may have been, this massage tool's fine craftsmanship reflects the revered position of its user. While most existing massage rollers in the imperial collection are made of glass beads, agate, and other stones, this tool features painted enamel. The Imperial Workshop (Zaoban chu) began producing painted enamelware in the late Kangxi period (1662–1722) after the technique reached China from Europe through the port of Canton (present-day Guangzhou). Enamelware designs were enhanced by the expertise of Western court painters assigned to the workshop. The smooth surface of this massage tool is wreathed in a variety of flowers—including peonies, hibiscus, and day lilies—that together symbolize wealth, longevity, and fertility. (DS)

1 Massage tools were among the seventieth-birthday gifts from Qianlong to his mother, Empress Dowager Chongqing. E'ertai and Zhang Tingyu (1769) 1987, *juan* 18.

2 Yuan Hongqi and Zhang Shiyun 1994, 279–80.

PLATE 35

清中期　黃地緙絲鳳梧牡丹圖
紫檀木刻字柄團扇

Leaf-shaped fan with phoenix, paulownia tree, and peonies

Probably Imperial Silk Manufactory, Suzhou
Early 19th century
Silk tapestry (*kesi*), polychrome silk and metallic-wrapped threads and pigments; handle: *zitan* wood, ivory, copper alloy with gilding, and silk tassels
Cat. 87

PLATE 36

清乾隆　米色紗貼絹桃樹
仙鶴圖烏木雕花柄團扇

Lobed fan with cranes, peaches, and rocks

Qianlong period, 1736–95
Appliqué, silk fabric on silk gauze with pigments; handle: wood and ivory
Cat. 88

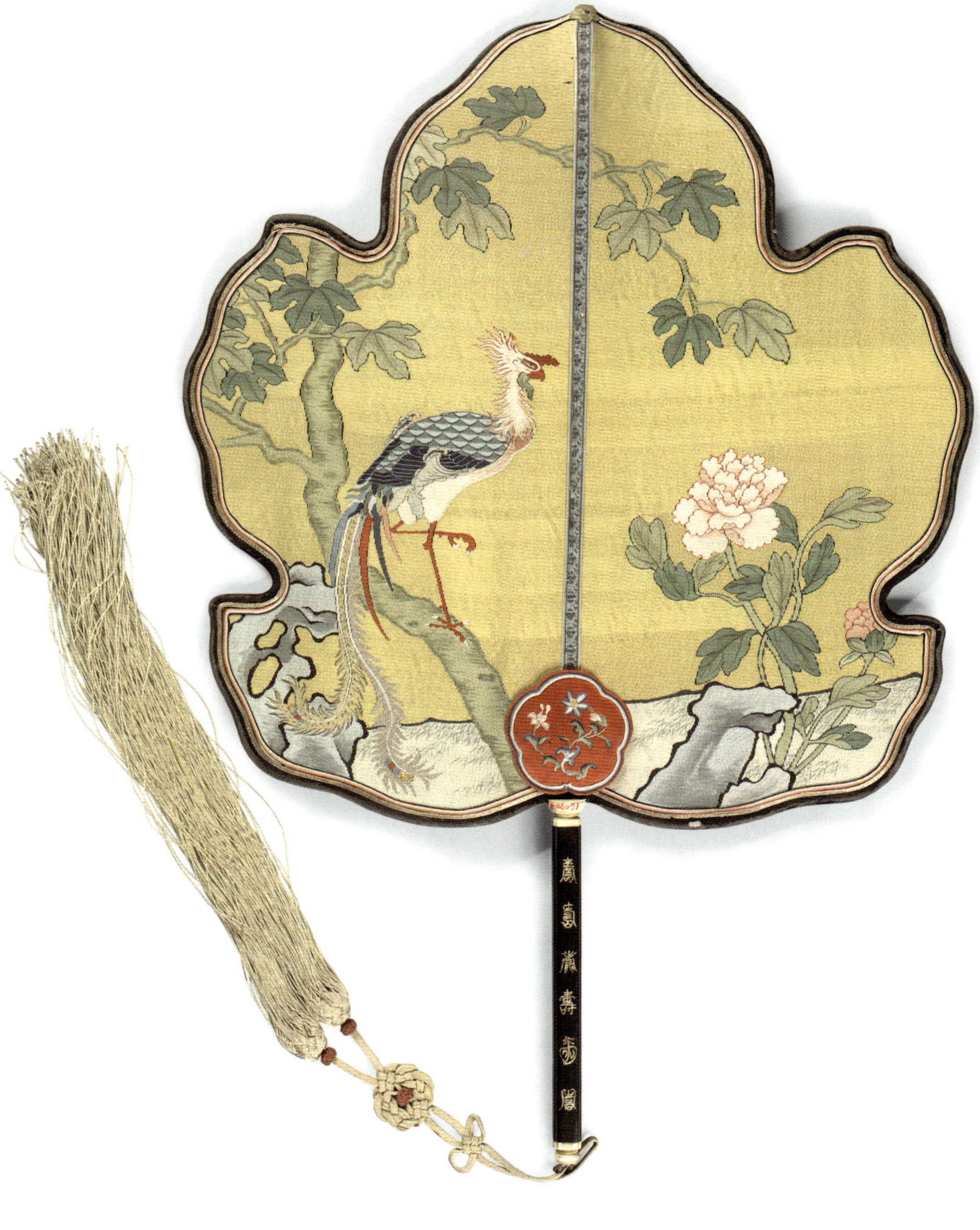

PLATE 35

In court paintings Qing empresses and other palace women are often depicted holding round, foliated, or oval fans. Men also used these fans, particularly toward the end of the dynasty. These fans entered the court from two main sources: gifts from officials and commissions by emperors. The Imperial Silk Manufactories in Suzhou, Hangzhou, and Nanjing and the Wood Workshop of the Imperial Household Department (Neiwu fu) in Beijing handled imperial commissions.[1]

The fan with the phoenix (pl. 35) is the product of extraordinary technical mastery: it features identical silk tapestry designs on both sides, which required the weaver to make the back as neat as the front, trimming or concealing loose threads like an embroiderer. When the fan is waved, the user would be able to view the exquisite decoration on both sides. The lobed fan with cranes (pl. 36) features appliquéd elements created by covering pieces of paper with silk and attaching them to the translucent gauze background, creating a low-relief effect. Minute details such as the crane's plumage were painted to add color and texture. The same design is precisely laid out on the other side of the fan.

As with much Qing art, auspicious symbols abound. The tip of the central rod of the fan with cranes is decorated with the head of a wish-granting scepter (*ruyi*), suggesting that whoever held the fan would enjoy currents of good fortune as well as cool air. The crane was considered an immortal bird and thus an emblem of longevity. The message of long life was enhanced by the tree bearing peaches above. In Chinese mythology, the Queen Mother of the West owns an orchard with special peaches that ripen every 3,000 years; whoever eats them attains immortality. High-status Qing imperial women often associated themselves with this goddess, expressing their desire to enjoy a long, healthy life—thus providing more opportunity for influence, seniority, and status in the imperial family. (XL; trans. DYW)

1 Xie Li 2013.

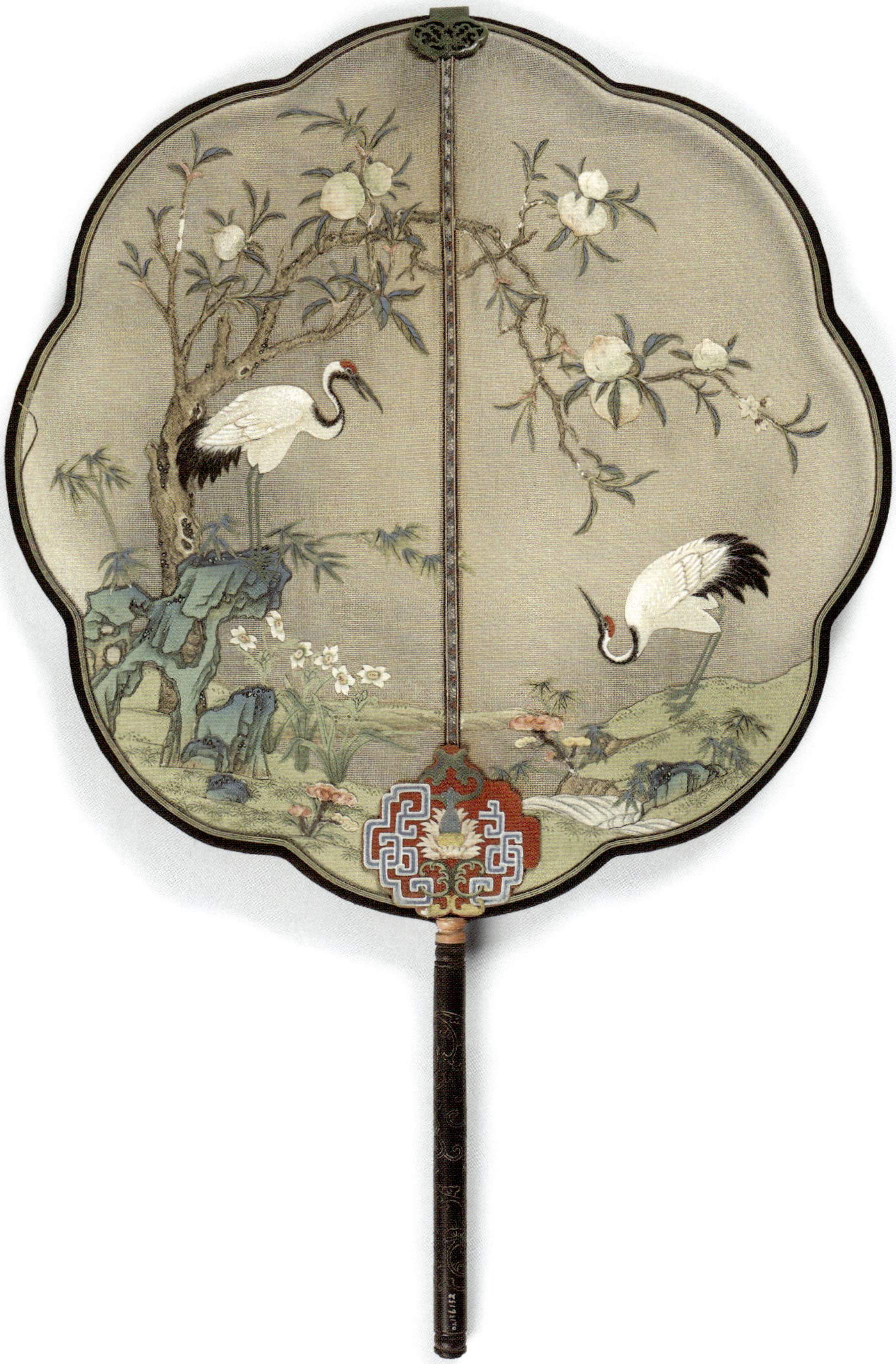

PLATE 36

PLATE 37

清乾隆　金髮塔

Stupa containing Empress Dowager Chongqing's hair and Amitayus Buddha

Imperial Workshop, Beijing
Qianlong period, 1777
Gold and silver alloy with coral, turquoise, lapis lazuli, and other semiprecious stones, and glass; pedestal: *zitan* wood
Cat. 179

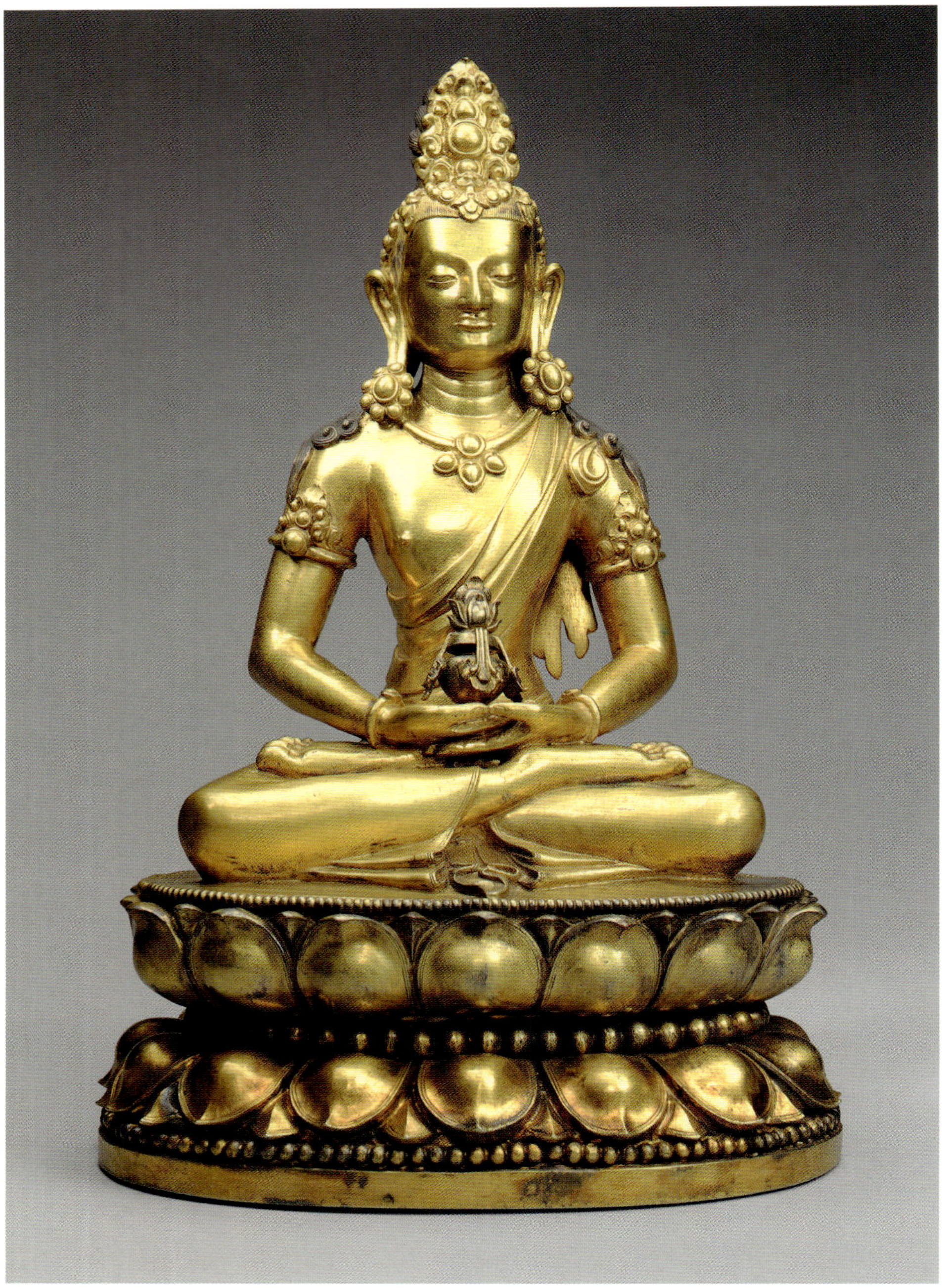

DETAIL, AMITAYUS BUDDHA

In Buddhism, stupas enshrine the relics or possessions of the Buddha or other holy persons. Soon after Empress Dowager Chongqing's death in early 1777, her son, the Qianlong emperor, commissioned this monumental stupa to commemorate her. It was placed in the East Buddhist Chamber at her residence the Palace of Longevity and Health (Shoukang gong). Inside is a gold box that contains Chongqing's hair. In China, hair was considered a precious and enduring part of the human body and therefore could be saved as a memento of the deceased.[1] Along with Chongqing's hair is a statuette of Amitayus, Buddha of Limitless Life who presides over the Western Paradise where souls are reborn. This stupa not only suggests the deified status of Chongqing but also conveys the wish for her rebirth. Buddhist symbols such as the *vajra* (a magic weapon and ritual scepter symbolic of power and indestructibility), lotus petals, and guardian lions adorn the stupa and its wooden pedestal.

While mourning his mother, the Qianlong emperor conveyed some twenty orders specifying the size, thickness of the gold walls, materials, design, and placement of the stupa.[2] An outstanding example of Qing court metalwork, it consists of nearly 100 components joined together piece by piece and layer by layer, with repoussé and chased decoration and inlaid coral and semiprecious stones. Because Qianlong demanded that it be bigger and taller, the height of the finished stupa is twice that of the original design. This required a substantial amount of gold and silver, and a number of items from Chongqing's residences—including an investiture book (recording her conferred title), a seal, a snuff bottle, washbasins, and dining utensils—were inventoried and melted down for the stupa; the Bureau of Privy-Purse under the Imperial Household Department (Neiwu fu) provided additional metal. The finished work weighs 237 pounds (107.5 kg), making it the largest gold stupa in the Palace Museum's collection. (XQX and LGL; trans. DYW)

1 Hair has been an important memento mori in many cultures and eras, including in the West during Victorian times.

2 ZGDYLSDAG 2005, 40:403–12.

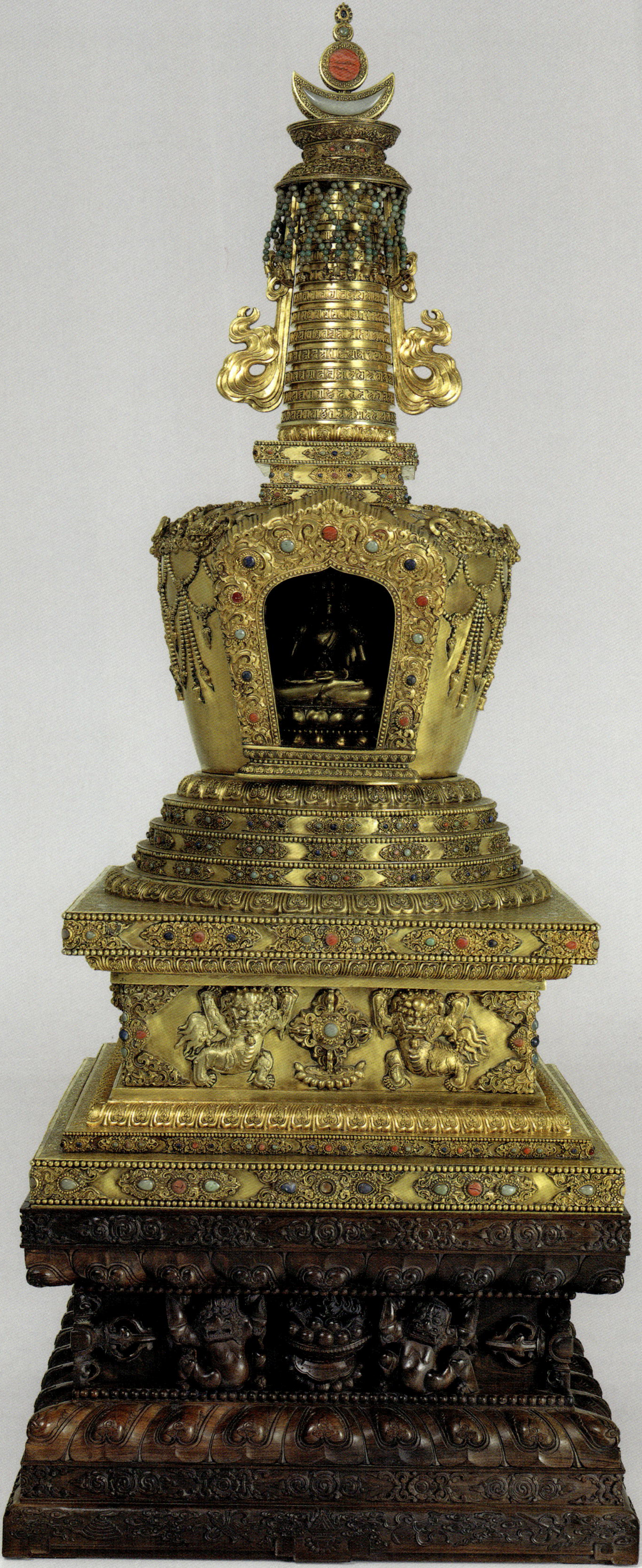

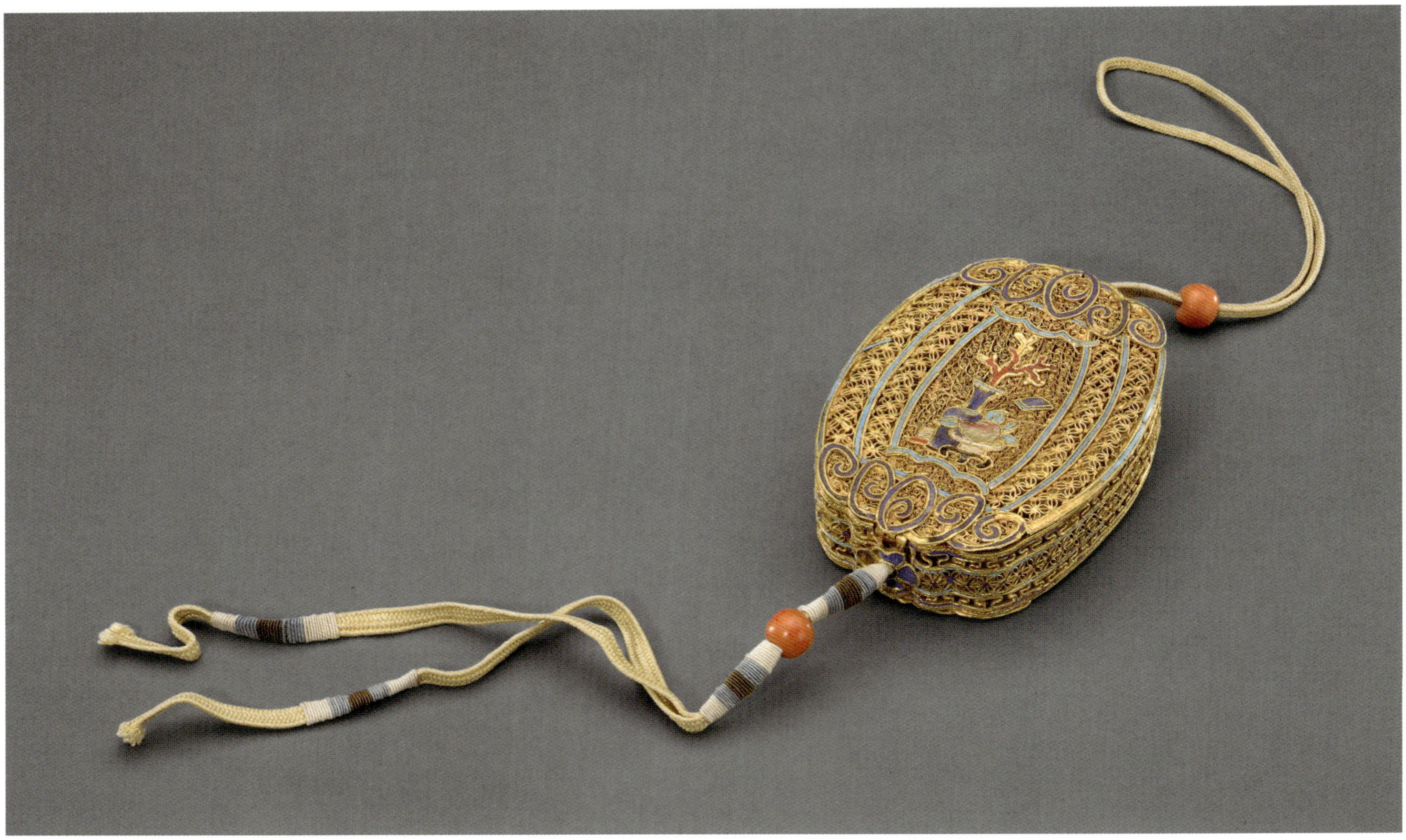

PLATE 38

清　金點翠清供圖花囊

Aromatic case with incense burner, vase, and chime

18th or 19th century
Gold alloy with kingfisher and other feathers, coral, and silk cords
Cat. 90

This intricate filigree case can be opened to hold fresh flower petals or small bags of other fragrant mixtures. Unlike the smaller embroidered silk pouches designed to be carried on one's person, this case was hung from a silk cord on a special stand to provide pleasant aromas throughout a room.[1] The body features a *gu*-shaped vase with peacock feathers, a square incense burner, a chevron-shaped stone chime (*qing*), and a double ring (see detail). Together they suggest the act of appreciating antiquities, a favorite pursuit of empresses and other consorts. The objects also create a message. The double-ring motif, for example, symbolizes ideas of betrothal, permanence, and continuous generations of the family.

Gold filigree is a complex technique. First, fine gold alloy wires are nipped into tiny patterned units, and these units are then joined together to form larger sections. These sections are placed on top of a three-dimensional mold and pressed into the desired form. The latticed gold top of this case features feather inlays of three colors—blue, green, and lavender—forming color contrasts that highlight the delicate design of the case. The brilliant hue of these plumes does not fade over time, making blue kingfish feather, for example, a prized material for headdresses (see pl. 14), hairpins (see pls. 27 and 29), and other precious objects of imperial women. (DS)

1 Meng Hui 2008.

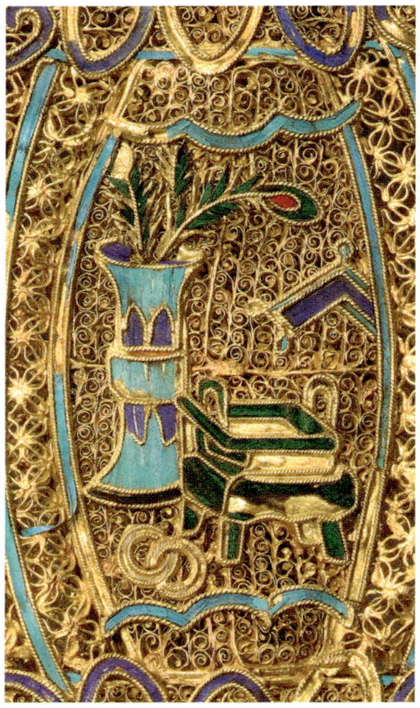

DETAIL, REVERSE

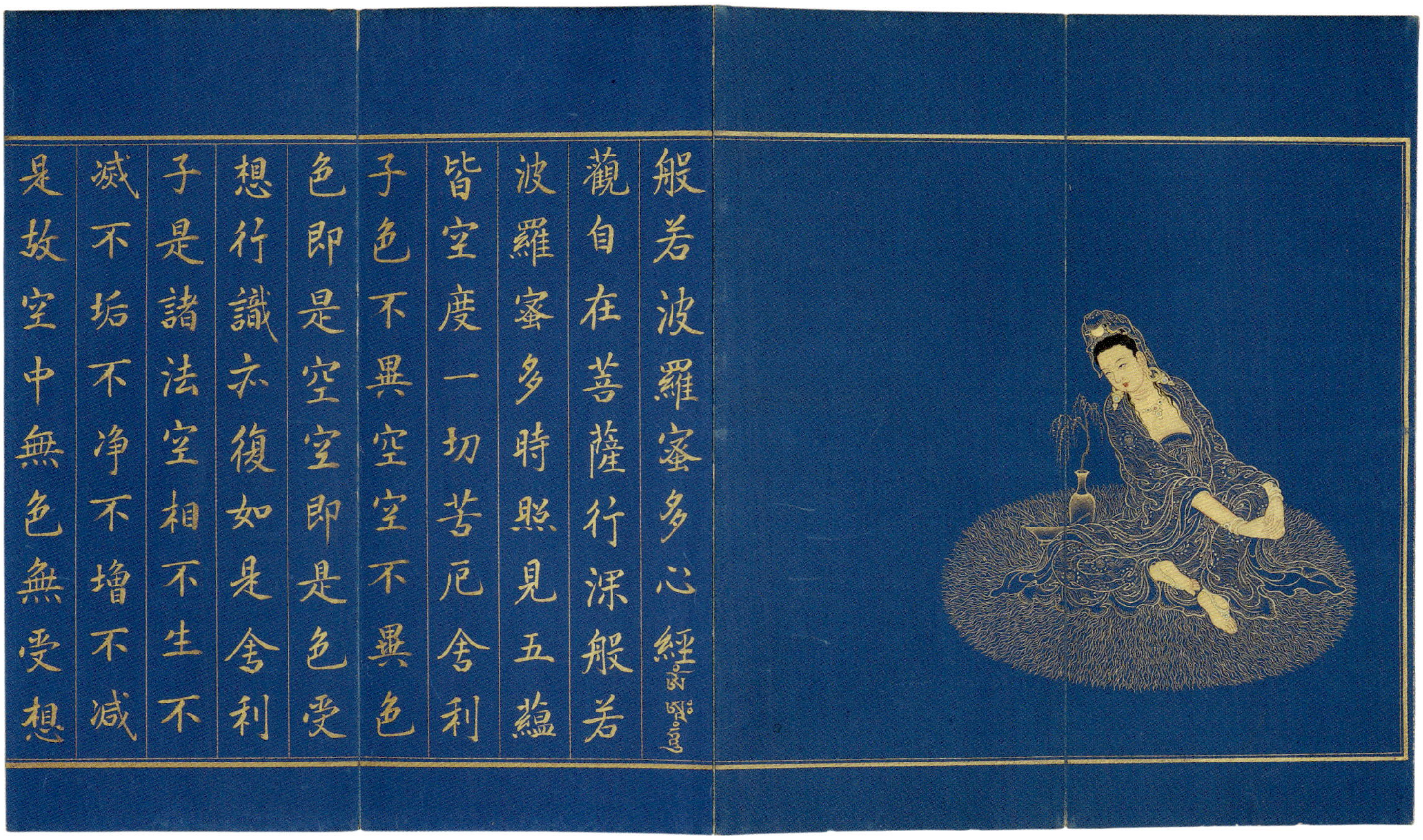

PLATE 39

清康熙　聖祖玄燁泥金寫本《般若波羅蜜多心經》

Heart of the Perfection of Wisdom Sutra (*Prajnaparamitahrdayasutra*)

The Kangxi emperor (1654–1722)
Kangxi period, 1702
Album, gold and color on paper
Cat. 176

Buddhist devotees, including Qing emperors, considered copying scriptures a sacred act that transmitted Buddhist teachings, accumulated merit, and invoked blessings—as well as cultivating the mind and body. Over 1,000 sutras copied by Qing emperors on birthdays, festivals, and other special occasions survive.[1]

On the birthday of Empress Xiaohui (Empress Dowager Renxian; 1641–1717) in 1702, the Kangxi emperor used powdered gold to copy the *Heart of the Perfection of Wisdom Sutra*, one of the most important of all Buddhist scriptures in China. The "perfect wisdom" in this sutra refers to the knowledge of emptiness as the nature of ultimate reality, a key tenet of Buddhism. The sutra text is flanked by paintings of Avalokiteshivara (Guanyin), known as the bodhisattva of compassion, and the guardian figure Skanda (Weituo). On the day he copied this sutra, Kangxi was on an inspection tour in a city away from Xiaohui; in order to convey his wishes for her longevity, he lit incense and respectfully copied this sutra to be presented to her.

Born to a Mongol noble family, Empress Xiaohui was a grandniece of the powerful Empress Xiaozhuang. She was installed at the age of thirteen as the second empress of the Shunzhi emperor, replacing his deposed first empress. However, her fame and position were overshadowed by her husband's attachment to his favorite consort from the Donggo clan (1639–1660), and Xiaohui risked being demoted. When her husband died, Xiaohui was only twenty and childless. She soon received the title of empress dowager because of her marriage to Shunzhi. Although she was not Kangxi's birth mother, they formed a close relationship. After Kangxi's birth mother died, Xiaohui became a focus of his filial attention. He took her on extensive inspection tours in southern China, sent her delicacies when he was traveling, and staged grand celebrations on her sixtieth and seventieth birthdays.[2] Kangxi was the first Qing emperor to copy sutras on the birthday of an empress dowager, and his filial devotion, as illustrated by this work, served as an inspiration for his grandson, the future Qianlong emperor. (YGP and LY; trans. DYW)

1 Zhang Guangsheng and Lu Ying 2013, 144.
2 Yang Zhen 1994, 51–78.

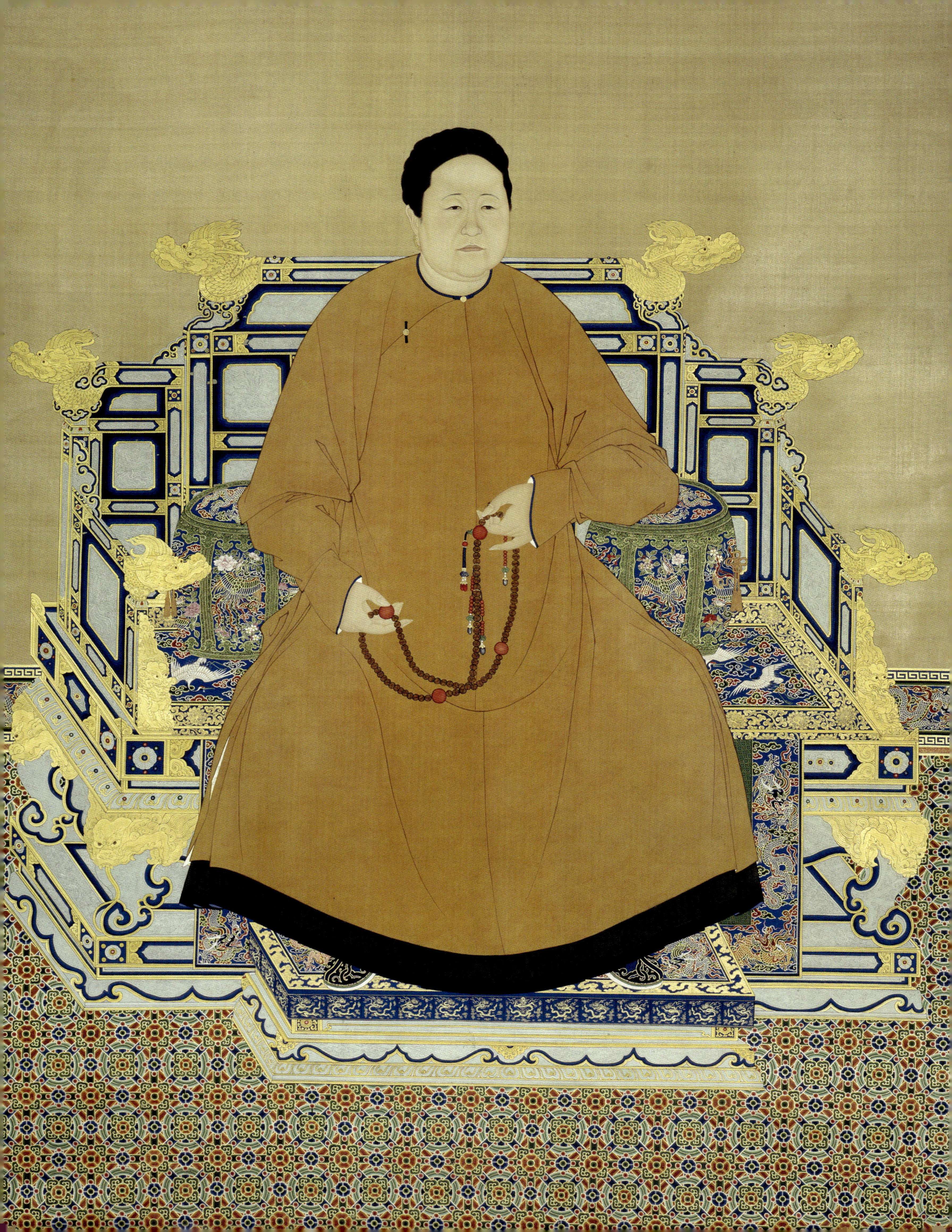

PLATE 40

清乾隆　孝莊文皇后像軸

Empress Xiaozhuang

Probably Giuseppe Castiglione (Lang Shining; Italy, 1688–1766) and other court painters, Beijing
Qianlong period, about 1750
Hanging scroll, ink and color on silk
Cat. 8

This portrait of Empress Xiaozhuang, the mother of the Shunzhi emperor and the grandmother of the Kangxi emperor, differs from Qing portraiture for ancestral worship in several ways. Though the empress is shown seated on a throne, as in ancestor portraits, her figure is not fully frontal but slightly inclined toward the viewer's right, so she lacks the "iconic gaze" found in imperial paintings used for ancestral sacrifices. Just as notable is the fact that she is not wearing the formal attire (*chaofu*) customary in ancestral portraits. Her robe is a "regular robe" (*changfu*) with sleeves that end in the horse-hoof-shaped cuffs as prescribed for Manchu dress. The robe is relatively plain and features a cloud design rather than the embroidered or woven court robe emblazoned with dragons and the vest that was de rigueur for ancestor paintings, suggestive of notions of frugality, for which Xiaozhuang was known. Also absent is such court regalia as the phoenix-topped headdress and pearl earrings. Instead, she wears three plain gold hoops. Further, she holds the court necklace in her hands rather than wearing it around her neck.

If this portrait was not intended for ancestral rituals, for what purpose was it commissioned? Its enormous size strongly suggests it was intended for display within the palace, and its mounting as a scroll allowed it to be rolled up and stored, suggesting it might have been brought out only for special occasions. In the end, however, we can only speculate as to the motives behind creating this unusual portrait. Regardless of his intent, the artist captured the firm and determined spirit of the Mongol noblewoman who was an influential figure during the Shunzhi and Kangxi reigns. (ESR)

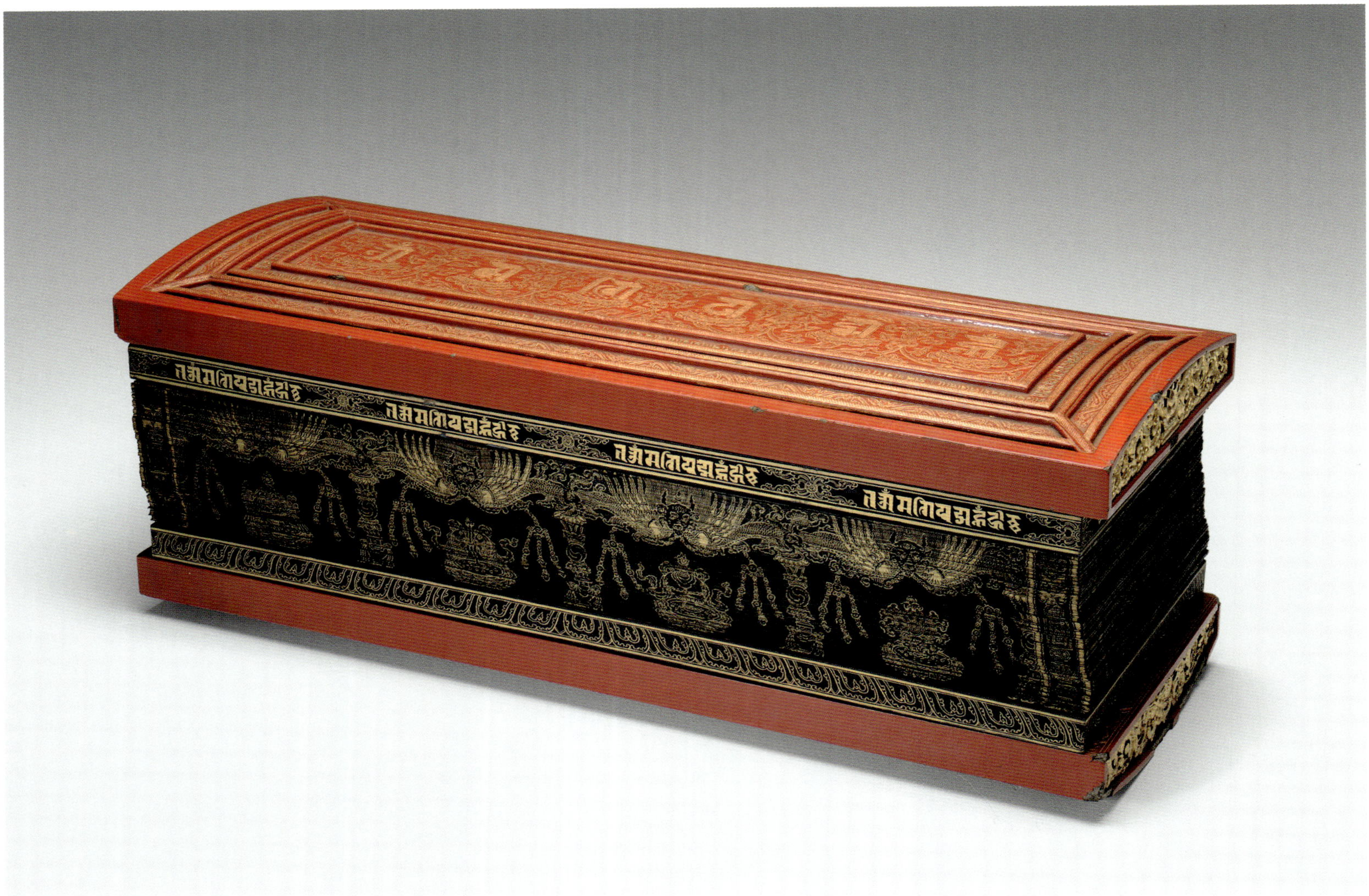

PLATE 41

清乾隆　甘珠爾經

One volume from the 108-volume Kanjur Sutra

Imperial Workshop, Beijing, and workshop, Suzhou
Qianlong period, 1767–70
Gold on paper; covers: lacquer and gold on wood core, silk tapestry (*kesi*), ink and color on paper, gold, pearls, coral, lapis lazuli, turquoise, and silk cords
Cat. 178

The Tibetan word *Kanjur* refers to scriptures attributed to the Buddha. Various versions contain different numbers of texts, most likely based on Sanskrit originals or translations into other languages. This volume is from a large and lavish Kanjur commissioned in 1767 by the Qianlong emperor in anticipation of the eightieth birthday of his mother, Empress Dowager Chongqing, in 1771.[1] It is handwritten in gold on rectangular sheets of indigo paper, with each volume held within wooden covers featuring recessed areas decorated with Sanskrit and Tibetan texts as well as images of Buddhist figures richly embellished with gold and other precious materials. When closed for storage, the indigo leaves and inner covers are wrapped in fine silk and further secured by red lacquer outer covers that are bound together by silk cords. This format originated in Indian bark or palm-leaf manuscripts and was adopted for Tibetan books.

The Qianlong emperor modeled this Kanjur on a handwritten edition dated 1669 that the Kangxi emperor commissioned at the decree of Empress Xiaozhuang (see Luk Yu-ping's essay, pp. 110–27). Qianlong's artisans made a few modifications, notably adding a sutra the emperor believed belonged with the scriptures.[2] Thus, this holy book not only reflects Qianlong's understanding of Buddhist writings but also acknowledges his filial piety; his respect for his grandfather, the Kangxi emperor; and the role Empress Xiaozhuang played in the development of Tibetan Buddhism at the Qing court. Once it was completed, this Kanjur was most likely kept in the Pavilion of Compassion and Shelter (Ciyin lou) within the Garden of the Palace of Compassion and Tranquility (Cining gong huayuan), which served as a center for Chongqing's religious activities.[3] (LYP)

1 Ninety-six of the 108 volumes are in the Palace Museum, Beijing; the remainder are in Taiwan.
2 This is the *Surangama Sutra*. See Weng Lianxi 2013, 4; Berger 2003, 88.
3 Gugong bowuyuan 2015b, p. 164, no. 11.

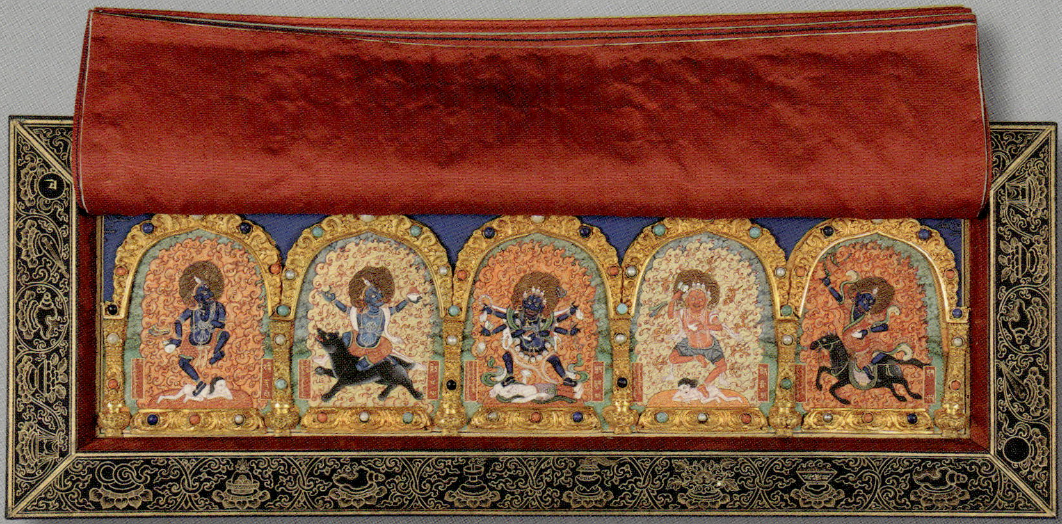

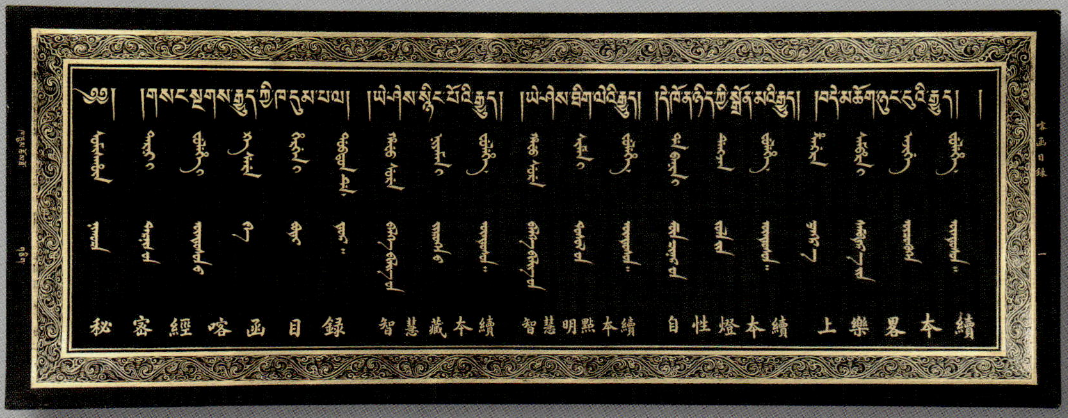
秘密經喀函目録
智慧藏本續
智慧明點本續
自性燈本續
上樂畧本續

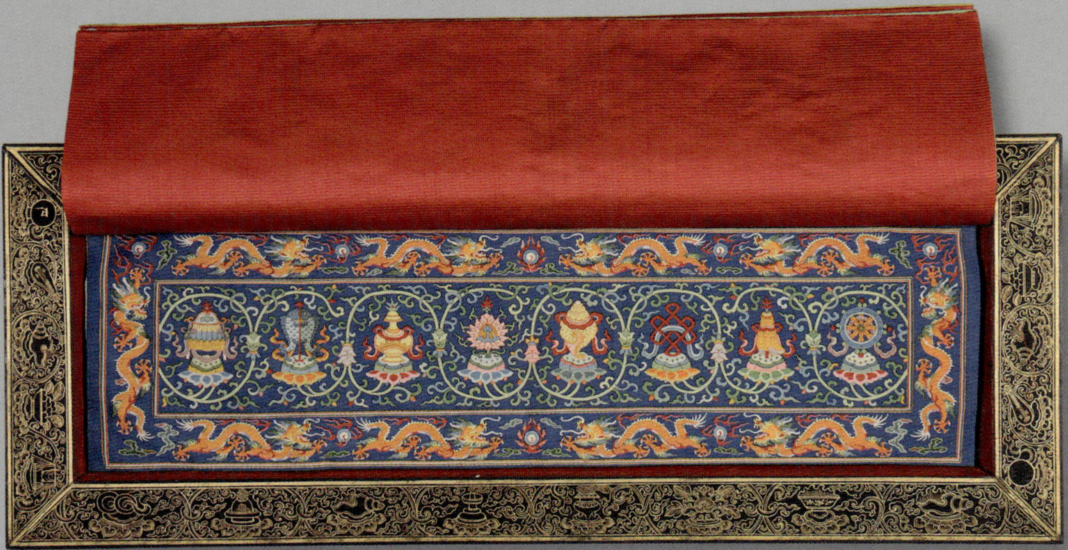

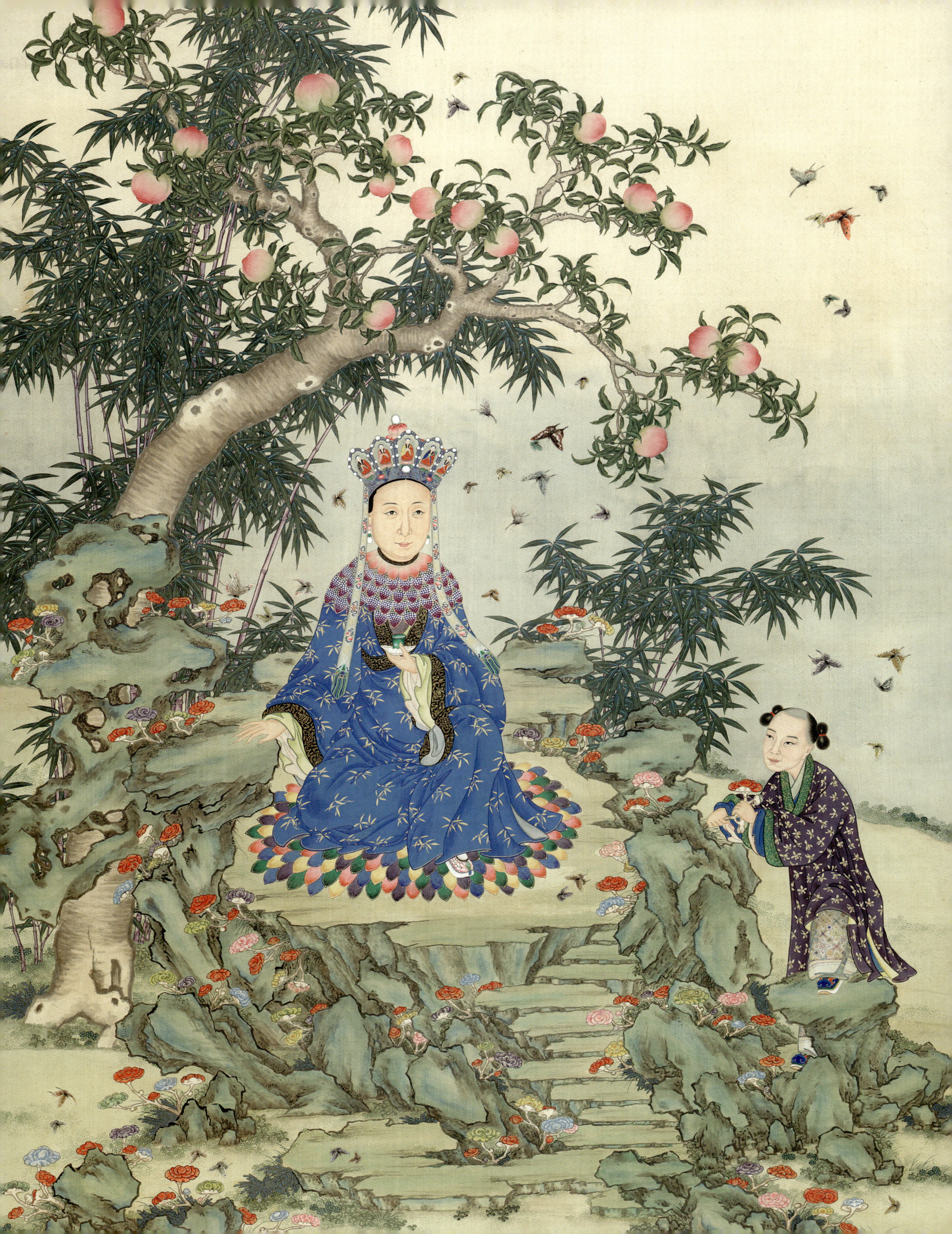

PLATE 42

清光緒　慈禧皇太后扮觀音像軸

Empress Dowager Cixi in the guise of the bodhisattva Avalokiteshvara (Guanyin)

Court painters, Beijing
Guangxu period, 1875–1908
Hanging scroll, ink and color on silk
Cat. 173

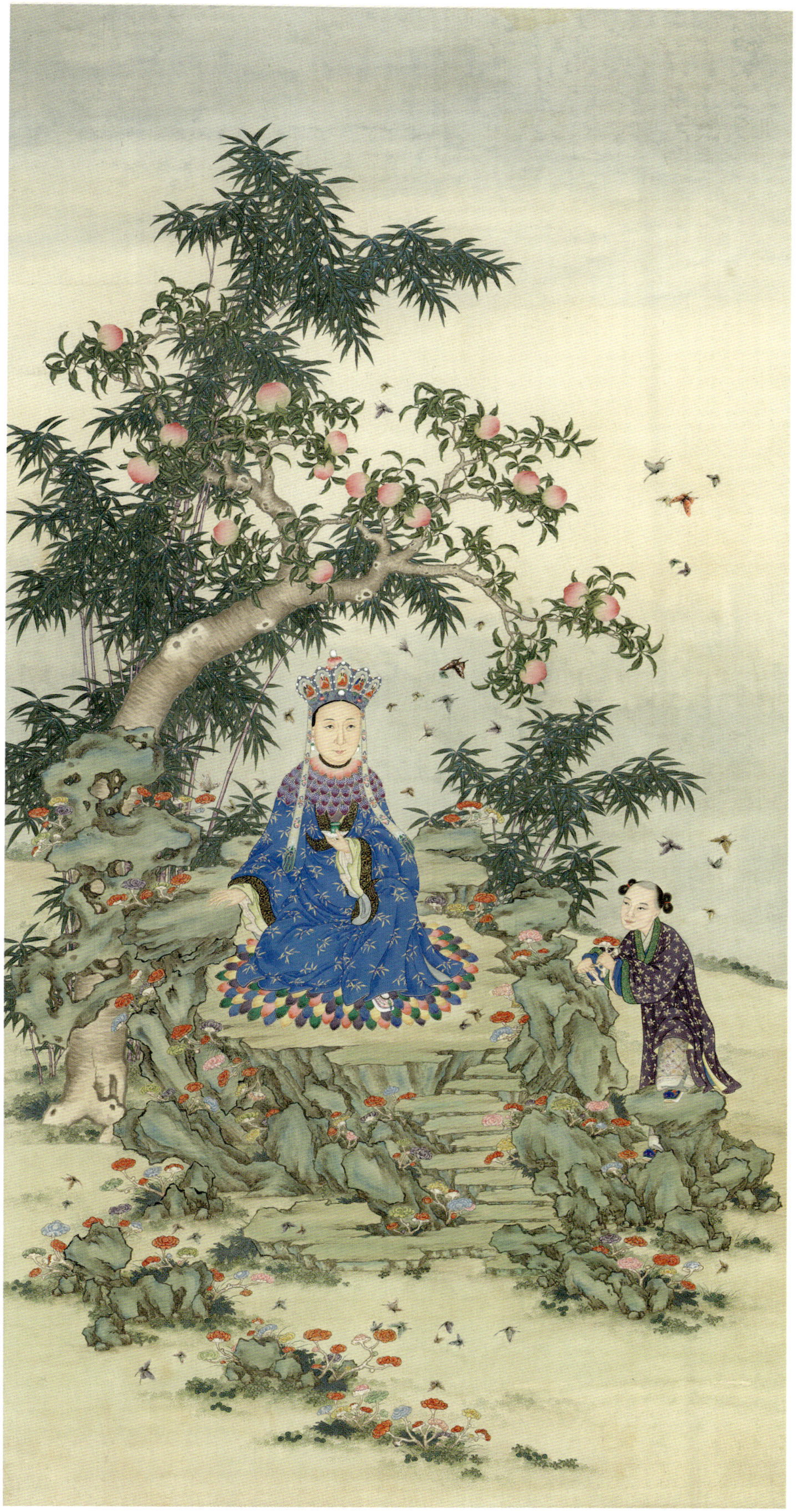

Since the early Qing, emperors had been endorsed by Dalai Lamas as the incarnation of the bodhisattva Manjusri. The Yongzheng and Qianlong emperors both commissioned portraits posing as this deity in works that followed Buddhist iconography so rigorously that sacred image and secular identity sometimes merged.[1] True to form, Empress Dowager Cixi adapted this tradition to her own taste and ends, appearing in several paintings and photographs in the guise of the bodhisattva Avalokiteshvara, or Guanyin. This example features Cixi seated under a peach tree laden with fruit. She wears a blue robe decorated with golden bamboo, a pearl mantle in the shape of lotus petals, and a five-Buddha diadem. Seated on a large rock, she holds a green jade cup and white jade saucer in the form of a lotus petal. As in other visual representations of Cixi-as-Guanyin, a strong connection with theatrical performance can be detected in this painting. The empress dowager's costume, for instance, resembles Qing stage costume rather than the white robe most commonly seen in depictions of this deity.

To her left stands a smaller male figure in a dark purple robe picking an auspicious mushroom and offering it to the deity. According to Buddhist iconography, this figure is Sudhana (Shancai), a young male devotee of Guanyin, but his physiognomy here suggests the figure is Cixi's top eunuch, Li Lianying (1848–1911), who also appeared in photographs of Cixi embodying Guanyin.[2] Incorporating a servant into a portrait of this nature was unprecedented in Qing court art. His presence, along with that of the auspicious mushroom, the peach tree, and butterflies—all popular motifs of longevity for birthday celebration—transform this painting from a serious embodiment of the empress dowager's sacred identity to a performance by Cixi. (YCP)

1 Henss 2001.
2 Li Yuhang 2011, 192.

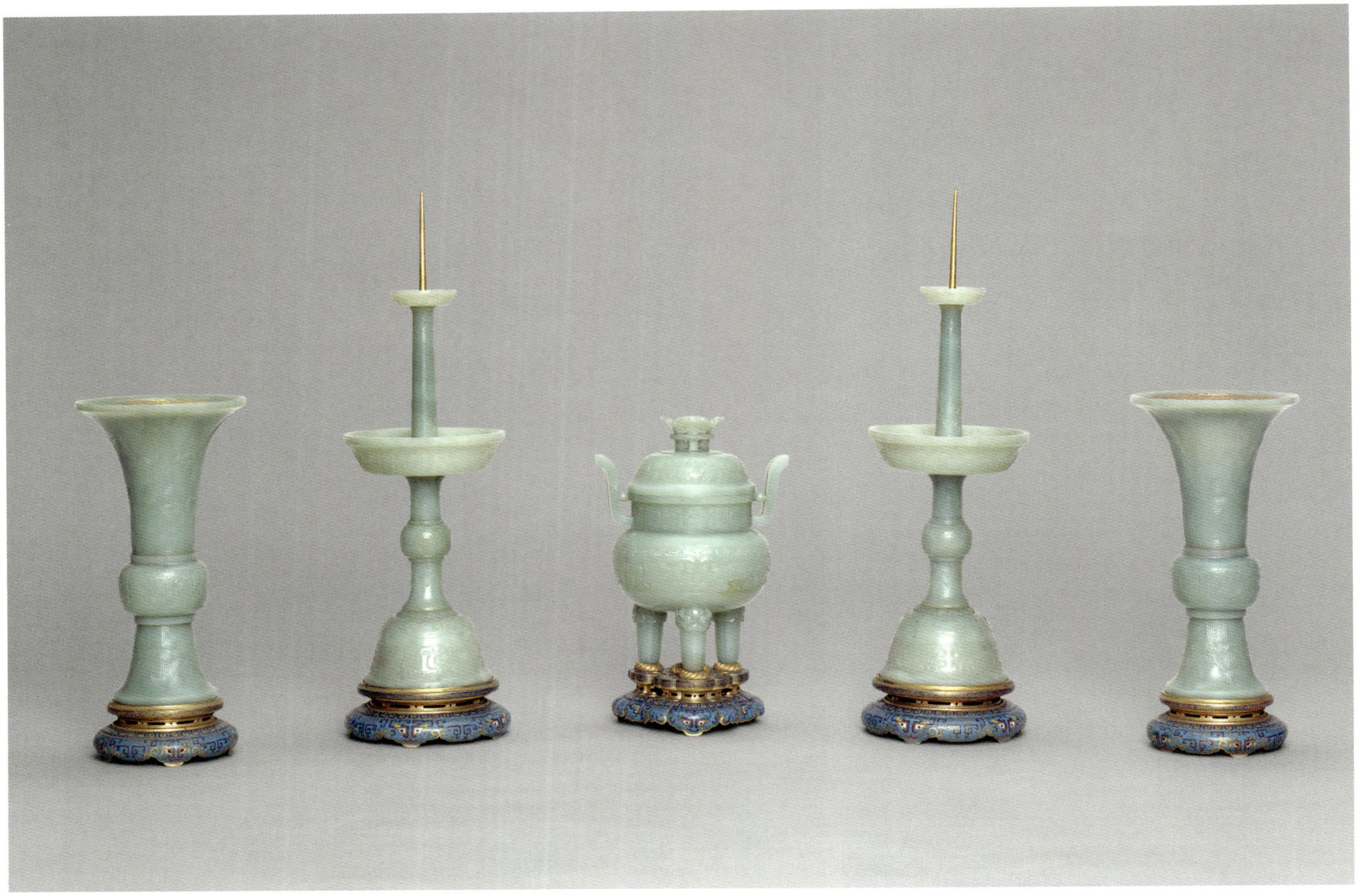

PLATE 43

清乾隆　青玉雙耳萬壽獸面紋三足蓋爐、青玉壽字勾雲紋燭臺、青玉壽字蕉葉紋花插

Altar garniture: incense burner, two candle stands, and two vases with animal masks and the character for longevity

Qianlong period, 1736–95
Jade (nephrite); stands: cloisonné, copper alloy with polychrome enamels and gilding
Cat. 153

The liturgical array known as the "Five Offerings" (*wugong*)—often called a garniture—consists of an incense burner, candle stands, and vases. It emerged as a standard feature of Buddhist altar tables in China during the sixteenth century. This set is believed to have come from the Palace of Compassion and Tranquility (Cining gong), where imperial consorts practiced Buddhist rites. It was most likely placed before images of Tibetan Buddhist deities. Sets of the Five Offerings at the palace were made from a variety of materials, such as bronze and enameled porcelain.[1] This one is made from a particularly fine soft-colored, translucent jade from Hetian, a town in western China renowned for its high-quality nephrite. Each of these pieces sits on a custom-made cloisonné stand that further unifies the grouping as a coherent whole. This set of the Five Offerings makes clear that Qing empresses had access to the finest materials and imperial craftsmanship and suggests the lavish spaces in which they worshipped.

The covered incense burner here is carved with animal masks and the character for longevity (*shou*). The candle stands have lotus patterns, clouds in the shape of *ruyi* (wish-granting) mushrooms, *shou* characters, and archaic dragon motifs. The vases likewise carry *shou* characters and archaic dragon motifs as well as banana-leaf patterns. These carved designs reference ancient ritual bronzes, a common feature in decorative arts of the Qianlong period. The repeated use of the auspicious character for longevity on these pieces suggests they were made to celebrate the birthday of the Qianlong emperor's mother, Empress Dowager Chongqing. (LYP)

1 See examples in Gugong bowuyuan 2015a, 46–47, 114–15.

PLATE 44

清晚期　雕核桃羅漢紋十八子手串

Rosary-bracelet with beads decorated with *luohan* and pendants

Probably 19th century
Walnut shell, coral, lapis lazuli, turquoise, seed pearls, copper alloy with gilding, and silk tassels
Cat. 97

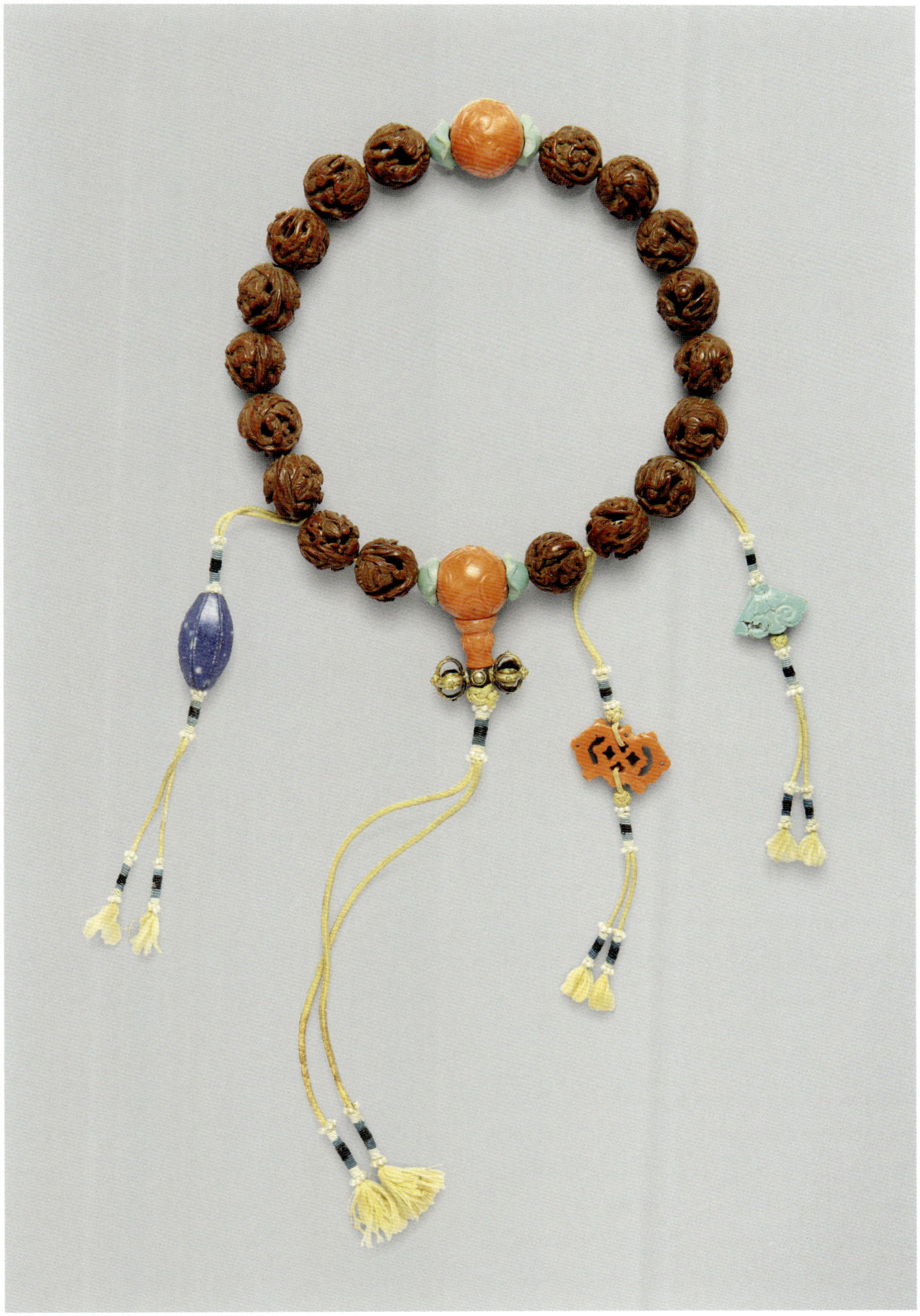

This bracelet is at once a rosary, a talisman, and an ornament. The form originated in Buddhist prayer beads fingered by adherents to keep count of the number of recitations made in the course of a worship service or meditation session. It consists of eighteen beads made of walnut shell, each featuring miniscule carved openwork depicting a *luohan*, a person who, in Buddhism, had attained spiritual perfection. Often portrayed in groups of eighteen, *luohan* were understood to have a key role in protecting Buddhist teaching.

The bracelet's protective power was emphasized by the presence of a double-sided gilt *vajra*, a magic weapon and a symbol of power. The *vajra* was commonly used as a ritual object in Tibetan Buddhist liturgies to symbolize the sudden and powerful enlightenment Buddhist practice can bring. The turquoise beads on either side of the coral orbs are shaped like lotus leaves, which are associated with purity and rebirth in Buddhism, while the three dangling pendants convey auspicious meanings: the one of turquoise, for example, represents a stone chime (*qing*), a homophone for "celebration" in Chinese.

The walnut beads were carefully carved and polished to add tactile interest, and the user's fondling would have further smoothed them. While the material and format of court jewelry for formal occasions was strictly regulated, this type of bracelet was informal and intimate, meaning it could be worn in a variety of ways and contexts and took diverse forms. A wide range of decorative techniques and precious materials—aromatic woods, rare seeds, gold, semiprecious stones—were used to make large quantities of such bracelets for imperial use as they gained popularity in the second half of the nineteenth century. Buddhist devotees in the Qing imperial family, such as Empresses Dowager Cixi and Ci'an and the Guangxu emperor, were portrayed wearing bracelets like this, often hung from a button on their robe, coat, or vest.[1] (DYW)

1 Chen Xiasheng 2006.

PLATE 45

清乾隆　銅無量壽佛

Amitayus Buddha in a niche

Workshop, probably Tibet
Qianlong period, 1771
Copper alloy with gilding and pigments;
niche: *zitan* wood with silk damask
Cat. 182

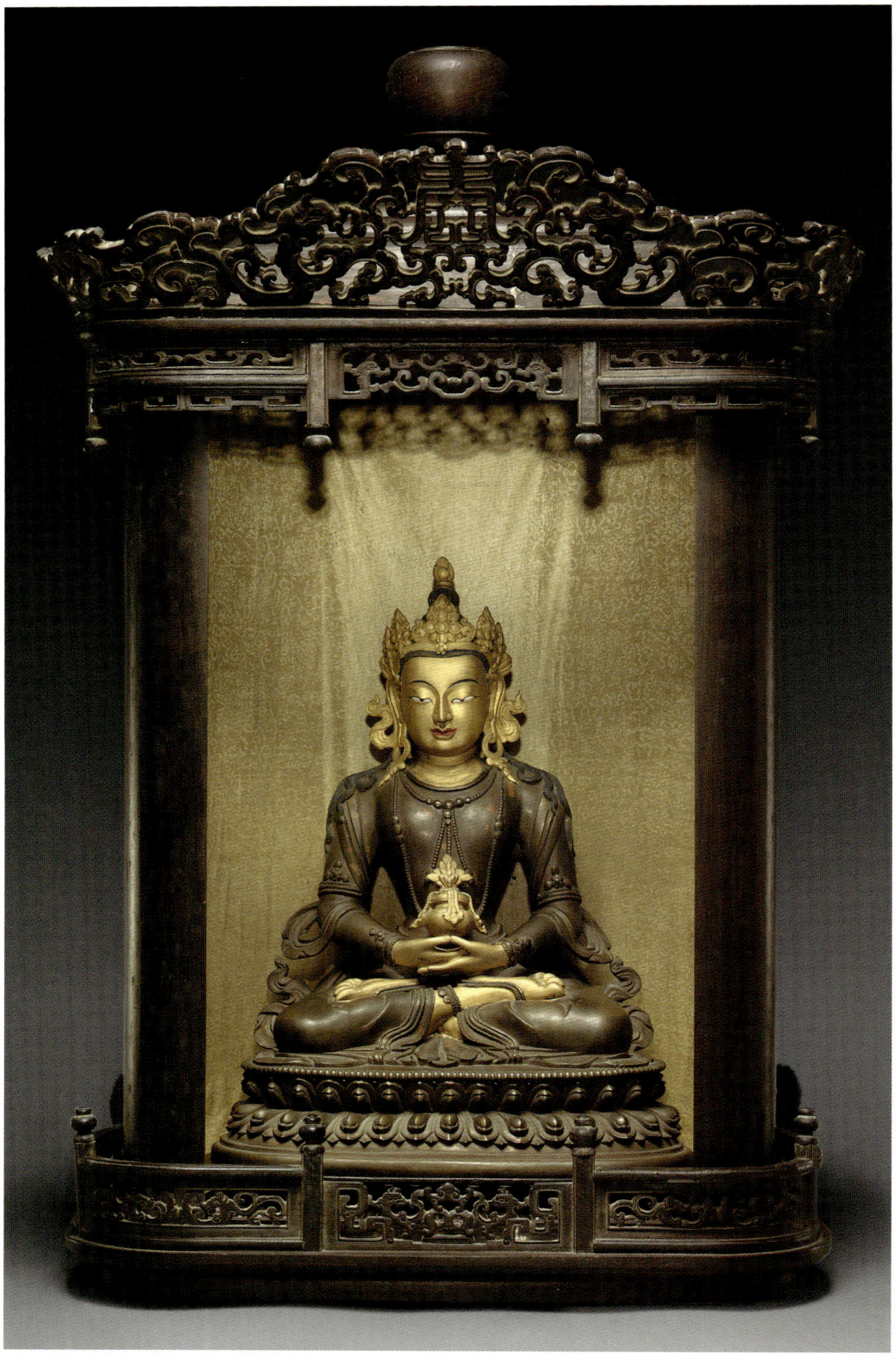

In Tibetan Buddhism, Amitayus, Buddha of Limitless Life, is venerated for his healing powers and ability to prolong life. Figures of this deity were popular during the Qianlong reign, and the emperor himself regularly gave his mother, Empress Dowager Chongqing, statues of Amitayus for her birthday—a particularly appropriate gift given the empress's piety and long life and Qianlong's manifest filial devotion.[1]

Qianlong commissioned this bronze statue for Chongqing's eightieth birthday.[2] It represents Amitayus's familiar attributes: seated in a meditative pose on a lotus pedestal, blue hair falling on his shoulders from beneath a crown, he holds an ambrosia vase bearing the leaves of the *ashoka* tree symbolizing a long life without care.[3] The statue rests in a carved wooden niche that features details that further underscore the auspiciousness of the figure: Prominently displayed at the top of the niche is the character for longevity (*shou*). On the back, carved in the four official languages of the Qing court (Chinese, Mongolian, Manchu, and Tibetan), are transliterations of the names of Amitayus as well as an inscription stating that Qianlong ordered a lama to oversee production of this work in 1771.

After this statue was presented to Empress Dowager Chongqing, it was kept and venerated with other Tibetan Buddhist objects in the Pavilion of Compassion and Shelter (Ciyin lou) in the Garden of the Palace of Compassion and Tranquility (Cining gong huayuan).[4] The Qianlong emperor renovated this garden and its buildings to serve as a place of worship for his mother. (LYP)

1 Berger 2003, 43; Gugong bowuyuan 2015a, 82.

2 The inscription on the niche gives the date of the twenty-eighth day of the eleventh month of the thirty-sixth year of the Qianlong reign (1771), suggesting the statue was made for the eightieth birthday of Empress Dowager Chongqing.

3 Chandra 2008, 36.

4 Gugong bowuyuan 2015a, 158–59.

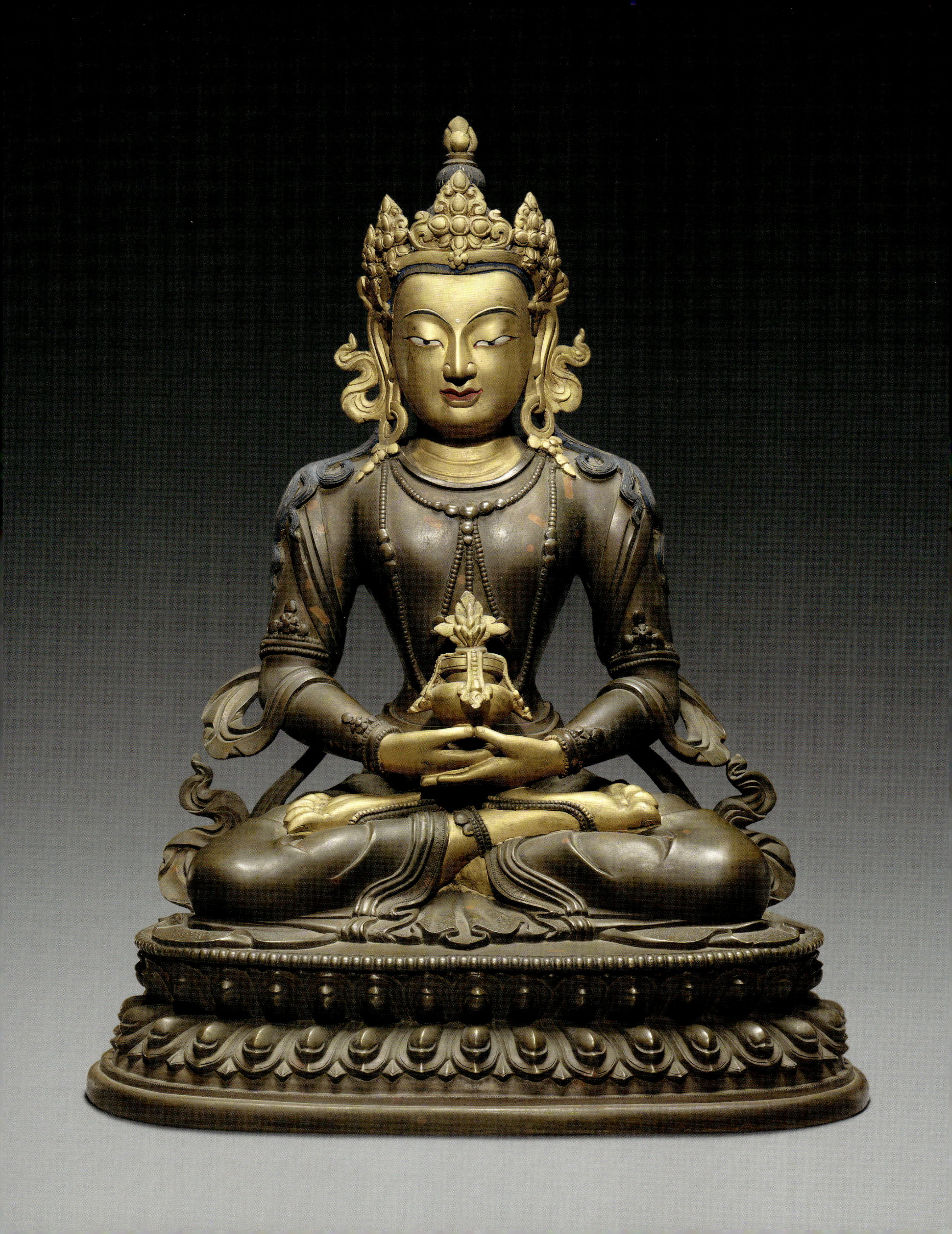

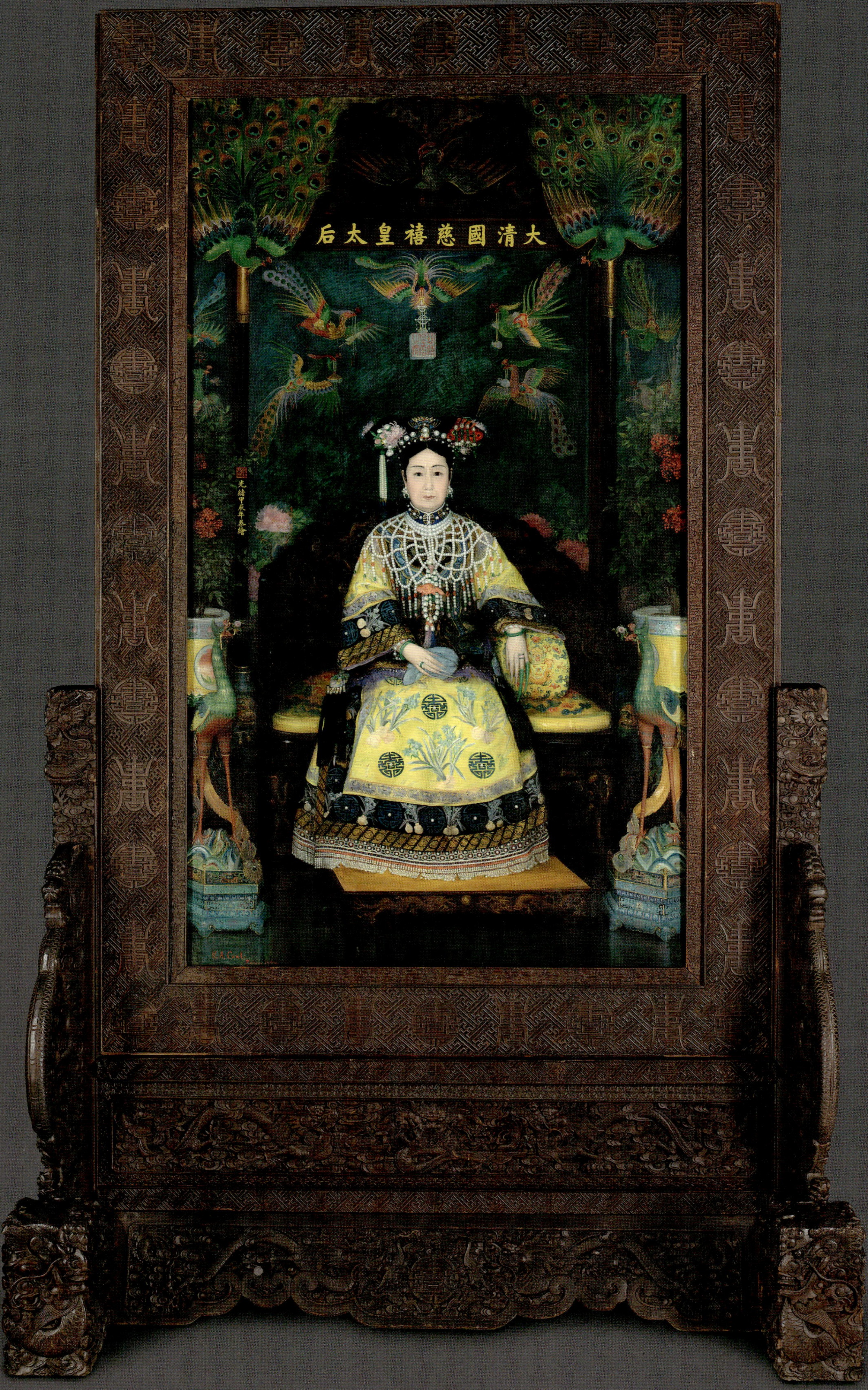
大清國慈禧皇太后

PLATE 46

慈禧皇太后油畫像屏

Empress Dowager Cixi

Katharine A. Carl (United States, 1865–1938)
Guangxu period, 1903
Painting: oil on canvas; frame: camphor wood
Transfer from the Smithsonian American Art Museum, Arthur M. Sackler Gallery
Cat. 42

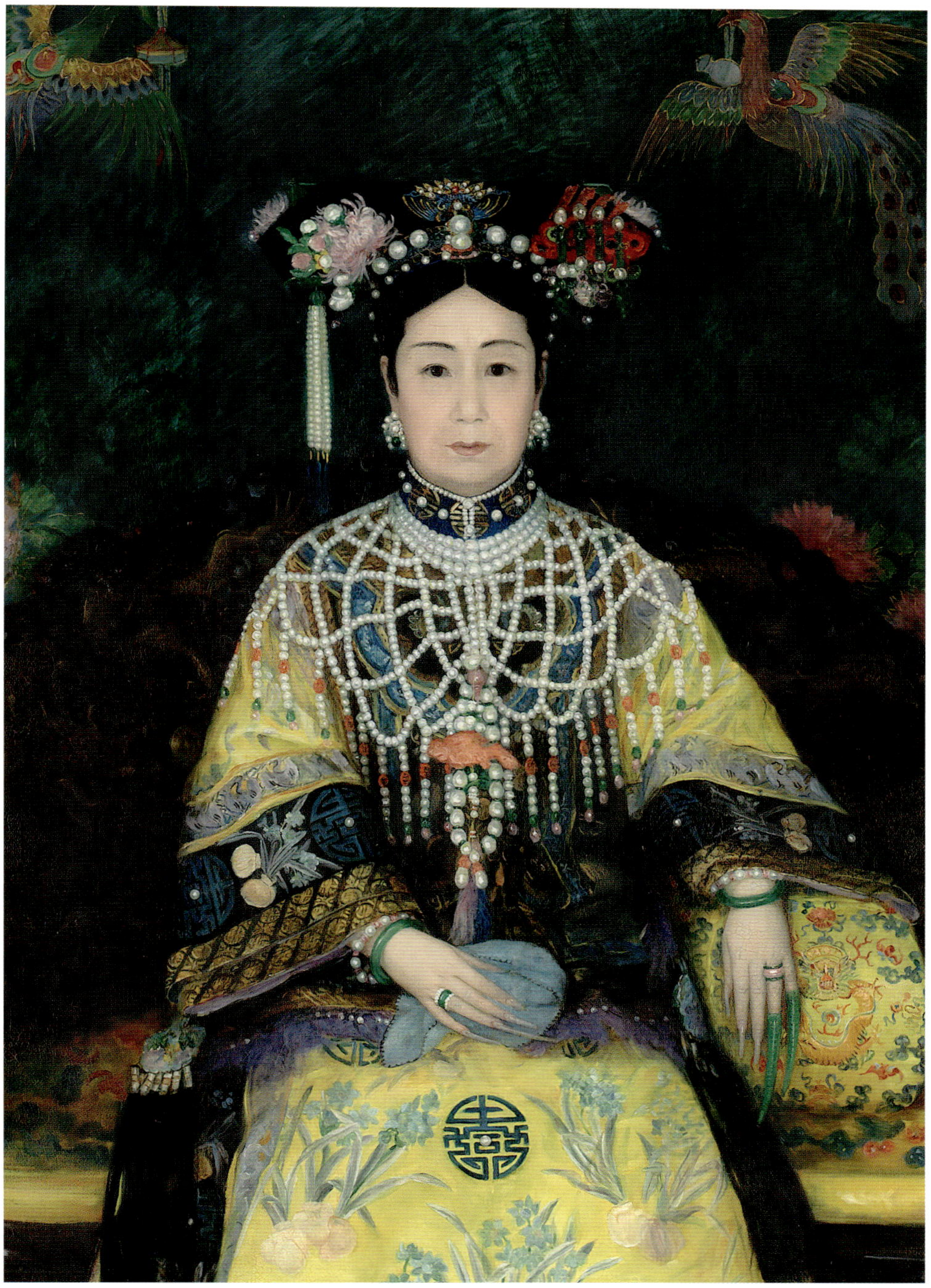

DETAIL

This monumental oil portrait, displayed at the St. Louis Exposition in 1904, marked Empress Dowager Cixi's unprecedented decision to publicize her image beyond the Forbidden City.[1] She commissioned this painting at the suggestion of Sarah Conger (1843–1932), the wife of the US ambassador to China, and it was painted by American artist Katharine A. Carl. Following the tradition of formal portraiture in China, Cixi is depicted in a frontal view with little facial expression. She wears a mantle of pearls and a bright yellow robe decorated with roundels of the longevity character (*shou*) and narcissus flowers. Her official title—"Empress Dowager Cixi of the Great Qing"—is written in Chinese on the frame of the screen behind her, and a vertical line of smaller characters on the handle of the peacock feather fan to her left indicates the year of the painting's production.

The portrait is imbued with symbols of imperial power. Cixi directed Carl to paint nine phoenixes—icons representing the empress's power—on the screen as if they were hovering about her; the central one holds the empress dowager's official seal. (The painter complained that she had never seen a phoenix, let alone painted one realistically.[2]) The color yellow, symbolizing royalty in China, dominates the picture, yet Cixi chose not to wear her most formal court attire with dragons—a gesture perhaps intended to downplay the lingering rumor that she had attempted to kill the Guangxu emperor to assume the throne (see Ying-chen Peng's essay, pp. 128–41).

Cixi also supervised the design of the portrait's elaborate wooden frame, which was intended to further augment the impact of the painting. This tactic may have backfired, as some American journalists commented that the gigantic frame was inappropriate and prevented them from appreciating the painting.[3] (YCP)

1 After its display in St. Louis, the portrait was presented as a state gift to President Theodore Roosevelt in 1905 and stored in the Smithsonian Institution. It was loaned to Taiwan in 1966. In 2011 it was shipped back to the Smithsonian for conservation. *Empresses of China's Forbidden City, 1644–1912* is its first public display since its return to the United States. Leng 2015.

2 Carl 1905, 238.

3 "An Imperial Portrait," *New York Times*, June 27, 1904.

PLATE 47

民國　金交龍紐皇后之寶

Seal of empress with double-headed dragon with box, tray, lock, key, and plaques

Imperial Workshop, Beijing
Republican period (1912–49), 1922
Gold alloy with silk tassels
Cat. 162

PLATE 48

清同治　壽山石翔鳳四靈紋紐
慈禧皇太后御覽之寶

Seal of Empress Dowager Cixi with phoenix and dragon

Tongzhi period, 1862–74
Shoushan stone
Cat. 146

PLATE 49

清乾隆　青玉交龍紐孝莊仁宣誠憲恭懿至德純徽翼天啟聖文皇后之寶

Seal of Empress Xiaozhuang

Qianlong period, 1736
Jade (nephrite) with silk tassels
Cat. 145

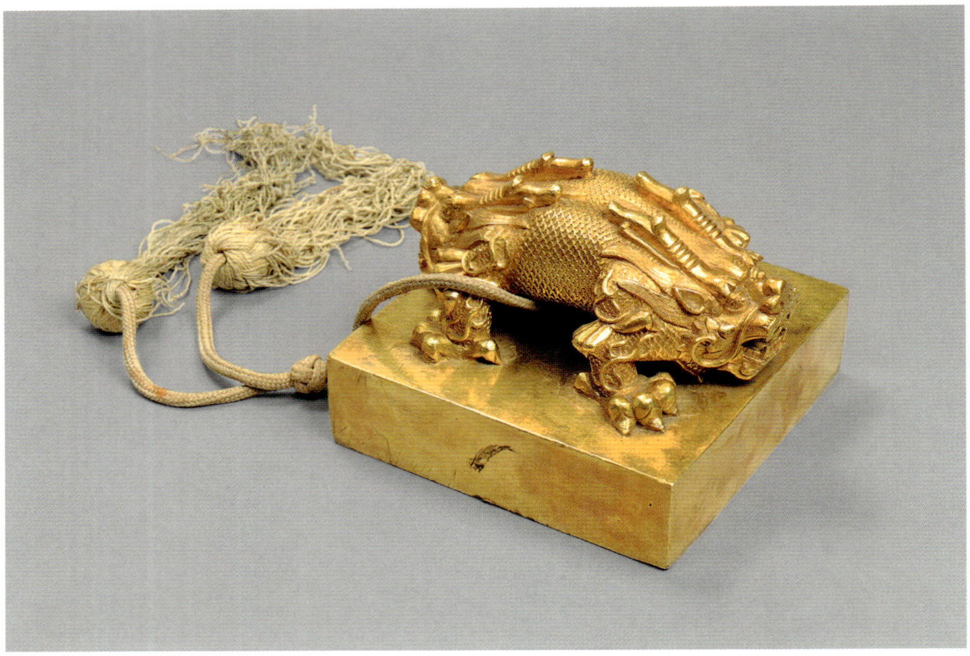

PLATE 47

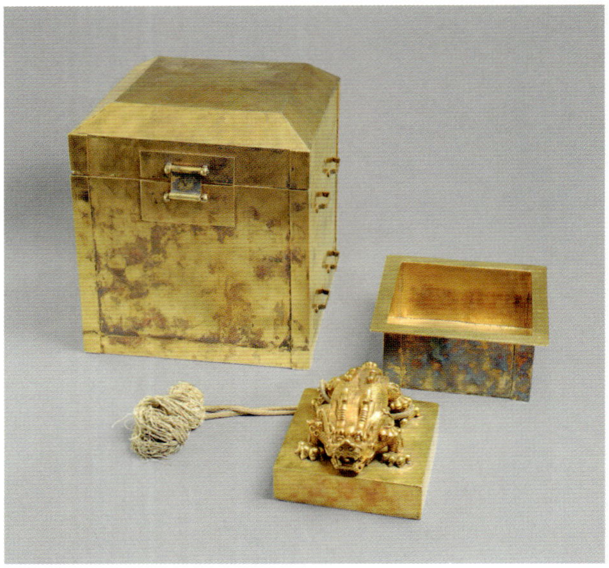

PLATE 47

SEAL MARK, PLATE 47

In the Qing dynasty seals served as badges of office, from district magistrates up to imperial consorts and the emperor. The conferral of seals in solemn public rituals signified the assumption of authority and made a prince an emperor, a bride an empress, and a mother an empress dowager. New seals were created whenever a consort was promoted in rank or received a new honorific title (*huihao*). Seals also recorded posthumous names. Whenever an emperor, empress, empress dowager, or other high-ranking imperial consort died, he or she was given a posthumous name (*shihao*) and a temple name (*miaohao*). These would then be inscribed on his or her spirit tablet and seal, which were installed in the Temple of the Ancestors (Tai miao) in Beijing and served as objects of veneration.

Weighing nearly forty pounds, the large gold seal (pl. 47) was bestowed upon Empress Xiaoke on the occasion of her wedding in 1922 to mark her investiture as empress. The dragon, a symbol associated with only the most supreme of positions, signifies her authority and identity, as do the Chinese and Manchu texts reading "seal of empress" cast on the base. Seals of earlier empresses were often melted down and repurposed. This one survives because

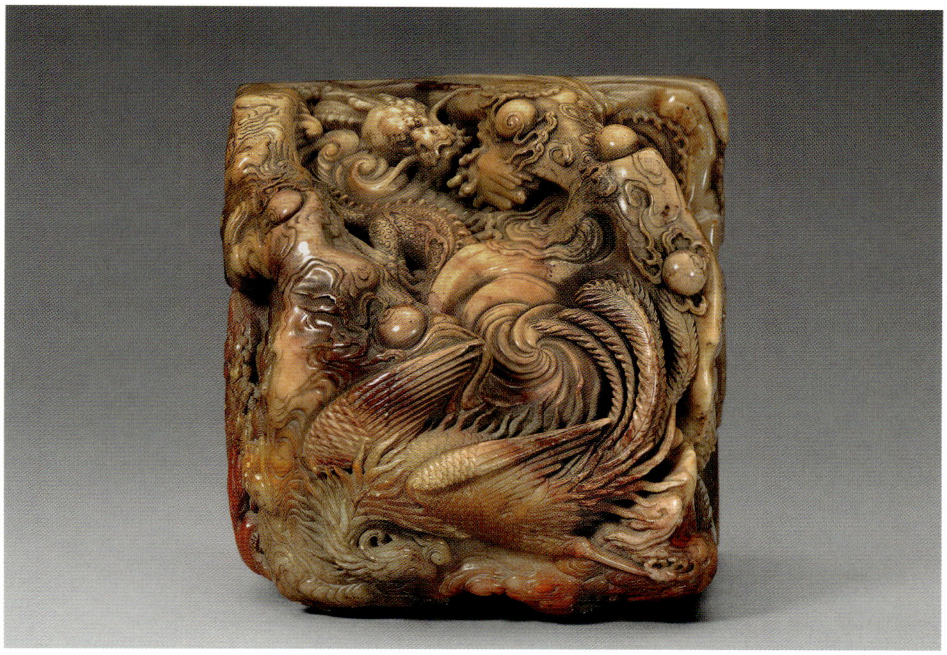

PLATE 48

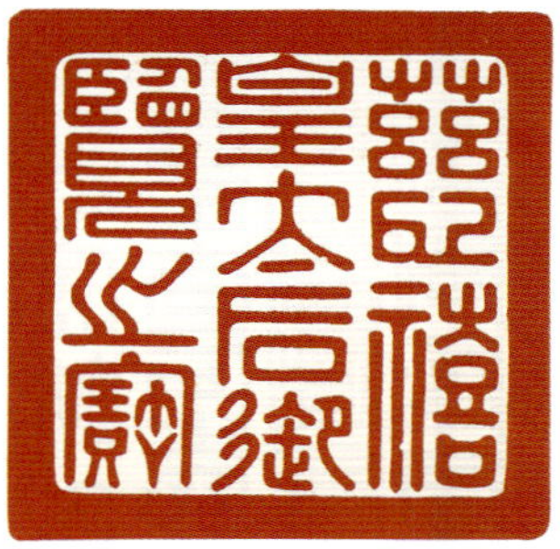

SEAL MARK, PLATE 48

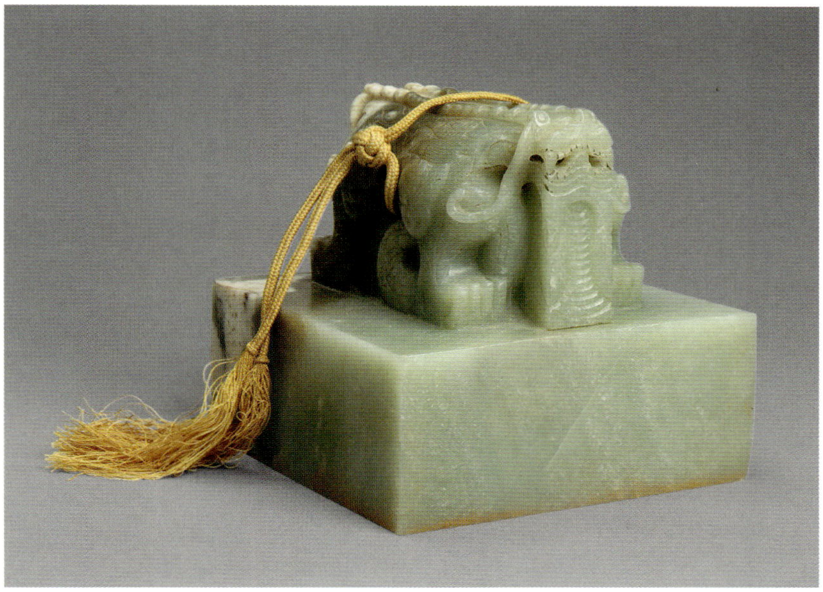

PLATE 49

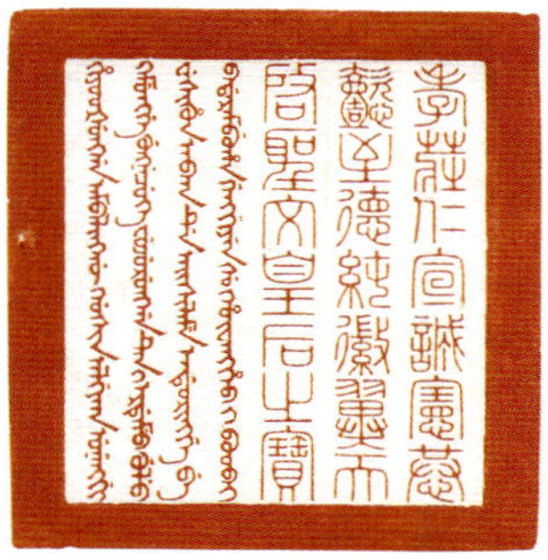

SEAL MARK, PLATE 49

Xiaoke was the last empress. She and her husband—the Xuantong emperor (Puyi), the last Qing monarch—were expelled from the Forbidden City only two years after their wedding. They left this seal behind.

The inscription on the jade seal with the double-headed dragon (pl. 49), written in both Manchu and Chinese, bears the honorific titles of Empress Xiaozhuang. These honorific titles, generally two characters in length, were bestowed on the occasion of a national celebration, an imperial wedding, the empress's birthday, or a great military victory. Every new title required a public investiture ceremony that featured newly carved tablets (*ce*) and seals (*bao*) bearing the new titles. This process of adding titles continued until the total number of honorifics reached sixteen.

Seals were also used by wealthy educated individuals (mostly men) as a mark of connoisseurship. They commissioned artisans to carve stone seals in intaglio (*yinwen*) or relief (*yangwen*) bearing their "studio names" (*hao*) and used these seals to leave their mark on paintings and calligraphy.[1] A scholar-connoisseur might have multiple studio names and hence multiple seals. The inscription on the seal decorated with a phoenix, dragon, and *qilin* (pl. 48) reads: "Seal [indicating that] Empress Dowager Cixi viewed [this]."[2] More so than previous Qing empresses, Cixi actively engaged in scholarly and artistic pursuits. She also employed instructors and "ghost artists" to help her produce artworks, which she stamped with her personal seal and occasionally bestowed as presents on officials and foreign dignitaries. (ESR)

1 Literati males commonly adopted a name they used in writing poems and acts of connoisseurship.

2 A mythical Chinese creature, the *qilin* was said to appear with the arrival or passing of a sage or virtuous ruler; it was thus an auspicious imperial symbol.

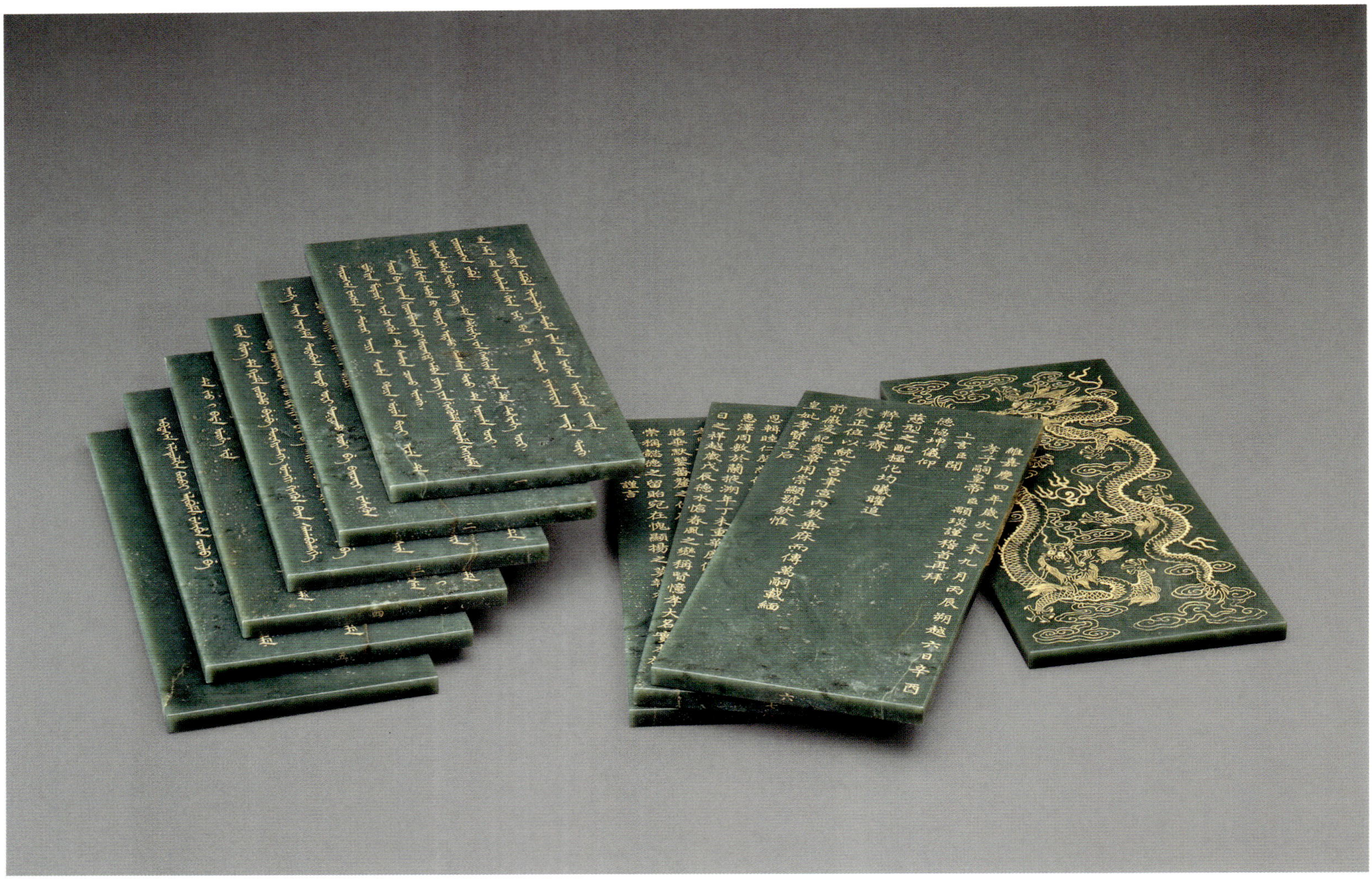

PLATE 50

清嘉慶　青玉孝賢純皇后謚冊

Jade book with dragons and eulogy for Empress Xiaoxian

Jiaqing period, 1799
Jade (nephrite) with gold
Cat. 147

This "jade book" (*yuce*) is really a mortuary tablet bearing the posthumous name of Empress Xiaoxian, wife of the Qianlong emperor. It was commissioned by the Jiaqing emperor in 1799, long after the empress's death in 1748. To understand the context in which the tablet was commissioned, we must delve into Qing funerary customs.

The Chinese belief in an existence that extended beyond the grave led to elaborate rituals for the dead at the Qing court. An empress (like an emperor) received a posthumous name (*shihao*) that was usually drafted by the court's chief ministers. The posthumous name was inscribed (in Manchu and Chinese) on silk that was burned during funerary rites; a set of tablets and a seal inscribed with the name would be buried with the empress's coffin; and a set of similarly inscribed jade tablets—like this one—and a seal were placed in the Temple of the Ancestors (Tai miao), located just south of the palace in Beijing. Jade, highly prized from ancient times onward, was judged to be an appropriate material to commemorate a name (and identity) that the Chinese believed would endure for eternity.

Sacrifices to a deceased empress were addressed to her posthumous name. However, since Xiaoxian predeceased her husband, her first posthumous name lacked one final, essential component: *his* posthumous name. When the Qianlong emperor died in 1799, the character for "great" (*chun*) was selected as his posthumous name. Henceforth, Xiaoxian would be called "Xiaoxian Chun huanghou." When "Chun" was added to her posthumous name, new tablets and seals were carved. (ESR)

PLATE 51

清同治　孝貞顯皇后璇闈日永圖軸

Empress Dowager Ci'an

Court painters, Beijing; calligraphy by the Tongzhi emperor (1856–1875)
Tongzhi period, about 1872–73
Hanging scroll, ink and color on paper
Cat. 16

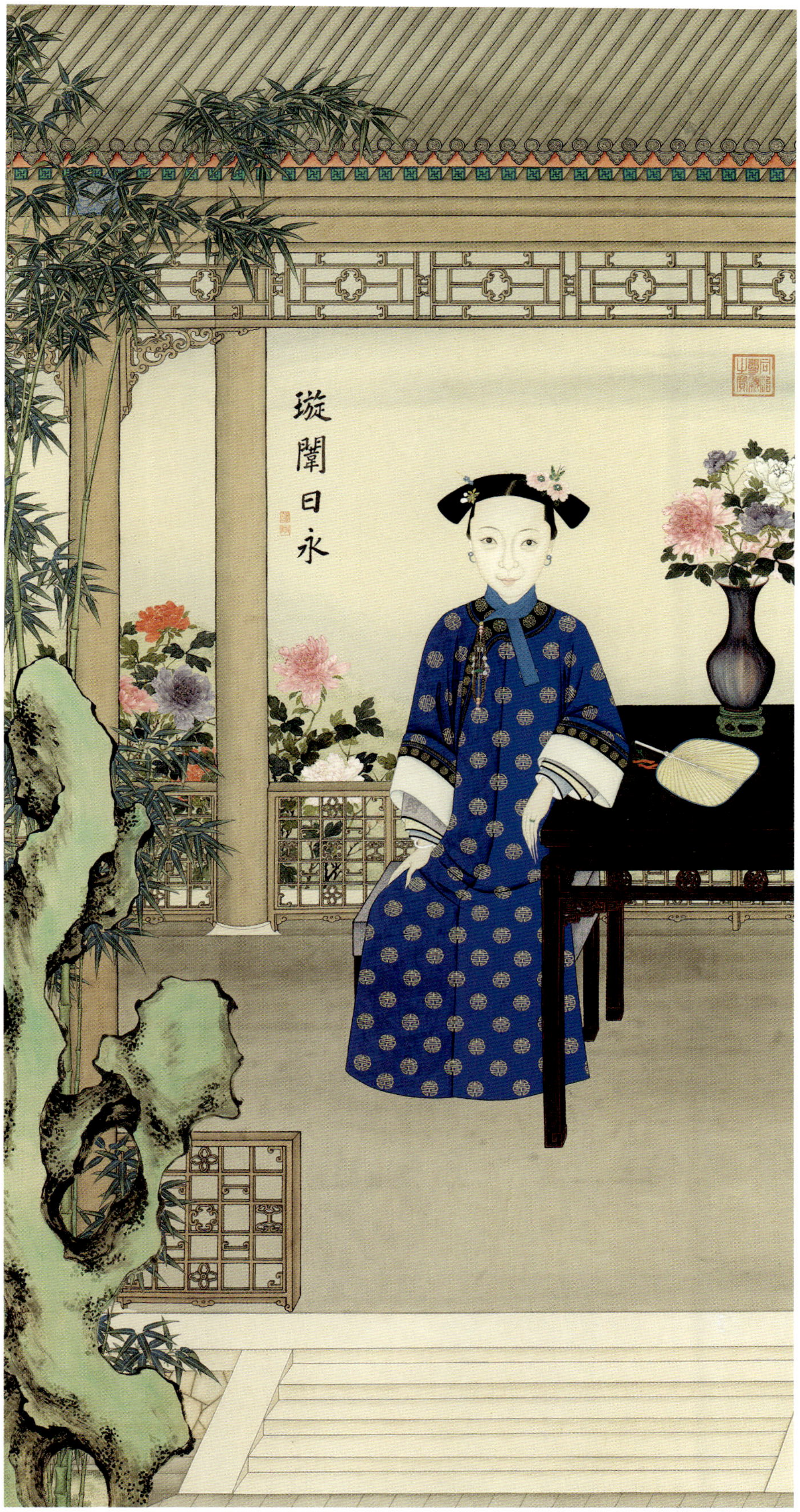

She may have carried the impressive title of senior empress dowager regent, but Empress Dowager Ci'an was overshadowed by her co-regent, the junior empress dowager, Cixi. This painting is one of the few portraits of Ci'an that offers insight into her personality, which can be summed up by the word "propriety." Its ambience bespeaks the traditionally held ideal qualities of an imperial woman: gentle, feminine, and motherly. Seated by a table in a garden pavilion, Ci'an smiles mildly and peacefully. Her dark blue robe is decorated with golden roundels with a stylized *shou* character for longevity and follows the dress code for widows in the Qing dynasty.[1] The fan on the table was a common accessory for women. The peonies in the vase and blooming in the garden behind Ci'an symbolize her supreme status as they were said to be the "king of flowers."

The painting contains hints of the Tongzhi emperor's affectionate relationship with Ci'an. The seal above the vase reads "Tongzhi's seal of respecting parents" (*Tongzhi zunqin zhibao*), and the four-character inscription to Ci'an's right reads "May the sun forever shine in women's residences" (*Xuanwei riyong*)—a common wish for mothers' birthdays. Filial intimacy of this sort is intriguingly missing from portraits of Cixi, the Tongzhi emperor's birth mother, a contrast that helps define Ci'an's demure persona as a regent who showed less concern about matters beyond the inner court. As the senior empress dowager, Ci'an had the status of being Tongzhi's nominal, or formal, mother.

A garden setting was common in informal portraiture of the Qing court. Here, the painter employed Western techniques to enhance the realistic depiction of the environment. The treatment of the steps, columns, balustrades, table, and eaves reflects his attempt to incorporate linear perspective into the composition, and the arrangement of the large green scholar's rock and bamboo in the foreground and the peonies in the background further enhances this sense of depth. (YCP)

1 Peng 2014, 100–01.

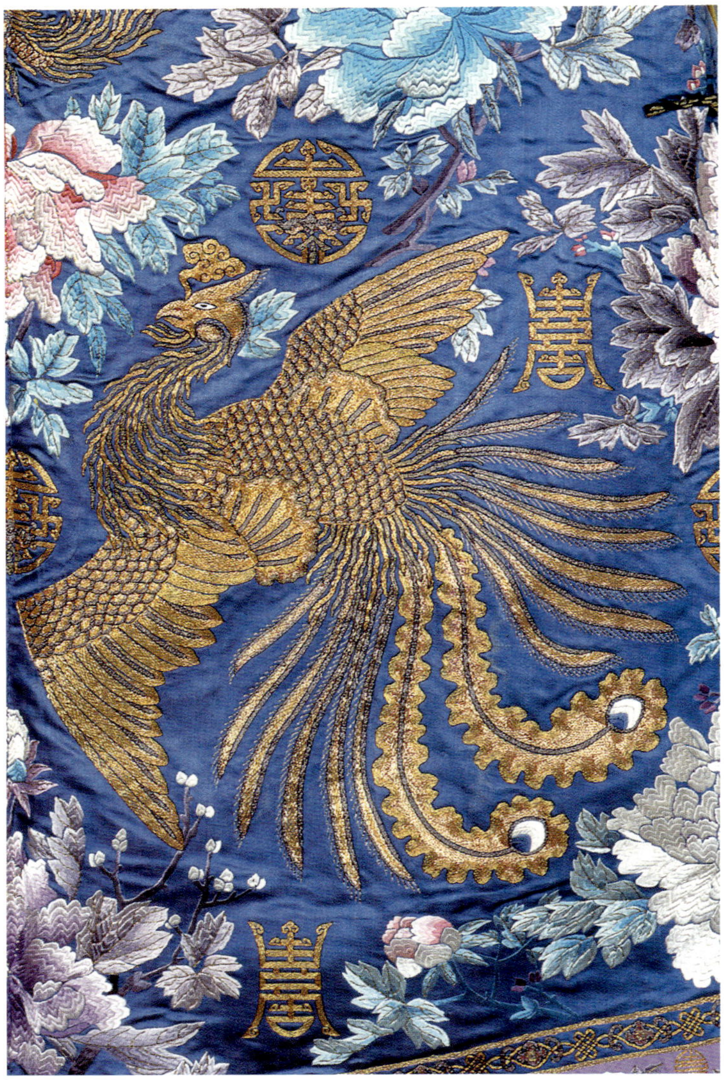

DETAIL

PLATE 52

清光緒　寶藍色緞繡鳳穿牡丹
壽字紋襯衣

Woman's robe with phoenixes, peonies, and the character for longevity

Guangxu period, 1875–1908
Embroidery, polychrome silk and metallic-wrapped threads on silk satin
University of Alberta Museums, Mactaggart Art Collection
Cat. 64

Toward the end of the Qing dynasty, a type of robe called *chenyi* for everyday use gained great popularity among imperial women. Because it was not regulated by official codes, *chenyi* offered more possibilities for new styles, motifs, and colors than did formal garments (see pls. 20 and 21). The design and placement of the decoration—in this instance, the auspicious and powerful symbol of the phoenix, reserved for imperial women of the highest rank—still followed certain conventions of court attire, but the short, wide sleeves reference the style of Han Chinese dress, which formal court garments eschewed as an expression of Manchu identity. Intense new colors such as bright purple were in favor at the Qing court thanks to the introduction of synthetic aniline dyes from Europe in the late nineteenth century.[1] (DYW)

1 Cao Zhenyu 2008.

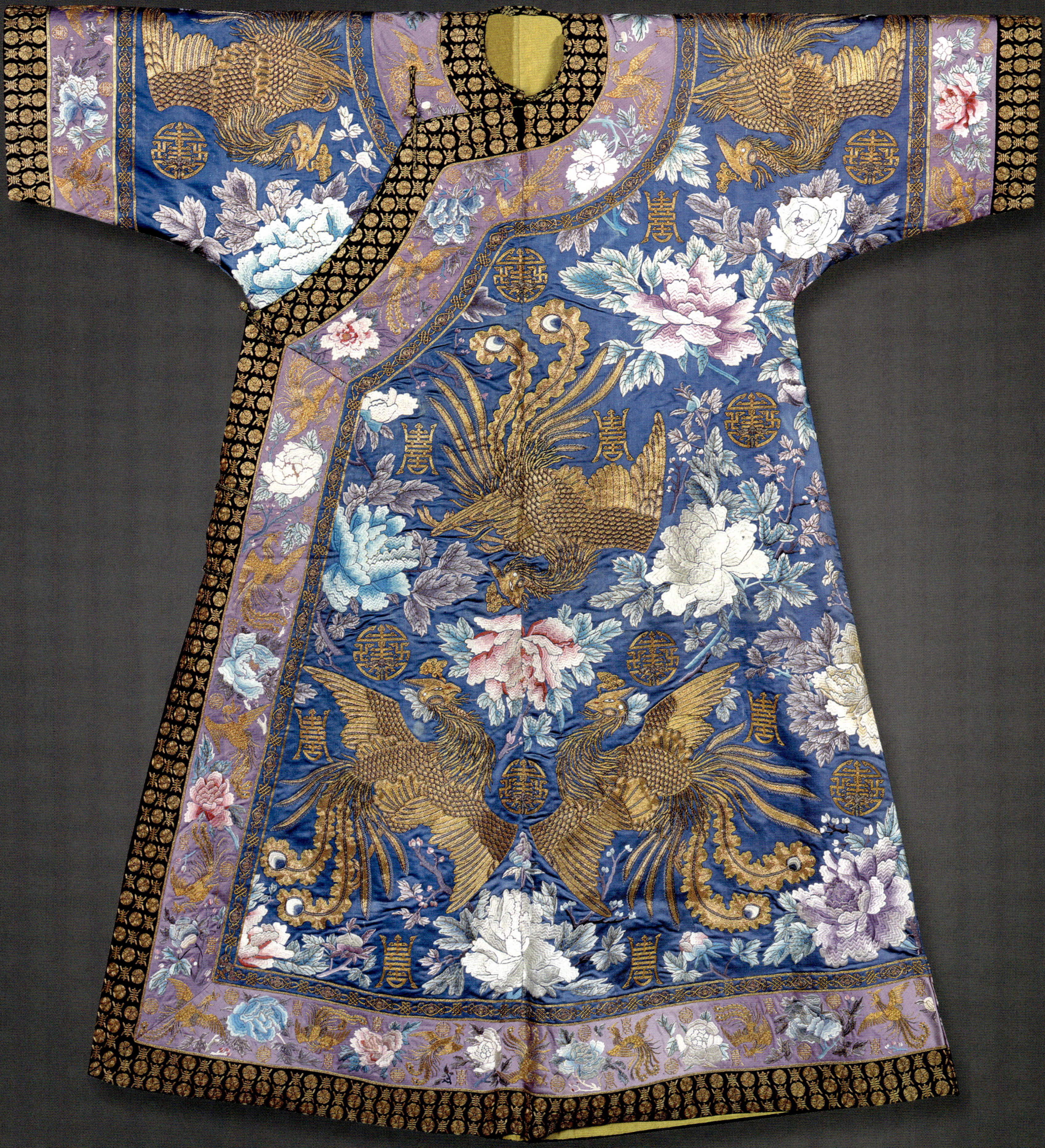

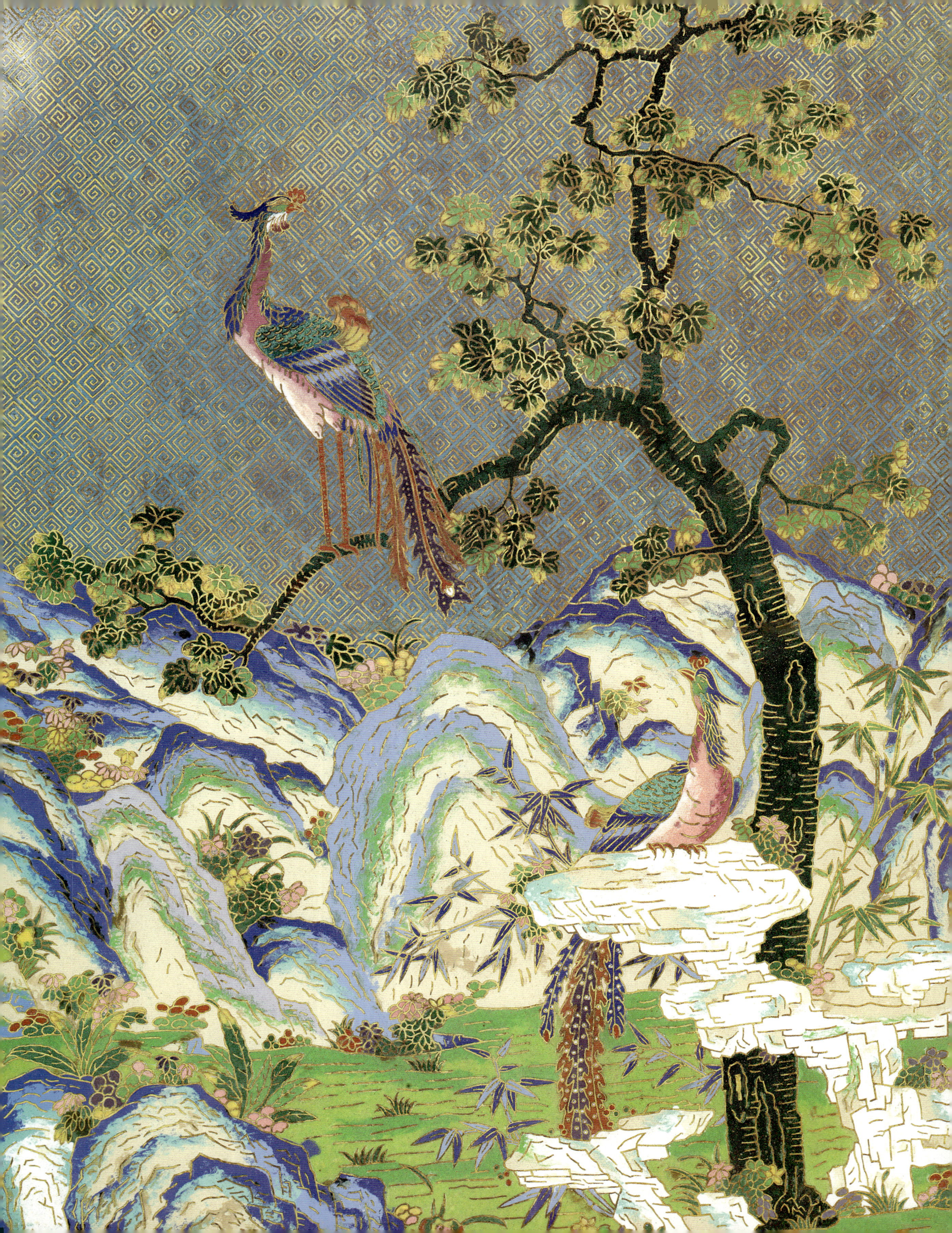

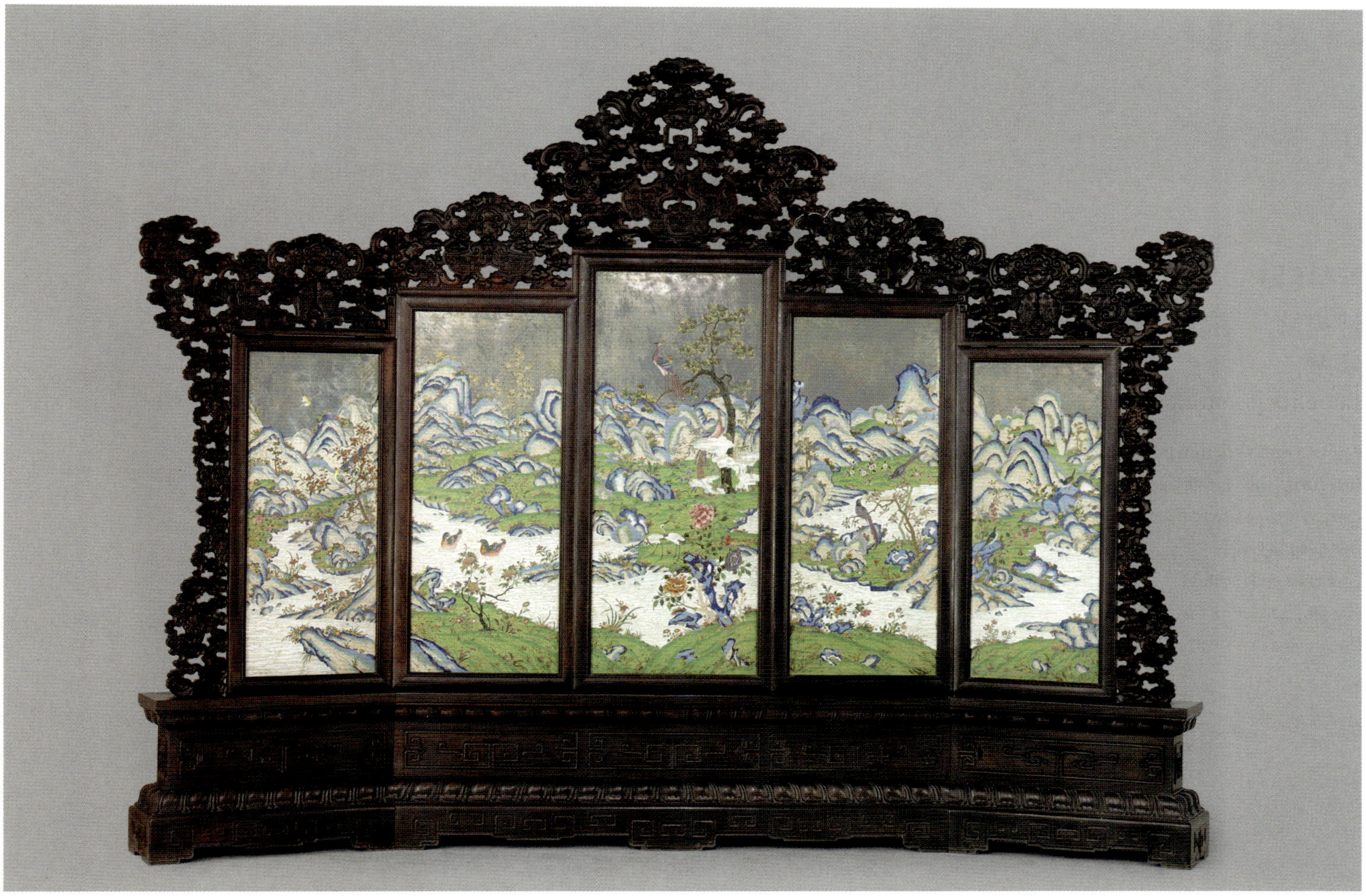

PLATE 53

清乾隆 紫檀木嵌琺琅山水花卉百鳥朝鳳圖圍屏

Five-panel screen with phoenixes and birds in landscape

Workshop, probably Guangzhou
Qianlong period, probably 1775 or earlier
Panels: cloisonné, copper alloy with polychrome enamels and gilding; frame: *zitan* wood and *nan* wood
Cat. 117

This screen features a pair of phoenixes (*fenghuang*) in the central panel. These mythical creatures were said to alight on paulownia trees only during times of just and proper rule. As sovereigns of the avian world, the phoenixes are surrounded by various species of auspicious birds paying them homage. Cranes represent longevity, while the mandarin ducks on the river communicate a message of marital harmony. This scene also symbolizes the five basic human relationships—between ruler and minister, father and son, husband and wife, senior and junior, and among friends—critical to maintaining familial and social order according to Chinese philosophy. For example, the phoenix represents the ruler, and the crane is the minister. The screen thus creates a picture of a peaceful, prosperous, and harmonious world.[1]

While they were not always associated with women, the phoenixes here may allude to the exalted status of the screen's recipient as a "sovereign" among palace women. Its history and decoration also suggest its connection with high-ranking imperial ladies and birthdays. References to those annual celebrations abound: The openwork wooden frame features upside down bats (*fu*), a rebus for the arrival of good fortune. Each bat holds either a stone chime (*qing*), a homophone for celebration, or a pair of fish, a Buddhist symbol for compassion and wisdom as well as a pun for abundance (*yu*). Five wooden panels on the back of the screen are embellished with roundels of the longevity character (*shou*), enhancing the screen's association with birthdays. The screen was once in the inventory of the Palace of Longevity and Peace (Shou'an gong), a residence of widowed Qing consorts.[2] It was likely a tributary gift from Debao (1719–1789), the Imperial Inspector of Guangdong, to the court a few months before Empress Dowager Chongqing's eighty-fourth birthday in 1775.[3] The style of carving and the combination of cloisonné and champlevé decoration are consistent with other works produced in Guangzhou, a bustling southern port city full of foreign traders and missionaries as well as Chinese artisans who quickly absorbed outside influences, including enameling techniques imported from Europe. (DWY)

1 Li Jiufang 2002, 141.
2 My thanks to Lin Shu for providing information about the screen's reference number, which indicates its location during the survey of the palace collection conducted between 1924 and 1930.
3 ZGDYLSDAG 2005, 39:153.

PLATE 54

清光緒　慈禧皇太后指畫鳳凰圖軸

Phoenix perching in a paulownia tree

Painting and signature by Empress Dowager Cixi (1835–1908); calligraphy by Quan Zhong (active 19th–early 20th centuries) and Xu Fu (1836–1908)
Guangxu period, 1888
Hanging scroll, ink on paper
Cat. 21

Signed by Cixi, this painting alludes to the empress dowager's power and ambition as China's de facto ruler. It was created at a time, early 1888, when she faced a challenge. The upcoming wedding of her nephew the Guangxu emperor would mark the maturity of his rulership, meaning he would no longer be required to retain Cixi's services as his regent and adviser. But Cixi, ever the savvy politician, determined to maintain her influence and engineered a marriage between the emperor and her own niece.

How does this painting allude to her imperial might? The key lies in its subject: the phoenix. In Chinese mythology, this mythical creature brings order, justice, and prosperity to the world—just as a wise ruler does. At the Qing imperial court, the phoenix represented empresses, just as the dragon represented emperors, and it was a favorite motif in paintings, decorative arts, and costumes created by or for Cixi. Further, a poem above the painting on pink paper exalts the phoenix as it forcefully and joyously soars the tens of thousands of miles to reach the heavenly palace. A red square seal mark at the top right of Cixi's signature along the left side of the painting proclaims her mandate to govern the country by following the "principles of heaven," understood to be the source of political power for male rulers in dynastic China.

Did Cixi actually create the painting? Continuing a practice of Qing emperors of enhancing their authority through art, Cixi employed court artists, both male and female, to tutor and ghost paint for her.[1] She is the only Qing empress to have left a significant body of signed artworks, and the several hundred surviving paintings and calligraphy pieces attributed to her vary greatly in style, pointing to the presence of multiple hands in their making. This painting is unique among the works attributed to her in that it was created using fingertips and other parts of the hand instead of the brush commonly used in Chinese painting. Faint fingerprints are visible in the ink along the left border of the inscription she supposedly wrote, imparting a personal touch and a tangible imperial presence. (DYW)

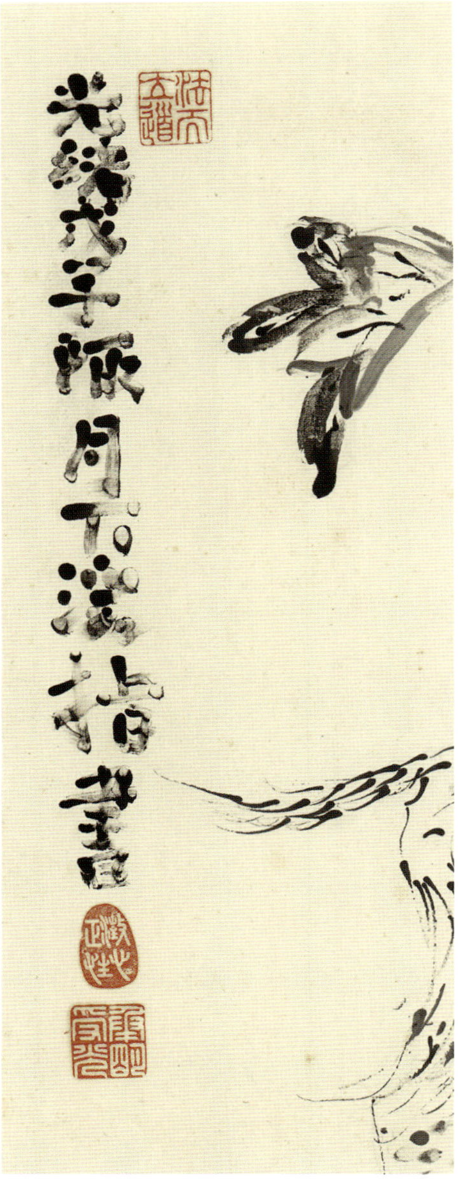

DETAIL, EMPRESS DOWAGER CIXI'S SIGNATURE LINE

1 Li Shi 2008, 181–89.

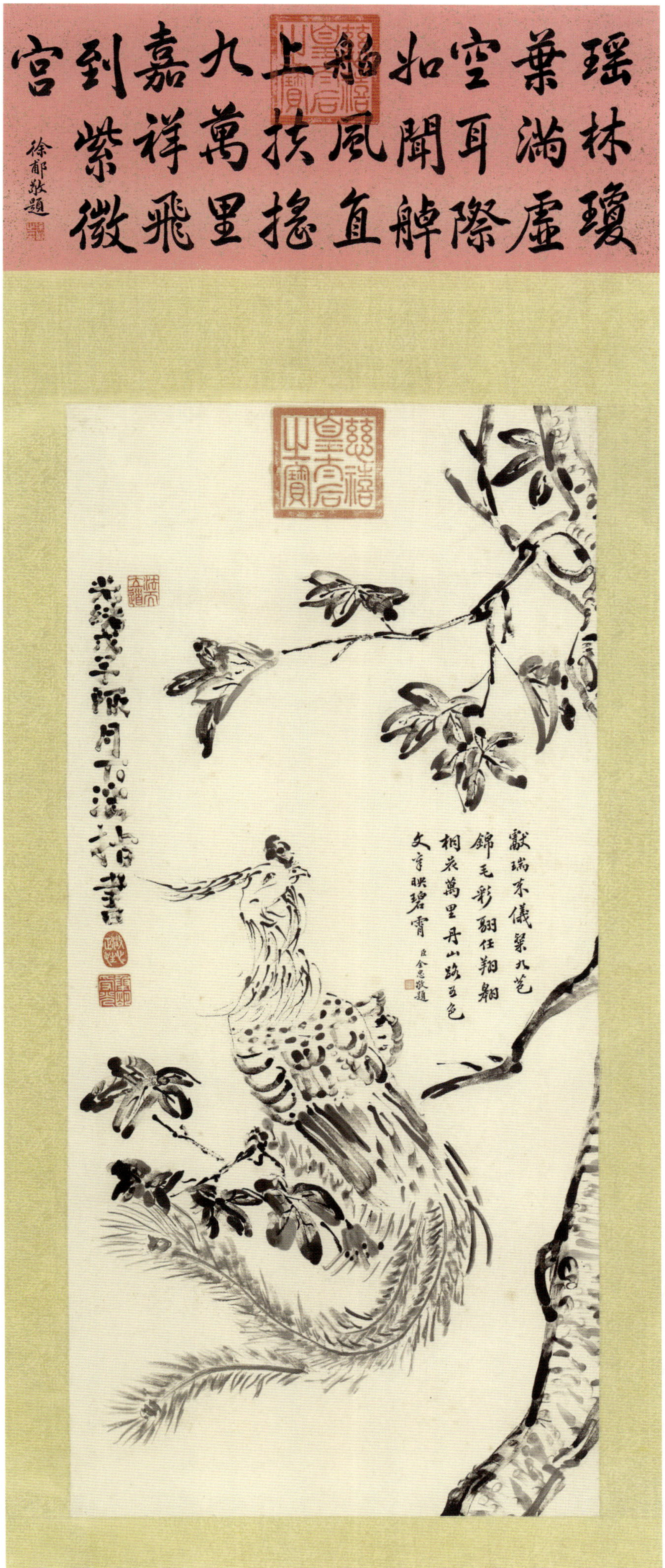

PLATE 55

清光緒　粉彩牡丹花鳥紋長方花盆

Flowerpot with peonies and birds

Imperial Porcelain Factory, Jingdezhen
Guangxu period, 1875 or 1876
Porcelain with enamels over colorless glaze
Cat. 131

PLATE 56

清光緒　牡丹花鳥紋長方花盆圖樣

Sketch of peonies and birds for porcelain flowerpot decoration

Court painters, Beijing
Guangxu period, 1875 or 1876
Ink and color on paper
Cat. 132

The Tongzhi emperor's ambitious scheme to rebuild the Garden of Perfect Brightness (Yuanming yuan) as the Garden of Myriad Springs (Wanchun yuan) for Empress Dowager Cixi was initiated in 1873 but soon came to an ominous end. Troubled by corruption, the project was fiercely opposed by Qing officials, who forced Tongzhi to cancel it the next year.[1] Four months later the emperor was dead. While the endeavor was still active, however, Cixi was determined to decorate her imperial complex lavishly and commissioned an extensive set of porcelain objects from the Imperial Porcelain Factory. These ceramics were already in production when the larger venture was abandoned, making them the only part of the project that was realized.

Cixi repeatedly demanded that the imperial kiln in Jiangxi province complete the commission (they were finally shipped to Beijing in batches in 1875 and 1876) and personally reviewed the designs.[2] For example, she would have approved the layout of elements on this flower pot, with its blooming peonies and colorful birds—two at rest and another flying above. The sketch for this vessel bears a red tag indicating it is the eighteenth design in a group and a yellow tag detailing the number and sizes of pots to be produced. The resemblance between the pot and the drawing shows how closely the potters followed these instructions. The inscription and seal in red enamel on one side of the pot are symbols of Cixi's ownership. The inscription "Daya zhai" refers to her personal painting studio, the Studio of Utmost Grace, and the seal reads "Whole world celebrating as one family" (*Tiandi yijiachun*), also the name of the palace in the Garden of Myriad Springs where Cixi had planned on living. (YCP)

1 Liu Dunzhen 1933, 301–02.
2 Zhang Xiaorui 2004.

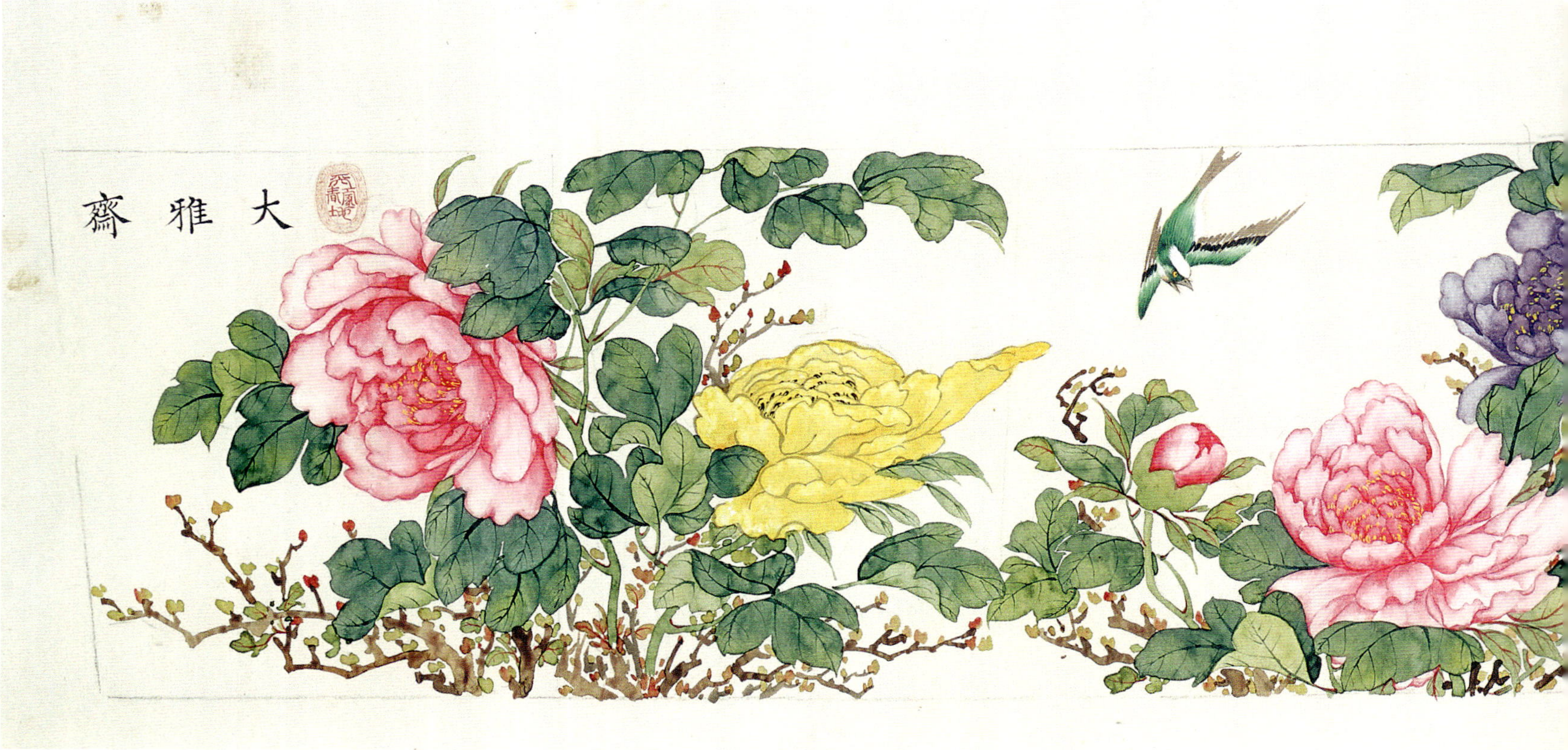

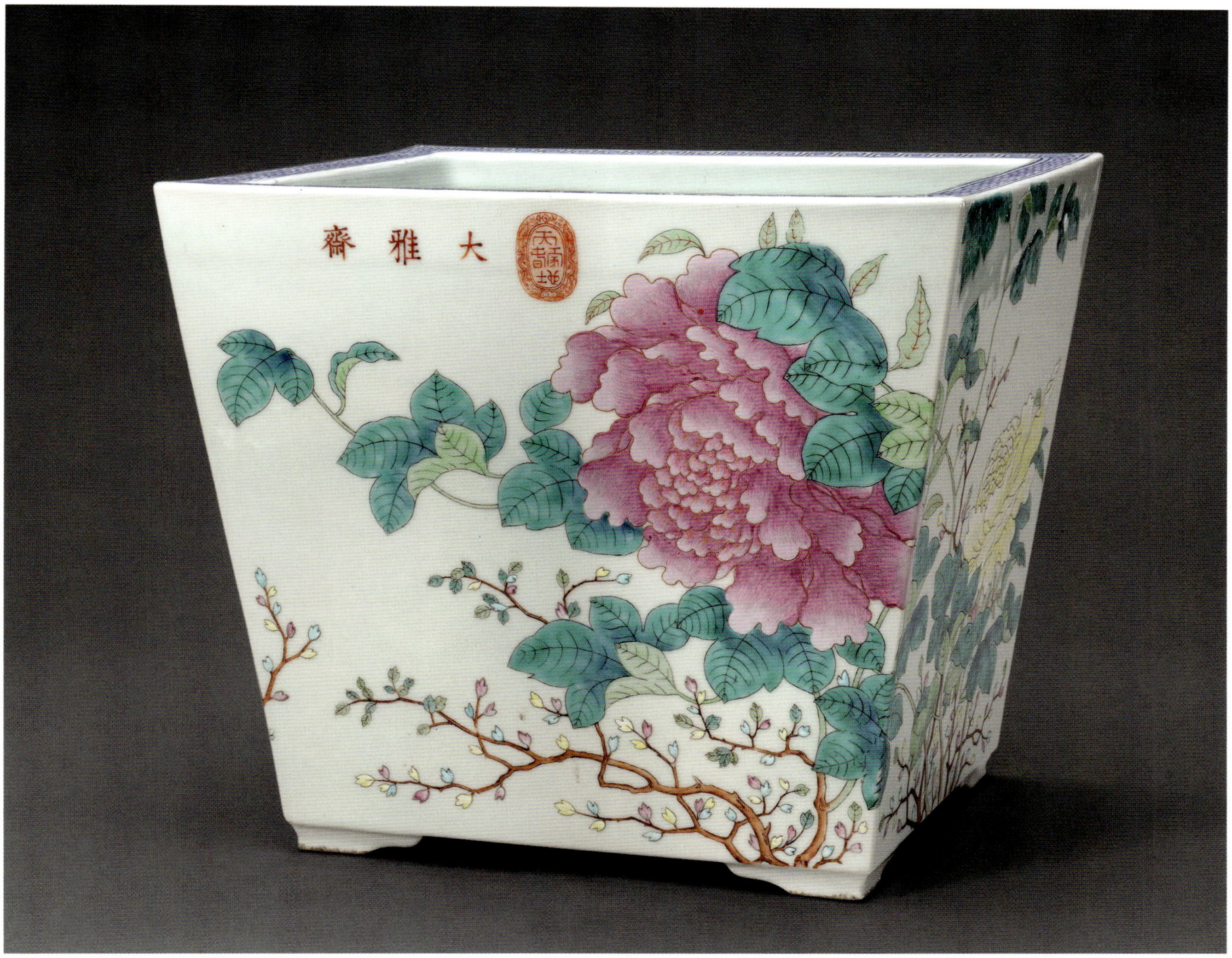

PLATE 55

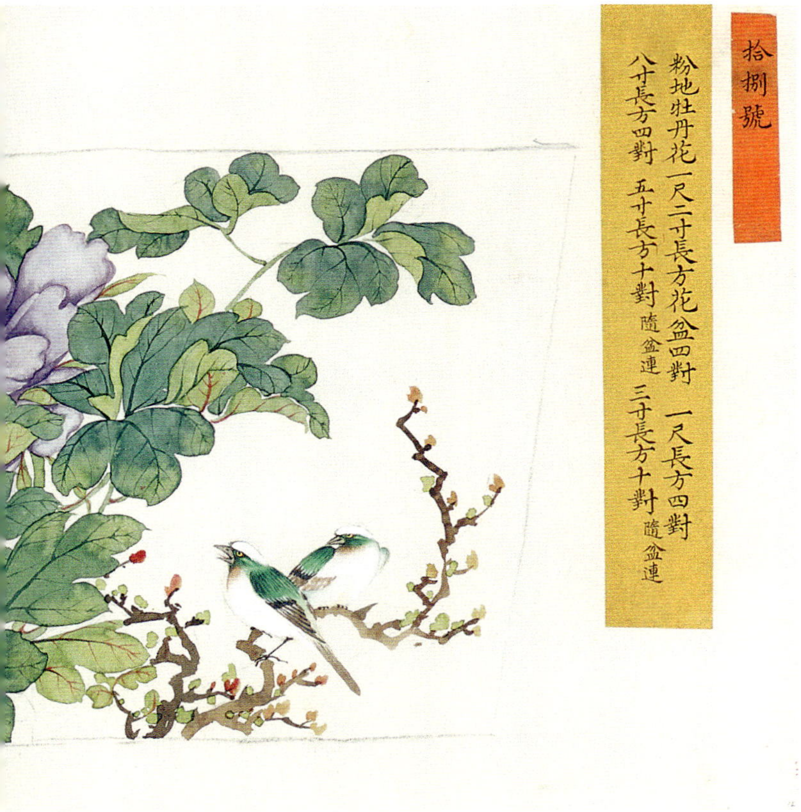

PLATE 56

PLATE 57

1860 年清漪園智慧海蛋白照片

The Great Imperial Porcelain Palace, Yuen Ming Yuen [Yuanming yuan], October 1860/Pekin

Felice Beato (Italy, 1832–1909)
1860
Albumen print
Peabody Essex Museum
Cat. 185

This is one of the earliest photographic images of the Garden of Clear Ripples (Qingyi yuan), known today as the Summer Palace, in northwest Beijing. In 1750 the Qianlong emperor commissioned this imperial resort—consisting of palaces, landscaped grounds, and a large lake—and made it a sixtieth-birthday gift for his mother, Empress Dowager Chongqing, who frequently enjoyed living and traveling outside the Forbidden City. In addition to its many scenic spots, the Garden of Clear Ripples featured numerous Buddhist temples designed for Chongqing, a devotee. This photograph shows the Sea of Perfect Wisdom (Zhihui hai), a Buddhist hall on the crest of Longevity Hill (Wanshou shan) in the Garden of Clear Ripples. Its exterior is completely covered with glazed tiles of brilliant yellow and green that form thousands of glistening niches in which are seated Buddhist deities. The hall was once home to a sculpture depicting Amitayus, Buddha of Limitless Life, the deity associated with longevity and birthday celebrations at the Qing court.

Felice Beato captured this view in October 1860 when he accompanied troops entering Beijing during the Anglo-French expedition to China during the Second Opium War.[1] During this conflict soldiers burned the imperial complex at the Garden of Clear Ripples, which remained abandoned for almost thirty years. But the Sea of Perfect Wisdom, being constructed entirely of masonry rather than timber, survived. In the 1880s, in an effort to erase the stigma of China's defeat by Western powers and to emulate Chongqing's status and lifestyle, Empress Dowager Cixi launched a project to restore and expand the Garden of Clear Ripples, which would then become her main residence. In 1889, facing a financially strapped imperial treasury, Cixi embezzled a large sum (intended to strengthen the Chinese navy) in order to restore the garden's splendor in the name of her nephew the Guangxu emperor as an example of his filial devotion.[2] The garden was again vandalized in 1900 when an international coalition from eight nations occupied Beijing in response to the antiforeign and anti-Christian Boxer Uprising, which was supported by Cixi. (DYW)

1 For more on nineteenth-century photography of the garden, see Harris 1999, 93, 151; and Pearce 2005, 113.
2 ZGDYLSDAG 2015, 974–76.

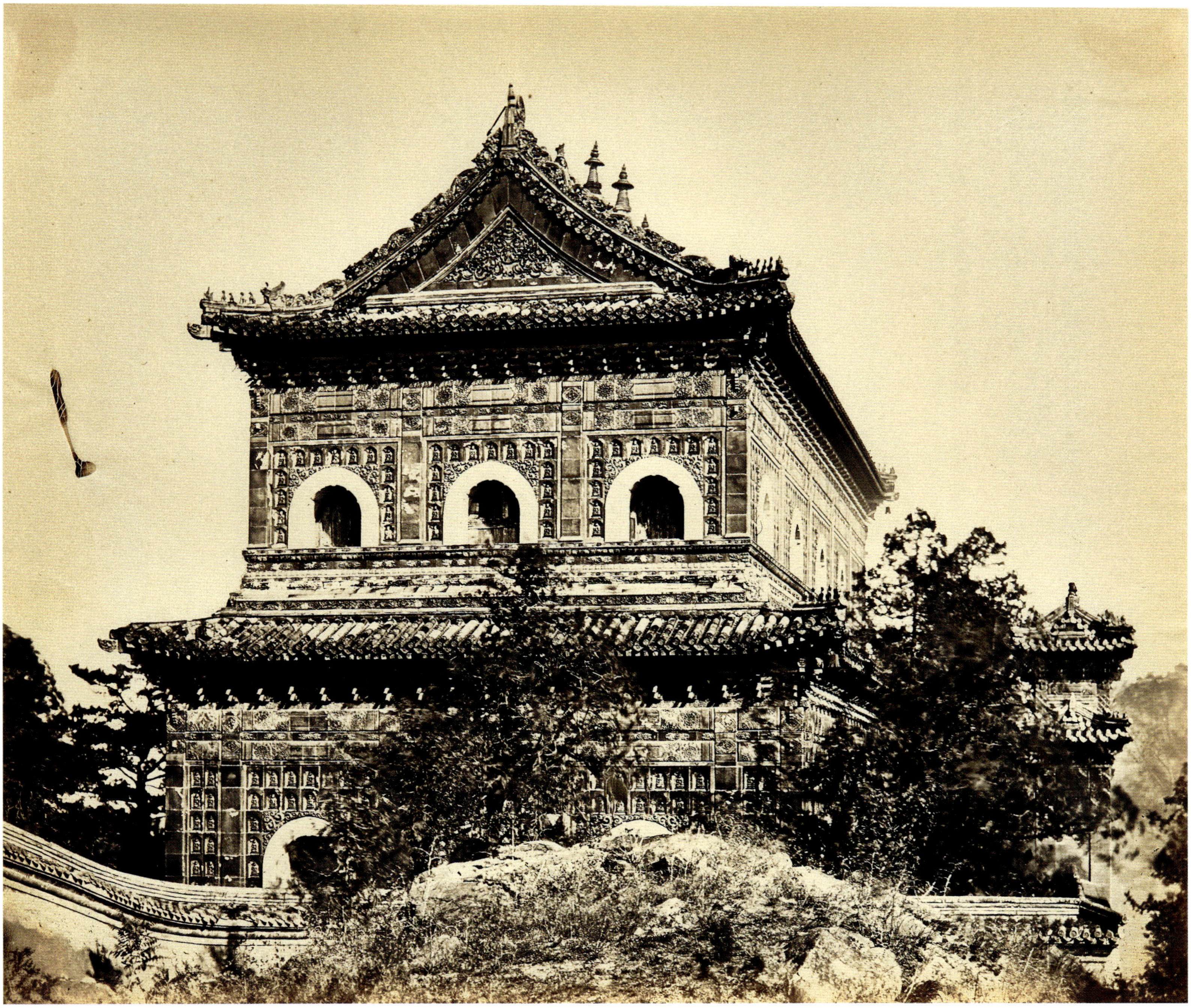

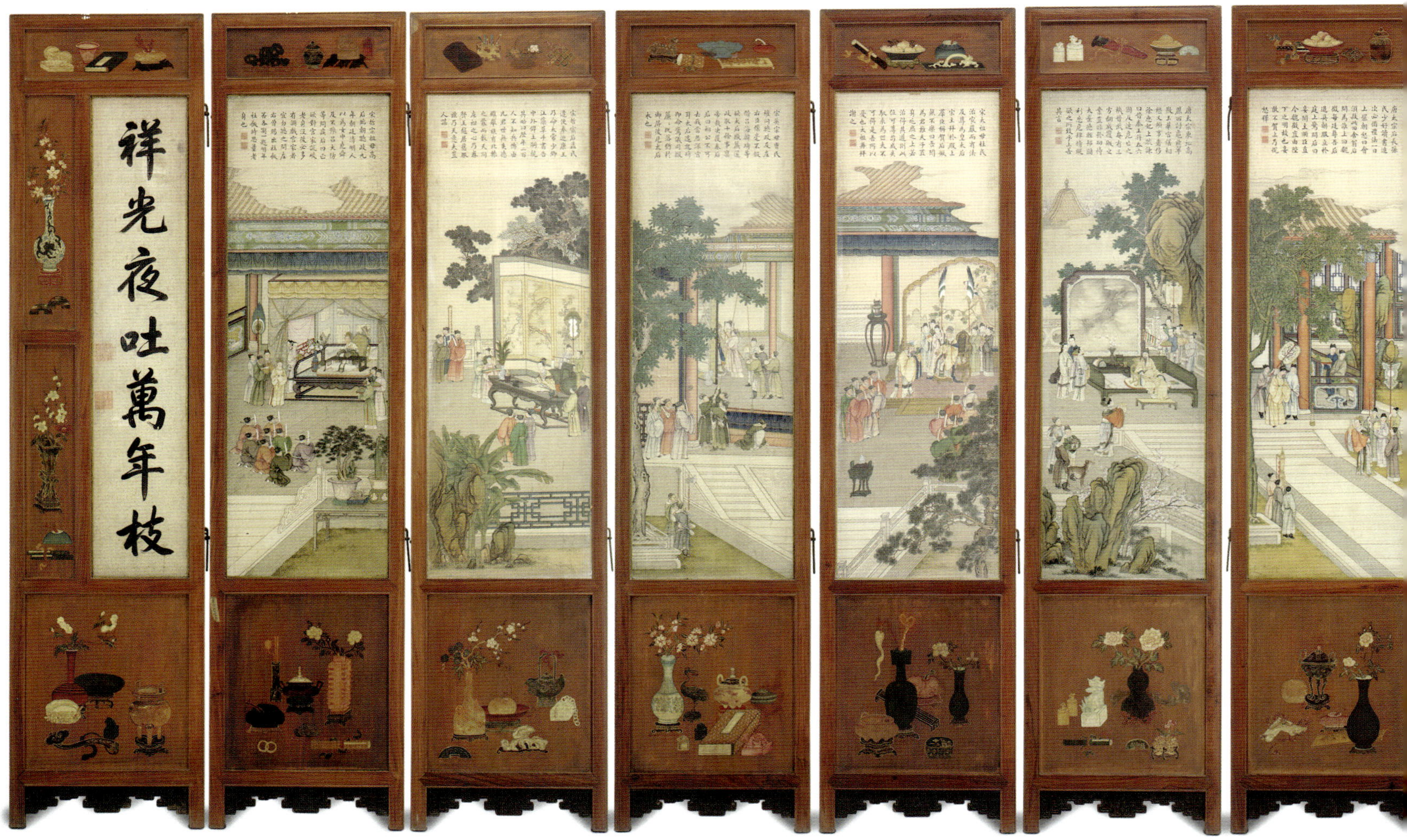

PLATE 58

清乾隆　花梨木邊歷朝賢后圖十二扇炕屏

Twelve-panel screen with stories of virtuous empresses and empresses dowager in successive dynasties

Court painters at the Imperial Painting Academy (Huayuan chu), Beijing

Qianlong period, 1737

Panels: ink and color on silk; frame: *huali* wood and *zitan* wood with pigments and gold

Cat. 118

This screen features images of empresses and empresses dowager throughout Chinese history whose virtuous conduct Qing imperial women were called on to emulate. Empress Jiang of the Western Zhou dynasty (1050–771 BCE) is shown removing her hairpin and earrings and asking to be punished for failing to keep her husband, Emperor Xuan (r. 827–782 BCE), from indulging his sensual desires and neglecting state affairs (detail A). These actions awakened the emperor to his misdeeds, and he thereafter became a diligent and successful ruler. Empress Deng (81–121 CE) of the Eastern Han dynasty (25–250 CE) was known for an erudition unusual in women of her time (detail B). She could read at age six and knew such Chinese classics as the *Book of Poetry* and the *Analects* at twelve. She was filial, respectful, and proper as well as a brilliant stateswoman and intellectual, and she became a regent.[1] Flanking the ten paintings are two panels with lines from a poem referring to the phoenix, the mythical bird often associated with high-ranking imperial women.

The screen was intended to be placed on a heated platform in the residence of Empress Dowager Chongqing, the Palace of Longevity and Health (Shoukang gong), completed in 1736 (see Lin Shu's essay, pp. 78–87). Each painting of an imperial woman is accompanied by a poem inscribed by her son, the Qianlong emperor, a personal touch emphasizing his devotion to his mother. Based on a handscroll attributed

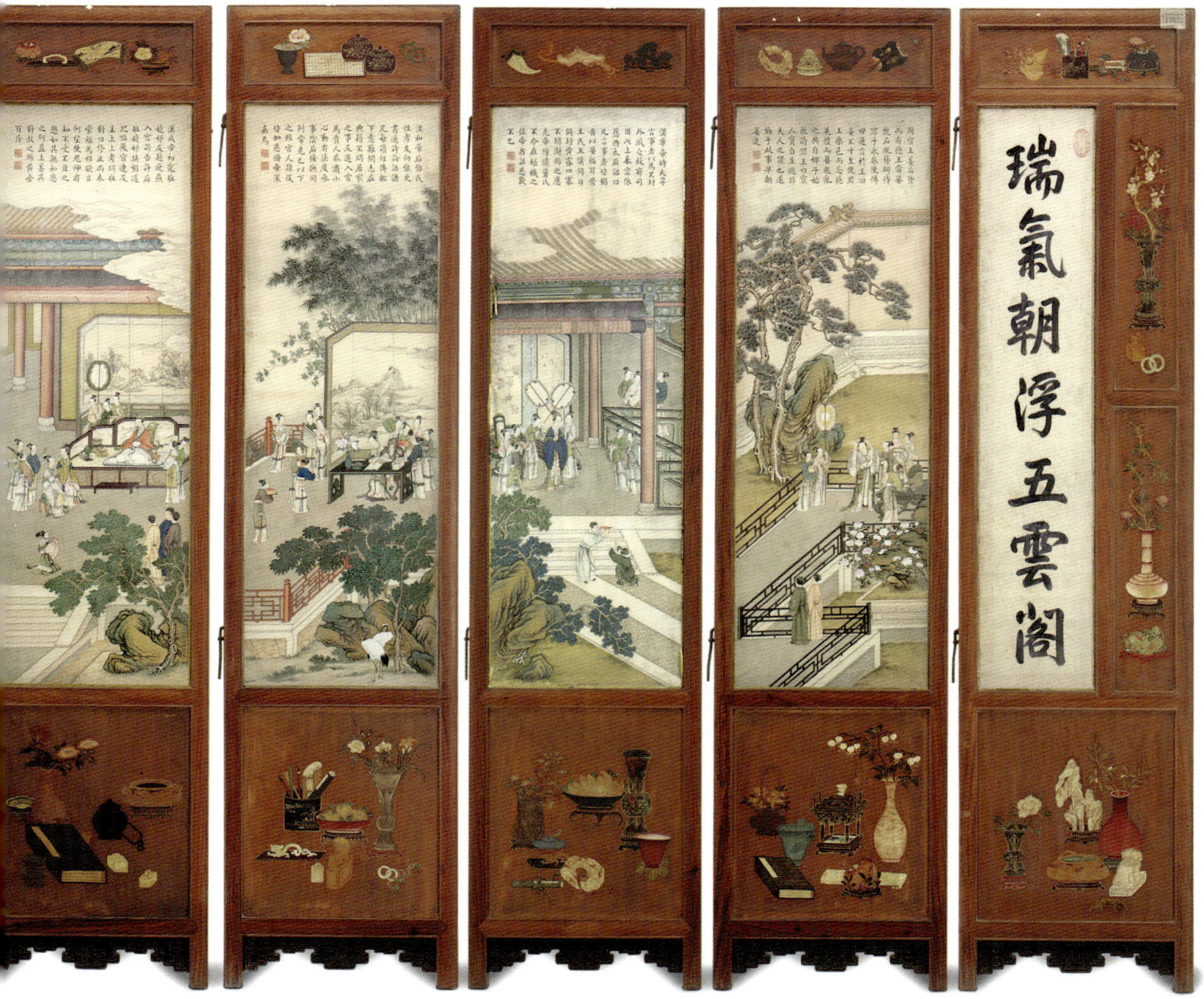

to the renowned painter Wang Zhenpeng (active 1280–1329) in Chongqing's collection, the paintings were executed by court artists from the Imperial Painting Academy (Huayuan chu).[2] (ZYY; trans. DYW)

1 McMahon 2013, 103–05.
2 ZGDYLSDAG 2005, 7:775–76.

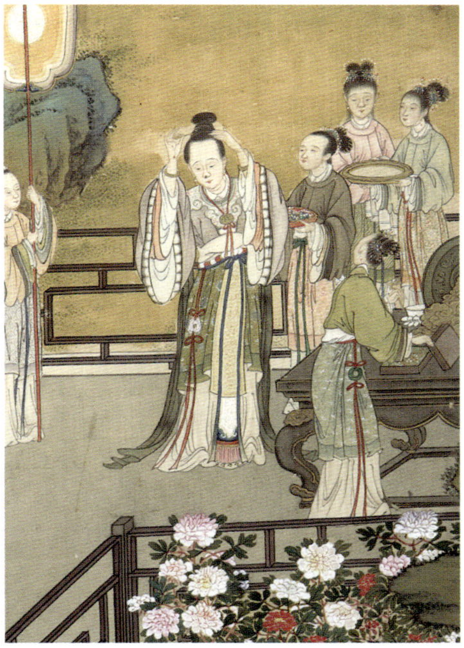

DETAIL A, EMPRESS JIANG REMOVING HER HAIRPIN AND JEWELRY

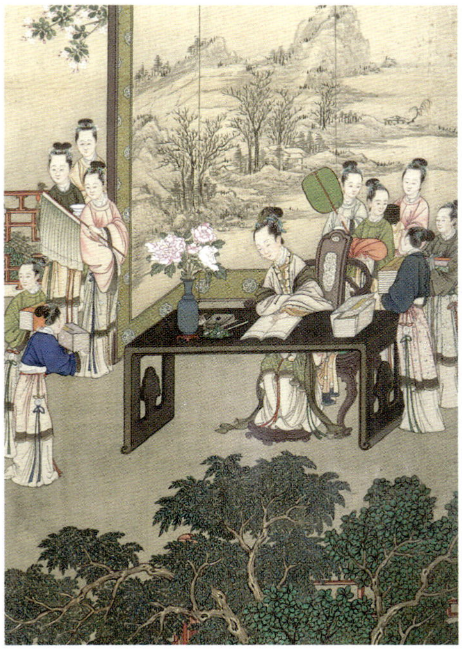

DETAIL B, EMPRESS DENG ENGAGED IN SCHOLARLY ACTIVITIES

CATALOGUE OF THE EXHIBITION

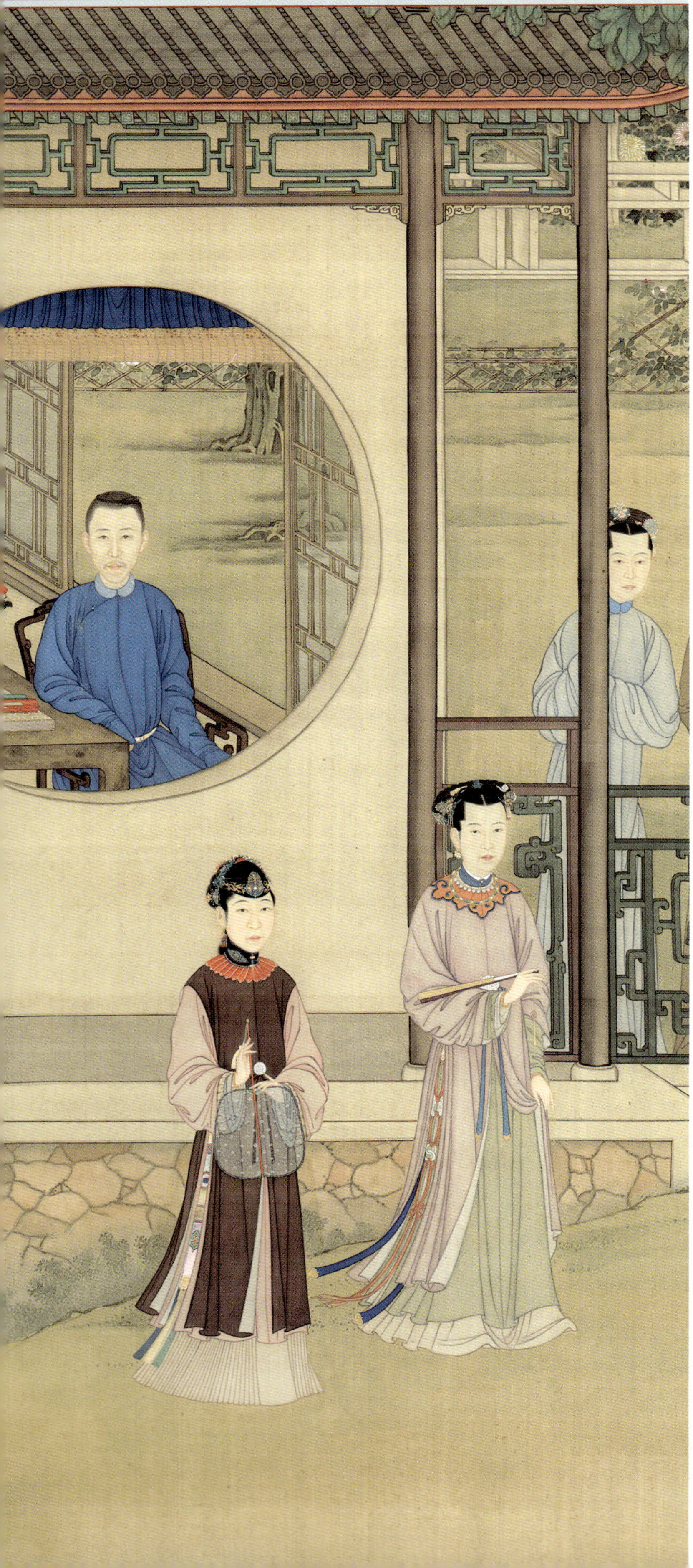

All works were made in China during the Qing dynasty (1644–1912) and are lent by the Palace Museum, Beijing, unless otherwise noted.

Objects are organized by media, format, and date.

Workshop names and locations are provided if known; omission of this information does not imply that the object is not the product of a workshop.

Dimensions are given height before width before depth, with diameter (diam.) and circumference (circum.) noted as necessary. In paintings, calligraphies, and photographic prints, dimensions are provided for the image proper (without the mounting) unless otherwise noted.

Venues at which objects appear are given as PEM and F|S.

PAINTING AND CALLIGRAPHY: HANGING SCROLLS

1 **Yinzhen and Consorts**
Court painters, Beijing
Kangxi period, early 18th century
Hanging scroll, ink and color on silk
61 13/16 × 27 15/16 in. (157 × 71 cm)
Palace Museum, Gu6440
F|S

2 **Drinking Tea *from* Yinzhen's Twelve Ladies**
Court painters, Beijing, possibly including Zhang Zhen (active late 17th–early 18th century) or his son Zhang Weibang (about 1725–about 1775)
Kangxi period, 1709–23
Hanging scroll, ink and color on silk
72 7/16 × 38 9/16 in. (184 × 98 cm)
Palace Museum, Gu6458-7/12
PEM

3 **Looking at Plum Blossoms *from* Yinzhen's Twelve Ladies**
Court painters, Beijing, possibly including Zhang Zhen (active late 17th–early 18th century) or his son Zhang Weibang (about 1725–about 1775)
Kangxi period, 1709–23
Hanging scroll, ink and color on silk
72 7/16 × 38 9/16 in. (184 × 98 cm)
Palace Museum, Gu6458-8/12
PEM

4 **Listening to Magpies *from* Yinzhen's Twelve Ladies**
Court painters, Beijing, possibly including Zhang Zhen (active late 17th–early 18th century) or his son Zhang Weibang (about 1725–about 1775)
Kangxi period, 1709–23
Hanging scroll, ink and color on silk
72 7/16 × 38 9/16 in. (184 × 98 cm)
Palace Museum, Gu6458-3/12
F|S

5 **Flitting Butterflies *from* Yinzhen's Twelve Ladies**
Court painters, Beijing, possibly including Zhang Zhen (active late 17th–early 18th century) or his son Zhang Weibang (about 1725–about 1775)
Kangxi period, 1709–23
Hanging scroll, ink and color on silk
72 7/16 × 38 9/16 in. (184 × 98 cm)
Palace Museum, Gu6458-10/12
F|S

6 **Consort of the Qianlong emperor with a hairpin**
Probably Giuseppe Castiglione (Lang Shining; Italy, 1688–1766) and Jin Tingbiao (d. 1767)
Qianlong period, probably 1750s or 1760s
Hanging scroll, ink and color on silk
$39\frac{3}{4} \times 36\frac{1}{4}$ in. (101×97.2 cm)
Palace Museum, Gu6524-2/2
PEM

7 **Lady with a Hairpin**
Jin Tingbiao (d. 1767)
Qianlong period, mid-18th century
Hanging scroll, ink and color on silk
$87\frac{3}{8} \times 51\frac{3}{8}$ in. (222×130.5 cm)
Palace Museum, Gu5272
F|S

8 **Empress Xiaozhuang**
Probably Giuseppe Castiglione (Lang Shining; Italy, 1688–1766) and other court painters, Beijing
Qianlong period, about 1750
Hanging scroll, ink and color on silk
$103\frac{1}{8} \times 71\frac{1}{2}$ in. (262×181.6 cm)
Palace Museum, Gu6379
Plate 40
F|S

9 **Empress Dowager Chongqing at the Age of Sixty**
Probably Giuseppe Castiglione (Lang Shining; Italy, 1688–1766) and other court painters, Beijing
Qianlong period, about 1751
Hanging scroll, ink and color on silk
$91\frac{3}{4} \times 55\frac{11}{16}$ in. (233×141.5 cm)
Palace Museum, Gu6454
PEM

10 **Empress Dowager Chongqing at the Age of Seventy**
Probably Giuseppe Castiglione (Lang Shining; Italy, 1688–1766) and other court painters, Beijing
Qianlong period, about 1761
Hanging scroll, ink and color on silk
$90\frac{3}{4} \times 55\frac{5}{8}$ in. (230.5×141.3 cm)
Palace Museum, Gu6452
PEM

11 **Empress Dowager Chongqing at the Age of Eighty**
Ignatius Sichelbarth (Ai Qimeng; Bohemia, 1708–1780), Yi Lantai (active about 1748–86), and Wang Ruxue (active 18th century)
Qianlong period, 1771
Hanging scroll, ink and color on silk
$89\frac{13}{16} \times 55\frac{5}{16}$ in. (228.1×140.5 cm)
Palace Museum, Gu6453
F|S

12 **Empress Xiaoxian**
Ignatius Sichelbarth (Ai Qimeng; Bohemia, 1708–1780), Yi Lantai (active about 1748–86), and possibly Wang Ruxue (active 18th century)
Qianlong period, 1777, with repainting possibly in 19th century
Hanging scroll, ink and color on silk
$99\frac{1}{8} \times 45\frac{3}{8}$ in. (251.8×115.2 cm)
Peabody Essex Museum, gift of Mrs. Elizabeth Sturgis Hinds, 1956, E33619
PEM, F|S

13 **Empress Xiaomu**
Court painters, Beijing
Daoguang period, 1850
Hanging scroll, ink and color on silk
$91\frac{5}{8} \times 44\frac{1}{4}$ in. (232.7×112.4 cm)
Peabody Essex Museum, gift of Mrs. Elizabeth Sturgis Hinds, 1956, E33618
PEM

14 **The Daoguang emperor and the Imperial Noble Consort Quan with imperial family members in an autumn garden with joy**
He Shikui (active first half of 19th century)
Daoguang period, 1833–34
Hanging scroll, ink and color on paper
$71\frac{1}{4} \times 79\frac{3}{4}$ in. (181×202.5 cm)
Palace Museum, Gu6564
PEM

15 **Empress Dowager Ci'an in a garden with rocks, bamboo, and peonies**
Court painters, Beijing
Tongzhi period, about 1872–73
Hanging scroll, ink and color on paper
$51\frac{3}{8} \times 26\frac{9}{16}$ in. (130.5×67.5 cm)
Palace Museum, Gu8764
PEM

16 **Empress Dowager Ci'an**
Court painters, Beijing; calligraphy by the Tongzhi emperor (1856–1875)
Tongzhi period, about 1872–73
Hanging scroll, ink and color on paper
$66\frac{3}{4} \times 35\frac{7}{16}$ in. (169.5×90.3 cm)
Palace Museum, Gu6596
Plate 51
F|S

17 **Empress Dowager Cixi in a garden with rocks and bamboo**
Court painters, Beijing
Tongzhi or Guangxu period, probably 1870s
Hanging scroll, ink and color on paper
$51\frac{3}{16} \times 26\frac{9}{16}$ in. (130×67.5 cm)
Palace Museum, Gu8766
PEM

18 **Empress Dowager Cixi playing Chinese chess (*weiqi*)**
Court painters, Beijing
Tongzhi or Guangxu period, 1862–1908
Hanging scroll, ink and color on silk
$91 \times 56\frac{1}{8}$ in. (231.1×142.6 cm)
Palace Museum, Gu6594
F|S

19 **Empress Xiaoqin**
Court painters, Beijing
Guangxu period, about 1908
Hanging scroll, ink and color on silk
$99\frac{5}{8} \times 43\frac{1}{2}$ in. (253×110.5 cm)
Palace Museum, Gu6599
F|S

20 The character for longevity with Queen Mother of the West and immortals in birthday celebration
Zhang Kai (active 1867–95), Liang Derun (active second half of 19th century), Zhang Weiming (active second half of 19th century)
Guangxu period, 1883
Hanging scroll, ink and color on silk
83 × 59¾ in. (210.8 × 151.8 cm)
Palace Museum, Gu257526
PEM

21 Phoenix perching in a paulownia tree
Painting and signature by Empress Dowager Cixi (1835–1908); calligraphy by Quan Zhong (active 19th–early 20th century) and Xu Fu (1836–1908)
Guangxu period, 1888
Hanging scroll, ink on paper
97⅞ × 45⅝ in. (248.6 × 116 cm)
Palace Museum, Gu248300
Plate 54
F|S

22 Chrysanthemums
Painting and signature by Empress Dowager Cixi (1835–1908); calligraphy by Lu Runxiang (1841–1915)
Guangxu period, 1905
Hanging scroll, ink and color on silk
51 1/16 × 20 9/16 in. (129.7 × 52.3 cm)
Museum of Fine Arts, Boston, gift of Sarah Buchan Jewell, 1991, 1991.100
PEM

23 Peaches of Immortality
Empress Dowager Cixi (1835–1908)
Guangxu period, 1875–1908
Hanging scroll, ink and colors on silk
50 3/16 × 24 15/16 in. (127.4 × 63.4 cm)
Purchase—Smithsonian Collections Acquisition Program and partial gift of Richard G. Pritzlaff, Arthur M. Sackler Gallery, S1991.52
F|S

24 Character for longevity
Empress Dowager Cixi (1835–1908)
Guangxu period, 1902
Ink on paper with gold
71 × 36¼ in. (179.5 × 92 cm)
Museum of Fine Arts, Boston, gift of Sarah Buchan Jewell, 1991, 1991.105
PEM

PAINTING AND CALLIGRAPHY: HANDSCROLLS

25 Elegy for the Deceased Empress
The Qianlong emperor (1711–1799)
Qianlong period, 1748
Handscroll, ink on paper
11¼ × 102 in. (28.6 × 259.1 cm)
Palace Museum, Gu238723
PEM

26 Expressing My Grief
The Qianlong emperor (1711–1799)
Qianlong period, 1748
Handscroll, ink on paper
11¼ × 52 13/16 in. (28.5 × 134.2 cm)
Palace Museum, Gu247908
Plate 2
F|S

27 The Admonitions of the Instructress to Court Ladies
The Qianlong emperor (1711–1799), after a painting attributed to Li Gonglin (1049–1106)
Qianlong period, 1747
Handscroll, ink on paper
11⅛ × 237⅜ in. (28.2 × 603 cm)
Palace Museum, Gu247926
PEM

28 Splendid Palaces Filled with Joy, *scroll four of* Celebrating Empress Dowager Chongqing's Birthday
Ding Guanpeng (active 1726–1770), Zhang Gao (active 18th century), Zhang Tingyan (1735–1794), Wu Weiqian (active 18th century), Chen Zhaolong (active 18th century), and other court painters, Beijing and Suzhou
Qianlong period, 1751–61
Handscroll, ink and color on silk
25 9/16 × 1,093 11/16 in. (65 × 2,778 cm)
Palace Museum, Gu8618-4/4
Plate 8
F|S

29 The Qianlong Emperor and an Imperial Woman Hunting a Deer
Court painters, probably at the Wish-Fulfilling Studio (Ruyi guan), Beijing; frontispiece by the Qianlong emperor (1711–1799)
Qianlong period, probably 1760–79
Handscroll, ink and color on paper
14 13/16 × 77 in. (37.6 × 195.5 cm)
Palace Museum, Gu9205
Plate 15
F|S

30 Auspicious Scene of the Moon Festival
Court painters, Beijing
18th–19th century
Handscroll, ink and color on silk
11⅞ × 126 in. (30.2 × 320 cm)
Palace Museum, Gu6298
PEM

PAINTING AND CALLIGRAPHY: ALBUMS

31 **Virtuous Empresses and Empresses Dowager in Successive Dynasties**
Jiao Bingzhen (about 1660–1726)
Kangxi or Yongzheng period, early 18th century
Album leaves, ink and color on silk
12 × 14⅝ in. (30.5 × 37.2 cm) each
Palace Museum, Gu5632
PEM (eight leaves), F|S (four leaves)

32 **Paintings Illustrating the Poems of Ten Palaces**
Painting by Leng Mei (1670–1742);
calligraphy by Liang Shizheng (1697–1763)
Yongzheng period, 1735 or earlier
Album leaves, ink and color on silk
13 1/16 × 13 1/16 in. (33.2 × 33.2 cm) each
Palace Museum, Gu5186
PEM (eight leaves), F|S (two leaves)

33 **The Pursuit of Pleasures in the Course of the Seasons**
Painting by Chen Mei (1697–1745); calligraphy by
Liang Shizheng (1697–1763)
Painting, Yongzheng period, 1723–35; calligraphy,
Qianlong period, 1738
Album leaves, ink and color on silk
14 9/16 × 12½ in. (37 × 31.8 cm) each
Palace Museum, Gu9224
PEM (four leaves), F|S (four leaves)

34 **Scenes of Bliss and Celebration**
Jin Tingbiao (d. 1767) and other court painters, Beijing
Qianlong period, 1761–71
Album leaves, ink and color on silk
38 9/16 × 63¾ in. (98 × 162 cm) each
Palace Museum, Gu9198-3/8, 5/8, 7/8, and 8/8
PEM

35 **Illustrated Precedents for the Ritual Paraphernalia of the Qing Imperial Court**
Leng Jian (active 18th century), Huang Men (active 18th century),
and other court painters, Beijing
Qianlong period, probably 1772
Album leaves, ink and color on silk
16⅛ × 31½ (41 × 80 cm) each
Palace Museum, Gu6116-70/92; leaves 1 and 7
Plate 13
F|S

36 **The Grand Imperial Wedding of the Guangxu Emperor**
Qing Kuan (1848–1927) and other court painters, Beijing
Guangxu period, about 1889
Album leaves, ink and color on silk
24 × 43 11/16 in. (61 × 111 cm) each
Palace Museum, Gu5887
PEM (ten leaves), F|S (five leaves)

OTHER PAINTINGS

37 **Empress Xiaoxian**
Probably Giuseppe Castiglione (Lang Shining; Italy, 1688–1766)
and other court painters, Beijing
Qianlong period, about 1736
Panel, oil on paper; frame: wood covered with silk brocade
20⅞ × 16 in. (53 × 40.5 cm)
Palace Museum, Gu6520
Plate 1
F|S

38 **Dragon Boat Festival in the Fifth Lunar Month *from* The Yongzheng Emperor Enjoying Himself throughout the Twelve Months**
Court painters, Beijing
Yongzheng period, 1723–35
Panel, ink and color on silk
73 13/16 × 40 3/16 in. (187.5 × 102 cm)
Palace Museum, Gu6441-5/12
F|S

39 **Double-Seventh Festival in the Seventh Lunar Month *from* The Yongzheng Emperor Enjoying Himself throughout the Twelve Months**
Court painters, Beijing
Yongzheng period, 1723–35
Panel, ink and color on silk
73 13/16 × 40 3/16 in. (187.5 × 102 cm)
Palace Museum, Gu6441-7/12
PEM

40 **Enjoying the Moon in the Eighth Lunar Month *from* The Yongzheng Emperor Enjoying Himself throughout the Twelve Months**
Court painters, Beijing
Yongzheng period, 1723–35
Panel, ink and color on silk
73 13/16 × 40 3/16 in. (187.5 × 102 cm)
Palace Museum, Gu6441-8/12
PEM

41 **Consort of the Qianlong emperor and the future Jiaqing emperor in his boyhood**
Probably Giuseppe Castiglione (Lang Shining; Italy, 1688–1766)
and other court painters, Beijing
Qianlong period, probably 1760s
Painting originally mounted on a wall (*tieluo*), ink and color on silk
128½ × 73¼ in. (326.5 × 186 cm)
Palace Museum, Gu6539
Plate 3
F|S

42 **Empress Dowager Cixi**
Katharine A. Carl (United States, 1865–1938)
Guangxu period, 1903
Painting: oil on canvas; frame: camphor wood
117 × 68¼ in (297.2 × 173.4 cm)
Transfer from the Smithsonian American Art Museum,
Arthur M. Sackler Gallery, S2011.16.1-2a-ap
Plate 46
PEM, F|S

43 Panorama of the Garden of Nurturing Harmony
Guangxu or Republican period, probably early 20th century
Painting originally mounted on a wall (*tieluo*), ink and color on paper
$48\frac{1}{4} \times 99\frac{3}{8}$ in. (122.6 × 252.4 cm)
Peabody Essex Museum, gift of Dorothea Reynolds Hanson in memory of Dorothea Jordan Reynolds, 2015, 2015.28.1
PEM

COSTUMES AND TEXTILES

44 Court robe with dragons and clouds
Imperial Silk Manufactory, Suzhou (embroidery), and Imperial Workshop, Beijing (tailoring)
Yongzheng period, 1723–35
Embroidery, polychrome and metallic-wrapped silk threads on silk gauze and coral
$50\frac{13}{16} \times 69\frac{5}{16}$ in. (129 × 176 cm)
Palace Museum, Gu41902
PEM

45 Court robe with dragons and clouds
Imperial Silk Manufactory, Suzhou (embroidery), and Imperial Workshop, Beijing (tailoring)
Yongzheng period, 1723–35, or Qianlong period, 1736–95
Embroidery, polychrome and metallic-wrapped silk threads on silk satin and coral
$57\frac{1}{2} \times 67$ in. (146 × 170.2 cm)
Palace Museum, Gu43478
PEM, F|S

46 Court robe for the Tongzhi emperor with dragons and clouds
Probably Imperial Silk Manufactory, Suzhou (silk and embroidery), and Imperial Workshop, Beijing (tailoring)
Tongzhi period, probably 1860s
Embroidery, polychrome and metallic-wrapped silk threads on silk tabby with sable
$35\frac{7}{16} \times 48\frac{13}{16}$ in. (90 × 124 cm)
Palace Museum, Gu43554
PEM

47 Court vest with dragons and clouds
Imperial Silk Manufactory, Suzhou (embroidery), and Imperial Workshop, Beijing (tailoring)
Yongzheng period, 1723–35
Embroidery, polychrome and metallic-wrapped silk threads on silk gauze
$56\frac{11}{16} \times 46\frac{7}{16}$ in. (144 × 118 cm)
Palace Museum, Gu43482
PEM

48 Court vest with dragons and clouds
Imperial Silk Manufactory, Suzhou (embroidery), and Imperial Workshop, Beijing (tailoring)
Qianlong period, 1736–95
Embroidery, polychrome and metallic-wrapped silk threads on silk satin with coral buttons
$56\frac{1}{4} \times 49\frac{1}{2}$ in. (142.9 × 125.7 cm)
Palace Museum, Gu43483
PEM, F|S

49 Vest with cranes and clouds
Qianlong period, 1736–95
Embroidery, polychrome, metallic-wrapped, and peacock-filament-wrapped silk threads on silk satin
$52 \times 46\frac{7}{8}$ in. (132 × 119 cm)
Palace Museum, Gu43472
F|S

50 Festive robe with eight dragon roundels
Imperial Silk Manufactory, probably Nanjing (weaving)
Shunzhi period, 1644–61
Patterned silk gauze with metallic and polychrome silk threads and coral
$53\frac{15}{16} \times 71\frac{5}{8}$ in. (137 × 182 cm)
Palace Museum, Gu41737
Plate 20
PEM

51 Festive robe with dragons and clouds
Probably workshop, Nanjing (weaving)
Kangxi period, 1662–1722
Brocaded silk satin with metallic and polychrome silk threads
$54\frac{5}{16} \times 75\frac{9}{16}$ in. (138 × 192 cm)
Palace Museum, Gu42568
F|S

52 Festive robe for a princess with dragons, clouds, and the character for longevity
Probably workshop, Jiangsu or Zhejiang province (weaving)
Kangxi period, 1662–1722
Silk satin, silk and metallic threads
$24\frac{13}{16} \times 35\frac{7}{16}$ in. (63 × 90 cm)
Palace Museum, Gu41684
PEM

53 Festive robe with eight roundels of baskets with lotuses
Probably Imperial Silk Manufactory, Suzhou (appliqué and embroidery), and Imperial Workshop, Beijing (tailoring)
Yongzheng period, 1723–35
Appliqué and embroidery, silk satin and polychrome silk threads on silk gauze
$56\frac{11}{16} \times 70\frac{1}{16}$ in. (144 × 178 cm)
Palace Museum, Gu42934
PEM

54 Festive robe with bats, clouds, and the character for longevity
Probably Imperial Silk Manufactory, Nanjing (weaving), and Imperial Workshop, Beijing (tailoring)
Qianlong period, 1785 or earlier
Patterned silk satin and embroidery, polychrome silk and metallic-wrapped threads on silk fabric
$56\frac{5}{16} \times 70\frac{1}{16}$ in. (143 × 178 cm)
Palace Museum, Gu42136
Plate 11
PEM

55 Festive robe with flowers in vases and butterflies
Imperial Silk Manufactory, Suzhou (weaving and embroidery), and Imperial Workshop, Beijing (tailoring)
Qianlong period, 1736–95
Embroidery, polychrome silk threads on silk satin
$59\frac{7}{16} \times 68\frac{1}{2}$ in. (151 × 174 cm)
Palace Museum, Gu42151
Plate 21
F|S

56 Festive robe with eight roundels of dragons and clouds
Qianlong period, 1736–95
Embroidery, polychrome and metallic-wrapped silk threads on silk gauze
$58\frac{1}{16} \times 68\frac{1}{2}$ in. (147.5 × 174 cm)
Palace Museum, Gu42158
F|S

57 Festive robe with bats, lotuses, and the character for longevity
Probably Imperial Silk Manufactory, Suzhou (embroidery), and Imperial Workshop, Beijing (tailoring)
Jiaqing period, 1796–1820
Embroidery, polychrome and metallic-wrapped silk threads on silk tabby
$56 \times 71\frac{1}{5}$ in. (142 × 181 cm)
Palace Museum, Gu43302
PEM

58 Festive robe with dragons, clouds, and twelve imperial symbols
Probably Imperial Silk Manufactory, Suzhou
19th century
Silk tapestry (*kesi*), polychrome and metallic wrapped threads
56 × 74 in. (142.2 × 188 cm)
Private property of Shirley Z. Johnson on long-term loan to the Arthur M. Sackler Gallery, LTS2015.5.43
F|S

59 Festive robe with eight dragon-phoenix roundels and twelve imperial symbols
Imperial Silk Manufactory, Suzhou (embroidery), and Imperial Workshop, Beijing (tailoring)
Guangxu period, about 1888–89
Embroidery, polychrome and metallic-wrapped silk threads on silk tabby
$56\frac{11}{16} \times 71\frac{11}{16}$ in. (144 × 182 cm)
Palace Museum, Gu44219
PEM, F|S

60 Surcoat with eight dragon roundels
Imperial Silk Manufactory, probably Nanjing (weaving), and Imperial Workshop, Beijing (tailoring)
Yongzheng period, 1723–35
Patterned silk gauze with polychrome and metallic silk threads
$55\frac{1}{8} \times 69\frac{5}{16}$ in. (140 × 176 cm)
Palace Museum, Gu42344
PEM

61 Imperial noblewoman's summer surcoat
Probably Imperial Silk Manufactory, Suzhou
Probably late Daoguang or Tongzhi period, 1821–74
Embroidery, silk and metallic-wrapped threads on silk gauze
$53\frac{1}{4} \times 57\frac{3}{8}$ in. (135.3 × 145.7 cm)
Purchase—funds provided by an anonymous donor, Arthur M. Sackler Gallery, S1992.7
F|S

62 Informal robe with peonies and the character for longevity
Guangxu period, 1875–1908
Embroidery, polychrome and metallic-wrapped silk threads on silk tabby
$53\frac{3}{4} \times 52$ in. (136.5 × 132 cm)
Palace Museum, Gu45925
F|S

63 Informal robe with butterflies and the character for double happiness
Probably Imperial Silk Manufactory, Suzhou (embroidery), and Imperial Workshop, Beijing (tailoring)
Guangxu period, about 1888–89
Embroidery, polychrome and metallic-wrapped silk threads on silk gauze
$52\frac{3}{16} \times 45\frac{11}{16}$ in. (132.5 × 116 cm)
Palace Museum, Gu44574
PEM

64 Woman's robe with phoenixes, peonies, and the character for longevity
Guangxu period, 1875–1908
Embroidery, polychrome silk and metallic-wrapped silk threads on silk satin
$51\frac{3}{16} \times 51\frac{3}{8}$ in. (130 × 130.5 cm)
University of Alberta Museums, Mactaggart Art Collection, gift of Sandy and Cécile Mactaggart, 2005, 2005.5.250
Plate 52
PEM

65 Informal robe with goldfish, wisteria, and aquatic plants
Probably Imperial Silk Manufactory, Suzhou
Guangxu period, 1875–1908
Silk tapestry (*kesi*), polychrome and metallic-wrapped silk threads
53 × 64 in. (134.6 × 162.6 cm)
Peabody Essex Museum, gift of Mrs. Delia G. Tyrwhitt, 1982, E72788
PEM

66 Informal robe with chrysanthemums
Probably Imperial Silk Manufactory, Suzhou (embroidery), and Imperial Workshop, Beijing (tailoring)
Guangxu period, 1875–1908
Embroidery, polychrome and metallic-wrapped silk threads on silk satin
$51\frac{3}{16} \times 53\frac{9}{16}$ in. (130 × 136 cm)
Palace Museum, Gu45719
PEM

67 Theatrical robe with flowers and butterflies
Imperial Silk Manufactory, Suzhou (embroidery)
Qianlong period, 1736–95
Silk tapestry (*kesi*), embroidery, and painting, polychrome silk and metallic-wrapped threads and pigments on silk satin
$49\frac{5}{8} \times 78\frac{1}{8}$ in. (126 × 198.5 cm)
Palace Museum, Gu214371
Plate 9
F|S

68 Theatrical robe with peaches, butterflies, bats, and clouds
Imperial Silk Manufactory, Suzhou (embroidery)
Qianlong period, 1736–95
Embroidery, polychrome and metallic-wrapped silk threads on silk satin
$54 \times 91\frac{1}{4}$ in. (137.5 × 231.8 cm)
The Minneapolis Institute of Art, The John R. Van Derlip Fund, 42.8.115
PEM

69 Theatrical jacket and skirt with dragons and clouds
Imperial Silk Manufactory, Suzhou (embroidery)
Qianlong period, 1736–95
Embroidery, polychrome and metallic-wrapped silk threads on silk satin with silk velvet and metal studs
Jacket: $29\frac{3}{4} \times 65$ in. (75.5×165 cm); skirt: 33 in. (84 cm) H.
The Minneapolis Institute of Art, The John R. Van Derlip Fund, 42.8.127A,B
PEM

ACCESSORIES

70 Court hat with phoenixes
Probably Imperial Workshop, Beijing
18th or 19th century
Sable, velvet, silk floss, pearls, tiger's-eye stone, lapis lazuli, glass, birch bark and metal with gilding, and kingfisher feather
$14\frac{1}{2} \times 10\frac{3}{5}$ in. (37×27 cm)
Palace Museum, Gu60084
PEM, F|S

71 Festive headdress with phoenixes and peonies
Probably Imperial Workshop, Beijing
Tongzhi or Guangxu period, probably 1872 or 1888–89
Silver with gilding, kingfisher feather, pearls, coral, jadeite, ruby, sapphire, tourmaline, turquoise, lapis lazuli, and glass; frame: metal wires with silk satin, velvet, and cardboard
$7\frac{3}{4} \times 11\frac{7}{8} \times 8\frac{1}{2}$ in. ($19.6 \times 30.2 \times 21.6$ cm)
Palace Museum, Gu59708
Plate 14
PEM

72 Festive headdress with phoenixes and peonies
Probably the second half of 19th century
Metal with gilding, kingfisher feather, jadeite, tourmaline, coral, pearls, and glass; frame: metal wires with silk floss and satin
$6 \times 11\frac{1}{2} \times 11$ in. ($15.2 \times 29.2 \times 27.9$ cm)
Rhode Island School of Design Museum, gift of Mrs. John D. Rockefeller, Jr., 1937, 37.125A–D
PEM, F|S

73 Ceremonial sash with grains, lantern, and bats
Probably Imperial Silk Manufactory, Suzhou
18th or 19th century
Embroidery, polychrome silk threads on silk tabby with metal, seed pearls, coral, agate, lapis lazuli, turquoise, jade (nephrite), and kingfisher feather
$40\frac{1}{2} \times 9$ in. (102.9×22.9 cm)
Palace Museum, Gu251061
PEM, F|S

74 Ceremonial sash with flower basket, bats, and Daoist symbols
Probably Imperial Silk Manufactory, Suzhou
18th or 19th century
Embroidery, polychrome silk threads on silk satin with gold, silver, rubies, jadeite, jade (nephrite), tourmaline, turquoise, coral, mother-of-pearl, pearls, and goldstone
$42\frac{1}{8} \times 5\frac{15}{16}$ in. (107.5×15 cm)
Palace Museum, Gu12162
PEM

75 Pair of boots with phoenixes, peonies, and lotuses
Workshop, probably Jiangsu or Zhejiang province
Kangxi period, 1662–1722
Embroidery, polychrome and metallic-wrapped silk threads on silk satin; soles: wood core covered with cotton, leather trim, felted paper
$16\frac{1}{2} \times 9\frac{1}{4} \times 5\frac{7}{8}$ in. ($41.91 \times 23.5 \times 14.94$ cm) each at calf
Palace Museum, Gu60211
Plate 16
PEM, F|S

76 Pair of boots with butterflies
Workshop, probably Jiangsu or Zhejiang province
Kangxi period, 1662–1722
Embroidery, polychrome and metallic-wrapped silk threads and seed pearls on silk satin; soles: wood core covered with cotton, leather trim
$18\frac{1}{2} \times 9\frac{7}{16} \times 3\frac{9}{16}$ in. ($47 \times 24 \times 9$ cm) each
Palace Museum, Gu60310
PEM

77 Pair of shoes with dragons and clouds
Workshop, probably Jiangsu or Zhejiang province
Kangxi period, 1662–1722
Embroidery, polychrome silk threads on woven plant fiber; soles: wood core covered with cotton, silk brocade
$3\frac{3}{4} \times 8\frac{11}{16} \times 3\frac{9}{16}$ in. ($9.5 \times 22 \times 9$ cm) each
Palace Museum, Gu60597
PEM

78 Pair of shoes with phoenixes
Workshop, probably Jiangsu or Zhejiang province
Kangxi period, 1662–1722
Embroidery, braided and metallic-wrapped threads on silk satin with seed pearls; soles: wood core covered with cotton, leather trim
$3\frac{9}{16} \times 10\frac{13}{16} \times 3\frac{9}{16}$ in. ($9 \times 27.5 \times 9$ cm) each
Palace Museum, Gu61703
Plate 18
PEM, F|S

79 Pair of platform shoes with lotuses and flower baskets
Guangxu period, 1875–1908
Embroidery, polychrome silk threads on silk satin with silk tassels; platforms: wood core covered with cotton, glass beads
$6\frac{7}{8} \times 8\frac{7}{16} \times 3\frac{15}{16}$ in. ($17.5 \times 21.5 \times 10$ cm) each
Palace Museum, Gu61391
PEM, F|S

80 Pair of platform shoes with tiger heads, the character for longevity, and bats
Guangxu period, 1875–1908
Appliqué, silk satin; platforms: wood core covered with cotton, glass beads
$6\frac{7}{8} \times 8\frac{1}{4} \times 3\frac{15}{16}$ in. ($17.5 \times 21 \times 10$ cm) each
Palace Museum, Gu61568
Plate 17
PEM

81 Pair of socks with phoenixes and clouds
Workshop, probably Jiangsu or Zhejiang province
Kangxi period, 1662–1722
Embroidery, polychrome and metallic-wrapped silk threads on silk tabby and silk damask
$18\frac{5}{16} \times 9\frac{7}{16}$ in. (46.5×24 cm) each
Palace Museum, Gu61788
PEM

82 Pair of socks with phoenixes and other birds
Workshop, probably Jiangsu or Zhejiang province
Kangxi period, 1662–1722
Embroidery, polychrome, metallic-wrapped, and peacock-filament-wrapped threads on silk satin with silk damask and silk lining
$19\frac{1}{16} \times 9\frac{5}{8}$ in. (48.5 × 24.5 cm) each
Palace Museum, Gu61795
Plate 19
PEM, F|S

83 Folding fan with day lilies and a poem
The Qianlong emperor (1711–1799)
Qianlong period, 1760
Ink on paper; frame: bamboo
$11\frac{7}{16} \times 18\frac{1}{2}$ in. (29 × 47 cm)
Palace Museum, Gu236814
PEM

84 Folding fan with day lilies, rocks, and a poem
The Qianlong emperor (1711–1799)
Qianlong period, 1762
Ink and color on paper; frame: bamboo
$11\frac{1}{4} \times 18\frac{1}{8}$ in. (28.5 × 46 cm)
Palace Museum, Gu236818
PEM

85 Fan with lotuses and a poem
The Qianlong emperor (1711–1799)
Qianlong period, 1762
Ink and color on silk; handle: *zitan* wood with jade (nephrite)
$15\frac{3}{8} \times 7\frac{11}{16}$ in. (39 × 19.5 cm)
Palace Museum, Gu236987
F|S

86 Lobed fan with chrysanthemums and butterflies
Probably Imperial Silk Manufactory, Suzhou
Jiaqing or Daoguang period, 1796–1850
Embroidery, polychrome silk threads on silk satin with ivory; handle: bamboo
$18\frac{7}{8} \times 12\frac{3}{16}$ in. (48 × 31 cm) overall with handle
Palace Museum, Gu135713
PEM

87 Leaf-shaped fan with phoenix, paulownia tree, and peonies
Probably Imperial Silk Manufactory, Suzhou
Jiaqing or Daoguang period, early 19th century
Silk tapestry (*kesi*), polychrome silk and metallic-wrapped threads, and pigments; handle: *zitan* wood, ivory, copper alloy with gilding, and silk tassels
$19\frac{1}{4} \times 13\frac{1}{4}$ in. (48.9 × 33.7 cm) overall with handle
Palace Museum, Beijing, Gu136091
Plate 35
F|S

88 Lobed fan with cranes, peaches, and rocks
Qianlong period, 1736–95
Appliqué, silk fabric on silk gauze with pigments; handle: wood and ivory
$19\frac{3}{16} \times 13\frac{1}{16}$ in. (48.8 × 33.2 cm) overall with handle
Palace Museum, Gu136152
Plate 36
PEM

89 Perfume bottle with watch
Artists in France
18th century
Glass, enamel, and copper alloy with gold
$4\frac{1}{4} \times 1\frac{3}{4} \times 1$ in. (10.8 × 4.5 × 2.5 cm)
Palace Museum, Gu184105
PEM, F|S

90 Aromatic case with incense burner, vase, and chime
18th or 19th century
Gold alloy with kingfisher and other feathers, coral, and silk cords
$9\frac{1}{16} \times 2\frac{9}{16}$ in. (32 × 6.5 cm) overall
Palace Museum, Gu11656
Plate 38
F|S

JEWELRY

91 Court necklace
Probably Imperial Workshop, Beijing
18th or 19th century
Coral, lapis lazuli, sapphire, pearls, tourmaline, metal with gilding, kingfisher feather, and silk cords
$18 \times 13\frac{1}{4} \times 49\frac{5}{8}$ in. (45.7 × 33.7 × 126 cm)
Palace Museum, Gu71693
PEM, F|S

92 Torque
Probably Imperial Workshop, Beijing
18th or 19th century
Gold alloy with lapis lazuli, rubies, sapphires, red glass, pearl, kingfisher feather, and silk cords
$17\frac{3}{4} \times 5\frac{15}{16}$ in. (45 × 15 cm)
Palace Museum, Gu12017
PEM, F|S

93 Bracelet with the character for double happiness
Imperial Workshop, probably Guangzhou or Beijing
Probably Guangxu period, about 1888–89
Coral, lapis lazuli, jadeite, pearls, and silk cords
$11\frac{13}{16} \times 13\frac{3}{4}$ in. circum. (30 × 35 cm circum.)
Palace Museum, Gu9878
PEM, F|S

94 One of a pair of bracelets with dragons and pearls
Probably 19th century
Gold with pearls
$3\frac{1}{8}$ in. (8 cm) exterior diam.; $2\frac{1}{4}$ in. (5.8 cm) interior diam.
Palace Museum, Gu11970-2/2
Plate 30
PEM, F|S

95 One of a pair of bracelets with the character for longevity
Probably 19th or early 20th century
Coral with pearls
$2\frac{3}{8}$ in. (6 cm) interior diam.
Palace Museum, Gu9810-1/2
Plate 32
PEM, F|S

96 Pair of bracelets with bats, peaches, and flowers
Probably 19th or early 20th century
Tortoiseshell with coral, kingfisher feather, pearls, ruby, jadeite, tourmaline, and silver with gilding
$2\frac{7}{16}$ in. (6.2 cm) interior diam.
Palace Museum, Gu10371
Plate 31
PEM, F|S

97 Rosary-bracelet with beads decorated with *luohan* and pendants
Probably 19th century
Walnut shell, coral, lapis lazuli, turquoise, seed pearls, copper alloy with gilding, and silk tassels
$11\frac{7}{16}$ in. (29 cm) overall height
Palace Museum, Gu71820
Plate 44
PEM, F|S

98 Rosary-bracelet with the character for longevity
Workshop, probably Guangzhou
Probably 19th century or early 20th century
Agarwood with gold-alloy inlay
$11 \times 10\frac{1}{16}$ in. circum. (28 × 25.5 cm circum.)
Palace Museum, Gu71814-4/10
PEM, F|S

99 Ring with peaches
19th or early 20th century
Jadeite
$\frac{5}{8}$ in. (1.6 cm) interior diam.
Palace Museum, Gu9699
PEM, F|S

100 Pair of earrings with endless-knot decoration
19th or early 20th century
Jade (nephrite)
$1\frac{3}{8}$ in. (3.5 cm) diam. each
Palace Museum, Gu71601-2/16
PEM, F|S

101 Hairpin with phoenix finial
Ming dynasty (1368–1644)
Jade (nephrite)
$8\frac{11}{16} \times 1\frac{1}{4} \times \frac{13}{16}$ in. (22 × 3.2 × 2 cm)
Palace Museum, Gu98897
Plate 28
PEM, F|S

102 Hair ornament with bats and the character for longevity
Probably Imperial Workshop, Beijing
Qianlong or Jiaqing period, 1805 or earlier
Kingfisher feather, pearls, imitation pearls, glass, and silver with gilding
$2\frac{13}{16} \times 5\frac{5}{16}$ in. (7.2 × 13.5 cm)
Palace Museum, Gu10178
PEM, F|S

103 Hair ornament with basket of lotuses
Daoguang period, 1831 or earlier
Kingfisher feather, pearl, imitation pearls, glass, tourmalines, and silver with gilding
$3\frac{15}{16} \times 3\frac{3}{16}$ in. (10 × 8.5 cm)
Palace Museum, Gu10226
PEM, F|S

104 Hairpin with crab and reed
Daoguang period, 1834 or earlier
Jade (nephrite), kingfisher feather, pearls, ruby, and silver with gilding
$7\frac{7}{8} \times 2\frac{3}{4}$ in. (20 × 7 cm)
Palace Museum, Gu10223
Plate 29
PEM, F|S

105 Hairpin with figure and vase
18th or 19th century
Pearls, sapphire, coral, turquoise, kingfisher feather, and silver with gilding
$5\frac{3}{8} \times 2\frac{1}{8}$ in. (13.7 × 5.4 cm)
Palace Museum, Gu10130
Plate 27
PEM, F|S

106 Hair ornament with pair of dragons
Probably 19th century
Pearls, coral, kingfisher feather, and silver with gilding
$2\frac{3}{8} \times 10\frac{5}{8}$ in. (6 × 27 cm)
Palace Museum, Gu10104
PEM, F|S

107 Hairpin with plum blossoms
Probably 19th century
Coral
$7\frac{7}{8} \times 1$ in. (20 × 2.5 cm)
Palace Museum, Gu71363-1/14
PEM, F|S

108 Hairpin with hand-shaped finial
19th or early 20th century
Jadeite, pearls, and gold alloy
$6\frac{11}{16} \times \frac{1}{8}$ in. (17 × 2.8 cm)
Palace Museum, Gu9640
PEM, F|S

109 Hairpin with adjoining rings
Deyu Workshop
19th or early 20th century
Gold alloy with pearl
$7\frac{11}{16} \times 1\frac{1}{8}$ in. (19.5 × 2.8 cm)
Palace Museum, Gu12039
PEM, F|S

110 Hair ornament with peonies
19th or early 20th century
Jade (nephrite) with tourmaline and jadeite
$1\frac{3}{16} \times 12\frac{13}{16} \times \frac{3}{8}$ in. (3.0 × 32.5 × 1 cm)
Palace Museum, Gu98969
PEM, F|S

111 **Hair ornament with dragons and the character for longevity**
Workshop, probably Guangzhou
19th or early 20th century
Agarwood with seed pearls and gold-alloy inlay
$1\frac{5}{16} \times 12\frac{15}{16} \times \frac{3}{8}$ in. (3.3 × 32.8 × 1 cm)
Palace Museum, Gu225542
Plate 33
PEM, F|S

112 **Fingernail guard with bat and the character for longevity**
19th century
Silver with gilding, pearl, pigment, and kingfisher feather
$3\frac{5}{8} \times \frac{9}{16}$ in. diam. (9.2 × 1.4 cm diam.)
Palace Museum, Gu225578
PEM, F|S

113 **A set of hairdressing tools in box**
Workshop, probably Guangzhou
19th or early 20th century
Ivory with lacquer and gold
Box: $13\frac{3}{8} \times 12\frac{5}{8} \times 1\frac{7}{16}$ in. (34 × 32.1 × 3.7 cm)
Palace Museum, Gu173473
PEM, F|S

FURNISHINGS AND FURNITURE

114 **Cushion cover with phoenixes, peonies, and bats**
Imperial Silk Manufactory, Suzhou
Yongzheng or Qianlong period, first half of 18th century
Silk tapestry (*kesi*), polychrome silk threads
$40 \times 41\frac{1}{2}$ in. (101.5 × 104.9 cm)
The Art Institute of Chicago, restricted gift of Russell Tyson, 1958, 1958.305
PEM

115 **Pendants with phoenixes and clouds**
Qianlong period, 1736–95
Patterned silk brocade, polychrome silk and metallic threads
1936.130a: $106\frac{3}{8} \times 7\frac{1}{2}$ in. (270.3 × 19.2 cm); 1936.130b: $106\frac{1}{4} \times 7\frac{1}{2}$ in. (269.8 × 19.2 cm); 1936.131a: $107 \times 8\frac{3}{8}$ in. (271.7 × 21.3 cm); 1936.131b: $106\frac{1}{4} \times 8\frac{1}{4}$ in. (269.8 × 20.8 cm)
The Art Institute of Chicago, gift of the Orientals, 1936, 1936.130a–b, 1936.131a–b
PEM

116 **Six-panel wall hanging with phoenixes and birds in landscape, Daoist immortals, and the character for longevity**
Imperial Silk Manufactory, Suzhou
Qianlong period, 1736–95
Embroidery and appliqué, polychrome and metallic-wrapped silk threads on silk satin, silk fabric, and pigments
144 × 196 in. (365.8 × 497.8 cm)
Peabody Essex Museum, gift of William F. Spinney, 1933, E21173.A–F
PEM

117 **Five-panel screen with phoenixes and birds in landscape**
Workshop, probably Guangzhou
Qianlong period, probably 1775 or earlier
Panels: cloisonné, copper alloy with polychrome enamels and gilding; frame: *zitan* wood and *nan* wood
$116\frac{15}{16} \times 151\frac{3}{16} \times 12\frac{3}{16}$ in. (297 × 384 × 31 cm)
Palace Museum, Gu210730
Plate 53
PEM, F|S

118 **Twelve-panel screen with stories of virtuous empresses and empresses dowager in successive dynasties**
Court painters at the Imperial Painting Academy (Huayuan chu), Beijing
Qianlong period, 1737
Panels: ink and color on silk; frame: *huali* wood and *zitan* wood with pigments and gold
$60\frac{1}{4} \times 15\frac{3}{8}$ in. (153 × 39 cm) each
Palace Museum, Gu210802
Plate 58
F|S

119 **One of a pair of "precious treasures" display cabinets**
Yongzheng or Qianlong period, 1723–95
Lacquer with gold on wood core, metal with gilding, and ivory
$63\frac{3}{8} \times 34\frac{1}{16} \times 13\frac{9}{16}$ in. (161 × 86.5 × 34.5 cm)
Palace Museum, Gu207580
Plate 24
PEM, F|S

120 **Banquet table with cranes in landscape**
Qianlong period, 1736–95
Lacquer and pigments on wood core
$13\frac{3}{8} \times 42\frac{1}{2} \times 30\frac{5}{16}$ in. (34 × 108 × 77 cm)
Palace Museum, Gu206709
PEM, F|S

121 **Basin stand with figures**
Guangxu period, 1875–1908
Hongmu wood
$72\frac{13}{16} \times 21\frac{7}{16} \times 23\frac{1}{4}$ in. (185 × 54.5 × 59 cm)
Palace Museum, Gu209048
PEM, F|S

122 **Dressing case with mirror stand and handheld mirror**
Qianlong period, mid- to late 18th century, with later repairs
Lacquer with gold and polychrome decoration on wood core, *zitan* wood, *suanzhi* wood, mother-of-pearl, bone, metal with gilding; wood-framed mirror with embroidered silk case
$16\frac{3}{4} \times 16\frac{1}{4} \times 16\frac{1}{4}$ in. (42.5 × 41.3 × 41.3 cm) with the case closed
Palace Museum, Gu180527
Plate 26
PEM, F|S

123 **Dressing case and mirror with flowers, bats, birds, and insects**
Late 18th or 19th century
Wood with sapphire, tourmaline, jadeite, pearls, lapis lazuli, ruby, glass, and copper alloy with gilding
$18\frac{7}{8} \times 11\frac{5}{8} \times 8\frac{1}{2}$ in. (48 × 29.5 × 21.6 cm)
Palace Museum, Gu9826
PEM, F|S

CERAMICS

124 Dish with incised dragons
Imperial Porcelain Factory, Jingdezhen
Kangxi period, 1662–1722
Porcelain with cobalt reign mark beneath colorless glaze (on base) and yellow enamel over colorless glaze
1⅝ × 9 13/16 in. diam. (4.2 × 25 cm diam.)
Palace Museum, Gu157564-1/4
PEM, F|S

125 Dish with dragons
Imperial Porcelain Factory, Jingdezhen
Kangxi period, 1662–1722
Porcelain with cobalt reign mark beneath colorless glaze (on base) and cobalt ground under colorless glaze with yellow enamels over colorless glaze
2½ × 12 11/16 in. diam. (6.4 × 32.2 cm diam.)
Palace Museum, Gu146984-1/6
PEM, F|S

126 Dish with dragons
Imperial Porcelain Factory, Jingdezhen
Kangxi period, 1662–1722
Porcelain with cobalt reign mark on base under colorless glaze and green and aubergine enamels on the biscuit (unglazed clay)
1⅞ × 9 13/16 in. diam. (4.7 × 24.9 cm diam.)
Palace Museum, Gu146973
PEM, F|S

127 Lobed vase with flowers and poems
Imperial Porcelain Factory, Jingdezhen
Qianlong period, 1736–95
Porcelain with cobalt under colorless glaze and polychrome enamels and gold over colorless glaze
25½ × 8¾ in. diam. (64.7 × 22.2 cm diam.)
Palace Museum, Gu154673
PEM, F|S

128 Vase with boys at play
Imperial Porcelain Workshop, Jingdezhen
Qianlong period, 1736–95
Porcelain in joined-colors (*doucai*) technique, cobalt under colorless glaze and polychrome enamels over the glaze, with gold
8 7/16 × 2 15/16 in. diam. at foot (21.5 × 7.4 cm diam. at foot)
Palace Museum, Gu154747
Plate 6
PEM, F|S

129 Flagon with dragon-shaped handle and phoenix-shaped spout
Imperial Porcelain Factory, Jingdezhen
Qianlong period, 1736–95
Porcelain with enamels over colorless glaze and gold
18½ × 5⅜ in. (47 × 13.7 cm)
Palace Museum, Gu152677
PEM, F|S

130 Scene of sericulture *from volume 4 of* Pictures of Tilling and Weaving with poems by the Qianlong emperor
Imperial Porcelain Factory, Jingdezhen; binding: Imperial Workshop, Beijing
Qianlong period, 1736–95
Porcelain with gray, black, and red enamels over colorless glaze; silk damask binding
4 5/16 × 3⅜ × 4¾ in. (11 × 8.5 × 12 cm) folded
Palace Museum, Gu154828
PEM, F|S

131 Flowerpot with peonies and birds
Imperial Porcelain Factory, Jingdezhen
Guangxu period, 1875 or 1876
Porcelain with enamels over colorless glaze
9 1/16 × 10⅝ × 8⅝ in. (23 × 27 × 21.9 cm)
Palace Museum, Gu157098
Plate 55
PEM, F|S

132 Sketch of peonies and birds for porcelain flowerpot decoration
Court painters, Beijing
Guangxu period, 1875 or 1876
Ink and color on paper
15¼ × 43⅞ in. (38.8 × 111.4 cm)
Palace Museum, Shu3414
Plate 56
F|S

133 Cup with magpies and plum blossoms
Imperial Porcelain Factory, Jingdezhen
Tongzhi period, 1868–72
Porcelain with polychrome enamels and gold over colorless glaze
1½ × 2½ in. diam. (3.8 × 6.3 cm)
Peabody Essex Museum, The Conger Collection, gift of Mrs. Sarah B. Jewell, 1991, E76765
PEM

134 Bowl with dragons, phoenixes, gourds, and the character for double happiness
Imperial Porcelain Factory, Jingdezhen
Guangxu period, probably 1888–89
Porcelain with polychrome enamels over colorless glaze
3 9/16 × 7 11/16 in. diam. (9 × 19.5 cm diam.)
Peabody Essex Museum, The Conger Collection, gift of Mrs. Sarah B. Jewell, 1991, E76744
PEM

LACQUERWARE

135 Peach-shaped box with peaches and bats
Workshop, Suzhou
Yongzheng period, 1723
Red lacquer with gold on wood core
6½ × 19 11/16 in. (16.5 × 50 cm)
Palace Museum, Gu113491-2/9
PEM

136 Lidded peach-shaped box with landscape and characters for boundless longevity
Probably Qianlong period, 1736–95
Gold with polychrome lacquer on wood core
7 3/8 × 12 1/2 × 13 3/8 in. (18.7 × 31.7 × 34 cm)
Palace Museum, Gu114026
PEM, F|S

137 Lidded box with plants, flowers, fruits, vessels, and stone chime
Probably workshop, Suzhou
Qianlong period, 1736–95
Brown and black lacquer on wood core with carved red lacquer, jade, turquoise, amber, ivory, coral, tourmaline, glass, and gold
5 1/8 × 15 9/16 × 15 9/16 in. (13 × 39.5 × 39.5 cm)
Palace Museum, Gu115381
PEM, F|S

138 Lidded foliated box with phoenixes, peonies, cranes, and clouds
Qianlong period, 1736–95
Polychrome lacquer with engraved and gold-filled decoration on wood core
5 15/16 × 12 13/16 in. diam. (15 × 32.5 cm diam.)
Palace Museum, Gu108244
PEM, F|S

139 Lidded oblong box with phoenixes, peonies, and bats
Qianlong period, 1736–95
Polychrome lacquer with engraved and gold-filled decoration on wood core
5 13/16 × 15 1/16 × 9 7/16 in. (14.7 × 38.3 × 24 cm)
Palace Museum, Gu112753
PEM

140 Tray with boys at play
Workshop, Suzhou
Qianlong period, 1742–43
Carved polychrome lacquer on wood core
2 3/16 × 23 1/8 × 12 7/8 in. (5.6 × 58.7 × 32.7 cm)
Palace Museum, Gu108653
Plate 5
PEM, F|S

141 Standing screen with boys at play
Probably workshop, Suzhou
Qianlong period, 1736–95
Carved red lacquer on wood core
19 1/2 × 23 7/16 × 8 3/8 in. (49.5 × 59.5 × 21.3 cm)
Palace Museum, Gu108955
PEM

142 Tray with hare in moon pounding the elixir of immortality
Probably workshop, Suzhou
Qianlong period, 1736–95
Carved red lacquer and painted polychrome lacquer with engraved and gold-filled decoration on wood core
6 1/2 × 8 1/2 × 1 7/16 in. (16.5 × 21.6 × 3.7 cm)
Palace Museum, Gu108987
PEM, F|S

143 Portable box of tableware with floral decoration
Qianlong period, 1736–95
Black and red lacquer with gold on wood core
15 3/16 × 17 13/16 × 11 15/16 in. (41.1 × 45.2 × 30.3 cm)
Palace Museum, Gu115596
PEM, F|S

144 Hand warmer with landscapes
Probably workshop, Suzhou
Qianlong period, 1736–95
Lacquer with gold and pigments on metal core
5 1/2 × 7 1/4 × 5 1/16 in. (14 × 18.4 × 12.9 cm)
Palace Museum, Gu113194
Plate 25
PEM, F|S

JADES AND OTHER STONES

145 Seal of Empress Xiaozhuang
Qianlong period, 1736
Jade (nephrite) with silk tassels
4 5/8 × 4 15/16 × 4 15/16 in. (11.7 × 12.6 × 12.6 cm)
Palace Museum, Gu166330
Plate 49
PEM, F|S

146 Seal of Empress Dowager Cixi with phoenix and dragon
Tongzhi period, 1862–74
Shoushan stone
4 3/4 × 4 1/16 × 4 1/16 in. (12 × 10.4 × 10.4 cm)
Palace Museum, Gu167338
Plate 48
PEM, F|S

147 Jade book with dragons and eulogy for Empress Xiaoxian
Jiaqing period, 1799
Jade (nephrite) with gold
11 5/16 × 5 × 1/4 in. (28.7 × 12.7 × 0.7 cm) each
Palace Museum, Gu167228
Plate 50
PEM, F|S

148 Chime with phoenixes and peonies
Probably workshop, Suzhou
Qianlong period, 1761
Jade (nephrite) with gold
12 5/8 × 23 5/8 × 1 7/16 in. (32 × 60 × 3.6 cm)
Palace Museum, Gu169306
PEM, F|S

149 A set of pendants with flowers representing the twelve months
Probably workshop, Suzhou
Qianlong period, 1736–95
Jade (nephrite)
Center disc: 4 7/16 in. diam. × 5/16 in. (11.3 × 0.8 cm); surrounding pendants: 2 1/2 × 2 1/16 × 1/4 in. (6.4 × 5.5 × 0.7 cm) each
Palace Museum, Gu92344
PEM

150 **Lidded box with bats and the character for longevity**
Probably workshop, Suzhou
Qianlong period, 1736–95
Jade (nephrite)
3 3/8 × 5 13/16 in. diam. (8.6 × 14.8 cm diam.)
Palace Museum, Gu98620
PEM

151 **Lobed bowl with flowers and poems**
Probably workshop, Suzhou
Qianlong period, 1761 or later
Jade (nephrite) with gold
2 5/8 × 5 15/16 in. diam. (6.7 × 15 cm diam.)
Palace Museum, Gu103657
PEM, F|S

152 **Bowl on lotus-shaped stand with Buddhist figures**
Probably workshop, Suzhou
Probably Qianlong period, 1736–95
Jade (nephrite)
3 3/16 × 4 5/8 in. diam. (8.1 × 11.8 cm diam.)
Palace Museum, Gu98259
PEM, F|S

153 **Altar garniture: incense burner, two candle stands, and two vases with animal masks and the character for longevity**
Qianlong period, 1736–95
Jade (nephrite); stands: cloisonné, copper alloy with polychrome enamels and gilding
Candle stands: 21 1/4 × 6 3/8 in. diam. (54 × 16.2 cm) each; burner: 9 15/16 × 7 11/16 in. diam. (25.3 × 19.5 cm diam.); vases: 11 5/16 × 6 5/16 in. diam. (28.8 × 16 cm diam.) each
Palace Museum, Gu93897
Plate 43
PEM, F|S

154 **Walking stick with bird-shaped finial**
Workshop, probably Suzhou
Qianlong period, 1770s or 1780s
Bamboo with jade (nephrite) and metal fitting
47 1/16 in. (119.5 cm) overall height
Palace Museum, Gu120537
Plate 10
PEM, F|S

155 **Wish-granting scepter (*ruyi*) with image of the God of Wealth and transcription of a poem by the Qianlong emperor**
Qianlong period, mid-18th century
Bamboo, jade (nephrite), and silk tassels
3 1/8 × 19 5/16 × 4 7/8 in. (8 × 49 × 12.4 cm)
Palace Museum, Gu120738-2/3
F|S

156 **Wish-granting scepter (*ruyi*) with bats and chrysanthemums**
Probably Guangxu period, after 1888
Jade (nephrite) with silk tassels
15 1/16 in. (38.2 cm)
Palace Museum, Gu99604
PEM, F|S

METALWORK

157 **Ewer with dragons and clouds**
Probably Imperial Workshop, Beijing
Qianlong period, 1736–95
Gold alloy
12 3/8 × 7 11/16 in. (31.5 × 19.5 cm)
Palace Museum, Gu11455
PEM, F|S

158 **Pot with dragons for milk tea**
18th to 19th century
Silver with gilding
11 1/8 × 16 9/16 × 4 5/8 in. diam. at foot (28.2 × 42 × 11.8 cm diam. at foot)
Palace Museum, Gu140977
PEM, F|S

159 **Pair of chopsticks**
Probably Qianlong period, 1736–95
Gold with agate and *zitan* wood with silver and gold inlay
11 in. (27.9 cm) each
Palace Museum, Gu10728
PEM, F|S

160 **Portable censer with phoenixes, gourds, and the character for double happiness**
Imperial Workshop, Beijing
Tongzhi period, 1872 or earlier
Gold alloy with *zitan* wood and silk tassel
Censer: 9 1/8 × 6 1/2 in. (23.2 × 16.5 cm); rod: 41 × 3 in. (104.1 × 7.6 cm)
Palace Museum, Gu11663
Plate 12
PEM, F|S

161 **Wish-granting scepter (*ruyi*) with the character for double happiness and a scroll with the character for dragon**
Imperial Workshop, Beijing
Guangxu period, about 1888–89
Gold alloy with silk tassels; hanging scroll, ink on silk
Scepter: 11 7/16 × 3 15/16 in. (29 × 10 cm); scroll: 8 3/4 × 7 3/16 in. (22.3 × 18.2 cm)
Palace Museum, Gu11355
PEM (scepter), F|S (scepter and calligraphy)

162 **Seal of empress with double-headed dragon with box, tray, lock, key, and plaques**
Imperial Workshop, Beijing
Republican period, 1922
Gold alloy with silk tassels
Seal: 4 × 5 1/2 × 5 1/2 in. (10 × 14 × 14 cm)
Palace Museum, Gu167075
Plate 47
PEM, F|S

ENAMELWARE

163 Ewer with lady and boy in garden on two sides
Imperial Workshop, probably Beijing
Qianlong period, probably 1760s or 1770s
Cloisonné and painted enamel, copper and gold alloy with polychrome enamels and gilding, coral, turquoise, and lapis lazuli
$15\frac{3}{8} \times 11$ in. (39×28 cm)
Palace Museum, Gu11450
Plate 4
PEM, F|S

164 Massage tool with flowers
18th century
Painted polychrome enamels on copper-alloy core with gilding
$3\frac{3}{4} \times 2\frac{3}{16}$ in. (9.5×5.6 cm)
Palace Museum, Gu116454
Plate 34
PEM, F|S

165 Lidded cup and lobed tray with phoenixes and peonies
Imperial Workshop, Beijing
Qianlong period, 1736–95
Painted polychrome enamels on copper-alloy core with gilding
Cup: $3\frac{1}{4} \times 4\frac{5}{16}$ in. diam. (8.3×11 cm diam.); tray: $8\frac{7}{8}$ in. (22.5 cm) diam.
Palace Museum, Gu116518
PEM, F|S

166 Lidded jar with lady and boy
Imperial Workshop, Beijing
Qianlong period, 1736–95
$7\frac{7}{16} \times 2\frac{1}{16}$ in. diam. (18.9×5.3 cm diam.)
Painted enamel, polychrome enamels on copper-alloy core with gilding
Palace Museum, Gu116801
PEM, F|S

167 Basin with phoenixes and birds in landscape, dragons, and flowers
Workshop, Guangzhou
Qianlong or Jiaqing period, 1736–1820
Painted enamel, polychrome enamels on copper-alloy core
$4\frac{5}{8} \times 17\frac{3}{4}$ in. diam. (11.8×45.1 cm diam.)
Palace Museum, Gu118098
PEM, F|S

168 Mirror with landscape and mirror case with chrysanthemums, the character for longevity, and phoenixes
Probably Imperial Workshop, Beijing
Qianlong period, 1736–95
Mirror: cloisonné, polychrome enamels on copper-alloy core with gilding; mirror case: embroidery, silk threads on silk satin with gold; kingfisher feather, seed pearls, coral, and silk cords
Mirror: $\frac{1}{4} \times 3\frac{7}{8}$ in. diam. (0.6×9.9 cm diam.)
Palace Museum, Gu119547
PEM, F|S

169 Duck-shaped vessel
Imperial Workshop, Beijing
Qianlong period, 1736–95
Cloisonné, polychrome enamels on copper-alloy core with gilding
$12\frac{3}{16} \times 9\frac{7}{16}$ (31×24 cm)
Palace Museum, Gu118956
PEM, F|S

170 Snuff bottle with woman and child
Qianlong period, 1736–95
Painted enamel, polychrome enamels on copper-alloy core with gilding; stand: ivory
$2\frac{3}{4} \times 1\frac{9}{16} \times \frac{13}{16}$ in. ($7 \times 4 \times 2$ cm)
Peabody Essex Museum, Museum purchase, 1988, E82696
PEM

BUDDHIST ART

171 Four-armed bodhisattva Avalokiteshvara (Guanyin)
Probably Imperial Silk Manufactory, Suzhou
Qianlong period, probably 1743–44 or earlier
Silk tapestry (*kesi*), polychrome and metallic-wrapped silk threads with pigments
$90\frac{15}{16} \times 32\frac{1}{4}$ in. (231×82.5 cm)
Palace Museum, Gu72734
F|S

172 Four-armed bodhisattva Avalokiteshvara (Guanyin)
Probably Imperial Silk Manufactory, Suzhou
Qianlong period, 1743–44 or earlier
Silk tapestry (*kesi*), polychrome and metallic-wrapped silk threads with pigments
$146 \times 49\frac{3}{4}$ in. (371.1×126.2 cm) overall
The Art Institute of Chicago, gift of Ma Chang Kee to the Buckingham Collection, 1932, 1932.874
PEM

173 Empress Dowager Cixi in the guise of the bodhisattva Avalokiteshvara (Guanyin)
Court painters, Beijing
Guangxu period, 1875–1908
Hanging scroll, ink and color on silk
$85\frac{5}{8} \times 45\frac{7}{8}$ in. (217.5×116.5 cm)
Palace Museum, Gu6603
Plate 42
F|S

174 Empress Dowager Cixi in the guise of the bodhisattva Avalokiteshvara (Guanyin)
Probably court painter, Beijing
Guangxu period, 1875–1908
Hanging scroll, ink and color on silk
$50\frac{3}{8} \times 25\frac{3}{8}$ in. (128×64.5 cm)
Chazen Museum of Art, University of Wisconsin–Madison, Walter A. and Dorothy Jones Frautschi Endowment Fund, Ineva T. Reilly Endowment Fund, and Earnest C. and Jane Watson Endowment Fund purchase, 2016, 2016.3
PEM, F|S

175 **Sutra on Medicine Buddha (*Bhaisajyaguru*)**
The Kangxi emperor (1654–1722)
Kangxi period, 1698
Album, ink and color on silk
$10\frac{3}{4} \times 326$ in. (27.3 × 828.1 cm)
Palace Museum, Shu9491
PEM

176 **Heart of the Perfection of Wisdom Sutra (*Prajnaparamitahrdayasutra*)**
The Kangxi emperor (1654–1722)
Kangxi period, 1702
Album, gold and color on paper
$11\frac{5}{8} \times 53\frac{5}{8}$ in. (29.5 × 136.2 cm)
Palace Museum, Shu7768
Plate 39
F|S

177 **Sutra Displaying the Land of Bliss (*Sukhavativyuhasutra*)**
The Qianlong emperor (1711–1799)
Qianlong period, 1761
$12 \times 4\frac{13}{16} \times 1\frac{1}{16}$ in. (30.4 × 12.3 × 2.7 cm) closed
Album, gold on paper
Palace Museum, Shu9500-1/2
PEM

178 **One volume from the 108-volume Kanjur Sutra**
Imperial Workshop, Beijing, and workshop, Suzhou
Qianlong period, 1767–70
Gold on paper; covers: lacquer and gold on wood core, silk tapestry (*kesi*), ink and color on paper, gold, pearls, coral, lapis lazuli, turquoise, and silk cords
$11\frac{7}{16} \times 30\frac{5}{16} \times 10\frac{5}{8}$ in. (29 × 77 × 27 cm)
Palace Museum, Shu28249
Plate 41
PEM, F|S

179 **Stupa containing Empress Dowager Chongqing's hair and Amitayus Buddha**
Imperial Workshop, Beijing
Qianlong period, 1777
Gold and silver alloy with coral, turquoise, lapis lazuli, and other semiprecious stones, and glass; pedestal: *zitan* wood
Stupa: $60\frac{1}{4} \times 27\frac{9}{16} \times 27\frac{9}{16}$ in. (153 × 70 × 70 cm);
stand: $27\frac{9}{16} \times 27\frac{9}{16}$ in. (70 × 70 cm)
Palace Museum, Gu11866
Plate 37
PEM, F|S

180 **Four-armed bodhisattva Avalokiteshvara (Guanyin)**
Imperial Workshop, Beijing
Qianlong period, 1748
Gold alloy with coral, sapphires, rubies, lapis lazuli, turquoise, and pearls
$35\frac{13}{16} \times 18\frac{5}{16} \times 14\frac{5}{16}$ in. (91 × 46.5 × 36.3 cm)
Palace Museum, Gu11759
PEM, F|S

181 **Vajradhara**
Probably workshop, Tibet
Qianlong period, 1771
Copper alloy with gold and turquoise
$5\frac{1}{2} \times 4\frac{1}{16}$ in. (14 × 10.3 cm)
Palace Museum, Gu203044
PEM, F|S

182 **Amitayus Buddha in a niche**
Workshop, probably Tibet
Qianlong period, 1771
Copper alloy with gilding and pigments; niche: *zitan* wood with silk damask
Sculpture: $13 \times 10\frac{1}{4}$ in. (33 × 26 cm); niche: $28\frac{3}{8} \times 16\frac{9}{16} \times 11\frac{7}{16}$ in. (72 × 42 × 29 cm)
Palace Museum, Gu203040
Plate 45
PEM, F|S

183 **Ritual bell with *vajra* (thunderbolt)**
Probably Qianlong period, 1736–95
Copper alloy with gold
$7\frac{1}{16} \times 3\frac{13}{16}$ in. diam. (18 × 9.7 cm diam.)
Palace Museum, Gu203179
PEM, F|S

184 **Diadem with Sanskrit seed syllables and sashes with dragons**
Probably Imperial Silk Manufactory, Suzhou (embroidery)
Qianlong period, 1736–95
Gold, pearls, coral, lapis lazuli, and turquoise on silk velvet and satin
Diadem: $7\frac{1}{2} \times 22\frac{3}{4}$ in. (19 × 57.8 cm); sashes on left: $19 \times 6\frac{1}{2}$ in. (48.3 × 16.5 cm); sashes on right: 19 × 7 in. (48.3 × 17.8 cm)
Palace Museum, Gu59382
F|S

PHOTOGRAPHY

185 **The Great Imperial Porcelain Palace, Yuen Ming Yuen [Yuanming yuan], October 1860/Pekin**
Felice Beato (Italy, 1832–1909)
1860
Albumen print
$9\frac{13}{16} \times 11\frac{5}{8}$ in. (24.9 × 29.5 cm)
Peabody Essex Museum, gift of Howard Corning, 1930s, PH2.40
Plate 57
PEM

186 **Summer Palace (Wan shoushan)**
Thomas Child (United Kingdom, 1841–1898)
1870s
Albumen print
$9 \times 7\frac{3}{8}$ in. (22.9 × 18.8 cm)
Peabody Essex Museum, Phillips Library, Ward Collection
PEM

187 **Boy on horseback with attendants**
Tongzhi or Guangxu period, 1870s
Albumen print
8⅝ × 11 in. (21.8 × 27.9 cm)
Peabody Essex Museum, Phillips Library, Ward Collection
PEM

188 **Prince Chun and his sons**
Attributed to Liang Shitai (active about 1870s–1880s)
Guangxu period, about 1886–88
Albumen print
8⅛ × 10⅞ in. (20.6 × 27.7 cm)
Peabody Essex Museum, museum purchase, 1997, PH23.3
PEM

189 **Portrait of Prince Kung [Gong], Brother of the Emperor of China; Who Signed the Treaty, 1860**
Felice Beato (Italy, 1832–1909)
1860
Albumen print
6⅛ × 4 9/16 in. (15.5 × 11.6 cm)
Peabody Essex Museum, gift of Howard Corning, 1930, PH2.53
PEM

190 **Her Imperial Majesty, the Empress Dowager of China**
Yu Xunling (1874–1943)
Guangxu period, about 1903
Hand-colored silver gelatin print
9⅛ × 6¾ in. (23.1 × 17.2 cm)
Museum of Fine Art, Boston, gift of Sarah Buchan Jewell, 1991, 1991.134
PEM

191 **Empress Dowager Cixi in the guise of the bodhisattva Avalokiteshvara (Guanyin)**
Yu Xunling (1874–1943)
Guangxu period, 1903
Print from glass plate negative
9½ × 7 in. (24.1 × 17.8 cm)
Freer Gallery of Art and Arthur M. Sackler Gallery Archives, Smithsonian Institution, Washington, DC, purchase, FSA A.13 SC-GR-246
F|S

192 **Postcards of the Palace of Gathered Elegance (Chuxiu gong) and the Bower of Enchanting Scenery (Lijing xuan) in the Forbidden City**
Republican period (1912–49), 1920s
Silver gelatin print
3¼ × 5¼ in. (8.3 × 13.3 cm)
Peabody Essex Museum, Phillips Library, purchase with Scott Offen Funds, 2009–2012, DS795.8 .F67, Nos. 1–3, 6–8
PEM

BOOKS AND ALBUMS

193 **Views of Jehol, the Seat of the Summer Palace of the Emperors of China**
Matteo Ripa (Italy, 1682–1746)
Kangxi period, 1714
Book with leaves of copperplate engravings; ink on paper
12¾ × 7½ × ⅝ in. (32.4 × 19 × 1.6 cm)
Peabody Essex Museum, Phillips Library purchase, Frederick Townsend Ward Memorial Fund, 1963, 915.1-R588
PEM

194 **Imperial Consort in Qing Dynasty Attire**
Painters in Guangzhou
Qianlong period, 1745
Album, ink and color on paper
16 × 12 in. (40.6 × 30.5 cm)
Peabody Essex Museum, museum purchase, 1996, AE85315.22
PEM

195 **Illustrated Description of Famous Places in China *(Morokoshi meisho zue)*, vol. 1**
Okada Gyokuzan (Japan, 1737–1812), Oka Yugaku (Japan, 1762–1833), Ohara Toya (Japan, 1771–1840)
Published by Kawachiya Kichibe, Osaka, Japan, 1805
Thread-bound book, woodblock prints
10 × 7 × ½ in. (25.5 × 17.8 × 1.3 cm)
Peabody Essex Museum, Phillips Library purchase, Herbert Offen Research Collection, 2004, DS708-.O33-1805-V.-1
PEM

196 **With the Empress Dowager of China**
Katharine A. Carl (United States, 1865–1938)
Published by Century Co., New York, 1906
Book with cloth cover
8½ × 5¾ × 1½ in. (21.6 × 14.6 × 3.8 cm)
Peabody Essex Museum, Phillips Library purchase, Frederick Townsend Ward Memorial Fund, 915.1-C278
PEM

197 **Court Life in China: The Capital, Its Officials and People**
Isaac Taylor Headland (United States, 1859–1942)
Published by Fleming H. Revell Company, 1909
Book with cloth cover
8⅜ × 5⅞ × 1⅝ in. (14.9 × 21.3 × 4.1 cm)
Peabody Essex Museum, Phillips Library purchase, DS710.H5-1909
PEM

198 **Two Years in the Forbidden City**
Princess Der Ling (Yu Deling, 1885–1944)
Published by Moffat, Yard and Company, New York, 1912
Book with cloth cover
8½ × 6 × 1½ in. (21.6 × 15.2 × 3.8 cm)
Peabody Essex Museum, Phillips Library purchase, Frederick Townsend Ward Memorial Fund, 1963, DS763.T8-D43-1912-C2
PEM

GLOSSARY OF SELECTED NAMES AND TERMS

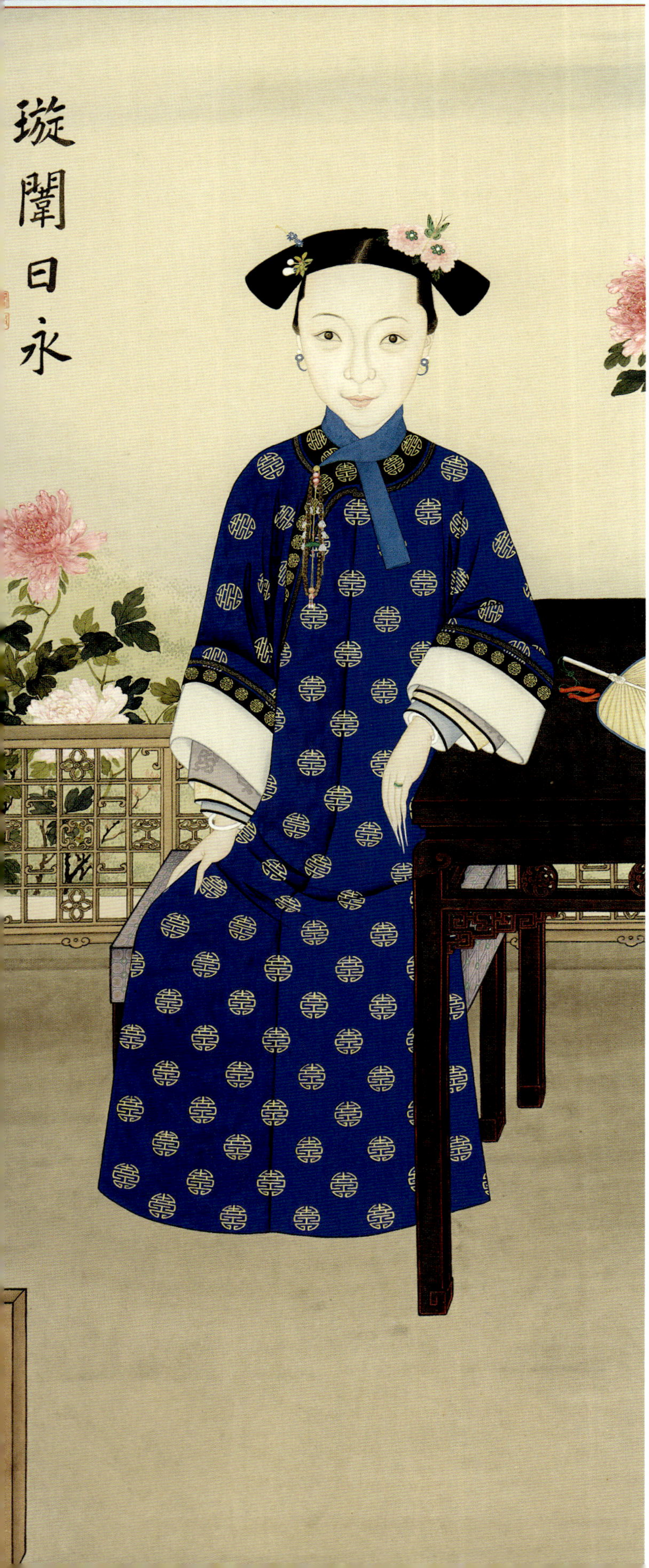

Note: Romanized Chinese, Manchu, Sanskrit, and Tibetan names and terms are included with their Chinese character equivalents.

Ai Qimeng 艾啓蒙 (Ignatius Sichelbarth)
Aisin Gioro 愛新覺羅
Aixin jueluo zongpu 愛新覺羅宗譜
Amitayus 無量壽佛
Baiyi dabei wuyinxin tuoluonijing 白衣大悲五印心陀羅尼經
Baiyun guan 白雲觀
baizi tu 百子圖
banzhao li 頒詔禮
bao 寶
Bao Chao 鮑超
Baohe dian 保和殿
baomu 保姆
Baxian gong 八仙宮
Beijing 北京
beile 貝勒
Bixia yuanjun 碧霞元君
cai 才
ce 冊
cefei 側妃
Chang Cun 常存
Changchun gong 長春宮
Changchun yuan 長春園
Changchun yuan 暢春園
changzai 常在
chaofu 朝服
chaojian li 朝見禮
chen 臣
Chen Guanquan 陳觀泉
Chen Mei 陳枚
Chen Zhaolong 陳兆龍
Chen Zuzhang 陳祖璋
Chengde 承德
Chenghua 成化
Chengqian gong 承乾宮

chenyi 襯衣
Chongqing 崇慶
Chuxiu gong 儲秀宮
Ci'an 慈安
Cining gong 慈寧宮
Cining gong huayuan 慈寧宮花園
Cixi 慈禧
Ciyin lou 慈蔭樓
cizhu yanqing 慈竹延清
Dabaoen yanshou si 大報恩延壽寺
Da fotang 大佛堂
Da Qing huidian 大清會典
Da Qing tongli 大清通禮
Da Qing yudie 大清玉牒
dahun 大婚
Dalai 達賴
Daoguang 道光
Daya zhai 大雅齋
daying 答應
dazheng li 大征禮
Debao 德保
Deng huanghou 鄧皇后
Deng Sui 鄧綏
dGe lugs pa 格魯派
dianzi 鈿子
die 蝶 / 瓞
Ding Guanpeng 丁觀鵬
Dong liu gong 東六宮
Dong Qichang 董其昌
Donggo 董鄂
Donghua men 東華門
Dorgon 多爾袞
doucai 鬥彩
duobaoge 多寶格
Eidu 額亦都
Fangwai guan 方外觀
fei 妃
fenghuang 鳳凰
Fengxian dian 奉先殿
Foxiang ge 佛香閣
fu 福 / 蝠
Fuca 富察
Fuheng 傅恒
fujin 福晉
furong 婦容
Galdan 噶爾丹
Gao Rentong 高仁峒
gege 格格
gongfen 宮分
gongnü 宮女
gongxun tu 宮訓圖
gongyi 宮衣
gu 觚
Gu Kaizhi 顧愷之
Gu Pengnian 顧彭年
Guandi 關帝
Guangdong 廣東
Guangren zi 廣仁子
Guangxu 光緒
Guangzhou 廣州
Guanyin 觀音
guifei 貴妃
Guifei zuijiu 貴妃醉酒
guining li 歸寧禮
guiren 貴人
guzhuang 古裝
Han 漢
Hanjun 漢軍
Hanqing zhai 含清齋
hao 號
he 荷 / 合 / 和
Heilongjiang 黑龍江
Hejia cun 何家村
Hetian 和田
Hong Taiji 皇太極
Hongloumeng 紅樓夢
Hou san gong 後三宮
huali 花梨
Huang Men 黃門
Huangchao liqi tushi 皇朝禮器圖式
huangguifei 皇貴妃
huanghou 皇后
huanghuali 黃花梨
Huangji dian 皇極殿
huangtaihou 皇太后
Huayuan chu 畫院處
huihao 徽號
ji 戟 / 吉
Jiajing 嘉靖
Jiaqing 嘉慶
Jiangnan 江南
Jiangxi 江西
Jianzhou 建州
Jiao Bingzhen 焦秉貞
Jiaotai dian 交泰殿
jifei 繼妃
jifu 吉服
Jilin 吉林
Jin 金
Jin Tingbiao 金廷標
Jinchuan 金川
Jing guifei 靜貴妃
Jingdezhen 景德鎮
Jingju 京劇
Jingling gong 景靈宮
Jingren gong 景仁宮
Jingshan 景山
Jingyang gong 景陽宮
Jinyu zuo 金玉作
Junji chu 軍機處
Jurchen 女真
kang 炕
Kangxi 康熙
Kanjur 甘珠爾
kesi 緙絲
Kunning gong 坤寧宮
Kunqu 崑曲

Lan 蘭
Lang Shining 郎世寧 (Giuseppe Castiglione)
Laofoye 老佛爺
Leng Jian 冷鑒
Leng Mei 冷枚
Leshou tang 樂壽堂
li 禮
Li Bingzhi 李秉直
Li Gonglin 李公麟
Li Hongzao 李鴻藻
Li Lianying 李蓮英
Liang Shizheng 梁詩正
Liaoning 遼寧
Lijing xuan 麗景軒
Ling fei 令妃
Liu Chengyin 劉誠印 (Liu Suyun 劉素雲)
long 龍
Longyu 隆裕
Lu Ji 陸機
Luo Xuedan 羅學旦
luohan 羅漢
ma 馬
Mangguri 莽鵠立
Manzhou jishen jitian dianli 滿洲祭神祭天典禮
meiren hua 美人畫
Miaofeng shan 妙峰山
miaohao 廟號
miaojian li 廟見禮
Mingde 明德
Mulan 木蘭
nacai li 納彩禮
Nanjing 南京
Nanyuan 南苑
neidan 內丹
neiting 內廷
neiting zhengwei 內廷正位
Neiwu fu 內務府
Ningshou gong 寧壽宮
Niohuru 鈕祜祿氏
Niulang 牛郎
Nurhaci 努爾哈赤
Nüshi zhen tu 女史箴圖
Oboi 鰲拜
pin 嬪
ping'an 平安
Pingfu tie 平復帖
Puyi 溥儀
"Qi Yue" 七月
Qianlong 乾隆
Qianqing gong 乾清宮
Qichun yuan 綺春園
qilin 麒麟
Qin'an dian 欽安殿
qing 磬 / 慶
qinghe yanyan li 慶賀筵宴禮
Qingning gong 清寧宮
Qingshi gao 清史稿
Qingyi yuan 清漪園
Qintianjian 欽天監
Qiqiao 乞巧
Quan Zhong 全忠
Quanzhen 全真
Qufu 曲阜
Rehe 熱河 (Jehol)
Renxian 仁憲
Rong 容
Rong fei 容妃
ruyi 如意
Ruyi guan 如意館
Sansuo 三所
Shancai 善財
shengmu 聖母
shengrong 聖容
shengzi 生子
shenpai 神牌
shenwei 神位
Shenwu men 神武門
Shenyang 沈陽
shenyu 神御
shenzhu 神主
Shiduo 世鐸 (Li qinwang 禮親王)
shihao 謚號
Shijing 詩經
shinü tu 仕女圖
Shiqu baoji 石渠寶笈
shizui 試晬
shou 壽
Shou'an gong 壽安宮
Shouhuang dian 壽皇殿
Shoukang gong 壽康宮
shufei 庶妃
Shunzhi 順治
Siyong zhai 思永齋
Soni 索尼
suanzhi 酸枝
sui 歲
Su Shi 蘇軾
Suzhou 蘇州
Tai miao 太廟
Taihe dian 太和殿
Taihe men 太和門
Taihou dian 太后殿
Taiji dian 太極殿
Tanzhe si 潭柘寺
Tian'an men 天安門
tieluo 貼落
Tiren ge 體仁閣
tongjing hua 通景畫
tonglao hejin li 同牢合巹禮
Tongwen guan 同文館
Tongzhi 同治
Tongzhi zunqin zhibao 同治尊親之寶
Tuota 托塔
Ula Nara 烏拉那拉
waichao 外朝
Wanchun yuan 萬春園
Wang Ruxue 王儒學
Wang Youxue 王幼學
Wang Zhenpeng 王振鵬
Wanli 萬曆
Wanshou shan 萬壽山
Wanshou si 萬壽寺
weiqi 圍棋
Weituo 韋馱
Weng Tonghe 翁同龢
Wu men 午門

Wu Weiqian 吳維乾
wugong 五供
Wutai shan 五台山
wuyi 舞衣
xi 喜
Xi liu gong 西六宮
Xi'an 西安
Xianfeng 咸豐
Xianfu gong 咸福宮
xianghui 香會
Xianruo guan 咸若館
xiao 孝
Xiao Hanzhen 蕭漢振
Xiaocheng 孝誠
Xiaoci 孝慈
Xiaoding 孝定
Xiaoduan 孝端
Xiaogong 孝恭
Xiaohe 孝和
Xiaohui 孝惠
Xiaojing Xian 孝敬憲
Xiaomu 孝穆
Xiaoqin 孝欽
Xiaosheng 孝聖
Xiaosheng Xian 孝聖憲
Xiaoxian 孝賢
Xiaoxian Chun huanghou 孝賢純皇后
Xiaoyi 孝儀
Xiaozhe 孝哲
Xiaozhen 孝貞
Xiaozhuang 孝莊
Xihua men 西華門
Xinjiang 新疆
Xiong Xuepeng 熊學鵬
xiunü 秀女
Xu Fu 徐郙
Xuantong 宣統
xuanwei riyong 璇闈日永
Yaji shan 丫髻山
yang 陽
Yang Yuhuan 楊玉環
yangwen 陽文
Yangxin dian 養心殿
Yangxin dian dong nuange 養心殿東暖閣
Yangxing dian 養性殿
Yanhui ge 延暉閣
Yanxi gong 延禧宮
Yanxi tang 燕禧堂
Yao Wenhan 姚文瀚
Yehe Nara 葉赫那拉
Yi fei 懿妃
Yi guifei 懿貴妃
Yi Lantai 伊蘭泰
Yihe yuan 頤和園
Yihuan 奕譞 (Chun qinwang 醇親王)
Yikuang 奕劻 (Qing qinwang 慶親王)
Yikun gong 翊坤宮
Yili 儀禮
yin 陰
yinwen 陰文
yingtang 影堂
Yinzhen 胤禛
Yixin 奕訢 (Gong qinwang 恭親王)
Yonghe gong 永和宮
Yonghe gong 雍和宮
Yongshou gong 永壽宮
Yongxing 永瑆
Yongyan 永琰 / 顒琰
Yongyou dian 永佑殿
Yongzheng 雍正
yu 魚 / 餘
Yu huayuan 御花園
Yu Xunling 裕勛齡
Yuan Ying 袁瑛
Yuanfei 元妃
Yuanming yuan 圓明園
yuce 玉冊
Yueshi lou 閱是樓
Yuhua ge 雨花閣
yuhuchun ping 玉壺春瓶
yurong 御容
Zaifeng 載灃 (Chun qinwang 醇親王)
Zaoban chu 造辦處
Zhang Gao 張鎬
Zhang Tingyan 張廷彥
Zhang Weibang 張為邦
Zhang Yuanxuan 張圓璿
Zhang Zhen 張震
Zhao Mengfu 趙孟頫
Zhaodai xiaoshao 昭代簫韶
Zhen fei 珍妃
Zhejiang 浙江
Zhihui hai 智慧海
Zhinü 織女
Zhongcui gong 鍾粹宮
Zhonghe dian 中和殿
Zhongzheng dian 中正殿
Zhou Ben 周本
zitan 紫檀
Zongli yamen 總理衙門
Zunghar 準噶爾
Zuo Shu'e 左書諤

SELECTED BIBLIOGRAPHY

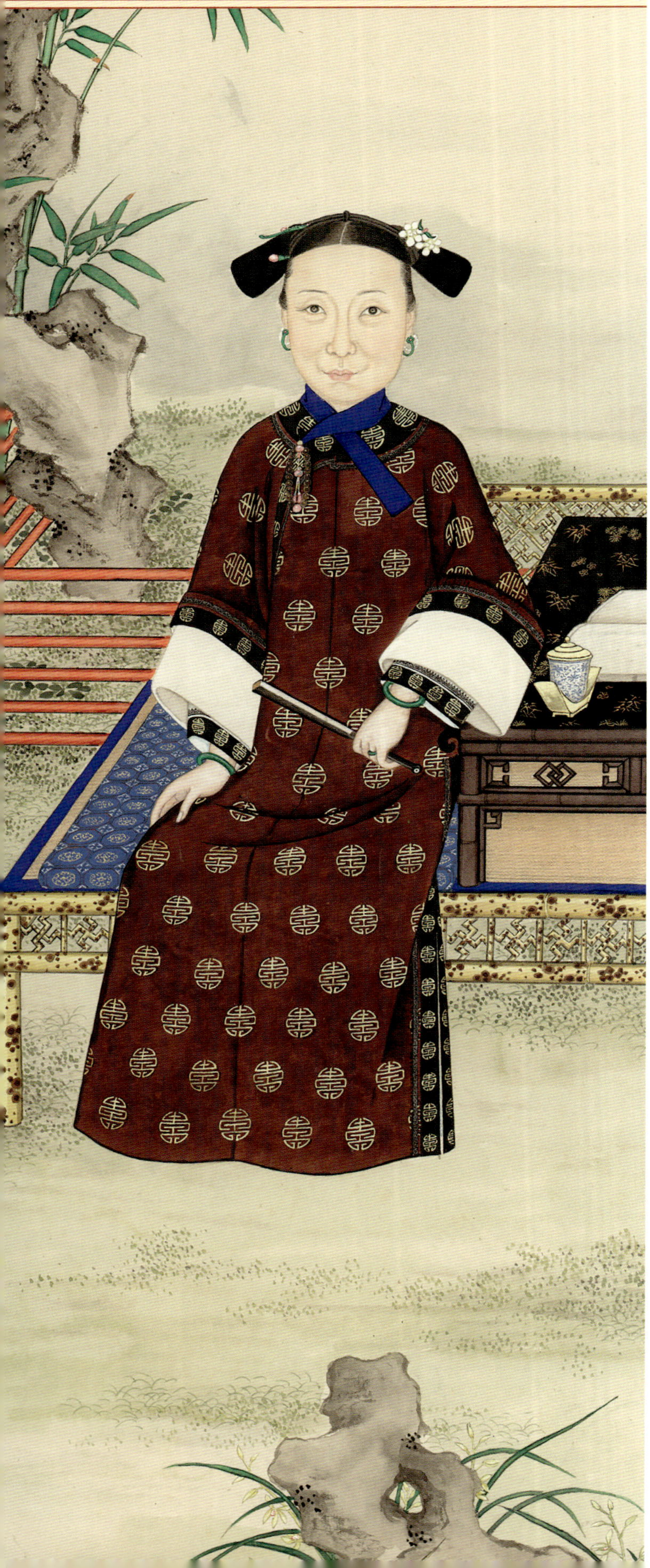

ARCHIVAL AND PRIMARY SOURCES

Note: The short-form abbreviation for Zhongguo diyi lishi dang'an guan (First Historical Archives of China) is ZGDYLSDAG.

AJZP.
Aixin jueluo zongpu 愛新覺羅宗譜 [Genealogy of the Aisin Gioro]. Edited by Jin Songqiao 金松喬 et al. Fengtian, 8 vols., 1937–38.

Carl 1905.
Carl, Katharine A. *With the Empress Dowager*. New York: Century, 1905.

Conger 1909.
Conger, Sarah Pike. *Letters from China: with Particular Reference to the Empress Dowager and the Women of China*. Chicago: McClurg, 1909.

Der Ling 1911.
The Princess Der Ling. *Two Years in the Forbidden City*. New York: Moffat, Yard, 1911.

Dezong shilu 1963.
Dezong shilu 德宗實錄 [Veritable records of the Guangxu emperor]. In *Qing shilu* 清實錄 [Veritable records of the Qing dynasty], 47:37–38. Taibei: Huawen shuju, 1963.

E'ertai and Zhang Tingyu (1769) 1987.
E'ertai 鄂爾泰 and Zhang Tingyu 張廷玉, eds. *Guochao gongshi* 國朝宮史 [History of the Qing imperial court]. 1769; Beijing: Beijing guji chubanshe, 1987.

Fuheng et al. 1760.
Fuheng et al. 傅恆等. *Zou wei huangtaihou wanshou shengjie xiuqi Xihuamen zhi Xizhimen liangbang jiedao shi* 奏為皇太后萬壽聖節修葺西華門至西直門兩傍街道事 [Court memorial regarding the renovation of the streets from the West Gate of Glory to the West Straight Gate in preparation for the celebration of the empress dowager's birthday], dated the fourth day of the twelfth lunar month of the twenty-fifth year of the Qianlong reign [1760]. File no. 05-0185-007. Zhongguo diyi lishi dang'an guan, Beijing.

Gaozong shilu 1968.
Gaozong shilu 高宗實錄 [Veritable records of the Qianlong emperor]. In *Qing shilu* 清實錄 [Veritable records of the Qing dynasty], *juan* 22. Taibei: Huawen shuju, 1968.

Guangxu dahun dianli hongdang 光緒大婚典禮紅檔 [Archives of the grand imperial wedding of the Guangxu emperor], *juan* 18. Zhongguo diyi lishi dang'an guan, Beijing.

Guangxu dahun yizhu 光緒大婚儀註 [On the rites of the grand imperial wedding of the Guangxu emperor], 1889, *ce* 3. Palace Museum, Beijing.

Haiwang 1735.
Haiwang 海望, "Zouwei xiuli Cining gong nei dongnan weifang zhiling qianliang shizhe" 奏為修理慈寧宮內東南圍房支領錢糧事折 [Memorial on receiving funds for renovating the southeast buildings of the Palace of Compassion and Tranquility], dated the third day of the eleventh lunar month of the thirteenth year of the Yongzheng reign [1735]. *Zouxiao dang* 奏銷檔. File no. 190-025-1. Zhongguo diyi lishi dang'an guan, Beijing.

Haiwang 1737.
———. “Zouwei qingzhi jiang xinjian Shoukang gong jiaming ji gaocheng riqi zhihui neige zairu huidian shi” 奏為請旨將新建壽康宮嘉名及告成日期知會內閣載入會典事 [Memorial on requesting the emperor’s permission to inform the cabinet to record the name and completion date of the Palace of Longevity and Health in the *Administrative Code of the Great Qing Dynasty* (*Da Qing huidian*)], dated the tenth day of the sixth lunar month of the second year of the Qianlong reign [1737]. *Zhou’an* 奏案. File no. 05-0013-028. Zhongguo diyi lishi dang’an guan, Beijing.

Loti 1902.
Loti, Pierre. *The Last Days of Pekin*. Translated by Myrta L. Jones. Boston: Little, Brown, 1902.

Manzhou jishen jitian dianli 滿州祭神祭天典禮 [Manchu rites for sacrifices to the spirits and to heaven], 1781. Reprint, Shenyang: Liaohai shushe, 1934.

Neiwu fu 1750a.
Neiwu fu 內務府 [Imperial Household Department]. *Cheng wei gonghui liezu shengrong dan* 呈為恭繪列祖聖容單 [List of respectfully painted portraits of deceased Qing emperors], dated the twenty-first day of the twelfth lunar month of the fifteenth year of the Qianlong reign [1750]. File no. 05-0111-023. Zhongguo diyi lishi dang’an guan, Beijing.

Neiwu fu 1750b.
———. *Cheng wei gonghui liehou shengrong dan* 呈為恭繪列后聖容單 [List of respectfully painted portraits of deceased Qing empresses], dated the twenty-first day of the twelfth lunar month of the fifteenth year of the Qianlong reign [1750]. File no. 05-0111-024. Zhongguo diyi lishi dang’an guan, Beijing.

Qinding da Qing huidian: Guangxu chao 欽定大清會典 光緒朝 [Administrative code of the Great Qing dynasty: Guangxu period edition], *juan* 1180. Zhongguo diyi lishi dang’an guan, Beijing.

Qinding da Qing huidian: Jiaqing chao 欽定大清會典 嘉慶朝 [Administrative code of the Great Qing dynasty: Jiaqing period edition], *juan* 74, 369, 662, 891. Zhongguo diyi lishi dang’an guan, Beijing.

Qinding da Qing huidian: Yongzheng chao 欽定大清會典 雍正朝 [Administrative code of the Great Qing dynasty: Yongzheng period edition], *juan* 97. Zhongguo diyi lishi dang’an guan, Beijing.

Qinding gongzhong xianxing zeli 欽定宮中現行則例 [Imperially commissioned current palace regulations]. Photoreproduction of 1856 ms. with this title in *Jindai Zhongguo shiliao congkan* 近代中國史料叢刊. Edited by Shen Yunlong 沈雲龍, vols. 621–24. Taibei: Wenhai, 1979.

Qinding shiqu baoji xubian 欽定石渠寶笈續編 [The precious collection of the stone moat], *juan* 19, vol. 2. Chinese Text Project database. http://ctext.org/.

Qinding zongguan neiwufu tang xianxing zeli 欽定總管內務府堂現行則例 [Imperially commissioned regulations on the office of the Ministers of the Imperial Household Department], 4 *juan*, 1884 preface.

Qing Gaozong shilu 清高宗實錄 [The veritable records of the Qing dynasty: the Qianlong emperor]. Zhongguo diyi lishi dang’an guan database.

Qing Gaozong yuzhi shiwen quanji 清高宗御製詩文全集 [Complete collection of the Qianlong emperor’s prose and poetry], 10 vols. Beijing: Zhongguo renmin daxue chubanshe, 2013.

Qingshi shanhou weiyuanhui (1925) 2004.
Qingshi shanhou weiyuanhui 清室善後委員會 [Committee for the Disposition of the Qing Imperial Possessions]. *Gugong wupin diancha baogao* 故宮物品點查報告 [Inventories of objects in the palace], 10 *juan*. 1925. Reprint, Beijing: Xianzhuang shuju, 2004.

“Shoukang gong dengchu shuji guazhou shoujuan ceye shumu qingce” 壽康宮等處《書籍掛軸手卷冊頁數目清冊》[Inventories of books, hanging scrolls, handscrolls, and albums at the Palace of Longevity and Health and other places], dated the forty-second year of the Qianlong reign [1777]. Zhongguo diyi lishi dang’an guan, Beijing.

Tongzhi dahun dianli hongdang 同治大婚典禮紅檔 [Archives of the grand imperial wedding of the Tongzhi emperor], *juan* 23. Zhongguo diyi lishi dang’an guan, Beijing.

Wenyuan ge siku quanshu 文淵閣四庫全書 [Complete library in four sections: Wenyuan ge edition], Ji bu, Bieji lei, Yuzhi shiji, *ji* 4, *juan* 32, 1775–84. Taibei: Taiwan shangwu chubanshe, 1983–86.

Xianghuangqi hujunying 1872.
Xianghuangqi hujunying 廂黃旗護軍營 [The Division of Imperial Guards of the Bordered Yellow Banner]. *Chengbao sui huangtaihou qu Shouhuang dian hujun canling geyuan dan shi* 呈報隨皇太后去壽皇殿護軍參領各員單事 [On the list of the imperial military officers who escorted Empress Dowager Cixi to visit the Hall of Imperial Longevity], dated the twelfth day of the tenth lunar month of the eleventh year of the Tongzhi reign [1872]. File no. 05-0864-062. Zhongguo diyi lishi dang’an guan, Beijing.

Yi Min-hwan (1573–1649) 1978.
Yi Min-hwan 李民寏, “Jianzhou wenjianlu” 建州聞見錄 [Records of what I saw and heard in Jianzhou]. In *Zhazhong rilu jiaoshi, Jianzhou wenjianlu jiaoshi* 柵中日錄校釋-建州聞見錄校釋 [Annotated diary behind the bars and annotated records of what I heard and saw in Jianzhou]. Edited by Liaoning daxue lishixi. Shenyang: Liaoning daxue lishixi, 1978.

Zhang Rong 2012.
Zhang Rong 張榮, comp. 養心殿造辦處史料輯覽 *Yangxindian zaoban chu shiliao jilan* [Selected historical records from the Imperial Workshop of the Hall of Mental Cultivation]. Beijing: Gugong chubanshe, 2012.

Zhao Erxun 1960.
Zhao Erxun 趙爾巽, ed. *Qingshi gao* 清史稿 [Draft history of the Qing]. Hong Kong: Xianggang wenxue yanjiushe, 1960.

ZGDYLSDAG 1991.
Zhongguo diyi lishi dang’an guan 中國第一歷史檔案館 (First Historical Archives of China), comp. *Yuanming yuan* 圓明園 [Garden of Perfect Brightness]. Shanghai: Shanghai guji chubanshe, 1991.

ZGDYLSDAG 2002.
Zhongguo diyi lishi dang’an guan 中國第一歷史檔案館 (First Historical Archives of China), comp. *Qianlongdi qiju zhu* 乾隆帝起居註 [Diaries of activity and repose of the Qianlong emperor]. Guilin: Guangxi shifan daxue chubanshe, 2002.

ZGDYLSDAG 2005.
Zhongguo diyi lishi dang'an guan 中國第一歷史檔案館 (First Historical Archives of China) and the Xianggang Zhongwen daxue wenwuguan 香港中文大學文物館 (Art Museum of the Chinese University of Hong Kong), comps. *Qinggong neiwufu zaoban chu dang'an zonghui* 清宮內務府造辦處檔案總匯 [Comprehensive archival records from the Qing Imperial Household Department's workshops]. 55 vols. Beijing: Renmin chubanshe, 2005.

ZGDYLSDAG 2015.
Zhongguo diyi lishi dang'an guan 中國第一歷史檔案館 (First Historical Archives of China) and Beijingshi Yihe yuan guanlichu 北京市頤和園管理處 (Management office of the Garden of Nurturing Harmony of the municipality of Beijing), comps. *Qinggong Yihe yuan dang'an: yingzao zhizuo juan* 清宮頤和園檔案: 營造制作卷 [Archives of the Garden of Nurturing Harmony in the Qing dynasty: building construction, restoration and object manufacture]. Beijing: Zhonghua shuju, 2015.

Zhu Saihong 2013.
Zhu Saihong 朱賽虹, ed. *Gugong bowuyuan cang Qinggong chenshe dang'an* 故宮博物院藏清宮陳設檔案 [Archives of Qing imperial objects for display in the collection of the Palace Museum]. Beijing: Gugong chubanshe, 2013.

Zhuang qinwang Yunlu et al. 1738.
Zhuang qinwang Yunlu et al. 莊親王允祿等. "Zouwei zunzhi yifu Shouhuang dian dengchu anfeng benchao lidai dixiang" 奏為遵旨議覆壽皇殿等處安奉本朝歷代帝像 [Court memorial regarding the placement of imperial portraits of the Qing and previous dynasties at the Hall of Imperial Longevity and other sites according to the imperial order], dated the second day of the twelfth lunar month of the third year of the Qianlong reign [1738]. File no. 05-0025-002. Zhongguo diyi lishi dang'an guan, Beijing.

Zongguan neiwu fu 1777a.
Zongguan neiwu fu 總管內務府. "Zouwei chaqing Cining gong Shoukang gong suoyou chenshe wupin shi" 奏為查清慈寧宮壽康宮所有陳設物品事 [Memorial on inventorying the objects in the Palace of Compassion and Tranquility and the Palace of Longevity and Health], dated the sixth day of the fourth lunar month of the forty-second year of the Qianlong reign [1777]. *Zou'an* 奏案. File no. 05-0331-068. Zhongguo diyi lishi dang'an guan, Beijing.

Zongguan neiwu fu 1777b.
———. "Cheng nijiao gechu wujian qingdan" 呈擬交各處物件清單 [Proposal to submit an inventory of objects from all relevant locations], dated the sixth day of the fourth lunar month of the forty-second year of the Qianlong reign [1777]. *Zou'an* 奏案. File no. 05-0331-072. Zhongguo diyi lishi dang'an guan, Beijing.

SECONDARY SOURCES

Bao Chengguan 1980.
Bao Chengguan 寶成關. *Yixin Cixi zhengzheng ji* 奕訢慈禧政爭記 [The political conflicts between Yixin and Cixi]. Changchun: Jilin wenshi chubanshe, 1980.

Berger 2003.
Berger, Patricia Ann. *Empire of Emptiness: Buddhist Art and Political Authority in Qing China.* Honolulu: University of Hawai'i Press, 2003.

Bray 2013.
Bray, Francesca. *Technology, Gender and History in Imperial China: Great Transformations Reconsidered.* New York: Routledge, 2013.

Cahill 1996.
Cahill, James. "Three Zhangs, Yangzhou Beauties, and the Manchu Court." *Orientations* 27 (9): 59–68.

Cahill 2010.
———. *Pictures for Use and Pleasure: Vernacular Painting in High Qing China.* Berkeley: University of California Press, 2010.

Cahill, Handler, and White 2013.
Cahill, James, Sarah Handler, and Julia M. White. *Beauty Revealed: Images of Women in Qing Dynasty Chinese Painting.* Berkeley: University of California, Berkeley Art Museum and Pacific Film Archive, 2013.

Cao Xueqin 1973.
Cao Xueqin, *Hongloumeng* 紅樓夢 [The Story of the Stone]. Translated by David Hawkes. Harmondsworth, UK: Penguin, 1973.

Cao Zhenyu 2008.
Cao Zhenyu 曹振宇. "Zhongguo jindai hecheng ranliao shengchan ji ranse jishu fazhan yanjiu" 中國近代合成染料生產及染色技術發展研究 [A study of synthetic dye production and the development of dye technology in modern China]. PhD diss., Donghua University, 2008.

Chandra 2008.
Chandra, Lokesh. *Tibetan Art.* New Delhi: Niyogi Books, 2008.

Chang Jianhua 2016a.
Chang Jianhua 常建華. "Kangxi di xunyou Wutaishan rizhi" 康熙帝巡遊五台山日誌 [Diary of the Kangxi emperor's visit to Mount Wutai]. *Zijincheng* 紫禁城 5 (2016): 132–43.

Chang Jianhua 2016b.
———. "Qifu: Kangxi di xunyou Wutaishan xintan" 祈福：康熙帝巡遊五台山新探 [Offering prayers: A new exploration of the Kangxi emperor's patronage of Mount Wutai]. *Lishi yanjiu* 歷史研究 2 (2016): 90–105.

Chen Huixia 2010.
Chen Huixia 陳慧霞. "Yongzheng chao de yangqi yu fangyangqi" 雍正朝的洋漆與仿洋漆 [Yongzheng-period court lacquer—foreign and imitation of foreign styles]. *Gugong xueshu jikan* 故宮學術季刊 28 (1): 142–95.

Chen Huixia 2016.
———. "Qingdai gongting funü zanshi zhi liubian" 清代宮廷婦女簪飾之流變 [The development of court ladies' hairpins and accessories during the Qing dynasty]. *Jindai Zhongguo funüshi yanjiu* 近代中國婦女史研究 28 (2016): 53–124.

L. Chen 2012.
Chen, Liana. "The Empress Dowager as Dramaturg: Reinventing Late Qing Court Theatre." *Nan Nü* 14 (1): 21–46.

Chen Pao-chen 2011.
Chen Pao-chen. "An Analytic Reading of Portraits of Emperor Qianlong and His Consorts." In *Bridges to Heaven: Essays on East Asian Art in Honor of Professor Wen C. Fong*, edited by Jerome Silbergeld, Dora C. Y. Ching, Judith G. Smith, and Alfreda Murck, 335–62. Princeton, NJ: Princeton University Press, 2011.

Chen Xiasheng 2006.
Chen Xiasheng 陳夏生. "Zaitan Qingdai fushi zhong de chaozhu yu shouchuan" 再談清代服飾中的朝珠與手串 [On court necklaces and rosaries—bracelets in Qing costume]. *Gugong wenwu yuekan* 故宮文物月刊 274 (2006): 92–96.

Y. Chen 1994.
Chen, Yiyun. "Out of the Traditional Halls of Academe: Exploring New Avenues for Research on Women." In *Engendering China: Women, Culture, and the State*. Translated by S. Katherine Campbell, edited by Christina Gilmartin et al., 69–79. Cambridge, MA: Harvard University Press, 1994.

Chen Yong 2013.
Chen Yong. *Confucianism in Religion: Controversies and Consequences*. Leiden and Boston: Brill, 2013.

W. Cheng 2014.
Cheng, Wen-chien. "Idealized Portraits of Women for the Qing Imperial Court." *Orientations* 45 (4): 87–99.

Cheng Zijin 2016.
Cheng Zijin 程子衿, ed. *Zijincheng yuedu Shier meiren* 紫禁城悅讀十二美人 [Enjoyable readings from the Forbidden City about the *Twelve Beauties*]. Beijing: Gugong chubanshe, 2016.

Chiang 2013.
Chiang, Nicole Ter-chuang 蔣得莊. "Qianlong huangdi shoucang zaisikao" 乾隆皇帝收藏再思考 [Revisiting the Qianlong emperor's collection]. *Gugong wenwu yuekan* 故宮文物月刊 368 (2013): 34–43.

Chong Yi 1982.
Chong Yi 崇彝. *Dao Xian yilai chaoye zaji* 道咸以來朝野雜記 [Miscellaneous notes on life in and outside the court since the Daoguang and Xianfeng reigns]. Reprint, Beijing: Beijing guji chubanshe, 1982.

Chou 2014.
Chou Wen-shing. "Reimagining the Buddhist Universe: Pilgrimage and Cosmography in the Court of the Thirteenth Dalai Lama (1876–1933)." *Journal of Asian Studies* 73 (2): 419–45.

Chun Hua 2011.
Chun Hua 春花. "Xiaozhuang taihou zunfo yijing dui Qingdai zongjiao zhengce de yingxiang" 孝莊太后尊佛譯經對清代宗教政策的影響 [The effect of Empress Dowager Xiaozhuang's veneration of Buddhism and translations of sutras on the religious policies of the Qing dynasty]. *Shenyang gugong bowuyuan yuankan* 瀋陽故宮博物院院刊 11 (2011): 56–63.

Chung 1975.
Chung, Sue Fawn. "The Much Maligned Empress Dowager: A Revisionist Study of the Empress Dowager Tz'u-Hsi in the Period 1898 to 1900." PhD diss., University of California, Berkeley, 1975.

Crossley 1990.
Crossley, Pamela K. *Orphan Warriors: Three Manchu Generations and the End of the Qing World*. Princeton, NJ: Princeton University Press, 1990.

Crossley 1997.
———. *The Manchus*. Oxford: Basil Blackwell, 1997.

Crossley, Siu, and Sutton 2006.
Crossley, Pamela K., Helen F. Siu, and Donald S. Sutton, eds. *Empire at the Margins: Culture, Ethnicity, and Frontiers in Early Modern China*. Berkeley: University of California Press, 2006.

Dennerline 2002.
Dennerline, Jerry. "The Shun-chih Reign." In Peterson 2002, 73–119.

Di Cosmo 1999.
Di Cosmo, Nicola. "Manchu Shamanic Ceremonies at the Qing Court." In *State and Court Ritual in China*, edited by Joseph McDermott, 352–98. Cambridge: Cambridge University Press, 1999.

Ding Wenfu 2012.
Ding Wenfu 丁文父. *Zhongguo gudai xiuqi jiaju: shi zhi shiba shiji zhengju de yanjiu* 中國古代髹漆傢具: 十至十八世紀證據的研究 [Chinese lacquer furniture: research based on examples from the tenth to the eighteenth centuries]. Beijing: Wenwu chubanshe, 2012.

Ding Yizhuang 1999.
Ding Yizhuang 定宜莊. *Manzu de funü shenghuo yu hunyin zhidu de yanjiu* 滿族的婦女生活與婚姻制度的研究 [A study of the life and marriage customs of Manchu women]. Beijing: Beijing daxue chubanshe, 1999.

Du Fangqin 1996.
Du Fangqin 杜芳琴. *Faxian funü de lishi—Zhongguo funüshi lunji* 發現婦女的歷史—中國婦女史論集 [The discovery of women's history—collection of theses on Chinese women's history]. Tianjin: Tianjin shehui kexueyuan chubanshe, 1996.

Duindam 2016.
Duindam, Jeroen. *Dynasties: A Global History of Power, 1300–1800*. Cambridge: Cambridge University Press, 2016.

Ebrey 2003.
Ebrey, Patricia Buckley. *Women and the Family in Chinese History*. London: Routledge, 2003.

Elisseeff 2017.
Elisseeff, Danielle. "Empresses and Concubines." In *La Cité Interdite à Monaco: Vie de Cour des Empereurs et Impératrices de Chine*, edited by Jean-Paul Desroches, 168–71. Monaco: Grimaldi Forum, 2017.

Elliott 1999.
Elliott, Mark C. "Manchu Widows and Ethnicity in Qing China." *Comparative Studies in Society and History* 41 (1): 33–71.

Elliott 2001.
———. *The Manchu Way: The Eight Banners and Ethnic Identity in Late Imperial China*. Stanford, CA: Stanford University Press, 2001.

Elliott 2009.
———. *Emperor Qianlong: Son of Heaven, Man of the World*. New York: Longman, 2009.

Esherick 1987.
Esherick, Joseph W. *The Origins of the Boxer Uprising*. Berkeley: University of California Press, 1987.

Fang Hongjun, Yan Yong, and Wan Jun 2007.
Fang Hongjun 房宏俊, Yan Yong 嚴勇, and Wan Jun 萬鈞. "Dui Qingdai batuan caiyun jinlongwen jifu de zairenshi" 對清代八團彩雲金龍紋吉服的再認識 [New light on festive robes with eight roundels with gold dragons and polychrome clouds in the Qing dynasty]. *Gugong bowuyuan yuankan* 故宮博物院院刊 3 (2007): 80–93.

Farquhar 1978.
Farquhar, David M. "Emperor as Bodhisattva in the Governance of the Ch'ing [Qing] Empire." *Harvard Journal of Asiatic Studies* 38 (1): 5–34.

Feng and Lu 2015.
Feng Mingzhu 馮明珠 and Lu Xueyan 盧雪燕, eds. *Shusheng yinyuan: Neifu nijin xieben Zangwen Longzangjing tansuo* 殊勝因緣：內府泥金寫本藏文龍藏經探索 [A wondrous occasion predestined: Unveiling the Tibetan-language Kanjur Sutra copied in gold produced in the Kangxi reign]. Taibei: Guoli gugong bowuyuan, 2015.

Fong, Qian, and Zurndorfer 2004.
Fong, Grace S., Nanxiu Qian, and Harriet Thelma Zurndorfer. *Beyond Tradition and Modernity: Gender, Genre, and Cosmopolitanism in Late Qing China.* Leiden: Brill, 2004.

Garrett 1994.
Garrett, Valery M. *Chinese Clothing: An Illustrated Guide.* Hong Kong: Oxford University Press, 1994.

Garrett 1997.
———. *A Collector's Guide to Chinese Dress Accessories.* Singapore: Times Editions, 1997.

Greenwood 2013.
Greenwood, Kevin. "Yonghegong: Imperial Universalism and the Art and Architecture of Beijing's 'Lama Temple.'" PhD diss., University of Kansas, 2013.

Gu Xinchun 2012.
Gu Xinchun 谷新春. "Luoyang Baimasi cang yuan Beijing Da Nengrensi fojiao zaoxiang kao" 洛陽白馬寺藏原北京大能仁寺佛教造像考 [Study of Buddhist figures in Luoyang's White Horse Monastery, originally from Beijing's Great Forbearance and Compassion Monastery]. *Wenwu shijie* 文物世界 6 (2012): 31–36.

Gu Xinchun 2015.
———. "Cining gong Dafotang nei de sanzuo fota" 慈寧宮大佛堂內的三座佛塔 [Three Buddhist pagodas in the Great Buddha Hall of the Palace of Compassion and Tranquility]. *Zijincheng* 紫禁城 7 (2015): 34–41.

Guan Jing 2015.
Guan Jing 觀靖. "Chengqi yinggan; Qin'an dian daochang" 誠祈應感：欽安殿道場 [Responses to sincere prayers: The Daoist ritual space of the Hall of Imperial Peace]. *Zijincheng* 紫禁城 5 (2015): 83–102.

Gugong bowuyuan 2007.
Gugong bowuyuan 故宮博物院 (Palace Museum). *Guanyang yuci—Gugong bowuyuan cang Qingdai zhici guanyang yu yuyaociqi* 官樣御瓷—故宮博物院藏清代製瓷官樣與御窯瓷器 [Qing porcelain designs and imperial porcelain wares in the collections of the Palace Museum]. Beijing: Zijincheng chubanshe, 2007.

Gugong bowuyuan 2010.
———. *Qinggong fushi tudian* 清宮服飾圖典 [Costumes in the collection of the Palace Museum]. Beijing: Zijincheng chubanshe, 2010.

Gugong bowuyuan 2011.
———. *Gugong falang tudian* 故宮琺瑯圖典 [Enamels in the collection of the Palace Museum]. Beijing: Zijincheng chubanshe, 2011.

Gugong bowuyuan 2012.
———. *Qinggong houfei shoushi tudian* 清宮后妃首飾圖典 [Jewelry of empresses and imperial consorts in the collection of the Palace Museum]. Beijing: Zijincheng chubanshe, 2012.

Gugong bowuyuan 2015a.
———. *Cining gong huayuan* 慈寧宮花園 [Garden of the Palace of Compassion and Tranquility]. Beijing: Gugong chubanshe, 2015.

Gugong bowuyuan 2015b.
———. *Putian tongqing: Qingdai wanshou shengdian* 普天同慶：清代萬壽盛典 [The world rejoices as one: Celebrating imperial birthdays in the Qing dynasty]. Beijing: Gugong chubanshe, 2015.

Gugong bowuyuan and Shoudu bowuguan 2013.
Gugong bowuyuan 故宮博物院 (Palace Museum) and Shoudu bowuguan 首都博物館 (Capital Museum). *Gugong zhencang Cixi de ciqi* 故宮珍藏慈禧的瓷器 [Empress Dowager Cixi's porcelains in the collections of the Palace Museum]. Beijing: Shoudu bowuguan, 2013.

Halsey 2015.
Halsey, Stephen R. *Quest for Power: European Imperialism and the Making of Chinese Statecraft.* Cambridge, MA: Harvard University Press, 2015.

Hansen 2003.
Hansen, Valerie. "The Hejia Village Hoard: A Snapshot of China's Silk Road Trade." *Orientations* 34 (2): 14–19.

Harris 1999.
Harris, David. *Of Battle and Beauty: Felice Beato's Photographs of China.* Santa Barbara, CA: Santa Barbara Museum of Art, 1999.

Hayter-Menzies 2011.
Hayter-Menzies, Grant. *The Empress and Mrs. Conger: The Uncommon Friendship of Two Women and Two Worlds.* Hong Kong: Hong Kong University Press, 2011.

He Li 2014.
He Li. Entry for *Twelve Beauties.* In Li Jian, He Li, Sung Hou-mei, and Ma Shengnan 2014, 124.

Headland 1909.
Headland, Isaac Taylor. *Court Life in China: The Capital, Its Officials, and People.* New York: Revell, 1909.

Henss 2001.
Henss, Michael. "The Bodhisattva-Emperor: Tibeto-Chinese Portraits of Sacred and Secular Rule in the Qing Dynasty." *Oriental Art* 47 (3): 2–16.

Hershatter, Honig, Mann, and Rofel 1998.
Hershatter, Gail, Emily Honig, Susan Mann, and Lisa Rofel, eds. *Guide to Women's Studies in China.* Berkeley: Institute of East Asian Studies, University of California, Berkeley, 1998.

Hinsch 2011.
Hinsch, Bret. *Women in Early Imperial China.* Lanham, MD: Rowman and Littlefield, 2011.

Ho 1998.
Ho, Chuimei. "Food for an Emperor: Qianlong and His Entourage." In Ho and Jones 1998, 73–94.

Ho and Bronson 2004.
Ho, Chuimei, and Bennet Bronson. *Splendors of China's Forbidden City: The Glorious Reign of Emperor Qianlong.* Chicago: Field Museum of Natural History, 2004.

Ho and Jones 1998.
Ho, Chuimei, and Cheri A. Jones, eds. "Life in the Imperial Court of Qing Dynasty China," *Proceedings of the Denver Museum of Natural History*, 3rd ser., vol. 15 (1998).

Hogge 2010.
Hogge, David. "Empress Cixi: Scanned and Discovered," Smithsonian Institution Archives blog, June 3, 2010, https://siarchives.si.edu/blog/empress-cixi-scanned-and-discovered.

Hogge 2011.
———. "The Empress Dowager and the Camera." *Visualizing Cultures* (blog), Massachusetts Institute of Technology. https://ocw.mit.edu/ans7870/21f/21f.027/empress_dowager/cx_essay03.html.

Holmgren 1991.
Holmgren, Jennifer. "Imperial Marriage in the Native Chinese and Non-Han State, Han to Ming." In Watson and Ebrey 1991, 58–97.

Hong Kong Heritage Museum 2016.
Hong Kong Heritage Museum and Gugong bowuyuan 故宮博物院 (Palace Museum). *Gong xi: Qingdi dahun qingdian* 宮囍: 清帝大婚慶典 / *Ceremony and Celebration: Grand Weddings of the Qing Emperors*. Hong Kong: Hong Kong Heritage Museum, 2016.

Hsieh 2003.
Hsieh Ming-liang 謝明良. "Qianlong de taoci jianshang guan" 乾隆的陶瓷鑑賞觀 [The Qianlong emperor's ceramic aesthetics]. *Gugong xueshu jikan* 故宮學術季刊 21 (2): 1–38.

Huang Chongwen 2014.
Huang Chongwen 黃崇文. "Yonghegong *Lüdumu buxiuxiang* de yishu fengge" 雍和宮「綠度母補繡像」的藝術風格 [The artistic style of the *Embroidered Image of Green Tara* in the Lama Temple]. *Zhongguo zongjiao* 中國宗教 1 (2014): 57–59.

Hummel 1943.
Hummel, Arthur W., ed. *Eminent Chinese of the Ch'ing Period (1644–1912)*. 2 vols. Washington, DC: US Government Printing Office, 1943.

Hyer 1981.
Hyer, Paul. "The Dalai Lamas and the Mongols." *Tibet Journal* 6 (4): 3–12.

Idema 2017.
Idema, Wilt L., trans. *Two Centuries of Manchu Women Poets: An Anthology*. Seattle: University of Washington Press, 2017.

Jagou 2009.
Jagou, Fabienne. "The Thirteenth Dalai Lama's Visit to Beijing in 1908: In Search of a New Kind of Chaplain-Donor Relationship." In *Buddhism between Tibet and China*, edited by Matthew T. Kapstein, 349–77. Boston: Wisdom Publications, 2009.

Jin Lei 2008.
Jin Lei 金磊. *Zoujin Beijing simiao* 走進北京寺廟 [Going into temples in Beijing]. Tianjin: Tianjin daxue chubanshe, 2008.

Jin Yi and Shen Yiling 2010.
Jin Yi 金易 and Shen Yiling 沈義羚. *Gongnü tanwang lu* 宮女談往錄 [Reminiscence of palace women]. Beijing: Zijincheng chubanshe, 2010.

Kahn 1967.
Kahn, Harold L. "The Politics of Filiality: Justification for Imperial Action in Eighteenth-Century China." *Journal of Asian Studies* 26 (2): 197–203.

Kahn 1971.
———. *Monarchy in the Emperor's Eyes: Image and Reality in the Ch'ien-lung Reign*. Cambridge, MA: Harvard University Press, 1971.

Kessler 1976.
Kessler, Lawrence D. *K'ang-hsi and the Consolidation of Ch'ing Rule, 1661–1684*. Chicago: University of Chicago Press, 1976.

Kleutghen 2015.
Kleutghen, Kristina. *Imperial Illusions: Crossing Pictorial Boundaries in the Qing Palaces*. Seattle and London: University of Washington Press, 2015.

Ko 1994.
Ko, Dorothy. *Teachers of the Inner Chambers: Women and Culture in Seventeenth-Century China*. Stanford, CA: Stanford University Press, 1994.

Ko 1998.
———. "The Emperor and His Women: Three Views of Footbinding, Ethnicity, and Empire." In Ho and Jones 1998, 37–48.

Ko 2004.
———. "High Heels and Platform Shoes." In Ho and Bronson 2004, 70–71.

Ko, Haboush, and Piggott 2003.
Ko, Dorothy, JaHyun Kim Haboush, and Joan R. Piggott. *Women and Confucian Cultures in Premodern China, Korea, and Japan*. Berkeley: University of California Press, 2003.

Kwong 1984.
Kwong, Luke S. K. *A Mosaic of the Hundred Days: Personalities, Politics, and Ideas of 1898*. Cambridge, MA: Council on East Asian Studies, Harvard University, 1984.

Lee 2010.
Lee, Hui-shu. *Empresses, Art, and Agency in Song Dynasty China*. Seattle: University of Washington Press, 2010.

Leng 2015.
Leng, Shujie 冷書傑. "Cixi xiuhuren" 慈禧修護人 [Repairers of Cixi]. *Jiemian* 界面, June 11, 2015. www.jiemian.com/article/302085.html.

Li Baowen 2011.
Li Baowen 李保文. "Xiaozhuang taihuangtaihou yu Kangxichao *Nijin xieben Zangwen Longzangjing*" 孝莊太皇太后與康熙朝泥金寫本藏文龍藏經 [Empress Xiaozhuang and the Tibetan-language Kanjur Sutra copied in gold produced in the Kangxi reign]. *Gugong wenwu yuekan* 故宮文物月刊 335 (2011): 8–17.

Li Jian, He Li, Sung Hou-mei, and Ma Shengnan 2014.
Li Jian, He Li, Sung Hou-mei, and Ma Shengnan. *Forbidden City: Imperial Treasures from the Palace Museum, Beijing*. Richmond: Virginia Museum of Fine Arts, 2014.

Li Jiufang 2002.
Li Jiufang 李久芳, ed. *Jinshu tai falang qi gugong bowuyuan cang wenwu zhenpin quanji* 金屬胎珐瑯器 故宮博物院藏文物珍品全集 [Enamelware with metal core, the complete collection of treasures of the Palace Museum, Beijing]. Hong Kong: Commercial Press, 2002.

Li Shi 2008.
Li Shi 李湜. *Ming Qing guige huihua yanjiu* 明清閨閣繪畫研究 [Study of paintings of gentry women in the Ming and the Qing dynasties]. Beijing: Zijincheng chubanshe, 2008.

Li Shi 2017.
———. "Qing yiming 'Xiaomu huanghou chaofuxiang' yu Shouhuang dian yurong" 清佚名《孝穆皇后朝服像》與壽皇殿御容 [The portrait of Empress Xiaomu in court attire and imperial portraits in the Hall of Imperial Longevity]. *Gugong bowuyuan yuankan* 故宮博物院院刊 1 (2017): 38–50.

Li Yuhang 2011.
Li Yuhang. "Gendered Materialization: An Investigation of Late Imperial Chinese Women's Artistic and Literary Reproductions of Guanyin." PhD diss., University of Chicago, 2011.

Li Yuhang 2012.
———. "Oneself as a Female Deity: Representations of Empress Dowager Cixi as Guanyin." *Nan Nü* 14 (1): 75–118.

Li Zhi'an 2012.
Li Zhi'an 李芝安. "Qingdai houfei toushi—dianzi" 清代后妃頭飾 – 鈿子 [Hair accessories of Qing dynasty empresses and imperial consorts—dianzi]. In *Qinggong houfei shoushi tudian* 清宮后妃首飾圖典 [Jewelry of the empresses and imperial consorts in the collection of the Palace Museum]. Edited by Gugong bowuguan 故宮博物院, 19–24. Beijing: Gugong chubanshe, 2012.

Li Zhi'an 2013.
———. "'Qincantu' huagui yu Qianlong di de xiancanli shulun"《親蠶圖》畫櫃與乾隆帝的先蠶禮述論 [On the cased set of paintings on *Offering to the Sericulture Ancestor* and the sericulture ritual developed by the Qianlong emperor]. *Gugong xuekan* 故宮學刊 2 (2013): 354–63.

Lin Shih-Hsuan 2011.
Lin Shih-Hsuan 林士鉉. "*Longzangjing* yu Qingchu Man Meng lianyin—Jianshu Xiaozhuang Wen huanghou de zhengjiao taidu" 院藏龍藏經與清初滿蒙聯姻—兼述孝莊文皇后的政教態度 [The Dragon Sutra in the museum's collection and early Qing marriage alliances between the Manchu and Mongols—with discussion of Empress Xiaozhuangwen's attitude toward politics and religion]. *Gugong wenwu yuekan* 故宮文物月刊 341 (2011): 116–27.

Lin Shu 2015a.
Lin Shu 林姝. "Chongqing huangtaihou de wanshou qingdiantu" 崇慶皇太后的萬壽慶典圖 [Paintings depicting the birthday celebrations of Empress Dowager Chongqing]. *Zhijincheng* 紫禁城 10 (2015): 44–55.

Lin Shu 2015b.
———. "Chongqing huangtaihou huaxiang de xin faxian—Yao Wenhan hua Chongqing huangtaihou baxun wanshou tu" 崇慶皇太后畫像的新發現—姚文瀚畫崇慶皇太后八旬萬壽圖 [A rediscovered painting of Empress Dowager Chongqing: new light on the painting celebrating her eightieth birthday by Yao Wenhan]. *Gugong bowuyuan yuankan* 故宮博物院院刊 4 (2015): 54–66, 160.

Lin Shu 2015c.
———. "Fengyang dongchao zhi suo de xingjian: Shoukang gong de zhaojian shimo" 奉養東朝之所的興建：壽康宮的肇建始末 [Building the residence of the empress dowager: The story of how the Palace of Longevity and Health was built]. *Zijincheng* 紫禁城 7 (2015): 42–57.

Lin Shu 2015d.
———. "'Shi'er meiren tu' wei Yongqinwang fujinxiang kao" 十二美人圖為雍親王福晉像考 [A study to attest that the women depicted in the set of paintings "Twelve Beauties" are Prince Yong's consorts]. In *Gugong bowuyuan shinian lunwenxuan (2005–2014)* 故宮博物院十年論文選 (2005–2014) [Selected essays from the publications of the Palace Museum (2005–2014), vol. 3]. Beijing: Gugong chubanshe, 2015.

Lin Shu 2015e.
———. "Shoukang ruxi meng chengjing—Shoukang gong yu Chongqing huangtaihou" 壽康如昔夢成境—壽康宮與崇慶皇太后 [Palace of Longevity and Health and Empress Dowager Chongqing]. *Zhijincheng* 紫禁城 7 (2015): 60–71.

Little et al. 2000.
Little, Stephen, et al. *Taoism and the Arts of China*. Chicago: Art Institute of Chicago; Berkeley: University of California Press, 2000.

Liu Dunzhen 1933.
Liu Dunzhen 劉敦楨. "Tongzhi chongxiu Yuanming yuan shiliao" 同治重修圓明園史料 [Archives of the reconstruction of the Garden of Perfect Brightness during the Tongzhi reign]. In *Liu Dunzhen wenji* 劉敦楨文集 [Collected writings of Liu Dunzhen], 287–390. 1933. Reprint, Nanjing: Zhongguo jianzhu gongye chubanshe, 1982.

Liu Housheng 1997.
Liu Housheng 劉厚生, ed. *Aixin jueluo jiazu quanshu 5: Jiafa liyi* 愛新覺羅家族全書 5: 家法禮儀 [The complete books on the Aisin Gioro family 5: family customs and rituals]. Jilin: Jilin renmin chubanshe, 1997.

Liu Lu 1997.
Liu Lu 劉潞. "Qingdai huanghou celi yu baqi daxing shizu" 清代皇后冊立與八旗大姓氏族 [The investiture of empresses and the major clans of the Eight Banners in the Qing dynasty]. *Gugong bowuyuan yuankan* 故宮博物院院刊 1 (1997): 52–65.

Liu Lu 2004.
———. "Yibu guifan Qingdai shehui chengyuan xingwei de tupu: Youguan Huangchao liqi tushu de jige wenti" 一部規範清代社會成員行為的圖譜—有關《皇朝禮器圖式》的幾個問題 [Several questions concerning *Illustrated Precedents for the Ritual Paraphernalia of the Qing Imperial Court*]. *Gugong bowuyuan yuankan* 故宮博物院院刊 4 (2004): 130–44.

Liu Xingliang 2012.
Liu Xingliang 劉興亮. "Lun Songdai de yurong ji fengsi zhidu" 論宋代的御容及奉祀制度 [Imperial portraits of the Song dynasty and related regulations and veneration practices]. *Lishi jiaoxue* 歷史教學 3 (2012): 20–26.

Liu Xun 2004.
Liu Xun. "Visualizing Perfection: Daoist Paintings of Our Lady, Court Patronage, and Elite Female Piety in the Late Qing." *Harvard Journal of Asiatic Studies* 64 (June 2004): 57–115.

Luk 2015.
Luk Yu-ping. *The Empress and the Heavenly Masters: A Study of the Ordination Scroll of Empress Zhang* (1493). Hong Kong: The Chinese University Press, 2015.

Luk 2016.
———. "Heavenly Mistress and the Nine-Lotus Bodhisattva: Visualizing the Celestial Identities of Two Empresses in Ming China." In *Women, Gender and Art in Early Modern Asia, c. 1500–1900*, edited by Melia Belli Bose, 63–90. London: Routledge/Ashgate, 2016.

Luk 2018.
———. "Collecting Chinese Jewellery at the V&A." *Transactions of the Oriental Ceramics Society* (forthcoming 2018).

Mann 1997.
Mann, Susan. *Precious Records: Women in China's Long Eighteenth Century*. Stanford, CA: Stanford University Press, 1997.

Mann 2011.
———. *Gender and Sexuality in Modern Chinese History*. Cambridge: Cambridge University Press, 2011

Manxue yanjiuhui 1989.
Manxue yanjiuhui 滿學研究會 (Society of Manchu Studies), ed. *Qingdai diwang houfei zhuan* 清代帝王后妃傳 [Biographies of emperors, empresses, and imperial consorts of the Qing dynasty]. Beijing: Zhongguo huaqiao chuban gongsi, 1989.

Mao 2007.
Mao Liping 毛立平. *Qingdai jiazhuang yanjiu* 清代嫁妝研究 [Studies of dowry culture in the Qing dynasty]. Beijing: Beijing renmin daxue chubanshe, 2007.

McCarthy and Chase 2003.
McCarthy, Blythe, and Ellen Salzman Chase. "Feathers of Blue on a Field of Gold: Chinese Ornament with Kingfisher Feather Cloisonné." In *Scientific Research in the Field of Asian Art: Proceedings of the First Forbes Symposium at the Freer Gallery of Art*, edited by Paul Jett, 15–25. London: Archetype; Washington, DC: Freer Gallery of Art, Smithsonian Institution, 2003.

McDermott 1999.
McDermott, Joseph Peter. *State and Court Ritual in China*. Cambridge: Cambridge University Press, 1999.

McMahon 2013.
McMahon, Keith. *Women Shall Not Rule: Imperial Wives and Concubines in China from Han to Liao*. Lanham, MD: Rowman & Littlefield, 2013.

McMahon 2016.
———. *Celestial Women: Imperial Wives and Concubines in China from Song to Qing*. Lanham, MD: Rowman & Littlefield, 2016.

Meng Fanren 2010.
Meng Fanren 孟凡人. *Mingdai gongting jianzhu shi* 明代宮廷建築史 [History of court architecture in the Ming dynasty]. Beijing: Zijincheng chubanshe, 2010.

Meng Hui 2008.
Meng Hui 孟暉. "Yongzheng de huaxiang" 雍正的花香 [Aroma of the Yongzheng emperor's flowers]. *Zijincheng* 紫禁城 5 (2008): 188–93.

Millward, Dunnell, Elliott, and Foret 2004.
Millward, James A., Ruth W. Dunnell, Mark C. Elliott, and Philippe Foret, eds. *New Qing Imperial History: The Making of Inner Asian Empire at Qing Chengde*. London and New York: Routledge, 2004.

Mokros 2012.
Mokros, Emily. "Reconstructing the Imperial Retreat: Politics, Communications, and the Yuanming Yuan Under the Tongzhi Emperor, 1873–4." *Late Imperial China* 33 (2): 76–118.

Mullaney 2012.
Mullaney, Thomas S. "Critical Han Studies: Introduction and Prolegomenon." In *Critical Han Studies: The History, Representation, and Identity of China's Majority*, edited by Thomas S. Mullaney, James Leibold, Stéphane Gros, and Eric Vanden Bussche, 1–20. Berkeley: University of California Press, 2012.

Naquin 1992.
Naquin, Susan. "The Peking Pilgrimage to Miao-feng Shan: Religious Organizations and Sacred Site." In *Pilgrims and Sacred Sites in China*, edited by Susan Naquin and Chün-fang Yü, 333–77. Berkeley: University of California Press, 1992.

Naquin 2008.
———. *Peking: Temples and City Life, 1400–1900*. Berkeley: University of California Press, 2008.

Nie Chongzheng 1996.
Nie Chongzheng 聶崇正. *Qingdai gongting huihua* 清代宮廷繪畫 [Court paintings of the Qing dynasty]. Hong Kong: Commercial Press, 1996.

Nie Chongzheng 2004.
———. "Qingdai gongting huihua gaoben shukao" 清代宮廷繪畫稿本述考 [Description and examination of the drafts made for Qing court paintings]. *Gugong bowuyuan yuankan* 故宮博物院院刊 3 (2004): 75–91.

Nie Chongzheng 2008.
———. *Qinggong huihua yu xihua dongjian* 清宮繪畫與西畫東漸 [Qing court paintings and influences of Western painting]. Beijing: Zijincheng chubanshe, 2008.

Oxnam 1970.
Oxnam, Robert B. *Ruling from Horseback: Manchu Politics in the Oboi Regency, 1661–1669*. Chicago: University of Chicago Press, 1970.

Pan Cunjuan 2012.
Pan Cunjuan 潘存娟. "Cixi yu Xi'an Baxiangong" 慈禧與西安八仙宮 [Cixi and the Palace of Eight Immortals in Xi'an]. *Zongjiaoxue yanjiu* 宗教學研究 2 (2012): 66–69.

Pang 2005.
Pang, Laikwan. "Photography, Performance, and the Making of Female Images in Modern China," *Journal of Women's History* 17 (4): 56–85.

Pearce 2005.
Pearce, Nick. *Photographs of Peking, China 1861–1908: An Inventory and Description of the Yetts Collection at the University of Durham—Through Peking with a Camera*. Lewiston, NY: Edwin Mellen Press, 2005.

Peng 2002.
Peng Ying-chen 彭盈真. "A Palace of Her Own: Empress Dowager Cixi (1835–1908) and the Reconstruction of Wanchun Yuan." *Nan Nü* 14 (2002): 47–74.

Peng 2006.
———. "Wuming hua zhong de youming wu: Luetan 'Shenliu dushutang meiren hua' de zhenwan" 無名畫中的有名物—略談"深柳讀書堂美人畫"的珍玩 [Famous antiquities in anonymous painting: an examination of the antique treasures in a beauty painting for the Deep Willow Study]. *Gugong wenwu yuekan* 故宮文物月刊 284 (2006): 80–95.

Peng 2012.
———. "Sanhai yishi: Cixi taihou de 'Zhonghai ban Guanyin' paizhao shimo" 三海遺事: 慈禧太后的 '中海扮觀音' 拍照始末 [Forgotten matters from the Three Lakes: the story of photographing Empress Dowager Cixi as Guanyin at the Central Lake]. *Zijincheng* 紫禁城 6 (2012): 32–39.

Peng 2013.
———. "Lingering between Tradition and Innovation: Photographic Portraits of Empress Dowager Cixi." *Ars Orientalis* 43 (2013): 157–75.

Peng 2014.
———. "Staging Sovereignty: Empress Dowager Cixi (1835–1908) and Late Qing Court Art Production." PhD diss., University of California, Los Angeles, 2014.

Peng 2017.
———. "Reconfiguring Patriarchal Space: Empress Dowager Cixi (1835–1908) and the Reconstruction of the Garden of Nurturing Harmony." In *Gender, Continuity and the Shaping of Modernity in East Asian Art, 16th–20th Centuries*, edited by Kristen L. Chiem and Lara C. W. Blanchard, 191–233. Leiden: Brill, 2017.

Peterson 2002.
Peterson, Willard J., ed. *The Ch'ing Dynasty to 1800*. Vol. 9, pt. 1, of *The Cambridge History of China*. Cambridge: Cambridge University Press, 2002.

Porter 2016.
Porter, Jonathan. *Imperial China, 1350–1900*. New York: Rowman & Littlefield, 2016.

Pruitt 1979.
Pruitt, Ida. *Old Madam Yin: A Memoir of Peking Life*. Stanford, CA: Stanford University Press, 1979.

Qinghua 2000.
Qinghua daxue jianzhu xueyuan 清華大學建築學院 [School of Architecture at the Qinghua University]. *Yihe yuan* 頤和園 [Garden of Nurturing Harmony]. Beijing: Zhongguo jianzhu gongye chubanshe, 2000.

Qu 1970.
Qu Hongji 瞿鴻機. *Shengde jilüe* 聖德紀略 [Abbreviated record of the sage's virtues]. Taibei: Wehnhai chubanshe, 1970.

Quette 2011a.
Quette, Béatrice. "The Emergence of Cloisonné Enamels in China." In Quette 2011b, 14–15.

Quette 2011b.
——, ed. *Cloisonné: Chinese Enamels from the Yuan, Ming, and Qing Dynasties*. New York: Bard Graduate Center; Paris: Musée des Arts Décoratifs; New Haven, CT: Yale University Press, 2011.

Rawski 1988.
Rawski, Evelyn S. "The Imperial Way of Death: Ming and Ch'ing Emperors and Death Ritual." In *Death Ritual in Late Imperial and Modern China*, edited by James L. Watson and Evelyn S. Rawski, 228–53. Berkeley, Los Angeles, and London: University of California Press, 1988.

Rawski 1991.
——. "Qing Imperial Marriage and Problems of Rulership." In Watson and Ebrey 1991, 170–203.

Rawski 1996.
——. "Reenvisioning the Qing: The Significance of the Qing Period in Chinese History." *Journal of Asian Studies* 55 (1996): 829–50.

Rawski 2004.
——. "The Empress's Silkworms." In Ho and Bronson 2004, 72–79.

Rawski 2009.
——. *The Last Emperors: A Social History of Qing Imperial Institutions*. Berkeley: University of California Press, 2009.

Rawski and Rawson 2006.
Rawski, Evelyn S., and Jessica Rawson. *China: The Three Emperors, 1662–1795*. London: Royal Academy of Arts, 2006.

Ren Wanping 2004.
Ren Wanping 任萬平. "Qingdai huangdi dahun lisu shulun" 清代皇帝大婚禮俗述論 [Ceremonies and custom of the grand weddings of Qing emperors]. In *Ming Qing luncong* 明清論叢 5 (2004): 438–48.

Ren Wanping 2011.
——. "Kenmeina kisaki to shitoyakana kisaki—kindai izen no Chūgoku ni okeru josei no mohan" 賢明な后と淑やかな妃 – 近代以前の中国における女性の模範 [Virtuous empresses and imperial consorts—exemplary women in premodern China]. In *Pekin Kokyū Hakubutsuin ten: Chijō no tengū* 地上の天宮 – 北京故宮博物院展 / *The Palace of Heaven on Earth: Works from the Palace Museum in Beijing*, 32–42. Tokyo: Tokyo Fuji Art Museum, 2011.

Rhoads 2000.
Rhoads, Edward J. M. *Manchus and Han: Ethnic Relations and Political Power in Late Qing and Early Republican China, 1861–1928*. Seattle: University of Washington Press, 2000.

Rojas 2008.
Rojas, Carlos. *The Naked Gaze: Reflections on Chinese Modernity*. Cambridge, MA: Harvard University Asia Center, 2008.

Rowe 2009.
Rowe, William T. *China's Last Empire: The Great Qing*. Cambridge, MA: Belknap Press, 2009.

Rudolph 2008.
Rudolph, Jennifer M. *Negotiated Power in Late Imperial China: The Zongli Yamen and the Politics of Reform*. Ithaca, NY: East Asia Program, Cornell University, 2008.

Ruggles 2000.
Ruggles, D. Fairchild, ed. *Women, Patronage, and Self-representation in Islamic Societies*. Albany, NY: State University of New York Press, 2000.

Schorkowitz and Chia 2017.
Schorkowitz, Dittmar, and Chia Ning, eds. *Managing Frontiers in Qing China: The Lifanyuan and Libu Revisited*. Leiden: Brill, 2017.

Shang Hongkui 1982.
Shang Hongkui 商鴻逵. "Qingdai Xiaozhuang Xiaoqin lianghou biping" 清代孝莊孝欽兩后比評 [Comparison of Qing dynasty Empresses Xiaozhuang and Xiaoqin]. *Gugong bowuyuan yuankan* 故宮博物院院刊 3 (1982): 23–30.

Silleras-Fernandez 2008.
Silleras-Fernandez, Nuria. *Power, Piety, and Patronage in Late Medieval Queenship: Maria de Luna*. New York: Palgrave Macmillan, 2008.

Smith 2015.
Smith, Richard J. *The Qing Dynasty and Traditional Chinese Culture*. Lanham, MD: Rowman & Littlefield, 2015.

Song Wen 2015.
Song Wen 宋文. "Cong Kunninggong de bianhua kan Qingdai tongzhizhe de Manzu jianshou yu duoyuanhua rentong" 從坤寧宮的變化看清代統治者的滿族堅守與多元化認同 [The Qing rulers' adherence to Manchu ethnicity and multiple identities from the perspective of changes in the Palace of Earthly Tranquility]. Master's thesis. Zhongguo shehui kexueyuan, 2015.

Spence 2013.
Spence, Jonathan D. *The Search for Modern China*. 3rd ed. New York: Norton, 2013.

Storey 2017.
Storey, Matthew. "Portraits of the Princesses." In *Enlightened Princesses: Caroline, Augusta, Charlotte, and the Shaping of the Modern World*, edited by Joanna Marschner with David Bindman and Lisa L. Ford, 229–31. New Haven, CT: Yale University Press, 2017.

Stuart 1998.
Stuart, Jan. "Imperial Pastimes: Dilettantism as Statecraft in the 18th Century." In Ho and Jones 1998, 55–65.

Stuart 2001.
——. "Realism and the Iconic Pose." In Stuart and Rawski 2001, 75–92.

Stuart 2006.
——. "Images of Imperial Grandeur." In Rawski and Rawson 2006, 64–75.

Stuart 2011.
——. "Timely Images: Chinese Art and Festival Display." In *Proceedings of the British Academy, Volume 167, 2009 Lectures*, edited by Ron Johnson, 295–348. Oxford: Oxford University Press, 2011.

Stuart and Rawski 2001.
Stuart, Jan, and Evelyn S. Rawski. *Worshiping the Ancestors: Chinese Commemorative Portraits*. Washington, DC: Freer Gallery of Art; Stanford, CA: Stanford University Press, 2001.

Tang Bangzhi 1967.
Tang Bangzhi 唐邦治. *Qing huangshi sipu* 清皇室四譜 [Four genealogies of the imperial family]. In *Jindai Zhongguo shiliao congkan* [Collectaneum of modern Chinese history], edited by Shen Yunlong 沈雲龍, vol. 71. Taibei: Wenhai, 1967.

Tian Jiaqing 1999.
Tian Jiaqing 田家青. *Fenghua zaixian: Ming Qing jiaju tezhan* 風華再現：明清家具特展 [Splendor of style: classical furniture from the Ming and Qing dynasties special exhibition]. Taibei: Guoli lishi bowuguan, 1999.

Tierney 1999.
Tierney, Helen, ed. *Women's Studies Encyclopedia*. Revised and expanded edition, vol. 1. Westport, CT: Greenwood Press, 1999.

Tong Wen'e 2006.
Tong Wen'e 童文娥. "Qing yuanben 'Qincantu' de yanjiu" 清院本《親蠶圖》的研究 [Research into the Qing palace version of the "Painting of the Sericulture Ritual"]. *Gugong wenwu yuekan* 故宮文物月刊 278 (2006): 71–78.

Urban Council of Hong Kong 1995.
Urban Council of Hong Kong. *Jinxiu luoyi qiaotiangong* 錦繡羅衣巧天工/ *Heavens' Embroidered Cloths: One Thousand Years of Chinese Textiles*. Hong Kong: Hong Kong Museum of Art, 1995.

Walthall 2008.
Walthall, Anne, ed. *Servants of the Dynasty: Palace Women in World History*. Berkeley: University of California Press, 2008.

Wan Xiufeng 2013.
Wan Xiufeng 萬秀鋒. "Qing qianqi gongting shiyong qie'nan xiang shulue" 清前期宮廷使用伽南香述略 [A brief description of the use of agarwood at the court in the first half of the Qing dynasty]. *Lishi dang'an* 歷史檔案 129 (2013): 135–38.

Wan Yi 1985.
Wan Yi 萬依, "Cong Cixi shengzi kan Qing gong louxi" 從慈禧生子看清宮陋習 [The bad customs of the Qing palace as seen from Cixi's birthing experience]. In *Xitaihou* 西太后 [Empress Dowager Cixi], edited by Yu Bingkun 愈炳坤 et al., 63–70. Beijing: Zijincheng chubanshe, 1985.

Wan Yi 2016.
——, ed. *Gugong cidian* 故宮辭典 [Annotated dictionary of the Forbidden City]. Expanded edition. Beijing: Gugong chubanshe, 2016.

Wang Baizhong 2007.
Wang Baizhong 王柏中. "Qinghuangjia neimiao jizu wenti tanxi" 清皇家內廟祭祖問題探析 [On issues of ancestor worship in the inner imperial temple in the Qing dynasty]. *Guangxi minzu xueyuan xuebao* 廣西民族學院學報 29 (2007): 60–63, 105.

Wang Cheng-hua 2012a.
Wang, Cheng-hua 王正華. "Going Public: Portraits of the Empress Dowager Cixi, Circa 1904," *Nan Nü* 14 (2012): 119–76.

Wang Cheng-hua 2012b.
———. "Zouxiang 'gongkaihua': Cixi xiaoxiang de fengge xingshi zhengzhi yunzuo yu xingxiang suzao" 走向「公開化」: 慈禧肖像的風格形式、政治運作與形象塑造 [Going public: the stylistic form, political function, and image construction in Cixi's portraits]. *Meishushi yanjiu jikan* 美術史研究集刊 32 (2012): 239–316, 320.

Wang Chutong 1988.
Wang Chutong, ed. 王初桐. *Lian shi* 奩史 [History of female toilette], *juan* 70, *Chaichuan mensan* 釵釧門三 [hairpins and bracelets, no. 3]. Reprinted in *Beijing tushuguan guji zhenben congkan* 北京圖書館古籍珍本叢刊 [Series of rare books in the collection of the Library of Beijing], *juan* 72. Beijing: Shumu wenxian chubanshe, 1988.

Wang Jiapeng 1991.
Wang Jiapeng 王家鵬. "Zhongzheng dian yu Qinggong Zangchuan fojiao" 中正殿與清宮藏傳佛教 [The Hall of Central Uprightness and Tibetan Buddhism at the Qing court]. *Gugong bowuyuan yuankan* 故宮博物院院刊 3 (1991): 31, 58–71.

Wang Jiapeng 2014.
———. "Cining gong Dafotang diaocha ji" 慈寧宮大佛堂調查記 [Record of investigation into the Great Buddha Hall of the Palace of Compassion and Tranquility]. In *Da xile yu da yuanman: Qingzhu Tan Xiyong xiansheng bashi huadan Han Zang foxue yanjiu lunji* 大喜樂與大圓滿：慶祝談錫永先生八十華誕漢藏佛學研究論集 [Great joy and great completion: Essays in Buddhist studies to celebrate the eightieth birthday of Mr. Tan Xiyong], edited by Shen Weirong 沈衛榮, 441–68. Beijing: Zhongguo zangxue chubanshe, 2014.

Wang Liping and Feng Jian 2016.
Wang Liping 王莉萍 and Feng Jian 馮建. "Gugong Cining gong Dafotang wenwu diaobo Luoyang diaochaji" 故宮慈寧宮大佛堂文物調撥洛陽調查記 [Investigation into the transfer to Luoyang of artifacts from the Great Buddha Hall of the Palace of Compassion and Tranquility at the Palace Museum]. *Wenwu tiandi* 文物天地 3 (2016): 14–21.

Wang Peihuan 1993.
Wang Peihuan 王佩環. *Qinggong houfei* 清宮后妃 [Empresses and imperial consorts of the Qing dynasty]. Shenyang: Liaoning daxue chubanshe, 1993.

Wang Peihuan 2014.
———. *Qingdai houfei gongting shenghuo* 清代后妃宮廷生活 [The lives of Qing empresses and imperial consorts at court]. Beijing: Gugong chubanshe, 2014.

Wang Qi 2004.
Wang Qi 汪亓. "Kangxi huangdi xiaoxianghua jiqi xiangguan wenti" 康熙皇帝肖像畫及其相關問題 [A tentative discussion of portraits of the Kangxi emperor and related questions]. *Gugong bowuyuan yuankan* 故宮博物院院刊 1 (2004): 40–57.

Wang Qiuju 2017.
Wang Qiuju 王秋菊. "Qing Qianlong neifu Zangwen nijin xieben 'Ganzhuer' jing" 清乾隆內府藏文泥金寫本《甘珠爾》經 [The Tibetan-language Kanjur Sutra copied in gold commissioned by the Qianlong emperor of the Qing dynasty]. *Wenwu tiandi* 文物天地 4 (2017): 68–70.

S. Wang 2004.
Wang, Shuo. "The Selection of Women for the Qing Imperial Harem." *Chinese Historical Review* 11 (2): 212–22.

Wang Yanyun 2008.
Wang Yanyun 王艷雲. "Jindai yurong ji feng'an zhidu" 金代御容及奉安制度 [Imperial portraits of the Jin dynasty and related regulations and veneration practices]. *Gugong bowuyuan yuankan* 故宮博物院院刊 5 (2008): 79–88.

Wang Zilin 2014.
Wang Zilin 王子林. "Cining gong Dafotang kao" 慈寧宮大佛堂考 [Study into the Great Buddha Hall of the Palace of Compassion and Tranquility]. *Gugong bowuyuan* yuankan 故宮博物院院刊 4 (2014): 70–90.

Watson 1986.
Watson, Rubie S. "The Named and the Nameless: Gender and Person in Chinese Society." *American Ethnologist* 13 (1986): 619–31.

Watson and Ebrey 1991.
Watson, Rubie S., and Patricia Buckley Ebrey, eds. *Marriage and Inequality in Chinese Society*. Berkeley: University of California Press, 1991.

Wen Ming 2015.
Wen Ming 文明. "Cining gong huayuan zongshu" 慈寧宮花園綜述 [Survey of the Garden of the Palace of Compassion and Tranquility]. In Gugong bowuyuan 2015a, 9–32.

Weng Lianxi 2013.
Weng Lianxi 翁連溪. "Qing Qianlong neifu Zangwen nijin xieben Ganzhuer xiehui zhizuo kaoshu" 清乾隆內府藏文泥金寫本甘珠爾寫繪製作考述 [Study into the text and painting production of the Tibetan-language Kanjur handwritten in gold in the Qing Qianlong imperial collection]. In *Diyijie Qinggong dianji guoji yantaohui lunwenji: Tianlu zhencang* 第一屆清宮典籍國際研討會論文集:天祿珍藏 [Precious collection: The first international symposium on books in the collection of the Qing palace], compiled by Gugong bowuyuan, 1–16. Beijing: Gugong chubanshe, 2013.

Wolf 1972.
Wolf, Margery. *Women and the Family in Rural Taiwan*. Stanford, CA: Stanford University Press, 1972.

Wong et al. 2017.
Wong, Belinda S. L. 黃秀蘭 et al. *Wanshou zaide Qinggong dihou danchen qingdian* 萬壽載德—清宮帝后誕辰慶典 / Longevity and Virtues: Birthday Celebrations of the Qing Emperors and Empress Dowagers. Hong Kong: Hong Kong Museum of History, 2017.

Wright 1957.
Wright, Mary C. *The Last Stand of Chinese Conservatism: The T'ung-Chih Restoration, 1862–1874*. Stanford, CA: Stanford University Press, 1957.

Wu Hung 1996.
Wu Hung. *The Double Screen: Medium and Representation in Chinese Painting*. Chicago: University of Chicago Press, 1996.

Wu Hung 1997.
———. "Beyond Stereotypes: The Twelve Beauties in Qing Court Art and the 'Dream of the Red Chamber.'" In *Writing Women in Late Imperial China*, edited by Ellen Widmer and Kang-i Sun Chang, 307–65. Stanford, CA: Stanford University Press, 1997.

Wu Meifeng 2007.
Wu Meifeng 吳美鳳. *Sheng Qing jiaju xingzhi liubian yanjiu* 盛清家具形制流變研究 [Studies in the evolution of furniture forms during the high Qing]. Beijing: Zijincheng chubanshe, 2007.

Wu Meifeng 2015.
———. "Ming Qing houfei zhidu lüekao" 明清后妃制度略考 [A brief study on Ming and Qing systems of imperial consorts]. *Gugong xuekan* 故宮學刊 1 (2015): 124–58.

S. Wu 1979.
Wu, Silas H. L. *Passage to Power: K'ang-hsi and His Heir Apparent, 1661–1722*. Cambridge, MA: Harvard University Press, 1979.

Wu Xiangxiang 1969.
Wu Xiangxiang 吳相湘. *Wan Qing gongting yu renwu* 晚清宮廷與人物 [Late Qing court and its people]. Taibei: Zhuanji wenxue chubanshe, 1969.

Wu Xiaoqun 2005.
Wu Xiaoqun 吳效群. "Huanghui: Qingmo Beijing minjian xianghui de zuigao zhuiqiu" 皇會: 清末北京民間香會的最高追求 [Imperial association: the greatest aspiration for folk incense associations in late Qing Beijing]. *Minjianwenhua luntan* 民間文化論壇 3 (2005): 39–45.

Y.-L. Wu 2010.
Wu, Yi-Li. *Reproducing Women Medicine: Metaphor, and Childbirth in Late Imperial China*. Berkeley: University of California Press, 2010.

Xiaodong Xu and Tong Yu 2017.
Xiaodong Xu and Tong Yu. "The Arts of *Leisi* and Kingfisher Blue in Ancient China." *Arts of Asia* 47, no. 4 (July–August 2017): 42–53.

Xie Li 2013.
Xie Li 謝麗. "Qingdai gongting chengshan gailun" 清代宮廷成扇概論 [An introduction to Qing court fans]. In *Qingfeng xulai: Gugong bowuyuan cang Qingdai gongting chengshan* 清風徐來：故宮博物院藏清代宮廷成扇 [Here comes the gentle breeze: Qing court fans in the Palace Museum collection], edited by Xie Li, 21–23. Beijing: Zijincheng chubanshe, 2013.

Xin 1992.
Xin Xiuming 信修明. *Lao taijian de huiyi* 老太監的回憶 [Remembrances of an old eunuch]. Beijing: Beijing yanshan chubanshe, 1992.

Xu Che 1994.
Xu Che 徐徹. *Cixi dazhuan* 慈禧大傳 [Grand biography of Cixi]. Liaoning: Lianshen shushe, 1994.

Xu Guangyuan 2016.
Xu Guangyuan 徐廣源. *Qingchao ershiliu houfei* 清朝二十六后妃 [Twenty-six empresses and imperial consorts of the Qing dynasty]. Beijing: Xinshijie chubanshe, 2016.

Xu Jin 2015.
Xu Jin 徐瑾. "Qingdai huangdi yurong anfeng zhidu tanxi" 清代皇帝御容安奉制度探析 [Regulations regarding the placement of Qing imperial portraits]. *Gugong xuekan* 故宮學刊 2 (2015): 192–214.

Yan Chongnian 1993.
Yan Chongnian 閻崇年. "Qingdai gongting yu saman wenhua" 清代宮廷與薩滿文化 [The Qing court and shamanic culture]. *Gugong bowuyuan yuankan* 故宮博物院院刊 2 (1993): 55–64.

Yan Qianpei 2011.
Yan Qianpei 顏千佩. "Shier meiren tu" 十二美人圖 [Twelve "beauty" paintings]. In *Guoli Taibei yishudaxue meishushi yanjiusuo Zhongguo meishushi zu jiangyi fenzi* 國立臺北藝術大學美術史研究所中國美術史組議藝份子第十六期 [National Taipei University of the Arts' Art History Research Center's Chinese art history series], no. 16 (March 2011): 29–54.

Yang Boda 1984.
Yang Boda 楊伯達. "Qingdai Huizhuang pinfei xiang" 清代回裝嬪妃像 [Portraits of a Qing dynasty consort in Uyghur dress]. *Zijincheng* 紫禁城 1 (1984): 1, 6–9, 22.

Yang Xin 2013.
Yang Xin 楊新. "Yinzhen weiping *meirentu* tanmi" 胤禛圍屏美人圖探秘 [Deciphering Yinzhen's screen of the beautiful ladies]. *Zijincheng* 紫禁城 5 (2013): 94–118.

Yang Zhen 1994.
Yang Zhen 楊珍. *Kangxi huangdi yijia* 康熙皇帝一家 [The Kangxi emperor's family]. Beijing: Xueyuan chubanshe, 1994.

Yang Zhishui 2014.
Yang Zhishui 揚之水. *Zhongguo gudai jinyin shoushi* 中國古代金銀首飾 [Historical gold and silver jewelry in China]. 3 vols. Beijing: Gugong chubanshe, 2014.

Ye Zhiru and Tang Yinian 1986.
Ye Zhiru 葉志如 and Tang Yinian 唐益年. "Guangxu chao Sanhai gongcheng yu Beiyang haijun" 光緒朝三海工程與北洋海軍 [Constructions of Sanhai during the Guangxu reign and the Beiyang Fleet]. *Lishi dang'an* 歷史檔案 4 (1986): 110–18.

Yi Jo-lan 2014.
Yi Jo-lan. "Gender and Sericulture Ritual Practice in Sixteenth-Century China." *Journal of Asian History* 48, no. 2 (2014): 281–302.

Yin Zhihua 2010.
Yin Zhihua 尹志華. "Qingmo Beijing Baiyunguan fangzhang Gao Rentong xingshi" 清末北京白雲觀方丈高仁峒行實 [The life of Gao Rentong, abbot of the White Cloud Monastery in late Qing Beijing]. *Hongdao* 弘道 42, no. 1 (2010): 45–49.

Yu Bingkun 1985.
Yu Bingkun 俞炳坤, "Cixi rugong shijian, shenfen he fenghao" 慈禧入宮時間、身份和封號 [On the date of Empress Dowager Cixi's entry into the imperial palace and her identity and title]. In Yu Bingkun et al. 1985, 55–62.

Yu Bingkun et al. 1985.
Yu Bingkun et al., eds. *Xitaihou* 西太后 [Empress Dowager Cixi]. Beijing: Zijincheng chubanshe, 1985.

Yu Minzhong (about 1785) 1983.
Yu Minzhong 于敏中. *Rixia jiuwen kao* 日下舊聞考 [Study of ancient accounts heard in the precincts of the throne]. About 1785. Beijing: Beijing guji chubanshe, 1983.

Yuan Hongqi and Zhang Shiyun 1994.
Yuan Hongqi 苑洪琪 and Zhang Shiyun 張世芸. "Cixi yu zhongyao meirong" 慈禧與中藥美容 [Empress Dowager Cixi and Chinese medicinal cosmetology]. In *Houfei meirong shu* 后妃美容術 [The cosmetology of empresses and consorts], edited by Lu Yanzhen, Zhang Shiyun and Yuan Hongqi, 278–87. Beijing: Zhongyang minzu daxue chubanshe, 1994.

Yun Limei 2011.
Yun Limei 惲麗梅. "Guanyu Qingdai hou fei ce bao de jige wenti" 關於清代后妃冊寶的幾個問題 [Several issues regarding the investiture tablets and seals of Qing empresses and consorts]. *Manzu yanjiu* 滿族研究 3 (2011): 70–76.

Zhang Guangsheng and Lu Ying 2013.
Zhang Guangsheng 張廣生 and Lu Ying 魯穎. "Yubi xiejing" 御筆寫經 [Buddhist sutras hand-copied by Qing emperors]. *Zijincheng* 紫禁城 9 (2013): 143–49.

Zhang Guobin 2016.
Zhang Guobin 張國斌. "Qinggong xinyang yu Shengjing gongdian" 清宮信仰與盛京宮殿 [Belief at the Qing court and the palace complex at Shenyang]. *Zhongguo wenhua yichan* 中國文化遺產 5 (2016): 42–49.

Zhang Guoqing 1993.
Zhang Guoqing 張國慶. "Qidan Liaodi de zaoxiang yu jizu" 契丹遼帝的造像與祭祖 [Images of Khitan emperors and ancestor veneration in the Liao dynasty]. *Heilongjiang minzu congkan* 黑龍江民族叢刊 34 (1993): 85–89.

Zhang Naiwei 1988.
Zhang Naiwei 張乃煒. *Qinggong shuwen* 清宮述聞 [Jottings on the Qing palace]. 1937. Reprint, Beijing: Beijing guji chubanshe, 1988.

Zhang Peng 2016.
Zhang Peng 張鵬. "Meishushi yanjiu zhong de Song Liao yurong wanglai" 美術史研究中的宋遼御容往來 [Imperial portrait exchange between the Song and the Liao imperial courts in art history]. *Gugong bowuyuan yuankan* 故宮博物院院刊 3 (2016): 86–98.

Zhang Qiong 2004.
Zhang Qiong 張瓊. "Guanyu Qingdai dihou chaofu yu chaofuxiang de jidian kanfa" 關於清代帝后朝服與朝服像的幾點看法 [On Qing emperors' and empresses' court attire and portraits of Qing emperors and empresses in court attire]. *Gugong bowuyuan yuankan* 故宮博物院院刊 3 (2004): 60–74.

Zhang Rong 2011.
Zhang Rong. "Cloisonné for the Imperial Courts," In Quette 2011b, 163–67.

Zhang Xiaorui 2004.
Zhang Xiaorui 張小銳. "Qinggong dang'an jiekai Daya zhai ciqi niandai zhi mi" 清宮檔案揭開大雅齋瓷器年代之謎 [Unveiling the myth over the date of Dayazhai ware through archives of the Qing court]. *Zijincheng* 紫禁城 5 (2004): 122–23.

Zhao Zhongfu 1970.
Zhao Zhongfu 趙中孚 ed. *Weng Tonghe riji paiyinben* 翁同龢日記排印本 [A typeset edition of the diary of Weng Tonghe], vol. 2. Taibei: Chengwen chubanshe, 1970.

Zhao Zhongnan et al. 2010.
Zhao Zhongnan 趙中南 et al. *Mingdai gongting dianzhi shi* 明代宮廷典制史 [The history of court ceremonial regulations during the Ming dynasty]. Beijing: Zijincheng chubanshe, 2010.

Zhu 1986.
Zhu Jiajin 朱家溍. "Guanyu Yongzheng shiqi shier fu meirenhua de wenti" 關於雍正時期十二幅美人畫的問題 [Concerning the questions of Yongzheng's twelve "beauty" paintings]. *Zijincheng* 紫禁城 3 (1986): 45.

Zhu 2008.
——. *Ming Qing gongting shinei chenshe* 明清宮廷室內陳設 [Interior decoration in the palaces of the Ming and Qing]. Beijing: Zijincheng chubanshe, 2008.

Zou Ailian 1996.
Zou Ailian 鄒愛蓮. *Qinggong saman jisi de xingshuai yu yanbian* 清宮薩滿祭祀的興衰與演變 [The rise, decline, and development of shamanic rituals at the Qing court]. Beijing: Zijincheng chubanshe, 1996.

Zuo Shu'e 1993.
Zuo Shu'e 左書諤. *Cixi taihou* 慈禧太后 [Empress Dowager Cixi]. Changchun: Jilin wenshi chubanshe, 1993.

Zurndorfer 1999.
Zurndorfer, Harriet Thelma. *Chinese Women in the Imperial Past: New Perspectives*. Leiden: Brill, 1999.

INDEX

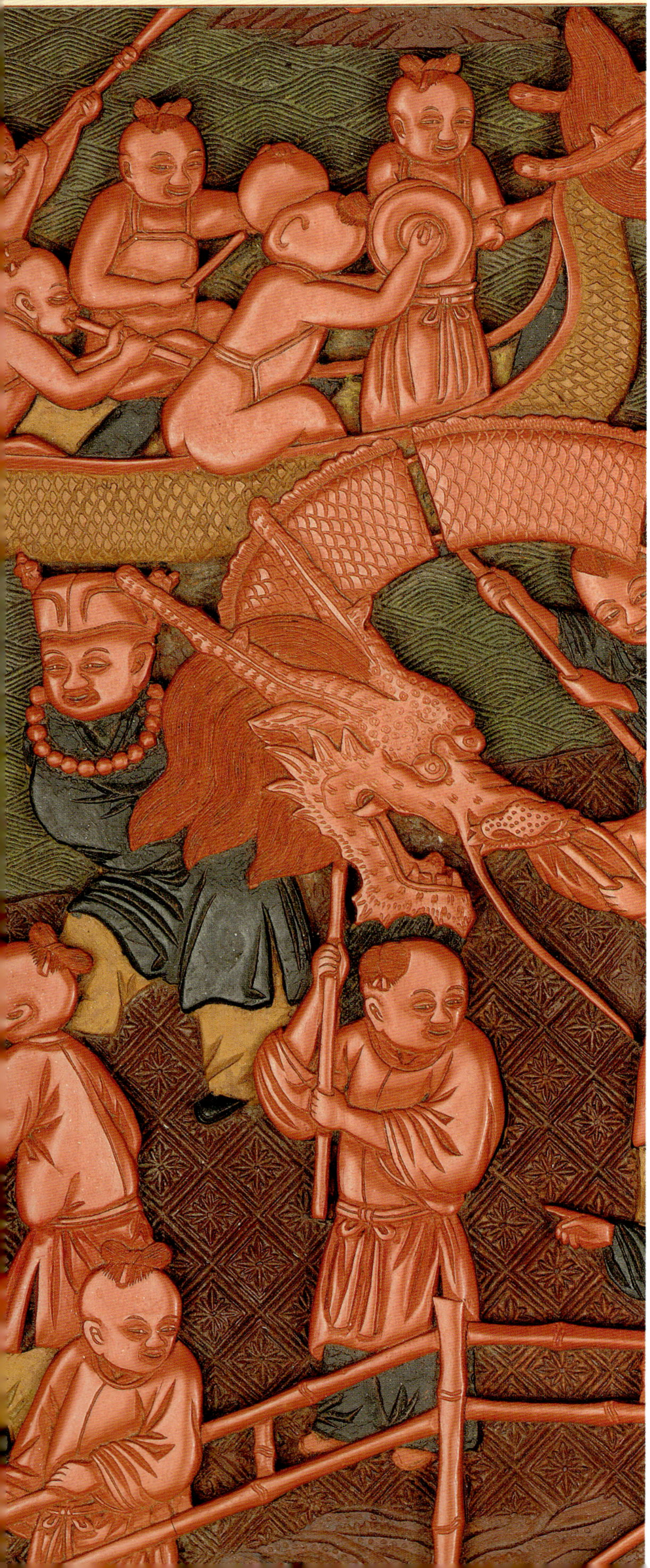

Page numbers in **boldface** indicate plates; page numbers in *italics* indicate figures.

CREDITS

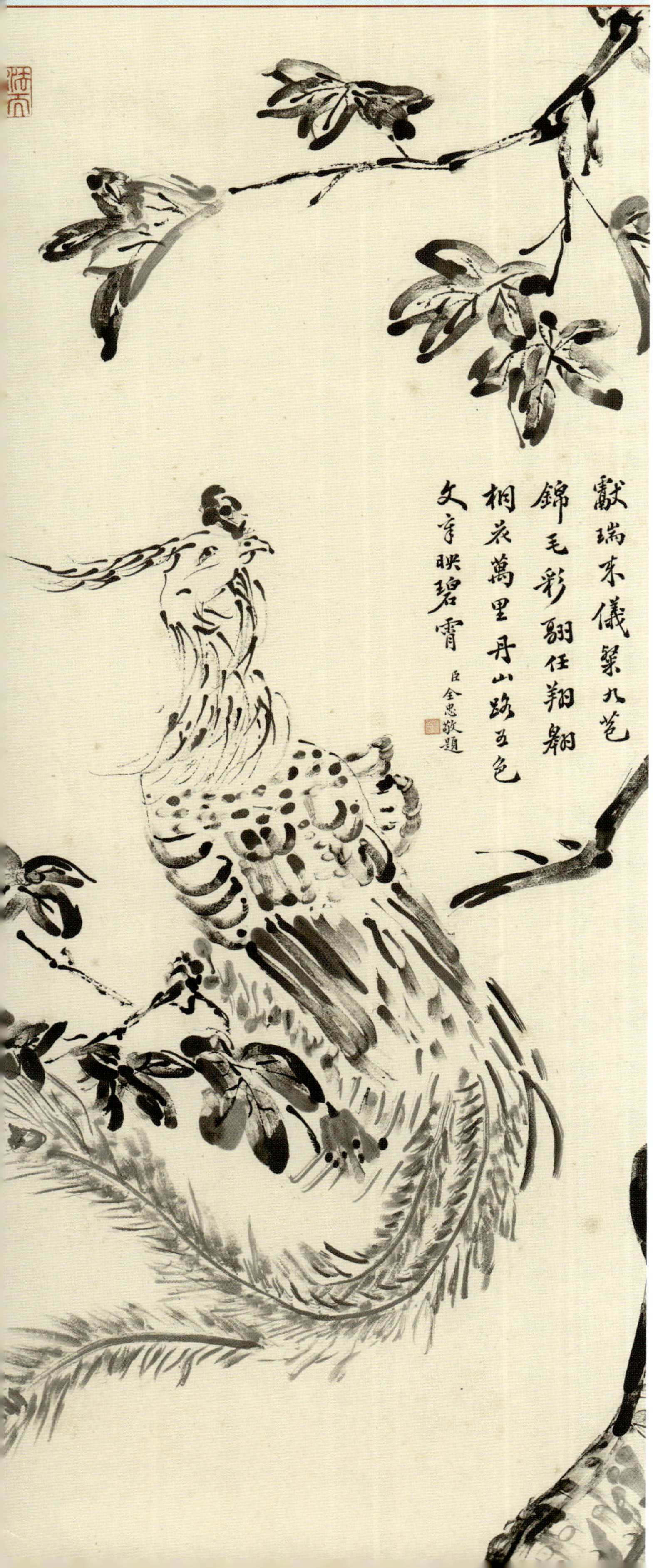

Unless otherwise indicated below, all photographs in this book were generously provided by the Digital Information Department of the Palace Museum. Special thanks to photographer Wang Jin.

Map based on illustration by Chiu Kwong-chiu, Design and Cultural Studies Workshop, Hong Kong: pp. 30–31

© The Cleveland Museum of Art: p. 103

Courtesy of Freer Gallery of Art and Arthur M. Sackler Gallery, Smithsonian Institution, Washington, DC: pp. 206–07

Courtesy of Freer Gallery of Art and Arthur M. Sackler Gallery Archives, Smithsonian Institution, Washington, DC: pp. 26, 47, 120, 136, 138–39

Courtesy of Li Shi: p. 104 (left)

© The Metropolitan Museum of Art. Courtesy of Art Resource, NY: p. 44

© 2018 Museum of Fine Arts, Boston: p. 93 (right)

Courtesy of Palace of Harmony and Peace, Beijing: pp. 110, 119

© 2018 Peabody Essex Museum. Photo by Bob Packert: pp. 39, 117

Peabody Essex Museum. Photo by Walter Silver: pp. 70 (left), 88, 90, 94 (all), 97 (all), 105 (right)

Peabody Essex Museum. Photo by Kathy Tarantola: pp. 45, 135

Peabody Essex Museum. Photo by Allison White: p. 221

Phillips Library, Peabody Essex Museum. Photo by Bob Packert: p. 137

Courtesy of Potala Palace, Lhasa: pp. 124–25

Courtesy of Shanghai Museum: p. 65

Courtesy of University of Alberta Museums: pp. 212–13

Courtesy of White Cloud Monastery, Beijing: p. 122 (all)

Empresses of China's Forbidden City, 1644–1912 accompanies the exhibition *Empresses of China's Forbidden City* organized by the Peabody Essex Museum in Salem, Massachusetts, the Freer|Sackler, Smithsonian Institution, in Washington, DC, and the Palace Museum in Beijing, China.

EXHIBITION ITINERARY

Peabody Essex Museum
August 18, 2018–February 10, 2019

Freer|Sackler, Smithsonian Institution
March 30–June 23, 2019

Library of Congress Control Number: 2018010720

ISBN: 978-0-300-23708-5 (hardcover)
ISBN: 978-0-875-77235-6 (softcover)

First published in the United States of America in 2018 by

Peabody Essex Museum
East India Square
Salem, Massachusetts 01970-3726
www.pem.org

Freer|Sackler, Smithsonian Institution
1050 Independence Avenue SW
MRC 707, P.O. Box 37012
Washington, DC 20013-7012
www.freersackler.si.edu

Distributed by

Yale University Press
302 Temple Street
P.O. Box 209040
New Haven, Connecticut 06520-9040
www.yalebooks.com/art

Edited by Tom Fredrickson
Designed and produced by Joan Sommers and Amanda Freymann, Glue + Paper Workshop, Chicago
Index by Siobhan Drummond
Color separations by Professional Graphics, Rockford, Illinois
Printed in China through Asia Pacific Offset on 150 gsm Lumi matte

Typeset in HTF Requiem and Ideal Sans

2018 2019 2020 2021 / 10 9 8 7 6 5 4 3 2 1

Details:
Page 1: detail of pl. 53
Page 2: detail of fig. 1, p. 62
Page 3: detail of pl. 21
Page 4: detail of fig. 14, p. 68
Page 5: detail of cat. 157
Page 6: detail of pl. 40
Page 8: detail of pl. 36
Page 10: detail of pl. 14
Page 13: detail of fig. 6, p. 67
Page 14: detail of pl. 42
Page 18: detail of pl. 22
Page 20: detail of pl. 8
Page 26: detail of fig. 9, p. 138
Page 32: detail of pl. 15
Page 51: detail of fig. 9, p. 59
Page 60: detail of fig. 12, p. 69
Page 78: detail of pl. 7
Page 88: detail of fig. 1, p. 90
Page 110: detail of fig. 7, p. 119
Page 128: detail of fig. 5, p. 134
Pages 142–43: detail of pl. 8
Page 224: detail of fig. 3, p. 36
Page 240: detail of pl. 51
Page 244: detail of fig. 3, p. 133
Page 256: detail of pl. 5
Page 262: detail of pl. 54
Page 264: detail of Respectfully escorting the empress's phoenix palanquin to exit the Gate of Supreme Harmony, leaf 10, volume 6, from The Grand Imperial Wedding of the Guangxu Emperor. Qing Kuan (1848–1927) and other court painters, Beijing, Guangxu period, about 1889, album leaf, ink and color on silk, cat. 36.

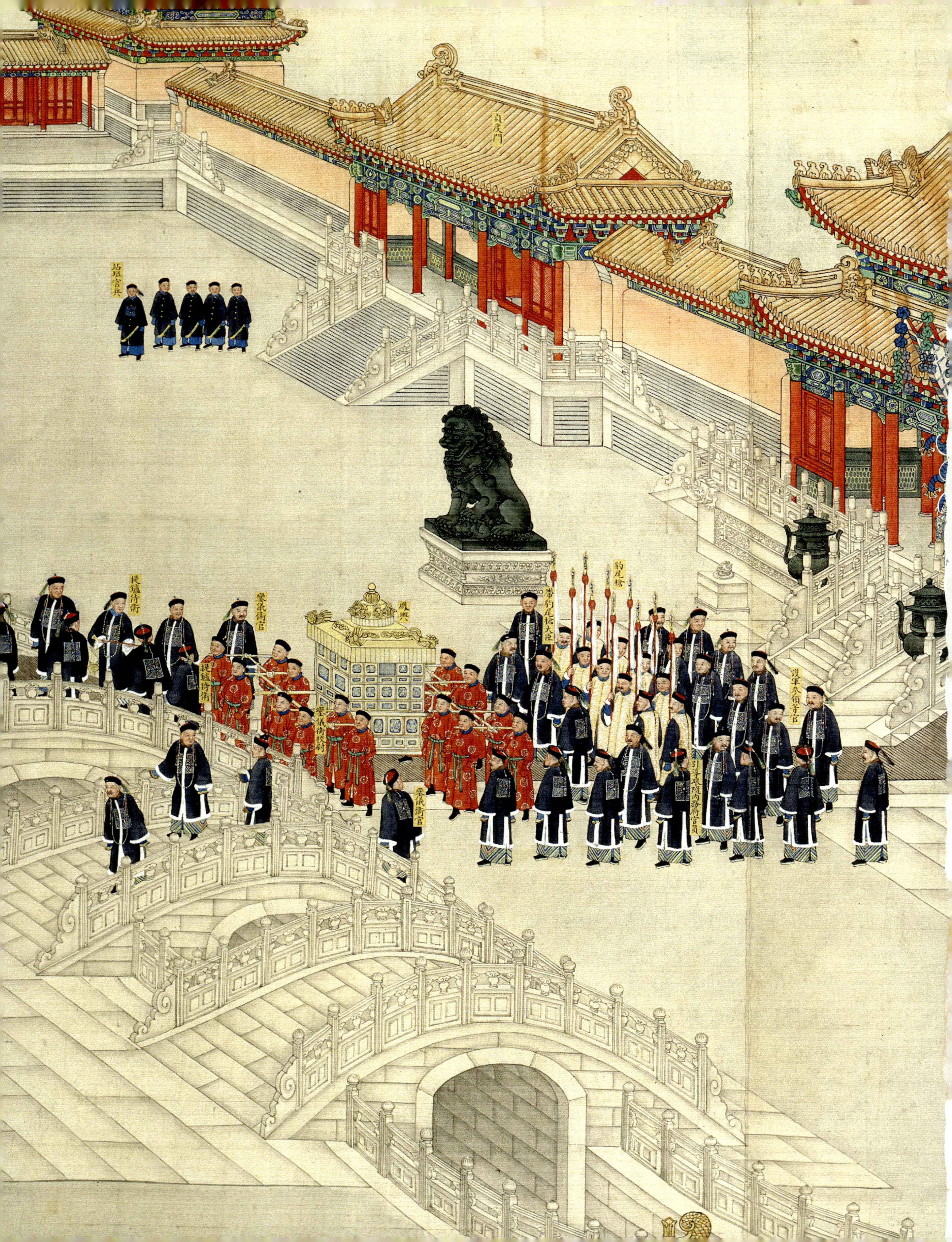
貞度門
站班官兵
提爐侍衛
鑾儀衛官
鳳輿
提爐侍衛
鑾儀衛校尉
鑾儀衛官
豹尾槍
帶豹尾槍大臣
護軍參領等官
引導跟隨內務府官員